THE AGE OF ROOSEVELT

The Coming *of*
the New Deal

BOOKS BY
ARTHUR M. SCHLESINGER, JR.

Orestes A. Brownson:
A Pilgrim's Progress

The Age of Jackson

The Vital Center

The General and the President
(with Richard H. Rovere)

The Age of Roosevelt
I. The Crisis of the Old Order, 1919-1933
II. The Coming of the New Deal
III. The Politics of Upheaval

The Politics of Hope

A Thousand Days:
John F. Kennedy in the White House

The Bitter Heritage:
Vietnam and American Democracy, 1941-1966

The Crisis of Confidence:
Ideas, Power and Violence in America

The Imperial Presidency

Robert Kennedy and His Times

The Cycles of American History

The American Heritage Library

THE AGE OF ROOSEVELT

THE COMING OF THE NEW DEAL

Arthur M. Schlesinger, Jr.

Houghton Mifflin Company · Boston

For information about permission to reproduce selections
from this book, write to Permissions, Houghton Mifflin Company,
2 Park Street, Boston, Massachusetts 02108.

Library of Congress Cataloging-in-Publication Data

Schlesinger, Arthur Meier, date.
 The coming of the New Deal / Arthur M. Schlesinger, Jr.
  p. cm. — (The American Heritage library) (The Age of Roosevelt)
 Bibliography: p.
 Includes index.
 ISBN 0-395-48905-9 (pbk.)
 1. United States—History—1933–1945. 2. New Deal, 1933–1939.
3. Depressions—1929—United States. 4. Roosevelt, Franklin D. (Franklin
Delano), 1882–1945. I. Title. II. Series. III. Series: Schlesinger, Arthur Meier,
date. Age of Roosevelt.
E806.S344 1988 88-8209
973.917—dc19 CIP

Printed in the United States of America

S 10 9 8 7 6 5 4 3 2 1

KIN

FOR
MY MOTHER AND FATHER

"There is nothing more difficult to carry out, nor more doubtful of success, nor more dangerous to handle, than to initiate a new order of things."

MACHIAVELLI

Foreword to
the American Heritage Library Edition

THE FIRST THREE VOLUMES of *The Age of Roosevelt*, now reissued in the American Heritage Library, were published a generation ago: *The Crisis of the Old Order* in 1957, *The Coming of the New Deal* in 1958, and *The Politics of Upheaval* in 1960. These volumes cover the life and times of Franklin Roosevelt through the election of 1936. Their emphasis, reflecting FDR's own priorities during these years, is on the New Deal and domestic affairs.

The next volume was scheduled to deal with FDR and foreign affairs in the 1930s. But in 1960 many essential foreign policy documents were under official lock and key, protected by government classification from scholarly inquiry. I saw no choice but to suspend *The Age of Roosevelt* until I could gain access to the files. Then, for a number of years thereafter, I was drawn into other matters, political and scholarly.

In these years also the American and British archives were gradually opened to the end of the Second World War (and now well beyond). The fourth volume of *The Age of Roosevelt*, covering FDR and the coming of the war, is at last in the making. More volumes will follow in due course. I regret the delay but take solace in the example of my putative ancestor George Bancroft, who published the first volume of his *History of the United States* in 1834 and, after spirited and interesting digressions into politics and public service, published the tenth (and final) volume in 1874—and then added a two-volume *History of the Formation of the Constitution of the United States* in 1882 (at the age of eighty-two).

When I wrote *The Crisis of the Old Order*, FDR had been dead for hardly more than a decade. His presidency had stirred vivid and intense emotions. Like all great American presidents, he had been a divisive figure in his own time. Most Americans revered him. Some detested and reviled him. Change always provokes resentment and anger, especially on the part of those who benefit from the old order. The passions of the 1930s had not much abated by the 1950s. Many Americans still actively loved Roosevelt. A not inconsiderable number still actively hated him.

Moreover, the 1950s, like the 1920s thirty years before and the 1980s thirty years after, fell in the conservative phase of the political cycle. (In the same way, times of liberalism, reform, and affirmative government come along every thirty years: Theodore Roosevelt and the Progressive era in 1901, FDR and the New Deal in 1933, John Kennedy and the New Frontier in 1961.) The reputation of liberal presidents declines in conservative swings of the cycle, as the reputation of conservative presidents declines in liberal swings.

In any case, presidential reputations tend to be at low ebb in the years shortly after a president's death. When I went to college in the 1930s, Theodore Roosevelt, who died in 1919, and Woodrow Wilson, who died in 1924, were only beginning to emerge from the fashionable judgment that one was an adolescent braggart and the other a Presbyterian fanatic. The combination of the conservative phase of the cycle with the recency of FDR's death accounts for the somewhat defensive tone the reader may find in the foreword to *The Crisis of the Old Order*.

Today, nearly half a century after Roosevelt's death, the bitter passions of the 1930s and 1940s have pretty well subsided. Periodic polls of historians and political scientists routinely rank Roosevelt as one of the three greatest American presidents, with Lincoln and Washington. FDR reshaped scholarly conceptions and popular expectations about the presidency, and his towering personality and astute management of the office have haunted all his successors, as William Leuchtenburg reminded us in his excellent book of 1985, *In the Shadow of FDR*. Even during the conservative 1980s, when the most conservative president since Herbert Hoover mounted a counterrevolution against FDR's New Deal, Ronald Reagan nevertheless spoke with affection and respect of Franklin Roosevelt himself, perhaps because, when younger and possibly wiser, he had cast his first *four* presidential votes for FDR.

But history should never be an exercise in reverence. Franklin

Roosevelt had superb qualities of leadership, superb instincts for the crucial problems of his age, superb ability to select and manage vigorous subordinates, enormous skill as a public educator, and enormous ability to lift the spirits of the republic and to mobilize national energies. He was, however, far from infallible. He made mistakes both in policy and in politics. He had his moments of deviousness, craftiness, vanity, undue casualness, and insouciant cruelty. He combined soaring idealism with tough and sometimes petty realism. He was, in other words, a human being, somewhat larger than life but hardly exempt from human infirmity, frailty, and error.

   Those vigorous subordinates in FDR's supporting cast add color and excitement to the age of Roosevelt. When these volumes were first published, their names and personalities—Hopkins, Ickes, Wallace, Hull, Morgenthau, Frankfurter, Tugwell, Berle, Frances Perkins, Tom Corcoran and Ben Cohen, Jimmy Byrnes and Jesse Jones, Robert Jackson and Francis Biddle, Sumner Welles and David Lilienthal—were still well known. What a formidable and dashing group they were! Few of them, alas, are household words today. Still I trust that these pages contain enough about their characters and contributions to explain their impact on those turbulent and agitated times. I had the great luck to know and interview a good many of them, and I hope that their testimony will impart a certain directness to the narrative.

   Indeed, the determination to take advantage of living witnesses was an important motive in my decision to attempt *The Age of Roosevelt.* When I was preparing to write *The Age of Jackson,* I benefited greatly, as have all Jackson scholars, from James Parton's wonderful *Life of Andrew Jackson.* In his preface Parton discussed the problems of discovering information "respecting a man whom two thirds of his fellow-citizens deified, and the other third vilified, for a space of twelve years or more." To find out what Jackson was like, Parton, conducting his research a decade after Jackson's death, "conversed with politicians of the last generation, who have now no longer an interest in concealing the truth." He roamed around the country eliciting "the recollections of men and women, bond and free, who knew him well, knew him at all periods of his life, lived near him, and with him, served him and were served by him. . . . Thus it was that contradictions were reconciled, that mysteries were revealed, and that the truth was made apparent."

I cannot pretend to the journalistic skills or literary graces of James Parton. But I was struck by his methods. I was struck too by the frustrations that attend those methods, for the questions Parton asked of his witnesses were not always the questions to which future historians have sought answers. At any rate, I was inspired by his example to talk to FDR's friends, associates, and adversaries (no one was more generous and helpful than the fine man he trounced in 1936, Alfred M. Landon). I do not suppose that I was any more successful than James Parton in asking the questions that will interest scholars of the future, but I hope that at least testimony may have been preserved that might otherwise have perished with the witnesses.

Since these books were published, a very considerable literature has appeared on many facets of the age of Roosevelt. I do not believe that the outpouring of scholarly books, monographs, and articles changes the main outline of the story told in these volumes, but some float ingenious theories and others add valuable details. I will take account of this rich literature in the volumes of *The Age of Roosevelt* yet to come.

The Roosevelt years were above all a battlefield of ideas—ideas about the American past and the American future; ideas about the role of government in guaranteeing the economy and protecting the forgotten man (and woman); ideas about isolationism and internationalism and America's relationship to the world beyond; ideas articulated with uncommon vehemence and ardor and often with authentic brilliance; ideas that intersected with power and helped shape the destiny of the United States and the world.

Today, I believe, a new cyclical change impends in American politics. If the rhythm holds, the nation can be expected to move from the energetically conservative 1980s into an energetically progressive new decade. I would like to think that in this coming period new generations will find power and resonance in the memory of Franklin Roosevelt and the New Deal. Of course the problems of the 1990s will be very different from the problems of the 1930s. But the spirit of experiment, idealism, and concern with which the republic defeated the worst depression and won the greatest war in American history remains, I think, a precious resource as we confront the darkly unpredictable future.

ARTHUR M. SCHLESINGER, JR.

May 21, 1988

Foreword

THE CRISIS OF THE OLD ORDER, the first volume of *The Age of Roosevelt*, described the impotence of the reigning leadership in the United States during the economic breakdown which began in 1929. This second volume, *The Coming of the New Deal*, shows how the American people began in the first presidential term of Franklin D. Roosevelt to respond to the crisis. The events recounted in this volume take place in the main in 1933 and 1934, though in certain instances it has seemed appropriate to continue the stories until a later date. Foreign affairs (except for the London Economic Conference, which was an organic episode in the evolution of domestic policy) are reserved for discussion in subsequent volumes.

May I say again, as I said in the foreword to *The Crisis of the Old Order*, that I will greatly welcome corrections or amplifications of anything I have written in this text. And I want again to thank the busy persons whose generous assistance contributed so much to the pleasure of writing the book as well as to the improvement of the result. I owe more than I can say to my father and mother, Arthur M. Schlesinger and Elizabeth Bancroft Schlesinger, who read the entire manuscript with a care and conscience which did not permit parental sympathy to restrain critical judgment. To my friends Seymour Harris and John Kenneth Galbraith I am endlessly indebted for their willingness not just to read the text but to discuss problems which must have seemed as elementary to them as they seemed complicated to me; if economic solecisms persist, it is the consequence of my obtuseness, not of their counsel. I am under heavy obligation to the following who read portions of the manuscript (but who bear no responsibility for the result): Arthur J. Altmeyer, Emily Morison Beck, Adolf A. Berle, Jr., John D. Black, Benjamin V. Cohen, Thomas G. Corcoran, Chester Davis, John Dunlop, Herbert Feis, James Lawrence Fly, Jerome Frank, Ruth Harris, Leon Henderson, Gardner Jackson, Barbara Wendell Kerr, Leon Keyserling, James M. Landis, Arthur Maass, Raymond Moley, Paul A. Porter, Blackwell Smith, Rexford G. Tugwell, James P. Warburg, Aubrey Williams. Herman Kahn not only subjected the manuscript to exceptionally acute and informed criticism but, as Director of the Franklin D. Roosevelt Library at Hyde Park, offered, along with his admirable staff, the most generous and efficient cooperation. My fellow Roosevelt scholars, John M. Blum, Frank Freidel, Richard H. Rovere, Basil Rauch, James M. Burns, Robert Jacoby, and Earle W. Newton, have responded more than generously to all appeals. I am grateful to Helen Phillips, Anne Barrett, and Paul Brooks of the staff of Houghton Mifflin for valuable suggestions. I am particularly in the debt of Adolf A. Berle, Jr., Francis Biddle, McGeorge Bundy (for the papers of Henry L. Stimson), Mary Dewson, Herbert Feis, Mrs. Lilla Levitt (for the papers of J. P. Moffat), Raymond Moley, Henry Morgenthau, Jr., Blackwell Smith, Rexford G. Tugwell, and James P. Warburg for permission to examine and quote personal papers. All students of contemporary American history owe much to the initiative of the Oral History Research Office at Columbia University. I could not have completed this work without the unremitting aid and cooperation of Paul H. Buck, Robert Haynes, and the staff of the Harvard University Library. Donald Born kindly helped in reading the proofs.

I am happy to express particular obligation to E. G. Shinner and the Shinner Foundation for a generous research grant which came at a most opportune moment and has been of inestimable assistance. Julie Armstrong Jeppson has responded to every crisis of research, typing, and office management with invariable charm, good humor, and generosity. And I want to express special appreciation to my wife Marian Cannon Schlesinger for the fortitude with which she bore the agonies of composition and for the gaiety with which she lights so many other areas of my life.

ARTHUR M. SCHLESINGER, JR.

March 10, 1958

Contents

The Coming *of* the New Deal

1. Prologue: The Hundred Days

SATURDAY, MARCH 4, 1933. "This nation asks for action, and action now. . . . We must act, and act quickly." The great mass before the Capitol, huddling in the mist and wind under the sullen March sky, responded with a burst of applause. The new President moved on to his conclusion. "In this dedication of a Nation we humbly ask the blessing of God. May He protect each and every one of us. May He guide me in the days to come." Then the flourish of cavalry bugles, and the call to the inaugural parade, and Franklin Delano Roosevelt, his face still set and grim, entered his car to review the marchers from the stand in front of the White House.

Through the country people listened to their radios with a quickening hope. Nearly half a million of them wrote letters to the White House in the next few days. People said: "It was the finest thing this side of heaven"; and "Your human feeling for all of us in your address is just wonderful"; and "It seemed to give the people, as well as myself, a new hold upon life." "Yours is the first opportunity to carve a name in the halls of immortals beside Jesus," wrote one. "People are looking to you almost as they look to God," wrote another.

But others could not suppress anxiety. Eleanor Roosevelt called the inauguration "very, very solemn and a little terrifying" — terrifying "because when Franklin got to that part of his speech when he said it might become necessary for him to assume powers ordinarily granted to a President in war time, he received his biggest demonstration." What could this mean for the baffled

and despairing nation? "One has a feeling of going it blindly,"
she said, "because we're in a tremendous stream, and none of us
knows where we're going to land." [1]

II

In the morning the members of his cabinet had prayed with
Roosevelt at St. John's Episcopal Church across from the White
House, Endicott Peabody of Groton conducting the services. Late
in the afternoon, as the streets of Washington fell silent after
the excitements of the day, the cabinet foregathered with him once
again, now in the Oval Room of the White House. There they
stood, a quiet, serious group, inexplicably brought together by the
crisis: — Cordell Hull, Secretary of State, grave, pale and fragile;
William Woodin, Secretary of the Treasury, dark with anxiety
over the banking collapse; Harold Ickes, the Secretary of the
Interior, with his square, stubborn face, and Henry Wallace, the
Secretary of Agriculture, earnest and intent, and Frances Perkins,
the Secretary of Labor, with her brisk, womanly determination;
and, beside them, the political professionals, ready for anything,
Attorney-General Homer Cummings, Secretary of Commerce
Daniel C. Roper, Postmaster-General James A. Farley, and the
service secretaries Claude Swanson and George Dern. As Justice
Benjamin N. Cardozo administered the oaths, precedents fell:
never before had a cabinet been sworn at a single stroke, never
before had the swearing-in occurred at the White House. Roosevelt, with a smile, called it a "little family party" and handed
each his commission of office.

So the first day ended in suspense. And on the next, the new
President (as he later recalled it), wakening with a pressing sense
of work to be done, ate an early breakfast and had himself wheeled
over to his new office. There, seated for the first time in the
presidential chair, he found himself suddenly alone in an empty
room. The desk was empty, the drawers were empty, the President could not even find pencil and pad to make a note. He
looked for buzzers on the desk, but found no button to push,
no way to signal the outside world. He sat for a moment, the
great chamber echoing and silent, the center of action cut off

from the nation at the moment of crisis. At last he bestirred himself and gave a mighty shout, which brought Missy LeHand and Marvin McIntyre running from adjacent rooms. For others, the story, as he used to tell it, seemed a skit on his physical helplessness. For himself — or so at least Rexford G. Tugwell surmised — the predicament was a parable of the national helplessness, extending for a dreadful moment even to what Wilson had called "the vital place of action in the system."

It was hard to understate the need for action. The national income was less than half of what it had been four short years before. Nearly thirteen million Americans — about one quarter of the labor force — were desperately seeking jobs. The machinery for sheltering and feeding the unemployed was breaking down everywhere under the growing burden. And a few hours before, in the early morning before the inauguration, every bank in America had locked its doors. It was now not just a matter of staving off hunger. It was a matter of seeing whether a representative democracy could conquer economic collapse. It was a matter of staving off violence, even (at least some so thought) revolution.

Whether revolution was a real possibility or not, faith in a free system was plainly waning. Capitalism, it seemed to many, had spent its force; democracy could not rise to economic crisis. The only hope lay in governmental leadership of a power and will which representative institutions seemed impotent to produce. Some looked enviously on Moscow, others on Berlin and Rome; abroad there seemed fervor, dedication, a steel determination. Could America match this spirit of sacrifice and unity? "What does a democracy do in a war?" said Al Smith, the former governor of New York, who had been the Democratic party's candidate for President in 1928. "It becomes a tyrant, a despot, a real monarch. In the World War we took our Constitution, wrapped it up and laid it on the shelf and left it there until it was over." "Even the iron hand of a national dictator," said Alfred M. Landon of Kansas, "is in preference to a paralytic stroke. . . . If there is any way in which a member of that species, thought by many to be extinct, a Republican governor of a mid-western state, can aid [the President] in the fight, I now enlist for the duration of the war." [2]

III

The first priority was the banking system. Before anything else could be done, it seemed imperative to clear the financial arteries of the economy. The outgoing President had asked the President-elect in February to join with him in meeting the banking crisis. But Herbert Hoover had stipulated that cooperation was to be on his own terms; this meant, as he privately confided to a friend, the ratification by Roosevelt of "the whole major program of the Republican Administration" and "the abandonment of 90% of the so-called new deal." Roosevelt, angered at the proposal that he renounce the policies on which he had won the election, broke off negotiations. Last-minute attempts to bring the two men together just before the inauguration failed. Avoiding responsibility without power, now, on March 5, Franklin Roosevelt had both.

He had already settled on the main lines of his attack. Before arriving in Washington, he had rough drafts of two presidential proclamations: one calling a special session of Congress; the other declaring a bank holiday and controlling the export of gold by invoking forgotten provisions of the wartime Trading with the Enemy Act. On Saturday night, a few hours after the inauguration, Secretary of the Treasury Woodin agreed to have emergency banking legislation ready for Congress when it convened on Thursday, March 9. After lunch on Sunday, Roosevelt called the cabinet together to complete the program of action. Woodin, after a morning of conferences, reported that the bankers, hastily summoned from across the country, had no plan of their own. Attorney-General Cummings then gave his official assent to the use of the Trading with the Enemy Act. This prepared the way for the two proclamations, and they were issued in the next four hours.

With the declaration of the bank holiday, the administration bought time — eighty hours until Congress reconvened — to work out a plan for reviving the banks. Old officials and new labored together day and night in the Treasury. Ogden Mills, Hoover's Secretary of the Treasury, exhorted the group to produce a program; if they couldn't, let "the President and Mr. Woodin tell us to get the devil out of here and get some men who can." We had "forgotten to be Republicans or Democrats," wrote Raymond Moley, the chief of Roosevelt's campaign brain trust, now an Assistant Secretary of State. "We were just a bunch of men trying to save the banking system."

The decision to save the system rather than to change it had come about almost by inadvertence. The first problem, as the President saw it, was to banish fear. If he was to restore confidence in the system, he had to offer policies which bankers themselves would support. And he had no real alternative to the restoration of the existing structure. It is true that Rexford G. Tugwell, another member of the campaign brain trust, now Assistant Secretary of Agriculture, had a scheme by which the postal savings system would take over the deposit and checking transactions of banks, while separate corporations would assume the job of commercial credit; but Tugwell's advice was not sought in the banking crisis. Indeed, as Tugwell later acknowledged, Wall Street and the orthodox economists had a monopoly of *expertise* in this area. America had no one outside the charmed circle, like John Maynard Keynes in Britain, who might have conceived a genuine reform.

There was restiveness in Congress about the President's approach. "I think back to the events of March 4, 1933," Senator Bronson Cutting of New Mexico later wrote, "with a sick heart. For then . . . the nationalization of banks by President Roosevelt could have been accomplished without a word of protest. It was President Roosevelt's great mistake." On the night before Congress convened, Senators Robert M. La Follette, Jr., of Wisconsin and Edward P. Costigan of Colorado, two leading progressives, called at the White House to urge Roosevelt to establish a truly national banking system. But they found Roosevelt's mind made up. "That isn't necessary at all," La Follette later recalled Roosevelt saying. "I've just had every assurance of cooperation from the bankers." The very moneychangers, whose flight from their high seats in the temple the President had so grandiloquently proclaimed in his inaugural address, were now swarming through the corridors of the Treasury.[8]

IV

For the country, the proclamation of the holiday ushered in almost a springtime mood. The closing of the banks seemed to give the long economic descent the punctuation of a full stop, as if this were the bottom and hereafter things could only turn upward. Anything was better than nagging uncertainty. Now everyone knew where he stood. People enjoyed the sense of a common plight. They made jokes and wrote out checks and accepted scrip and adjusted themselves with good cheer to the bankless economy.

But Washington, where the banking system was to be saved, could not be so philosophical. The ever approaching deadline stretched already taut nerves to the breaking point. Phones rang incessantly with excited calls from distant cities. The corridors of the Treasury echoed with rumor, fear, and fantasy. Bankers went to pieces under the pressure, and brain trusters showed the strain. Yet the old Treasury team, led by Mills and his Undersecretary, Arthur A. Ballantine, remained cool; and the new Treasury chief was displaying unexpected qualities of poise and endurance.

Woodin, whose pointed chin and delicate triangular face inevitably provoked the adjective "elfin," hid strength beneath his guileless surface. The stories about him were disarming but not particularly relevant to the banking crisis: he was addicted to bad puns; he liked to strum the zither or the guitar; he was the composer of "Raggedy Ann's Sunny Songs." Sixty-four years old, in poor health, soft-spoken and self-effacing, he seemed hardly the man to dominate a melee of panic-stricken bankers. Still the crisis found him clearheaded. He demanded what he called "swift and staccato action"; he was ready to accept responsibility and enforce decision; and he moved through turbulence with serenity.

By Monday a variety of proposals were under discussion at the Treasury. Many bankers demanded that the government issue scrip as it had during the panic of 1907. This idea assumed that the banks had too little currency on hand to meet national needs on reopening. The Hoover administration, in one of its last acts, had actually prepared a joint resolution to provide for the issuance of currency by clearinghouses. But, on reflection, the Treasury group, now reinforced by George L. Harrison of the New York Federal Reserve Bank and George W. Davison of the Central Hanover Bank, turned against this proposal. They favored instead a plan devised by Dr. E. A. Goldenweiser of the Federal Reserve Board whereby currency could be issued under the Federal Reserve Act against bank assets. If the first essential was to restore confidence, then Federal Reserve notes would be far less disturbing than clearinghouse scrip. Woodin, after spending Monday evening, so it was said, dozing and strumming his guitar, adopted the Goldenweiser idea.

For the rest, the banking bill, as it took shape in the next frenzied days, gave the Secretary of the Treasury power to prevent gold hoarding and to take over gold bullion and currency in exchange for paper; and it provided for the review and reopening of the closed banks under a system of licenses and "conservators." In the Treasury, men worked around the clock to translate the broad plan into legislative language, pausing only for coffee, a shower, or a snatch of sleep. On Wednesday afternoon a draft went to the White House. That evening Roosevelt presented the legislation to a conference of congressional leaders from both parties. A newspaperman asked Woodin whether the bill was finished. "Yes, it's finished," said Woodin wryly. "My name is Bill and I'm finished too."

On Thursday, March 9, at noon, a breathless five days after the inauguration, Congress convened. Almost at once it received a message from the President: "I cannot too strongly urge upon the Congress the clear necessity for immediate action." Chairman Henry B. Steagall of the Banking and Currency Committee read aloud the only available copy of the proposed banking legislation. Debate was limited to forty minutes, and even before this time expired members began calling "Vote! Vote!" Shortly after four o'clock, the House passed unanimously and without a roll call the bill few of its members had ever seen. In the meantime, the Senate, which had been awaiting printed copies, decided to substitute the House version and open its own debate. Huey Long of Louisiana, trying to amend the bill, succeeded only in provoking Carter Glass of Virginia, once Secretary of the Treasury under

Woodrow Wilson, into white-faced rage; Long's amendment was shouted down. Just before seven-thirty, the Senate passed the bill 73 to 7. An hour later, it was at the White House. The whole affair, from the first introduction to the final signature, had taken less than eight hours.

Not for years had Congress acted with such speed and decision. And already, before the passage of the bill, the Secretary of the Treasury had issued regulations permitting urgent transactions to go ahead. Though technical hitches prevented banks from reopening on Friday, March 10, as Roosevelt wished, the basic procedures were nonetheless now established. Gold and deposits were flowing back into the system. After the weekend, the people could look forward with assurance to orderly reopening.[4]

v

Roosevelt had first thought of putting through the emergency banking legislation and sending Congress home. But the momentum generated by the banking bill now seemed too valuable to waste. On Wednesday night Henry Wallace and Rex Tugwell raised the possibility of keeping Congress in session long enough to enact a farm program. And, even more insistently, Roosevelt's budget director, Lewis W. Douglas, argued that the President should seize the opportunity to do something about government economy.

In these early weeks, Lew Douglas was emerging as an increasingly influential figure. He was thirty-eight years old, lean and friendly, with an easy grin, candid brown eyes, an open manner, and a facile tongue. A member of the Arizona copper-mining family, he had gone to Amherst (where his class yearbook described him as "Dirty Doug, the slippery sleuth from the desolate wastes of Arizona"), served with distinction in the Argonne and Flanders during the First World War, and, after mining and citrus ranching in his native state, had entered politics. From the Arizona legislature he moved on in 1927 to the House of Representatives in Washington. There he won national attention by his fight for government economy, even daring to stand up against the veterans' lobby — a deed considered by politicians almost as heroic as the one for which he had earned a citation from General Pershing in France.

Douglas's passion for economy was part of his larger belief that economic order — indeed, civilization itself — rested on fiscal credit. "The country's future depends upon it," he exclaimed, " — upon a balanced budget and an end to wild extravagance." Under the spendthrift Hoover administration, Douglas declared, America had been going "the identical way that Germany went in the years just after the war." The only hope was a drastic reversal in government fiscal policy. "If we fail to practice economy, if we do not balance the budget, then we shall have created a malevolent wheel which is revolving constantly in an adverse direction and which inevitably means the complete economic collapse of the United States. . . . It would mean plunging the whole world into darkness."

Nor did Douglas want to balance the budget by increasing taxes. A larger tax burden, he felt, would have economic effects almost as deplorable as deficit spending itself. The solution was to cut government spending — taper off subsidies to farmers, to business, to public works, to veterans, even to national defense. "To those who say, 'You must not cut the army, for instance,'" Douglas declared, "I say, which is more important? A national defense which is perfectly futile, if the credit of the government collapses, or an unimpaired credit of your government? For myself, I say 'An unimpaired credit of the government.' For it is upon that, that all human values of our people ultimately rest."

For Douglas, the essence of the Roosevelt program was the pledge, rashly made in a speech at Pittsburgh during the 1932 campaign, to reduce the cost of government 25 per cent — to move toward what Roosevelt had then called "the one sound foundation of permanent economic recovery — a complete and honest balancing of the Federal budget." Once the budget was balanced, Douglas believed, confidence would return, frozen loans would thaw out, credit would expand, and recovery would be assured. But his experience in the House had convinced him that Congress could never bring itself to cut government spending. The only way to effect genuine retrenchment, he had come to think, was through the delegation of power to the Executive. During the interregnum, Roosevelt and Douglas had discussed the wartime grants of authority which Congress had made to Woodrow Wilson. Now in the first week of power, with Congress in a mood of unwonted acquiescence, it seemed the right time to request such delegations again.

On Thursday night, March 9, only an hour after he had signed the Emergency Banking Act, Roosevelt outlined an economy program to congressional leaders. With bland amiability, Roosevelt presented his proposals: reorganization of the veterans' pension system and reduction of pensions, to be accomplished through delegation of authority to the President; a reduction of congressional salaries; a reduction of Federal salaries — all designed to save the budget half a billion dollars. The politicians listened with incredulity. Undeterred, Roosevelt drove his argument home in his special message to Congress the next day. "For three long years," he said, "the Federal Government has been on the road toward bankruptcy." The existence of the staggering deficit of five billion dollars had increased economic stagnation, multiplied the unemployed, and contributed to the banking collapse. Employment and economic health could only rest on national credit. "Too often in recent history," the President warned sententiously, "liberal governments have been wrecked on rocks of loose fiscal policy." [5]

VI

Roosevelt spoke with deep sincerity. His fiscal notions were wholly orthodox. He saw little difference so far as budgets were concerned between a household or a state government on the one hand and the federal government on the other. In either case, Micawber was right: more income than expenditure — happiness; more expenditure than income — misery. Moreover, Roosevelt was much impressed by his new Budget Director. Early in April he told Colonel Edward M. House, the onetime friend of Wilson's, still active behind the scenes in the party, that Lewis Douglas was "in many ways the greatest 'find' of the administration." To Moley, Roosevelt observed, "In twelve years he would be a good Democratic candidate for President." In May, Arthur Krock of the

New York Times could refer to the Budget Director as "the real head of the Roosevelt Cabinet." Rex Tugwell complained in his diary that the President "had got far too dependent on Douglas," adding, "it is so easy to like Douglas that his biases tend to be forgotten."

For a moment, however, the economy bill seemed to break the presidential spell. In the House, the Democratic caucus declined to support the President. Some Democrats were doubtless motivated by old obligations to the veterans' lobby or by old fears of its retaliatory power. Yet others honestly — and plausibly — believed that it made no sense to cut government spending when the overriding economic need was for more spending everywhere in the economy. A number of liberal Democrats — Gordon Browning of Tennessee, Wright Patman of Texas, John Rankin of Mississippi, Fred Vinson of Kentucky, James Mead of New York, John McCormack of Massachusetts — abandoned the President. However, the conservative Democrats, led by John McDuffie of Alabama, maintained parliamentary control; and, with the expert assistance of an economy-minded Republican, John Taber of New York, McDuffie was able to get the bill through the House on Saturday by a vote of 266–138, two days after the banking bill, one week after the inauguration.

The second Sunday of the Roosevelt administration was no day of rest for the President. Over supper at the White House Roosevelt remarked, "I think this would be a good time for beer." Louis Howe produced a copy of the Democratic platform; and, late in the evening, Roosevelt wrote a brief message based on the platform calling for the modification of the Volstead Act in order to legalize beer and light wines. On Monday the 13th, Congress received the new message; on the same day, the economy bill passed its first test in the Senate. On Tuesday the House, ignoring the Anti-Saloon League and the Women's Christian Temperance Union, voted for 3.2 beer. On Wednesday the Senate voted 62 to 13 for economy and on Thursday 43 to 30 for beer: the two most powerful lobbies in Washington — the veterans and the prohibitionists — were now in rout. A Treasury bond issue on March 13 was oversubscribed in a single day. On the 15th, the securities markets, closed during the bank holiday, reopened in a bullish mood. In the meantime, banks were reopening, and deposits were exceeding withdrawals. The acute panic was evidently at an end.[6]

VII

And the President during these days spoke not only to Congress. He also addressed himself directly to the people. The day before Congress convened, he held his first presidential press conference. Over a hundred skeptical reporters crowded into the executive office. They found, not the dour irritability to which White House correspondents were accustomed, but a gay and apparently open friendliness. The President hoped, he told the press, that these meetings could be enlarged additions of the "very delightful family conferences I have been holding in Albany." "No more written questions," he said; no more "presidential spokesmen." Instead he proposed a free exchange between the Executive and the newsmen, to be made the more effective by defining some information as "background," not for attribution to the White House, and by putting other remarks "off the record" entirely. "I am told that what I am about to do will become impossible," Roosevelt said, " but I am going to try it." As he launched into a frank discussion of the banking crisis, his enjoyment of the give-and-take with the press was obvious. When the conference ended, the newspapermen broke into spontaneous applause.

On Sunday evening, March 12, at the conclusion of the first week, Roosevelt made even more direct contact with the nation in the first of what came to be called his "fireside chats." His purpose was to reassure people that their savings in closed banks were secure. Charles Michelson wrote a draft, which he submitted for technical vetting to Ballantine and others in the Treasury. Then he gave it to Roosevelt, who read it over, "lay on a couch" (in Michelson's words) "and dictated his own speech." With Grace Tully taking his words down, the President looked at the blank wall, trying to visualize the individuals he was seeking to help: a mason at work on a new building, a girl behind a counter, a man repairing an automobile, a farmer in his field, all of them saying, "Our money is in the Poughkeepsie bank, and what is this all about?" In plain language Roosevelt analyzed the banking crisis and forecast the steps which lay ahead. "Let us unite in banishing fear," he concluded. ". . . It is your problem no less than it is mine. Together we cannot fail." The President took a complicated subject like banking, said Will Rogers, and made everybody understand it, even the bankers.

The fireside chat was the climax of a week of resurgent hope. "America hasn't been so happy in three years as they are today, no banks, no work, no nothing." Again it was Will Rogers, reviewing the first week. ". . . They know they got a man in there who is wise to Congress, wise to our so-called big men. The whole country is with him, just so he does something. If he burned down the capitol we would cheer and say 'well, we at least got a fire started anyhow.' We have had years of 'Don't rock the boat,' go and sink if you want to, we just as well be swimming as like we are."

Even conservatives joined in the applause. After all, Roosevelt had saved the old banking system, cut government spending, struck at prohibition, and displayed no evidence of radicalism. Henry L. Stimson, Hoover's Secretary of State, who had heard the inaugural address with much suspicion, now wrote the President, "I am delighted with the progress of your first week and send you my heartiest congratulations." William Randolph Hearst said, "I guess at your next election we will make it unanimous." Hamilton Fish proudly pronounced the new regime "an American dictatorship based on the consent of the governed without any violation of individual liberty or human rights." Newton D. Baker described Roosevelt as "a providential person at a providential moment." Cardinal O'Connell called him "a God-sent man."

The sense of motion in a capital too long sunk in apathy and gloom was reawakening the nation. "At the beginning of March," as Walter Lippmann summed it up, "the country was in such a state of confused desperation that it would have followed almost any leader anywhere he chose to go. . . . In one week, the nation, which had lost confidence in everything and everybody, has regained confidence in the government and in itself." [7]

VIII

Above all, the presidential mansion itself embodied the new
spirit. Colonel Starling, head of the President's Secret Service detail, took the Hoovers to the railroad station on Inauguration
Day. When he returned a few hours later, he found the White
House, he said, "transformed during my absence into a gay place,
full of people who oozed confidence." Rudolph Forster, the digni-
fied and self-contained Executive Clerk who had served every President since McKinley, later said, "I would not have believed that
twenty-four hours could make the difference that those did when
the last people moved out of here and these new ones moved in."
Where once glumness and formality had ruled, there was now a
mixture of levity and high seriousness, of solemnity and exhilara-
tion; the public business went on, but one seemed to hear in the
distance barking dogs and voices of children. "There is no more
resemblance between the citadel of aloofness which Mr. Hoover
built," wrote a *New York Times* reporter, "and the friendly, welcoming air of the Executive Offices now than there would be between a formal embassy tea and old-home week at Hyde Park."
"The President reigned," wrote Tugwell, "in an informal splendor
which shed its glow over all Washington."

The day before inauguration, Roosevelt, making a ceremonial
visit at the White House, had suggested that the outgoing President need not return his call. Hoover had coldly replied, "Mr.
Roosevelt, when you are in Washington as long as I have been, you
will learn that the President of the United States calls on nobody."
But Hoover's Washington vanished in the new informality. Only
five days after Hoover made his remark, Felix Frankfurter reminded Roosevelt that it was Oliver Wendell Holmes's ninety-
second birthday. Before March 8 was over, the President had taken
enough time from the banking crisis to negotiate the steep stairs
at I Street and pay his personal respects. "We face grave times,"
Roosevelt said to the old Justice. "What is your advice?" The Civil
War veteran replied without hesitation: "Form your ranks and
fight!" ("A second-class intellect," Holmes said of Roosevelt
later, " — but a first-class temperament!")

An even more striking contrast with his predecessor came in May when a second installment of the Bonus Expeditionary Force descended on Washington. The Roosevelt tactic, instant and instinctive, was to kill by kindness. Instead of the shacks at Anacostia and the hostility of police and Army, Roosevelt offered the veterans an Army camp, three meals a day, endless supplies of coffee, and a large convention tent, where the leaders could orate to their hearts' content. The Navy Band played for the veterans; Army doctors ministered to their ills; dentists pulled their teeth; the President conferred with their leaders; and, as a climax, Mrs. Roosevelt and Louis Howe drove out one rainy spring day in a blue convertible. While Howe dozed in the car, Mrs. Roosevelt walked through ankle-deep mud and led the vets in singing "There's a long, long trail a-winding." "Hoover sent the Army," said one veteran; "Roosevelt sent his wife." In two weeks, most of the veterans went affably into the Civilian Conservation Corps, and the Second B.E.F. had met a painless Waterloo.

The White House staff, composed of old friends, heightened the atmosphere of informality and high spirits. Louis Howe, shrewish and sardonic, his clothes more rumpled than ever, was chief secretary. Two other veterans of the 1920 campaign — the hard-boiled and efficient Steve Early and gentle Marvin McIntyre — handled press relations and appointments. Marguerite LeHand and Grace Tully headed his stenographic corps. As for the President, the pattern of his day was soon set: breakfast in bed; a quick skimming of half a dozen morning newspapers; then a nine o'clock bedside conference to discuss the day's urgencies. Howe and the other secretaries would lead off; but the most influential men on policy questions at this period were Moley and Douglas.

Then the day widened out into a vast variety of appointments, conferences, phone calls, letters read and answered, memoranda studied, decisions made, accomplishments miraculously pulled out of chaos. Only the sense of pressure remained constant. Small groups of men, their mandates vague, their lines of authority obscure, their composition often accidental, even their office space insecure and fluctuating, drafted, tore up, redrafted, wrangled over proposed bills, and worked until dawn in silent government buildings or in cramped Georgetown houses.

Somehow Roosevelt kept all the reins in his hand. He seemed

to thrive on crisis. Reporters took from his press conferences images of urbane mastery, with the President sitting easily behind his desk, his great head thrown back, his smile flashing or his laugh booming out in the pleasure of thrust and riposte. He saw agitated congressmen, panicky businessmen, jealous bureaucrats; he kidded the solemn, soothed the egotistical, and inspired the downhearted. There remained too a sense of ambiguity and craftiness. He could be hard and frightening when he wanted to be, and he played the political game with cold skill. Charm, humor, power, persuasion, menace, idealism — all were weapons in his armory.[8]

IX

The first explosive week, which saw the Emergency Banking Act, the economy drive, the attack on prohibition, and the dramatic display of presidential leadership, was only the beginning. As yet, Roosevelt had done nothing to carry out the New Deal he had proclaimed during the campaign. On Thursday, March 16, the administration took a new turn. On that day Roosevelt sent Congress a message calling for the national planning of agriculture. This was the first of a series of proposals designed to reorganize one after another the basic aspects of American economic life. In the next weeks the New Deal proper began to unfold.

And, with the New Deal came the New Dealers. The old capital did not know what to make of the invasion. "A plague of young lawyers settled on Washington," wrote George Peek, the veteran farm leader, sourly. "They all claimed to be friends of somebody or other and mostly of Felix Frankfurter and Jerome Frank. They floated airily into offices, took desks, asked for papers and found no end of things to be busy about. I never found out why they came, what they did or why they left."

This was one view, and certainly the change was startling. Depression, by cutting off normal outlets in law practice or in the universities, had made men of intellectual ability available as never before; and government had never been so eager to hire them. Like circles beyond circles, both the legal network and the academic network were limitless. With each prominent New Dealer acting as his own employment agency, Washington was deluged with an endless stream of bright young men. "If ability could be measured in a tin bucket," Willard Kiplinger wrote in the journal of the United States Chamber of Commerce in 1934, "I should say that the Roosevelt administration contained more gallons of ability than any of its recent predecessors." They brought with them an alertness, an excitement, an appetite for power, an instinct for crisis and a dedication to public service which became during the thirties the essence of Washington. "No group in government," said Arthur Krock, "has ever been more interesting, dull, brilliant, stupid, headstrong, pliable, competent, inefficient; more honorable in money matters, more ruthless in material methods." Their *élan*, their bravado, their sense of adventure, their cocky assurance, their inexhaustible activism were infectious. They often were irritating, but they always were alive. "The Filii Aurorae make me actively sick at my stomach," Judge Learned Hand said early in 1934; "they are so conceited, so insensitive, so arrogant. But on the whole the Old Tories are intellectually so moribund . . . so stupid and emit such dreary, hollow sounds."

The sounds of the New Dealers were rarely dreary or hollow. They altered the whole tempo and tone of Washington as a community. The capital had never seemed so much like a real city; at last, said Anne O'Hare McCormick, it had been annexed to the United States. "They have transformed it," Ray Tucker reported in *Collier's*, "from a placid, leisurely Southern town, with frozen faces and customs, into a gay, breezy, sophisticated and metropolitan center." Everything was now lively and informal. "In times of relaxation," said Krock, "they are a merry group, the New Dealers. They like singing and dancing and a fair amount of drinking. They are hearty eaters and colossal workers." Above all, they talked. Henry James had called Washington "the City of Conversation" a quarter-century before — "one of the most thorough, even if probably one of the most natural and of the happiest cases of collective self-consciousness that one knows." But never had the city conversed so fiercely, so hilariously and so recklessly. "All the members of the brain trust," a veteran State Department official noted in his diary with admiration, "have got an exceptional fluency in self-expression. . . . One and all can present a case with the utmost convincingness." "The common characteristic of all up-lifters," said Peek, "is an unquenchable thirst for conversation. They were all chain talkers." Chat after dinner no longer consisted of tedious anecdotes about quail shooting and golf. Instead, it dealt in issues and ideas and went on till early in the morning. "It's exciting and educational," said Ray Tucker, "to be alive and asked out in Washington these days."

Who were the New Dealers? They represented all classes — from the wellborn, like Franklin Roosevelt, Averell Harriman, Francis Biddle, to the sons of poverty, like Harry Hopkins — but they were predominantly middle class. They represented a variety of occupations; but they were mostly lawyers, college professors, economists, or social workers. They came from all parts of the land and from both city and country, though most of them had been educated in state universities or in Ivy League colleges, and many had their first political experience in the fight for decent city government. They were all ages, though most of them were born between 1895 and 1905. But the common bond which held them together, as Herman Kahn has acutely noted, was that they were all at home in the world of ideas. They were accustomed to analy-sis and dialectic; and they were prepared to use intelligence as an instrument of government. They were more than specialists. As Kahn has further pointed out, they were — or considered them-selves — generalists, capable of bringing logic to bear on any social problem. They delighted in the play of the free mind.

They were by no means of a single school. Indeed, they repre-sented divergent and often clashing philosophies. The laissez-faire liberalism of the Democratic party, dedicated, in the tradi-tion of Grover Cleveland, to sound money, fiscal orthodoxy, and tariff reduction, found its voices in Lewis Douglas and Cordell Hull and its first victory in the Economy Act. The agrarian tradition, stronger in the Congress than in the administration, harking back to William Jennings Bryan and demanding monetary inflation as a means of turning the terms of trade more favorably to the farmer, soon expressed itself in the Thomas amendment to the Agricultural Adjustment Act and in the devaluation policy. The trust-busting liberalism of the Brandeis-Wilson school, seeking to liberate the economy from business bigness, spoke especially through Professor Felix Frankfurter of Harvard and shortly achieved the Securities and Glass-Steagall Acts. And to these traditional Democratic strains there was now added an infusion of the Theodore Roosevelt-Herbert Croly Progressivism of 1912, finding advocates from Raymond Moley on the right to Rexford Tugwell on the left, and seeking to counter the anarchy of competition by government-business collaboration.

What Roosevelt gave the New Dealers was an opportunity to put ideas to work. Motives, of course, were mixed. For some, it was a job, or a passing enthusiasm, or a road to personal power. But for the best of them, the satisfaction lay, as Francis Biddle once put it,

> in some deep sense of giving and sharing, far below any surface pleasure of work well done, but rooted in the relief of escaping the loneliness and boredom of oneself, and the unreality of personal ambition. The satisfaction derived from sinking individual effort into the community itself, the common goal and the common end. This is no escape from self; it is the realization of self.

They often suffered frustration and disillusion. They worked to the edge of collapse. They had moments when they hated Washington and government and Roosevelt. Yet for most of them this was the happiest time and the deepest fulfillment they would ever know. "It was one of the most joyous periods in my life," wrote Thomas L. Stokes as a newspaperman covering Roosevelt's arrival in Washington. "We came alive, we were eager." It was, said Tugwell in retrospect, a "renaissance spring" when men were filled with courage beyond natural instincts, with hopes beyond reasonable expectation, with a belief in human possibility which it would take a good deal of betrayal to break down — "a time of rebirth after a dark age." The memories would not soon fade — the interminable meetings, the litter of cigarette stubs, the hasty sandwich at the desk or (if there was time) the lazy lunch along sun-drenched wharves by the Potomac, the ominous rumor passed on with relish, the call from the White House, the postponed dinner, the neglected wife, the office lights burning into the night, the lilacs hanging in fragrance above Georgetown gardens while men rebuilt the nation over long drinks, the selflessness, the vanity, the mistakes, the achievement. At his worst, the New Dealer became an arrant sentimentalist or a cynical operator. At his best, he was the ablest, most intelligent, and most disinterested public servant the United States ever had.[9]

X

In the three months after Roosevelt's inauguration, Congress and the country were subjected to a presidential barrage of ideas and programs unlike anything known to American history. On adjournment on June 15, 1933, the President and the exhausted 73rd Congress left the following record:

March   9 — the Emergency Banking Act

March 20 — the Economy Act

March 31 — establishment of the Civilian Conservation Corps

April 19 — abandonment of the gold standard

May 12   — the Federal Emergency Relief Act, setting up a national relief system

May 12   — the Agricultural Adjustment Act, establishing a national agricultural policy, with the Thomas amendment conferring on the President powers of monetary expansion

May 12   — the Emergency Farm Mortgage Act, providing for the refinancing of farm mortgages

May 18   — the Tennessee Valley Authority Act, providing for the unified development of the Tennessee Valley

May 27   — the Truth-in-Securities Act, requiring full disclosure in the issue of new securities

June 5   — the abrogation of the gold clause in public and private contracts

June 13 — the Home Owners' Loan Act, providing for the refinancing of home mortgages

June 16 — the National Industrial Recovery Act, providing both for a system of industrial self-government under federal supervision and for a $3.3 billion public works program

June 16 — the Glass-Steagall Banking Act, divorcing commercial and investment banking and guaranteeing bank deposits

June 16 — the Farm Credit Act, providing for the reorganization of agricultural credit activities

June 16 — the Railroad Coordination Act, setting up a federal Coordinator of Transportation.

This was the Hundred Days; and in this period Franklin Roosevelt sent fifteen messages to Congress, guided fifteen major laws to enactment, delivered ten speeches, held press conferences and cabinet meetings twice a week, conducted talks with foreign heads of state, sponsored an international conference, made all the major decisions in domestic and foreign policy, and never displayed fright or panic and rarely even bad temper. His mastery astonished many who thought they had long since taken his measure. Norman Davis, encountering Raymond Fosdick outside the presidential office, expressed the incredulity of those who had worked with him during the Wilson administration: "Ray, that fellow in there is not the fellow we used to know. There's been a miracle here." "Many of us who have known him long and well," wrote Oswald Garrison Villard, the editor of the *Nation,* "ask ourselves if this is the same man."

Roosevelt had moved into the White House as if he were repossessing a family estate. He now spoke for and to the nation with dignity and ease and evident enjoyment. "The truth is," Tugwell noted in his diary, "F.D. really loves the appurtenances of the job. He savors completely the romance and significance of each experience. He works hard and honestly, though, and I am glad he does get such a kick out of it." The combination of power and delight was irresistible to people used to neither in the White

House; it gave Americans new confidence in themselves. Roosevelt pressed home the recovery of morale. "When Andrew Jackson, 'Old Hickory,' died," he said in July, "someone asked, 'will he go to Heaven?' and the answer was, 'He will if he wants to.' If I am asked whether the American people will pull themselves out of this depression, I answer, 'They will if they want to.' "

Before March 4, America was in a state of extreme shock. No one would ever know, General Hugh S. Johnson later said, "how close were we to collapse and revolution. We could have got a dictator a lot easier than Germany got Hitler." "I do not think it is too much to say," wrote Tugwell, "that on March 4 we were confronted with a choice between an orderly revolution — a peaceful and rapid departure from past concepts — and a violent and disorderly overthrow of the whole capitalist structure." "At the end of February," wrote Walter Lippmann, "we were a congeries of disorderly panic-stricken mobs and factions. In the hundred days from March to June we became again an organized nation confident of our power to provide for our own security and to control our own destiny."

By bringing to Washington a government determined to *govern*, Roosevelt unlocked new energies in a people who had lost faith, not just in government's ability to meet the economic crisis, but almost in the ability of anyone to do anything. The feeling of movement was irresistible. Washington, Arthur Krock reported, was experiencing the sensation of a man traveling on a life-and-death errand thousands of miles away who suddenly found himself switched from an ox cart to an airplane. "Never was there such a change in the transfer of government." Justice Harlan Stone of the Supreme Court wrote his old friend Herbert Hoover two months after the shift in administration, "To judge by the rapidity of changing events, as many decades might have passed." And there could be no question, Krock added, who was responsible: "The President is the boss, the dynamo, the works."

For a deceptive moment in 1933, clouds of inertia and selfishness seemed to lift. A despairing land had a vision of America as it might some day be. "For the first time since we can remember," said Frances Perkins, "we are trying to be a unified people." Anne O'Hare McCormick described the response as "the rising of a nation." "It's more than a New Deal," said Harold Ickes. "It's a new world. People feel free again. They can breathe naturally. It's like quitting a morgue for the open woods." "We have had our revolution," said *Collier's,* "and we like it." The clouds would come back, as they always had through the long travail of history. But, in this moment of clarity, the American people threw off a sick conviction of defeat and began to believe in themselves again. And, as they did, they rekindled hope elsewhere in the world. "The courage, the power and the scale of [Roosevelt's] effort," wrote an English observer, "must enlist the ardent sympathy of every country, and his success could not fail to lift the whole world forward into the sunlight of an easier and more genial age." Like Roosevelt himself, the Englishman saw the effort in the long perspective of history. "For in truth," said Winston Churchill, "Roosevelt is an explorer who has embarked on a voyage as uncertain as that of Columbus, and upon a quest which might conceivably be as important as the discovery of the New World." [10]

I

The Fight for
Agricultural Balance

2. Emergence of a Farm Policy

THE FIRST BUSINESS of the Hundred Days had been the banks. But another problem lay urgently on Roosevelt's mind that March: this was the problem of the farmers. No group in the population, except perhaps the Negro workers, was more badly hit by depression. The realized net income of farm operators in 1932 was less than one-third what it had been in 1929 — a dizzying collapse in three years. Farm prices had fallen more than 50 per cent; and the parity ratio — the ratio of prices received by farmers to the prices they paid — had plummeted from 89 in 1929 down to 55 in 1932 (in terms of 1910–14 as 100). The seething violence in the farm belt over the winter — the grim mobs gathered to stop foreclosures, the pickets along the highways to prevent produce from being moved to town — made it clear that patience was running out. In January 1933, Edward A. O'Neal, the head of the Farm Bureau Federation, warned a Senate committee: "Unless something is done for the American farmer we will have revolution in the countryside within less than twelve months."

Roosevelt knew this. And he knew too that there was little chance of general recovery so long as so large a part of the population had lost its buying power. "That's the fellow you've got to build up," he told visitors, "the farmer." In the expiring lame-duck session of President Hoover's Congress, Roosevelt had accordingly instructed his supporters to give new agricultural legislation priority. Hope of action had perished in the legislative acrimonies of January and February, but the special session still offered a new chance to do something before spring planting. On March 8,

1933, when Henry Wallace and Rex Tugwell, his new Secretary and Assistant Secretary of Agriculture, urged Roosevelt to hold Congress long enough to pass a new farm program, they found a receptive listener.[1]

II

Henry Agard Wallace, looking younger than his forty-five years, was beginning his first large administrative job. But he could hardly be said to be facing a new challenge; like Roosevelt entering the White House, Wallace must have felt in a sense that he was coming home when he entered the Department of Agriculture. He sat in the same room his father had occupied as Secretary under a Republican administration a decade before. One of the first things he did was to bring the elder Wallace's portrait out of exile and hang it on the oak-paneled wall opposite his desk. Family piety was deep in the Wallaces; it carried young Henry back perhaps even more intimately to his grandfather, still another Henry Wallace, who might have been Secretary too under McKinley and again under Taft, but who preferred life as editor of *Wallace's Farmer* and as an elder statesman of the middle border.

The Wallace heritage was one of devotion to the soil and to those who labored on it. All this was bred into young Henry Wallace — the smell of damp earth in the spring, the green spears of corn breaking through the black ground, the golden blaze of an Iowa cornfield in autumn — all this, and also the monotony and hardship of the farmer's condition, and the interminable struggle against the inscrutable mercies of markets beyond his control. The editorial sanctum of *Wallace's Farmer* could not escape being, in part, a farmer's wailing wall; and the shy, serious, hard-working youth was reared in an atmosphere vivid with a sense of the glories and the grievances of agricultural life.

From an early age he applied himself to both the science and the economics of farming. As a boy, he was taught to recognize stamens and pistils in grass flowers by a gangling Negro named George Washington Carver, who had shown up at the Iowa State Agricultural College at Ames. Before he went on to the State College himself, young Henry had begun to experiment in plant genetics and especially in the breeding of hybrid corn. By the time of the First World War he was accounted a remarkable plant geneticist, a competent agricultural statistician, a valued contributor to *Wallace's Farmer,* and a worthy heir of the Wallace tradition.

When Henry C. Wallace joined Harding's cabinet, young Henry — "H.A." — took over the paper. During the next decade he became an important figure in the agrarian uprising. His role was less central or dramatic than that of George Peek or Chester Davis; but he struck distinctive notes. One of his favorite themes was the improvement of agricultural productivity; another was the better utilization of land. He was especially concerned with leveling out the agricultural surplus through what he called, borrowing a phrase from Confucius, a "constantly normal" (later "ever normal") granary. And he was much interested in the changed international role of the United States as a consequence of its shift after the First World War from a debtor to a creditor nation.

What seemed the persecution of his father in Harding's cabinet soured young Henry on the Republicans, especially on Hoover, who as Secretary of Commerce had appeared the particular foe both of the older Wallace and of all projects to improve farm prices. In 1928 H.A. abandoned his family's party to support Al Smith. And in 1932, when Rex Tugwell introduced him into the Roosevelt circle, the intense idealism which lay beneath Wallace's diffidence impressed the President-elect. So this solidly built man, two inches under six feet in height, his hair rumpled, his mouth sensitive and almost tremulous, his blue gray eyes some times alive with interest or passion, sometimes glazed and wandering, his manner occasionally warm and cordial, often absent and preoccupied, now rather surprisingly sat in Franklin Roosevelt's cabinet.

III

The concrete and utilitarian mingled in Wallace with much that was vague and dreamy. His interest in crop genetics, in agricultural prices, in banking and credit were the expression of a practical and exact intellectual curiosity. Yet, at a certain point, his mind seemed almost to break through a sonic barrier and transform itself, so that hardheaded analysis passed imperceptibly into rhapsodic mysticism.

Underneath the passion for science and statistics, Wallace was deeply religious. "You must not expect to be a really big man," his grandfather once told him, "unless you live a sincere, earnest religious life. . . . We are really in a great big world, the servants of a God who is infinitely bigger than we can possibly comprehend." Wallace felt the divine presence, immanent as well as transcendent. Once, attending a Roman Catholic service, he had a sudden impulse to cross himself, genuflect and kneel in silent adoration. In the end, unable either to go to Rome or to accept the austerities of Iowa Presbyterianism, he struck a compromise in High Church Episcopalianism. For a time, be became an acolyte and, donning cassock and surplice, assisted at the eight o'clock mass.

This sense of closeness to what he called "that blissful unmanifested reality which we call God" gave him his mission in life. Nothing moved him more than the Old Testament prophets. The vision of Micah was forever in his mind, when swords were beaten into plowshares and spears into pruninghooks, when nations no longer warred against nations, and every man sat under his vine and his fig tree, and none made them afraid. Nor had he any doubt where the prophets would have stood on contemporary issues. "It happens, fortunately it seems to me," he once said, not altogether humorously, "that the Biblical record is heavily loaded on the side of the Progressive Independents." Micah and Jeremiah, Elijah and Amos were almost as real to him as Senator Norris; he cited their views as he might those of elder liberal statesmen with whom he lunched the day before.

If it was, as he said, a time for prophets, "for their passionate thunderings, their intense longings, their visions of ultimate purposes," Wallace fell easily into the prophetic stance himself. He lived an ascetic life, rising at dawn, walking two and a half miles through Rock Creek Park to work, exercising with violence, denying himself tobacco, liquor, and, for periods, meat, and at times committing himself to revolting diets of rutabagas, soybeans, or cottonseed meal. He felt a sense of impending religious revival; the hour was approaching, he believed, for "great spiritual changes in the United States . . . of lasting significance not only to this country, but to the whole world." Such a spiritual reawakening would offer mankind the moral unity of early Christianity or of the Middle Ages — men and women joined together everywhere ("the world is one world," he wrote in 1934) in a common passion for social justice.[2]

IV

Wallace's search for unity through religion soon carried him beyond the bounds of Christian orthodoxy. Like Ralph Waldo Trine, whose works greatly influenced him, he sought to be in tune with the infinite. The occult fascinated him. He saw special significance in the Great Seal of the United States, with its phrase *E Pluribus Unum* and its conception of unity out of diversity; even more in the reverse of the Seal — the incomplete pyramid, with its thirteen levels of stone and the apex suspended above in the form of an all-seeing eye, surrounded by the inscription *Annuit Cœptis . . . Novus Ordo Seclorum.* "Those who are devout believers in the prophecies of the Bible and who also have great depth of feeling concerning the founding and destiny of this country," Wallace once wrote, might well wonder whether the reverse of the Great Seal did not prefigure the Second Coming of the Messiah. Though he remained noncommittal about the extent of his own belief, Wallace did induce the Secretary of the Treasury to put the Great Pyramid on the new dollar bill in 1935. He sold this to Secretary Morgenthau on the prosaic ground that *Novus Ordo* was Latin for New Deal, and for years afterward Morgenthau was beset by people who assumed that the appearance of the Great Pyramid on the currency signified his own attachment to some esoteric fellowship.

His susceptibility to the occult had drawn Wallace in the late twenties into the orbit of a White Russian mystic in the tradition of Blavatsky named Dr. Nicholas Roerich. A painter and an associate of the Moscow Art Theater and the Diaghilev Ballet, a friend of Stravinsky and of Rabindranath Tagore, this small, bald man, with his soft voice and white beard, billing himself as the exclusive representative of the White Brotherhood of the East, spun out before adoring disciples ideas about the essential oneness underlying all diversity. Wallace occasionally called on him at the Roerich Museum on Riverside Drive in New York. The friendship continued after Wallace went to Washington. Roerich had long striven for an international pact under which nations in case of war would pledge themselves to refrain from destroying cultural treasures marked by a Banner of Peace. Sponsors of this laudable project included such non-mystics as Senator Pat McCarran of Nevada, Governor Eugene Talmadge of Georgia, Governor Floyd Olson of Minnesota, and James M. Beck. "I believe so profoundly in things for which the Banner of Peace stands," Wallace told Roerich, "that I am only too happy to offer you any cooperation in my personal capacity to help make your efforts along this line successful." He particularly admired the Banner itself with its three spheres, symbolic of the Trinity, enclosed within a larger circle. "This design," Wallace wrote in his book *New Frontiers,* "has great depths of meaning." The "imagined circle of unifying freedom" represented for him the realization of individual diversity within the limitations of the whole.

"Just why Wallace has been so interested and why he has pressed Mr. Hull so hard," one State Department official wrote in his diary, "remains a matter of mystery." Wallace's insistence in time resulted in the signing of the Roerich Pact by twenty-two nations at the White House in April 1935. In the meantime, he found private solace in a strange and protracted correspondence with Roerich and certain of his disciples. The letters, some addressing Roerich as "Dear Guru," contained cabalistic references to "the Flaming One" or "the Wavering One" or "the Mediocre One," by which he seems to have meant Roosevelt, "the Sour One" (Cordell Hull), "the Dark Ones" or "the Tigers" (the Soviet Union), and mystic allusions to the chalice with the flame above it and to the descent of America into the depths of purifying fires. On one occasion, Wallace even rashly wrote Roosevelt in language derived from Arthur Hopkins's *The Glory Road* as well as from Roerich, that, while they stood on the verge of a New Era,

I feel for a short time yet, that we must deal with the "strong ones," the "turbulent ones," the "fervent ones," and perhaps even with a temporary resurgence, with the "flameless ones" who with one last dying gasp will strive to re-animate their dying giant "Capitalism."

Mr. President, you can be the "flaming one," the one with an ever upward-surging spirit to lead us into the time when the children of men can sing again. But I feel, Mr. President, that the perils concerning which I spoke to you last Wednesday must be successfully passed before we can enter safely into the time of the infinite unselfish expansion of the spirit.

The "perils" of last Wednesday had been the possibility of the recognition of Russia, which Wallace, perhaps influenced by Roerich's White Russian passions, sternly opposed. It is not clear whether Wallace and Roerich had already begun to discuss an expedition to the Gobi Desert, ostensibly in search of drought-resistant grass but perhaps also to carry on anti-Soviet intrigues or even to seek out indications of the Second Coming. In any case, Roerich did leave the country the next year on such a mission from the Department of Agriculture. He never returned.

Roosevelt, who could not make head or tail of these moods of rapture, dismissed Wallace amiably in this aspect as "a kind of mystic" and preferred to talk with him about crops, land, and water, on which his information was firm and his analysis substantial. And it is hard, indeed, to evaluate the nature of Wallace's interest in the Roerich cult. Wallace was, in Westbrook Pegler's phrase, a "spiritual window-shopper," moved both by the experimental curiosity which interested a William James in psychical research and by the prairie mysticism which led so many of his fellow Iowans into weird sects when they retired to California. Without fully believing it all, he probably found release (or refuge) in Roerich's theosophical potpourri as other men might in sex or liquor.

What particularly appealed to him, perhaps, was the hope that the vision of spiritual unity might enable him to join together the two halves of his own personality. For, as both scientist and mystic, both politician and prophet, both opportunist and idealist, Wallace was split down the middle. This interior division produced not creative tension but a wavering and tormented dissociation which he sought constantly to exorcise by mysticism or to bridge by rhetoric. When contradictions existed, in himself or in the world, they could always be resolved, he appeared to feel, by higher — which ordinarily meant foggier — formulations. "It seems to me," he once wrote in a characteristically hortatory moment, "that it should be a fundamental objective with all of us to discover constructive formulae that will unify our efforts instead of critical formulae which tend to split us among ourselves."

But neither mysticism nor rhetoric could abolish the fissure, the emptiness, at the core of his own personality. He rarely made contact with others, perhaps because it was so hard for him to make contact with himself. His associates speculated whether he had any capacity for human affection. At times it seemed as if he had a greater sense of intimacy with plants ("The Strength and the Quietness of Grass" was the title of a radio talk he gave as Secretary of Agriculture). And in his public life his inner division led to evasiveness and vacillation. Confronted by choice, he was always inclined to cut things in half and split the difference, mistaking eclecticism for synthesis. The quest for personal integration consumed him. It led him down strange byways in both religion and politics. In the end, neither yogis nor commissars would produce a satisfactory answer.[3]

v

Wallace was an awkward figure in Washington — no airs, no polish, no small talk, no wit, no front; as Sherwood Anderson summed it up, "no swank." Before inauguration, Tugwell had taken him to Saks Fifth Avenue to make sure that he would at least dress like a cabinet officer; but an obstinately rustic air lingered on. He remained out of place in the smart apartment at the Wardman Park, where his father had lived before him; ill at ease at capital cocktail parties or official dinners; uncomfortable even in his own office, where, unable to get used to buzzing for secretaries, he walked to the door and called them. In conference, he would sit slumped in his chair, eyes half closed, vest unbuttoned, feet propped on the wastebasket, head resting on hand. Sometimes he disconcerted people by the apparent vacancy of his gaze or by his nervous grin and giggle. "He gives me an eerie feeling that he really isn't listening when I talk with him," said one of his writers. Before an audience, he was often fumbling and obscure. An old-time politician observed, "Henry's the sort that keeps you guessing as to whether he's going to deliver a sermon or wet the bed."

But talking agriculture, Wallace could be exceedingly crisp, hard-hitting, and impressive. For all his turmoil within and his vagaries without, the fact remained that few Americans in 1933 were so steeped in the agricultural crisis, or had brooded over it so thoughtfully, or brought to it such acute and informed judgment. To his genuine knowledge Wallace added a shyness and modesty which won the protective adoration of his subordinates and the respect of many of his colleagues. "He was the most cooperative of all Cabinet members," Donald Richberg later wrote. . . . He had less pride of opinion than any man meeting heavy responsibilities with whom I have had any dealings, and certainly no pride of position." His essential desire, it seemed, was to get the job done — to restore the farmers' position in the national economy.

"When former civilizations have fallen," Wallace said shortly after he assumed office, "there is a strong reason for believing that they fell because they could not achieve the necessary balance between city and country." This view, buttressed by his reading of Flinders Petrie and of Guglielmo Ferrero, lay at the bottom of Wallace's agricultural philosophy. In America, the city-country balance had been upset, as he saw it, by the economic vulnerability of agriculture. Businessmen, when confronted by reduced demand, could protect themselves by reducing output and maintaining price levels; farmers, when confronted by reduced demand, apparently had no choice but to maintain their individual output and watch prices collapse. "In agriculture," said Wallace succinctly, "supply sets the price. In industry, price sets the supply."

Since the war, agriculture had been dealt two grave blows — first by the disappearance of foreign markets in the twenties, then by the depression. Given the inflexibility of industrial prices, agriculture had had to bear the brunt of the price readjustments since 1929, and this process had only accentuated the imbalance. "The price structure we have let grow here," Wallace once put it in a striking phrase, "is half of steel and half of putty." The result was that the farmer's dollar, based on wheat, corn, hogs, and cotton, bought only half as many city products as it used to, while the city dollar, based on gold, bought more farm products than before.

If the balance were to be re-established, it would require, by this analysis, the increase of prices and reduction of output in the flexible-price sector, and the reduction of prices and increase of output in the rigid-price sector. Four main steps seemed urgent — the reduction of crop acreage through the domestic allotment plan; the scaling down and refinancing of farm indebtedness; the expansion of the means of payment through what Wallace frankly termed "controlled inflation" — whether by devaluing the dollar or, as proposed by Dr. George F. Warren of Cornell, by increasing the price of gold; and the search for new foreign markets by means of reciprocal trade agreements.[4]

VI

Of these measures, the most pressing, as Wallace viewed the problem in March 1933, was the domestic allotment plan. This plan, devised in 1929, proposed in effect to offer the farmer a price subsidy in return for his tacit agreement to limit output. For some time, farm leaders, disliking production control, had resisted the plan. But depression eroded old prejudices. By 1932 most farm leaders, including Ed O'Neal and the powerful Farm Bureau, were ready to accept the need for a direct attack on surpluses. In considerable part this change was due to a professor at Montana State College named M. L. Wilson.

Wilson was a man of varied agricultural experience — as a student at Ames (where he had known young Henry Wallace) ; as a homesteader in Montana before the First World War; as head of the Division of Farm Management in the Department of Agriculture in the twenties; and as one of those who, along with John D. Black and Beardsley Ruml, had helped develop the domestic allotment plan just before the crash. He was a gentle, shaggy zealot, forty-eight years old, combining a farmer's passion for the soil with an ideologue's conviction that civilization rested on its agricultural base. The determination to save the republic by saving agriculture gave his advocacy of the new plan missionary zeal. Hardly able to afford Pullman fare or a two-dollar hotel room, Wilson traveled, corresponded, and spoke without rest through 1931 and 1932. An early convert was Henry I. Harriman, president of the

United States Chamber of Commerce, who owned hundreds of thousands of acres of ranch land in Montana and saw in domestic allotment the agricultural counterpart of his own project for central industrial planning. And there were others: Henry Wallace, who told Wilson in 1932 that the plan would work if the country was headed toward state socialism, adding that that was just where the country seemed to be headed; Mordecai Ezekiel, who had served in the Department since the Harding administration and was now arguing for domestic allotment within the Farm Board; Rex Tugwell, who, in a manner of speaking, sold the idea to Roosevelt just before the Chicago convention; and the Farm Bureau leaders.

In the spring of 1932, two agrarian Republicans, Clifford Hope of Kansas and Peter Norbeck of South Dakota, introduced a domestic allotment bill in Congress. Wilson, who had worked on the bill along with Black and Ezekiel, testified for it before congressional committees, and pleaded on its behalf before farmers' groups. By now, the plan had changed somewhat from Black's original proposal. It focused on four major surplus crops — wheat, hogs, cotton, tobacco. Every farmer agreeing to regulate his production in accordance with the government plan would receive payments; noncooperating farmers would gain from the general price increase, but, if benefit payments were properly calculated, the cooperator would get a larger income from reducing production than the noncooperator would get from increasing it. Stanley Reed, counsel of the Federal Farm Board, had said that the plan would be unconstitutional unless based on the taxing power; and H. I. Harriman proposed that the government collect an excise tax at the first point of processing — the flour mill, the textile mill, the packing house — with the proceeds to be distributed among the cooperating farmers. The amount of the processing tax, in the earlier versions, was intended to be enough to make the tariff effective; in later versions the standard for fair returns to the farmer shifted to "parity" — that is, restoring to farm products their prewar power to command industrial goods in exchange. (Both the processing tax and the concept of parity grew out of McNary-Haugen ideas of an "equalization fee" and a "ratio price.")

In its operations — and on this point Wilson was particularly emphatic — the plan had to be decentralized and democratic. A large majority of the farmers involved in any commodity program would have to agree by referendum before it could go into effect, and day-to-day administration should be as much as possible on a county basis and in the hands of the farmers themselves. But although decentralized in administration, it was to be centralized in policy. The plan frankly envisaged the farmer as part of the national economy and assigned the federal government the decisive role in protecting farm income. "This plan," said Wilson in 1932, "applies to agriculture fundamental ideas of adjusting production to consumption, as exemplified in industry by the Swope plan and the plan of the United States Chamber of Commerce for stabilization and continuity in business." [5]

VII

As for the new President, his New York experience had given him clear-cut views about land-use planning; but he knew little at first hand about the problems of grain and cotton surpluses. During the campaign, in a speech at Topeka to which Ezekiel, Wilson, and Wallace contributed, he had laid down general specifications for a farm program which plainly implied the domestic allotment approach. In December 1932, when about forty farm representatives met with Morgenthau and Tugwell in Washington, it became apparent that opinion was flowing more powerfully than ever toward domestic allotment. While Wallace wholly sympathized with this, he also feared that commitment to a single method of farm relief would increase both political resistance and administrative inflexibility. So he proposed in March that the administration offer a bill which would authorize a variety of methods and leave the choice among them to the Secretary.

The farm leaders themselves, summoned to Washington by Wallace for a conference on March 16, had noted approvingly the broad delegations of authority in the banking bill. With government and farm organizations thus in independent agreement over the theory of the measure, the Washington meeting was, in the words of Clifford V. Gregory of the *Prairie Farmer*, "the most harmonious farm meeting I ever attended." In the next frantic days, Wallace, along with Ezekiel, Frederic P. Lee, one of the old agricultural pros, and Jerome Frank, a city lawyer, set out to draft the bill.

The essence of the bill, as they saw it, was "agricultural adjustment," by which they meant not simple curtailment of output but an attempt to achieve balance by shifting production out of surplus lines. Though domestic allotment, induced by benefit payments and financed by the processing tax, remained the core of the bill, a wide variety of other powers were proposed for the Secretary. Probably never in American history had so much social and legal inventiveness gone into a single legislative measure. There was the residue of McNary-Haugenism — the power to control the quantity of commodities released for sale through marketing agreements and quotas, and the power to stimulate exports through subsidies. And there were new devices — the power to reduce production through leasing farm land and withdrawing it from cultivation; the power to maintain prices through government loans on storable crops or through direct government purchase; the power to enforce compliance through the licensing of processors. The measure was, said Wallace, "a contrivance as new in the field of social relations as the first gasoline engine was new in the field of mechanics." For another quarter-century, agricultural policy came up with very little which was not provided for one way or another in the Agricultural Adjustment Act.

When Wallace and Tugwell took the bill over to the White House, they brought along a draft message to Congress. But Roosevelt, warming to the boldness of the new plan, had already scribbled his own message in longhand on a sheet of paper. His words were few, plain and cogent. "I tell you frankly," he warned the Congress, "that it is a new and untrod path, but I tell you with equal frankness that an unprecedented condition calls for the trial of new means." [6]

3. Organization of Agricultural Adjustment

THE AGRICULTURAL ADJUSTMENT BILL was essentially a leadership measure, devised by farm economists, sold by them to farm organization leaders, sold again by economists and farm leaders in combination to the President, but lacking any basis in public understanding. For the conservatives particularly, the bill was a rude shock. Suddenly perceiving in the proposals the planning heresies of Roosevelt's speeches before the Chicago convention, they awoke quickly from the complacency with which they had regarded the first week of the New Deal. "Seldom, if ever," exclaimed the New York *Herald Tribune*, "has so sweeping a piece of legislation been introduced in the American Congress." "The bill before the House," declared Representative Fred Britten of Illinois, "is more bolshevistic than any law or regulation existing in Soviet Russia." "We are on our way to Moscow," cried Representative Joseph W. Martin of Massachusetts. And the instinctive dislike among conservatives for any sort of government planning was compounded in this case by the very specific and fierce objections of canners, millers, and the food industry to the processing tax. In short order, the processors' lobbyists began to deploy around Capitol Hill.

And the farmers themselves, preoccupied with immediate problems of debt and mortgage, uneasy at the suggestion of curtailing their planting, could not quickly grasp the full implications of the complicated new proposals. Some of their spokesmen in Washington, moreover, continued to view the whole idea of agricultural adjustment with suspicion. Thus the Farmers' Union leaders, backed by some senators, including George Norris, demanded that government assure the farmer his cost of production — a standard which remained too elusive, however, to be of convincing practical use. More influential were the farm senators who advocated the time-honored solution of inflation. If the President wanted to play around with devices for agricultural adjustment, they were prepared to let him go ahead; but they did not want him to forget that the cheapening of the currency was, as they saw it, the sure way to lighten the dead weight of debt and to redress the unfavorable terms of trade between countryside and city.

In the House of Representatives, where debate could be limited, the administration succeeded in pushing through the agricultural adjustment bill without difficulty. But in the Senate inflationist sentiment could not be so easily contained. By now, at least three different techniques of inflation had acquired ardent supporters. Some inflationists, like Burton K. Wheeler of Montana and Huey Long of Louisiana, wanted, in the phrase of the day, to "do something" about silver. Others, like Tom Connally of Texas, favored general devaluation. Still others, like Elmer Thomas of Oklahoma, proposed, in a straightforward way, to enlarge the currency through the printing of paper money. All agreed in regarding the administration farm bill as fatally defective in its disregard of monetary remedies.

The demand for inflation evoked a wide response. Too many of the actions of March — especially the closing of the banks and the Economy Act — had been deflationary in their effect; the dollar was continuing to climb against the value of goods; and unemployment seemed still to be increasing. In the Senate the smooth and voluble Thomas was emerging as the head of the inflation bloc. A veteran of the free-silver fight of '96, he had incessantly urged inflationary remedies from the start of the depression. His theoretical analysis was rudimentary. Money, so far as he was concerned, was legal-tender currency and very little more; bank deposits he rejected as a fictitious substitute for money, acceptable in place of the real thing in times of financial confidence but of small consequence in depression. Therefore the way to revive the economy was to enlarge the legal currency: "We must have more money in circulation. I care not what kind — silver, copper, brass, gold or paper." Without inflation, he direfully predicted, even Wall Street would decay and its great edifices become "the abode of bats and owls." The choice, he said, lay between "reflation" — as the inflationists, perhaps under the influence of Amos 'n' Andy ("I'se regusted"), had disarmingly rebaptized their nostrum — and revolution. In this conviction, Thomas now combined the main inflationist techniques — silver, devaluation, and fiat money — into a single package and brought forward the Thomas amendment designed to be tacked on to the agricultural adjustment bill.

The administration watched the inflationist drive with alarm. On April 17, Wheeler's silver amendment came up for vote. In January, a similar amendment had received a mere 18 votes; this time, it received 33. Could the White House expect to sit on the lid much longer? After the defeat of the silver amendment, Elmer Thomas promptly introduced his omnibus amendment authorizing the President to issue greenbacks, to remonetize silver, and to alter the gold content of the dollar. It was apparent that the Thomas proposal would unite all inflationists and very likely command a majority of the Senate. Over the bitter opposition of his orthodox advisers, Roosevelt, preferring permissive inflationary legislation to mandatory, decided to accept a qualified version of the Thomas amendment in the hope of turning aside the inflationist drive.[1]

II

Already discontent was flaring in the farm belt. In mid-March the Farmers' Holiday Association, speaking through its chief, Milo Reno, had threatened a farm strike if Congress did not accept its demands by May 3. The Farmers' Holiday people denounced the domestic allotment scheme as "worse than silly." They wanted a guaranteed cost of production for farm products, mortgage relief, and, above all, inflation. Reno declared it "an undisputed fact that our trouble is not overproduction, but underconsumption, [brought about] by the monopolization and manipulation of our circulating medium." With the farm bill bogged down in the Senate, farmers began to take things into their own hands, as they had the previous autumn. They stopped eviction sales, denounced foreclosures, intimidated the agents of banks and insurance companies. On April 27 over five hundred farmers crowded the courtroom in Le Mars, Iowa, to demand that Judge Charles C. Bradley suspend foreclosure proceedings until the state courts had

passed on recently enacted state legislation. When Bradley turned
the farmers down and rebuked them for wearing hats and smoking in the presence of the court, a sullen murmur rose from the
crowd. A Farmers' Holiday leader later described the reaction:
"That's not his courtroom. We farmers paid for it with our tax
money and it was as much ours as his. The crowd had a perfect
right there." As the judge continued to scold the throng, men
stepped forward, their faces masked in blue bandanas, and dragged
him from the bench. In a fury they slapped him and mauled him,
placed a blindfold around his eyes and threw him on a truck. Some
shouted, "Get a rope! Let's hang him!" A mile from the city, they
stopped, tossed a rope over a telegraph pole, fastened one end
about his neck and tightened the knot till he nearly lost consciousness. Someone removed a hub cap from the truck and put
it on his head, while others pushed him to his knees and told him
to pray. Crowned with the cap, grease running down his face,
thrust to the ground, he looked at the angry men around him and
prayed: "Oh Lord, I pray thee, do justice to all men." And still
he refused to pledge himself not to foreclose mortgages on their
farms. They threw dirt on him, then tore off his trousers and
smeared them with grease and dirt, till, weary and perhaps abashed,
they went away.

At Denison, Iowa, in the same week, a crowd of farmers attacked a collection of agents and special deputies trying to foreclose J. F. Fields's farm. Alarmed by the new surge of violence, Governor Clyde L. Herring placed half a dozen counties under martial
law and moved in the National Guard. A farmer and a *New York
Times* reporter watched trucks pushing through the spring mud,
soldiers in khaki, rifles on their backs, clinging to the sides; the
Army was looking for the farmer's son. "I guess this is Russia
now," the farmer said. In the end, nearly one hundred and fifty men
were arrested in Plymouth and Crawford Counties. Near Sioux
City, a young farmer told Frazier Hunt that if the government did
not stop foreclosures and raise prices their would be revolution.
Hunt asked what kind of revolution he meant. "I suppose we'd
be foolish if we started anything away from home," the farmer
said unsmilingly; "you know a rooster can fight best on his own
dunghill. Maybe we'll just sit around under a tree with a shotgun
in our lap and wait. Anyway, they're not going to keep putting

us off our land." "For all of the loose talk in America about red revolution and menaces of the kind that exist only in the hysterical imaginations of patrioteers," said the New York *World-Telegram,* "Americans are slow to understand that actual revolution already exists in the farm belt. . . . When the local revolt springs from old native stock, conservatives fighting for the right to hold their homesteads, there is the warning of a larger explosion."

The farmers had been through too much — their crops crushed by hailstorm and withered by drought and consumed by plagues of grasshoppers, their hard labor brought to naught by falling farm prices, their homes and livelihood menaced by the banks and insurance companies, their recourse to legislation now threatened by nullification in the courts and apathy in the Congress. "It was more than a mere coincidence," wrote Harlan Miller of the *Times,* "that the Le Mars riots occurred at precisely the moment when the farm bill . . . seemed to waver." [2]

III

And still the debate dragged on in Washington. The administration farm plan had been repugnant enough; the Thomas amendment, piling inflation on top of regimentation, compounded the horror. It was, said Senator Arthur H. Vandenberg of Michigan, "the most revolutionary proposal that has ever been presented in the history of the government." Carter Glass, with tears in his eyes, pleaded with the Senate not to give the President authority to cut the gold content of the dollar. Senator Reed of Pennsylvania called on the country to reject "this insane plan." Ogden Mills, back in Washington to organize the Republican opposition, said the bill would lead to uncontrolled inflation, predicting credit expansion to the amount of sixty billion dollars.

But the clamor for action was too great. The Senate passed the bill by a vote of 64 to 20, and on May 12 it went to Roosevelt for signature. It now contained three parts. Title I was the Agricultural Adjustment Act; Title II was the Emergency Farm Mortgage Act; Title III, concerned with monetary issues, included the Thomas amendment. As Roosevelt signed, the Farmers' Holiday Association, under pressure also from Olson of Minnesota and other midwestern political friends, agreed to postpone its strike to give the new program a chance.

The mortgage question was causing more immediate unrest than anything else; and the administration had already moved with vigor to relieve the situation. At the end of March, Roosevelt reorganized the hodgepodge of federal agricultural credit instrumentalities into a single new agency, the Farm Credit Administration, and made his Dutchess County neighbor Henry Morgenthau, Jr., its head. Under the fast-moving direction of Morgenthau and his deputy, William I. Myers of Cornell, the new agency took quick action to stave off the sheriff. Its powers confirmed by the Emergency Farm Mortgage Act and supplemented in June by the Farm Credit Act, FCA refinanced farm mortgages, inaugurated a series of "rescue" loans for second mortgages, developed techniques for persuading creditors to make reasonable settlements, set up local farm debt adjustment committees, and eventually established a system of regional banks to make mortgage, production, and marketing loans and to provide credits to cooperatives. It loaned more than $100 million in its first seven months — nearly four times as much as the total of mortgage loans to farmers from the entire land-bank system the year before. At the same time it beat down the interest rate in all areas of farm credit. "Damn you, old moneybags," John Garner, the Uvalde banker, growled to Morgenthau one day at cabinet. "Until you came along, Mrs. Garner and I averaged 16 per cent on our money, and now we can't get better than 5." Though anger still rumbled in the farm belt, FCA gave every evidence of getting at least the emergency debt problem under control.[3]

IV

Problems on the agricultural adjustment front were more complicated, however, and progress less certain. The broad design was clear: to help correct the imbalance between industry and agriculture by raising farm prices; and to raise farm prices through the curtailment of production, the regulation of marketing, and a variety of other devices. And there was general agreement on the mechanism: the establishment of a new agency within the

Department of Agriculture, to be called the Agricultural Adjustment Administration. But the immense discretion conferred on the Executive under the AAA law left many crucial decisions for the future. Much would therefore depend on the men summoned to conduct what Mordecai Ezekiel pronounced "the greatest single experiment in economic planning under capitalist conditions ever attempted by a democracy in times of peace."

The very audacity of the experiment called for conservatism in the selection of the administrator. With political shrewdness, Wallace and Roosevelt determined on Bernard Baruch as their first choice, confident that his appointment would quiet doubts both on Capitol Hill and among farm capitalists. But, with equal shrewdness, Baruch dodged the assignment, recommending in his place his old War Industries Board associate and the inventor of McNary-Haugenism, George Peek. From the administration's point of view, this idea too had much in its favor: Peek was considered a "practical" man on the Hill, while at the same time he was wholly identified with the cause of agricultural equality. After the War Industries Board, he had gone to Illinois to help put the Moline Plow Company on its feet. "That is what I was doing in 1920 when the rest of the country started putting the screws on agriculture," Peek recalled on the day of his appointment. "Then I got mad and came out of my hole to fight." In 1922 Peek and Hugh Johnson, his associate both in the War Industries Board and at Moline, set forth the basic ideas later incorporated in the McNary-Haugen bill, and thereby defined the terms of the farm battle of the twenties.

Peek's selection did, however, raise problems. He was a man — *the* man — of the older generation in the agricultural fight. He was now sixty, and doubt existed whether he had enough flexibility for the shifting issues he would face in AAA. This doubt was compounded by Peek's gruff, narrow, and pugnacious personality. Having got mad in 1920, he had stayed mad ever since. He looked with testy mistrust on later ideas devised by the farm intellectuals — "Boys with their hair ablaze!" he would snort. "The job's simple. It's just to put up farm prices." The intellectuals returned his mistrust, mingling it, though, with respect for a man they viewed as a monument of an earlier stage in the fight. "We saw Peek plodding down the street," Tugwell wrote later in a vivid impression, "bandy-legged, walking flat-footed like an Indian, red-faced and blunt . . . a little stupid but shrewd, like an English squire."

So far as policy was concerned, McNary-Haugenism remained for Peek the ultimate in agricultural wisdom. "He plowed just one furrow," said Russell Lord, "and plowed it straight." The farm problem, Peek believed, was "primarily a tariff problem." The elements of a sound policy, as he analyzed it, were a two-price system, a high tariff to save the American market for the American farmer, marketing agreements to control the flow of farm products into the home market, a government-supervised export program to find markets at any price abroad for what could not be sold at the protected price at home — and no pro-duction controls. The idea of curtailing output was repugnant to Peek; it was the farmer's sin against the Holy Ghost. The point, he kept insisting, was "control of supply rather than control of production." There was no such thing as overproduction for Peek, so long as there remained a market anywhere in the world into which the American surplus could be dumped.

His policy, therefore, pointed ultimately in quite different directions from that of Wallace, Wilson, and Tugwell, who believed that, for the moment, the volume of production had to be reduced and that dumping was no longer a realistic solution. Still, in the emergency of 1933, Peek conceded more to these views than his theory would allow, or than he would himself later admit. Thus, when Senator Cotton Ed Smith of South Carolina asked him during hearings on the agricultural adjustment legislation, "You don't mean to advocate, in order to maintain prices, the destruction of crops that are already produced, do you?" Peek stoutly replied, "I would destroy them before I would let the slight surplus destroy our whole national economy; yes, sir." And, while sticking by the high tariff for the present, he told Roosevelt in March that "eventually we may be required to lower tariffs generally." Though he plainly pinned his major faith on market-ing agreements and on the unloading of exports, he still seemed in April 1933 to diverge from Wallace more on questions of emphasis than of principle. Tugwell, summarizing his own and

Wallace's feelings in a diary jotting early in April, wrote that Peek, for all his drawbacks, was forceful and able, that he carried weight on the Hill and would bring along the Baruch faction. "We do not like this crowd particularly and would rather have a hard-boiled progressive. But this is a new thing and much depends upon cooperation amongst the processors. . . . He will not want to look to us for advice, probably, but we shall have to make out as best we can."

The question of crop control was still unresolved. Early in May, Wallace, hoping to nail matters down, arranged a meeting at the White House with the President. Here Wallace and Tugwell urged the case for acreage reduction; Peek dissented, though making an exception for cotton. The President listened attentively, but nothing very definite emerged in the way of policy clarification. On the day AAA became law, Wallace reiterated his position, telling Peek in a formal letter, "It seems to me entirely clear that we ought to undertake acreage reduction in both cotton and corn." Peek thus knew Wallace's views perfectly well, but he evidently counted on modifying or circumventing them; and this intention perhaps underlay his insistence, at Baruch's prodding, on "direct access" to the President — i.e., on not having to report to the President through the Secretary of Agriculture. The prospect of his old subordinate at Moline, Hugh Johnson, reporting directly to the President as head of the agency charged with industrial recovery, probably also made Peek wish AAA to have equivalent status. In any case, Roosevelt, convinced that he needed the political symbolism of Peek's appointment, accepted his condition. Wallace had no alternative but to go glumly along, foreseeing trouble in the future. "It is becoming clear to me," he complained to Roosevelt by the middle of May, "that Mr. Peek's insistence on using you as an umpire between him and myself will . . . prove to be a fundamental handicap to unified administration of the Farm Adjustment Act."

In June, Roosevelt personally confirmed the decision that major emphasis should go to production adjustment rather than to marketing agreements. Peek acquiesced; but in the meantime he staffed the new agency as much as possible with men who had fought with him in the battle of the twenties. For co-administrator, he selected (with Wallace's enthusiastic support) Charles J. Brand, an old pro who had been close to Wallace's father. Chester Davis, who had stood shoulder to shoulder with Peek for McNary-Haugen but was more open-minded on the question of new farm policies, came in as chief of the Production Division; M. L. Wilson became chief of the Wheat Division. In addition Peek stated publicly that he would look to Baruch and Frank Lowden, a former Republican governor of Illinois and senior agricultural statesman, for advice. All this was reassuring to those who feared that AAA would fall into the hands of presumed social experimenters like Tugwell and Ezekiel. But the liberals were not totally worsted. In particular, they had captured one position of great strategic importance — the office of the General Counsel.[4]

V

The new General Counsel, Jerome N. Frank of New York and Chicago, represented, so far as Peek and his friends were concerned, an alien world. He was forty-four years old in 1933, and had been a successful corporation lawyer in Chicago, where he had also served as special municipal counsel in the protracted traction litigation of the early twenties; in 1930, he had moved to an even more successful practice in New York. He was an intellectual, omnivorous in curiosity, sharp and skeptical of mind, pungent in expression, forever worrying problems to their roots. His book of 1930, *Law and the Modern Mind,* was an audacious essay in the new jurisprudence, setting forth the theses of legal realism with dash and abandon. When the New Deal began, Jerome Frank, yearning for public service, arrived in Washington armed with letters from Felix Frankfurter and asked what he could do.

Wallace, looking for a Solicitor for the Department of Agriculture, seized upon him; but Jim Farley, confusing the name and convinced that Frank's father-in-law was a political enemy in New York, succeeded in blocking the appointment. Frank had no father-in-law, but it proved difficult to erase the misapprehension, so Frank was shifted instead to AAA. There he threw himself into the farm relief job with all the verve of a brilliant personality. Of medium height, spare, with a high, rather austere forehead and lively blue eyes, his bearing volatile and gay, he seemed never to stop working, talking, or thinking. "Being married to Jerome," his wife once said, "is like being hitched to the tail of a comet."

He searched the law schools and the great firms of New York and Chicago to make up his staff. Knowledge of farming was, from Frank's point of view, the least of requirements; he had a lawyer's confidence that men trained in the law could master anything. "What we need," he told Peek, "are brilliant young men with keen legal minds and imagination." In a short time he brought together a remarkable group — among them, Thurman Arnold and Abe Fortas from the Yale Law School; Adlai Stevenson of Chicago; and, from the Harvard Law School, Alger Hiss, Lee Pressman, John Abt, and Nathan Witt. He provided exciting leadership, fascinating his aides with his speed and lucidity, shaming them with his memory, resourcefulness, and limitless energy. The young men, dazzled by his example, worked twenty hours a day, slept on couches in their offices and hastily briefed themselves on the agricultural life.

Frank kept up the pace after hours, when after hours were possible. Night after night stray lawyers, economists, newspapermen, and innocent bystanders appeared at the house he shared with Tugwell and indulged heavily in conversation and bourbon. It was sometimes hard to tell which was the more intoxicating. (One overnight visitor, a friend of Frank's from business days, was shocked by Tugwell in a mood of early morning intensity and forthwith wired Frank: BEWARE COMMA JEROME BEWARE STOP THIS MORNING AT YOUR BREAKFAST TABLE I SAW THE FACE OF ROBESPIERRE. Frank showed the telegram to Tugwell that evening as they were driving home. Taken aback, Tugwell swung abruptly around a corner and grazed the curb, observing that it was a hell of a life when idiots dropped in for a look and then just repeated what they had read in the papers. "Well," Frank said, "you drive like Robespierre.")

The old agrarians looked on Frank's office as if it were a menagerie — "an entirely new species to me," said Peek. The farm specialists had long constituted a club, where everybody knew everybody else, and they resented this upsurge of strange urban types. There were too many Ivy League men, too many intellectuals, too many radicals, too many Jews. Nor were things helped when (according to a familiar story) Lee Pressman, attending a meeting to work out a macaroni code, asked belligerently what the code would do for the macaroni growers; or when (according to another story) an AAA lawyer on a field trip to the countryside saw his first firefly and exclaimed "Good God! What's that?" George Peek had opposed Frank from the start, remembering him perhaps as a member of the law firm which had liquidated the Moline Plow Company. When he could not stop Frank's appointment, Peek asked that his own salary as Administrator be paid to Frederic P. Lee to serve as his private counsel. From an early point, friction threatened between the General Counsel and the Administrator.

Frank and his lawyers found support in one other office in AAA — that of the Consumers' Counsel. Old Frederic C. Howe, veteran of so many liberal causes, his hope still unquenched at sixty-six, was now charged with the responsibility of making sure that the rise in farm prices would not gouge the consumer. Working with him was another militant liberal, a generation younger, Gardner Jackson, who had played a leading role in the Sacco-Vanzetti case and whose abundant sympathy, courage, and curiosity kept him in the middle of one fight after another for the underprivileged; "the underdog has him on a leash," a friend once said of Pat Jackson. And outside AAA the reformers, who had no scruples about going outside authorized channels, found strong support in the Department — from Tugwell, the Assistant Secretary, whom they inclined to look upon as their leader; from Paul Appleby, a newspaper editor and publisher whom Wallace had taken on as his assistant; from C. B. Baldwin, a self-confident Virginian who helped Appleby; from Mordecai Ezekiel, who had become Wallace's economic adviser; from Louis Bean, a master statistician; and, intermittently, from the Secretary himself.

Tugwell and Frank and their adherents had two things in common — a city background, which disposed them to think in terms not just of the farmers but of the impact of farm policies on consumers and the entire economy; and a passionate liberalism, which disposed them to think in terms not just of filling the farmer's purse but of reorganizing the system of agricultural production and distribution. From the viewpoint of Peek, who wanted to raise prices and nothing else, the offices of the General Counsel and Consumers' Counsel were filled with too many men who wanted to make America over. This was the Department of Agriculture, Peek used to say caustically, not the "Department of Everything." [5]

VI

It was certainly the department of more things than Tugwell or Frank knew. For the social militance of the office of the General Counsel provided a cover behind which operated more than simply the reformist liberalism of Jerome Frank. The smoldering discontent on the farm belt had long attracted the solicitous concern of the American Communist party. The party's agricultural expert was Harold Ware, the son of the veteran agitator Ella Reeve Bloor. Hal Ware had spent several years in the Soviet Union; his work there had won a good notice from Lenin; and when, as his fond mother put it, "the Russian farmers, already collectivized, no longer needed him as much as the American farmers did," he returned to take charge of the agrarian work of the American Communist party.

Ware was a discreet, earnest, quiet man, indistinguishable in a crowd, with rimless glasses on a plain midwestern face; Whittaker Chambers, who was one of his contacts in the party underground, remembered him "as American as ham and eggs." He became a consultant for the Department of Agriculture when Coolidge was President and remained on the Department books until the last year of the Hoover administration. In the fall of 1932, Ware and Mother Bloor tried to move in on the farm strikes in western Iowa. Returning to Washington in 1933, Ware encountered in AAA a number of actual or potential Communists, whom he soon organized into an underground group. Members of the group included Pressman, Witt, Abt, and according to some testimony Hiss.

It is evident that these men were in AAA, not because of any planned Communist infiltration of the Agriculture Department, but because of the accident that Jerome Frank had jobs to fill.

Some, like Nathaniel Weyl, an AAA economist, came to Washington as Communists; others, like Pressman (according to his own claim, in any case) were recruited into the party after coming to Washington. All were men, in their way, of conscience and zeal, persuaded that capitalism had reached the end of its tether, and eager to enlist in a crusade of social transformation. "The future looked black for my generation," Pressman said later. ". . . In my desire to see the destruction of Hitlerism and an improvement in economic conditions here at home, I joined a Communist group."

The two best-placed recruits, Pressman and (according to Chambers and Weyl) Hiss, had been classmates at the Harvard Law School. Though coming from contrasting backgrounds and possessing contrasting personalities, the penetrating and sardonic Jew and the handsome, cool, and reserved Anglo-Saxon were intimate friends. As Jerome Frank wrote Charles Brand in the summer of 1933 about Pressman, "I was reluctant to urge him to come to Washington but finally did so at the insistence of Mr. Hiss who has the highest regard for Mr. Pressman's ability and character." Pressman brought in Witt, and Frank hired Abt, whom he had known in Chicago.

The group met in great secrecy in a music studio on Connecticut Avenue run by Ware's sister. It was not illegal for Communists to work for the government; according to a Department of Agriculture ruling, "A man in the employ of the Government has just as much right to be a member of the Communist Party as he has to be a member of the Democratic or Republican Party." But concealment of party membership was necessary for anyone who wanted to get ahead. "If it had been known," said Weyl, looking back, "it would have wrecked their careers." Too many of their superiors disliked Communists. Jerome Frank was both philosophically and practically opposed to Communism. Tugwell had just been through a trying experience with a Communist instructor in the economics department at Columbia. Donald Henderson had been a student and protégé of Tugwell's; and, as a result of the episode with him, Tugwell "reached the conclusion that I would never again work with any Communist if I could avoid it. . . . If I had had any reason to think that our young lawyers were

signed-up party members, I should have refused them employment."
As for Wallace, he declared his "profound abhorrence for many
of the things for which the Communists stand. I detest," he continued, "the arousing of what amounts to religious fanaticism for
national or class interests, and the building up of bitterness between classes."

For these reasons, the young Communists had to operate in
darkness. The excitement of the emergency, the tremendous hurry
to get things done, the existence of a common enemy to the right,
all gave them protective coloration. Their superiors found them
useful on the job and were not aware of their private reservations,
their division of loyalty, their shrouded evening meetings, or their
secret scorn and contempt. And, indeed, the presence of Communists in AAA had its own futilities. While the cell was no
doubt constantly trying to figure out ways to help the cause, the
nature of the farm problem was such that it did not lend itself,
except in the most general and long-run way, to Communist purposes. No issue which confronted them could be manipulated
in a manner uniquely in the interests of the Communist party;
nothing of importance took place in AAA as a result of their
presence which the AAA liberals would not have done anyway.
For the Communist party, the AAA group was a staging area for
personnel, not a fulcrum for policy.[6]

4. The Politics of Agriculture

FROM THE START George Peek, while reluctantly accepting production control in cotton and wheat and later in corn and hogs, saw marketing agreements as the basic AAA weapon. If the object was to raise farm prices, this could be done most expeditiously, he contended, by making food processors pay higher prices to the farmers. The processors, especially if granted immunity from antitrust laws, could then pass on price increases to consumers. As higher prices stimulated new production, the surpluses could somehow be unloaded abroad. It was still, in short, the old formula, and it was still based on the conviction of the agrarian pros that the job of farm policy was to take care of the farmers while the rest of the economy took care of itself. What was new was the idea of cooperation with the farmer's traditional foe, the middleman. In his first public statement, Peck promised the food and textile industries that he would act "with as little interference with established institutions and methods — indeed with as little administration of any kind as is consistent with the fixed purpose of the law; namely, to raise farm prices."

Wallace, Wilson, Tugwell, Frank, and the others disagreed profoundly. They were wholly skeptical about the notion of dumping surpluses in foreign markets in a world of rising tariffs and multiplying quotas — "We ought to act for the moment," Wallace told Peek, "as if we were a self-contained agricultural economy." Believing this, they believed that the surplus problem had to be tackled at home. While some of them, notably Frank and Tugwell, saw possibilities in marketing agreements, they looked on them as devices for achieving balance throughout the economy, not as a means of filling the pockets of processors and farmers. Frank argued that the processors owed the government something in exchange for antitrust exemption, and that the way to prevent excessive price increases was through access to the company books. By this means, the spread between what the middleman paid the farmer and what he charged the consumer could be held to reasonable margins. As a result of these differences, a quiet but increasingly bitter struggle began in the summer of 1933 — Peek demanding the acceptance of a series of marketing agreements, Frank holding them up with searching questions, Fred Howe protesting them in the name of the consumer. On occasion Peek and Frank carried their disagreements to the harried Secretary, and Wallace sometimes decided one way, sometimes another.

In late September the Secretary encouraged the reformers by turning down a draft agreement devised by the sugar industry — an agreement which, as the Legal Division saw it, helped the refiners at the expense of the consumers without much benefiting the cane and beet growers. About the same time Wallace took up the question of processors' profits in frank terms at a meeting of the Special Industrial Recovery Board. The government could not indefinitely dodge the profit question, he said; "we can go ahead in the rush of getting people to work and getting prices for farmers and perhaps wink at these things for the time being, but once that rush is past I am inclined to think both the AAA and the NRA will have to insist on a complete look at the books because of the fact that capitalism, as I see it, inevitably takes out too much in the way of profits and does not pay out enough for labor and agriculture." If capitalism were to be saved, Wallace thought, it might even be necessary to limit profits and make sure that the rest was paid out to labor and to raw materials producers.[1]

II

Matters rose toward a climax in September in a controversy over a draft agreement for flue-cured tobacco. The agreement, to the outrage of the industry, proposed to limit price increases on processed tobacco. It also sought what the industry deemed undue access to company records. The representative of the Legal Division in the negotiations frightened the tobacco companies with what they considered his antibusiness zeal; and Peek who was beginning to perceive a sinister pattern in the general activity of the Legal Division, demanded a redraft of the agreement to meet industry objections. Other things worried Peek. About the same time, for example, Lee Pressman, working on milk marketing agreements, asked an attorney (according to a letter the attorney dispatched to Peek) whether the government could not take over the control of milk. When the attorney countered by saying then why not take over grocery stores and department stores, Pressman replied, "Why not?" But would this not be Communism? "Call it what you may," said Pressman, "this plan is failing, and government operation has to come." (This remark, it should be noted in connection with Communist operations in AAA, was plainly the smart-aleck comment of an arrogant young lawyer, and not at all what a genuine and effective conspirator would be saying to promote the objective contained in the words.) Convinced that a crew of "collectivists" — a term Peek applied loosely to such antagonistic figures as Tugwell and Frankfurter — was plotting to make AAA an instrument of radical change, Peek determined to carry the tobacco fight to the President. Roosevelt, after hearing the case, backed Peek on the merits (except on the issue of acreage control). But Peek continued to be thwarted in his efforts to get rid of Frank; and, so long as Frank was there, every marketing agreement promised a struggle.

At the same time, Peek continued to press the other half of his program — the attempt to promote exports. Through the export subsidy provisions of the Agricultural Adjustment Act, he was able in October to send considerable quantities of wheat from the Pacific Northwest to the Far East; and in November he tried to transfer half a million dollars from the processing-tax accounts to subsidize the export of butter to Europe. Wallace at this point was out of town, leaving Tugwell as Acting Secretary. Tugwell, after thoughtful consideration, rejected the proposal, partly perhaps because he felt the Peek problem had to be brought to a head, but essentially because the two-price system — selling abroad at a price lower than the market at home — seemed to him disastrous to the foreign economic relations of the United States. "This practice," Tugwell wrote Wallace, "has been condemned in every international conference; it was the subject of special treatment in our recent tariff truce agreement; it is recognized as provocative of retaliation. . . . A sound foreign trade must be based on equal exchange between countries."

For Peek this was the beginning of the end. If the marketing agreement and the foreign trade features of the Act were to be sabotaged, if production control were to be the main thing, he no longer wanted to administer the law; "I wanted to be on the outside fighting." In the meantime, Roosevelt, who had been unhappy about Tugwell's precipitate action, called him over to the White House. Tugwell was mad too; he told the President that he was taking the line the President would have to take in the end, and that those who were fighting his fight were being constantly let down by him; he could no longer avoid decision. "What shall I do?" Roosevelt mused. "Do I have to fire Peek?" Or would another job be possible? The Ministry at Prague, for example? Tugwell suggested that if Peek cared so much about developing foreign markets maybe he could do something in that area. "Lordy, Lordy," said Roosevelt, "how Cordell Hull will love that!" But it was, after all, a way out. A few days later Roosevelt summoned Peek, told him that there was important work to be done in the foreign trade field, and suggested that he might be more effective there. Peek handed in his resignation as AAA chief and accepted his new assignment.

And so Peek's stormy career in AAA came to an end. A man shaped by a decade of farm struggle to an iron fixity of purpose, he saw only that the farmer had been exploited too long; his single aim was to redress the balance of exploitation, at whatever cost to the balance of the economy. He did not look much beyond the farmer — to the consumer, to the domestic economy in general, to the place of the nation in the world economy. Moreover, construing the farmer as the large-scale commercial farmer or the landlord, he showed little concern within the rural economy for the tenant, the sharecropper, or the subsistence farmer. Bearing the imprint of another generation, he had preconceptions too narrow and rigid for the national economic crisis of the thirties. In frustration, he could only turn savagely against his opponents, characterizing them all indiscriminately as dupes or collectivists. The lack of discrimination in his rage was unfortunate. For, although Peek sensed in 1933 what Wallace and Tugwell and Frank did not sense — that some men in AAA were less interested in helping the farmer than in using his woes as a lever with which to discredit the system — the angry old man, in claiming Tugwell and Frank as part of the conspiracy, discredited whatever there was of soundness in his instinct.

In a few days, Wallace decided to make Chester Davis, Peek's old associate, his successor. In a final talk, Peek told Davis, "Get rid of Jerome Frank and the rest of that crowd as a condition to your acceptance." Davis, confident that he could control the situation, ignored the advice.[2]

III

In the meantime, for all the controversy on top, AAA had proceeded swiftly and effectively to put its crop control programs into operation. The first problem was cotton, where the carryover of stocks from previous years was eight million bales, almost three times as much as normal — enough, indeed, to satisfy the world market for American cotton for 1933 without the harvesting of a single new plant in the United States. By the time the act was passed in May 1933, forty million acres had been planted in cotton, and a bumper crop was in prospect. What could be done at this late date? "We were," as George Peek said, "working against the sun." Yet it was all too obvious that if the 1933 crop ever went on the market cotton, already down five cents a pound, would sink out of sight.

There was a single hope — to take part of the planted acreage out of production. But how could this be done? AAA, a confusion of desks, telephones, people, and conferences, was obviously in no state to undertake a campaign of mass education. Yet a reservoir of trained field personnel did exist. Under the Agricultural Extension Service of the Land Grant Colleges, most rural counties already had county agents — men charged with bringing the farmers information on improved agricultural techniques. The county agents knew the local problems; they had the confidence of the local people. Would they not be the ideal field staff for AAA?

So M. L. Wilson, with his passion for grass-roots participation, believed, and he proposed that the State Extension Directors be made the state AAA administrators. Tugwell disagreed. The Extension Service, he thought, was too much identified with the interests of the large farmers. "I haven't a damn bit of confidence in Extension Directors," he once whispered loudly to Wallace as he left an extension conference in the Secretary's office. For Tugwell saw behind the Extension Service the shadowy outline of the unofficial structure of power in the agricultural field — a structure of private power which might, in time, challenge the Department itself. In the early years of the Extension Service, local farm bureaus had been set up to support the county agents. The local bureaus, affiliating first on a state and then on a national basis, eventually became the American Farm Bureau Federation. The Extension Service, a presumably public body, and the Farm Bureau, a private lobby, thus had a long-standing morganatic alliance which few politicians would mention and none would criticize. Presiding benignly over this liaison were the Land Grant Colleges. Together, the three groups expressed the vested interests of commercial agriculture.

To use the Extension Service, then, would be to commit the future of AAA in considerable part to men who, while well qualified in technical and scientific knowledge, would think in terms of an agricultural *status quo* so far as ownership and the distribution of income were concerned. Still, what was the alternative? Where could AAA recruit trained men for a field force of its own except from the Extension Service and the Land Grant Colleges? Time was slipping by, crops were ripening, decisions could not be escaped, they were working against the sun. Wallace endorsed Wilson's solution.[3]

IV

In a whirlwind drive, the county agents now signed up hundreds of thousands of farmers for the cotton plow-up campaign. Steel plows behind tractors turned briskly to uprooting a quarter of the 1933 crop (where farmers only had mules, however, they found it hard to persuade the animals to walk on the rows of cotton). In return, the growers received over a hundred million dollars in benefit payments. It was an extraordinary development — "an epoch in American agriculture," even Peek was willing to exclaim in July. ". . . History has been made during these days." Henry Wallace was more rueful. The effort, he said, in its sweep and boldness "went beyond anything known to history," but the like of it, he added, "I hope we shall never have to resort to again. To destroy a standing crop goes against the soundest instincts of human nature."

The administration took other steps to strengthen cotton prices. Oscar Johnston, a Mississippi planter in AAA, suggested government loans to cotton farmers at a rate above the market price. Holding the cotton as security would keep the surplus from further depressing the market. If prices rose above the loan, then the grower could redeem his cotton; if not, then it remained in the possession of the government. On a fall afternoon, Roosevelt called Jesse Jones, chairman of the Reconstruction Finance Corporation, to the White House and said, "Jess, I want you to lend 10 cents a pound on cotton." With cotton at eight or nine cents, the ten-cent loan would obviously operate as a means of price support. Jones talked the matter over with his general counsel, Stanley Reed of Kentucky; and on October 16 they set up the Commodity Credit Corporation to operate the new program. With capital from the RFC, the CCC immediately made loans to cotton farmers who had agreed to participate in the 1934 reduction program. By the end of the year, cotton growers could look at future cotton prices with qualified hope instead of total despair. And the CCC introduced a brilliant new technique of price support, which the administration soon applied to corn, wheat, and other storable commodities.

Wheat was almost as urgent a problem as cotton. The carryover in 1933 was three and a half times as large as normal — 360 million bushels. Statisticians reported that the price of wheat had not been so low since the days of Queen Elizabeth. The United States, said Wallace, had "the largest wheat surplus and the longest breadlines in its history." But unfavorable weather conditions were expected to hold the 1933 yield down so it did not seem necessary to plow under growing wheat; as Wallace commented, "nature had already done it." Under the careful direction of M. L. Wilson, the wheat program thus developed on less of an emergency basis than cotton. AAA offered a three-year program of benefit payments in return for an agreement to reduce planting in 1934 and 1935 by percentages to be specified.[4]

V

Corn and hogs presented a peculiarly difficult problem. For a time, Wallace considered a plow-up campaign for corn, but finally decided against it and instead combined a Commodity Credit Corporation loan program with acreage adjustment. And, since most corn was marketed in the form of pork, AAA proposed at the same time large reductions in hog breeding for 1934. But could the corn belt survive the winter on $.35 corn and $2.50 hogs? Obviously some emergency action was required in addition. A National Corn–Hog Committee, representing local committees of corn and hog producers and including also the presidents of the Farm Bureau, the Grange, and the Farmers' Union, came up in the midsummer of 1933 with a startling recommendation: the only way to prevent a vast number of hogs from glutting the market over the next winter, they told the Department of Agriculture, was for the government to purchase and slaughter five or six million little pigs in the fall.

Wallace and the AAA officials anticipated the public shock at this idea, but they saw no alternative. Within the government, the hog program provoked much ribald kidding ("How are you getting on with your wholesale murder of hogs, George?" said Roosevelt one day at a meeting of the Executive Council. "I think we are progressing," Peek replied. "Wouldn't birth control be more effective in the long run?" asked the President, no doubt with a hearty laugh. "We think not," said Peek, a little grimly). Outside, it provoked widespread popular wrath and incredulity. No one felt the madness of the policy more keenly than Wallace himself. "The plowing under of 10 million acres of cotton in August, 1933, and the slaughter of 6 million little pigs in September, 1933," he wrote the next year, "were not acts of idealism in any sane society. They were emergency acts made necessary by the almost insane lack of world statesmanship during the period from 1920 to 1932."

What alternative was there, given the rules of the game? No doubt it could be said that there was no such thing as a food surplus so long as there was a single hungry Asian. "But these standpat sentimentalists who weep that farmers should practice controlled production," said Wallace bitterly, "do not suggest that clothing factories go on producing *ad infinitum*, regardless of effective demand for their merchandise, until every naked Chinaman is clad." No one had been morally indignant, the Secretary said, when American industry plowed under so much of its potential output between 1929 and 1933 — $20 billion worth of goods which might have fed, clothed, and housed cold and hungry Americans. Yet agriculture was now excoriated for reducing its output one tenth as much. How could anyone who granted industry the right to control its production deny the same right to agriculture? "We must play with the cards that are dealt," Wallace said. "Agriculture cannot survive in a capitalistic society as a philanthropic enterprise."

The logic was unanswerable. In a profit system, the farmer had to make profits too, or go under. If he planted for hungry Asians who could not buy his output, he would only destroy himself. "The people who raise the cry about the last hungry Chinamen are not really criticizing the farmers or the AAA, but the profit system." The destruction of pigs and cotton, said Wallace, made it possible for more people to eat in 1934 than if they had not been destroyed. And the special outcry about the baby pigs particularly exasperated the agricultural officials. Why was it more humane to kill a big hog than a little one? People seemed to contend, Wallace said, that "every little pig has the right to attain before slaughter the full pigginess of his pigness. To hear them talk, you would have thought that pigs were raised for pets." Nor, indeed, did the pigs die in vain. In October, Wallace, with Harry Hopkins and Harold Ickes, organized the Federal Surplus Relief Corporation which brought over 100 million pounds of baby pork to hungry people on relief.

At the same time Wallace emphasized that AAA's ultimate object was to produce not scarcity but balance. "Rationalize it any way we have to," Tugwell had said early in the Hundred Days, "we can't make a religion out of growing or making fewer goods with this whole country and the whole world in bitter need." AAA was thus a mechanism of control, to be used as required for curtailment or for expansion. As the economy came into balance and as demand was restored, Wallace observed, "we can take off the brakes and step on the gas." The "enforced meanness" of modern society would surely become in time insupportable; the "hard, hopeless" economics of Adam Smith would fade away, and a new Economics of Potentialities would arise. "Only the merest quarter-turn of the heart separates us from a material abundance beyond the fondest dreams of anyone present," he told a Des Moines audience in 1933. A new social machinery was in the making if only people could maintain sweet and kindly hearts toward each other. "Oh! how the world has been under the weight of that need to subsist, to keep body and soul together, in the past few years!" Wallace cried in a moment of emotion in 1934. "We can throw off the miserable burden. We can stand like free men in the sun." [5]

VI

For the moment these aspirations seemed far in the future. Indeed, the enthusiasm which greeted AAA in the spring of 1933 began to wear off as summer passed without miraculous improvements in the farmers' condition. Given the late enactment of the law, few AAA programs could affect prices before 1934; but the reasons for delay were not fully recognized in the farm belt. Moreover, in the early fall, farm prices which had shot up in June and July as a result of speculative buying began to decline, at just the time that the farm implement manufacturers and the mail order houses, responding to the National Recovery Administration drive, started to put their prices up. What good was an increase in farm prices if the ratio of farm to industrial prices was beginning to rise?

By September, the farm belt was watching prices with increasing irritation. "The political temper of the dairy and livestock farmers of the middle west at the present time," Wallace warned the President on September 11, "is far worse than you realize." The scrawl of an Indiana farmer to Roosevelt expressed a growing state of mind:

> I am a farmer. Have spent a lifetime building up a 200 acre farm, buildings and equipment. Am $1200 in debt but can hold on longer than 90% of the farmers. Last spring I thought you really intended to do something for this country. Now I have given it all up. Henceforward I am swearing eternal vengence on the financial barons and will do every single thing I can to bring about communism.

"Our feeling," said a Farmers' Holiday leader in Aberdeen, South Dakota, "is that down there in Washington they don't understand us right. We have asked for things, but they just ignore us. We have tried to help, but they won't even listen to us." The speaker had a 3000-acre farm, had his own grain elevator, until recently had kept twenty men at work. "The President, it seemed, wouldn't listen to anybody but Wallace and the 'Brain Trust,'" he continued. "Well, Wallace and the 'Brain Trust' haven't done much for us. . . . We have only one weapon left. We've exhausted our voices. All there is left for us is resistance."

The Farmers' Holiday Association was wasting no time in capitalizing on the spreading discontent. Milo Reno, returning to the battle with zest, shouted, "We've forgotten all about Mr. Wallace. And we'll forget the man in the White House too if he forgets us." John Simpson of the Farmers' Union joined the clamor. Farm congressmen added their voices. "The President drove the money-changers out of the Capitol on March 4th," cried William Lemke of North Dakota, "— and they were all back on the 9th." Elmer Thomas renewed his cry for inflation in mass meetings in the South and West. Talk of a new farm strike mounted.

In North Dakota Governor William Langer imposed an embargo on the shipment of wheat to market. In Wisconsin radical farm leaders staged a march on Madison and occupied the state Assembly chamber. In Iowa, farmers blocked roads, overturned trucks, set bridges on fire; once again, milk trickled along the cold cement roads. "They say there is over-production, that crops must be reduced," said Milo Reno. "As long as there are twenty-five million hungry people in this country, there's no overproduction. For the government to destroy food and reduce crops at such a time is wicked. The payments Washington proposes to make the farmers are nothing but a dole. The scheme won't work, and it would be wrong if it did."

Reno began to send wires to the President demanding the immediate enactment of the Farmers' Holiday program. ("I do not like to have anybody hold a pistol to my head and demand that I do something," Roosevelt said wrathfully to Henry Morgenthau.) The radicals now had a new wrinkle — the idea of a code for farmers, modeled on the NRA codes, with provisions guaranteeing farm income and fixing agricultural prices. As feeling mounted during the fall, five northwestern governors, led by the radical Farmer-Laborite, Floyd Olson of Minnesota, elaborated this idea; and in November they came to Washington to demand that the government adopt a plan for compulsory production control and price-fixing for basic farm commodities, to be enforced by licensing all farmers and processors. NRA codes, Olson pointed out, forbade manufacturers to sell below the cost of production. Why should the farmer alone be abandoned to the law of supply and demand? "Agriculture, the basic industry of the United States," said Olson, "is the only industry whose commodity prices are not protected in the public markets."

Wallace was dismayed at the regimentation such a program would involve; it would end, he suggested, with the licensing of every plowed field and the marketing of all grain and livestock by a ticket-punch system. But the governors were not deterred. Olson, for one, regarded Wallace as too cautious and detached. "Philosophers make good advisers but bad generals," the Minnesota governor advised Roosevelt later. When an AAA official ventured the opinion that the scheme might be unconstitutional, one governor cheerfully spoke the mood of the times, "Hell, what's the Constitution between friends?" After three days of conferences, the administration turned down the governors' proposals. As Roosevelt subsequently wrote Olson, "If the farmers want price-fixing and all that goes with it, I think their desire can be fulfilled effectively only through Congressional action. . . . It is still my earnest conviction that we should not try to impose compulsion on the farmers and that compulsion should not be adopted until farmers in general know all that is involved and willingly accept it."

Wallace himself, on a propitiatory speaking tour through the farm belt, announced the loan program for all farmers who would sign up for corn and hog control in 1934. At the same time, the administration began to explore new possibilities in monetary manipulation. As benefit payments, commodity loans and FCA mortgage refinancing contracts began to flow into the Middle West, as the depreciation of the dollar under the gold-purchase program began to quiet the inflationists, the agrarian excitement began to die away. In mid-November the President remarked that conditions were much improved in the West. By winter, the atmosphere was clearing, and AAA was coming into its own.[6]

5. The Ordeal of a Prophet

EVEN AS AAA BEGAN TO MOVE with confidence into 1934, it was suddenly confronted by a new and terrible phenomenon, which both complicated and simplified its operations. American agriculture in the thirties was paying the price for generations of careless cultivation. For too long farmers had plowed the plains soil and grazed their herds on plains grass, casually ripping away the thin, strong, protective cover of turf on which, without their knowing it, their fortunes depended. For it was the grass which held the water in the soil; it was the grass which kept the wind from blowing the soil away. Without the grass, nature's unending battle between wind and water could only end in desert. And so the cover of turf, broken by plows, scarred by the hoofs of sheep and cattle, torn by overgrazing, became sparse and fragile.

The twenties had been years of moisture in the Great Plains. The rains had fallen; the farmers had edged beyond the line of semi-aridity into land their fathers had considered too dry for cultivation. When the steady rains stopped coming after 1930, when the summer sun beat down without mercy and the summer cloudbursts only washed away the soil the faster, when the water level of the blue northern lakes sank by the height of a tall man, ominous shadows began to hang over the plains. There was drought in 1931, localized in area but big with portent of the future. And then the winds began to blow. The soil was parched and dried; and where the grass remained, it was yellow and withered and could not hold the soil; and the winds, like a sand-blast over the flat prairies, caught up the dust in great black clouds which darkened the sky and blotted out the sun.

II

There had been foretastes in 1931 and 1932, small dust storms in western Kansas and eastern Colorado. In 1933 Department of Agriculture agronomists and climatologists looked to the next year with mounting apprehension. They predicted drought; and, because of their predictions, the AAA decided not to plow under the wheat on the western plains. As the months wore on, apprehension deepened. Rex Tugwell, traveling that winter across the plains, sent back pessimistic word. The winter snows were light; but, even if the rains were to come, the land was too beaten to absorb it; now water, instead of resisting wind, would complete its work. The soil, Tugwell said, showed through the grass, and the wheat was thin, "like the stubble on an old man's chin."

And in the spring of 1934 only sun, and no rain; sun, at first, and then the winds. In May the dust storms began to blow. Rising first out of the Panhandle, the great clouds mushroomed into the sky, a powder of humus and colloids, the topsoil of the country blowing away. And still the sullen sun shone. The drought came to center in the Dakotas, but it burned across the Middle West and the central states as far south as Texas and as far east as the Alleghenies. As summer approached, the winds grew hotter and more fierce. The clouds of plains dust billowed in the sky, brown and yellow and acrid. Dust drifted like snow against barns and fences. Schools were closed, cars stalled by the side of the road, street lights shone at noonday. The dust sifted through the doors and windows of the farmhouses, through the wet rags stuffed into cracks and chinks, through the wet sheets hung over the windows, till the houses were dark with the burning, choking air. On and on the clouds whirled, some into the astonished East, spreading their baleful orange and amber aura, the smell of dirt and the taste of grit, until they passed on and fell at last into the Atlantic.

The winds swept topsoil from millions of acres of farm land. They seared the crops of two-dozen states. They left behind wheat and corn withered in the fields, ground baked hard as rock, dead trees lonely against the horizon. Cattle, without water to drink or grass to eat, their lungs strangling with dust, grew thin and lay down in fence corners to die. Some ate so much dirt as they scratched at the grass roots that they died from mudballs in their stomachs. And beyond the farmers, suffering the catastrophe of drought on top of the calamity of depression, beyond the baked crops and the emaciated livestock, lay the land itself, naked and vulnerable, tracking off into rills and gullies, yielding ever more of its fertility to wind and water, brown, barren, silent. "The country seems to brood," one observer wrote, "as though death were touching it." On the farms, men reacted in strange ways. Some saw in the drought and dust the judgment of God on men who had dared plow under cotton and slaughter baby pigs. A demand arose that AAA be abolished. Washington, confronted with the worst drought in the history of the republic, went into swift action, rushing seed and feed to the distressed areas, buying and removing livestock, and acting in other ways to see the farmers through the emergency. At the same time, the government began to develop plans for the protection of land and water over the longer run.

In the dust bowl, farmers responded with gratitude to positive government. "They were a hopeful people," wrote Franklin Roosevelt in 1934 after his first trip west of the Mississippi since 1932. "They had courage written all over their faces. They looked cheerful. They knew they were 'up against it' but they were going to see the thing through; whereas, in 1932, there was a look of despair." [1]

III

The black blizzards of 1934 had their major long-run impact in speeding the development of federal conservation policies. But they also had a direct effect on the workings of AAA. For they cut down production, particularly of wheat, with a deadly and harsh efficiency far surpassing the man-made efforts of the AAA administrators. The wheat crop, which had averaged 864 million bushels over the years 1928–32, sank to an average of about 567 million bushels for 1933–35; of this reduction, perhaps 20 million resulted from AAA and the rest from the weather. As a consequence, the wheat carryover was absorbed, wheat prices rose, and by 1935–36 the United States was actually importing wheat in material quantities.

The recovery in wheat prices following the reduction in output fully corroborated the economics of AAA. All along the agricultural front, AAA programs — through production control, benefit payments, CCC loans, the purchase of surpluses for distribution in relief channels, and the other weapons in the varied AAA arsenal — were having similar effects. In cotton, AAA could claim exclusive credit for price increases. In corn, both AAA and weather helped; but no one could question the results. "Corn is 70 cents on the farms in Iowa," Senator Louis Murphy wrote to Roosevelt. "Two years ago it was 10 cents. Top hogs sold at Iowa plants yesterday at $7.40, or $4.50 to $5.00 better than a year ago. Farmers are very happy and convinced of the virtue of planning. . . . Secretary Wallace can have whatever he wants from Iowa farmers."

Between 1932 and 1936, gross farm income increased 50 per cent, and cash receipts from marketing, including government payments, nearly doubled. Even more important was the striking improvement in the farmers' terms of trade. The ratio between prices the farmers received and the prices they paid, including interest and taxes, rose steadily from 55 in 1932 to 70 in 1934 and 90 in 1936. Farmers' prices increased by two-thirds in this period. All this was accompanied by a decrease of a billion dollars in the size of the farm debt, and a wholesome shift of creditors from private banks and insurance companies to federal agencies. The degree of agricultural recovery was all the more remarkable at a time when income and employment in the general economy still remained low.[2]

IV

AAA's contribution to raising farm income and redressing the balance of the economy was facilitated by the surprising smoothness of its administrative operation. So much had appeared to be against the agricultural experiment: the difficulty of adapting a national plan to the problems created by a diversity of crops and localities; the unacceptability of crop reduction to men and women whose pride lay in growing as much as they could; the improbability, in any case, of regulating the behavior of what was supposedly the most stubborn and independent-minded section of the population. Yet conditions turned out to be more propitious for planning than many anticipated. The desperate plight of the farmers had considerably diminished their objections to collective action. Moreover, the long travail of the countryside in the twenties had caused technical analysis to focus on agriculture as a national economic problem; and the decades of training in Land Grant Colleges and in the Extension Service had produced a corps of experts capable of carrying out whatever plans the economists might devise.

But the success of AAA derived above all from a brilliant administrative insight. Tugwell isolated the secret one day after a lunch with Wallace and Wilson at the Cosmos Club during the interregnum — during that quiet period, so long behind them all, when men still had time to think. "Under this plan," he noted, "it will *pay* farmers, for the first time, to be social-minded, to do something for all instead of for himself alone. We thus succeed, we think, in harnessing a selfish motive for the social good." Here was democracy's feasible middle way between a self-interest which meant anarchy and a coercion which might mean tyranny — planning by incentive, rather than planning by command. "We can even go further with this," Tugwell added: "we can make [the farmer] contribute toward a long-run program in this way. We can plan for him and with him."

If Tugwell tended to stress planning *for* the farmer, Wilson stressed planning *with* him. He insisted at every turn of the road that AAA adjustments should be made only as rapidly as farmers desired them. Wallace strongly shared this belief in what he called "economic democracy." Thus, with remarkable social ingenuity, AAA officials invented methods by which important decisions could be passed on to the farmer himself.

The "lifeblood" of AAA, in Tugwell's phrase, was furnished by the county production-control committees, made up of farmers who elected their own officers and actually administered many of the control programs. As the county committees made acreage allotments, as they checked the execution of the programs, the farmers subjected themselves to a novel process of economic self-government. Running their own show within a framework of national policy, they educated themselves in social discipline. "It is not possible for three million farmers to go through such experiences, it seems to me," wrote Wallace, "without a very real effect on whole communities in every corner of the nation."

An accompanying technique was the referendum, by which the producers themselves decided the character of the control programs. And, even after a vast majority of producers endorsed a program (as in the corn-hog referenda of 1934 and 1935 and the wheat referendum of 1935), AAA preferred to keep its programs on a voluntary basis. Pressure for compulsion, indeed, came not from Washington but from the farmers themselves. When AAA insisted on voluntary programs, Congress, responding to the desires of the grass roots, passed in 1934 the Bankhead Cotton Control Act and the Kerr-Smith Tobacco Control Act, both using the taxing power to force recalcitrant producers into the control system.

Looking back years later, Tugwell concluded that the cult of "grass-roots democracy" was largely an illusion. Its effect, he argued, was to deliver the power of agricultural decision to the agricultural hierarchy — the triple alliance of Extension Service, Farm Bureau, and Land Grant College — and thus to the rich farmers in every locality. County production associations could not, in any case, represent the interests of all the nation; only the government could do that; and, in practice, they were likely to represent the farmers who could afford to hire others to work their farms while they themselves attended committee meetings.

Although Tugwell was certainly correct in questioning the sentimentality which so often accompanied talk of grass-roots democracy, he perhaps did not do justice to the extent to which the vast apparatus of local committees — nearly four thousand of them by the middle of 1934 — actually did produce both popular education and popular consent. The issue he identified would cause increasing tension within AAA; and the results of the grass-roots approach would certainly fall far below the radiant Wallace-Wilson dream of "a new epoch, in which Democracy, embracing the economic as well as the political field, becomes for the first time a reality." Still, the effectiveness of that approach may have had a good deal to do with the fact that in 1935, Raymond Moley could safely describe the Agricultural Adjustment Administration as "the most successful and generally popular feature of the New Deal." [3]

V

For all the external success, interior tensions remained. Peek and Frank (and, behind Frank, Tugwell) had represented the opposite poles of old-school agrarianism and urban liberalism in AAA in 1933; and Wallace, by making Chester Davis chief of AAA, doubtless thought he was bringing in a skilled and patient conciliator who might compose the internal differences. A native of Iowa, a graduate of Grinnell, Davis had been a farm editor in Montana and then state commissioner of agriculture before he went to Washington in the twenties. Next to Peek himself, no man had been more identified with the McNary-Haugen fight than Davis. Yet, fourteen years younger than Peek and far less set in his ways, Davis had been among the first to abandon the McNary-Haugen hope that export dumping could solve the surplus problem. In the debates of the first year of AAA, he had sided with Wallace and Wilson on the crucial issue of production control. A short, sturdy, twinkling figure of a man, tough and humorous in manner, moderate and practical in approach, he seemed well qualified to mediate between the old school and the new.

Still Wallace, in choosing Davis, was making a decisive choice. For the realistic Davis was determined to work for the farmer within the existing structure of agricultural power. Davis was a man, in many respects, of broad social outlook; he often had reservations about the processors; he was often irritated by the triple alliance of Extension Service, Farm Bureau, and Land Grant College. But he did not consider it his duty as head of AAA to alter the conditions of his job. That job, as he saw it, was recovery, and to achieve recovery he was prepared to work with all the forces in the agricultural picture. In so doing, he could not help clashing with the reformers.

Though Tugwell remained the ultimate inspiration for the liberals within the Department, he had now almost no role in AAA. Wallace had not even consulted him on Davis's appointment, and Davis consulted him as little as possible thereafter. Within AAA Jerome Frank was more than ever the sparkplug of the reform drive, abetted by his staff of young lawyers, and aggressively supported by Fred Howe, Gardner Jackson, and the office of the Consumers' Counsel. As reformers, they wanted to take advantage of the emergency to tackle the more revolting evils in the agricultural economy — the chronic poverty of the sharecropper and the tenant farmer; the wretched conditions of farm labor; the excessive profit margins and restrictive marketing practices of the processors and distributors. For them AAA was not just a means of restoring farm income. It was also an opportunity to revise the distribution of income within the agricultural community. To achieve their objectives, the reformers often went over the head of Davis, their superior, and tried to amend or reverse his decisions by informal representations to the office of the Secretary.

The relations of the reform group with what they called "Henry's father's gang" were varied and fluctuating. There were able and devoted men in both camps, working hard together on problems of common concern, agreeing more often than they disagreed. Nonetheless both sides became increasingly aware of large and basic differences. As issues developed, the bureaucratic cold war, waged through obstruction and harassment inside the organization and through leaks to the press outside, steadily grew in intensity.

Friction continued over marketing agreements even after Peek's resignation. While Davis, unlike Peek, had no belief in marketing agreements as a sovereign remedy, he considered them a useful supplement to production control; moreover, marketing agreements provided a means of relief for farmers whose production of "non-basic" crops — fruits and vegetables — kept them out of the cash benefit system. Davis believed, in addition, that the success of the broad AAA program required a continuing effort to enlist the friendly cooperation of the processors. Tugwell and the reformers thought otherwise; and, in the summer of 1934, when Davis was engaged in confidential talks with large packers over raising farm prices, he was suddenly confronted by news of a speech delivered by Tugwell in Des Moines blasting certain packers by name for their refusal to open up their books. The packers, clouted by one part of the Department of Agriculture while they were chatting with another, felt themselves the victims of bad faith, and Davis, furious at seeing his negotiations undercut, complained to Wallace, who issued instructions that all speeches touching on AAA issues must thereafter be cleared with the Administrator. "The point at issue," as Paul Appleby defined it, "is a rather fundamental difference of opinion concerning the wisdom of attacking the processors. Chester believes that Earl Smith and Cliff Gregory are the best examples of successful farm leadership and they make it a point always to play with the big boys." Appleby added, speaking the mind of the Frank group, "My own feeling is that if we were to choose from a standpoint of political expediency between an attitude of continual pugnacity and continual playing with the big boys, I think, as Democrats, we certainly should choose pugnacity."

Milk presented a particular area of tension. "The toughest problem has been milk and dairy products," Davis told the National Emergency Council in February 1934. "In our own work, the milk problem worries me most," Tugwell wrote in his diary in April. No commodity was more essential to the nation's health; but in few fields was distribution more chaotic, or the middlemen's cut larger, or the middlemen themselves a more mixed lot. (As Jerome Frank had remarked on his return from a milk hearing in Chicago where gangsters were prominent in the audience, their artillery presumably under their overcoats, "And I thought agriculture was such a mild, pastoral calling.") The first milk marketing agreements had pretty much broken down by January 1934; and the big milk distributors had shown every disposition to run things in their own way in the future.

In a speech at Madison, Wisconsin, late in January, Henry Wallace condemned what he represented as the excessively high profit margins enjoyed by distributors in the large milksheds. At the same time, AAA liberals, especially in the office of the Consumers' Counsel, were arguing that milk should be declared a public utility and even proposing experiments with municipal milk processing and distribution. Roosevelt himself rather liked — indeed, may have suggested — the notion of trying out municipal milk projects; and planning progressed to the point where a city — Milwaukee, with its Socialist mayor — was selected for the experiment. The milk industry, for its part, decided to fight back. Pat Jackson, the Assistant Consumers' Counsel, brought Wallace the story of a secret industry meeting in Philadelphia where it was decided to go after the AAA liberals. Wallace listened in reverie.

"I don't understand you," he said at last, "— you and your friend Justice Brandeis. When you see something you think is wrong, you want to do something about it right away. You want to act quickly. I'm not like that. I'd rather sit under a tree and let the cycle of time help heal the situation." Here he made a broad circular motion with his right arm. Then: "I know in Rex and Chester I've got two ill-matched horses in harness together. I may have to let one of them go when we get a bit further down the road. I can't tell now which it will be." [4]

VI

In the meantime, a fresh issue entered the situation. This was the problem of the southern sharecropper, suddenly thrust into public attention by the effect of the cotton plow-up program of 1933 on croppers and tenant farmers. The first question involved was the division of the benefit payments handed out in exchange for the plowed acreage. The cotton contract was a land rental contract, which meant that the payment of the rental went to the person who controlled the land. The only benefit the cropper could expect was the increased price he received on his half of the crop, plus half of such "parity" payments as were made. This meant that the planters received about 90 per cent of the government payments. In addition, as cotton acreage contracted, many cropper families were cast off their farms to go on relief or to shift pitifully for themselves. The ones who had fallen farthest behind were ordinarily turned loose first.

An AAA survey, conducted by Professor Calvin B. Hoover of Duke University, underlined the human pathos of the situation. But, as Chester Davis saw it, there was all too little AAA could do. A procedure was set up for the investigation of complaints; but it took an unusually defiant cropper to bring charges against his own landlord. To have weighted the program by requiring arbitrary payments to share tenants would have merely invited the substitution of day labor for tenancy. The basic problem, in Davis's analysis, was the overconcentration of labor in the cotton states, and AAA could do little or nothing about that.

Nevertheless, Davis held up the 1934–35 cotton contract for several weeks in his office in order to work out with Hoover a clause giving tenant farmers more protection under the provisions for acreage control — a clause inserted in the contract over the implacable opposition of such representatives of the planters themselves as Oscar Johnston. Alger Hiss represented the Legal Division in this discussion; and language was eventually agreed upon binding the landlord as far as possible to keep the same number of tenant units that he had in 1933 and assuring the tenant continued possession of his cabin, garden land, access to wood lots, and other things necessary for family maintenance. At the same time, the contract seemed clearly to recognize that while the landlord could be made to keep the same *number* of tenants he could not pledge himself to keep the same tenants, any more than the tenant himself could be pledged to the same landlord.

"They cannot move people off the farms as a result of this campaign," Davis said early in 1934. But this prediction proved optimistic. Landlords dominated the local administration of the act; and the displacement of tenants continued. In the meantime, their plight was attracting national attention. The Southern Tenant Farmers' Union was organized. Norman Thomas led the way in condemning the inequitable results of AAA in the South. While the outside agitation unquestionably exaggerated the actual amount of displacement, it also hardened the determination of the AAA liberals to try to correct the balance. The means eventually hit upon was a reinterpretation of the tenant provision of the AAA contract. A new opinion, written by Alger Hiss and approved by Frank, declared — in line with the demands of the Southern Tenant Farmers' Union — that every individual tenant had the right to continue in his place during the life of the contract. This opinion, the reformers believed, would bring AAA operations more in line with the larger objectives of the farm program and the New Deal. While Davis was on a field trip early in 1935, Frank prevailed upon the Acting Administrator, without consultation with Davis or other top AAA officials, to send out the Hiss reinterpretation as a new AAA directive.

On his return, Davis in cold fury canceled the directive both as intolerable administrative insubordination and as a wholly unjustified reversal of the basis on which the cotton contracts had been administered through their first year. It put AAA into the reform business, he thought, under conditions which might lead to revolutionary outbreaks in the South. If the reinterpretation had been carried out, Davis said later, "Henry Wallace would have been forced out of the Cabinet within a month." Going to Wallace, Davis bluntly demanded a showdown. The Secretary would have to choose: either Jerome Frank would get out, or Davis himself. Wallace, who had so long avoided the ultimate decision, finally agreed that the reformers had gone too far. "I am convinced that from a legal point of view, they had nothing to stand on," he later noted in his diary, "and that they allowed their social preconceptions to lead them into something which was not only indefensible from a practical agricultural point of view but also bad law." But what to do now? Stay out of the picture for twenty-four hours, said Davis, and let me handle it. How? By abolishing the office of General Counsel and firing the troublemakers in AAA — and here Davis named several headed by Frank, Pressman, Howe, and Jackson. Alger Hiss was oddly not on Davis's purge list, though Davis had complained particularly of him to Wallace; but Davis, who considered Hiss honest and hard-working, evidently felt that this eager young lawyer had been misled by Frank and Pressman. No one discussed ulterior motives in connection with the dismissals, though fifteen years later Davis remembered Wallace's apparently irrelevant remark that he could not go along with Communists; they didn't believe in God.

The next morning curt dismissal letters signed by Davis began to descend on selected desks in AAA. In the afternoon, the purgees, tense and angry, met in Jerome Frank's office to discuss what should be done, and to await an appointment with Henry Wallace. With them were others, like Hiss, who, though not fired, had said they would resign. Frank, rising from his desk at frequent intervals to pace the room, sucking deeply on one cigarette after another, talking with fervent emotion, announced his continuing faith in Henry Wallace. After all, they were simply carrying out Wallace's own ideals. Frank talked on, reassuring the others with his torrent of eloquence. Only Lee Pressman, self-contained and sardonic, dissented, asking in mocking tones how Frank could be so naïve as to rely on Wallace.

Finally word arrived that Wallace would see two of the rebels.

Jerome Frank and Alger Hiss were chosen to go. Frank was still full of hope as they went out the door and down the long corridor. When they entered the Secretary's office, Wallace greeted them, his hand outstretched, his face filled with emotion. He told Frank that he and the others had been the best fighters in a good cause that he had ever worked with, but that he had to fire them. Frank asked why he had not told them so himself. Wallace hesitated a moment, then said softly that he had just not been able to face them.

Rex Tugwell, who had been on vacation in Florida, returned hastily to Washington. He talked to Harry Hopkins, who was outraged, to Louis Howe, who was sympathetic, to Wallace, who seemed halting and abashed, and to the President. Tugwell saw the purge as part of a studied plan to drive all liberals out of the Department and turn control over to the conservative farm leaders and to the processors. Basic issues of the New Deal were involved, he told Wallace and Roosevelt; the purgees had been fighting the New Deal fight. Tugwell added that he had about decided to resign himself. "The Secretary makes no decisions," he observed dispiritedly to the President, "and when I make decisions he is quite as likely to back up the person decided against as he is to back up me. I have been told that I am to have nothing to do with AAA policies and I do not feel that I can function properly as things are."

Roosevelt responded that he would take it as a personal favor if Tugwell would sit tight and wait until he could work the situation out. The President had no choice but to back Wallace and Davis. Still, he had high regard for Jerome Frank (whom he immediately placed in the RFC) and great fondness for Pat Jackson. When Senator Costigan expressed concern over the purge, Roosevelt replied, "I sympathize much with your thought about the Agriculture changes." Then he added thoughtfully, "Sometimes situations arise in an administrative organization where two or more people simply do not seem to get on with each other. In most cases neither side is at fault. Nevertheless, when situations like that arise, the first thing to do is to try to smooth out the troubles and if that does not work the next thing to do is to remove one side or the other from the picture! . . . All I can tell you is that I am sorry and have the highest respect for all parties concerned." [5]

VII

For Wallace, the process of choosing was difficult, but the choice was predestined. On the one side, there was the ultimate hope of the New Deal — the vision of social reconstruction which Wallace, in his prophetic mood, so deeply shared. On the other, there were the hard practicalities of politics, not so ultimate, perhaps, but more insistent. While one lobe of Wallace's brain responded avidly to idealism, the other responded even more avidly to the Farm Bureau, the Extension Service, and Senator Joe Robinson of Arkansas. And Washington had developed new appetites in Wallace. From 1935 on — or at least so friends of Wallace like Tugwell and La Follette came to believe — the Secretary of Agriculture was dominated by the mounting ambition to be the successor to the President. And, even apart from this, Wallace was not, like Tugwell and Frank, a city slicker; at bottom, he had emerged from the same environment as Chester Davis and George Peek.

So Frank, rather than Davis, went in February 1935. Yet Wallace still aimed at riding conservative and liberal horses; and he did it with continuing personal skill. Davis and Tugwell alike were more clearheaded and categorical than Wallace. He owed much of his reputation to the calm competence with which Davis ran AAA and to the courage with which Tugwell reorganized and streamlined the rest of the Department. In addition both knew well the extent to which the Secretary was preserved from foolishness by the vigilance of his own staff, particularly by the astute Appleby and later by the irresistible and penetrating Kentuckian Paul A. Porter. Yet for all the dreaminess, for all the Roerich nonsense, for all the Navajo medicine men who still occasionally enticed him, there remained a personal power in Wallace, vague but compelling, to which even Davis, even Tugwell, with their clarity and certitude, could not but defer.

It was partly Wallace's large and brooding sense of his job. He knew by birthright all the stock responsibilities of the Secretary of Agriculture. He added to this an expert's respect for experts. Economists and scientists had never felt so direct a contact with the making of agricultural policy. And, beyond this, he had a passion for the life and needs of the Department — a passion that spread a new excitement among those who had worked so long in limited jobs for limited objectives. The past was never enough for Wallace; and the future required new insights and new convictions. Thus he imported sages to tone up the staff — George Russell, Æ, the Irish poet; and the miscellany of philosophers and anthropologists collected by M. L. Wilson. Much of this was show; but much stuck, and it charged routine assignments with a sense of mission. Wallace had little talent for administration as such; but, for all the confusion and friction which arose as his Department took on new and sometimes ill-defined functions, its morale had not been so high for a generation.

Nor had its purposes been so concerted. For Wallace had a conception of agriculture as a national problem, its special aspects — from corn to cotton, from apples in Oregon to grapefruit in Florida — all parts of the larger whole; and this national problem, as he saw it, had to be met in national terms. Thus embodying the idea of a national solution for agriculture, he conducted an effective campaign of education in the Congress and among the public and, almost as important, among the farm organizations and within the agricultural hierarchy.

He had a sound instinct for emerging needs. He was aware in 1935 that AAA, in its original form, was beginning to play out. Acreage reduction was breaking down in certain areas, partly because too many farmers (as in wheat) were staying outside the system, partly because increases in productivity nullified the effect of reducing acreage. The Act was under challenge in the courts, too, particularly from the processors; and Wallace, as he told Henry Morgenthau on a walk to work on a fall morning in 1935, would be glad enough to have the processing tax declared unconstitutional, so that AAA would thereafter get its money from the general tax funds. It was clear to him, and even clearer to Howard R. Tolley, head of the Program Planning Division, that AAA would have to evolve in new directions. Beginning in 1934, the Department's planners thought more than ever of realizing Wallace's old dream of an "evernormal granary" through a system of price supports based on government loans for storable commodities.

And it was equally clear that AAA by itself would not be enough. An adequate national agricultural policy would have to do more than control production; it would have to go behind the problem of production into the question of the land itself, and it would have to go beyond the problem of production into the question of consumption.

Much of vital importance was started in 1933 and 1934 looking toward the conservation of natural resources, especially after the dust storms shocked the nation into a recognition of the need. Wallace gave this movement hearty support, and a good deal of it took place in his own Department. As for an increase in consumption, this depended, in the first instance, on industrial recovery. Beyond this, there lay the hope of getting more farm products consumed through developing healthier national food habits. Wallace and his associates started to think about programs which would promote and subsidize consumption, providing nutritious diets for families which could not otherwise afford the right foods. In these terms, the surplus removal programs could take on a new and more positive function. If the American people, particularly in the low-income groups, were to eat all they needed, the Department estimated, the agricultural surplus would largely disappear.[6]

VIII

In addition, Wallace never abandoned the hope that foreign markets might open up once again for the American agricultural surplus. He knew that dumping could never pry them open; and, in the first year of the farm program, he insisted that foreign markets should play no material part in AAA calculations. But for the long run he sharply opposed the idea of national self-sufficiency. After brooding on the subject, he expressed his thoughts in a pamphlet of the spring of 1934 called *America Must Choose*.

Thoroughgoing nationalism, he contended, would have dangerous implications: the retirement of 40 to 100 million acres of farm land; the licensing of the rest; base and surplus quotas for every farmer for every product for every month of every year; compulsory control of marketing. Nor would regimentation necessarily stop there. It might indeed, Wallace wrote, "go farther and faster here than anywhere else, if we once took the bit in our teeth and set up for a 100 percent American conformity in everything. We are a people given to excesses." He recalled the Liberty Loan drives; he mentioned the demands from the farmers themselves that AAA programs be made compulsory. "Under such conditions the traditional American spirit would soon be, it seems to me, as a spring, tightly coiled, and ready to burst out dangerously in any direction. I wonder if we could stand the strain."

What about the internationalist alternative? This would require, Wallace said, the purchase from abroad of nearly a billion dollars more goods than in 1929, which would mean the radical reduction of tariffs and the retirement of some of America's protected industries. Obviously he considered this preferable to "the pain of a pinched-in national economy"; but he felt it called for too much in the way of rapid readjustment. With his penchant for solving problems by splitting the difference, he ended by advocating a planned middle course which would retract good agricultural land by 25 million acres and lower tariffs enough to bring in annually another half-billion dollars' worth of goods.

America Must Choose had an instant impact. Its prose was vigorous and colloquial; and its analysis seemed sharp and to the point (even if, after beginning by implying that America "must" choose between nationalism and internationalism, Wallace characteristically ended by showing that the choice could be evaded). And the argument had an appealing prophetic resonance. The keynote of the new age, Wallace wrote, was the overwhelming realization that mankind now had "such mental and spiritual powers and such control over nature that the doctrine of the struggle for existence is definitely outmoded and replaced by the higher law of cooperation." The vision of Isaiah and the insight of Christ, he suggested, were on their way toward fulfillment.

In six months over 100,000 copies of *America Must Choose* were in type. It was widely reprinted in the United States and abroad. It seemed almost as if the prophet had found his voice. The fight to save agriculture from collapse was ending by making Henry Wallace a national figure.[7]

II

Experiment in
Industrial Planning

6. The Birth of NRA

THE FIGHT TO SAVE the banking system opened the Hundred Days; the fight to save the farmers opened the New Deal proper. But throughout the sleepless days and nights of March 1933 a major gap in the recovery program became increasingly vivid and disconcerting. For the heart of the American economy was neither finance nor agriculture but industry; and that heart was only beating faintly. By the Federal Reserve Board index, manufacturing production declined from 110 in 1929 to 57 in 1932 — almost 50 per cent. The total value of all finished commodities at current prices had fallen even more — from $38 billion to $17.5 billion. Private construction had crashed from $7.5 billion to a dismal $1.5 billion. As General Hugh Johnson contended to Raymond Moley on the New York train five days after the inauguration, a rise in farm prices without a corresponding stimulation of industrial activity would be fatal to recovery.

But how to go about stimulating industry? Johnson and Moley agreed on one thing: that the industrial program would have to be carried out in a framework of business-government partnership. The General, who had helped mobilize industry for war fifteen years earlier, now advocated a comparable national effort to mobilize industry for recovery. He had always believed that the War Industries Board contained lessons for peace. "If cooperation can do so much," he had reflected after the war, "maybe there is something wrong with the old competitive system." In a report of December 1918 he wrote that although detailed central controls might not be necessary, the peacetime economy could attain full efficiency only by permitting planning through trade associations in areas where joint action was forbidden under the antitrust laws. In 1919 he tried with Peek to establish what he called "self-government in industry under government supervision" through the short-lived Industrial Board. Business experience in the twenties only confirmed his dislike of unrestrained competition. Depression perfected the indictment. The antitrust acts, Johnson declared, had failed the nation in every crisis. They had to be suspended during the war to enable the country to defend itself. When they were restored in 1919, they set the stage for 1929. They fed the inflation, and they fostered the crash. Unchecked competition had no place in a mechanized and integrated society. "The very heart of the New Deal," he asserted, "is the principle of concerted action in industry and agriculture under government supervision looking to a balanced economy as opposed to the murderous doctrine of savage and wolfish individualism, looking to dog-eat-dog and devil take the hindmost."

Johnson's personal patron and old War Industries Board chief lent the force of his own presumably supernatural economic wisdom to this general view. Bernard Baruch too had favored coordination through trade associations under public supervision in 1919. As early as the spring of 1930, he called for suspension of the antitrust laws to permit collaborative business action against depression. On May 20, 1933, he denounced the Sherman Act, invoked the WIB example, and renewed his call for industrial planning.[1]

II

In the meantime, business itself had gone far to provide "self-government" an organizational basis. The key instrumentality, as Johnson and Baruch had argued in 1919, was the trade association; this was, said Raymond Moley, "the natural means which economic life has sought to find a way out of chaos." (In 1922 Franklin D. Roosevelt himself had become president of one such association, the American Construction Council.) Throughout the twenties, the Federal Trade Commission not only stimulated the spread of these associations but encouraged them to promulgate "codes of fair competition" for their industries. About 150 such codes were adopted between 1926 and 1933. And by 1931 business leaders — especially

Henry I. Harriman of the Chamber of Commerce and Gerard Swope of General Electric (another War Industries Board veteran) — were calling for national economic planning through the trade associations.

Beyond the general proposals of Harriman and Swope for all industry, the cry for planning arose with special urgency in industries confronting particularly chaotic internal conditions. Oil, for example, was greatly overdeveloped in terms of existing demand as a result of the tapping of new pools between 1926 and 1931. When depression came, the industry itself tried to allocate production, first through voluntary agreements and then through state legislation. As these controls broke down, industry leaders by early 1933, seeing anarchy ahead, began to plead for a federal oil dictator.

In other unstable industries, like coal and the needle trades, the demand for planning came from organized labor. Here the trade association was bypassed in favor of direct resort to government. In the case of coal, which had been a sick industry through the twenties, the United Mine Workers early developed a plan to stabilize the industry through federal licensing, control of production, suspension of antitrust laws, a thirty-hour week and the guarantee of collective bargaining. After the onset of depression, it became apparent to John L. Lewis, the Mine Workers' president, that coal could not be stabilized apart from the rest of the economy. Accordingly he began to urge the extension of these principles to the economy as a whole. (Some coal operators had more drastic views, urging a federal coal dictator and even telling the Secretary of Labor that they would "sell the mines to the government at any price fixed by the government. Anything so we can get out of it.")

The garment industry, with a long history of destructive competition, had similarly produced labor leadership interested in stabilizing production and employment. Like Lewis, Sidney Hillman of the Amalgamated Clothing Workers believed that the disease had spread beyond his own industry and that the time had come, as he said in 1933, for the establishment of "an instrumentality to coordinate the industries of this country and with power to put its planning at once into effect." [2]

III

There were, in addition, special labor interests at stake, which made even a conservative American Federation of Labor leader like Matthew Woll call for "national planning which will conceive of the economic activity of the nation as a whole rather than individual parts." In an unplanned system, labor seemed the first casualty of economic crisis. The obvious way to preserve profits was to cut costs; the firm which worked its labor longest and paid it least gained the greatest competitive advantages. "Cutthroat competition," as Hillman observed, "makes the unscrupulous employer the leader in each industry and the rest willingly or otherwise follow." (Businessmen who cut wages had the further satisfaction of knowing they were following the injunction of orthodox economics that the effort to maintain wage rates increased unemployment.)

With the worker — and the responsible businessman — thus at the mercy of the greedy, desperate or doctrinaire competitor, standards of wages and hours, attained after so many years of battle and negotiation, began to crumble away. No state laws existed to provide effective protection for wages; and, where laws regulated working hours, no state had a weekly limit as low as 44 hours even for women. Sweatshops were springing up on every side. Child labor was coming back. The Pennsylvania Department of Labor and Industry reported that half the women in the textile and clothing industries were earning less than $6.58 a week, and 20 per cent less than $5. In Fall River, Massachusetts, more than half the employees in a garment factory were getting fifteen cents an hour or less. At the same time, the work week in some states was lengthening to sixty, sixty-five, even seventy hours. There stretched ahead only the prospect of longer, grimmer work days and thinner pay envelopes.

In many cases, trade associations hoped through industry agreement to resist the attack on labor standards. But, when the Cotton Textile Institute resolved not to work women at night, 15 per cent of the manufacturers refused to comply, and the agreement broke down. How to protect the responsible employer in his effort to resist the pressure against wages and hours? In New York, laundrymen sought out the National Consumers' League and offered it

$10,000 a year if it would inspect and "white-list" laundries main-
taining fair wages and hours. But others simply gave up the voluntary effort. George W. Alger, impartial chairman of the cloak-and-
suit industry, declared, "I am convinced today that decent industry
needs help from law, which it never required before." As the
executive secretary of the chemical industry trade association put
it, the individual selfishness of employers left legislation as the
only method by which unfair practices could be eliminated.

Even before his inauguration, Molly Dewson, once of the Consumers' League, more recently of the Women's Division of the
Democratic party, urged on Roosevelt the importance of wages
and hours legislation to arrest the downward spiral. When New
York passed a minimum-wage law in April 1933, Roosevelt called
on governors of a dozen other states to take similar action. But would
state action solve a nationwide problem? Hillman had already recommended that the federal government set up labor boards to control wages and hours in all industries where self-government had
broken down. And the American Federation of Labor, unwilling
to go quite that far, now threw its support to a measure introduced into the Senate by Hugo Black of Alabama — a bill prohibiting interstate shipment of goods produced by men working
more than thirty hours a week.

The case for a limitation on working hours had received its most
effective statement in *Jobs, Machines and Capitalism,* a book by
Arthur Dahlberg published in 1932. It had won some support in
business circles: thus Ralph Flanders of the Jones and Lamson machine tool company wrote that it was "difficult to disagree with
Dahlberg's arguments" (though by 1933 both Dahlberg and Flanders concluded that the depression had become too severe to respond
to the thirty-hour remedy). From Dahlberg, Black took the theory
that technological progress would create a permanent labor surplus unless work was in some manner spread among the entire
labor force. And, in addition, Black argued that the thirty-hour
week was essential in the present emergency; it would halt the
attack on labor standards and, by forcing employers to hire more
workers, would reduce unemployment and increase mass purchasing
power. Black put no minimum-wage provisions in the bill, apparently in the belief that the Supreme Court had outlawed federal

regulations of wage rates; also perhaps because of the American Federation of Labor's continued opposition to minimum-wage legislation. He was confident that as the shorter week tended to create a labor shortage the increase in labor's bargaining power would push wages up. His bill, he predicted, would put six million men back to work, give new strength to organized labor, and provide a permanent means of absorbing the consequences of technological progress.

Organized labor agreed. If Congress did not enact the bill, William Green, the AF of L president, told a Senate committee, labor would exercise its "economic force"; he spoke ominously of a general strike. "Which would be class war, practically?" said Black. "That is the only language that a lot of employers ever understand," said Green; " — the language of force." [3]

IV

The movement for industrial coordination had still another source: the proponents of concentration and control who traced their inspiration back to the New Nationalism of Theodore Roosevelt. Thus a veteran of the Bull Moose crusade like Donald Richberg had never abandoned the dream of what he had termed in 1917 the "democratization of industry." "There might grow, out of our present spreading commercial empires," he wrote in 1929, "a group of industrial republics within our national boundaries"; this, he said, would give democratic government "a new birth in state and nation." The grand objective, as he saw it, was "self-government in industry."

Depression made Richberg call with new vehemence on government to take the lead in bringing about industrial reorganization. "While not advocating the permanent socialization of business or property," he told a Senate committee, "we believe that an emergency governmental control is now as essential to the national welfare as it would be in a time of war. . . . No man with sufficient intelligence to be worthy of any attention can deny that a planned control of the great essential industries is absolutely essential." When someone asked how far he would extend that control, Richberg answered quickly, "Practically as far as necessary to put the employees back to work by whatever means were necessary. . . . A nationally planned economy is the only salvation of our present situation and the only hope for the future." He proposed a national planning council on top of a pyramid of industrial councils. He differed from Harriman and Swope in resting industrial self-government not on trade associations but on councils made up of managers, investors, and workers and in visualizing a larger measure of federal intervention.

Richberg advanced these ideas in a mood of extreme radicalism. The planning solution, he said bitterly, would probably be intolerable to the masters of industry because of their "insensate greed." "Although the conspicuous money-makers who presume to advise you have proved their ability to make themselves wealthy," he told the senators, "it is far more important for this committee to realize that they have also proved their ability to make millions of people very poor." His only concern, Richberg added, was whether an effective program could be put into effect "before too large a percentage of the people have been starved into either hopeless resignation or desperate revolt."

Within Roosevelt's own circle, Moley favored what he called "a policy of cooperative business-government planning" to combat economic instability and social insecurity. Tugwell had a particularly comprehensive conception of government-business planning. "Self-government in industry" by itself, Tugwell thought, would only benefit the individual industry. What was necessary was rather "a forced balance among all industries." In *The Industrial Discipline* in 1933 he advanced the idea of coordination through an Industrial Integration Board. Each trade association would have its own planning apparatus; and the Board would reconcile the plans of the affiliated industries with the basic plan laid down by government. Only in this way, Tugwell felt, could the private collectivism created by the new technology be reliably harnessed to the public interest. Nor would he recoil from the War Industries Board model; after all he once favorably described the War Industries Board as "America's War-Time Socialism."

Jerome Frank, Tugwell's ally in the Department of Agriculture, had similar views. He felt that the key mass-production industries should be treated frankly as monopolies and made to adopt intelligent policies; and he contended that the solution of the problems of a profit economy lay in *"an intensification of coordination between all parts of the economy."* "Just as America took an important step forward when it rejected political anarchy and integrated this continent into one nation," wrote Frank, "so it needs now to press forward to a deliberate economic integration." Like Tugwell, Frank would strive for this integration through a new central agency.

The planning philosophy had support in the Senate, notably from Robert F. Wagner of New York and Robert M. La Follette, Jr., of Wisconsin. No member of the Senate had been so consistently alert to the problems of industrial society as Wagner. Even before the depression, he had argued that government had the responsibility and could have the power to maintain employment and stability. In 1931 he called for a public works program, a federal employment stabilization board, and a federal system of unemployment insurance. La Follette at the same time had contended for large public works and relief programs as well as for a national economic council. With the new administration, both Wagner and La Follette were determined to press for new initiative in the industrial field.[4]

V

And so, from diverse sources — from recollections of the war mobilization of fifteen years before, from business hopes for protection of prices and profits, from trade union hopes for protection of labor standards, from liberal hopes for creative national planning, from a collective revulsion against a competitive system which competed at the expense of human decency — opinion was converging on a broad approach to the problem of industrial recovery. With past policies of exhortation and drift discredited, with state socialism undesired and politically excluded, there remained the prospect of a mighty attempt, organized by government, to halt the decline through a massive experiment in national cooperation. Even a writer like John T. Flynn, so soon to be an impassioned critic of the result (and to blame it all on the United States Chamber of Commerce), called in March 1933 for the establishment "without delay" of an Economic Council to "take measures for bal-

THE BIRTH OF NRA

anced production through the organization of trades under government supervision."

The nation was more than ready. Many people had an anguished
sense of crisis. For some, society itself seemed confronted by the
specter of dissolution. "It is no wonder," said Bernard Baruch,
"that the whole of industry seems to have risen *en masse* to find
some way to check it as a matter of stark self-preservation." Alexander Sachs of the Lehman Corporation, a close friend of Hugh
Johnson's, summed up the feeling when he said that the entire
Western economic order was threatened "not by the destructive
impact of external or natural forces, but by a spontaneous disintegration from within." This was not, Sachs said, normal economic
depression; it was *"economic nihilism, which, from a national point
of view, cannot be permitted to go on."* The crisis did appear, in a
phrase of the day, worse than war. For a moment, all bets were
off, all antagonisms adjourned; Americans, it seemed, had to work
together or else they would founder together.

The President, preoccupied with banking, agriculture, and relief, did little in his first month to face up to the industrial problem. Then the unexpected passage by the Senate of the Black
thirty-hour-week bill on April 6, 1933, ended administration lethargy. "It's the first constructive measure yet passed dealing with
unemployment," said William Green with satisfaction. But Frances
Perkins, upon whom the burden of policing the measure would
fall, was a good deal less satisfied. And the President was particularly repelled by the bill's rigidity: "there have to be hours
adapted to the rhythm of the cow," he remarked, thinking of its
irrelevance to the dairy industry. In addition, he considered the
bill unconstitutional. Yet he sympathized with its objectives; and he
did not want to embarrass the Democrats who had voted for it.
Above all, he must have sensed the rising demand in the nation for
action on the industrial front. "It was," Ernest K. Lindley wrote
of the Black bill, "revolution boiling up from the bottom."

In the meantime, a separate clamor had arisen in the Senate for a
federal public works program. This was led by Wagner, La Follette, and Costigan and backed by many in the administration (including Miss Perkins, Ickes, Dern, Tugwell, and Richberg, but
definitely excluding Douglas, who was strongly opposed). The

convergence of the Black bill and the public works drive meant that the administration could no longer put off thinking about a comprehensive plan for industry to parallel its program for agriculture. For some time, plans for industrial recovery had been indiscriminately dumped in the busy office of Raymond Moley at the State Department. Roosevelt now told Moley to get in touch with the people working on business-government cooperation plans around town and come up with some recommendations.[5]

VI

By this time several groups were working independently on the general problem. Because they had shifting and overlapping membership and engaged in a continual process of cross-consultation, it is difficult to reconstruct the sequence of developments; and the recollections of participants in this respect have proved as confusing as the events themselves doubtless were. It seems evident that two groups were especially important. One centered in Senator Wagner's office on Capitol Hill, the other in the office of John Dickinson, the Undersecretary of Commerce.

Wagner, of course, had been concerned with employment planning ever since arriving in the Senate. In his group, David Podell, a trade association lawyer, proposed modifying the Antitrust Act through codes of fair competition in the interests of business self-government; Gilbert H. Montague was an expert on the law of business association; Robert M. La Follette, Jr., emphasized public works and national planning; W. Jett Lauck of the United Mine Workers spoke both for the interests of labor and for the UMW approach to economic planning; and Harold Moulton of the Brookings Institution brought an economist's judgment to the reconciliation of the various suggestions. The Dickinson group drew primarily on the ideas and resources of the Executive Branch; along with Dickinson himself, Tugwell, Jerome Frank, and Frances Perkins were its active members. From the start, the two groups were in contact. Thus young Leon Keyserling, a Harvard Law School graduate whom Tugwell brought to Washington in March, came into the discussion as a lawyer on Frank's staff. His contribution at an early meeting impressed Wagner, who then invited

Keyserling to come to the Hill as his legislative assistant. After a time, the Wagner and Dickinson groups in effect joined forces and went to work on a common draft.

Moley, who was flooded with other responsibilities, was finding industrial expansion one project too many. At just this point, Baruch and Hugh Johnson, fresh from a hunting trip in South Carolina, showed up in Washington. Moley, running into Johnson in the lobby of the Carlton late in April, begged him to get into the picture: "Nobody can do it better than you. You're familiar with the only comparable thing that's ever been done — the work of the War Industries Board." Johnson needed no urging. He went over to Moley's office that afternoon, took off his coat and tie, unbuttoned his collar, and went to work with furious energy. A year of discussion with Alexander Sachs on the agenda of industrial re vival, on top of his own varied business experience, convinced him that he knew exactly what should be done. On only one point did he feel weak — the problem of labor. Then someone spoke of Donald Richberg. Johnson called him in, and they appeared to hit it off from the start.

By early May, there were two main drafts — a Johnson draft, written originally on a couple of sheets of legal-size foolscap, based on a tough government licensing system; it bore the endorsement of Moley, Douglas, and Richberg; and a Dickinson draft, more legalistic, complex, and cautious, looking to industrial self-government through trade associations, and bearing the endorsement of Frank and of the Wagner group. Tugwell liked much in the Dickinson-Wagner draft, but he was also attracted by the fact that Johnson had more power in his bill, with clearer compulsions. Henry I. Harriman, who was in and out of the discussions, preferred the Dickinson-Wagner draft because it made greater use of trade associations; but he also felt, like Tugwell, that the sanctions of the Johnson draft ought to be included. Frances Perkins regarded the public works provisions of both drafts as inadequate.

The President awaited the results of the interminable meetings with impatience. As early as April 12 he had hinted to his press conference about the possibility of a plan designed to secure "the regulation of production or, to put it better, the prevention of foolish over-production." When the United States Chamber of

Commerce met in Washington in early May, he called on business to work with government "to prevent over-production, to prevent unfair wages, to eliminate improper working conditions." (The convening businessmen could hardly have been more enthusiastic about the prospect. Of the forty-nine speakers, twenty-seven came out for more government direction of industry. "If we are to save our traditional freedom for the future," said Paul W. Litchfield of Goodyear Tire and Rubber, ". . . we must make substantial concessions to what we have in the past classified as the more radical school of thought.") And in his second fireside chat, on May 7, Roosevelt talked about "a partnership in planning" between government and business, with government having the "right" to "prevent, with the assistance of the overwhelming majority of that industry, unfair practices and to enforce this agreement by the authority of Government." (While they were working on this speech, Moley said, "You realize, then, that you're taking an enormous step away from the philosophy of equalitarianism and laissez-faire?" Roosevelt, silent a moment, replied with great earnestness, "If that philosophy hadn't proved to be bankrupt, Herbert Hoover would be sitting here right now. I never felt surer of anything in my life than I do of the soundness of this passage.")

Three days later, with Johnson and Dickinson still unable to reach agreement, a meeting was called at the White House. Here Roosevelt, after listening to the competing arguments, issued his familiar order that the group lock itself in a room until it could come out with a single proposal. Then Dickinson, Johnson, Wagner, Tugwell, Richberg, Frances Perkins, and Douglas moved over to Douglas's office for the final agony of drafting. There were unpleasant moments: Douglas made a last effort to knock out public works; Dickinson became biting and arrogant toward Johnson; but Tugwell, siding with Johnson in his demand for sanctions, helped resolve the dispute. By May 15, the long struggle was over, and a bill was ready for Congress.[6]

VII

The bill was divided into two main parts. Title I, "Industrial Recovery," proclaimed the intent of the Congress "to promote the organization of industry for the purpose of cooperative action among trade groups." Sections providing for codes of fair competition and for exemption from the antitrust laws embodied the trade association program; a provision for the federal licensing of business showed the influence of the national planners; and Section 7a, pledging collective bargaining, maximum hours, and minimum wages, fulfilled the hopes of labor and the promise of the Black bill. Title II, "Public Works and Construction Projects," calling for the establishment of a Public Works Administration with an appropriation of $3,300,000,000, satisfied the public works advocates. The Act was to be in effect for two years.

The House passed the bill with few changes in just over a week. Most important was a determined attempt, pressed by William Green, to strengthen Section 7a. This section had already had a precarious passage through the drafting process. The trade association group, evidently feeling that organization was a privilege to be accorded only to employers, accepted the idea of 7a with reluctance; even the more liberal among them, like Harriman and Swope, had made no provision for organized labor in their own plans. As a result, 7a was constantly on the verge of being defined out of existence. Only the vigilance of Jerome Frank, Leon Keyserling, and Senator Wagner and the fear of provoking labor opposition kept it in. Now Green took advantage of the House hearings to persuade the Ways and Means Committee to plug possible holes. Language taken over bodily from the Norris-La Guardia Act made explicit the protection of workers from coercion by anti-union employers, and other changes in phraseology specifically exempted workers from having to join company unions as a condition of employment.

In the Senate, however, the bill in general and 7a in particular had a stormier time. The National Association of Manufacturers and the Chamber of Commerce both assailed the labor provisions; and Senator Bennett C. Clark of Missouri came up with an amendment stating that "nothing in this title shall be construed to compel a change in existing satisfactory relationships between the employees and employers of any particular plant, firm, or corporation." The Senate liberals, led by George Norris, were quick to denounce this as an attempt to favor company unions, if not to legalize yellow dog contracts. Clark then astonished the opposition by explaining that Donald Richberg, who had been present during discussions of the amendment, had said he thought it very beneficial. But the liberals, unmoved at this revelation, said that Richberg could not have understood what he was endorsing and voted down Clark's proposal.

The more important part of the Senate discussion, however, turned on another question — the significance of the suspension of the antitrust laws. William E. Borah of Idaho led the attack on the bill from the viewpoint of an old-fashioned antitruster, with cogent support from Burton K. Wheeler and Hugo Black; and Wagner, courteous, wearily patient, ever resourceful, defended the measure. The debate, conducted on an uncommonly high level, opened up basic issues. Borah contended that the suspension of the antitrust acts would infallibly promote the concentration of wealth and power. Wagner replied that the urgent need was to outlaw sweatshops, long hours, and low wages, and that this could only be done by allowing business cooperation. The issue quickly reduced to the question: Could industry be trusted to combine for fair standards for wages, hours, and working conditions without at the same time combining for pools and price-fixing? [7]

VIII

The question of price-fixing rapidly assumed critical importance. It was already clear that many businessmen — including, for example, the Chamber of Commerce group — believed that the bill conferred on industry the power to fix prices and restrict production. Businessmen wired Borah that if the bill did not do this it would be just a labor measure, and they wanted no part of it. Richberg, testifying before the House Committee, said that price-fixing would be permitted. But Wagner, who saw clearly the implications of uncontrolled price-fixing, stated vigorously in the Senate debate, "It is not contemplated that prices shall be fixed, because the fixation of prices is not in conformity with the preservation of fair competition." The bill was not designed, he said, to end competition but to lift its standards — "to make sure the best judgment and the highest ideals of the industry govern its competitive activities, replacing the now low standard of sweat-shop, cutthroat competition. . . . The bill does not abolish com-petition; it purifies and strengthens it."

Yet even Wagner made exceptions: sales below cost should be forbidden in the interests of preserving small enterprises against their chain competitors; moreover, cooperation might be neces-sary to prevent harmful price fluctuations. For these reasons Wagner opposed a Borah amendment flatly prohibiting price-fixing. The real danger, said Wagner, was "monopolistic price fixing"; and this was forbidden in the bill. "What the Senator fears," Wagner said, "can result only from a faithless and disloyal administration of the act." To this Borah, Wheeler, and Black responded in effect that suspension of the Sherman Act made a faithless and disloyal administration inevitable. "Do you mean to tell me," said Black, ". . . that they would meet and agree on minimum wages and maximum hours and never discuss, to any extent whatever, the questions of the price at which they were to sell their goods?" The big interests, added Borah, would always dominate code-making, whatever the language of the bill. But how else, except through the codes, Wagner responded, to outlaw sweatshops and to store up the crumbling position of labor? "I do not think we will ever have industry in order," he said, "until we have nationally planned economy, and this is the first step toward it."

It was a close argument. Given the presumption that a direct federal attack on wages and hours was unconstitutional, the only way that competition could be stopped from grinding labor stand-ards down to ever more squalid levels was through covenants en-forceable throughout the industry. Yet, if agreement were permit-ted on wages and hours for the benefit of labor, how to prevent agreement on prices and production for the benefit of monopoly? Opinion in the Senate swayed back and forth as the debate pro-gressed. Thus Black voted against Title I, for the bill, and finally against the conference report; La Follette, Norris, Wheeler, Costigan, Cutting, and other progressives voted for Title I and the bill, and then against the conference report; Huey Long, after denouncing the bill in unmeasured terms ("The Democratic Party dies tonight, Mr. President. We will bury it"), voted for it and then against the conference report. But the Senate finally adopted the conference report on June 13 by 46 to 39, and the bill was rushed to the President.

The purpose of the bill, the President said on June 16, was to put people back to work. It was to raise the purchasing power of labor by limiting hours and increasing wages. It was to elevate labor standards by making sure that no employer would suffer competitive disadvantages as a result of paying decent wages or establishing decent working conditions. Above all, it represented an historic experiment in government partnership with business. "It is a challenge to industry," Roosevelt emphasized, "which has long insisted that, given the right to act in unison, it could do much for the general good which has hitherto been unlawful. From today it has that right."

"History probably will record the National Industrial Recovery Act," Roosevelt added, "as the most important and far-reaching legislation ever enacted by the American Congress." [8]

7. The Blue Eagle

HUGH JOHNSON had not wasted a moment while the industrial recovery bill was going through Congress. Working sixteen to eighteen hours a day, he nursed the bill on the Hill, held conferences with businessmen and labor leaders, launched work on industrial codes, prepared organization charts, recruited personnel, talked on the long-distance phone with Bernard Baruch, and checked everything with the President. In the end, his devotion and his vigor were irresistible. One day, as they were going over an outline of the proposed organization, Roosevelt told him, "Hugh, you've got to *do* this job."

Under the tutelage of Alexander Sachs, the General had come to see Titles I and II of the act as inseparable. The reactivation of the capital-goods industry, he believed, was the lever of recovery; and only a great government public works effort could bring this about. If, for example, the public works program went into operation fast enough, it might increase purchasing power sufficiently for the rise in sales volume to absorb new labor costs without price increases. Johnson liked to think of the National Industrial Recovery Act as a giant organ through which he could play on the economy of the country. For this purpose, the Public Works Administration seemed an indispensable part of the keyboard.

II

But Roosevelt began to develop qualms over giving both responsibilities to Johnson. The General, for all his energy and capacity, was impetuous and sometimes irresponsible. Moreover, either industrial control or public works was a full-time job in itself. And they seemed to the President to be quite clearly separate jobs. Roosevelt saw the National Recovery Administration as the means for a long-run reform and reorganization of the economy; public works was an emergency program and at that point did not bulk large in his calculations. Accident bound the two titles together in a single statute; but common sense, in his judgment, prescribed two independent administrators.

The President raised the question of separating the two agencies in a cabinet meeting on June 16. The cabinet members, happy at the chance to whittle down a noncabinet rival, enthusiastically agreed. "It will be hard on Johnson," mused the President. "He won't like it, but I think it is the best thing to do." "Well," the President continued, "who shall it be?" After a quick look at her colleagues, Frances Perkins made a hesitant suggestion: "Why not the Secretary of the Interior?" The President replied, "I am against creating so many independent agencies. We ought not to create any more if we can help it. Is there any department or anybody better than the Secretary of the Interior?" Ickes then broke a long silence by saying dryly, "This is so sudden, Mr. President, but I think I have at least the negative and austere qualities which the handling of so much public money requires."

Johnson was then called in. As he greeted the cabinet around the long mahogany table, he thought that one or two of them had the expression of the cat which had just swallowed a canary. Roosevelt, never more charming, told Johnson that he was about to sign the bill and appoint him administrator. Johnson, beaming, made an appropriate response. Then Roosevelt, still smiling, went on to say that he felt that administering both titles would impose an inhuman burden on one man and that he had decided to make different arrangements for Title II.

Johnson's smile vanished. His face grew red, then purple. Finally he said, his tones low and strangled, "I don't see why. I don't see why." The President affecting not to notice, terminated the meeting. Then he beckoned Frances Perkins over. "Stick with Hugh," he said. "Keep him sweet. Don't let him explode." As for Johnson, he had already decided that NIRA could not possibly succeed. "Unless Title I and Title II could move abreast in perfect coordination the whole economic basis of the plan as we had proffered it was changed." He saw no course but resignation. As they moved out the door, Frances Perkins linked arms with him. Johnson, in a daze, mumbled, "He's ruined me."

When Miss Perkins tried to cheer him, he ignored her. "I've got to get out, I can't stay," he said. Determined to keep him from the newspapermen, she led him to her car. They drove slowly for miles around Washington as she tried to calm him down. "Don't pull out," she said. "It's terrible, it's terrible," was his distraught reply. In time her charm and persistence won the day. As Johnson later described the episode, Frances Perkins was "so understanding, friendly, kindly, and persuasive that there was hardly a choice but to agree with her and . . . very fatuously, I did." [1]

III

The episode was characteristic of Johnson. This emotional, pungent, truculent figure saw all life as melodrama slightly streaked with farce; he was forever rescuing the virtuous, foiling the villains, chewing the carpet in moods of excitement or despair, and mingling it all with a fusillade of insults, wisecracks, and picturesque phrases. Square-jawed, thick-necked, red-faced, profane, he combined the qualities of a top sergeant, a frontier editor, and a proconsul. When news of his appointment broke, he said typically, "It will be red fire at first and dead cats afterward. This is just like mounting the guillotine on the infinitesimal gamble that the ax won't work."

Temperament condemned him to excesses — of admiration, of scorn, of work, of language, of relaxation. He was a hero worshipper — Wilson, Baruch, now for a moment Roosevelt. No one in Washington labored so long, shouted so loudly, smoked so many cigarettes, or drank so much liquor. His hard, weary face was marked with lines; pouches were deepening under his fierce blue eyes: his voice seemed to grow every day more gruff, his jaw more flinty and uncompromising, his whole bearing more bellicose. Out the words would tumble in a cavalryman's tirade, blunt expletives varied by ingenious and sulphurous formulas of denunciation — critics "in whose veins there must flow something more than a trace of rodent blood," "perfumed guys from the State Department," merchants of bunk, guff, and hooey. Yet, when people hated Johnson most, he could suddenly become most disarming. There would well up the sentimentality which led him to weep over arias from *Madame Butterfly*, the slow, sleepy, abashed smile, the rueful self-criticism, the quotations from Scripture, the excesses of humility which followed the excesses of egotism.

His abilities were considerable. The campaign had shown that he had not only copious literary style and a talent for invective, but also a vast amount of more or less exact information about the workings of the American economy and a capacity to condense complex problems into simple and telling statements. Sometimes he pretended a disdain for general ideas ("I'm not going into any of that blah-blah," he said when a female interviewer asked him about the social philosophy behind NIRA); but he was, in fact, well read and even, on occasion, thoughtful. He won the job on his merits, not because Baruch recommended him for it. Actually, Baruch observed sourly later in the year, "He didn't even ask about Johnson. He just took him." Indeed, Baruch, who was not seeing Roosevelt at the time because of their disagreement over gold policy, actually warned Frances Perkins against Johnson. "I think he's a good number-three man, maybe a number-two man," Baruch said, "but he's not a number-one man. He's dangerous and unstable. He gets nervous and sometimes goes away for days without notice. I'm fond of him, but do tell the President to be careful." Baruch knew Johnson well — not only the bluster but the inner uncertainties it concealed, the incapacity to sustain decisions, the panicky escape into drunken sprees.

For his own number-two man, Johnson had already settled on Donald Richberg. Johnson wanted him as general counsel because he was an able lawyer and a sincere and persuasive exponent of the NIRA idea. He wanted him too because he assumed that Richberg had the confidence of labor and the liberals. A veteran of reform movements for a quarter of a century, Richberg, now fifty-two, was a year older than Johnson — a tall, bulky man, with a big and mostly bald head, large features which mingled benevolence with cunning, and an unexpected litheness of movement. Like Johnson,

Richberg was sensitive and emotional; but, unlike Johnson, he usually succeeded in masking his feelings under a smooth, bland, and almost diffident exterior. He had a sly, cynical humor, great ambition, and an immense capacity for adjustment. Friends knew well his high-pitched, giggling laugh when describing some legal or tactical success.

His writings — his novels, poems (largely unpublished) and his autobiography of 1930 — disclosed romantic and restless yearnings. He liked to see himself in stances of martyrdom, defying sinister and conspiratorial forces around him. Few progressives exceeded him in the passion with which he assailed the leaders of American business. He continually inveighed against the "traders, pawn-brokers and slave-drivers who have sought the mastery of the world for the witless purpose of squeezing more money out of more men." Yet how much was pose and how much reality? Harold Ickes, who had practiced law with him in Chicago, did not trust him. But then, Ickes trusted no one except himself. Still, certain ambiguities in Richberg's performance during the incubation of NIRA — his apparent acquiescence in price-fixing, his implication in the effort to dilute 7a — disturbed other old friends. In the meantime, Richberg took care that his position as Johnson's sub-ordinate would not shut him off from direct access to the President — an access which Roosevelt welcomed and Johnson reluctantly accepted.[2]

IV

On June 20, a short four days after the bill passed, Johnson was able to announce the formation of the National Recovery Administration. Already NRA personnel were taking over unfurnished offices in the new Commerce Building, of which Herbert Hoover was so proud ("the worst-planned and least efficient modern office building in the world," Johnson called it; its offices, he said, reminded him of the pay toilets in the Union Station). Johnson and Richberg immediately confronted a basic decision on the conception of the NRA job. If the code was the NRA's chosen instrument — the means by which industry pledged itself to shorter hours, higher wages, better trade practices, and better labor relations — then the critical questions were, first, how to get each industry under a code, and, second, how to make sure that code provisions were enforced.

From the viewpoint of the national planners, NRA at last provided the mechanism for straight-out government direction of the economy. The National Industrial Recovery Act "did not fix the design," Tugwell noted, "— the farm bill did that — but it carried it out even more perfectly." The only problem was to make sure that, in return for exemption from the antitrust laws, each industry met its obligations to the public welfare; and this called for hard-boiled code negotiations and a determined use of the licensing power. If it worked, Tugwell thought, each industry would end with a government of its own, under which it could promote its fundamental purpose ("production, rather than competition"). NRA could have been administered, Tugwell later wrote, so that a "great collectivism" would have channeled American energy into a disciplined national effort to establish a secure basis for well-being.

But from Johnson's seat it did not appear so simple. Though his memories were of the quasi-dictatorship of the War Industries Board, and though he himself had written tough sanctions into the Act, Johnson now found himself hamstrung by doubts concerning the constitutionality of his new power. Sachs, whom Johnson brought to Washington as head of the Research and Planning Division, was convinced that the Act was unconstitutional; and his arguments shook the confidence of his chief. In any case, Johnson, wondering whether legal compulsion would stand up in court, began to feel that he had no choice but to substitute social compulsion and thus to gamble on a voluntary approach to industrial planning. "The Act was of such nature," he said in a few months, "to be absolutely unenforceable without a strong surge of public opinion behind it." This feeling was strengthened by a report that, if the Act did not work out to their liking, a group of leading industrialists meant to take it to the courts. Faced with this possibility, Johnson decided that everything else had to be subordinated to winning the uncoerced assent of major industries to the codes. In this way, he could bypass the constitutional issue. NRA could not therefore be an agency of direction. It had to be a forum of bargaining. The licensing powers written so hopefully into the bill could not be invoked (and, indeed, never were).

The pressure on Johnson to take the road of persuasion rather than command was further increased by Roosevelt's amputation of the Public Works Administration. From the start, the President had NRA and PWA report to separate cabinet committees; and he never gave Ickes any special orders to keep in touch with Johnson. As for Ickes, who opposed Johnson's appointment, the PWA chief actually directed his subordinates not even to consult the General. For Ickes, the public works problem was not to spend money fast but to spend it honestly. While Johnson raced over the country, whipping businessmen into codes, Ickes sat at his desk in Interior examining projects with stingy and meticulous care. Given this wary approach to spending, PWA trickled money into the economy at too slow a pace to give much initial push to NRA. (One New Deal official had a recurrent dream according to which Roosevelt had made Johnson head of PWA and Ickes head of NRA. Johnson was spending money by the billions; he had galvanized state and local officials into prodigies of activity; the nation was humming with revival. Meanwhile Ickes, careful and suspicious, was still poking around in industry. No code had yet been signed, but Ickes had decided what the government had to do to make codes work and was prepared to enforce the public authority. Alas, only a dream.)

The disappearance of PWA meant, as Johnson saw it, that NRA had lost its engine of expansion. All it could do now, he believed, was to redistribute existing income among a larger number of workers in the hope that, if wage increases were not canceled out by higher prices, new purchasing power might gradually induce expansion. "Once deprived of the second lung," wrote Sachs, "the economy had to bear too great a burden on the NRA lung — inasmuch as the PWA was scarcely palpitating for almost half a year after the NRA was organized." As Johnson realized he could not offer the immediate physical stimulus of public works, he began to wonder whether he could substitute a moral stimulus that might induce expansion through a sheer upsurge of national emotion. If this were worth a try, it meant that he was more than ever dependent on winning the spontaneous support of industry.

Circumstances thus impelled Johnson to think in terms of winning cooperation rather than of exerting control. "How are we going to do it?" he said. "Public opinion." "I want to avoid even the smallest semblance of czarism," he said on another occasion. "It is industrial *self-government* that I am interested in. The function of this act is not to run out and control an industry, but for that industry to come to this table and offer its ideas as to what it thinks should be done." NRA's job was not to impose codes, but to accept them. Defining for Richberg the difference between AAA and NRA, Johnson wrote, "AAA thinks that government should run business. NRA thinks that business should run itself under government supervision." As he told the National Association of Manufacturers, "NRA is exactly what industry organized in trade associations makes it." He characteristically added that, before NRA, the trade associations had about as much effectiveness as an Old Ladies' Knitting Society; "now I am talking to a cluster of formerly emasculated trade associations about a law which proposes for the first time to give them potency." [3]

V

The General could not, of course, subdue his roar and bluster. But beneath the iron glove there usually lay a velvet hand. So the process of code-making turned from an exercise in overhead government planning into a series of protracted bilateral negotiations. And in these government was handicapped by a difficult bargaining position. In his initial statements, the President had made clear his belief that the codes should concentrate on the wages and hours provisions. This meant that each negotiation began with automatic concessions *from* industry — concessions which meant an increase in costs. The next phase, in other words, would naturally seem concessions *to* industry; and industry did not overlook this advantage. Thus Johnson had hoped to get the ten big industries under codes as rapidly as possible — textiles, coal, petroleum, steel, automobiles, lumber, garments, wholesale trade, retail trade, and construction. In only one case did he strike a quick response, and even here he had to compromise on basic NRA principles before he got his code.

This was the cotton textile industry, where the trade association had long striven for industry-wide agreements which might bring order into production and decency into working conditions. Because of this experience, the association had a draft code ready on the day the Act passed. The code contained the necessary provisions for maximum hours, minimum wages, and collective bargaining. Johnson thought that it should have, in addition, an express denunciation of child labor. The industry at first demurred, arguing that in practice the minimum-wage provisions would bring child labor to an end. But Johnson insisted; and, after an emergency meeting, the cotton textile people agreed to outlaw child labor by name — a decision which produced roars of applause when announced in the hearing room and instantly caught the imagination of the country.

By ending child labor in the cotton mills, NRA secured overnight what decades of reform agitation had failed to achieve. Who could have supposed that within four years of the bitter Gastonia strike the cotton mills would recognize unions and end sweatshops? Roosevelt said of child-labor abolition, "That makes me personally happier than any other one thing which I have been connected with since I came to Washington." If, in view of the new minimum wages, this renunciation was no great economic sacrifice for the mill-owners, it nevertheless seemed to offer a promising glimpse of the brighter world into which NRA might lead American business. But the Cotton Textile Code also illustrated the hazards of code negotiation. The wage provisions meant an increase in the substandard textile wages; this meant that manufacturing costs rose too. To ease this burden, NRA felt that it had to give in to industry demands for the authority to limit production. The first code thus contained unfortunate precedents which other industries were quick to insist on for themselves.

As the merciless summer sun beat down on Washington, code hearings began in a variety of industries. "We are going to do this whole job in a goldfish bowl," Johnson said. Baffled businessmen, mopping their foreheads in heat and perplexity, flocked down the long corridors of the Commerce Building to find out the methods of procedure. Coatless and perspiring, they teetered on gilt chairs in the ballrooms of Washington hotels to wrangle over the details of industrial reorganization, business glaring at labor, labor glaring back, and both chafing under the cold eye of the NRA deputy administrator. It was a slow process. After six weeks, cotton textiles was still the only major code.

Johnson remained an unquenchable center of energy and conviction. Seated in his plain, uncomfortable office in Commerce, surrounded by a litter of papers and Old Gold cigarette butts, coat off and blue shirt open at the neck, clothes baggy from four hours' night sleep on the office sofa, he received a steady stream of callers, sometimes over a hundred a day. Bruce Bliven described him in action — cajoling, wheedling, bullying, pounding with his fist, roaring with sudden laughter, now and then rushing off by airplane to make a speech. In his outside office sat Frances Robinson, the ubiquitous Robbie, the General's secretary and assistant, a trim, aggressive, pert girl in her late twenties, becoming, through her efficiency and her increasing intimacy with the General, a growing power in NRA. There was an incessant air of motion and excitement. But, as the weeks passed by without result, Johnson, the furious activist, grew more and more unhappy.[4]

VI

There were compelling reasons for his disquiet. Production and employment had risen steadily from March to July; but part of the revival, it was becoming apparent, was due to a spurt of forward manufacturing and purchasing before the imposition of the codes increased costs; and another part was a purely speculative reaction to the hope of monetary inflation. A sudden collapse of the stock market on July 19 underlined the insubstantial character of the business upturn. With codification bogging down, Johnson was coming to believe that some grand new effort would be necessary to recapture the momentum of recovery.

Moreover, the NRA officials now realized that there was competition between industries as well as within them, and that non-codified business obviously had competitive advantages over a business which responded to patriotism and came in quickly. Something plainly had to be done to reduce the incentive for procrastinating on codification. Something had to be done too for industries which were not sufficiently organized to submit codes. And some wanted to do something to bring local workers, not involved in interstate commerce, into the national pattern. Above all, something had to be done to rouse public opinion, both to facilitate the job of code enforcement, and to give the faltering business revival a new injection of confidence. What NRA should become, Johnson concluded in mid-July 1933, was a mass movement. Why not a nationwide campaign to pledge all employers to a blanket agreement to uphold NRA standards on wages and hours — that is, to promise a minimum wage of $12 or $13 a week for forty hours of labor; this agreement to be in effect until more formal codification could be completed? But the Special Industrial Recovery Board — the cabinet committee to which Johnson was supposed to report — received the idea with gloom. "I am just scared to death," said Tugwell. "I am afraid of the commitment and of getting the President into this. If we strike what a number of us anticipate, which is a flattening out of markets and maybe a precipitous drop right in the midst of a ballyhoo campaign, we will look like ten cents." John Dickinson felt that Johnson's emergency program "would almost certainly destroy at the outset the great advantages which may be expected from organizing the industries of the country one by one." Get the big boys first; the corner groceries and barber shops could wait. Moreover, what if, after all the hullabaloo, not enough people signed up? It was not wartime, added Homer Cummings; "if you start out to get the whole nation to sign the pledge, you are going to run into enormous difficulty."

"I have said right along that it is a gamble," Johnson replied. "I think it is a good gamble. I think I can put this thing over." After all, he said, the European war had been less real for most Americans than the depression. "Almost every individual has either suffered terribly, or knows of friends and relatives who have; so there is waiting here to be appealed to what I regard as the most fertile psychology that you could imagine. . . . I think this has anything that happened during the War backed off the board." [5]

VII

The Board remained unconvinced, as did much of the NRA staff. But Roosevelt, warming to Johnson's boldness and doubtless sensing the popular need for action, told him to go ahead. On July 21 Johnson launched the new campaign. Three days later, in his third fireside chat, Roosevelt set forth the idea of the blanket agreement and called for nationwide cooperation to stop "the continuing descent into the economic hell of the past four years." In a few days copies of the President's Re-employment Agreement, with its emergency stipulations on wages and hours, were in the mails to employers throughout the country.

In the meantime, Johnson laid out the psychology of the campaign. One day, after talking with Henry Wallace about thunderbirds, the General sketched a figure modeled on the old Indian ideograph. Suitably retouched by a professional, this grew into a Blue Eagle. Bearing the legend "We Do Our Part," it became NRA's symbol of compliance. The symbolism was not a new idea; the War Industries Board had had something like it, and Baruch suggested it in his speech of May 1933. "In war, in the gloom of night attack," as the President explained in his broadcast, "soldiers wear a bright badge on their shoulders to be sure that comrades do not fire on comrades. On that principle, those who cooperate in this program must know each other at a glance."

Under the standard of the Blue Eagle, Johnson now launched a furious assault on the nation's conscience and eardrums, moving around in an aura of mass meetings, motorcades, cheering crowds, and brass bands, using every device of appeal and persuasion to enlist support. "When every American Housewife understands that the Blue Eagle on everything that she permits to come into her home is a symbol of its restoration to security," he said, "may God have mercy on the man or group of men who attempt to trifle with this bird." He was stern in his attitude toward noncooperators.

Those who are not with us are against us, and the way to show that you are a part of this great army of the New Deal is to insist on this symbol of solidarity exactly as Peter of the Keys drew a fish on the sand as a countersign and Peter the Hermit

exacted the cross on the baldric of every good man and true.
This campaign is a frank dependence on the power and the
willingness of the American people to act together as one person
in an hour of great danger.

Richberg seconded the drive with comparable ardor. In so urgent
a crisis, he said, there could be "no honorable excuse for the slacker
who wastes these precious moments with doubting and debate —
who palsies the national purpose with legalistic arguments." He
added, with vehemence,

> There is no choice presented to American business between
> intelligently planned and controlled industrial operations and
> a return to the gold-plated anarchy that masqueraded as
> "rugged individualism." . . . Unless industry is sufficiently
> socialized by its private owners and managers so that great
> essential industries are operated under public obligation ap-
> propriate to the public interest in them, the advance of political
> control over private industry is inevitable.

The response fulfilled Johnson's predictions and justified his
audacity. The new emblem became the focus of moral and civic
pressure. Parades celebrated it. Speeches praised it. Throughout
the land merchants put the Blue Eagle in their windows and
stamped it on their products. Over two million employers signed
up. Consumers signed a pledge of their own (among the signers was
Herbert Hoover, who had not yet decided that NRA was fascism).

The climax came with the Blue Eagle parade in New York City
early in September. In the greatest march in the city's history, a
quarter of a million men and women streamed down Fifth Avenue,
while a million and a half more lined the streets, watching and
cheering. On the reviewing stand were General Johnson and Governor Lehman with W. Averell Harriman, the NRA state chairman.
Johnson could not get over the gaiety of the crowd, so different, he
felt, from the metallic hilarity of 1929, which he remembered as
"the hectic laughter of a dance-hall hostess, slightly tight." Now
he saw a new and healthier America. After sunset, the lights of
Fifth Avenue, amber for the occasion, bathed the street in a golden

glow. Still the marchers came — CCC boys in olive drab; life insurance men and telephone linemen; stock brokers and chorus girls; brewers walking under red flares and bands playing "Happy Days Are Here Again." On it went till midnight in a pandemonium of ticker tape, enthusiasm, and fellowship. The flight of the Blue Eagle had reached its zenith.[6]

VIII

The national surge around the Blue Eagle helped break the log jam in Washington. Draft codes began to pour in to NRA — 144 in the last half of July, 546 in August — and Johnson armed with new sanctions in public opinion, now intervened with boldness and impatience to push the final codes through. Shipbuilding and wool textile came in during the last week of July; electrical manufacturing and the coat and suit trades in the first week in August. Yet oil, coal, automobiles, lumber, and steel still held out.

The problem with oil was bitter disagreement among the operators. By midsummer, the petroleum industry had become, in Johnson's contemptuous phrase, "a discouraged and disorganized mob." The operators had a vague yearning for a czar, but they differed over the content of the czardom, and, after repeated failures, had shown themselves hopelessly incapable of agreeing on a code. If any progress were to be made, the government would have to make it; so, with Roosevelt's backing, Johnson wrote a final draft, presented it to the industry, and added coldly that they had twenty-four hours to register protests. "We will now pass copies of the code," Johnson said. "The meeting is adjourned." When the oilmen rushed toward the pile of mimeographed documents, Johnson shouted, "Please sit down. Sit down or I'll stop it immediately." Cowed, they retreated to their chairs. Johnson, leaving the distribution to flunkies, put on his hat and strode out.

Steel, a proud and powerful industry, combined a reflex of automatic resistence to NRA with specific objection to the labor provisions. The draft submitted by the Iron and Steel Institute provided for company unions. The steelmen fought bitterly before finally accepting language along the lines of Section 7a; they obtained a bundle of concessions on price policy in exchange. In the end the President called Myron C. Taylor of United States Steel and Charles M. Schwab of Bethlehem to the White House. When Schwab said he could not accept the code because of his obligations to the Bethlehem stockholders, Roosevelt asked amiably whether he had been looking after his stockholders when he paid those million-dollar bonuses to Eugene Grace and allowed his miners to live in coke ovens. To another visitor later that day, the President said with satisfaction, "I scared them the way they never have been frightened before and I told Schwab he better not pay any more million dollar bonuses."

Lumber provided another tough problem, and again NRA mingled threats and concessions to get it under the tent. On August 19, just before midnight, Roosevelt signed the codes for oil, steel, and lumber. But there were still two major industries to go: automobiles and coal. The problem in Detroit was Henry Ford. Suspicious and independent as ever, Ford had always stayed out of the National Automobile Chamber of Commerce; and he showed no greater disposition to join the other companies in working out an NRA code. Fearing that Ford's refusal would give him competitive advantages, the rest of the industry stalled. Johnson, thinking that a direct approach might work, decided to talk to Ford personally. "I'm here to button this thing up," he snapped at the Detroit airport, and for a moment he thought he had. But, though Ford directed his representatives to help draft the code, he backed out at the end. He would sign no code which obliged him to bargain collectively with the representatives of his workers. (In addition, he soon came to believe, as he jotted in one of his pocket-size reminder books, "Our competitors are behind all tax and NRA plans with the bankers' international and they are running all the governments in the world.") Johnson, tired of delay, decided to organize the industry without Ford. A newspaperman asked him how long it would be before he cracked down on the holdout. "I think maybe the American people will crack down on him," Johnson replied, "when the Blue Eagle is in other cars and he does not have one."

The automobile industry, minus Ford, came along on August 27. This left the most confused and dispiriting situation of all — coal. Here there were not only regional divisions within the industry, but also a schism, drenched in blood and history, between the mineowners and labor. From the start, chances of agreement on a national plan seemed slim. John L. Lewis's massive determination to cash in on 7a and resuscitate the near-moribund United Mine Workers further complicated negotiations. Still Johnson persisted, hammering away at labor and management in a series of endless conferences, backed by speechmaking forays into coal territory. Roosevelt also called the owners into the White House, warned them that they were riding a "dying horse," and told them their tactics were only helping Communism. In August and September there was a new flare-up of strikes. Company police shot miners, and the UMW organized slowdowns to force the operators into the code. Roosevelt once again summoned the owners, and gave them twenty-four hours to reach an agreement. On September 18, the Bituminous Coal Code was finally approved.

It had been a fantastic three months, and it exacted its price. Johnson had paid a large price himself. He had labored without stint, mastered the details of a dozen complex industries, managed an increasingly baffling and incoherent organization, traveled madly around the country, harangued mass meetings, abandoned sleep; and it was now evident that even his wild energy had its limits. And NRA paid a price too, for Johnson, in transforming a government agency into a religious experience, had put over all too well a millennial vision of rising wages, spreading work, and six million new jobs by Labor Day. Johnson, indeed, had pretty much shouldered the rest of the recovery program out of the picture. People identified the whole recovery effort with NRA. If Johnson was overextended, NRA was overpromised. "There is no task-master," reflected Richberg, "like a multitude on the march." [7]

8. The Conundrum of Price

IN AUGUST, JOHNSON OUTLINED his strategy to the Special Industrial Recovery Board. The first necessity, he said, was to get industry under the code; "we have gone to extreme measures to get them under it in some cases." During the period of signing up, it was "wise not to press too harshly the disciplinary measures on the one hand and investigations on the other." Once the bear's claw was in the trap, then NRA could concentrate on the second phase — revision and enforcement. The first phase, Johnson predicted, should be over by September 15. "About that time the phase of disciplining these people begins."

"What will happen to objectors who won't go along with the code?" someone asked Johnson while he was lunching on lamb chops and beer. "They'll get a sock right on the nose," Johnson shot back, wiping the suds off his lips. But inducing compliance was not, alas, so easy, particularly when the Department of Justice questioned the enforceability of the President's Re-employment Agreement, and when Johnson himself recoiled from anything that might bring the Recovery Act into court. There was never any crackdown on Henry Ford (who in any case observed code provisions for wages and hours, thereby confounding the Compliance Division at a time when other employers with Blue Eagles in their windows were violating the provisions).[1]

II

Johnson's main weapon against what he called the chiselers was social compulsion, triggered, he hoped, by the removal of the Blue

Eagle. An employer who trifled with the chance to lift the country out of economic hell, Johnson said, was "guilty of a practice as cheap as stealing pennies out of the cup of a blind beggar." NRA would take away his badge of public faith, break his bright sword of commercial honor under the eyes of his neighbors, and throw the fragments in scorn at his feet. Such a penalty, Johnson predicted, would be "a sentence of economic death. It will never happen. The threat of it transcends any puny penal provision in the law."

In the meantime, he relied on exhortation, calling on businessmen to behave justly toward their neighbors and denying that the wage and hour provisions would do anyone any harm. "Men have died and worms have eaten them," said Johnson, "but not from paying human labor thirty cents an hour." When homily and sarcasm failed, he turned to invective. "Al Capone," he told fifteen thousand people in Minneapolis, "was a poor ignorant Sicilian piker next to those rugged individualists who wanted to prolong the dark ages of human relationships." And, at Atlanta, with magnificent grandiloquence:

> Away slight men! You may have been Captains of Industry once, but you are Corporals of Disaster now. A safe place for you may be yapping at the flanks but it is not safe to stand obstructing the front of this great army. You might be trampled underfoot — not knowingly but inadvertently — because of your small stature and of the uplifted glance of a people whose "eyes have seen the glory" and whose purpose is intent on the inspired leadership of your neighbor and friend Franklin Roosevelt.

Still, for all Johnson's minatory thunder, it became evident by the early fall that the NRA enthusiasm was slackening. On the one hand, NRA had not achieved its economic objectives of reemployment and recovery; on the other, it had not always succeeded in holding people to its social objectives in wages, hours, and labor organization. Everywhere there was discontent over enforcement. George Leighton, visiting four states for *Harper's* late in 1933, reported that the codes were being violated, evaded, and ignored, and that NRA's apparatus of local compliance boards was lax and ineffectual. "Any supposition that business intends to 'govern itself' in the spirit of the New Deal," observed Leighton, "is preposterous. The profit motive is still solidly in the saddle." Lorena Hickok, after months of travel around the country, wrote despondently to Harry Hopkins:

> Oh, I've kidded myself along, trying to believe that the codes were working, at least in the big industries — that the textile people, for instance, were complying probably to the extent of 60%. But I wonder. I'll bet you right now that 99% of American big businessmen are trying to beat them and succeeding. And the little fellows aren't even pretending to live up to them. They can't. The whole damned outfit are simply grabbing everything they can for themselves out of improved business stimulated by the Government priming and public confidence in the President. They're not contributing anything.

By November criticism was widespread. Hearst condemned NRA as "absolute state socialism" and suggested that the initials stood for "No Recovery Allowed." "The excessive centralization and the dictatorial spirit," said Walter Lippmann, "are producing a revulsion of feeling against bureaucratic control of American economic life." Even early sponsors were losing faith. Henry I. Harriman, referring waspishly to the NRA offices as "the bedlam that they have over there," remarked that six months ago business was 100 per cent behind NRA; but "I know of no representative group of businessmen today in which some do not question the whole program." And on November 1, 1933, Gerard Swope proposed that NRA be replaced by a National Chamber of Commerce and Industry, centering in the United States Chamber of Commerce and based on a super-organization of the trade associations. NRA powers, in short, would be removed from government and turned over to business.

Disappointments focused on two issues. One was the price policy of NRA: businessmen were angry when NRA obstructed their efforts to raise prices; consumers were angry that NRA had given industry as much power over prices as it had. The other was NRA's labor policy: many businessmen hated Section 7a with its guarantee of the rights of collective bargaining; many labor leaders felt that Johnson and Richberg were themselves chiseling on 7a. These two issues dominated the NRA problem for the rest of its life.[2]

III

Franklin Roosevelt defined the price problem in his statement on the enactment of the Recovery Act. "The aim of this whole effort," he said, "is to restore our rich domestic market by raising its vast consuming capacity. If we now inflate prices as fast and as far as we increase wages, the whole project will be set at naught. We cannot hope for the full effect of this plan unless, in these first critical months, and, even at the expense of full initial profits, we defer price increases as long as possible." General Johnson in his first statements laid similar stress on the importance of preventing price increases from whirling away new purchasing power. "We are going to ask something in the nature of an armistice on increased capacity and prices," he told the press, "until we get this thing started." A few days later he warned, "This is a deadly serious matter — this danger of runaway prices. . . . This administration simply will not stand for that."

But words — even General Johnson's — were not enough, especially at a time when industry expected a *quid pro quo* in the codes in exchange for the NRA stipulations on wages, hours, and collective bargaining. For years, trade associations had been seeking, within the law and without, to "stabilize" competition through the private control of production and price. A model code sponsored by the National Association of Manufacturers now actually called for the assignment of production quotas by the code authority; and most of the trade associations were demanding a wide variety of price-fixing powers. In the scramble, industries began to vie with each other in pursuit of price protection; "whenever any industry received approval of a new type of [protective] clause," observed C. F. Roos, a conservative NRA economist, "others rushed to see if they also could get it." The price-fixing passion was increased, as Richberg suggested, by the "universal hunger for profits after a long depression fast." It soon became, as Alexander Sachs suggested, a panacea for American business, like the brazen serpent in the Book of Numbers which restored to health all those who had been bitten in the wilderness.

Indeed, the cold eye that Johnson first cast toward price stabilization so aroused the trade associations that in a few days he was forced to retreat. On June 23, he announced that the codes might include agreements not to sell below cost of production; "but if they use the code to fix extortionate prices," he added bravely, "I should have to step in immediately in conformance with the law." Yet Johnson, despite his theoretical awareness of the price problem, was soon so involved in the Blue Eagle drive that the drama of the codes came to seem to him more important than their details. In this mood, he was ready to sacrifice a good deal in the interests of speedy adoption. (The General, observed Jerome Frank with a backward glance at 1917, was suffering from a code in the head acquired in the draft.)

During the summer of 1933 the chief resistance to the business community's drive for price-fixing came less from NRA itself than from the Special Industrial Recovery Board. Of the Board members, Rex Tugwell, sitting in as deputy for the Secretary of Agriculture, had the most clear-cut price philosophy. For all his belief in overhead planning, Tugwell retained an old-fashioned faith in a functioning price mechanism. "One test of the goodness of business," he liked to say, "is the lowness of its prices." The reluctance of businessmen in the twenties to reduce prices in line with increased productivity, he thought, had been a major cause of the depression; and, even in a planned economy, the price system could play a basic role in clearing or clogging the economic process. His concern for agriculture further strengthened his determination to prevent industrial prices from getting out of hand. The intent of price-fixing was obviously to keep prices higher than they would be otherwise. The result by Tugwell's analysis would be to cancel out purchasing power (and thus the gains of AAA and the wages and hours provisions of NRA) and hold back consumption; and this, of course, would have the effect of holding back production. As Tugwell saw it, price policy was the key to whether NRA would play a restrictive or expansionist role in the economy.

From the beginning, he nagged Johnson about the price situation. As early as June 29, he apologized for growing "tedious" in calling the Administrator's attention once again to "the central importance to you of the problem of price." In meeting after meeting he stressed the importance of price policy in protecting purchasing power and promoting expansion. The adoption of the lumber code with provisions against selling below the cost of production spurred him to a new attack. Henry Wallace, at a Board meeting on August 21, pointed out that in agriculture, at least, cost-of-production formulas were practically impossible to compute; moreover, they tended to be based on high rather than low costs and thus to preserve the inefficient producer and to increase prices. "We cannot restore prosperity by giving consumers more money," Wallace told Roosevelt later, "if that money buys less than before." [3]

IV

But Johnson perceived another dimension in the price problem. The practice of selling below the cost of production, for example, seemed to him part of the bad old order in which businessmen competed at the expense of social decency. The principle of "low prices at any sacrifice," he told the Board, was vicious because the sacrifice always came from one place, "out of the hours and living conditions of labor." No one, he said, was "entitled to low prices achieved by the degradation of human labor." And competitive price-slashing would not only drive down labor standards, but, by wiping out small enterprise, it would hasten the trend toward monopoly. The more it was practiced, the more it would accelerate the downward plunge of the whole economy. Both recovery and humanity, in Johnson's view, required the end of "destructive price-cutting." In the interests of labor, of small business, and of general economic stability, Johnson concluded (and Richberg with him) that NRA must erect defenses against "suicidal" price warfare; it must abolish "economic murder." The problem, as they saw it, was to devise techniques which would raise prices enough to maintain decent wages and hours without raising them so much as to dry up purchasing power, restrict production, or introduce new rigidities into the economy. Restraining vicious competitive practices, they argued, was one thing; establishing monopoly was something quite different.

This search for a middle way dominated code-making. By the beginning of 1935, 568 out of the over 700 codes had one form or another of minimum-price provision. Of the many techniques for price defense, the most popular was the prohibition of sales below cost. This prohibition appeared in various forms in two-thirds of the first three hundred codes; by January 1935 it was in 420 codes. By this latter date, 203 codes had provisions for fixing minimum prices in emergencies; 122 prohibited price-cutting in general terms; and a dozen granted the code authorities power to set minimum prices without reference to cost. In addition, 416 of the codes had provisions for open price filing — that is, for the public posting throughout the industry of proposed price changes, generally with waiting periods before new prices could go into effect; and 507 had provisions for uniform accounting methods of cost formulas. Five codes specifically endorsed the basing point system, which made it easy to control price competition by assuring uniform delivered prices for each producer.

Beyond these direct techniques for price control, over 120 codes offered industry indirect power over prices by providing or contemplating control of production and capacity. Some industries had production quotas. Other codes regulated hours of machine operation, imposed restrictions on new plant or equipment, refused entry where overcapacity existed, or ruled that output could not exceed a certain ratio to inventory.

These price and production controls did not go nearly so far as the business community desired. On this point, there could be no question. As Ralph Flanders, himself a businessman, observed of the price-fixing and production-control features of NRA, "Our legislators and administrators cannot be blamed for them. It was our businessmen who were most thoroughly sold on the idea that recovery and prosperity depended on the restraint of competition." "Such price-fixing and production control regulations as found their way into the codes," said Ickes, "got there almost exclusively at the demand of businessmen themselves." "The government, had it been so minded," said Mary Harriman Rumsey, "would never have dared propose so many laws interfering with business discretion as are being urged upon the government by businessmen themselves." And NRA itself stated, "None of the more restrictive provisions approved remotely approached the stringency of proposals which were offered, demanded and battled for by a large number of industrial groups of fully representative character." As Eugene Grace of Bethlehem Steel observed more generally of NRA, "One of its chief benefits has been to relieve industry from the shackles of the antitrust laws." Far from wanting restrictionist provisions, NRA in the main accepted what it considered the minimum it could get away with to protect labor standards or to persuade industry to accept the codes.

Still, as device piled on device, the result was evidently to bestow formidable powers on the code authorities, and this meant, in effect, on the trade associations. For, though the code authority exercised public powers, it was not a public body. It was, as Johnson put it, "an agency of the employers in an industry"; only in exceptional cases did the authority even have labor or public representation. To these private agencies, then, the NRA delegated wide powers over price and production — powers that had been intended by the Congress to be exercised by government itself.[4]

v

The Special Industrial Recovery Board watched the trend with growing unhappiness. What had begun as an effort to check the downward spiral seemed now to turn in the hands of code authorities into a monstrous new apparatus by which business could keep production down and prices up. In the end, it was thought, the business community, in its pursuit of profits and security for each separate industry, might well create a situation where recovery for all would be impossible.

So the Board began to fear; but the Board's role in NRA was visibly declining. Johnson, who had always resented its very existence, resented more than ever its spasmodic efforts to review NRA policy; and the Board members, all of whom had full-time jobs of their own, hardly had time and energy left to take on the General. Nevertheless, toward the end of 1933, Tugwell and the others made a final effort. Watching the new structure of private price control growing up under the codes, Tugwell urged that the only hope for NRA was to induce business to forgo quick profits and commit itself to a low-price, large-volume program. "Profits," he said, "will have to follow from new efficiencies. To put them first is to put the cart before the horse" — it would be to mow down the new purchasing power before it could become operative.

How to keep prices down? "As the Model Code is now set up and as a good many of the codes now in operation are constituted," Tugwell told the Board, "there has been a complete abrogation of either protection to the public from price increases by competition, or by public authority, so that to all intents and purposes industries are now free to set up what prices they please." Let alone, they would only end by choking on their own high prices. The solution? If competition were not to be permitted to keep prices down, then "it would mean that the industries would logically be forced to accept full public control over their prices." The Federal Trade Commission, deeply exercised over the Steel Code, reported to the President in similar vein: if the public was not to be protected through price competition, the only alternative was "protection through government price-fixing. There is no middle ground discernible."

But for Johnson, government price-fixing was politically out of the question. He had expended himself enough as it was in repelling industry demands for even greater power of private price determination. In December, he deferred sufficiently to the Board to appoint public members to some of the code authorities. But he found the Board's harping on the price issue increasingly exasperating. When the Board proposed that NRA codes be brought to it before final adoption, this was too much. The General stormed to the President and demanded its dismissal.

For a number of reasons, Roosevelt was inclined to go along with Johnson. After all, the General had the operating responsibility, and he had done a unique job in putting NRA over. The President, with a prejudice for the player as against the kibitzers, was therefore disposed to discount the Board. Moreover, Roosevelt did not have any particular horror of price-fixing. He liked room for maneuver; and concessions on such points as sales below cost did not seem to him an unreasonable trade for the labor provisions. Possibly he saw industry as a whole in terms of the areas he knew best — natural resources, like coal and oil, and public utilities — where rate-making and price-fixing had a tradition and a use. Above all, he was still hopeful that businessmen would not abuse the powers granted them under NRA. Was not Johnson right therefore in wanting to establish broad principles quickly and tidy up details later? Given these views, Roosevelt yielded readily to Johnson's insistence and transferred the Board's functions to a remote co-ordinating body for all recovery programs, the National Emergency Council.[5]

VI

As the Special Industrial Recovery Board faded out, the main burden of resisting restrictionist pressure fell to a weak but scrappy agency within NRA, the Consumers' Advisory Board. Johnson, in designing the original NRA structure, had established industrial, labor, and consumers' advisory boards to assure representations of the three interests in the code-making process. In practice, the Industrial Advisory Board generally seconded the recommendations of the trade association, and the Labor Advisory Board too often lost interest once labor demands had been met. This left the Consumers' Advisory Board as the one voice to speak up for the public.

The Consumers' board owed its existence in great part to Mary Harriman Rumsey, daughter of E. H. Harriman, the railroad builder, and older sister of W. Averell Harriman. This slim, dark-eyed woman, sensitive and gay, had been her father's favorite child and constant companion. To his largeness of vision, she added a social conscience of her own. "When I was a young girl," she once said, "I began to realize that competition was injuring some, and I dreamed of a time when there would be more cooperation." In this spirit she founded the Junior League in 1901 as a means by which society girls could engage in settlement work. She became active in the Women's Trade Union League and in the Community Councils of New York, while at the same time she rode, hunted, and raised blooded livestock on her farm near Middleburg in Virginia.

"His period," Mary Rumsey said in 1933 of her father, "was a building age, when competition was the order of the day. Today the need is not for a competitive but a cooperative economic system." In the development of such a system, she believed, the consumer would play an active part. And the establishment of the

Consumers' Advisory Board in NRA, along with its counterpart in AAA, brought forward for a moment a new economic panacea — consumerism. During the winter of 1933–34, there was rising agitation for the establishment of a Department of the Consumer. The consumer mystique had many roots — in John Dewey's *The Public and Its Problems;* in the work of Stuart Chase, especially his book *Your Money's Worth,* written with F. J. Schlink in 1927; in Schlink's organization, Consumers' Research, and in his best-seller of 1933, *100,000,000 Guinea Pigs,* which he wrote in collaboration with Arthur Kallet. Schlink, who freely denounced the "pseudo-consumer, society-woman leadership" of the Consumers' Advisory Board, represented the radical wing of those who wished to orient the business system around the consumer instead of around the producer. The most systematic development of the consumer thesis came in a book of 1936 entitled *Guinea Pigs No More,* written by J. B. Matthews, then stopping off at Consumers' Research in transit from the far left to the far right. Matthews saw the solution of the social crisis in the establishment of a "consumers' society" as an alternative both to the rule of business and to a workers' state.

In its higher flights, consumerism verged on fantasy. Yet there was clearly a real economic issue involved. Gardiner Means analyzed the problem in 1934. So long as the market place was the effective regulator of economic activity, competition kept businessmen from programs of low output and high prices. But, with economic concentration, the market grew less important, and businessmen gained much more "administrative" control over production and price. The question now was whether consumers could develop enough strength to restrain the producer from succumbing to the temptation to raise prices and limit output. If so, the organized consumer could become the key to increased production and thus to the restoration of economic balance. Still, as Means carefully warned, wishing would not make it so, nor would even the ritual of appointing consumer representatives to government bureaus do it. "The consumer will get nothing for which he does not fight, however socially minded the agents of Government may be. . . . If there is no pressure on Government from people as consumers, there is little likelihood that their interests as consumers will be effectively represented."

Means stated the Consumers' Advisory Board dilemma with exactitude. Where the Industrial Advisory Board had the backing of the trade associations and the Labor Advisory Board had the backing of the trade unions, the Consumers' Advisory Board had no organized support at all; its representatives were, in a phrase of Tugwell's, "spearheads without shafts." Yet it did have compensating qualities — in particular, a rather dashing leadership, and a zealous and expert technical staff. Mary Rumsey knew everybody — the Roosevelts, Frances Perkins, with whom she shared a house, Hugh Johnson, who was an adoring friend — and she feared nobody. After a blowup in August 1933, when her executive director, W. F. Ogburn of Chicago, resigned because of her first amateurish sallies in consumer leadership, she brought in as Ogburn's successor Dexter Keezer, an economist who had been attacking NRA's consumer policy in influential articles in the Baltimore *Sun*. Both her direction and her organization became steadily more professional. For a time Paul H. Douglas of Chicago headed the Board's Bureau of Economic Education and tried to organize local consumer councils. Corwin Edwards, Walton H. Hamilton, Thomas Blaisdell, Stacy May, Robert S. Lynd, and Robert A. Brady also served the Board at various stages.[6]

VII

The Board was soon playing an aggressive role in the battle of NRA. General Johnson, despite his friendship for Mary Rumsey, found its intervention in the code-making process increasingly irritating. "Who is the consumer? Show me a consumer," he barked at those who claimed to speak in the consumers' interest; he referred disdainfully to "academicians" in "horn-rimmed glasses," knowing they predominated in the Board as nowhere else in the organization; and he later wrote, "I never heard of the Consumers' Advisory Board supporting anything in NRA."

He was in this mood one Saturday night in December when Mrs. Rumsey led a delegation of consumer leaders into his office. The group had come from a consumers' conference, the very conception of which led the outraged General to shout at them and to pound vigorously upon his desk. Then, to the astonishment of all, a member of the delegation shouted back equally loudly and pounded back equally hard, rattling the objects on the desk under the General's nose. This was Leon Henderson of the Russell Sage Foundation. Johnson, at first taken aback, was soon enchanted by Henderson's display of pugnacity. "If you're so god-damned smart," he said, "why don't you come down here and be my assistant on consumer problems?" Henderson took the dare. In a few weeks more, Johnson was enough further impressed to make Henderson head of the Research and Planning Division and NRA's chief economist.

The Consumers' Advisory Board meanwhile stepped up its pressure on price policy. Paul Douglas wanted to abolish price-fixing altogether; he thought that the grade-labeling of products according to quality standards might be a way of checking vicious price-cutting. The growing dissatisfaction eventually induced the NRA in January 1934 to hold hearings on price policy. Arthur D. Whiteside of Dun and Bradstreet, an old-time trade association man, was the most persuasive champion of price-fixing in NRA; and he conducted the hearings on ground rules designed to keep the findings as obscure as possible. But some criticisms found their way into a speech delivered a few days later in the Senate by Gerald Nye.

Quoting from the Board's reports on price policy, Nye declared that NRA had become the breeder of monopoly. In steel, in electronics, in cement, in pulp and paper, the big concerns, Nye charged, were using the power acquired under codes they themselves had written to discriminate against their small competitors. Borah, rising quickly to the antitrust bait, proposed an amendment to the Recovery Act terminating the suspension of the antitrust laws. General Johnson confronted the rising storm with a characteristic mixture of blandishments and threats. The antitrusters, he said, "have really nothing to support them but the width of their mouths and the volumetric capacity of their lung power." But he added quickly (he was speaking before the National Retail Dry Goods Association): "If I had only nine words with which to address you, I would rise here and say: 'Keep prices down — for God's sake, keep prices down.' " The plea was heartfelt. Prices nevertheless continued to rise.

As the pressure increased, Johnson convened a meeting of members of code authorities in March 1934 to review NRA policy. The Consumers' Advisory Board welcomed the four thousand representatives descending on Washington with a crisp report calling for a thorough overhauling of price policies. President Roosevelt, addressing the opening session, reiterated his faith in business and NRA. "You and I," he told the assembled delegates, "are now conducting a great test to find out how the business leaders in all groups of industry can develop capacity to operate for the general welfare. Personally I am convinced that with your help the test is succeeding." He went on to suggest that the test might succeed even better if business would keep prices down, reduce working hours, and increase wages. The audience listened without undue enthusiasm.

Johnson's concluding speech was another virtuoso performance. He reminded his audience that a year before they, the industrial and banking leadership of the country, had been in "complete and utter disrepute." He told them that Roosevelt had given them their chance for rehabilitation. He flattered them: "We have to plan our way out of this mud hole and that must be done by hard-boiled businessmen and not by academicians." He challenged them with the historic significance of the NRA experiment: "Nothing like it has ever happened in the history of the world. It is as important as the Council of Nicea or the Treaty of Verdun." He scolded them, shamed them, threatened them, and ended by exhorting them, in the language of the boys' stories he used to write, to "play the game." They listened with pleasure. Still prices rose.[7]

VIII

The Nye critique of NRA and the March conference produced one concrete result. This was the formation of the National Recovery Review Board to investigate monopolistic tendencies in the codes. The Board was set up in March in an atmosphere of mutual congeniality. Nye himself was permitted to nominate five of the six members; and Richberg first proposed the name of Clarence Darrow, the veteran criminal lawyer, as chairman. Johnson, in what he later described as "a moment of total aberration," enthusiastically seconded the idea.

Darrow, the great advocate, was now nearly seventy-seven years old, a tall man, stooped from many battles, experienced and quizzical, but still animated by a candid and youthful radicalism. Many memories stretched behind him, the dramatic moments of more than half a century at the bar — the Debs strike case; Moyer, Haywood, and Pettibone in Idaho, the McNamara brothers and the Los Angeles dynamite case; Loeb and Leopold in Chicago; the duel with Bryan over evolution in Dayton, Tennessee; the Fortescue-Massie case in Honolulu. The National Recovery Administration was, in a sense, Darrow's last case. He proposed to give it everything he had.

They brought the old man to Washington for the NRA review conference. He was, he allowed, much impressed by the utterances of big businessmen; he had not realized before, he said, how much the rich really loved the poor. "They should do so," he added, as if in afterthought. "They have lived off them for many years." When Hugh Johnson offered him offices next to his own, Darrow declined; he preferred to work out of the Willard Hotel. "Supposing we find the codes are not all right?" he asked Johnson. "Then you report to me," said Johnson pointing to himself. "I am the big cheese here." But Darrow preferred to report directly to Roosevelt.

Darrow, his associates and his staff, headed by Lowell Mason, a Washington lawyer, worked day and night. In four months they held nearly sixty public hearings, considered about three thousand complaints, inquired into thirty-four codes, and turned out a bundle of reports. The first, early in May, set the tone. It was no measured appraisal of the program, but rather a scathing attack on NRA as the instrument of monopoly. The document had certain discrepancies. On page 24, for example, it declared, "All competition is savage, wolfish and relentless; and can be nothing else. One may as well dream of making war ladylike as of making competition fair." On page 67, on the other hand, "A return to the antitrust laws for the purpose of restoring competition, we believe to be one of the great needs of the times." Then a supplementary report, signed only by two Board members, Darrow and his former law partner William O. Thompson, added that a return to unregulated competition was impossible; "the choice is between monopoly sustained by government, which is clearly the trend in the NRA; and a planned economy, which demands socialized ownership and control." The philosophical confusion was all too typical of a random, slapdash, and prejudiced investigation.

Over at NRA, Johnson and Richberg read the Darrow report with indignation. It is just what one might expect, Richberg commented, when "a noted socialist who advocates complete government control of business [is chosen] to write a report for philosophic anarchists, who apparently oppose any government control of anybody, including criminals." Johnson wrote Roosevelt, "A more superficial, intemperate and inaccurate document than the report, I have never seen." "Bloody old Jeffries at the Assizes," Johnson observed in a more reflective mood, "never conducted any hearings equal to those for cavalier disposal of cases." As for Darrow:

> Nobody in the world was ever more adept in convincing twelve men that another man who had bombed somebody, or poisoned somebody, or taken a kanaka for a ride in the most approved gangster style, or, with psychopathic urge, taken a little boy into the Michigan dunes and beaten the life out of him, hadn't either bombed, or poisoned, or ridden or beaten anybody. . . . It's a great gift.

Both Johnson and Richberg took far too much creative satisfaction out of invective to resist the temptation to thunder away at Darrow, and their indiscriminate abuse overshadowed their legitimate criticisms.

Darrow, who had dealt with major league polemicists for fifty years, gave as good as he got. For a few weeks, all Washington shook with the exchange of verbal fusillades. NRA's Labor Advisory Board joined in with enthusiasm. In prose that bore internal evidence of having been composed by another master, John L. Lewis, the labor leaders cursed out the Darrow Board for having secured its information from "irresponsible malcontents, sweatshop employers and business interests which had lost special privileges." Darrow, the labor leaders said, "has pandered to the worst elements in our political and economic life." On it went; yet in the midst of the hullabaloo, Darrow came one afternoon to call on Johnson. Together they rode in Johnson's car to Arlington as dusk fell, talking quietly about anthropology, comparative religion, whether murderers revisited the scenes of crimes, and whether man had a soul.[8]

IX

It is easy to sympathize with the fury of men who had worked long and hard to bring order out of industrial chaos at having their achievements traduced on the basis of erratic and *ex parte* hearings. Yet, with all its excesses, the Darrow Board brought violently into the open the issues which had been worrying the Special Industrial Recovery Board and the Consumers' Advisory Board for many months behind the scenes.

After the first Darrow report, Gerald Nye now returned to the attack on NRA restrictive policies in a series of exaggerated but impressive speeches in the Senate. At the same time, AAA continued fearful that rising industrial prices would nullify its attempts to raise agricultural prices; the Federal Trade Commission grew more worried than ever about monopoly; and the Public Works Administration was developing a concern over the impact of NRA price policies on construction costs. The price issue could no longer be evaded. Late in March, Roosevelt, after reading George Terborgh's report for the Brookings Institution on *Price Control Devices in NRA Codes,* appointed a cabinet committee under Frances Perkins to consider the long-run implications of price policy.

About the same time Johnson moved at last to give price policy top-level attention within NRA. Blackwell Smith, the associate general counsel, drafted a directive barring price-fixing under any conditions; Johnson diluted it to permit the setting of minimum prices in "emergencies" and issued it early in June as Office Memorandum 228. Business protest, even at this qualified ban, was so prompt and vehement that Johnson was obliged to add the next day that this ruling did not affect codes already approved — an exception which spared about 90 per cent of industry under NRA. Yet for all the dilutions, Memorandum 228 pointed to new directions in the future. With Smith and Henderson at the controls, the discretionary authority was rarely invoked; when prices were set, they were too low to be of fighting interest. Codes might still prickle with uniform price provisions, but the era of large-scale price regulation was plainly drawing to an end.[9]

9. The Conundrum of Labor

THE OTHER — and more significant — field of NRA controversy was labor. The principles of Section 7a of the National Industrial Recovery Act were not new. During the First World War, the National War Labor Board, on which Franklin Roosevelt had served, developed the doctrine that workers were entitled to choose their own representatives by majority vote. The Transportation Act of 1920 and the Railway Labor Act of 1926 (drafted by Donald Richberg and David Lilienthal) gave railroad workers the right to be represented by organizations of their own choosing; and the preamble of the Norris-La Guardia Act proclaimed similar aspirations for all workers. What the Recovery Act did was to give the tendencies of twenty years explicit legislative status, extending guarantees of self-organization and collective bargaining to all workers in interstate commerce.

In so doing, it brought about a fundamental change in the practical position of trade unions. While labor's right to organize had been recognized under law for nearly a century, so too had been management's right to resist labor organization. Employers had been free (apart from the railroads) to fire workers for union activity. or even for union membership; they could impose company unions on unwilling employees; they could use every means short of criminality to check labor agitation or to smash labor organization. Section 7a now greatly circumscribed the legal right of business to exterminate trade unionism. On the other hand, the nature of the guarantees extended to labor remained enigmatic.

> Employees shall have the right to organize and bargain collectively through representatives of their own choosing, and shall be free from the interference, restraint, or coercion of employers of labor, or their agents, in the designation of such representatives . . . no employee and no one seeking employment shall be required as a condition of employment to join any company union or to refrain from joining, organizing, or assisting a labor organization of his own choosing.

Did the right of collective bargaining compel employers to recognize unions? What specific types of employer action were now prohibited? Did the section require conferences and written agreements? How were employees empowered to select their representatives? What did 7a mean for the company union? for the closed shop? The section's words expressed an intent. But they did not precisely define a policy.[1]

II

The meaning of 7a, in short, would be determined in large part not by the words of the act but by the pressures management and labor could bring to bear on the process of interpretation. No one understood better that labor's position under the Act depended on its power — and thus on its success in exploiting the new government-sponsored organizing possibilities — than John L. Lewis. Lewis, who was fifty-three years old in 1933, had been the elected president of the United Mine Workers since 1920. He was an impressive figure, deep-chested and powerful, with massive head, upswept brush of dark rebellious hair, immense, shaggy eyebrows, startling blue eyes. He had the majestic presence of a veteran ham actor; and his manner, as well as his rhetoric, altered with his mood and his audience. In private, no one could be more captivating. He could discourse endlessly in mellow reminiscence; or tell stories on himself, with genial rumbles of laughter; or, in a scholarly frame of mind, quote Shakespeare or claim that his life had been shaped by the *Panchatantra,* an oriental book of animal fables. Leaning forward, his eyes candid and gentle, his hand laid confidingly on his visitor's knee, he was all directness, simplicity, wit, charm.

But on occasions of state he was transformed into a remote and heroic being. Expressions chased themselves across his face like clouds across a stormy sky — it was now beaming and radiant, as if at dawn; now somber and tinged with melancholy, as if at sunset; now black and threatening, like thunder. His eyes burned with fire and contempt; and his great voice, rolling out the sentences in the tone of a Welsh evangelist, declaimed, bewailed, taunted, condemned in a series of stately and pounding periods. It was a superb act. No one enjoyed it more than its author, who resisted all suggestions that he humanize this forbidding public personality. "He who tooteth not his own horn," he liked to say, "the same shall not be tooted."

The competitive chaos of the coal industry in the twenties had meant a time of troubles for the United Mine Workers. The rise of new coal fields, the shift of output to non-union areas, the spread of mechanization (encouraged by Lewis, who was prepared to trade reduced employment for higher wage rates) — all this struck at the power of the union. From time to time, internal factions tried to make the union more militant and introduce more "progressive" policies. Lewis, fighting for survival, methodically crushed rebellion. He denounced his rivals as Communists, hired hoodlums to beat them up, and clamped down an iron personal machine on what was once a lively and democratic organization. But the more he consolidated his grip, the smaller his kingdom became. The United Mine Workers dwindled from over 400,000 members in 1920 to probably fewer than 100,000 in 1933.

Politically Lewis remained a faithful Republican, backing Hoover even in 1932. But the depression eroded his old laissez-faire rejection of the state. Gradually he came to accept government, first as regulator of the economy, now as possible patron of labor. Motives mingled curiously in him: greed for personal power was all too evident; but he also had a bitter memory of the sufferings of his Iowa childhood and a proud identification with the woes of the miners. Perceiving the chance now to serve both himself and the working class, he fought hard in 1933 to get labor guarantees into the recovery bill.

"From the standpoint of human welfare and economic freedom," Lewis said of the National Industrial Recovery Act, "we are con-

vinced that there has been no legal instrument comparable with it
since President Lincoln's Emancipation Proclamation." The
United Mine Workers Journal added that Congress had given labor
"the greatest opportunity it has ever had to work out its own
destiny." But, the *Journal* warned, the law would not be self-
enforcing. "The bill will only be helpful to those who help themselves." Lewis proposed to waste no time. Reaching down deep into
the treasury of the international union, he staked the UMW's
survival on a summer organizing campaign. An army of organizers deployed through the coal fields, directed by such UMW veterans as Philip Murray and Van A. Bittner. They carried the gospel
of unionism into Kentucky, West Virginia, Pennsylvania, and Illinois, blaring their message on sound trucks, dispensing free beer in
the summer sun. They invaded the bloodstained battlegrounds of
coal unionism — Harlan County, Mingo County, the Connells-
ville coke region — and planted the union flag. Everywhere they
invoked the magic authority of the New Deal. "The President
wants you to unionize. It is unpatriotic to refuse to unionize. Here
is your union. Never mind about the dues now. Just join up!" A
Kentucky State Federation of Labor handbill was typical:

> The United States Government Has Said LABOR MUST
> ORGANIZE. . . . Forget about injunctions, yellow dog con-
> tracts, black lists and the fear of dismissal. The employers
> cannot and will not dare to go to the Government for privi-
> leges if it can be shown that they have denied the right of
> organization to their employees. ALL WORKERS ARE
> FULLY PROTECTED IF THEY DESIRE TO JOIN A
> UNION.

In Alabama the miners sang:

> In nineteen hundred an' thirty-three,
> When Mr. Roosevelt took his seat,
> He said to President John L. Lewis,
> "In union we must be."

In union they would be; and they crowded into grimy halls,
listened intently to organizing speeches and joined with passion
in the old union songs. When employers rejected the UMW, the

miners went out on strike; and, when company guards shot down strikers (as outside the Frick mines in Pennsylvania), the determination to win only redoubled. In the first months after NRA, over 100,000 miners flocked back; by November the union was virtually up to its strength of 1920.[2]

III

Few other labor chiefs saw the opportunity with Lewis's clarity. Most old-line AF of L leaders, reared in the voluntaristic tradition of Samuel Gompers, looked on government with mistrust. They could hardly get over the fact that depression had driven them to the point of tolerating such statist ideas as unemployment insurance and the NRA; the conception of the government as a partner in an organizing drive was too much. Moreover, where Lewis, as head of an industrial union, thought instinctively in terms of a single drive for each great industry, most of the Federation, committed to the craft idea, thought of organization, not by industry, but by skill. The automotive industry, for example, was to be organized, not in a single union, but in as many different unions as crafts were involved in making a car. So one night in the spring of 1933, when Lewis (according to his recollection) urged Bill Green to throw the Federation into a drive to organize the unorganized in automobiles, steel, rubber, shipbuilding, all Green could reply was, "Now John, let's take it easy."

Lewis found his best support in the needle trades of New York. Sidney Hillman, president of the Amalgamated Clothing Workers, had already displayed qualities of breadth and imagination unusual in the labor movement. Born in Lithuania in 1887, thrown into Russian prisons after the Revolution of 1905, Hillman came to the United States at the age of twenty. He went to Chicago and worked briefly as an apprentice cutter in the Hart, Schaffner and Marx factory. A bright, sensitive boy, avid for knowledge and for recognition, he haunted public libraries, reached out for new ideas, and became prominent in union activity. At this early stage, too, he began to distinguish himself from more rough-hewn colleagues by his appreciation of the power of people outside the movement, notably of social workers and intellectuals. Soon transforming himself from a worker to a union official, he lived for a time at Hull-House in Chicago and enjoyed the patronage of Jane Addams; and, when he moved to New York just before the war, he appeared under the sponsorship of Louis D. Brandeis. By 1914, at the age of twenty-seven, he was president of the Amalgamated. During the First World War, as a member of the Board of Control and Labor Standards for Army Clothing, he acquired a taste for Washington and an understanding of the potentialities of benevolent government.

In the next years, while organizing the clothing markets in leading cities, he engaged in dark and sometimes ambiguous battles with Communists, gangsters, and other disruptive elements within the union. Despite his taste for uplift, Hillman was quite ready, if need be, to fight his enemies with their own weapons. It was in this period that Louis Buchalter, the notorious Lepke of Murder, Inc., had his mysterious relations with the Amalgamated. Still, if Hillman consorted with labor racketeers like Abraham Beckerman and Philip Orlofsky in the afternoon, he spent his evening in the more edifying company of Leo Wolman and Felix Frankfurter. And he made his union much more than an agency for improving wages and working conditions; indeed, such mundane preoccupations seemed at times the least of his concerns. The Amalgamated became rather the model of the "New Unionism" — an organized attempt to better the lives of the workers on every front, overflowing with research departments (under Wolman), banks, insurance companies, schools, housing projects, singing circles, art classes, and newspapers in seven languages. Hillman even visited the Soviet Union in the early twenties and talked with Lenin about problems of economic reconstruction. His reputation among liberals and reformers steadily expanded. They fell for his igratiating personality, and they saw in his theory of unionism a higher form of labor statesmanship.

With the depression, Hillman was an early and ardent champion of economic planning. Like Lewis, he welcomed NRA; and both Hillman and Wolman joined Lewis on the Labor Advisory Board. Lewis, much impressed by Hillman, soon arranged for the admission of the Amalgamated to the AF of L. Hillman meanwhile launched his own drive in the men's clothing industry, and he gave full support to another New York labor leader, David Dubinsky, in a campaign to organize the women's garment trade.

Dubinsky, who became president of the International Ladies' Garment Workers in 1932, was five years younger than Hillman and had emigrated to America four years later, after union activity in Poland and a period of imprisonment in Siberia. Tough and alert, Dubinsky was colloquial where Hillman tended toward rhetoric and sardonic where Hillman tended toward piety; and he was much more concerned with making gains for his union in New York than with labor statesmanship in Washington. But, working for a moment in harmony, Hillman and Dubinsky made an irresistible team. In the next months, the ILGWU trebled its membership, and the Amalgamated, which had declined less under the depression, increased by 20 per cent. And, in the wake of Lewis, Hillman, and Dubinsky, a stirring of American workers began to make itself felt across the land.[3]

IV

For many employers, the drive for unionization seemed to strike at the very foundation of the system. Some went to any extreme to preserve themselves from the contaminating contact. One day, for example, the presidents of six steel companies — among them, Eugene Grace of Bethlehem, William A. Irwin of United States Steel, Ernest T. Weir of National Steel, and Tom Girdler of Republic Steel — walked into Frances Perkins's office to discuss the steel code. Miss Perkins, faced with the problem of labor representation in an unorganized industry, had asked William Green to sit in on the talks as a general representative of the steelworkers. When the steel magnates found themselves confronted by the mild and beaming countenance of the president of the American Federation of Labor, they recoiled as if from the head of Medusa. Not even permitting themselves to be introduced to Green, they backed away into the corner, in Miss Perkins's phrase, "like frightened boys." Miss Perkins took them aside and showed them Green's prepared remarks — warm praise for NRA and genial approval for the steel code. But even this did not reassure them; if they consented to acknowledge Green's existence, they felt, it would excite the steelworkers into new excesses of defiance. In the end, Green, perceiving that all was not well between himself and the tycoons, left the meeting in disgust.

Lewis took a more lordly attitude toward employers. In NRA hearings over the soft coal code, where General Patrick J. Hurley, formerly Secretary of War under Hoover, appeared as counsel for two Illinois coal companies, Hurley eloquently proclaimed his sympathy for the miners, pointing out that as a youth he himself had held a card in the UMW. Lewis rose, his face stony, and declared, "It is a matter of pride to a member of the United Mine Workers to see a man of that organization go out into the highways and byways of national politics and make a name for himself that is recognized throughout the country. [*Pause*] But it is a matter of sorrow and regret to see a man betray the union of his youth — [*Pause*] — for thirty lousy pieces of silver." Hurley, enraged, rushed at Lewis, shouting objections. Without turning his head, Lewis, sublimely nonchalant, said to Leon Henderson, who was chairing the hearings: "Strike out 'thirty pieces of silver.' Let it stand 'betray the union of his youth' " On another occasion, when the Alabama coal operators threatened to nullify the hours and wages provisions of the code, Lewis observed, "If they feel that way, the United Mine Workers are ready within fifteen days to furnish the President with twenty army divisions to force them to comply with the law." As Forney Johnston tried to reply for the southern operators, Lewis opened up the full force of his sarcasm and wrath, until Johnston, tormented beyond endurance, offered to "settle the question outside." "How charming!" said Lewis. "How novel! But I'm afraid it would not add to the gaiety of nations."

In Washington the labor-employer conflict was sometimes played as comedy. In industrial towns it was drama and sometimes tragedy. Frances Perkins glimpsed this when she toured western Pennsylvania early in August 1933. At Homestead, a company town, she had been permitted to speak to a group of steelworkers at a public hall. After the meeting, she learned that other workers, denied entrance to the hall, were waiting to speak to her outside. Turning to the mayor, she asked that they be invited in. "No, no, you've had enough," said the mayor. "These men are not any good.

They're undesirable Reds." Miss Perkins then started to speak to the men from the front steps. The mayor, appearing at her heels, shouted, "You can't talk here! You are not permitted to make a speech here." Miss Perkins suggested a public park nearby. "You can't do that," said the mayor, now red-faced and spluttering. Then Miss Perkins's indomitable eye caught the American flag waving in the breeze over a building across the square. She led the crowd into the post office, stood up on a chair and asked for questions about the steel code. . . . The incident called attention to the probable fate of free speech in company towns when the personalities involved were less exalted than the Secretary of Labor.[4]

V

In the meantime, employers were losing no time in mounting a counteroffensive. If the Recovery Act promised workers the right to organize, the law still remained vague about the form organization should take. Many businessmen decided that the best way to meet the terms of the Act without unduly strengthening labor was to set up company unions.

The company union — or the "employee representation plan," as its advocates more euphoniously termed it — was nothing new. Such unions existed typically in a single plant or, at most, in a single company. Isolation kept each bargaining unit weak and made industry-wide bargaining impossible. Moreover, workers ordinarily had to choose their representatives from among their fellows in the plant. Men whose future was dependent on the employer across the table obviously could not put the labor case with the freedom of an outsider or with the technical skill of a professional. (Employers themselves organized on an industry-wide basis and summoned outside aid for negotiations; but this was somehow different.) In addition, company unions were rarely permitted to accumulate enough funds to finance a strike.

Some employers had turned to the company union in earlier years in a sincere effort to preserve a spirit of neighborliness in management-labor relations which they feared would be destroyed by the injection of "walking delegates" from outside. But any company unions established from this motive were in existence, of course, well before 1933. What was new was the resort to company unions by employers who before NRA had resisted labor organization in any form. Since the effect of the company union was to create a bargaining tableau without creating anything approaching equality of bargaining power, it was an ideal instrument for any who sought to fulfill the letter and frustrate the spirit of the Recovery Act. So in the summer and fall company unions suddenly sprang up all over the country. The National Industrial Conference Board reported in November 1933 that nearly two-thirds of existing employee representation plans had been installed *after* NRA. Most of these plans were drawn up by the employer and imposed on the workers. If the workers were allowed to vote at all, the balloting took place under company supervision and without opportunity for debate. From labor's point of view, the company union was a form of fake representation forced on the workers by economic blackmail. They regarded it as a betrayal of Section 7a.

For labor, 7a thus meant protection of the right to organize independent unions; for management (or, at least, for a vocal and powerful part of it), it meant the right to install company unions. When the two interpretations clashed, the result was very often a strike. In June 1933 the Bureau of Labor Statistics reported 137 new strikes, in July 240, in August 246; by September nearly 300,000 workers were out. As trouble spread, it began to seem as if work stoppages might threaten the recovery program itself.

General Johnson had already made his share of statements on the union question without notably clarifying the issue. His attitude toward labor, as toward most other things, was complex and emotional. He had a hearty sympathy with individual workers and a personal liking for most labor leaders; he and John L. Lewis discovered a common enthusiasm for Napoleon and military strategy and even warbled hoarse-voiced songs together as they came home from Labor Advisory Board meetings. On one occasion, when Johnson felt that some grass-roots union officials were being outtalked by high-priced industry lawyers, he adjourned the meeting, beckoned Leon Henderson aside, and told him to take the union men over to his office and give them better statistics and arguments. He believed, moreover, that the logic of NRA was toward a form of guild government, based on trade associations and industrial unions. Yet he also had a mistrust of organized labor as an institution, and a compulsive need to dash in and settle strikes as soon as he heard about them. The result in labor policy was vacillation punctuated by melodrama.

NRA, Johnson claimed in an early press conference, was "not going to be used as a machine for unionizing any industry." "We are not trying to unionize labor by federal command," echoed Richberg. But, whether government desired it or not, labor was evidently determined to unionize itself. As labor actively gathered momentum, and as employer resistance mounted, Johnson expressed growing irritation at the conflicting theories of 7a. "Management has just carved out of that Section the interpretations that suit their point of view and published it all over their plants," he complained to the Special Industrial Recovery Board in September, "and, on the other hand, the labor people have carved out of the President's speeches or simple statements I have made, or Richberg has made, whatever they like until the whole thing is in confusion." In general, he felt that "this law should bring about open shops"; on the other hand, "I do not believe it is possible to have anything but a closed shop in the coal mining industry." And, in the meantime, his activism thrust him repeatedly into strike situations; once, after a futile trip to the Pennsylvania coal fields in August, he commented ruefully, "I stuck my nose into something that was none of my business and I got what was coming to me." NRA's function, he ambiguously concluded, was "to maintain an attitude of perfect neutrality, to lend itself to no one theory, but to execute the law." [5]

VI

Obviously this could not be enough: before the law could be executed, it had to be interpreted. Early in August, Johnson, on the joint motion of his Industrial and Labor Advisory Boards, set up a new body, the National Labor Board, to handle labor disputes arising under the NRA. The NLB had three members from labor — Green, Lewis, and Leo Wolman — and three from industry — Gerard Swope, Louis Kirstein, and Walter C. Teagle — with Senator Wagner as chairman. Its mandate was vague, its procedures were undefined, and its direct power of enforcement, beyond appeal to public opinion, was nonexistent. But it had the advantage of Wagner's energy and prestige, and it set to with a will to bring order into the labor picture.

Its first contribution to the settlement of strikes and the clarification of Section 7a was what became known as the Reading Formula. This formula called for immediate termination of the strike, reinstatement of the striking workers, the holding of an election under NLB auspices to choose representatives for collective bargaining, and the agreement by both parties to submit differences to the NLB for final decision. The election was the crux of the NLB approach. If a company union and an AF of L union both claimed to speak for employees, the solution, as the NLB saw it, was to let the workers choose freely for themselves. And the NLB further tended to assume — though it did not make the doctrine explicit for some months — that the organization chosen by a *majority* of workers was qualified to act as the bargaining agent for *all* the workers. This principle of "majority rule" implied that only one organization should speak for the workers in a given plant, as against the doctrine of proportional representation by which several unions might be entitled to negotiate on behalf of various fractions of workers. If collective bargaining meant anything, the Board reasoned, it meant one organization on one side of the table and another organization — not half a dozen other organizations — on the other side: it meant that each bargaining agent should recognize the existence of the other; and it meant a serious effort on the part of both sides to reach an agreement.

The NLB doctrines of a free election, a secret ballot, and majority rule obviously made a strong *prima facie* appeal to American democratic traditions. "This is America," said Gerard Swope to one fuming millowner, "and that's the way we do things here." And, in the crisis atmosphere of the late summer and fall of 1933, the Board was able to move effectively into one labor dispute after another. October, for example, saw the Board end a series of bitter strikes — in the silk mills of Patterson and Allentown, in the tool and die shops of Detroit, in the soft coal mines of southern Illinois. It did nearly as well in November.

There was spreading business discontent, nonetheless. The NLB placed new and irksome obligation on employers. If a company union were challenged, the employer now had to allow the Board to poll his workers as to their wishes. If his workers freely selected an "outside" trade union as their representative, the employer was presumably bound to deal with that union and to make an honest attempt to work out a contract. And, throughout the process, the employer was denied the pleasure of discharging the union men in his plant or exercising the other forms of economic coercion he had used to such advantage in the past. As the sense of crisis receded during the fall, employers began to defy the Board. Some declined to appear at Board hearings. In November the National Association of Manufacturers launched a campaign against the Board. And in December two cases of outright defiance put the Board's whole position in jeopardy.

The first arose out of a protracted dispute in the Weirton Steel Company. Ernest T. Weir, a long-time opponent of labor organization, had deferred sufficiently to NRA to install a company union in July 1933. In September the refusal of the Weirton management to meet with representatives of the AF of L's Iron, Steel, and Tin Workers led to strikes, and the strikers brought the case to the NLB. The Board ended the strike under the Reading Formula, with Weir agreeing that an election should be held to determine whether the workers preferred the company or the independent union.

Weir was an old-fashioned paternalist. He had always paid relatively high wages; he had avoided wage reductions as long as possible during the depression; for years, he had kept his office in the mills and had tried to maintain contact with his workers. The AF of L leaders were, in his books, "a handful of men led by a few racketeers." He now obtained a postponement of the election and used the interval to bring new pressure on the workers in favor of the company union — a policy which flooded the Board with more complaints from the workers. Then, as the election approached, he announced that the company would not permit the workers to choose the union of their preference, but only to choose their own representatives under the company union plan. Wagner, getting nowhere with Weir, appealed to Johnson, who wired Weir:

"In my opinion you are about to commit a deliberate violation of federal laws." But Weir went ahead with his private election.

The Budd Manufacturing Company of Philadelphia undertook a similar defiance. With Weir and Budd leading the way, employers everywhere were emboldened to ignore the Board. In addition, a campaign developed to discredit Senator Wagner personally. "Thousands of employers," wrote Charles R. Hook of American Rolling Mills to General Johnson, ". . . are either lukewarm or openly hostile because they are mad at the Labor Board, and when you analyze their hostility you invariably find it is directed to the Senator himself." [6]

VII

To carry out its decisions, the Board had to rely on action through the NRA — such as removal of the Blue Eagle — or on prosecution through the Department of Justice. All this meant tedious delays which only invited new resistance. Wagner succeeded in getting a new Executive order defining the Board's authority in more specific language. But there were still no direct enforcement powers. By February 1934 the Board had become almost impotent. It continued to issue opinions; but the opinions were largely ignored. Moreover, its interpretation of Section 7a was diverging more and more from that of NRA, on which it was so largely dependent for enforcement.

When the President sought to strengthen the Board in February by new Executive orders, the result was only to widen the breach. The order of February 1 was accompanied by an unofficial comment to the press that the government was seeking to check the growth of company unions. This suggestion produced the usual storm from businessmen. Two days later Johnson and Richberg made a statement of their own, rejecting the doctrine of majority rule and declaring instead for a system of multiple representation, under which a company might negotiate separate contracts with a majority group, several minority groups and even individuals in the same plant. This was manifestly an anti-union doctrine; Johnson himself later conceded that he did not regard a majority and a minority union in the same shop as practicable, while still insisting that this was what the law said. The Board, on the other hand, felt that the Johnson-Richberg interpretation was not only impractical but also unnecessary. At the first opportunity, it came out squarely for the majority rule.

At this point Johnson himself seemed to waver again. In his March speech before the code authorities, he told the assembled businessmen that there was no law against a company union if the men freely chose it; "but 99 times out of 100, you and I know that this is not the case. Let's not kid ourselves. . . . Submit to the law and get it over quickly." "I would rather deal," Johnson added, "with Bill Green, John Lewis, Ed McGrady, Mike MacDonough, George Berry and a host of others I could name, than with any Frankenstein that you may build up under the guise of a company union."

But a few weeks later, Johnson exhibited his chronic weaknesses for Frankensteins — or at least for their monsters — when he intervened over the Board's head in a dispute in the automobile industry. Invoking the prestige of the White House, the General settled the dispute on terms which provided for proportional representation instead of majority rule and which, in addition, superseded the NLB's authority by setting up a new Automobile Labor Board. With this resounding repudiation of its policy as well as of its jurisdiction, the Board itself went into a final decline.

By this time, Senator Wagner, long since despairing of progress through the NLB, had begun work on a bill designed to establish by statute a new labor board with enforcement powers. Drafted under the direction of Leon Keyserling of Wagner's office, the bill was introduced in the Senate in March 1934. Its provisions authorized the new board to hold elections, to prohibit acts of coercion and restraint by the employer, and to require management to do business with the designated representatives of a majority of workers. Clearly this attempt to put teeth into 7a was unacceptable to those who regarded even a toothless 7a with horror. In the next weeks, new storms of business protest whirled around Wagner and his few supporters in the Senate. Roosevelt, still hoping for the business cooperation which might make NRA a success, declined to back the measure.

Yet a new outburst of strikes in April and May made some kind of action imperative. Finally the President decided to bypass the issues raised by the Wagner bill. In a White House conference early in June, he proposed a congressional resolution authorizing him to set up labor boards empowered to conduct elections but lacking other powers which Wagner had deemed essential to the proposed board's successful operation. When Public Resolution No. 44 came before the Senate, Wagner accepted it for the moment, while promising to fight for a stronger measure later. Other liberal senators — La Follette, Norris, Nye, Bronson Cutting — held out for the original, Cutting saying bitterly, "The New Deal is being strangled in the house of its friends." On June 29 Roosevelt established the National Labor Relations Board, with Dean Lloyd K. Garrison of the Wisconsin Law School as chairman. With this action, struggle for control over national labor policy entered a new phase.[7]

10. The Decline of NRA

Office Memorandum 228 and Public Resolution No. 44 only provided stopgap solutions for issues of price and labor policy. The conflict which continued to swirl around these questions signified the persistent inner tensions within NRA. These tensions were inevitable, no doubt, in the nature of NRA's job. But they were rendered the more acute and lurid by the character of NRA's personnel.

For Johnson, the strain was beginning to tell by the spring of 1934. He had overestimated his physical strength as well as his capacity to hold all the reins in a single hand. Power reacted ominously on him. Overwork, fatigue, and the intoxication of authority stretched taut his nerves. He saved no time for reflection, hated to seek counsel, and tended to meet all problems with great bursts of activity, which more often than not evaded the basic troubles. As he spent himself, his self-control, never notable, began to fray away. His explosions grew increasingly frequent, invective becoming at times almost an end in itself. When a group of workers, after an unsatisfactory conference with him in June 1934, called him a windbag who ought to try scorching "his summer pants before an open-hearth furnace," Johnson replied, "I have worn enough skin off that part of me that fits into a saddle — or used to — riding over the flat lands of Texas and the hills of Arizona to make a half-dozen critics such as they." Everybody was a rink-stink but Hughie Johnson, and he was still all right.

When life became too much for him, as it did increasingly, he took to drink. Sometimes he disappeared for a day or two to return sheepishly with bloodshot eyes behind heavy lids, his face splotched and his hair plastered down, while Frances Robinson, to the irritation of the staff, tried to run NRA in his absence. Robbie's importance had steadily increased. She was fond of Johnson, tried to keep him from drinking and became in effect his nurse as well as his assistant. (Once Johnson, justifying her salary, told the press that she was no mere secretary, which produced headlines of the "more than a stenographer" type. Johnson, aggrieved, said, "Boys, you're hitting below the belt" — a remark which delighted the newspapermen even more.) Others in the government felt she threw her weight around far too much; she was, said Ickes, "as obtrusive as a certain type of wife is in the private affairs of her husband." Richberg told Henry Morgenthau that, wanting to speak privately one day with the General, he locked the door of Johnson's office to keep Robbie out. Furious, Robbie accord- ing to Richberg — pounded on the door and shrieked that she must come in. Never, said Richberg, had he had such an experience.

To his conception of NRA, the General brought a passion that under strain, became almost insensate. "Organization of both Industry and Labor to the ultimate," he said, "is the only way to meet the serious economic problems with which we are faced." This would probably mean price-fixing (Johnson said he could visualize circumstances "in which outright price fixing is the lesser of evils") ; and it would certainly mean "regulation of production" ("an inevitable attribute of a permanent NRA"). In the end, he saw an agency which would absorb the Departments of Commerce and Labor and around which the American government and economy could eventually be rebuilt.

This conception of NRA had ambiguous potentialities. Johnson once presented Frances Perkins with a copy of Raffaello Vigli- one's *The Corporate State;* and, when he finally resigned, he invoked what he called the "shining name" of Mussolini in a farewell speech. He was, of course, no Fascist. But he was consecrated to a crusade. "To me," he said later, "the idea of NRA was the flower of everything I cherished, believed in as a religion, and was willing to fight for with all my heart"; it was "a holy thing." Miss Perkins, on whose shoulder Johnson periodically wept until she could stand it no longer, began at last to wonder whether this restless, goodhearted, neurotic, dictatorial figure "might be moving by emotion and indirection toward a dangerous pattern." [1]

II

Within NRA, his relations with his general counsel grew particularly tense. He had in Richberg a subordinate who was already sufficiently sensitive, suspicious, and ambitious on his own; and protracted exposure to the irascible General soon proved too much for Richberg's jangled nerves. By the spring of 1934, Richberg was well on his way to becoming a mass of self-pity, telling everyone who would listen that life with Johnson was a living hell. For his part, Johnson, with his boy's-book conception of loyalty, seems to have remained jovially oblivious of Richberg's resentments. "I had no secrets from him," he later wrote, "and I trusted him as I would have trusted my own brother." This was doubtless so. Yet Richberg noted that, when on occasion Johnson suggested that perhaps they both should get out and let the President go ahead with a new management, he tended to add thoughtfully, "But I don't see how I can resign just yet," leaving Richberg the impression Johnson saw no reason why his lieutenant shouldn't.

By the middle of 1934, Johnson's increasing incapacity began to rouse concern at the White House. Roosevelt, with his readiness to pay a price for executive qualities, had been inclined to overlook Johnson's irresponsibility in gratitude for his energy and knowledge. When there had been complaint about Johnson in the cabinet early in the year, the President said philosophically that every administration had to have its Peck's Bad Boy. By June the General was straining even the presidential tolerance. Temperamentally reluctant to make a direct approach, Roosevelt now hoped to persuade Johnson, through Baruch, to take a European trip, perhaps leaving Richberg in charge of NRA. When report of this reached Johnson, there was another explosion. This resulted in Richberg's sending his formal resignation to the President accompanied by broad hints that Johnson was really the one who should go.

Roosevelt managed to smooth things over before he himself departed on a Pacific cruise. He calmed down both Johnson and

Richberg, ordering Johnson to take a holiday and transferring
Richberg out of NRA into the presumably more powerful position
of director of the National Emergency Council. This only deferred
the showdown. On the President's return in August, NRA was still
the top item on his agenda. Richberg and Frances Perkins, now
supported by Morgenthau, Tugwell, and others, were telling him
that he could not dally with the Johnson problem any longer.
Roosevelt's fondness for Johnson and appreciation for his services
once again constrained him. When Johnson offered to resign in
mid-August, the President softheartedly asked him to stay on until
the reorganization was completed. "I need you," he said (according to Johnson), "and the country needs you." Johnson melted
under the flattery. "My feet are nailed to the floor for the present,"
he told newspapermen on leaving the White House. "I am not
going to resign." [2]

III

This was manifestly no solution at all. A few days later Johnson
was summoned back to the White House. Richberg and Miss Perkins
were present. Neither looked up when Johnson greeted them. There
flashed in the General's mind the memory of two peons skinning a
cow at the barred gates of Santa Rosalita Rancho during the Pershing campaign in Mexico: George Patton, at the head of an American patrol seeking two brigands, knew he had cornered his quarry
when neither peon raised his eyes as the patrol approached. "They
too," thought Johnson of Richberg and Miss Perkins, "had been
skinning a cow." "I am going to explode a bomb-shell," Roosevelt
said pleasantly: Would not the General head a commission to study
recovery in European countries? Johnson immediately demanded
to know what would happen to NRA. The President waved that
aside as a detail. Johnson, his face stiffening, said, "Mr. President,
of course there is nothing for me to do but resign immediately."
They talked a while longer, Roosevelt referring wearily to "all this
pulling and hauling" and the attendant publicity. That evening
Johnson sent the President a long and overwrought letter of resignation in which he summed up his relationship to NRA and expressed
both his affection for the President and his now bitter distrust of

Richberg. The letter was delivered by hand at the White House, and Roosevelt replied within the hour — an answer, Johnson later wrote, "so affectionate, kind, considerate, understanding, and long-suffering, that I felt lower and more ashamed of myself than ever." The President told Johnson to forget his own letter and come to the White House for a quiet talk.

In their next conference, the President asked Johnson to work out his reorganization ideas. In the meantime, he said, he wanted to take over NRA himself so that he could see at first hand what the problems were. From that moment, Johnson, though still nominally Administrator, was effectively shuffled out of the NRA picture. Roosevelt told Blackwell Smith, the new general counsel, and Colonel G. A. Lynch, the administrative officer, to run NRA in direct contact with him and not to talk to anyone else, by which he meant Johnson. For some time thereafter, Smith and Lynch held weekly conferences to discuss with the President "difficult or controversial matters requiring attention in immediate future." Smith, along with Leon Henderson, the economic adviser, made the basic NRA decisions.

Johnson still clung to the title, though, and Richberg continued to bombard the President with pleas to get rid of him. There was but "one obstacle," Richberg said, to the rehabilitation of NRA: "a team of horses can't be driven in harness with a wild bull." Unless that obstacle was removed, all planning was a waste of time. Richberg — and Tugwell too — urged that Johnson be replaced, not by another individual, but by a board in order to dramatize the end of one-man rule in NRA. For his part, Johnson continued to plunge ahead. He announced his own ideas for NRA reorganization in a radio speech in mid-September, leading Richberg to complain to Roosevelt again and to question darkly his superior's sanity. But, in time, Johnson found the NRA freeze-out unendurable and finally, on September 24, submitted his resignation. Roosevelt promptly accepted it, sending a warm letter in reply.

On October 1, 1934, NRA employees crowded in to the auditorium of the Department of Commerce. Johnson looked over the throng with tears in his eyes. "It just tore at my vitals . . . to give up a place in the ranks of such an army." The NRA, he told them, was "as great a social advance as has occurred on this earth since a gaunt and dusty Jew in Palestine declared, as a new principle in human relationship, 'The Kingdom of Heaven is within you.' " "If NRA were to be regarded as nothing more than a practical school of economic and philosophical theory," he added, "it has been the greatest educational force that has ever existed." Climaxing a characteristic torrent of sentiment and hyperbole, he quoted (in Italian) the last words of Madame Butterfly before she committed hara-kiri. When he finished, tears were streaming down his cheeks, and much of the audience was sobbing.[3]

IV

In place of Johnson, Roosevelt now appointed a National Industrial Recovery Board to administer NRA. The membership of the Board consisted of two businessmen — Clay Williams of Reynolds Tobacco and Arthur D. Whiteside — two college professors — Leon C. Marshall and Walton Hamilton — and one labor leader — Sidney Hillman. In addition, Leon Henderson and Blackwell Smith, as economic and legal advisers, were *ex officio* members. W. Averell Harriman was administrative officer of NRA under the new setup. Donald Nelson of Sears, Roebuck was brought in as code administration director. In the background, Richberg, as executive secretary of the Executive Council and executive director of the National Emergency Council, two presidential committees hopefully designed to introduce order into the recovery effort, continued to exert influence on NRA policy.

Some members of the National Emergency Council felt that the Board had to be strengthened further if NRA was to make a public comeback. Charles E. Wyzanski, Jr., of the Department of Labor and Ickes separately arrived at the idea of Robert M. Hutchins, President of the University of Chicago, as chairman of the Board and operating head of NRA. Roosevelt thought this an excellent idea; and Hutchins, obtaining the permission of his board of trustees, accepted the invitation. Richberg preferred Williams as chairman because he felt that "a strong conservative influence" was necessary "to hold down this mad tendency to make the business world over in a year." If Hutchins were now made head of NRA, Richberg warned Roosevelt, business confidence would be upset, Williams and Whiteside would probably get out, and industry as a whole might well walk out of NRA. His ostensible case was strengthened when most of the Board (among them college professors who had worked with Hutchins before) elaborately offered to resign in order to make a place for Hutchins. The appointment was repeatedly delayed until Hutchins in disgust asked that the negotiations be called off.

In the meantime, Williams, as chairman of the National Industrial Recovery Board, functioned as the nominal head of NRA. Compared to Johnson or Richberg, Williams, a courtly southerner, was a monochromatic figure; but his very colorlessness helped release NRA from its bondage to histrionics. While Johnson and Richberg had vied for headlines, the second level of NRA had produced a number of exceedingly able, disinterested, and effective public servants, whose essential commitment was to the job and not to the drama of power. Letting their superiors brawl and posture, they had thought hard about specific problems of control and recovery. Criticism of NRA from within was almost as intense as from without, and far better informed. Now, at last, they were having their opportunity to reconstruct NRA policy.

Of these public servants, the leader was NRA's chief economist, Leon Henderson. Henderson, it is true, was not without his own picturesque qualities. "I got my job by hollering," he once said, " — and no day passes but what I holler about something." But Henderson hollered because he was concerned about economic issues, not because he was concerned about himself. In 1934, he was thirty-nine years old, black-haired, black-eyed, and built like a barrel. He chewed gum and smoked cigars, occasionally at the same time, swore, spat, and affected an uncouthness of behavior which rivaled that of General Johnson. The son of a worker in a glass factory in Millville, New Jersey, he had worked his way through Swarthmore College, served in the Ordnance Department in the First World War, and ended as a captain in the War Industries Board. Thereafter he taught economics until Gifford Pinchot made him deputy secretary of the Commonwealth of Pennsylvania. From this he went on to the Russell Sage Foundation and then, following his concern over consumer matters, into NRA. Beneath his sloppy clothes and tough language and appar-

ent willingness to trade punches with passing taxi drivers there
lay an oddly sensitive nature, a capacity for quick mastery of economic detail, and inexhaustible drive and energy. His toughness
impressed even Johnson who, after their occasional collisions of
will, would say admiringly, "And they told me you were a social
worker." In Blackwell Smith's Legal Division and in the Consumers' Division, now under Thomas Blaisdell (following Mary
Rumsey's death in a riding accident in December 1934), Henderson found able allies.

The problem, as they saw it, was to withdraw the organization
from its exposed and untenable positions and to concentrate on
doing what could be done well. NRA, they believed, had bitten off
far more than it could chew. The codes sought to cover too many
industries, to enforce too many rules and to usurp too many decisions. Why have codes for the hog-ring industry or the wood-
plug manufacturers or the pin setters at bowling alleys? Why not
concentrate on major industries and strike out everything except
minimum standards covering wages, hours, collective bargaining,
child labor, and clearly defined unfair trade practices? To do this
would be to dismantle the haphazard structure of controls by which
NRA found itself regulating price and production, restricting ma
chine operation and productive capacity, and even limiting entry
into business. It was this apparatus of physical control which, in
the judgment of Smith, Henderson, and Blaisdell was raising the
main problems of compliance. It was also this which gave the
advantage to established firms and condemned NRA to policies of
scarcity.

As Henderson insisted in June 1934, "Most of NRA's energy
should be concentrated on positive stimulants to greater productivity." How to break with the philosophy of scarcity? Price
policy still seemed the critical issue. By holding prices at artificial
levels, industry, in its pursuit of short-run profits, prevented the
"increasing volume of goods and services" which alone could end
unemployment. In May, when the Durable Goods Industries Committee had recommended that industry be entrusted with price
control, Henderson told Johnson, "This is contrary to the public
interest. Price determination is not a proper function of industrial
self-government. In this field self-government would involve mon-

opoly power, with an interest to securing maximum profits. Prices should be determined either by free competition or else by an independent agency which is concerned with the welfare of consumers and employees as well as equity-holders. . . . Industry must never have government sanction for price control, unless we are prepared to adopt kartellization." NRA's first task, as Henderson saw it, was to set prices free. "By quiet, persistent effort in revising codes so as to reduce prices the basis for volume production would be laid." [4]

v

By the summer of 1934, NRA had begun to reverse itself on price policy. Of the codes adopted after Office Memorandum 228, a much smaller proportion contained price-fixing provisions; and such provisions in earlier codes were in many cases tapered off or rendered inoperative. It was, of course, a continuing struggle, and one replete with irony. For it was the businessmen who wished to turn their backs on the free market and set up a system of price and production control; and it was the New Dealers who opposed them at every turn and tried to move toward a functioning price system and a free market. If the business image of NRA had prevailed, the result would very likely have been in time to put the private economic collectivism thus created under detailed public regulation and thereby bring into existence the very bureaucratic regimentation which business accused the New Deal of seeking for itself.

As late as January 1935, when NRA held a new series of price hearings, of the 2000 businessmen on hand, reported *Time,* probably 90 per cent insisted on price protection. If NRA were to end price-fixing, said George A. Sloan of the Cotton Textile Institute, the agency "might as well turn us back to 1932 and go home." Without price-fixing, observed another business leader, the codes would collapse and "the whole Marine Corps would be unable to enforce the wage provisions." But the young New Dealers in NRA were resolved to push their back-to-the-free-market movement; and, as recovery proceeded, even a number of businessmen who had demanded controls at their moment of extremity began to regard them as irksome.

While the younger NRA officials sought to overhaul and simplify the codes, on the one hand, they also sought to restrict their application, on the other. Through 1934 there had been a spreading breakdown in the machinery of enforcement. The compliance problem centered in small business. General Johnson himself had come to feel that the extension of codes to local service trades had been a mistake. In the spring of 1933, with cutthroat competition forcing down standards of wages and labor, the cleaning, dyeing, and laundry trades were threatening to become one vast sweatshop; and NRA had stepped in to avert total squalor. But subsequent efforts to enforce codes against pant-pressers and beauty-shop operators only dramatized the picture of NRA as a giant bureaucracy persecuting the little fellow on the corner. On the other hand, any failure to attempt enforcement both discredited the codes and demoralized the NRA staff. Johnson, who estimated that 90 per cent of the complaints on noncompliance arose from the small service establishment, later felt that the Cleaning and Dyeing Code had singlehandedly killed the Blue Eagle. Now NRA hoped to cut its losses, proposing the consolidation and elimination of local codes, offering exemptions to small businessmen, and planning to concentrate enforcement on industries where compliance was a realistic possibility.

Under the Industrial Recovery Act, NRA was due to expire in June 1935. As the time for renewal approached, internal NRA policy was becoming restrained and modest. The organization was contracting its activities, retreating from the attempt to regulate price and production and stiffening in its attitude toward business arrangements of a monopolistic character. Instead of trying to plan the industrial life of the nation, it was concentrating increasingly on defining ground rules and establishing a framework for private decision. As early as the spring of 1934, Blackwell Smith and Averell Harriman worked out a program to divest NRA of the service codes; then Sidney Hillman and Secretary Perkins, fearing the effect on labor standards, succeeded in killing the idea. Henderson and Blaisdell were now wondering whether the code device itself had not outlived its usefulness and whether standards governing wages, hours, and collective bargaining might not better be written into substantive law. But the weight of opinion was still against this proposal. The codes seemed both a more flexible and a more clearly constitutional approach to the problems of industrial control. "Can we successfully write 7a and wages and hours into a statute and enforce it," asked Johnson, "or even maintain its constitutionality?"

The President himself raised searching questions about NRA in his fireside chat on September 30, 1934. It was time, he said, to review the codes; he sharply questioned the wisdom "of those devices to control production, or to prevent destructive price cutting which many business organizations have insisted were necessary." (If the codes, he added, had gone "too far in such matters as price fixing and limitation of production," it should be remembered that "the representatives of trade and industry were permitted to write their ideas into the codes.") Yet Roosevelt too, as the renewal decision approached, seemed to feel that it would be better to benefit from the experience of NRA than to forsake the whole conception.[5]

VI

As Hugh Johnson's star set over Washington, Don Richberg's rose. He had the ear and presumably the confidence of Roosevelt; and the White House had no more frequent visitor. His supposed role as coordinator of the recovery agencies gave him a newspaper reputation as "Assistant President." "He is steadily building up his own power," his old law partner, Harold Ickes, remarked in December 1934 with envy and disapproval, "and he acted today like the fair-haired boy of the Administration. He looked like the cat that had swallowed the canary."

Probably none of Roosevelt's early appointments had given more satisfaction to labor and the liberals than that of Richberg. For a time, no New Dealer celebrated the changes of 1933 with greater radical fervor. "The long discussed revolution," he said in 1933, "is actually under way in the United States"; and, as late as March 1934, "We seek a socially planned economy brought about and administered by a democratic organization of mass interests. . . . Modern trade and industry . . . must have a discipline, a control and a direction."

Yet Richberg seemed to be moving more and more into the conservative camp. Susceptible to flattery, he was delighted when businessmen confessed their surprise at finding him not a dangerous agitator but a charming and intelligent gentleman. "His bosom companions," said the always captious Ickes, "are the rich and the conservative." He seemed now to regard his labor and liberal affiliations as entanglements from another age. Once Henderson, trying to nerve him to a decision, said, "From your life as I followed it for many years, and from my own, we were both hoping that we might have a chance like this to do something for poor people." Richberg decided the other way. "I believe he never forgave me," Henderson later said, "for holding the mirror of the past before him." "It makes me writhe," Richberg said in anguish in 1934, "to see myself cartooned carrying a red flag." He appeared almost under a compulsion to demonstrate his freedom by leaning over backward against those with whom he had once been allied.

"He is as busy as a bull pup in fly time," remarked Ickes. And in the winter of 1934–35 he was operating with great adroitness and confidence. There were signs, however, that he was beginning to overreach himself. Other officials considered him sly and shifty, charging that he used his access to the White House first to mislead the President about a problem and then to mislead others about the President's reactions. His relations with labor were symptomatic. Early in 1935 NRA faced the problem of renewing the Automobile Code, which included the question of renewing the Automobile Labor Board. This Board, predicated on a pluralistic theory of representation, was counter to the majority rule thesis favored by the NLRB as well as by the AF of L. On the National Industrial Recovery Board, a majority — Marshall, Hamilton, and Hillman — backed by Henderson and Blackwell Smith, opposed the extension. A careful and detached report by Henderson and Isador Lubin on the industry — a report accepted by the NIRB — had recommended the replacement of the Automobile Labor Board by a board of the kind set up in other fields under Public Resolution No. 44, thereby bringing automobile labor policy in line with the rest of industry. The AF of L had already opposed renewal of the code and had gained — or so they thought — assurances that nothing would be done without further consultation with them. Richberg told everybody not to worry. But at the same time he quietly persuaded Roosevelt to ignore the majority vote of the National Industrial Recovery Board and sign the extension. "Mr. Richberg," said John L. Lewis wrathfully, "secretly conspired with the leaders of the automobile industry to deceive the President and bludgeon labor. Like medieval ruffians, they lay in secret during the day and emerged after nightfall to perpetrate their deeds and announce the consummation of their plot. One can imagine the giggling falsetto cackles of Mr. Richberg when the strain was over and the deed was done" — Richberg, as Lewis continued, who sprang from the loins of labor, "labor that nurtured him and whose breast he suckled."

On the other hand, if Richberg was powerful, he was also, as Ickes further said, "highly temperamental and nervous and likely to go off at half cock." The higher he rode, the more insecure and irritable he became. When he heard that Hugh Johnson was planning to serialize his NRA reminiscences — *The Blue Eagle from Egg to Earth* — in the *Saturday Evening Post,* he took to his bed and warned the *Post* that it would be held legally responsible if he were libeled. "Donald's agitation," Johnson promptly commented, "is just a symptom of the ants of conscience in his pants." Richberg, after two months of silence, then produced a joke about "the Blue Eagle from egg to egomania." Johnson, as usual, had the better of the exchange. "I was recently accused of being an egomaniac," he replied, "because I wrote a book about NRA in which Mr. Richberg was not the hero." [6]

VII

As the time for NRA renewal approached, it became essential to strengthen and revitalize NRA's internal organization. Clay Williams was a failure as chairman of the National Industrial Recovery Board. His pro-business position put him out of sympathy with those who felt that the trouble with NRA had been an excess of business domination; and within the Board he was engaged in a troubling feud with Sidney Hillman. Wishing for personal reasons to return to private life, he finally resigned in early March 1935. NRA now lacked a head. "The primary necessity of good administration and good legislation," Richberg told Marvin McIntyre in

March 1935, "is a Chairman of the Board with recognized authority, able to carry out the President's policy and knowing what it is." Until a successor was selected, NRA could only drift along in circumstances which lowered morale inside the organization and hampered its chances on the Hill.

Who might the new chairman be? The leading candidates were Arthur D. Whiteside and W. Averell Harriman. Richberg wrote later that he favored Whiteside; but at the time he told McIntyre that he considered it "highly questionable" whether the Whiteside solution would work. What then? "Hillman, the best informed, most level headed labor adviser," Richberg informed McIntyre modestly, "strongly urged today that I should be given and accept the active responsibility of heading NRA. I cannot recommend this. But I must say that I have practically that responsibility now without the power to fulfill it." Other labor leaders were less enthusiastic about Richberg, who, as they saw it, had become the stooge of diehard employers — the automobile manufacturers, the newspaper publishers, the steelmen. But Richberg proposed that Philip Murray of the United Mine Workers be added to the Board, thereby giving labor and industry equal representation. This sweetened the pill, and Green and Lewis signified to the President that they would go along with Richberg as temporary chairman. [7]

VIII

On February 20, 1935, Roosevelt asked Congress for a two-year extension of the Recovery Act. His message summed up the new tendencies within NRA. Codes, he suggested, were to be contracted and simplified. The privilege of cooperating to prevent unfair competition could not be transformed into a license to strangle fair competition; "monopolies and private price fixing within industries must not be allowed or condoned." But the federal government would not falter in its determination to establish minimum standards of fair competition or to bring about decent conditions for labor. "The fundamental purposes and principles of the Act are sound. To abandon them is unthinkable. It would spell the return of industrial and labor chaos."

The ringing words of the message implied a confidence which

the friends of NRA no longer felt. The criticisms from without, the feuding within, was bringing NRA down the home stretch in a condition of weariness and irresolution. Its champions were proud of its accomplishments but uncertain about its prospects. "The friends of NRA are half-hearted," commented the *New York Times*. "They are like people who have a tired bear by the tail and are not sure whether it is safe to let go or not." Even Donald Richberg conceded in December 1934 that the "experiment with industrial self-government demonstrated all too clearly that private business is not yet adequately organized for collective action and self-discipline." ("The responsibility lies with business," said Harold Ickes, somewhat more acidly. "The government failed only to the extent to which it misjudged the ability of business to govern itself.")

Public opinion was halfhearted too, no longer fervent in its enthusiasm for NRA, but still unprepared to face up to economic life without it. Nor did NRA, like AAA, have a sharply defined constituency of its own which, as a recipient of tangible benefits, could be counted on for political support. Such constituency as NRA had consisted of organized business and organized labor. On the whole, the trade associations and the trade unions stuck by to the end. The United States Chamber of Commerce voted for continuance by nearly four to one; and a nearly unanimous Business Advisory Council of the Department of Commerce endorsed NRA. As for labor, Green, Lewis, and Hillman led an all-out fight for renewal. "It is unthinkable on the part of labor," said Green, "that we should go back, after having taken such a forward step in economic planning." Indeed, Green actually wanted to broaden the scope of NRA to cover all workers. If NRA were not extended, added Hillman, "this country is going to face an unemployment situation even worse than in 1932." The *United Mine Workers Journal* still regarded NRA as "the greatest victory for labor that ever was achieved."

The theorists of the managed society also continued to consider an NRA as indispensable. "Until that time when we do devise a better mechanism than NRA," said Moley, "we must keep NRA going. . . . Industrial laissez-faire is unthinkable." Something had to be done "to satisfy the need for government intervention and industrial cooperation"; "the interests involved in our economic life are too great to be abandoned to the unpredictable outcome of unregulated competition." If there had been anything wrong with NRA, said Hugh Johnson, "I think I can show that such faults as arose were due to my bad administration rather than a bad law." If NRA were permitted to die in June, "I, for one," Johnson said, "would not like to go home to face the hornets' nest that this will stir up, with the blood of its destruction on my hands. . . . If we can't regulate this economic engine, it has already proved that it has no governor. The next step will be abolition of the profit system, and page Mr. Stalin."

The exponents of national planning knew that they faced mounting criticism — not only the trust-busting oratory of progressive senators, but the more sophisticated objections of the bright young men in the school of Mr. Justice Brandeis and Professor Frankfurter who regarded NRA as an administrative monstrosity suffering under the curse of bigness and dedicated to a policy of scarcity. Then too a rising group within the administration was arguing that the key to recovery lay not in the reorganization of economic structure but in fiscal policy and the increase in government spending. And over NRA there hung a crucial series of constitutional tests in the federal courts.[8]

IX

As for Congress, its great worry about NRA had to do with "monopoly." In this nontechnical setting monopoly could mean two things. It could mean big business crushing small business within an industry. Or it could mean industry as a whole exploiting the public through the artificial raising of prices and restriction of production.

Congress was mainly concerned about the first. In suspending the Sherman Act, the Recovery Act had desecrated the sepulcher of old-fashioned progressivism; by this single action, in the progressive view, NRA had stripped small business of its fundamental protection. The Darrow inquiry confirmed the suspicion western progressives like Nye and Borah had held from the start that NRA was a big-business racket. When Richberg, a few days after the presidential message, insisted that any new NRA bill must be flexible enough to distinguish between unfair business combinations and industrial cooperation for the general good, Borah replied, "You may just as well talk about good kidnappers and bad kidnappers." (Bruno Richard Hauptmann was standing trial at Flemington, New Jersey.) But Borah's plea for the full restoration of the antitrust laws threatened, in Richberg's view, to deny business all protection against unfair competition. When Richberg said this, Borah denounced him as "the greatest friend of monopoly and the most pronounced foe of labor and small business" to appear in public life for a long time.

There was plainly substance behind Darrow's charges. Even Johnson, testifying before the Senate Finance Committee in its 1935 hearings on NRA, conceded that some of Nye's criticism the year before had been justified. Certain code authorities, for example, manipulated price schedules within their industry — e.g., setting favorable prices for certain products and unattractive prices for other products — in ways which helped the companies dominating the code authority and hurt the rest. In the case of the Steel Code, which provoked an unusually large number of complaints, United States Steel and Bethlehem wielded over half the voting strength of the code authority. Yet the full accuracy of the monopoly charge remains hard to estimate. Part of it rested less on the actuality than on the potentiality of the price and production controls which trade associations had written into the codes. No one could deny that the codes appeared to give trade associations extraordinary powers over the competitive pattern of their industries, or that trade associations were ordinarily dominated by their most powerful members. Still, in hard fact, a good many of these controls were never operative. In the case of production control, for example, industrial quotas were often set so high that they had no restrictive effect. Many of the price stabilization provisions were dependent on official findings of an emergency which NRA was generally reluctant to make. Moreover, the vigilance of Henderson, Smith and the Consumers' Advisory Board often prevented code authorities from utilizing powers nominally assigned to them. And industry, after it began to get back a measure of confidence, began to see the undesirability of restrictive provisions. There was, thus, often a difference between the language in the codes and the actual operation under them. Much of the concern arose, Johnson suggested, not without plausibility, "from some theorist's conjecture of the harm they may do at a future day."

In the most critical area — price policy — it is hard to see that the code provisions were, beyond dispute, injurious to the small businessman, except in the broad sense that the tendency (as defined by Hugo Black) "to make it a crime to produce too much, and to sell too cheaply" held back general recovery. Lowell Mason, Darrow's counsel, stated the small man's case against price-fixing in the following terms. "The greatest burden of our complaint," he said, "was on the question of the monopolistic industries being able to set a price, a floor price, so high for their advertised products that it simply foreclosed the small manufacturer from getting any market at all for his unknown product." This may have been the result in some cases; but in many more the setting of uniform prices tended to help the less efficient producer, which usually meant the little fellow. The big businessman, of course, would still gain under price-fixing an assured share of the market, relief from price competition and higher profit margins; but uniform prices denied him what no less a friend of small business than Mr. Justice Brandeis had often described as the most potent weapon of monopoly — predatory price-cutting. Even Senator Borah, who whipped himself into passions of antimonopolistic oratory over the iniquities of NRA price policies, was himself on other occasions a champion of fair-trade and retail-price-maintenance laws — that is, laws which forbade retailers from selling articles below a uniform price.

Certainly small business was having its troubles. Yet a good many of the monopolistic practices under which it suffered had flourished in the good old days when the Sherman Act was in full force; they could hardly be blamed on NRA. And the basic sources of trouble — shortage of working capital and of demand — were things NRA had not caused and was not set up to remedy. Still, in the circumstances, and especially in view of the impression left by General Johnson that his organization could solve everything, NRA became a natural scapegoat for small enterprisers trying desperately to stay in business.

X

It remains hard to resist the conclusion that the picture of NRA as the oppressor of the small businessman was both misconceived and exaggerated. The small businessman was not so much oppressed by NRA as contemporary and subsequent myth had it; the real causes of his trouble went far deeper; and, when he was harried by NRA, it was not so much because he was bravely fighting monopoly as it was because he was trying to grind the faces of labor. One clear test of NRA's performance was the experience of the Industrial Appeals Board. Johnson set up this Board in August 1934 as a result of the Darrow furor and instructed it to give special attention to the complaints of the small businessman. Testifying before the Senate Finance Committee in 1935, Monsignor John A. Ryan of the National Catholic Welfare Conference, a member of the Board, said that small businessmen before the Board "sought relief in the great majority of cases because they could not afford to pay the minimum wages, not because they were oppressed by monopoly"; indeed, monopoly had not been charged in a single case.

It was this situation which led NRA officials to react to the idealization of the martyred small businessman with understandable ill-humor. "You have almost nothing before you of concrete substantiated evidence of a little fellow hurt by NRA," said Hugh Johnson, "except that little fellows don't like to pay code wages for code hours." "The sweat-shop operator," said Richberg, "is the main complainant against the NRA." "The man who can hold his place in the competitive system only by working women and children for long hours at low wages," added Averell Harriman, "has no right to survive. The National Industrial Recovery Act gives a clear mandate to bring an end to competition at the expense of labor." Nor did small business suffering seem excessive. According to figures cited by NRA, the failure of small businesses in 1934 constituted a smaller proportion of all failures than in any year since 1921; and there seems to have been no marked increase in the rate of economic concentration during the NRA years. "NRA," Johnson even dared claim, "is the greatest charter of economic salvation that small business ever had."

The external objection to NRA price policy thus rested on unconvincing charges that NRA was persecuting small business. The
internal objection, as expressed by Henderson and his allies within
NRA, was different and more sophisticated. It was that price increases, by preventing increases in volume production, promoted
scarcity and held back recovery. At this point the question of the
antitrust laws came up in another form. For Henderson wished to
use the antitrust laws not so much to defend small business against
large as to increase the over-all flexibility of business prices. And
here he ran into a fundamental difference of attitude on the part
of men like Johnson, Richberg, and Moley.

The question had arisen in 1934 when the Federal Trade Commission tried to use its authority to prevent the abuses of power by
the Steel Code Authority. As Moley defined the issue, the FTC was
established on a theory of regulating business by prosecution,
NRA on the theory of government-business cooperation. "There
cannot be two coordinate bodies," he wrote, "with antagonistic
policies as to the relation of government to business." Johnson, as
usual, was more dramatic. The FTC version of economic planning, he said, was "a Lion-Tamer with a blacksnake whip, a re-
volver and a strong-backed chair, standing in a cage with six great
jungle cats snapping and snarling on six star-spangled hassocks."
He soon insisted to Roosevelt that the government take "a clean-
cut decision" between the theory of the FTC and the theory of
NRA; "you can't escape the issue — cooperation or competition."
As for Richberg, while he disliked direct price-fixing, he frankly
told the Senate Finance Committee that the efforts "to enforce the
principles of the antitrust laws have been a deceitful failure and a
continuing public injury for forty-five years." "If NRA legislation
is sufficiently devitalized to conform to the anti-monopoly ideas of
Senators Borah and Nye," he wrote privately to Roosevelt, "it will
in my opinion be made so ineffective and unworkable that it would
be worse than no law."

Henderson had no desire to devitalize NRA. But, where Borah
and Nye saw the Antitrust Act as the principle of good and Richberg saw it as a principle of evil, Henderson regarded it prag-
matically as a useful weapon of government economic management.
It was one way, he thought, that government could stop business

from using its position under the codes to increase prices and promote scarcity; and he did not feel that the objective of business-government cooperation meant that government must refrain from forcing issues with business.[9]

XI

Henderson was plainly right on the broad question of restrictionalism versus expansionism. NRA always contained the possibility of becoming a conspiracy of organized business and (in certain industries) of organized labor against the public — a profit-wage conspiracy against the consumer. Under such pressures, NRA tended to promote scarcity and hold back recovery. To this degree, the conventional critique of NRA seems justified. Yet insofar as this critique made price policy the central issue, it surely misunderstood the character of the economic problem which NRA confronted. Indeed, it is hard to resist the conclusion that the question of price policy per se consumed far more time in NRA (and far more space in subsequent analyses of NRA) than its importance warranted.

Price policy preoccupied those who held in their minds the classical model of the competitive market. It speaks for the power of this model that men so iconoclastic in other economic views as Tugwell, Henderson, and Paul Douglas were nonetheless so transfixed by it. If the model had corresponded to reality, then price policy would have been worth all the excitement it created. But that model had been overidealized and was now largely obsolescent. The hard fact was that the causes of price rigidity went a great deal deeper than anything written by trade associations into NRA codes, and that its cure was beyond the power of NRA to achieve. As a consequence of the changes in the underlying structure of the market — changes already demonstrated by Berle and Means — NRA price-fixing could do nowhere near the damage its critics supposed; nor would purging the NRA codes of every word tainted with price protection have had the effect the critics predicted. The ending of NRA price-fixing would certainly not, for example, have induced much expansion. The problem here was not the level of price but the gross failure of demand, and this was something that NRA by itself could not reverse.

This is not, of course, to defend businessmen who demanded every sort of profit protection. The effect of multiplying self-serving rigidities in the system would have been fatal. But it is to suggest that the economic philosophy of NRA was by no means so mistaken as its conventional critics have assumed. Where Henderson and the others supposed that a return to flexible prices was possible, Johnson and Richberg accepted the logic of a system of administered prices and sought means of reconciling administered prices with the national welfare. For this purpose, they tried to establish principles of conduct on prices and wages; and they embodied these principles in the codes. This effort represented a departure from the classical theory of the market; but, far from being a betrayal of a market system in general, it represented an effort in many respects fumbling and premature to adapt free enterprise to a market where competition took other forms than price competition. Their failure lay not in the idea of price-fixing through codes but in permitting business to dominate that process. The real cure, as Henderson perceived in his non-Adam Smith mood, was to strengthen government, labor, and consumer representation in the process of code-making. NRA, in a sense, was the first abortive attempt to invent institutions to express the workings of what J. K. Galbraith later called "countervailing power."

In accepting the logic of the administered market, NRA accepted the responsibility for acting directly on the relationships of prices, wages, and profits. It rejected the supposition that general principles could solve specific relationships in an equitable or productive way. It presumed instead that the solution of these problems — and, beyond this, the use and allocation of resources through the economy — required a considerable integration of public and private planning, in which business, labor, and consumers as well as government should play a part. While its institutions were too sketchy and improvised, too distorted by special interest and too confused by melodrama, to come near realizing its objective, NRA still operated in terms of a fairly realistic picture of the modern market. Thus its apparatus of codes, for all their defects, did succeed in placing a floor under the wage-price spiral which threatened in 1933 to take everything to chaos. Richberg once described the downward plunge:

> When goods cannot be profitably sold at prevailing prices, the natural means adopted by a business man . . . to prevent bankruptcy is to lower wages and to reduce employment. But, when such a program is generally adopted, the inevitable effect is to diminish further the purchasing power of the masses of the people, and to narrow the markets for all products, with the result of again lowering prices, calling for further reductions in wages and employment — and so the vicious downward spiral of depression.

It is true that the price decline stopped before the actual introduction of the codes; but the codes made it impossible for what Johnson called the saturnalia of destruction to resume. The kind of free enterprise which John L. Lewis described as competition based on a test to see how little a worker could eat was brought to an end.

And, for a season in 1933, NRA actually helped generate employment. The shortening of hours and the consequent spreading of work under the President's Re-employment Agreement gave jobs to something like two million workers; and the general increase in wages meant a temporary lift to demand. Beyond this, however, NRA's strictly economic contributions to recovery were limited. It represented a holding action, not a positive stimulus. Indeed, insofar as it eventually held up prices and held down production, it constituted a hindrance to recovery. As William Saroyan said, hearing a radio announcer say that aspirin was a member of the NRA, "Maybe the NRA is a member of aspirin. Anyway, together they make a pretty slick team. They are deadening a lot of pain, but they aren't preventing any pain. Everything is the same everywhere."

The more enduring achievements of NRA lay not in the economic but in the social field. Here NRA accomplished a fantastic series of reforms, any one of which would have staggered the nation a few years earlier. It established the principle of maximum hours and minimum wages on a national basis. It abolished child labor. It dealt a fatal blow to sweatshops. It made collective bargaining a national policy and thereby transformed the position of organized labor. It gave new status to the consumer. It stamped out a noxious collection of unfair trade practices. It set new standards of eco-

nomic decency in American life — standards which could not be
rolled back, whatever happened to NRA. In doing these things, it
accomplished in a few months what reformers had dreamed about
for half a century. "Forty-one years ago," said Hugh Johnson, "Congress declared that human labor is not a commodity of commerce.
NRA is the only gesture Congress has ever made to make that
assertion anything more than a sterile but pious generality."

More than this, NRA helped break the chains of economic
fatalism which had so long bound the nation. The Blue Eagle
campaign changed the popular mood from despair to affirmation
and activity. The psychological stimulus gave people new confidence in their capacity to work out their economic salvation. "It
was," said Frances Perkins, "as though the community rose from
the dead." Of equal importance, NRA taught the people the meaning and implications of the national economy. It collected basic
industrial information, often for the first time; Richberg once
mentioned his astonishment at the discovery that "trade after trade
and industry after industry in this country has not had in its possession the fundamental facts." It accustomed the country to the
feasibility of government regulation and taught people to think
in terms of national policy for business and for labor. And it
trained personnel for the responsibilities of government service in
a time of crisis.[10]

XII

NRA has suffered much in the verdict of history — in part because the people who have written about it have taken the classical
model of the competitive market as the base line from which to
offer judgment. This dismissal of NRA has become an historian's and
economist's cliché. It is no doubt futile to suppose that this verdict
can now be altered. Yet NRA was surely neither so rigid nor so
ominous an undertaking as it has been conventionally depicted. Its
ends — economic stabilization and social decency — were necessary
and noble. Its assumption about the economy as more administered
than self-regulating was much closer to actuality than the assumption of its critics. If it approached its goals in a clumsy and cir-
cuitous way, it did so because in 1933 the choice of roads was
exceedingly limited. According to prevailing constitutional doc-

trine, the Congress lacked power to legislate directly on such matters as wages, hours, and collective bargaining. The choice was between tackling these things through the codes or not tackling them at all. With the descending spiral carrying all standards of work and wages into the pit of depression, the irresistible need was for action.

By responding too eagerly to every aspect of that need, NRA accumulated for itself a mass of multifarious administrative responsibilities under which the organization eventually broke down. Still, NRA gave the American people for a fleeting moment a tremendous sense of national solidarity. So long as the sense of emergency gave the public interest a chance to win out over special interests, NRA worked. With a touch of recovery, the sense of emergency receded, and private interests came to the fore; and the lack of clear economic conceptions in NRA's administration as well as of clear legal standards in the law tempted private groups to concentrate on what each could get for itself. In the end, NRA foundered on the problem of asserting a vague public interest against the specific and well-focused demands of self-serving private interests. If those interests were permitted to win control of NRA policy, a business-dominated NRA, dedicated to scarcity, would surely condemn the country to permanent depression. If, on the other hand, NRA decisions were to be made against the business community, either a political storm would overthrow NRA or else the government itself in self-defense would march faster on the road to statism.

And so, as the sense of crisis waned, so too did the psychological foundation for NRA. Yet the memory of solidarity remained; and the experience of solidarity prepared the nation for a greater and more arduous crisis, which, when it came, almost seemed an NRA reunion. The child of the War Industries Board, NRA was the father of the War Production Board. Leon Henderson, Donald Nelson, Sidney Hillman, Averell Harriman, William H. Davis, Isador Lubin, Edward R. Stettinius, Jr. — all had their training in national mobilization in the breathless days of 1933 and 1934. For all its defects, NRA represented an essential continuity which in face of crisis helped preserve American unity.

III

The Economics
of Nationalism

11. The First New Deal

MORE AND MORE the movement of things in 1933 favored those who contended that industrial growth had produced an organic economy requiring national control. When the President's farm message of March 16 called for the federal regulation of agriculture the planning philosophy prepared to take over one vital sector of the economy. When, two months later, Roosevelt called for the organization of industry and commerce under federal authority, the planners occupied the other vital sector. These decisions to seek central management of agriculture and industry determined the shape of what came to be known as the First New Deal.

The tenets of the First New Deal were that the technological revolution had rendered bigness inevitable; that competition could no longer be relied on to protect social interests; that large units were an opportunity to be seized rather than a danger to be fought; and that the formula for stability in the new society must be combination and cooperation under enlarged federal authority. This meant the creation of new institutions, public and private, to do what competition had once done (or was supposed to have done) in the way of balancing the economy — institutions which might well alter the existing pattern of individual economic decision, especially on investment, production, and price.

II

The spirit of this approach was familiar enough. "Combinations in industry are the result of an imperative economic law,"

Theodore Roosevelt had said a generation before. ". . . The way out lies, not in attempting to prevent such combinations, but in completely controlling them in the interest of the public welfare." Former Bull Moosers in the administration, like Harold Ickes and Donald Richberg, thus found the new mood congenial; Moley similarly traced his own adherence to it back to 1912 and to C. R. Van Hise's *Concentration and Control*. For Tugwell, the belief in coordination under government sponsorship went back to Simon Patten's theory of abundance and to Frederick W. Taylor's theory of scientific management; for Hugh Johnson and George Peek, to the War Industries Board. Others had been prepared for it by the social philosophers of the twenties with their faith in planning, John Dewey, Thorstein Veblen, and Charles A. Beard, or by the benevolent paternalism inherent in the ethos of social work and in the Social Gospel.

Yet in one aspect the mood was new. The depression introduced special elements — not alone a concern with unemployment and the business cycle (Theodore Roosevelt, after all, had called for federal public works to combat unemployment as early as 1915) but, more important, a sobering sense that the age of economic expansion had come to an end. The First New Deal thus tended to see the problem of institutional reorganization not in the context of economic growth which the New Nationalism had carelessly assumed but in the context of what became known as "economic maturity."

The idea of economic maturity was in part, of course, a natural reaction to the darkened factories and the wheat rotting in the fields. It seemed almost self-evident in 1933 that America's capacity to produce had outstripped its capacity to consume. History, economics, and demography combined to confirm this supposition. A generation of scholars after Frederick Jackson Turner had told the nation about the disappearance of the frontier, from which many had deduced the end of internal expansion. Nor could the sharpest eye detect new industries on the horizon likely to give the economy the stimulus it had received in the twenties from the automobile. Above all, population itself seemed to be nearing standstill; the most expert forecasters anticipated, in Tugwell's words, "a state of stationary or even declining population within a few decades."

All this appeared to mean an inevitable slowing-up in the rate of economic growth, an inherent tendency toward stagnation — unless offset by positive governmental policies. Adolf Berle had written into Roosevelt's Commonwealth Club speech the idea that America no longer needed its builders and promoters; the economics of the future would be concerned less with the production of more than with the administration of what there was. Tugwell similarly observed that the nation was moving from an era of "economic *development*" to one of "economic *maintenance*"; "we have come to the end of a prodigal childhood." America now had to husband its resources and organize its economic life: growth could continue only as a result of intelligent national management. "With the vanishing of the physical frontier," wrote Harold Ickes, "the necessity of a rational national plan has become more and more apparent." Moley, Berle and Tugwell all adhered to the basic proposition, though each gave it his own interpretation.[1]

III

For Moley, who had been Roosevelt's chief adviser during the campaign and was now Assistant Secretary of State, these were trying days. The interregnum had marked his high point of power. He later wrote that he meant to stay on for only a month or so after March 4. The new confusion disturbed him, as did the sense of unresolved purposes; so too perhaps did the feeling that each new official appointed, each new adviser welcomed at the White House, threatened his position and diminished his authority. And he felt ill at ease and isolated in his new setting at State. Though the President persuaded him to stay longer than he intended, Moley's discontent grew. By spring he was already in negotiation with Vincent Astor concerning the possible editorship of a newspaper or magazine.

Pacing his room at State with its mahogany walls and high ceilings, or ensconced in his suite at the Carlton, talking impatiently in what one observer called his "gleeful-depressed" way, sucking hard on his pipe, he sometimes poured out disgust in vivid streams of sarcasm and rancor. Old friends were alienated by what they considered a distressing new sense of self-importance. "To think

that Ray Moley used to hang outside of my office six months ago
with the hope that I would pass on some of his papers to Governor
Roosevelt," Sam Rosenman remarked to Henry Morgenthau. "This
morning he acted as if he was running the Government and that
Roosevelt was carrying out Moley's suggestions." A favorite Washington wisecrack was "Moley, Moley, Moley, Lord God Almighty."
His new mood seemed to carry him away from the idealisms of the
brain trust. "Ray was somehow in process of being quite lost to
me," Tugwell later wrote of this period; "and the greater the
efforts I made to maintain the old relationship the more obvious
their unreality became." In place of his old colleagues, he began
to turn to "practical" men — to businessmen and to conservative
politicians. This inclination soon affected his interpretation of
his policy of "cooperative business-government planning."

Moley had no question about the need for positive government.
It would be madness, he believed, for industry to accept the "state
of anarchy imposed by the antitrust laws"; "laissez faire may live
again in the meanderings of philosophy and in the sophistries of
political speechmaking, but the world which it once ruled is
gone — forever." Regulation of the Brandeis type was little better;
the effort to keep economic units small would only produce a "state
of warfare" among employers, workers and consumers. The march
"toward greater and greater concentration . . . cannot be checked."
The obligation of government was to supply the focal point where
economic problems could be integrated and resolved. Within the
pattern of business-government planning, however, Moley was increasingly accepting the notion that business knew best.

Though Berle, unlike Moley and Tugwell, had turned down a
regular job in Washington, he averaged nearly half of every week
there during the Hundred Days, serving as special adviser to the
RFC, especially on railroad and banking legislation. While advocating government direction of the economy, Berle was troubled
by the administrative problems involved in the government's "taking over" industrial functions. Like Moley, he was consequently
prepared to leave operations in the control of businessmen. He
differed from Moley, however, in arguing that it was necessary to
fasten upon businessmen responsibilities which they could be made
to fulfill. And he even suggested that when government had ac-

quired enough experience in creating organisms for direct economic activity "the arguments for public ownership are likely to become irresistible."

Berle's deeper interest was in developing a new moral climate. Business could no longer be primarily an affair of making profits; its object must now be to provide goods and services sufficient to allow people to live full lives. "When it does not do this, business is bankrupt. It is bankrupt morally in the first place, and it is bankrupt financially shortly thereafter." The economic structure could no longer be taken, as it had been in 1929, as an end in itself. "A credo of some kind is as necessary to keep an economic civilization going as it is a political or religious civilization. I do not know that it matters very much what the credo is, provided it is intrinsically spiritual." Unless business realized this, private ownership was doomed; but Berle, for all his moments of impatience and pessimism, had an abiding faith that, in time, the corporation would generate a conscience and a soul.

For Tugwell, who lacked this faith, there was little to stop the same analysis from driving him to more drastic conclusions. Because business could not achieve self-discipline, government direction had to be far-reaching and specific. For agriculture, Tugwell wanted national regulation of production through democratic planning; for industry, "our present effort is to bring business combinations into the open, sanction them fully, coordinate and control them for the public good. . . . The old sentiment of fear of big business has become unnecessary." With the farm bill and the National Industrial Recovery Act, "we have turned our backs on competition and have chosen control." Where Tugwell particularly went beyond the others was in the degree of government intervention envisaged. "I thought of industrial leaders meeting under government auspices and determining quotas, prices and schedules," he later wrote. "I thought, in other words, of competition modified, of speculation outlawed by formal agreement, of resources and materials marshalled and flowing toward uses determined on the principles of national need."

Moley thus thought essentially of a business-managed economy, with government serving as a clearinghouse of information and as a means of facilitating business coordination. Berle thought more of a government-business partnership, with government promulgating new social ideals and inspiring businessmen to a sense of ethical responsibility. Tugwell thought of a government-managed economy, with government making the key decisions and reorganizing economic institutions so as to produce a more fool-proof business order. Where Moley was ready to trust business leaders as they were, Berle could trust them only as they might be — only as a realization of their power and their responsibility might lead them to repentance and to an acceptance of new social obligations. To Tugwell, even Berle's vision of a regenerated business community seemed utopian. Thus Tugwell saw in the business cooperation of the spring of 1933 not a change of heart but only frightened men who would return to their old habits the moment they thought they could get away with it. Why expect businessmen to be any different so long as the business system remained the same?

Moley's ideas were close to those expressed in 1932 and 1933 by such businessmen as Gerard Swope and H. I. Harriman; Tugwell's were closer to those of such labor leaders as John L. Lewis and Sidney Hillman. But, whatever the differences — and they were already growing — Moley, Berle, and Tugwell shared the passionate belief that the economic order had to be conceived as an organism, and not as a battlefield. As Moley put it, the old-fashioned conservatives and the old-fashioned radicals were equally wrong when they regarded economic life as "in its essence a conflict of the most desperate character." "Planning begins," Tugwell liked to say, "where hatred ends." Modern technological society demanded not conflict but coordination.[2]

IV

And coordination had a further logic of its own. The politico-economic pattern formed by AAA and NRA implied above all the belief that if the cause of depression lay within America the cure lay in the reorganization of American economic institutions; the first attack on depression must therefore take place within the American economy. The United States was not unique, of course, in this self-absorption. Everywhere governments were building economic walls to seal off their lands from the global decline and to protect their national recovery programs from the export of other nations' depression. In looking homeward, the United States was sharing — as it had been for some years — in a world-wide movement toward economic nationalism.

Yet nationalism could take diverse forms; and the nationalism of the First New Deal was different from that of the preceding Republican administration. The nationalism of Herbert Hoover aimed to protect the domestic industrial and agricultural structure by raising the tariff. At the same time, however, it clung to the international gold standard. The nationalism of AAA and NRA, on the other hand, aimed to free the national economy from international monetary institutions which prevented domestic planning; at the same time, it saw little point in increasing tariff barriers. The conservative version of economic nationalism was thus nationalist in trade, internationalist in finance; the liberal version, internationalist in trade, nationalist in finance.

Two documents of 1933 pointed up the contrast. One was a book, *America Self-Contained* by Samuel Crowther, the old-time collaborator of Henry Ford and an economic sage for the *Saturday Evening Post*. The other was an article in the June *Yale Review* called "National Self-Sufficiency," by John Maynard Keynes. If both Crowther and Keynes called for nationalism, they could not have differed more in their prescriptions.

For Crowther, capitalism, once it safeguarded itself against foreign goods, could solve its economic problems without planning. For Keynes, however, the whole point of economic nationalism was precisely the opposite: it was to make planning possible. Keynes had not reached a nationalist position easily, and his evolution was symptomatic. Brought up, as he said, to regard free trade almost as part of the moral law, he had come in the twenties to find difficulties in the received doctrine. The free-trade philosophy had assumed a world organized on the basis of laissez-faire capitalism. But depression, by everywhere compelling government intervention, had underlined the obsolescence of laissez-faire. Given the economic crisis, Keynes said, every nation would like to have a try at working out its own salvation; "we all need to be as free as possible of interference from economic changes elsewhere, in order to make our own favorite experiments towards the ideal social republic of the future." The "necessary preliminary" to world recovery, in short, was national freedom of action; and this could be obtained only by a planned movement toward national self-sufficiency.

How was self-sufficiency to be achieved? For Crowther the answer was a "prohibitive" tariff backed when necessary by "absolute embargo." But Keynes, though he briefly advocated a revenue tariff for Britain in 1931, put little stock in tariff protection as a solution. The critical field for nationalism in his analysis lay elsewhere. So long, for example, as the British interest rate (or, as his American followers would have added, the American price level) was determined internationally, then Britain (or the United States) would be condemned to permanent depression. "Above all," Keynes concluded, "let *finance* be primarily national." [3]

V

Depression similarly drove Americans of the classical faith along the nationalist road. "If the economic system is to be organized and planned and managed," Walter Lippmann argued, "it follows inevitably that the system must be protected against external forces that cannot be controlled. This means economic nationalism." The American people were thus "rejecting free trade among the nations because they have set their minds and hopes upon establishing a much more deliberately managed economic society." As industrialization increased the diversity of domestic production, Lippmann added, every nation was more capable of meeting its own economic needs. International commercial competition was thus becoming both "impracticable and unnecessary."

Charles A. Beard, who had no classical principles to surrender, offered an even more drastic program in his book of 1934, *The Open Door at Home*. The attempt to restore prosperity by developing foreign markets, he said, would only lead to class rule at home and to war abroad. The way to absorb American surpluses was rather by building the home market; and this could be only done, he contended, through national planning. As for foreign trade, he would place it under a Foreign Trade Authority with full power to license all exports and imports. By such means, the nation could substitute an intensive cultivation of its own garden for wasteful and ineffectual measures of foreign economic expansion.

Economic nationalism was in rising flood. "The greatest delusion-chasers in the modern world," wrote John Chamberlain, "are those who think we can have freedom of movement for goods and still preserve the results of a hundred years of social service legislation." So venerated a free-trade prophet as Frank W. Taussig made public confession of error for having, as chairman of the Tariff Commission, recommended the most-favored-nation principle, by which tariff concessions to a single nation were generalized to all nations. Lippmann pronounced the principle "as dead as mutton." "In my view," said Dean W. B. Donham of the Harvard Business School, "not only can relative self-containment be the solution of our problem of depression, but it is the only possible solution."

Both the conservative and liberal wings of the New Deal reflected the nationalist upsurge. "I am in favor of having each nation do what it can for itself," Bernard Baruch liked to say, "and then after that see what nations can do for one another." Hugh Johnson saw "unlimited possibilities of expansion in the domestic market with promise so rich that, if we tripled our exports (which was out of the question) at the expense of domestic balance, we would be the loser." George Peek hoped to protect agricultural and industrial prices by a combination of tariffs, exchange controls, and managed foreign trading. "We are pursuing primarily an economic policy of national self-sufficiency," said Donald Richberg. Moley regarded the New Deal program as presupposing "a considerable insulation of our national economy from the rest of the world." Tugwell's views, as usual, were more complicated. He too wanted to protect the economy against uncontrollable international forces until there was a measure of recovery; the doors of the house had to stay closed to outsiders while the family dispute was still in progress. Yet he also disliked nationalism of the Smoot-Hawley type. Seeking a solution somewhere short of "the international anarchy we call free trade," he looked to a trading revival through the use of new international mechanisms — bilateral agreements, commodity conferences, import and export boards, and other devices for international economic planning.[4]

VI

But the New Deal was by no means irrevocably committed to economic nationalism. The campaign dispute over the tariff speech at Sioux City — when Roosevelt directed Moley to "reconcile" competing drafts by Hugh Johnson and Cordell Hull — suggested the internal split. And the most devoted exponent of economic internationalism was now, as Secretary of State, in a peculiarly favorable position to advance his faith.

Cordell Hull, sixty-two years old in 1933, was the embodiment of old-fashioned southern liberalism. He was born in a log cabin in Overton County, Tennessee, in the foothills of the Cumberland Mountains, a rolling land fragrant with laurel and hickory. He was a bookish boy; and his father, who was rising in the world as a country trader and moneylender, sent him on to high school and then to the Cumberland University Law School. Politics soon captured the young man. He was barely old enough to vote when he began his first term in the Tennessee legislature. After service in Cuba during the Spanish-American War, he returned to Tennessee and became in 1903 a state circuit court judge. In 1906, Judge Hull, as he was forever after known, was elected to Congress.

In political philosophy, he had two grand mentors. One was Jefferson. Young Hull memorized great parts of the Declaration of Independence and Jefferson's first inaugural: "the final achievement of the five hundred years' struggle for Anglo-Saxon liberty," he felt, "was written in these axioms and principles." His other hero was a Tennessee politician named Benton McMillin, who had waged a long fight in Congress for tariff reduction and for the income tax. Out of this combination Hull emerged a Gladstonian liberal with a mild but real admixture of southern agrarian progressivism. Northern business interests, as he saw it, were plundering the nation through a malign system of special privilege; the hope was to dismantle the apparatus of exploitation and return to the Jeffersonian faith in equal and exact justice for all men. In his maiden speech in Congress, he demanded the "suppression of lawless combinations and proper curbing of corporate wealth."

Wilson's New Freedom suited him down to the ground. He had disliked Theodore Roosevelt's conception of the government as regulator. Now he saw an opportunity to make government the equalizer of opportunity. The income tax became his particular issue. He turned into a quiet fanatic on the subject, collecting statistics, investigating tax laws in other countries, introducing bill after bill in the hope of forcing the Supreme Court to reverse its earlier decision against the tax, talking so incessantly on the question that men like Champ Clark and John Sharp Williams walked in other directions when they saw him approaching. In time his perseverance paid off. After the enactment of the Sixteenth Amendment in 1913, Hull became the author of the first federal income tax law. He followed this up by drafting the inheritance and estate tax legislation of 1916.

With the income tax out of the way, he moved on to what he had described in his maiden speech as "the king of evils" — the protective tariff. At first, he had opposed protection solely for domestic reasons — because it meant the taxation of the consumers to subsidize the manufacturers, and because it promoted monopoly. The First World War enlarged his views and placed the tariff problem in its international dimension. Trade barriers, he believed, held down living standards and thus bred hostility among nations; "economic wars," he told the House of Representatives in September 1918, "are but the germs of real wars." For the rest of his life he was dedicated to a crusade for world peace by eliminating trade retaliation and discrimination among nations.

Defeated in the Harding landslide of 1920, Hull served as chairman of the Democratic National Committee from 1921 to 1924. He was re-elected to the House in 1922. As the twenties passed on, he looked at the country with mounting discouragement. All the old battles seemed lost. "The spirit of paternalism, bureaucracy, centralization, and materialism is abroad in the land," he said. He became, as he later described himself, the "Cassandra of Congress," and everyone ignored his prophecies. By 1929 he was almost resolved to abandon politics. Then one of the Tennessee senators died; and Hull decided that he had a greater chance of effectiveness in the upper chamber. In 1930 he was elected to the Senate.

The depression now offered new opportunities. The Democratic party, Hull said in 1930, would be recreant to its mission unless it proceeded to "bring about a civil revolution and political reformation as did Jefferson in 1800, Jackson in 1828, and Wilson in 1912."

VII

To this end, he led the fight against Smith, Raskob, and the high-tariff, big-business wing of the party. He had known Franklin Roosevelt since the Wilson administration; and in the twenties Roosevelt customarily stopped off to visit with him on trips to and from Warm Springs. In 1928 Roosevelt favored Hull for the vice-presidential nomination. Now they worked together to liberalize the party; and Hull was a Roosevelt leader at Chicago. Roosevelt, liking and respecting him, responding too to his fervent internationalism, then made him Secretary of State.

Serious, meditative, gentle, frail, Hull had the appearance of a benign southern gentleman of the old school. He was given to general moral statements of an unimpeachable piety; and he seemed to believe that the enunciation of a lofty principle was three-quarters of the battle. Generalization was easy, decision painful. His slight lisp increased his air of harmless benevolence. "We must eliminate these twade baa-yuhs heah, theah and ev'ywheah" was a favorite Washington rendition of his most familiar maxim. His personal habits were austere: he never played a game of poker after the Spanish-American War, abruptly gave up cigars one day in 1927 after smoking fifteen a day for thirty-five years, and drank only a sparing rye-and-water. He shunned ostentation and had little use for Washington society. The homilies to which he was addicted seemed to bespeak the man — righteous, preachy, and good.

Yet he was more complicated than this. His righteousness often concealed a self-righteousness. His two volumes of memoirs never confessed retrospective doubt or error. What some felt as saintly rectitude others saw as pious stubbornness and vanity. He was always right, and his opponents were always actuated by ignoble motives. And he had darker strains. He had come out of the no man's land of middle Tennessee, over which Yankee and

Confederate guerrillas and bushwhackers had swept during the
Civil War, looting, burning, and murdering. Hull's own father
had been shot and blinded in one eye in a guerrilla raid instigated
by a spiteful neighbor. After the war, the old Hull hunted out the
man responsible for the attack and shot him down on the main
street of a small Kentucky town. Cordell Hull himself once remarked to a newspaperman, "In my little home town in Tennessee
I have seen a dozen street shootings."

This world of mountain vengeance was still alive for him beneath
the veneer of old-fashioned courtesy. Occasionally his temper
exploded in a geyser of Tennessee expletives, generally beginning
with the exclamation "Cwist!" ("Cordell was in a 'Cwist' mood
today," Roosevelt used to say with amusement, "and the old boy
was certainly good.") And sometimes his emotions crystallized in
a hatred as grim and a determination as implacable as that which
had led his father to track down Jim Stepp sixty years before. As
those who knew him well put it, Cordell Hull carried a long knife.

Hull brought to his crusade a peculiar combination of evangelism
and vindictiveness, of selflessness and martyrdom. "The practice
of the half insane policy of economic isolationism during the past
ten years, here and elsewhere," he said in 1932, "is the largest
single underlying cause of the present panic." Either America
must follow the "suicidal" policy of reducing domestic output to
domestic needs, or it must lower tariffs, accept foreign goods, and
"gird itself for world trade conquest." Economic internationalism
was not just the way to recovery; it was the way to peace and salvation. With all the conviction of a Tennessee fundamentalist,
Cordell Hull was determined to set his country on the glory road.[5]

VIII

The Department of State was ready to go along with its new
Secretary. Indeed, in the Economic Adviser, Herbert Feis, Hull
found an able economist who could give his preachments technical
relevance to the increasingly nationalistic world. And Hull was not
without supporters elsewhere in the administration. His most
effective cabinet ally was Henry Wallace, who could see no long-
run solution for American farming except through an increase in

exports and could see no increase in exports through an increase in imports. "Frankly," Wallace wrote Roosevelt in September 1933, "I am convinced that sooner or later, we must be prepared to lower our tariffs very radically." But Wallace remained perplexed about reconciling tariff reduction with AAA; Tugwell fought for his soul in one direction, Feis in the other.

Hull's most important friend, though by no means a simple or reliable one, was the President himself. Though deeply pragmatic in this as in most other things, Roosevelt remained at bottom a Wilsonian internationalist. He chose Hull knowing perfectly well what he was getting; and, even though he was far more ready than Hull to temper the internationalist creed, he clearly respected Hull's capacity to recall him to the true faith. "In pure theory," he once wrote Hull, "you and I think alike but every once in a while we have to modify principle to meet a hard and disagreeable fact!" For Roosevelt, Hull served in economic matters as a kind of internationalist conscience, not always heeded at the instant, but generally triumphant at the end.

Still, for all his Wilsonianism, Roosevelt, like most people in 1933, felt keenly the case for economic self-protection. When Hearst asked him his foreign trade views during the interregnum, Roosevelt frankly replied that he accepted Hearst's nationalism "for the present emergency" but disapproved of high tariffs and the "Buy American" campaign as long-term policy. "In the long run it would work against us and our world trade and our industry," he told Hearst's emissary. He repeated this distinction in his inaugural address. "Our international trade relations," he said, "though vastly important, are in point of time and necessity secondary to the establishment of a sound national economy. I favor as a practical policy the putting of first things first. I shall spare no effort to restore world trade by international economic readjustments, but the emergency at home cannot wait on that accomplishment." Believing that the economy was built beyond the present capacity to consume, he warned against "increasing our crop output and our factory output in the hope that a kind Providence will find buyers at high prices." Given the consequent need for control of production, he instinctively thought, as an old-time conservationist, in terms of national planning; "our national economy," he said, "must be expressed in terms of the whole rather than in terms of the unit." And he affirmed the need for institutional reorganization. "There is no doubt in my mind," he wrote the Socialist Paul Blanshard, "that although many changes are involved, we are headed toward a new form of social structure."

Yet, while finding much in the Moley-Tugwell-Johnson view which appealed to him, Roosevelt was never committed to a nationalist philosophy. For Moley and the others, national planning tended to be almost an end in itself; for Roosevelt, it was a means to an end. Seeing people and not ideologies — specific cases rather than general principles — Roosevelt freely indulged in contradictions which drove logical men to despondency. Thus Moley could never understand how Roosevelt could draw on Frankfurter, who believed in competition at home, or on Hull, who believed in free trade, as well as on the campaign brain trust, who believed in concentration and control. Tugwell found Roosevelt's readiness to pick one idea from Lewis Douglas, another from Frankfurter, another from himself as reasonable as "to use part of a cotton picker, part of a rolling mill, and perhaps part of a bottle filling machine, all together and all with the intent to produce automobiles."

Yet Roosevelt saw himself in a favorite simile as a quarterback in a football game. He could not say what the play after next was going to be until the next play was completed. "If the play makes ten yards," he told a press conference in April 1933, "the succeeding play will be different from what it would have been if they had been thrown for a loss. I think that is the easiest way to explain it." And, from his point of view, the Frankfurters and the Tugwells, the Johnsons and the Hulls represented alternative plays, not alternative strategies. Each ideological system, as he must have felt it, described certain aspects of American reality, each missed out on certain vital features, and effectiveness might therefore most probably lie not in taking one or the other but in combining and applying both to meet the needs of a particular situation.

Though Tugwell and the others believed in experimentation, Roosevelt was at bottom a far more consistent experimentalist. They were ready to experiment *within* their systems. But Roosevelt transcended systems for the sake of a more complex vision of America, which included elements of coordination and of decentralization, of nationalism and of internationalism, and thus also included means of preventing any system from being pushed to logical — and probably destructive — extremes. Where others saw the New Nationalism and the New Freedom in mortal conflict, Roosevelt could serenely define the New Deal as a "satisfactory combination" of both. In the internal conflicts of his administration, he held a flexible and often inscrutable balance.[6]

12. The Dollar Dilemma

THE FIRST STRUGGLE between nationalism and internationalism came in monetary policy. The President's proclamation of March 6, 1933, prohibiting the export and hoarding of gold, left the gold standard in a sort of limbo. "As long as nobody asks me whether we are off the gold standard or gold basis, that is all right," Roosevelt told his press conference, "because nobody knows what the gold basis or gold standard really is." Actually Roosevelt knew quite enough about the gold standard to want to avoid rigid commitment to it. During the 1932 campaign, though he had talked warmly about sound money, he had taken care not to identify this unimpeachable phrase with gold. Early in January 1933, he told the emissary from William Randolph Hearst that if the fall in commodity prices could not be checked "we may be forced to an inflation of our currency," possibly by decreasing the amount of gold in the dollar or even by bimetallism. His refusal to give Carter Glass a pledge against inflation was a factor in Glass's decision not to become Secretary of the Treasury.

The emergencies of early March crowded monetary policy only momentarily into the background. On the day of Roosevelt's inauguration, the index of wholesale commodity prices was at 59.6 per cent of its 1926 level, of farm commodities at 40.6 per cent. The dead weight of debts contracted at higher price levels threatened to collapse the whole economy — unless prices could somehow be increased. And, as Roosevelt realized, the New Deal in its first month was doing little to raise prices. Quite the contrary: as the President said on April 7, "So much of the legislation we have had this spring is of deflationary character, in the sense that it locks up money or it prevents the flow of money, that we are faced with the problem of offsetting that in some way. . . . We have not yet caught up with the deflation that we have already caused." The proper course seemed obvious enough. "It is simply inevitable," Roosevelt wrote Colonel House, "that we must inflate." And to John A. Simpson, the veteran inflationist of the Farmers' Union: "I am just as anxious as you are to give the dollar less purchasing power."

One wing of Roosevelt's advisers, however, could conceive nothing more horrifying. Their leader was Lewis Douglas, with his conviction that only retrenchment could restore prosperity. The vision of Germany in the twenties still obsessed him, and he persuaded himself that the United States in the spring of 1933, even with resources and labor so wildly unemployed, might nonetheless be a candidate for runaway inflation. As for the suggestion that government conduct a controlled inflation, this seemed to Douglas and to other representatives of orthodoxy about the most perilous idea of all. "People who talk about gradually inflating," said Bernard Baruch, "might as well talk about firing a gun off gradually. . . . Money cannot go back to work in an atmosphere filled with the threat to destroy its value." (Baruch, of course, was more than a man: he was an institution. And, as an institution, he took care to hedge his bets. While he talked sound money, his associate Herbert Bayard Swope was consorting with inflationists; and while Baruch talked tariff reduction, his associate George Peek worked for protection.)

Douglas took the most rigorously orthodox position; but he had able allies within the administration in the fight for economic chastity. One was James P. Warburg, an articulate and agreeable young New York banker brought to Washington by Moley, who had recently declined appointment as Undersecretary of the Treasury out of mistrust for Roosevelt's propensity toward monetary experiment. Though Warburg too feared an immediate slide into the abyss of inflation, his position was far more flexible than Douglas's. Douglas wanted to return to the old gold standard, but Warburg wanted to move on to a reformed gold standard with new parities. Another ally was the new Undersecretary of the Treasury, Dean G.

Acheson, a tall, urbane figure with flaring mustaches who combined personal elegance with incisive intelligence. (Couzens of Michigan challenged Acheson's confirmation on the ground that he was too close to the House of Morgan; but Tydings of Maryland was able to clear him of this incriminating charge by pointing out that he had represented the Soviet government before the Tariff Comission.) Acheson was relatively uninformed about monetary matters; and his views lay somewhere between those of Douglas and Warburg. Outside the administration, the Douglas position had the support of the New York financial community and a large number of academic economists.[1]

II

The other pole of the monetary question was located in Congress. Here, of course, inflation had been a hallowed tradition since the first Congress's enthusiasm for paper money had long ago produced the phrase "not worth a Continental." Depression, as usual, reawakened inflationist sentiment. Since 1930 the heirs of William Jennings Bryan, with more support in each new session, had been demanding a cheaper dollar. The introduction of the farm bill had only recently offered Elmer Thomas of Oklahoma an opportunity to sound every resonance of the issue.

But the inflation campaign was more than simply an atavistic reversion to Populism. Its intellectual antecedents were rather more sophisticated than if not nearly so respectable as Douglas's laissez faire. For some time, thoughtful economists had been dissatisfied with what Irving Fisher of Yale called the "money illusion" — the notion, that is, that the monetary unit was fixed in value, so that it could serve as the measure of other things but did not need to be measured itself. The value of money, Fisher noted, was fixed only in terms of gold; value in terms of what money bought was subject to consistent fluctuation. Why should not the monetary unit be held steady in terms, not of gold, but of commodities? The development of "index numbers," Fisher argued, made it possible at last to measure fluctuations in the buying and debt-paying power of the dollar. The prospect now existed of attaining a dollar of stable real value.

Fisher was not only America's most brilliant monetary theorist but a resourceful and persistent organizer. In 1921 he assembled a group of economists and businessmen interested in promoting the idea of a dollar stable in terms not of gold but of purchasing power. The result was the formation of the Stable Money Association. Henry A. Wallace was a vice-president of the group from its inception; John G. Winant was active in it, as were economists like William T. Foster, Waddill Catchings, and Wesley C. Mitchell. The idea of the "commodity dollar" received support from farmers and some from businessmen, if very little from bankers. Fisher commented, "They naturally rebel against being asked to run their business so as to stabilize the price level, instead of so as to make money." There were two notable exceptions, however: Frank A. Vanderlip, who had been Assistant Secretary of the Treasury under McKinley and was for many years president of the National City Bank of New York; and George LeBlanc, formerly of the Equitable Trust. It was LeBlanc who persuaded Father Charles E. Coughlin, the Detroit radio priest, to urge on his growing audience the virtues of devaluation, silver, and monetary expansion.

In the summer of 1932, Vanderlip brought together a group of businessmen to consider what could be done about the disastrous deflation. Their discussions led to the formation early in 1933 of the Committee for the Nation to Rebuild Prices and Purchasing Power, which became the heir of Fisher's stable-money efforts of the twenties. James H. Rand, Jr., of Remington, Rand, General Robert E. Wood and Lessing Rosenwald of Sears, Roebuck, and Frank Gannett of the Gannett papers were among its leaders; Fisher and Professor George Warren of Cornell were its consulting economists; and its executive secretary was a dubious figure named Dr. Edward A. Rumely, who had been in obscurity since his conviction as a German agent during the First World War.

The Committee for the Nation spoke for a mixed constituency. If some of its supporters earnestly believed that reflation through a commodity dollar was the only way to save the system, others saw speculative opportunities in inflation, especially through increasing the price of silver. Others represented new enterprise hoping that inflation would increase the supply of available capital and convinced that growth would soon absorb the new currency.

Still others, like Dr. William Wirt of Gary, Indiana, were monetary cranks of an apparently amiable American sort. On the fringe there were even more ambiguous types. The monetary nostrum has often attracted political extremists: the story of which the Committee for the Nation is a part goes back to Rumely's pro-Germanism in the First World War and continues through the Committee for Constitutional Government of the late thirties and the America First Committee. James Rand's designation of Douglas MacArthur as chairman of the board at Remington, Rand in 1952 was perhaps a concluding chapter.

In 1933, however, the ambiguities of the Committee for the Nation were well beneath the surface. Preparing its arguments with purposeful care, proposing a wide variety of measures, employing able economists as its spokesmen, the Committee lent a sort of pseudo respectability to the inflation drive.[2]

III

The agricultural adjustment bill gave the congressional inflationists their first major opening, and they took full advantage of it. It was soon evident they were on a rising tide. The vote in the Senate for Burton K. Wheeler's amendment providing for free coinage of silver at the old Bryan ratio of sixteen to one made it clear in mid-April that Elmer Thomas's omnibus inflation amendment, authorizing the President to issue greenbacks, to remonetize silver, and to alter the gold content of the dollar, would surely pass. Roosevelt had spoken of wanting inflation; now it was about to be forced upon him. The only question left, wrote Walter Lippmann, was "how inflation was to be produced and whether or not it would be managed and controlled."

In an impressive column on April 18, Lippmann supplied Roosevelt with the formulation which justified the President's own instincts on the issue. Every nation, Lippmann wrote, had had to decide since the summer of 1931 whether it would defend the gold standard or its own internal price level; "no nation has been able to do both." If the United States now elected the gold standard, then it might as well abandon thought of credit expansion or of public works. "The evidence is now, I believe, conclusive that a decision to maintain the gold parity of currency condemns the nation which makes that decision to the intolerable strain of falling prices." Between keeping up prices at home and keeping up the gold value of the currency abroad, there could be no question, Lippmann felt, which the President should do.

That evening a group gathered in the White House to discuss the long projected International Monetary and Economic Conference which Roosevelt had inherited from the Hoover administration. Douglas and Warburg were there, along with Secretaries Hull and Woodin, Herbert Feis, William C. Bullitt, Key Pittman of Nevada, chairman of the Senate Foreign Relations Committee, Charles Taussig, and Moley. Roosevelt wasted no time. He first said that the gold standard, in suspension since March 4, was now to be definitely abandoned. This astounded the Douglas group; none of them, Warburg later wrote, had "any idea" the President was seriously considering such a move. But Bullitt, Pittman, and Moley had already endorsed the decision; Feis agreed with it; and even Warburg accepted it as necessary and wise, though he objected to going off gold without expressing the clear intention of returning to a modernized gold standard when circumstances permitted. In any case, the decision was an accomplished fact, no longer a subject for discussion.

Then the President produced a copy of Elmer Thomas's amendment with its compendium of inflationary possibilities. "Have it thoroughly amended," he said, handing it to Moley with a flourish, "and then give them word to pass it." To the others he said, "Congratulate me." At that moment, Moley later wrote, "hell broke loose." The acceptance of the Thomas amendment, Warburg told the President, especially the section providing for the issuance of greenbacks, would be harebrained and irresponsible; it would mean "uncontrolled inflation and complete chaos." Roosevelt observed that unless he took something like the amendment Congress would make inflation mandatory. The conservatives retorted that permissive legislation, by making the monetary future uncertain, was just as bad. For two hours, Douglas, Warburg, and Feis pleaded and argued, even invoking once more the example of Germany. As Moley recalled it, they scolded the President as if he were a perverse and backward schoolboy, though other participants find this account grossly exaggerated. Roosevelt, imperturbable and a little amused, confined himself to good-humored replies. Pittman defended the President. Moley, according to Warburg, sat by in satanic calm, obviously delighted by the discomfiture of the orthodox advisers. Bullitt, who refused to regard monetary policy as important, was entertained as by a show. But Feis, indignant at the wide-open greenback clause in the current draft of the amendment, was shocked by what he considered the adolescent levity of the talk, Woodin was visibly unhappy, and Hull silent and depressed.

After the meeting, Douglas and Warburg went on to Moley's hotel room. For hours they expanded on their fears, their predictions of catastrophe resounding in the sweet spring night. At last Douglas pronounced his verdict. "This," he exclaimed with somber passion, "is the end of western civilization." [3]

IV

From the viewpoint of classical theory, Roosevelt's decision to abandon the international gold standard was, indeed, a wanton step. When Britain had left gold in 1931, it had at least done so because the pressure on its gold reserves left it no alternative. But, despite Roosevelt's professed fears about a raid on American gold by Dutch banking interests, United States gold stocks were, in fact, capable of meeting normal foreign demands. The presidential decision seemed therefore to have a more sinister implication. It meant that American monetary policy was no longer to be the quasi-automatic function of an international gold standard; that it was to become instead the instrument of conscious national purpose. More than that, the step involved the repudiation of obligations to pay in gold long written into the "gold clause" of public and private contracts — an act which damaged all creditors who had hoped to make a killing out of the increase in the value of the dollar.

Contemplation of these results filled many businessmen with deep indignation. Winthrop Aldrich told a congressional committee that nobody could possibly propose a repudiation of the gold contract written on every bond and every piece of Federal Reserve currency; "it is simply incredible." Even a Democrat like Baruch said, "We're raising prices for the benefit of a small proportion — 20 percent — of the population, the unemployed, debtor classes — incompetent,

unwise people." On the departure from gold he added almost hysteri-
cally, "It can't be defended except as mob rule. Maybe the country
doesn't know it yet, but I think we may find that we've been in a
revolution more drastic than the French Revolution. The crowd
has seized the seat of government and is trying to seize the wealth.
Respect for law and order is gone." When Congress early in June
approved a joint resolution abrogating the "gold clause" and making
legal tender acceptable in settlement of private debts and of government obligations, conservative outrage mounted still another notch.

Aldrich and Baruch did not, however, speak for the entire business community. The New Deal gold policy won the unexpected
support of the House of Morgan. J. P. Morgan himself made a rare
public statement welcoming the departure from gold as "the best
possible course under existing circumstances." "Your action in going
off gold saved the country from complete collapse," Russell Leffingwell of Morgan's told Roosevelt. "It was vitally necessary and the
most important of all the helpful things you have done."

As for the administration, the series of decisions on gold were
the beginning of a bold effort to win freedom of action from foreign
economic entanglements. Under the old system, when disequilibrium
arose between domestic and world prices, the domestic price level
had to bear the burden of readjustment until equilibrium was restored. Now domestic prices were no longer to be sacrificed to the
requirements of maintaining the gold value of the dollar abroad.
By this act, the administration freed itself for the active prosecution
of price-lifting programs at home. Moreover, at a moment when it
was considering a public works program, it guarded against the panic
flight of capital which some thought would be a consequence of
mounting budgetary deficits. Beyond this, some in the administration believed that the depreciation of the dollar would in itself induce price rises in the United States; at least, the abandonment of
gold had seemed to arrest the price decline in Britain. And, of course,
depreciation, by improving the American position in world markets,
would be expected to stimulate the export trade.

As yet this was not a monetary policy: it was only the invitation
to a policy. In the hurly-burly of the Hundred Days, the President
could only give a fraction of his attention to monetary questions. Indeed, his whole attitude toward finance betrayed casualness of mind

and a disrespect for the accepted wisdom — an attitude deeply distressing to his orthodox advisers. As Warburg later commented, the money question seemed often to bore the President. He declined to take it seriously. Still, at the same time, Warburg said, monetary policy exercised a curious fascination for him; he kept looking for some trick by which the whole thing could be juggled into place. "You were up against a compulsive drive to do something in this area without ever being able to pin the man down so that he would really think about it — a very odd experience."

And Roosevelt's attitude expressed something more. It expressed a deep conviction that the significance of technical detail was greatly exaggerated by those who mastered it — even a heretical feeling that on some issues Elmer Thomas might be nearer right than Lewis Douglas. In 1933 the presidential insouciance restored intellectual perspective. The money question, as the Douglas group conceived it, was just not that fateful: this was not quite the end of Western civilization.[4]

V

The monetary uncertainties were coming to focus above all in the preparations for the Economic Conference. Herbert Hoover, who had convinced himself by 1932 that no more could be done to achieve recovery by domestic means, thought that "the next great constructive step" lay in the international field. Having come to see the depression as essentially an international financial phenomenon, he concluded that the beginning of a cure lay in the stabilization of the world currency exchanges. Accordingly he welcomed the scheme for the Conference, which reflected the views of the conservative central bankers of Europe; and he even tried to have other economic questions, such as tariff rates, barred from the agenda. The objective, in the words of Hoover's representatives on the Preparatory Committee, should be "the restoration of the gold standard in the key countries, England and Germany."

Little could have been more remote from New Deal thinking, either in diagnosis or in prescription. When Moley and Tugwell stumbled onto the State Department's pre-Conference planning during the interregnum, they consequently begged Roosevelt to put off the whole thing indefinitely. Roosevelt, who had told Norman

Davis right after the election that the Conference could be made "of the utmost importance," was not so sure. Still, he was at least ready to broaden the agenda to include such questions as tariffs, commodity production, and trade. And he kept the preparation for the Conference in the hands of men who expressed the nationalist viewpoint — first Tugwell, then Baruch, then Moley.

Hull acquiesced in his peripheral role. He had indicated to Henry Stimson before assuming office that he accepted Roosevelt's intention of being his own Secretary of State. The Treasury, in addition, admittedly had a special interest in stabilization problems. So the Secretary of State contributed little beyond his familiar plea for an end to economic warfare among nations. The total money value of world trade, he liked to point out, was less than one third of what it had been in 1929, and the physical volume had fallen by at least one quarter. The drive toward economic nationalism, to which the Hoover administration had so greatly contributed, seemed to be gathering new force. The great hope in the proposed Conference, as Hull saw it, was for the United States, having helped move the world in the wrong direction, now to cooperate in putting it back on its feet.

The questions of detail fell more or less to Moley. Confronted with the Conference, Moley felt more than ever that he was the only honest man in a den of internationalists. Hull seemed to him fuzzy-minded and a doctrinaire, Undersecretary of State William Phillips a stuffed shirt, and the "white-spat boys" of the foreign service useless. He said he could not uncover in the Department "a single person who understood and sympathized with F.D.R's domestic and foreign objectives" enough to be trusted with the preliminary work. Instead, in his catch-as-catch-can way, he called on Warburg, Bullitt, and Feis to prepare a program for the Conference. Warburg, with his inexhaustible energy, now drafted a series of resolutions looking toward the removal of exchange restrictions, currency stabilization on new parities, and a modernized gold standard.[5]

VI

While American thinking was still in this rudimentary stage, European governments were insisting to Washington that the Conference could no longer be postponed. Accordingly, in early April Roosevelt invited the key nations attending the Conference to send representatives to Washington for an exchange of views.

The essential difference among these nations was between those who were still on gold and those who were not. The gold bloc, led by France and Italy, having stopped the decline in the value of their currencies with the utmost difficulty, were determined to defend themselves against depreciation. They pressed the thesis advocated by the Hoover administration — that the first priority was the restoration of an international gold standard. The non-gold nations, led by Great Britain, tended to feel with varying degrees of conviction that the gold standard was a worthy ultimate objective, but that it could not be achieved until the world price level had been raised. As for the new American government, it had moved far from Hoover's faith in the rigid stabilization of the exchanges in terms of gold. Still, while seeking leeway for its own domestic price-raising policies, it continued to think in terms of some sort of world economic cooperation, even perhaps in the form of stabilization. "One of the things we hope to do," said Roosevelt in mid-April, "is to get the world as a whole back on some form of gold standard." But this was looking to the future. For the present, Roosevelt (as he put it in his invitation) thought the Conference should seek to "supplement individual domestic programs for economic recovery by wise and considered international action." It was with this definition of priorities that the parade of foreign dignitaries to Washington began.

First to arrive was the British Prime Minister, Ramsay MacDonald. For MacDonald, in concluding stages of personal and political disintegration, the Conference assumed overwhelming emotional importance. He evidently saw in it the chance for a brilliant coup which might transform his political fortunes. While MacDonald was still in mid-Atlantic, however, Roosevelt took the United States off the gold standard. With one stroke he not only abolished the advantage which nations already off gold enjoyed over the United States in world markets but reversed the bargaining position between America and Britain. MacDonald had expected the United States to implore Britain to return to gold. He found instead rather less desire for exchange stabilization in Washington than in London.

Underneath the official courtesies, the British party was deeply annoyed. "The whole business," said the *Financial News* of London, "has been deliberately planned in cold blood as a piece of diplomatic blackmail." (This was by no means a unanimous British reaction. Winston Churchill, for example, who had rashly staked his political career on the gold standard in the twenties, now congratulated Roosevelt on an act of "noble and heroic sanity," adding only that he would have preferred "to see this equitable and splendid act taken with even greater vigor by a definite reduction in the gold content of the dollar.")

The Roosevelt-MacDonald talks were evasive on the subject of stabilization. In his confused way MacDonald emerged with the impression that Roosevelt favored immediate dollar-pound stabilization — an impression shared by no other participant and productive of misunderstanding later. In any case, the critical question was not the principle of stabilization but the rate; on this point, Roosevelt was notoriously mistrustful of British attempts to outwit the Americans. The joint statement following the talks brushed the topic off, saying vaguely that the "ultimate establishment" of equilibrium in the international exchanges "should also be contemplated." The statement laid major stress on "the necessity for an increase in the general level of commodity prices" as "primary and fundamental." It called for government spending and credit expansion; and its whole thrust was toward the vindication of national recovery efforts.

During the French discussions, the United States made its most audacious proposal (an idea of Bullitt's) — a tripartite stabilization fund designed to keep the dollar, the franc, and the pound in a stable relation; but the weak French government, fearful of domestic political repercussions, turned the idea down. The joint statement with France mentioned "the re-establishment of a normal financial and monetary situation" along with the "raising of world prices" as objectives; and the joint statement with Italy, while still emphasizing domestic public works, declared that the fixed measure of exchange value to be re-established "must be gold."

The progression of these communiqués reflected not just the pressure of the gold bloc but also the internal vacillations of United States policy. As the talks attained a momentum of their own, Hull,

Warburg, and the internationalists became more sanguine. The very act of inviting world statesmen to Washington gave Roosevelt the appearance of being a special patron of the Conference and thus an apostle of the international attack on the depression. With the Conference scheduled to open on June 12 in London, public expectations appeared to be rising to unwarranted heights.

Or, at least, so it seemed to Moley. As the shape of the domestic program began to emerge, the prospect of entangling international commitments seemed to him increasingly perilous. Certain that Roosevelt had no real intention of sacrificing his New Deal on the altar of laissez-faire internationalism, Moley felt an increasing obligation to deflate the pre-Conference euphoria. In newspaper articles and finally in a radio speech on May 20, Moley, with Roosevelt's approval, warned against supposing that the world was going to be transformed by what took place in London. A conference that tried to cure the depression solely by concerted international measures, Moley said, "would necessarily result in failure. Each nation must set its own house in order and a meeting of representatives of all of the nations is useful in large part only to coordinate in some measure these national activities. . . . Our domestic policy is of paramount importance." Things still could be accomplished in London, he concluded, but they would be of secondary significance.

This address, which Moley delivered without consultation with Hull, strained further the already tense relations between the two men. They differed much more than in policy. In a contemporary note a State Department associate discerningly portrayed them:

The Secretary — a ruminative mind which has pondered long on the economic and political history of U.S. and on international economics. But one which is unclear outside of this sphere, which has stopped taking ideas from others, and which when confronted with the obstacles and difficulties to his good intentions does not analyze them and figure out ways and means of licking them — but *preaches* merely against them.

Moley — An interested mind, which only exposes itself in jumps. A mind which does not seek systematic solutions or even systematic procedures, but catches at ideas and measures . . . He sometimes asks others *to think through;* he does not do so himself. He is too blithe on important matters, too ready to dispose by a jest. . . .

Hull operates in a vacuum of his own making — ruminating, repeating his general cry, but leaving all action on any point to M. who regards him as a voice crying in the wilderness.

And they mistrusted each other's motives. It was during this period that Moley called at Hull's apartment to assure the Secretary that, whatever he may have heard, Moley was not seeking his job. Hull, unmoved, commented later, "Moley at least has the subject on his mind." [6]

VII

As June 12 approached, the President could no longer delay selecting the American delegation. It is impossible to divine what Roosevelt had in his mind in making his choices. For chairman, he picked Hull. Though well aware of Hull's own strong views on foreign economic policy, the President made no attempt to acquaint him with the competing requirements of the domestic program. For vice-chairman, he picked James M. Cox of Ohio, his running mate of 1920. From the Senate, he took Key Pittman of Nevada, chairman of the Foreign Relations Committee, and from the House, Samuel D. McReynolds of Tennessee, chairman of the Foreign Affairs Committee. He tried hard to enlist Hiram Johnson of California, even saying he would have no objection if Johnson, a confirmed isolationist, refused to go along with what the Conference decided. When Johnson declined, he turned at the last moment to James M. Couzens of Michigan. For the sixth member, named the day before the delegation embarked, he chose Ralph W. Morrison, a Texas businessman who had raised money for the Democratic party and whom John Garner and Jim Farley deemed deserving of reward. Of the delegation, Hull, Cox, and McReynolds were generally in the Wilsonian tradition of internationalism and sound money. Pittman was a high-tariff man and a silver fanatic; Couzens was also a protectionist and inflationist. Morrison's views on the London issues, if he had any, were unknown. No member of the delegation had ever been to an international conference before.

Possibly the President hoped that this strange collection might be controlled by the staff; here Moley installed Bullitt as executive officer, Warburg as financial adviser, and Feis as chief technical adviser. In addition, Professor O. M. W. Sprague of Harvard, who had been adviser to the Bank of England, was to go for the Treasury; and George L. Harrison, governor of the New York Federal Reserve Bank, planned to help as he could on his own. It was further arranged (though Hull could never remember the arrangement) that Moley should go to London as a liaison man after the adjournment of Congress.

Moley called them the argonauts, departing in search of the golden fleece. Before they left, the President called the delegates in for a briefing session. For their instructions, he handed them the resolutions Warburg had drafted some weeks earlier. Neither the President nor the Secretary of State invited any discussion of the critical issues which each must have known lay between them. The attempts of Baruch and Moley to raise these issues were shoved aside in comforting generalities. Insouciance in monetary policy could be carried too far. The delegation left Washington in a fog much denser than anything it might encounter in the North Atlantic.[7]

VIII

By late May, Conference prospects looked increasingly dim. In London, Norman Davis, after a series of confidential talks, discovered that the British were almost as disunited as the Americans; the chief difference was perhaps that, as usual, confusion in Whitehall was better organized. "The British will talk about agreeing with us upon the broad policy of economic cooperation to be adopted at the World Conference," Davis reported, "but I fear that the Cabinet with the possible exception of MacDonald has now little real faith or interest in achieving this." MacDonald, it seemed, had about as little relation to policy in London as Cordell Hull had to policy in Washington. The Prime Minister's rhetoric provided an amiable façade of liberalism, but the hard-boiled National Government could be counted on to use its arsenal of preferential clauses and quotas to protect the sterling bloc. As for the French, they informed Washington in mid-May of their belief that it was no use convening the

Conference at all unless a pound-dollar-franc stabilization agreement was first achieved. In Washington, Herbert Feis wished for postponement, and Moley and Tugwell, regarding the whole business as ridiculously oversold, were sorry that the United States had ever become involved.

For a moment, Hull himself, oblivious of Davis's discouraging cables, oblivious of the differences with the President, oblivious of the activities of Moley, remained an exception to the prevailing pessimism. He said on departure, "There should be an agreement as to the fundamentals of the situation in a few weeks that should equally apply to currency stabilization as well as to trade barriers." But this prediction assumed the enactment in the special session of a reciprocal trade agreements bill, which he could show in London as an earnest of Washington's intention to reduce tariffs. At sea, he learned that the President had decided not to request action on the bill. Hull at once cabled the President that the Conference would surely constitute "the most outstanding single achievement of your Administration" if the tariff bill were passed, but that, without the bill, the American delegation could do nothing. Roosevelt replied that, in the drive for adjournment, it would be inadvisable and impossible to ask for tariff legislation. This message was a terrific blow to Hull. "I left for London with the highest of hopes," he later wrote, "but arrived with empty hands." So upset, indeed, was he that he seemed on the verge of resigning; and Cox and Bullitt urgently wired the President to send Hull a personal message to restore his morale. Roosevelt cheerfully complied ("I am squarely behind you"); but Hull was not much mollified.[8]

IX

In London all was confusion. Delegates from sixty-six lands milled around the Geological Museum at Kensington, strolling in and out of committee rooms, forming knots of conversation in the corridors, or retreating in despair to the seventy-foot bar on the lower floor to sip drinks of all nations. Of all the delegations, none was more confused than the American. Hull, still dejected over the trade agreements disappointment, could not bring himself to assert authority. Without a firm hand on top, the heterogeneous band felt free to indulge its fancies. The morning meetings turned into aimless, shapeless discussions, filled with gossip, backbiting, stump speeches, and irrelevance. "From the beginning," noted Feis, "the delegates have shown themselves unused to work; they do not read the documents circulated; they will not patiently follow committee discussions, or talk out with each other any subject."

James M. Cox, who became chairman of the Monetary Commission, retained some sense of responsibility. Warburg used to brief him in the mornings, standing by in Cox's bathroom while an English valet dried Cox's bulky pink figure. But Cox could hardly pick up the reins which Hull had dropped. Pittman was hard, tough, crude, irascible. He knew what he wanted and moved to get it with sharp willfulness; but, apart from silver, he could not care less, and he spent much of the Conference drinking and quarreling. On one occasion, he chased a technical adviser down the corridors of Claridge's with a bowie knife; the adviser, who was suspected of inadequate enthusiasm for silver, bought a gun for future protection. Couzens had moments of usefulness, but found it hard to work in harness and kept trying to resign. McReynolds and Morrison, who went along for the ride, could hardly bring themselves to attend meetings. Several of the delegates irritated each other excessively, and few troubled to conceal their irritation, even on public occasions. The delegation, in short, displayed neither leadership nor policy nor cohesion. The Conference would probably have failed with the best delegation in the world. It could never have succeeded with this one.

Nor could the technical staff make up for the defects of the delegation. Warburg was enthusiastic and indefatigable but temperamental; and Feis, worn out trying to keep together a program for Hull, was soon filled with despair. Bullitt, making his first appearance on the diplomatic stage since the bitter spring of 1919, had flashes of brilliance. Roosevelt, meeting him during the 1932 campaign, had been much taken by his effervescence, intelligence, and dash; and during the interregnum he had allowed Bullitt to travel in Europe as his representative. After the inauguration, Bullitt came to Washington in the hope of landing a job in the State Department. Though William Phillips, who remembered him with contempt as "disloyal" to Wilson, opposed his appointment, Moley finally forced through a designation as Special Assistant to the Secretary of State. Felix Frankfurter, running into Bullitt in this period, asked him, "Well, Bill, have you learned to keep your shirt on yet?" "Absolutely," Bullitt replied, "it is nailed down this time." But he was in many respects the same old Billy: the dictograph which obsessed him during the First World War was still in the heater. In London he angered Cox by suggesting that the American delegation rooms had been wired by the British; he angered MacDonald by taking his secretary out for dinner and trying to pry from her the secrets of Downing Street; and even Moley had to concede that for Bullitt's romantic mind foreign affairs were too full of "plots and counterplots." His love of intrigue completed the delegation's demoralization.[9]

13. Explosion in London

THE CONFERENCE OPENED on June 12 with appropriate ceremonies. George V greeted the delegates; and Ramsay MacDonald briskly launched the business proceedings on a note of bad faith by calling in his opening address for a reduction of the war debts. MacDonald's allusion was mild enough, but it violated the pre-Conference agreement excluding all discussion of the debts; and, as a consequence, it set American teeth on edge from the start. "I was simply aghast," Ambassador Robert W. Bingham wrote to Roosevelt, adding that MacDonald's compatriots loyally excused his performance by blaming it "upon his physical and mental condition."

Introductory remarks continued for several days until all sixty-six delegations had satisfied the requirements of national prestige. In the meantime, Hull, despite his setback on trade agreements, decided to make one more effort at breaking the tariff log jam. Under his direction Feis worked up a scheme for a general 10 per cent tariff reduction. In the confusion, this idea was presented to the secretariat of the Conference as if a formal proposal by the American delegation. Pittman now rose in his wrath and secured its withdrawal — an episode which convinced the Conference even more of the zaniness of the Americans. Hull then subsided: and the Conference shifted definitely from trade barriers to monetary issues.

II

The emergence of the monetary question was inevitable in any case, for the French continued to insist that nothing else could be discussed until something was done about stabilizing foreign exchanges. But exchange stabilization was, of course, only one side of the monetary question; the other side was the problem of internal price levels. A fundamental split rapidly developed among the major nations as to whether stabilization of foreign exchanges or stabilization of domestic prices should be the major objective.

For the gold countries, the answer was plain enough. They wanted stability in the exchanges and were wholly prepared to risk instability in domestic prices. For the United States, the answer was growing almost as plain. Committed to raising commodity prices at home, the American government was increasingly prepared to achieve this at the risk of continuing instability in the foreign exchanges. Britain, divided in its own councils and eager to play a conciliatory role, agreed with the United States that some price increase must take place before exchange stabilization would be possible; but it tended to agree with the gold countries that price-raising through inflation or through deficit spending should be avoided.

The first act revolved around an attempt to appease the French by working out a temporary stabilization agreement for the franc, the dollar, and the pound. This proposal, which had been negotiated before the Conference by representatives of the central banks of the three countries, was intended to provide a currency truce for the duration of the Conference. As the stabilization formula developed, however, its terms reflected both the anti-inflationist prepossessions of the French government and the British desire to keep the pound low in relation to the dollar. In particular, it set the dollar-sterling rate at about $4 per pound, and in effect it bound the President not to use his powers under the Thomas amendment. American representatives in London nevertheless urgently recommended that Roosevelt accept the agreement, Sprague pleading that "a failure now would be most disastrous" and Warburg adding that without stabilization "it would be practically impossible to assume a leading role in attempting [to] bring about a lasting economic peace."

The perspective of London with the insistent French was one thing; the perspective of Washington with the insistent inflationists another. As the American press began to carry London stories predicting imminent stabilization, there were adverse reactions in the

American markets. On June 15 security prices broke in New York, and some commodity prices began to decline. For a moment, it looked as if the price structure were in peril. "An agreement to stabilize now on the lines your boy friends in London are suggesting," Hugh Johnson told Moley, "would bust to hell and gone the prices we're sweating to raise." With the dollar rallying in foreign exchange and likely to be tied to the pound at a disadvantageous level the inflationists, relatively quiet since the Thomas amendment, resumed their clamor. A petition signed by nearly one-sixth of the members of Congress actually asked that Father Coughlin be sent to London as an adviser to the American delegation.

Against this background, Roosevelt quickly rejected the London proposal. He had three important and convincing objections. For one thing, the projected rate seemed to him disadvantageously high for the dollar: as he cabled Hull on June 17 (and as Colonel House told Lord Lothian as late as June 23), he was ready to stabilize, but at a rate around $4.25. For another, he could not accept the restraint on American domestic policy: if commodity prices fell, he told Hull, WE MUST RETAIN FULL FREEDOM OF ACTION UNDER THOMAS AMENDMENT IN ORDER TO HOLD UP PRICE LEVEL AT HOME. And he mistrusted the consequences of such an undertaking for the longer run: WHAT I FEAR, he told Hull, IS THAT IT MAY BE CONSTRUED BY US AS GENERAL AND PERMISSIVE IN SCOPE BUT IS SO WORDED THAT LONDON AND PARIS MIGHT LATER CHARGE US WITH BAD FAITH IF WE DECLINE LATER TO GO ALONG WITH THEIR INTERPRETATION OF IT.

Roosevelt's rather brusque cable was intended less to kill the stabilization idea than to goad the American negotiators into driving a better bargain and also to restore the delegation's sense of proportion. IT IS MY PERSONAL VIEW, he concluded, THAT FAR TOO MUCH IMPORTANCE IS BEING PLACED ON EXISTING AND TEMPORARY FLUCTUATIONS. REMEMBER, he cautioned Hull on June 20, THAT FAR TOO MUCH INFLUENCE IS ATTACHED TO EXCHANGE STABILITY BY BANKER-INFLUENCED CABINETS. Let the American delegation rather take the lead in demanding consideration of the permanent program looking toward a means of exchange among all nations. Hull accepted this position; and, for a moment, despite indignation by MacDonald and an explosion by Georges Bonnet, the French Finance Minister, the crisis seemed to have been overcome. But the delegation was still shaken. IF YOU LOVE US AT ALL, Cox cabled Roosevelt on June 22, DON'T GIVE US ANOTHER WEEK LIKE THIS ONE. Roosevelt blandly replied, DELIGHTED WAY THINGS ARE GOING . . . DO NOT WORRY ABOUT ATTITUDE OF A FEW PAPERS LIKE NEW YORK TIMES.

With Congress adjourning, the President prepared to rest up from the Hundred Days by taking a cruise on the schooner *Amberjack II* in New England waters. As the weekend row developed in London over the 10 per cent tariff cut, however, and as conditions in the delegation grew more chaotic, it seemed to Moley time for his own projected visit to the Conference. Roosevelt, while talking vaguely of Moley's trip, had never mentioned a date. Now Moley booked passage on the *Manhattan,* scheduled to leave the following Wednesday, June 20. In the next twenty-four hours, however, he began to develop last-moment doubts, which were encouraged by Marvin McIntyre and James F. Byrnes. Uncertain whether, after all, he should go, he decided to put the question directly to the President.

Boarding a Navy plane, Moley flew to Nantucket, where a destroyer brought him alongside the schooner off Pollock Light. There, with Roosevelt at the wheel, navigating the gently rocking *Amberjack*, Moley sat in the sun and discussed his proposed mission. Roosevelt, as Moley later recalled it, insisted on his going. There is other evidence that Roosevelt was somewhat irritated by Moley's dramatic descent on the *Amberjack*. Yet there can be no question that the President acquiesced in Moley's trip. Some days later, Eleanor Roosevelt told her husband that it was a mistake to let Moley go on the ground that it was belittling to Hull. Henry Morgenthau, Jr., who was present during the conversation, later noted in his diary, "FDR tried to explain to her that this was not so."

"The essential thing," Roosevelt told Moley, "is that you impress on the delegation and the others that my primary international objective is to raise the world price level." He cited a recent column in which Walter Lippmann had argued that international cooperation was a good idea if it resulted in concerted action but not if it merely produced a negative and impotent stability. Knowing that Lippmann was in London, Moley asked whether he should not talk to him and to Keynes as well. Roosevelt agreed that this might help educate the American delegation about the administration's

monetary objectives. Before departing, Moley left a memorandum
with the President, prepared the day before by Herbert Bayard
Swope, stating the case against rigid and arbitrary stabilization
proposals. It might be useful, Moley suggested, if there were more
importunities from London. In another twenty-four hours, while
the *Amberjack* scudded before the wind off Massachusetts, Moley
and the *Manhattan* plowed grimly across the North Atlantic.[1]

III

Roosevelt did his best to minimize the significance of Moley's
trip. He privately directed Moley to keep away from newspapermen, reminding him that he was "under the Secretary"; and he
publicly described him as merely a "messenger or liaison officer."
But these gestures did not deceive the press, which swiftly convinced
itself that Moley was at least bringing new presidential instructions
if not superseding Hull as head of the delegation or even as Secretary of State. London, mesmerized by the speculation and by now
prepared for anything from the Americans, began to feel that
nothing could be done until Moley arrived. The Conference thus
practically suspended business, waiting, so to speak, for Moley to
rescue it.

As for Hull, he watched Moley's progress with mounting indignation. The newspaper stories, with their suggestion that he himself
had failed, upset him; and he deeply resented the officials and delegates who queued up to greet Moley on his arrival. The reception
given to Moley seemed to the embittered Secretary to be surpassed
only by those given to kings. Ramsay MacDonald actually asked
Hull to send Moley over to see him, adding, as an afterthought,
"You can come too, if you like." "Prime Ministers and other top
officials of governments flocked after Moley as if he were the Pied
Piper," Hull later wrote in angry exaggeration (Moley saw no
Prime Minister except MacDonald). "I continued to keep in the
background as if I were the most insignificant individual hanging
about the conference."

Moley well saw how slights, fancied and real, were tormenting
Hull; and he devoted his first twenty-four hours in London to
reassuring him about the routine nature of the mission. He osten-

tatiously deprecated his own importance in appearances before the delegation and the press and considered that he had much success in restoring Hull's self-esteem. As Moley recalled it, "Hull made no attempt to conceal his appreciation." But Hull was more subtle than the confident Moley realized. "I decided to give him all the rope he might want," Hull later wrote, "and see how long he would last in that London situation."

Having, as he thought, fixed up the Hull problem, Moley now turned to the new financial crisis. Roosevelt's coldness to the stabilization negotiations had stopped the rise of the dollar in foreign exchanges, and American prices were resuming their upward path. As the dollar continued to fall in the last weeks of June, some of the gold countries claimed to fear that they too would be forced off gold. This fear gave the pressure for temporary stabilization something approaching panic proportions. The gold bloc, in a desperate effort to hold the line whence all but they had fled, now prepared a new monetary declaration which, they asserted, alone would save them.

Moley, who was handling the stabilization talks without consultation with Hull, found the proposed declaration surprisingly innocuous. It was in great part a reworking of one of Roosevelt's original instructions to the American delegation, subsequently introduced by Pittman in the Conference as a formal resolution. It committed the United States to nothing except general affirmations, to which it was already substantially committed anyway, in favor of stabilization (eventually), gold (ultimately), and the limitation of exchange speculation. Moreover, with the dollar-pound rate now oscillating around $4.40, Roosevelt's bargaining tactic of the week before seemed to have worked; and Moley, remembering his willingness to accept $4.25, could suppose that one of the presidential conditions for cooperation with the British was now fulfilled. Accordingly, Moley now urged the President to accept the declaration. In New York, where they were gathered around the sickbed of Secretary Woodin, Acheson, Baruch, and Douglas endorsed this recommendation.

IV

Roosevelt, receiving Moley's message in northern waters, could not have seriously objected to the content of the declaration per se. But his own views of the general issue had become more clear-cut since he had so casually passed on Warburg's resolutions to the delegation a month earlier — even since he had last talked to Moley in mid-June. For one thing, the operations of AAA and NRA in June made the philosophy of his domestic program far more concrete and compelling. As a State Department friend warned Feis in London, "You fellows must not expect to find America the same as it was when you left. These things are real." For another, the price jitters of mid-June convinced Roosevelt of the vital necessity of preserving the domestic price-raising policy at almost any cost. And the cruise on the *Amberjack II,* removing him from the hour-to-hour harassments of Washington, gave him for the first time a chance to think through the whole question of reconciling his domestic and foreign economic policies.

There were no doubt more specific influences. Colonel House had given him Sir Basil Blackett's new book, *Planned Money.* There he could have read: "Planned Money is vital to Planning, which is hardly conceivable under a monetary system in which the general level of prices is subject to violent fluctuations." And he would have sympathized with Blackett's plea for a constant price level, "a currency of which the purchasing power will remain stable from year to year and from decade to decade." He had been interested when told of the last chapter of Keynes's *Treatise on Money* with its suggestion of an international commodity dollar which might relieve the world of dependence on gold; and he had asked Moley to take up this possibility with Keynes in London. He had also discussed with George F. Warren the managed currency thesis advanced in his new book, *Prices;* Warren would soon warn him against any agreement in London that would reduce "our freedom to change the dollar any day." Moreover, he read — and discussed with Henry Morgenthau on the *Amberjack* — an article by Garet Garrett in the July 1 *Saturday Evening Post.* Garrett (who quoted Blackett's book) strongly argued that "the first problem is that of mending the internal economy of nations, each one to find how it shall balance its own budget, reemploy its own people, restore its own solvency." In addition, Roosevelt had it fixed in his mind that international bankers — especially his old friend Thomas W. Lamont of Morgan's — were trying to influence American representatives both in New York and London through Herbert Bayard Swope. (No doubt the bankers wished to exert such influence; but the evidence is that Swope was on the antistabilization side of this argument.) Moreover, the mere rumor of stabilization in New York was causing the dollar to rise and prices to fall.

Against this background, the new declaration, however innocent on its face, acquired for the President a larger symbolic importance. It expressed to him a preoccupation of the Conference he considered exaggerated and a direction of policy he considered wrong. In the context of the gold bloc pressure, he read the declaration as an attempt to force his hand on stabilization. As Feis noted in London on July 3, "The first plan of stabilization put up to the President was far-reaching in character and would have required renunciation of his monetary policy. This probably left a scare which the second proposal stirred up again." Even Moley, in a cable recommending acceptance of the declaration, mentioned to Roosevelt in connection with supporting action proposed by Sprague, the DANGER THAT EVEN SUCH A TEMPORARY PROJECT IF KNOWN MIGHT BE REGARDED AS THE BEGINNING OF PERMANENT STABILIZATION. "If this declaration be accepted," said the London *Times,* "it should be possible for the various governments eventually to decide upon stabilization of currencies on a gold basis."

Morgenthau, now with the President, noted in his diary on June 30 that Roosevelt was much preoccupied, as if trying to reach a decision. In New York and in London, in the meantime, tension was growing acute. On the afternoon of June 30, Moley and Sprague called the New York group at Woodin's house. While they were talking, Woodin suddenly fainted, and for a moment Baruch and Acheson thought he was dying. Moley had hoped to announce Roosevelt's approval that day to diplomatic dignitaries assembled for the purpose at 10 Downing Street. Instead, the meeting had to be dismissed, while Moley, smoking cigarette after cigarette, waited nervously in the Embassy until three o'clock Saturday morning. He sent a frantic cable the next morning to Roosevelt:

BELIEVE SUCCESS EVEN CONTINUANCE OF THE CONFERENCE DEPENDS
UPON UNITED STATES AGREEMENT.

V

Around three o'clock on Saturday afternoon, the President's
reply began to come through. Moley, who had been haunting the
delegation code room, needed only a glance to see that it was unfavorable. Without waiting for the full text, he rushed to find Hull,
who was just then leaving Claridge's to stay with Lady Astor at
Cliveden. "We've just got to do something about it," Moley cried
(at least as Hull remembered it). The Secretary turned angrily
on him. "You had better get back home," he said. "You had no
business over here in the first place." Then he walked to his car.
("I saw he had reached the end of his rope," Hull later wrote, "and
was through.")

When Moley returned to the Embassy, the text was awaiting him.
The President's message was an attack not so much on the proposed
declaration as on the gold-standard potentialities he discerned
within it. It would be unwise, the President said, to permit limitations to be imposed on our domestic action by other nations. THE
ECONOMIC CONFERENCE WAS INITIATED AND CALLED TO DISCUSS AND
AGREE ON PERMANENT SOLUTIONS OF WORLD ECONOMICS AND NOT TO
DISCUSS ECONOMIC POLICY OF ONE NATION OUT OF THE 66 PRESENT.
Britain, after all, had been off the gold standard for two years before seeking stabilization, France had not stabilized for more than
three years. Why should the United States now be expected to
stabilize in three months? A SUFFICIENT INTERVAL SHOULD BE ALLOWED
THE UNITED STATES TO PERMIT . . . A DEMONSTRATION OF THE VALUE
OF PRICE LIFTING EFFORTS WHICH WE HAVE WELL IN HAND.

Moley stared ironically at the wreckage of his hopes. For he
could see studded through Roosevelt's message phrases and
sentences taken from the Swope memorandum that he had left on
the *Amberjack* ten days before. The economic nationalist who had
become so singularly the hope of economic internationalism was
now impaled on his own doctrine. Gamely he cabled Roosevelt,
PERSONALLY BOW TO YOUR JUDGMENT WITH NO INCONSIDERABLE RELIEF.

The next day all was consternation in London. But the worst

was yet to come. While the American delegation labored to prevent the Conference from breaking up, Franklin Roosevelt, now
cruising south on the destroyer *Indianapolis,* took off his coat, sat
down at his desk for a couple of hours, and wrote a new message
to London — this one for release to the Conference. He read the
statement aloud to Henry Morgenthau and Louis Howe and then,
with a few changes of his own, sent it off just as he had written it.

The language was stern and almost contemptuous. It would be
a catastrophe amounting to world tragedy, the President said, if
the Conference let itself be diverted from a consideration of basic
problems "by the proposal of a purely artificial and temporary
experiment affecting the monetary exchange of a few nations only."
Such a tendency, he continued, showed "a singular lack of proportion and a failure to remember the larger purposes for which the
Economic Conference originally was called."

He denounced the "old fetishes of so-called international bankers." They were now being replaced, he said, "by efforts to plan
national currencies with the objective of giving to those currencies
a continuing purchasing power which does not vary greatly in
terms of the commodities and need of modern civilization. Let me
be frank in saying that the United States seeks the kind of a dollar
which a generation hence will have the same purchasing and debt
paying power as the dollar value we hope to attain in the near
future. That objective means more to the good of other nations
than a fixed ratio for a month or two in terms of the pound or
franc."

"The Conference," Roosevelt concluded, "was called to better
and perhaps to cure fundamental economic ills. It must not be
diverted from that effort." [2]

VI

The statement exploded over London with an impact which
won it the name of the "bombshell" message. Roosevelt's reaction
was certainly out of proportion to the immediate issue. Very little
would have happened to America or the New Deal if he had accepted the declaration. Moley is perhaps right in suggesting that
had he done so then the public message of July 3 would have been

more persuasive and effective. But Roosevelt, seeing the declaration
in a long setting of pressure toward *de facto* stabilization, feared
that it would be taken as implying subsequent commitments. Feeling the United States under intolerable pressure from a cabal of
gold nations and international bankers to force it into policies
contrary to its own interest, he was determined to call the maneuver
once and for all. "A little plain conversation," he later said,
"seemed to be the only way to make everybody understand what
everybody else was driving at in the Conference." His further purpose was to shock the Conference into turning away from what he
saw as its excessive concern with bankers' problems and toward
the underlying economic issues. I PURPOSELY MADE LANGUAGE OF MY
MESSAGE HARSH, he cabled Hull, BECAUSE I FELT AT THIS DISTANCE
THAT CONFERENCE WAS GETTING INTO STAGE OF POLITE RESOLUTIONS.
Beyond this, Roosevelt felt that the message would counteract an
impression he believed to be widespread through the country that
the United States came away the loser from every international
conference.

So far as London was concerned, the effect was to dramatize an
issue far more significant than the acceptance or rejection of the
declaration. Roosevelt was essentially throwing the gauntlet of a
nationally managed currency in the face of the gold standard. Thus
John Maynard Keynes congratulated him (in an article which the
Daily Mail headlined PRESIDENT ROOSEVELT IS MAG-
NIFICENTLY RIGHT) for cutting through cobwebs with such
boldness. The message, said Keynes, was "a challenge to us to
decide whether we propose to tread the old, unfortunate ways,
or to explore new paths; paths new to statesmen and to bankers,
but not new to thought." A group of Oxford economists, headed
by J. M. Meade and Roy Harrod, hailed the statement "with enthusiasm." In the House of Commons, a powerful voice rose to
taunt the gold bloc and defend the American President. What if
damage had been done to the prospects of the Conference? "Conferences exist for men," said Winston Churchill, "and not men for
conferences." How anyone watching the great American experiment could have imagined that Mr. Roosevelt would tie up to gold
out of love for France was "quite beyond human comprehension."
(The speaker evidently forgot he had done so himself a few years

earlier.) Let Britain live up to its own stated policies of price-raising and wage-raising. "The American navy has come over, as they did in the Great War, and although separate from us is steaming along the same course. . . . It may well be that the whole armada will be united at no distant date, and will move forward together in one majestic array." "The Roosevelt adventure," Churchill later said, "claims sympathy and admiration from all . . . who are convinced that the fixing of a universal measure of value not based upon the rarity or abundance of any commodity but conforming to the advancing powers of mankind, is the supreme achievement which at this time lies before the intellect of man."

Many Americans backed the decision. "To safeguard his program," said Walter Lippmann, "the President has wisely rejected all proposals which would interfere with it." Cordell Hull called the statement "able and courageous," and Moley cabled, "I consider your message splendid. It was the only way to bring people to their senses, and do not be disturbed by complaints about severity of language. It was true, frank and fair." "Until each nation puts its house in order by the same Herculean efforts that you are performing," declared Bernard Baruch, "there can be no common denominators by which we can endeavor to solve the problems. . . . There seems to be one common ground that all nations can take, and that is the one outlined by you." Russell Leffingwell of Morgan's said, "You were very right not to enter into any temporary or permanent arrangements to peg the dollar in relation to sterling or any other currency." [3]

VII

But the general European reaction to the message was violent. "A Manifesto of Anarchy," cried the Manchester *Guardian*. Philip Snowden summed it up in an article entitled "Roosevelt the Laughing Stock." "No such message," Snowden said, "was ever before sent by the head of a government to representatives of other nations. It will be filed for all times as a classic example of conceit, hectoring and ambiguity." George V approached an eminent American Republican at a royal garden party and spluttered with rage at Roosevelt for wrecking the Conference; even Queen Mary

complained to the visitor's wife. (The visitor, who had reason to
recall that Britain had cheerfully gone off gold in 1931 leaving the
United States in an exposed position, was not impressed. He later
urged MacDonald to warn the King against indulging such rages
in the future.)

As for MacDonald, he was a stricken man, incapable at first even
of indignation. All he could see ahead was the breakup of the
Conference. The result, he helplessly told Cox and Warburg,
would be universal disappointment, possibly social disorder, and
almost certainly the overthrow of his government. To Hull he
wrote a letter proclaiming "the most bitter resentment." To Moley
he turned a ravaged face and said, "This doesn't sound like the man
I spent so many hours with in Washington. This sounds like a
different man. I don't understand." Roosevelt, he said savagely,
reminded him of Lloyd George. Then, in a moment of pride and
pathos, he quoted the King's words to him: "I will not have these
people worrying my Prime Minister this way."

In the Conference itself, gold bloc delegates spoke of going home
at once. If the Conference broke up, blame for "wrecking" it
would obviously fall on the United States. The American delegation, rallying for a final effort, was determined to prevent this last
humiliation. One hope for forestalling adjournment lay in re-
stating Roosevelt's position in terms which might win the support
of other non-gold nations. Moley hastily brought together Keynes,
Lippmann, and Herbert Bayard Swope for this purpose, and together this remarkable team, working till three thirty in the morning, wrote an urbane and masterly rendition of the new American
policy. The result helped relieve the tension. In particular, it set
the stage for a sudden revival of activity on the part of Hull.

For the Secretary, indeed, the situation had radically changed.
The bombshell, after all, had injured Moley more than it had him
— a fact which no doubt helped reconcile him to Roosevelt's decision. In any case, he had never felt intense interest in exchange
stabilization. More than that, the anti-American campaign now
redefined his problem. Hull was no longer facing a challenge in
monetary policy — an area which he imperfectly understood and
which filled him with gloom. He was facing a challenge in parliamentary politics. The Tennessee politician who had served a

quarter of a century in the United States Congress, was now in familiar territory. Coming to life, Hull began to take command of his delegation. Reaching deep into his parliamentary bag of tricks, effectively seconded by Bullitt, he prevented hasty action, lobbied persuasively in the corridors, and, when the showdown came, delivered a moving appeal which swung the balance for continuance. The result was victory, and the Conference stayed in session for another three weeks.

But it was an empty victory. Prolonging the agony could only let the world down more gently. It could not disguise the fact of failure.[4]

VIII

Could London have succeeded? In retrospect, several different ideas were entangled in the conception of the Conference. One was the gold bloc's thesis that the Conference should concentrate on stabilizing the exchanges and restoring the international gold standard. Another was Hull's thesis that it should concentrate on reducing trade barriers. Another was Roosevelt's thesis that it should concentrate on raising world prices. Could the Conference have accomplished anything in 1933 on any of these bases?

The gold bloc very considerably dominated the Conference, and its tactics were single-minded and ruthless. Thus the panic which stampeded Moley into endorsing the temporary stabilization declaration turned out to be phony. Of the nations which Moley was solemnly assured were about to be driven off gold unless the United States signed the declaration, all stayed on gold for two or three more years after Roosevelt's message. France made it clear throughout the Conference that if she could not force through currency stabilization in terms of gold she did not propose to let the Conference accomplish anything else. As the economist Gustav Cassel, present as a delegate from Sweden, described the strategy, "The gold countries were not satisfied with remaining themselves on a gold basis but demanded that all other countries should submit to their rule. During the Conference this demand took a more and more dictatorial form, and the gold countries finally refused to take part in any monetary discussions if their terms were not accepted. It was this imperative attitude that at last wrecked the Conference."

If the tactics of the gold bloc were disturbing, the objectives were manifestly unachievable. For the United States, for example, stabilization on gold bloc terms would have put a serious crimp in the policies of the New Deal — a price that Roosevelt could not be easily expected to pay. It is not clear, in addition, how genuinely anxious even the British were to return to gold. By the fall, when Roosevelt raised the direct question through George L. Harrison ("in order to place England on record . . . and not because we intended or expected to go back"), both the Bank of England and the Treasury replied that they would not join the United States in stabilization in terms of gold.

Of the gold-standard approach to London, it can be said that it could not conceivably have produced agreement; and that the rigidity of its proponents was the main cause of the failure of the Conference to achieve anything in other possible areas of economic cooperation.

As for the Hull thesis, its main defect was that no one apart from Hull himself seemed really eager to tackle the trade barriers problem. After the breakdown of the monetary approach, Hull made one more valiant effort to induce the Conference to face up to tariffs. His own report to the President stated the reasons for failure. "In general," Hull wrote, "each country advocated the abolition or reduction of all barriers to its commerce . . . *except* of kinds which it is itself practicing to such a degree that it is estopped from urging the case; and, in general, each country either defended its own practices as just or as necessary, or indicated its willingness to abandon such practices *provided* other countries did this, that and the other before or simultaneously." Thus Neville Chamberlain of Britain argued that the British tariff structure was still in the making and hence British rates must be defended while excessive tariffs (i.e., tariffs in other countries) were being lowered. It seems most doubtful that the passage of the reciprocal trade agreements bill, on which Hull staked so much, would have altered this situation in the slightest. Far from it: as Leo Pasvolsky summed up the problem of commercial policy, "The whole London effort might have broken down on that vital issue."

Of the trade barriers approach to London, it can be said that there was no will in any nation to make it work; and that, had Hull succeeded in pressing the issue as he wished, it probably would have led to as complete a fiasco as did the gold-standard approach.[5]

IX

There remained the price-raising theory. In a sense, this was the most hopeful approach. Roosevelt and MacDonald had appeared to agree in their joint communiqué of April that an increase in commodity prices was "primary and fundamental." The American delegation at an early point introduced a resolution calling for "a synchronized program of governmental expenditure in the different countries along parallel lines." When Roosevelt talked about the synchronization of government spending, he seemed to be moving toward the position which Keynes had outlined in his pamphlet of the spring of 1933, *The Means to Prosperity* (where, in fact, War- burg and Feis, who had written the resolution, had picked up the idea). "For the Conference to occupy itself with pious resolutions concerning the abatement of tariffs, quotas and exchange restric- tions," Keynes had said, "will be a waste of time."

But this approach was doomed too. For all the assurances of the Roosevelt-MacDonald statement in April, the British suddenly an- nounced in early July that they would have nothing to do with pub- lic works; "we shall not reopen those schemes [of capital expendi- ture], no matter what may be done elsewhere." "The United States," the Manchester *Guardian* observed dryly, "is evidently not the only country to change its policy in the middle of the Confer- ence." Senator Couzens for the American delegation vainly urged that there could be "no stable increase in prices except as this is supported by increased employment, higher wages and increased consumption," and that the way to achieve these goals was through public works. Couzens later concluded that American policy in this respect was "in direct conflict with the principal ends pro- posed to be accomplished in the Economic Conference." London in his judgment was dominated by the creditor mentality. "The supreme aim is to collect debts and this is what a majority of the statesmen have in mind when they talk about increase in prices. . . .

Rarely do they mention wages, consuming power or the obvious necessity of better distribution of the world's wealth."

Even had the British come along, the gold countries would have flatly opposed an expansionist policy. As it was, the committee set up to consider the American resolution met only once and agreed on nothing.

A bitter conclusion can hardly be escaped. In 1933 the essential difference was between the countries for whom the domestic price level was the major problem and those for whom foreign exchange was the major problem. The United States was determined to let nothing hinder its drive for recovery. The gold countries were determined to let nothing hinder their drive for the gold standard. This difference was too great to be bridged by any form of economic or diplomatic legerdemain. The London Conference did not create the difference. It simply came along too late — or too early — to do anything about it.

One question remains. If agreement was impossible, might it not still have been better to join in virtuous if meaningless resolutions than to send bombshell messages and break up in acrimony? Unquestionably Roosevelt's day-to-day management of American policy at the Conference was deplorable. He came to understand only gradually what he wanted himself; and his delegation represented very little beyond their own whimsies and prejudices. All this contributed to the confusion. But it should have deceived no one about the controlling realities. Given the controlling realities, it is hard to see what purpose rhetorical piety would have served. As it was, the Conference did produce a sufficiency of resolutions on a range of subjects; one more resolution papering over a profound difference on monetary policy would have done no one any good. As J. W. Beyen, a Dutch delegate at London, later reflected, "The 1933 Conference was the last conference of its kind in the economic field; let us hope that the world has learned that the production of such resolutions is a waste of time. It is inevitable that such resolutions become words that do not bind any government in any respect."

The final irony of London was its one tangible achievement. Senator Key Pittman of Nevada, whose sprees had shamed his own delegation and scandalized London, emerged in the end the single victor. When he sailed for America, he had in his pocket, signed and ready for operation, an international agreement on silver.[6]

X

There was, perhaps, another victor. BEFORE YOU SAIL, Roosevelt cabled to Cordell Hull, I WANT YOU TO KNOW ONCE MORE OF MY AFFECTIONATE REGARD FOR AND CONFIDENCE IN YOU. In the last month at London, the Secretary of State had redeemed his reputation. Moley, who had come to save the Conference, as the special representative of the President, departed eight days later in humiliation as the man who, more than anyone else, the President had repudiated. It was Hull, the man whom Moley was supposed to outshine, who remained behind to rescue the Conference from collapse.

The approval of the President and the press was gratifying. But Hull still had unfinished business. Before Moley left London, they had held one final talk at which (in Moley's recollection) Hull expressed complete satisfaction over Moley's good faith. This was doubtless so. Then the mood of harmony was quickly shattered. Shortly after Moley's departure, someone placed on the Secretary's desk a copy of a cable labeled "from Moley to the President alone and exclusively, with no distribution in the Department." As Hull's eye ran down the text, his blood began to boil. ON PERSONAL SIDE, he read, PITTMAN IS ONLY MEMBER OF DELEGATION ABLE INTELLECTUALLY AND AGGRESSIVELY TO PRESENT YOUR IDEAS. . . . RECONSTITUTED DELEGATION WOULD BE HELPFUL IN VIEW OF DEVELOPMENTS.

Moley later explained that the cable was prompted by the new situation created by the bombshell message. Since no one except Pittman shared Roosevelt's views (Moley had meant, he said, to write "intelligently," not "intellectually"), it seemed reasonable to recommend that the delegation be reconstituted. But Hull was not in a reasonable mood. The cable seemed the final act of sabotage and treachery.

When Warburg came back to the hotel that night, he found a message on his door asking him to see Hull at once. Warburg found the old man in his dressing gown, trembling with anger. "That piss-ant, Moley," the Secretary cried (as Warburg later re-

called it), "here he curled up at mah feet and let me stroke his
head like a huntin' dog and then he goes and bites me in the ass!"
To Roosevelt he sent a letter as deeply felt if more decorous. He
found it "most painful," the Secretary wrote, ". . . to report an
attitude and course of conduct on the part of Professor Moley
which has been utterly dumbfounding to me." He then offered an
itemized and caustic indictment of Moley's behavior in London and
before. "While it so happened," said Hull, "that I was in the position of undertaking to deal with this crisis singlehanded, and was
lucky enough if I may say so to be the chief single factor in preserving the life of the Conference and in saving you from the outrage of being branded as its destroyer, Moley was secretly sending
code messages to you about my incapacity to function here. He was
at the same time pretending absolute loyalty of friendship and of
official attitude toward me." Hull's conclusion was bitter: "My
regret only equals my amazement to discover the deliberate attempt
of one I have implicitly trusted thus secretly to undermine and destroy me while openly professing both friendship and loyalty."

For his part, Moley returned to the United States with ample
bitterness of his own. "The rest of the world was thinking   and
saying — that I had been kicked in the face." Could not the President set the matter straight with the press? Or at least indicate
personal regret? Visiting the President shortly after arrival, Moley
wrote a warning to himself at the head of his notes: "Don't seem to
be offended by anything that happened." But Roosevelt, in great
good humor, showed no concern about London and no interest
in improving Moley's position in the newspapers. Moley interpreted
this as meaning that he was to take up his duties as before. But
when Charlie Michelson, who had been the delegation's press
attaché, saw the President, Roosevelt remarked that he planned to
send Moley to report on conditions of law enforcement in Hawaii.

When this was eventually broached to Moley, he would have none
of it. He now perceived clearly enough the trend of events. When
Roosevelt next proposed that he be detached to the Department
of Justice to study possible reforms in the administration of criminal
law, Moley accepted this assignment as an honorable exit. His
negotiations with Vincent Astor had now resulted in a plan to
establish a magazine in association with Mary Harriman Rumsey

and Averell Harriman. Roosevelt had told Astor in July that he would accede to Moley's leaving the administration. With plans for *Today* now well under way, Moley submitted his resignation. On hearing the news, Hull smoothly issued a laudatory statement, in the course of which he denied that he had ever in the slightest suggested that Moley should leave. ("Your prophecy regarding Moley," Sumner Welles wrote to Norman Davis, "has proved singularly accurate. I frankly did not believe that he would hang himself so soon. There has been an unanimous sigh of relief from everybody in the Department.")

A newspaperman summed up the episode. "Hull's gaunt figure and downcast eyes are enough to move one to tears," he said, "until one remembers the stiletto protruding from Moley's back." [7]

XI

One or two other loose ends remained to be tied up. In August, Roosevelt sent an affable letter to Ramsay MacDonald. "I am concerned by events in Germany," the President wrote, "for I feel than an insane rush to further armaments in Continental Europe is infinitely more dangerous than any number of squabbles over gold or stabilization or tariffs." In his reply, MacDonald adverted obliquely to the London imbroglio. "You have opportunities for experiment which we do not have here," the Socialist told the New Dealer. ". . . To pull out a brick, to see what is behind or to get at some rotten bit of structure, is as dangerous in the State as I have just found out it is in my own delightful old house which is beginning to show signs of its two centuries of years." And in November, Roosevelt wrote to King George, discoursing agreeably about stamps and naval affairs and expressing his hope that "both our peoples will reach an agreement when this nightmare of currency and 'stabilization' is more permanently settled." Baffled, George V turned the letter over to the Foreign Office, which composed a courteous but vague reply. And so London passed into history.[8]

14. Variations in Gold and Silver

THE BOMBSHELL MESSAGE accomplished the first step in the definition of a new monetary policy. The objective was now clear: higher prices at home rather than stabilization abroad. Still, if the liberation of the dollar from foreign exchanges made a national monetary policy possible, that act did little by itself to clarify the content of such a policy. The apostles of orthodoxy, set back in London, could still hope to recoup in New York.

Several different interests were involved in the struggle to shape monetary policy. The New York banking group wanted to reinstate the gold standard and return control over interest rates to the private financial community. Representing to a large degree a class which had already made its money, the New York bankers were primarily concerned with protecting the value of the dollar and maintaining high rates of return on savings. But this was by no means a unanimous business view. Outside New York, the businessmen of the South and West had another set of concerns. They were predominantly men on the make; their desire consequently was for an abundance of cheap money at low interest rates. If Lewis Douglas was the representative of the *rentier* class in Washington, Jesse Jones of the Reconstruction Finance Corporation was the representative of the entrepreneur-promoter class. The Jones group was ready to back the New Dealers in their determination to wrest control of monetary policy from Wall Street. The farmers, of course, were chronically on the inflationist side. The champions of orthodoxy thus had to contend with an alliance of farm belt, new business money, and government.

II

It was against this background that the fight over monetary policy resumed after London. Douglas, tacitly acknowledging Warburg as the most persuasive, even if slightly heterodox, defender of the conservative position, urged him on his return to continue the battle against the commodity-dollar group and the inflationists. Acheson, Sprague, and Woodin, Douglas said, could be counted on; even Moley, Douglas added, now claimed to be on the side of conservatism. Cheered by this bulletin, Warburg reopened the monetary problem with the President. He found Roosevelt — as he found the whole country — preoccupied with NRA and rather indifferent to the issues which had seemed so urgent in London. Nonetheless Warburg proposed that the President now appoint a monetary group to determine "the exact nature of the gold standard to which the United States returns in the autumn." Roosevelt listened genially. Then he said, "I want you to talk to Warren and Rogers."

George F. Warren, professor of farm management at Cornell and an expert in land use, had recently introduced a drastic new thesis into the discussion in his book *Prices* (with Frank A. Pearson). The initial argument was not startling: that the depression was essentially a phenomenon of price and could be cured by higher prices. His more distinctive theory was that the price of gold controlled the general price level, and that the most swift and effective mode of inflation was therefore through acting on the price of gold. A formidable array of charts and graphs purported to back up the contention that past movements of commodity prices varied proportionately with gold prices. As for the present, the depression, said Warren, was not due to extravagant living or to unsound business practices or to overproduction. "It is due to high demand for gold following a period of low demand for gold." The required action was to raise the price level by raising the price of gold — that is, by reducing the number of grains of gold in the dollar, which would mean the depreciation of the dollar in foreign exchange. This, in turn, could be achieved by raising the price at which the government bought gold. The ultimate objective was the "commodity dollar" — "a dollar that has a constant buying power, not for one commodity but for all commodities at wholesale prices, managed in accordance with a price index by manipulation of the gold content."

Roosevelt had known Warren from New York days. Indeed, he had found time for an appointment with Warren on the evening of the day after inauguration. Through the spring, however, Warren's Washington activity was chiefly on behalf of the Committee for the Nation. His theory was already acquiring disciples. "As I see it," General Robert E. Wood of Sears, Roebuck wrote Henry Wallace, "everything has worked out according to Warren's predictions." Wallace himself, a veteran of the "stable money" movement and a onetime collaborator with the Committee for the Nation, while not wholly believing in the Warren thesis, brought back Warren into the presidential picture in July.

As for James Harvey Rogers, he was a Yale professor and a student of Irving Fisher's who had come into association with Warren as a result of a common interest in the effects of gold. Actually Rogers, who was relatively moderate and sophisticated in his views, did not fully accept the Warren thesis either and regarded public works as the more relevant remedy.[1]

III

The President, confronted by two sets of advisers, thus followed his usual formula of telling them to get together. After an evening's talk, Warburg found himself more impressed by Warren than by Rogers; but, though disarmed by the Cornell professor's sincerity and disinterestedness, he remained unconvinced by his prescription. At the same time, he was increasingly disturbed by Roosevelt's apparent absorption in Warren's charts and by the presidential curiosity about techniques of gold purchase. When he tried to tell the President that a definite price must be set for gold if businessmen were to make future contracts, Roosevelt seemed unmoved. "Poppycock," Roosevelt replied. "The bankers want to know everything beforehand and I've told them to go to hell." On the other hand, Irving Fisher, the veteran monetary theorist, stopping by at Hyde Park, found Roosevelt informed and receptive. "The most satisfactory talk I ever had with a President," reported Fisher, who had talked with Theodore Roosevelt, Taft, Wilson, Harding, and Hoover. Yet Roosevelt was not quite ready to foreclose on ortho- doxy. He encouraged Warren and Rogers to take a European trip, which made Warburg feel better, and in a few days he authorized the formation of Warburg's long desired monetary group with Woodin as chairman and Douglas, Acheson, Warburg, and George Harrison among the members.

Woodin's chairmanship was nominal. As early as July 5, he had begun to try to resign as Secretary of the Treasury; and by August, as his health continued to decline, he was no longer capable of offering vigorous leadership in a field — monetary theory — with which he was at best dimly acquainted. The others labored val- iantly, spurred by the fear that, without stabilization, the remaining gold countries might be forced off gold, an eventuality which still meant for most of them the end of Western civilization.[2]

IV

In the meantime, the domestic price situation had taken its acute turn for the worst. The small boom in commodity prices of June and July had played itself out. When farm prices sagged in Sep- tember, the farm belt renewed the cry for inflation. By mid- September telegrams and letters were inundating the White House. Thus Sam Rayburn of Texas on September 14: PEOPLE OF WHOLE STATE ARE URGING EXPANSION OF CURRENCY TO BOLSTER PRICE OF COT- TON WHICH HAS DECLINED RAPIDLY IN THE LAST TEN DAYS   THIS DROP IN PRICES SPELLS TRAGEDY. Hugo Black and William B. Bankhead of Alabama, Kenneth McKellar of Tennessee, John Rankin of Mississippi, and Robert L. Doughton of North Carolina wired in similar vein. Elmer Thomas threatened a march of a million men on Washington. Even a hard-money Democrat like Pat Harrison of Mississippi, conservative chairman of the Senate Finance Com- mittee, declared on the steps of the White House: "Commodity prices have got to go up. I favor some sort of rational inflation. We've got to do more than we are doing. . . . If commodity prices don't rise, I don't know when we are going to get out of this de- pression." And Roosevelt well understood the personal anguish that lay behind these appeals — the ordinary men and women on farms through the country who for a moment had glimpsed a chance of getting their heads above water and now felt themselves being dragged under a third time. "The West is seething with unrest," he explained to his mother, "and must have higher values to pay off their debts."

Up to this point, the President had watched the debate between Warburg and Warren with amiable detachment, acting, as Warburg later wrote, as a "tireless, serene, and often amused referee." Now, as his sense of popular distress grew more vivid, he became increasingly impatient toward orthodox advice. He was annoyed at what seemed to him the intellectual sterility of the recommendations: whatever the crisis, the members of the group could think of nothing except stabilization and a return to gold. He was annoyed too at what he considered their lack of compassion: their only care seemed to be the woes of the international financial community. More and more he began to feel that the group was becoming the instrument of the New York bankers in their attempt to control the New Deal.

This last feeling was an injustice to public-spirited men. Warburg's Wall Street friends, for example, regarded him as a renegade and radical. Yet even Warburg, the most enlightened of the group, seemed to Roosevelt hopelessly blind to the human and political realities of the problem. On September 20 Warburg wrote Roosevelt that this was probably his last chance to forestall inflation and begged him to issue a statement opposing further depreciation of the dollar. This was all very pretty, the President told Warburg the next day, but how to keep prices advancing? How to relieve the debt burden? If wheat and cotton prices did not move forward, Roosevelt said, there would be "marching farmers." Warburg replied that further depreciation would mean limitless inflation. Roosevelt said that it might injure those living on fixed income, but that this was the lesser of two evils. When Warburg observed in attempted extenuation that the President was no doubt under heavy pressure from the inflationists, Roosevelt replied sharply that it was not a matter of pressure at all; it was his own conviction. "What would you do," he asked Warburg, "to raise prices?" The banker could only reply that he saw no short cut; the way out was the slow, painful process of rebuilding, and this could not begin until businessmen regained confidence in the currency.

A few days later the group formally told Roosevelt that it objected to further depreciation and desired a return to the gold standard. "I do not like or approve the report," the President curtly told Woodin, adding: "I wish our banking and economist friends would realize the seriousness of the situation from the point of view of the debtor classes, — i.e., 90 per cent of the human beings in this country — and think less from the point of view of the 10 per cent who constitute the creditor classes." He had a final word: "Tell the committee that commodity prices must go up, especially agricultural prices. I suggest that the committee let you and me have the recommendation of how to obtain that objective and that objective only." [3]

v

For this question the monetary committee had no answer. But on the same day he talked with Warburg, Roosevelt did receive a clear-cut answer from another source. "A rise in prices," George Warren wrote him, "is essential. The only way in which a rise can be brought about and held is by reducing the gold value of the dollar. . . . If the Treasury is ordered to buy a certain amount of new gold at a certain price, and if the price is raised at frequent intervals, this would probably accomplish the purpose." The President's orthodox advisers, in short, could tell him to do nothing but wait while the people suffered. His unorthodox advisers offered him an opportunity for action.

How put the Warren program into effect? As early as August 16, Roosevelt had mentioned to Morgenthau that he would like the Treasury to buy gold in the open market. "I think that this would do the trick," he mused, "but I do not know how it is to be done." (Morgenthau asked, "Whose idea is that?" Roosevelt replied, "Mine.") The thunder from the farm belt in September increased his determination to try a gold-purchase program. The question remained whether the government had the legal authority. Dean Acheson declared for the Treasury that the President lacked the power to purchase gold at a price above that fixed by statute, which was currently $20.67 per fine ounce. The Attorney-General supported Acheson. The President was not satisfied. What he wanted, he indicated, was a method of getting something done, not a statement that it was impossible.

On September 26 Morgenthau told him that his lawyers in the Farm Credit Administration thought he could buy gold. "Please let me know," said Roosevelt, "because I certainly would love to do it." A few days later Morgenthau showed Roosevelt a longhand memorandum from his general counsel Herman Oliphant suggesting various ways by which the President might buy gold through his executive powers. The President commented that he had a method of his own which might be simpler. "I think we can form a separate corporation under the RFC and let this corporation buy the gold and put it up as collateral against money loaned to it by the Treasury." Oliphant, digging into the recesses of his memory, recalled a Civil War statute which permitted the government to buy gold at changing prices; combined with the RFC Act, this seemed to give the President the power he needed. Stanley Reed, general counsel of the RFC, endorsed Oliphant's reasoning.

Acheson remained unconvinced: whatever other laws might say, he declared, the gold value of the dollar was itself set by law. The Oliphant-Reed plan would "open wide the door for any and every kind of manipulation for ulterior purposes." At the same time, the Warburg group continued to argue for "immediate" pound-dollar stabilization and the "earliest possible" return to gold. And in the Middle West Milo Reno was calling again for a farm strike.

Faced with what he called "agrarian revolt," the President displayed increasing resentment over what he regarded as banker pressure and Treasury sabotage. For weeks, he had been trying to get the Treasury to buy gold; it was, he said, "like punching your fist into a pillow." Finally on October 19 a climactic White House conference was held to discuss the legality of gold purchases. Despite Acheson's heated arguments (Warren, not an unbiased witness, described him as "nearly hysterical") most present agreed that the RFC had the power. Acheson asked for a written order from the President; Roosevelt replied grimly, "I say it is legal." Later that day, Acheson arrived at the meeting of the RFC Board, his mustaches bristling, his face scarlet, his jaws clamped together, looking (according to Morgenthau) like a thunder cloud.

He said, "Gentlemen, I have just come from the President. You know that I am opposed to our buying gold. The President has ordered me to do it. I will carry out his orders."

Three days later Roosevelt announced his decision in his fourth fireside chat. "Under the clearly defined authority of existing law," he said, "I am authorizing the Reconstruction Finance Corporation to buy gold newly mined in the United States at prices to be determined from time to time after consultation with the Secretary of the Treasury and the President. . . . My aim in taking this step is to establish and maintain continuous control. . . . We are thus continuing to move toward a managed currency." ("Talked with Lew Douglas on the 'phone," James P. Warburg noted in his diary a few days later. "He sounded hopelessly sunk and said that Acheson felt likewise. He agreed that the President had burned his bridges. . . . Announcement that the gold price was fixed at $31.36. Here we go!") [4]

VI

To what extent did the President really think that he could raise the price of commodities by raising the price of gold? The probable answer is, not very much. "I don't believe that Roosevelt ever accepted at face value the Warren theory," Ernest K. Lindley later wrote. "I heard him laugh over Warren's charts more than once while he was supposed to be under Warren's spell." Warburg agreed. What carried the day with Roosevelt, he always felt, was not conviction that the Warren theory was right so much as the fact that Warren offered a program of action at a time when the demand for action seemed irresistible. "I am the first to admit that those of us who opposed Warren had no equally spectacular alternative."

The gold-purchase policy, indeed, had no really convincing exact basis in theory or in fact. Warren's statistics proved everything except his specific conclusions. The more sophisticated economists among Roosevelt's advisers, like Tugwell and Berle, considered Warren's claims absurd. Probably because the President sensed what their reaction would be, he did not consult them. Yet, if one looked not at Warren's assertion that he could establish any desired price level by reducing the weight of the gold dollar but at the gold-purchase program in general, it was very much like programs already undertaken by the British and French for not dissimilar purposes. "We need not assume too excitedly," said Walter Lippmann, "that the United States is embarked on a policy the like of which was never known on land or sea." Moreover, who could tell, the Warren thesis might work! "There is no point in trying to bless it or damn it," as Lippmann said, "on purely theoretical grounds." Certainly, for Roosevelt, the Warren plan had one decisive advantage: it freed him from the intolerable necessity of sitting by and doing nothing while prices fell. "I have had the shackles on my hands for months now," he said, "and I feel for the first time as though I had thrown them off."

Starting on October 25, Henry Morgenthau and Jesse Jones met in the President's bedroom every morning to set the price of gold. Jones was there as head of the RFC, which did the buying; Morgenthau, because of his recent experience in helping maintain wheat prices through a government purchase program. Sometimes Warren himself joined them. While Roosevelt ate his eggs and drank his coffee, the group discussed what the day's price was to be. The precise figure each day was less important than the encouragement of a general upward trend. One day Morgenthau came in, more worried than usual, and suggested an increase from 19 to 22 cents. Roosevelt took one look at Morgenthau's anxious face and proposed 21 cents. "It's a lucky number," he said with a laugh, "because it's three times seven." Morgenthau, never sure when his leg was being pulled, later made the literal-minded notation in his diary, "If anybody ever knew how we really set the gold price through a combination of lucky numbers, etc., I think they would really be frightened." Actually the price might as well have been set through a combination of lucky numbers as any other way. As Jones pointed out, the rate of increase had to be unpredictable lest speculators figure out what was going on.[5]

VII

As for the Undersecretary of the Treasury, Acheson planned to resign when the gold-buying decision was taken. Mr. Justice

Brandeis, for whom he had once worked as law clerk, supported this resolution. But he had been induced to stay on the ground that he could at least stop things from growing worse. Now he was trying loyally to execute the policy which he so strongly disapproved. Unfortunately stories began to appear in the press hinting that some in the administration regarded the program as unconstitutional; and the impression grew at the White House that Acheson was the source. When Roosevelt was told this on October 27, he flushed with annoyance and said to Morgenthau, "I guess this boil has about come to a head, and you know me, Henry, I am slow to get mad, but when I do, I get good and mad."

Two days later he summoned all the officials engaged in the new program to the White House. He was in a coldly angry mood. "Gentlemen," he said, "I have called you together to inform you that the question of our buying gold is an administration policy. We are all in the same boat. If anybody does not like the boat, he can get out of it." His glance went slowly around the room. "I do not mean anybody in particular, but everybody in this room in general." Then he added, "Gentlemen, if we continued a week or so longer without my having made this move on gold, we would have had an agrarian revolution in this country."

Before long another series of stories broke in the newspaper. Roosevelt, furious, immediately wrote to Acheson requesting his resignation. Before Acheson received the letter, the President informed the press that the Undersecretary of the Treasury had resigned. Acheson, hearing the news from newspapermen, took it philosophically. A few days later, when his successor was sworn in, Acheson, urbane and imperturbable as ever, came to the ceremony. His appearance astounded the President. Then Roosevelt recognized the code of Endicott Peabody, which he and Acheson shared, and beckoned Acheson over. "I'm mad as hell at you," he said, "but for you to come here today is the best act of sportsmanship I've ever seen!" The Achesonian gallantry made a deep impression. When another Undersecretary of the Treasury left in a less sporting way, Roosevelt suggested that he ought to look up the case of Dean Acheson and learn how a gentleman resigns. Eventually, too, the White House learned that the source of the leaks which had so infuriated the President was not Acheson but, in all probability, Douglas.

On the day that Roosevelt decided to fire Acheson, he asked Morgenthau to stay for a moment after the bedside meeting. Woodin, he said, was too sick to come back; therefore he was appointing a new Acting Secretary of the Treasury. He paused. Then he said, "I have decided that that person is Henry Morgenthau, Jr. You made good for me in Albany, and you are one of the two or three people who have made an outstanding success here in Washington, so let's you and I go on to bigger things. . . . We will have lots of fun doing it together." [6]

VIII

In appointing Henry Morgenthau, Jr., to the cabinet, Roosevelt was bringing in a cherished friend, upon whose loyalty he knew he could count absolutely. Morgenthau, forty-two years old in 1933, was a tall, heavy-set, nearsighted, partly bald man, slow in speech, often hesitant in reaction, but possessed of great stubbornness and drive. In his private relations he was a person of delicacy and warmth; in public he tended toward worry and suspicion, displaying in official relations a pervading mixture of insecurity and aggressiveness which never quite fully interfered with his effectiveness.

This insecurity derived no doubt from a childhood under the domination of a powerful, adored, and irrepressible father. Henry Morgenthau, Sr. — Uncle Henry, as he was known throughout the Democratic party — had a notable career in business and diplomacy. He had been Wilson's ambassador to Turkey and, according to Josephus Daniels, had himself aspired to be Secretary of the Treasury. As his only son, young Henry carried the weight of heavy parental expectation. Life was not always easy for the boy until, barely turned twenty-one, he spent six weeks on a Texas ranch recuperating from illness. From that time farming became his passion, mainly because he loved land and horses and crops but partly too, perhaps, because agriculture offered a way of living where he knew he would stand or fall on his own merits.

In 1913 he bought a thousand-acre farm near Fishkill in Dutchess County. In the next years he met his Hyde Park neighbors, the Roosevelts. He took to Franklin instantly, as his intelligent and public-spirited wife Elinor took to Eleanor Roosevelt; and the two young couples became great friends. In the meantime, he began to

244 THE ECONOMICS OF NATIONALISM

become a figure in state agricultural circles. In 1922 he bought the *American Agriculturist* and, as publisher, turned it into a vigorous and influential organ of farm opinion. Roosevelt subsequently brought him to Albany as chairman of his Agricultural Advisory Commission and as his energetic Conservation Commissioner; then he took him to Washington as the liquidator of the Federal Farm Board and as governor of the Farm Credit Administration.

Morgenthau's inarticulateness, as well as the penchant for worry which so often darkened his face with apprehension, caused people to underrate him. In a succession of tough assignments he had shown solid administrative gifts. He chose good people, used them effectively, ran tight organizations, got results, and kept his mouth shut. His own views represented a mixture of orthodoxy in economics with humanitarianism in social policy; and he was prepared to press these views with pertinacity. At the same time, he was hospitable to new ideas.

Above all, his highest ambition was plainly not for himself. It was to serve Franklin Roosevelt. And the President, for his part, though he could never resist the temptation of teasing Morgenthau, especially a Morgenthau laden with gloom and tragedy, regarded him with deep affection born of long association. Once Roosevelt gave Mrs. Morgenthau a picture of himself and Morgenthau side by side in an automobile, inscribed "For Elinor, from one of two of a kind." [7]

IX

Morgenthau took over his new responsibilities at a stormy moment. The gold-purchase program had already set the financial community in an uproar. On November 18, 1933, the Chamber of Commerce demanded "early return to a gold basis, with complete avoidance of monetary experimentation." On November 21, Professor Sprague announced his resignation, warning of a "drift into unrestrained inflation" and of the threat of "complete breakdown of the credit of the government." A day or two later, Warburg publicly broke with the administration and launched an attack on its monetary policies. Forty orthodox economists, led by E. W. Kemmerer of Princeton, set up the Economists' National Committee on Monetary

Policy to refute soft-money heresies. Al Smith summed up the campaign in characteristic language: "I am for gold dollars as against baloney dollars. I am for experience against experiment."

The result was a national debate over monetary policy — the most intense since the Bryan campaign of '96. Farm leaders rushed to the administration's defense. The Committee for the Nation stepped up its activity. Hugh Johnson caustically dismissed Dr. Sprague (who, after all, had recently helped reconstruct the currency of Britain) as "a hitherto obscure professor" who "by a dramatic resignation, has obtained his little hour or two to strut across the stage." On November 27, fifteen thousand people crowded into the Hippodrome in New York to hear Elmer Thomas defend inflation and Father Coughlin inveigh against "Morganism" and "the British propaganda from the Tory bankers of lower Manhattan."

Roosevelt himself grew convinced that an organized drive was under way, led by New York bankers and spurred by Ogden Mills and the Republicans, to stampede the country back to gold. He was already exasperated at the bankers for what he regarded as a deliberate slowdown on the extension of credit to business. Now they seemed to be making a last great effort to recapture control of the nation's monetary policy. The departure of Sprague became in his mind the symbol of the clash between Wall Street and Washington (ironically Sprague himself was in fact a moderate liberal, with no qualms about an unbalanced budget and a conviction that the path to recovery lay through housing programs). In response to Sprague's letter of resignation, the President now composed a letter of his own which, though apparently never sent, left a vivid picture of his state of mind. "If you had not resigned," Roosevelt coldly began, "you would have been dismissed." You say, Roosevelt continued, you have not been consulted of late. "That is true, for the very good reason that when I did consult you you offered no suggestion towards the immediate alleviation of unemployment and of the debt burden. . . . If the Gov. had followed your do-nothing advice the nation would have slipped back to the conditions of last March." In a final sentence Roosevelt summed up his complaint against the bankers: "You place a former artificial gold standard among nations above human suffering and the crying needs of your own country."

While the debate raged, the gold-purchase program went into

effect. It proved clearly ineffective so long as it was confined to buying domestic gold. As soon as it went into the world gold market, however, it had marked success in depreciating the dollar and to some extent in stopping price declines. Its effect on prices was essentially due to the degree to which it served as a rather crude form of exchange depreciation. By cheapening the American dollar, it operated on the prices of both exports and imports and contributed somewhat to a revival of world trade as well as to an improvement in American prices. But it was soon evident that it would not have the precise and automatic effect on the general level of commodity prices which Warren had so confidently predicted. Indeed, wholesale commodity prices actually went down in November and December.

Though Warren wanted to continue raising the price of gold until it reached the legal limit of $41.34 an ounce, Roosevelt decided in January 1934 to consolidate what gains had been made, to realize the profits which would come to the Treasury from a new fixed price for gold and to liquidate the gold-buying experiment. In a message to Congress on January 15, he proposed the temporary stabilization of the dollar at a level somewhere between 50 and 60 cents, with the profits from devaluation to go into a fund to help stabilize the foreign exchanges. Congress passed the Gold Reserve Act of 1934 in the next fortnight. The President immediately fixed by proclamation the value of the dollar at 59.06 per cent of its last official gold value and established the price of gold at $35 an ounce.[8]

x

So perished the dream of a commodity dollar with the same purchasing power for generations. With this act, the gold policy of the administration was for the time being complete. For all the eccentricities which accompanied the development of that policy, it could now be seen to have had in its way a central consistency. In one step after another, the government gained authority to demand physical possession of gold, to prevent its export, to reduce the amount of gold in the dollar, to set aside the gold clauses in private and public contracts, and to fix the price of gold.

In the light of this broad program, the gold-purchase experiment had its place as an expedient. Its function was to enable Roosevelt to retain control of monetary policy. At a time when he was under great pressure from opposing sides — from the proponents of exchange stabilization and from the proponents of outright inflation — the gold-purchase theory gave him an opportunity to undertake positive action of his own and thus to keep the monetary initiative. The action he took was, on the whole, ineffectual, and it was based on a shallow and incorrect thesis. Yet, if there was debate as to its benefit, it certainly did no great harm — and it plainly was better for the nation than either of the courses to which he might have been forced had he had no alternative. "What a task you have," wrote Russell Leffingwell to Roosevelt in March 1934, "in your war against hunger and unemployment! between the deflationists who are sadists or radicals and want deflation to bring on revolution, the deflationists who are reactionaries, like Baruch, Al Smith, the Chamber of Commerce, and my beloved Carter Glass, who are still fighting the Bryan-McKinley campaign; and the extreme inflationists, like Father Coughlin, who can't know that that too means starvation and revolution. . . . Well, you are the Captain, and you have always managed somehow. No doubt you will continue to do so; and to find some middle road between these extremes."

Roosevelt, in his monetary program, was seeking more than a middle road. For the gold policy in a series of short, sharp blows severed one after another of the strands by which New York bankers had long controlled the nation's currency system. In the twenties, the national monetary policy had been run to a great degree in New York by Benjamin Strong and the New York Federal Reserve Bank. Decisions basic to the nation's economic future were made not by government officials accountable to the people but by bankers in Manhattan board rooms. In 1933, as a result of Roosevelt's gold policy — and even more, perhaps, of such reforms as the new banking legislation and the control of margins under the Securities Act — this situation came to an end. The nation asserted its control over its monetary policy. In this process, the financial capital of the United States began to shift from Wall Street to Washington — a development welcomed by the rising business of the West and South as well as by the officials of the federal government. "The real truth of the matter," Roosevelt wrote to Colonel House, "is, as you and I know, that a financial element in the larger centers has owned the Government ever since the days of Andrew Jackson — and I am not wholly excepting the Administration of W.W. The country is going through a repetition of Jackson's fight with the Bank of the United States — only on a far bigger and broader basis." [9]

XI

Congress, in the main, watched the evolution of the gold policy with indifference. But this indifference by no means extended to the currency question as a whole. The metal that aroused deeper passions on Capitol Hill, however, was not gold but silver. Indeed, the resurgence of silver sentiment as a consequence of the price decline of late 1933 gave fair warning to the Roosevelt administration that its currency program would not be complete until, in the traditional phrase, something could be done for silver.

If gold was for Herbert Hoover (as he once put it) a commodity enshrined in human instincts for ten thousand years, silver was for most southern and western congressmen a commodity enshrined in American political sanctity for well over half a century. "My boy," Senator Ashurst of Arizona once told Morgenthau, "I was brought up from my mother's knee on silver and I can't discuss that any more with you than you can discuss your religion with me." Older men could remember the "Crime of '73" when the government had discontinued the coinage of silver dollars. Many more recalled the bitter fight of the nineties to save mankind from crucifixion on a cross of gold. The cry of "free silver" evoked memories of the Great Commoner rallying the masses against the hard hearts and hard money of Wall Street. Gold was the rich man's metal, the creditor's metal, the banker's metal; silver, the poor man's metal, the debtor's metal, the worker's metal — and that had been true ever since the House of Rothschild in Populist folklore had begun a century before to drive silver out of the currencies of the world.

Now that gold had once again brought the people to their knees, did not salvation lie in restoring silver as part of the circulating medium? And the remonetization of silver, it was argued, would not only ease the debt burden at home but would increase the purchasing power of silver-using countries like China and India and open up great new markets for American products. In Congress no panacea had more friends. Concentrated in seven western states, the silver industry commanded a band of fourteen senators. Key Pittman incessantly demanded the purchase of silver by the Treasury. "The nation," said Burton K. Wheeler, "must adopt bimetallism or face bolshevism." By the spring of 1933, over forty bills were in the hopper proposing to enlarge the monetary use of silver.

A few serious people outside the seven states were to be counted in the silver ranks. Thus Winston Churchill and Bernard Baruch considered themselves silverites. Ray Moley declared it "unfair and unintelligent to try to laugh away the fundamental contentions of the silver advocates." But, on the whole, of all the monetary panaceas, none had less informed support. Economists warned, for example, that high silver prices, far from benefiting China, would drain her silver away and cause deflation and incalculable financial stress. They warned in vain.

The Thomas amendment with its provisions for silver remonetization represented the first silverite victory. This was not enough, however, especially when the President kept his discretionary powers on the shelf. The next step in "doing something for silver" came in London. Pittman's silver accord purported to even out the flow of silver into the world market by having the principal silver-producing and silver-using countries contract for the next four years to ration the sale of existing silver hoards and to absorb newly mined silver. But the fine print made it clear that Pittman had done little more than give his domestic silver program the specious glamour of an international agreement. Under the proposal the United States was committed to take care of 70 per cent of the silver to be absorbed — an amount slightly higher than total American silver production in 1933. Of the other nations signatory to the Pittman agreement, most of them were committed to doing nothing about silver which they would not have done anyway.[10]

XII

Roosevelt proceeded to stall on this agreement until December, when the renewal of inflationist pressure made it seem expedient to toss a morsel to the silver bloc. The Committee for the Nation, galvanized into new paroxysms of activity by the autumn price declines, was increasingly concentrating on silver. In the meantime, new silver prophets were emerging, of whom the most influential was Father Charles E. Coughlin. If the nation did something for silver, Coughlin wrote Roosevelt, "We would speed up our factories, consume our surplus wheat cotton and pork and get rid of that assinine [sic] philosophy propagated by Henry Wallace. . . . My dear Mr. President there is no superfluity of either cotton or wheat until every naked back has been clothed until every empty stomach has been filled. There is a superfluity in the minds of these men who with the deflationary policies are opposed to accepting good silver money."

Roosevelt tried to head off the mounting pressure. In his message on gold of January 1934, he noted that, while he looked for a greatly increased use of silver, he was withholding further recommendations until there could be more experience with the London agreement. The silver bloc was not so easily pacified. In a few days, to avert an amendment to the Gold Reserve Act virtually installing bimetallism, Roosevelt had to accept a permissive silver certificate amendment. And this was only the beginning. The larger silverite objective was to translate the four-year commitment of London into permanent domestic legislation. The favored method was a silver-purchase bill offered by an indefatigable second-term congressman from Texas named Martin Dies.

The administration now dug in and tried to fight. On March 15 Morgenthau announced that he opposed any further silver legislation that session. Four days later the House passed the Dies bill by a better than two-to-one vote, and three weeks later the Senate Agriculture Committee unanimously reported a modified version. On April 14 the President held a placatory conference with a group of silver senators. He announced his sympathy for silver but objected to mandatory legislation: "I don't want my hand forced." The silver bloc, remembering Roosevelt's refusal to use the per-

missive powers granted under the Thomas amendment and the
Gold Standard Act, remained unimpressed.

Conciliatory methods having failed, it seemed necessary to try
something else. In February, Morgenthau had launched an investigation of silver speculators. He now proposed to the President
that the moment had arrived to "spring our silver list." Roosevelt
agreed, even suggesting that the list be published in installments in
order to obtain full publicity. On April 24, 1934, publication began. The most interesting feature was the revelation that, while
Father Coughlin had been demanding the "mobilization of all
Christianity against the god of gold," his secretary had been
prudently investing the funds of the Father's Radio League of the
Little Flower in silver futures up to the point of half a million
ounces. Coughlin promptly denounced Morgenthau as a tool of
the international bankers and pointedly praised silver as a "gentile"
metal.

The uproar over the silver list, however, was short-lived.
Coughlin's own reputation was somewhat damaged, though there
was no proof that he was making personal profits. The drive for
silver was only momentarily interrupted. With the rest of his legislative program in jeopardy, Roosevelt decided to face the inevitable.
On April 27, he asked the advice of the cabinet. All those who had
an opinion recommended compromise. Will Woodin died early in
May; and on the train to his funeral, Roosevelt indicated that he
would study a new silver bloc proposal. The question whether the
purchase plan was to be mandatory or permissive remained an issue; but a pro-silver article by Walter Lippmann on May 15 helped
provide a formula which broke the deadlock. On May 22 the President sent a message to Congress asking for silver legislation which
would be in essence mandatory but would permit the Treasury
discretion in the timing and conditions of purchase. In another
month both Houses passed the Silver Purchase Act.

Roosevelt surrendered to political blackmail on the part of the
silver bloc. He had reason to fear that a silver filibuster might hurt
his legislative program, or that a silver veto might damage congressional prospects in the fall. In capitulating, he committed the
government to the unlimited purchase of silver at artificial prices
until government silver holdings reached a value equal to one-

third of government gold reserves. The Silver Purchase Act, in short, assured the producers of silver a lavish subsidy, while the government received in exchange growing stocks of a metal which it did not need and for which it had no use.

The silver policy represented the most remarkable — as well as the least remarked — special-interest triumph of the period. A minor industry, employing in 1939 less than five thousand persons, the silver industry, in effect, held the government to ransom, extorting nearly a billion and a half dollars in the fifteen years after 1934 — a sum considerably larger than that paid by the government to support farm prices over the same period. The silver acquired under the legislation played little part in the American monetary system, and the American silver policy only complicated the monetary problems of countries, like China and Mexico, where silver constituted part of the circulating medium. No legislation passed in New Deal years had less excuse. "Our silver program," Morgenthau confessed in 1935, "is the only monetary fiscal policy that I cannot explain or justify." [11]

15. The Triumphs of Reciprocity

THE MONETARY POLICY of the Roosevelt administration, except for the silver aberration, was designed to make money the instrument of public rather than of private purposes It seemed nationalistic insofar as it sought to replace the international gold standard by national monetary management. But it was by no means nationalistic in the sense that it required movement toward economic self-sufficiency. A managed monetary system could promote either trade or self-containment, depending on the objectives of the managers, indeed, while the Roosevelt administration was gaining freedom of national action in the monetary sphere, it was steadily moving away from isolation in the world of commerce.

II

Cordell Hull, above all, remained dedicated to the liberalization of commercial policy. Arguments over monetary standards left him indifferent. It was tariff policy which seemed to him "at the very heart of this country's economic dilemma." He saw in the expansion of foreign trade not only the "path to recovery" but the means of escape from domestic regimentation and the road to world peace. For his part, Roosevelt continued an economic internationalist in principle, if not always in tactics and timing. The presidential decision not to ask for reciprocal trade agreement legislation during the Hundred Days only deferred a major fight over the tariff.

On Armistice Day, 1933, at the State Department's suggestion,

Roosevelt appointed an interdepartmental Executive Committee on Commercial Policy to prepare a new bill for the next session of Congress. Under the chairmanship of Assistant Secretary of State Francis B. Sayre, a law professor and a son-in-law of Woodrow Wilson, and with the counsel of Herbert Feis and Harry C. Hawkins, the Committee worked out a draft. On March 2, 1934, Roosevelt sent a message to Congress requesting authority for the Executive to enter into commercial agreements with foreign nations and to revise rates in accordance with such agreements up to 50 per cent either way. The authority was to expire in three years. Industries affected by reduction were assured a hearing before the Tariff Commission.

The new bill obviously contemplated a revolution in tariff-making. By eliminating the fine old congressional sport of log-rolling, it diminished the power of Congress as well as of the lobbyists from protected industries. The Republicans, who liked the older methods, recoiled almost as a unit. Senator William E. Borah solemnly pronounced the bill unconstitutional and called for its rejection in the name of traditional American liberties. "This proposal," declared Arthur H. Vandenberg of Michigan, "is Fascist in its philosophy, Fascist in its objective"; it was "palpably unconstitutional," "economic dictatorship come to America," "a combination of surrenders which could not be more flagrant or subversive of the American constitutional system." "Mr. President," warned Warren Austin of Vermont, "we are at the parting of the ways." Defeat of the measure would keep American freedom alive; enactment would mean "another step away from free government." Henry L. Stimson, who had been awakened from his Hoover-administration flirtation with Smoot-Hawleyism by Henry Wallace's *America Must Choose,* tried to rally Republican support for the measure; but when Senator Pat Harrison alluded to Stimson's views on the floor of the Senate he was obliged to rebuke Stimson's fellow-Republicans for their snickers. In the House of Representatives only two Republicans supported the bill, while but a handful of Democrats opposed it; in the Senate, Democrats voted 51 to 5 for the bill, Republicans 28 to 3 against.

For Cordell Hull, the bill's steady progress through Congress was the climax of a lifetime. At nine-fifteen on the evening of

June 12, 1934, he watched the President sign the bill. "Each stroke of the pen seemed to write a message of gladness in my heart." [1]

III

Yet the message of gladness in Hull's heart, while genuine enough, had to be qualified. The passage of the Reciprocal Trade Agreements Act did not settle the question of the New Deal trade philosophy. Within the framework of the Act, two approaches to foreign trade were possible. Hull's approach envisaged the reduction of tariffs and steady progress toward multilateralism. The other approach envisaged the Act as an instrument for bilateral commercial bargaining, and this approach had the powerful support within the administration of that hardened battler, George N. Peek.

When Peek was eased out of AAA in December 1933, Roosevelt appointed him special presidential assistant on trade policy. A few months later, in March 1934, the President made him his Foreign Trade Adviser. Hull later wrote, "If Mr. Roosevelt had hit me between the eyes with a sledge hammer he could not have stunned me more." On the Executive Committee on Commercial Policy, Peek not only took an active part in the discussions leading up to the trade agreements bill but was personally responsible for the decision to make the bill short and general rather than long and complicated. Still, if he could collaborate with Hull and Sayre in developing the broad idea of reciprocal trade, he sharply differed from them in basic philosophy.

From Peek's point of view, Hull's hope for a freely trading world was an exercise in nostalgia and futility. The new protective devices — tariffs, exchange controls, quotas, two-price systems, bilateral agreements — were here to stay. "I believe," Peek wrote, "that this situation represents a permanent change in the character of international trade. . . . The whole problem is one of finding methods whereby mutually advantageous exchanges of goods may take place." The answer, he thought, lay in a system of government-managed trading — in which reciprocal trade agreements could serve as the mechanism for bilateral balancing of accounts. Where Hull saw the trade agreement program as a means of scaling down the whole tariff structure, Peek thus saw it as a means of pushing exports through "horse-trading," *quid pro quo,* nation by nation. The operational difference was the extent to which the trade agreement program implied the most-favored-nation principle. Peek called Hull's unconditional principle, which would automatically extend to all nondiscriminating nations concessions granted to the first nation, "unilateral economic disarmament." With this principle, said Moley, reciprocal treaties would not be reciprocal at all; they would be general tariff reductions. Instead, Peek and Moley favored a conditional principle, by which concessions would be extended only to nations which themselves granted concessions equivalent to those made by the first nation. (The hearings did not clarify this issue: Hull himself told a congressional committee, "Under this bill that matter is left open.") Henry Wallace summarized the differences in a letter to Roosevelt. "What Mr. Peek is proposing, as I understand it," Wallace wrote, "is that we proceed to play the same game that the other countries have been playing, and try to get as large a share of the winnings as possible. What Mr. Hull has in mind, on the other hand, is that we do our best to change the rules of the game, so that . . . the world may gradually shift back to a freer exchange of goods."

And the dispute had larger implications. From the viewpoint of a man like Moley, the Hull doctrine represented an attempt to undo the planning program of the New Deal; it was incompatible, he wrote, "with the idea of a managed national economy." "These low-tariff principles," said Moley, "are an integral part of a still more ominous policy of internationalism which is threatening the integrity and unity of the New Deal on every side." Charles A. Beard similarly considered Peek "the realist among the administration men engaged on the foreign trade side." Indeed, the rationale of the new program remained ambiguous. If its purpose, as its advocates later contended, was to enable the United States to adjust to its position as a creditor nation, then the act ought logically to have aimed at increasing imports *into* the United States. But its preamble expressly defined its goal as that of "expanding foreign markets for the products of the United States." While this was to be done by increasing American purchase of foreign goods, such goods were to be admitted only in

accordance with the "needs" of American business. During the
debate Sayre stated the purpose of the bill as that "of making
possible larger sales abroad"; "the very foundation of such a program," he added, "must be avoidance of undue injury to American
producers." Cordell Hull himself declared, "The policy of the proposed bill is to supplement our almost impregnable domestic
markets with a substantial and gradually expanding foreign
market for our more burdensome surpluses. . . . Its support is only
urged as an emergency measure to deal with a dangerous and
threatening emergency situation."

The legislative history shows that the State Department mainly
sold the bill as something which would help recovery through the
promotion of exports. Peek, in short, had considerable justifica-
tion in regarding the Act not as a congressional commitment to
general tariff reduction but as a bargaining mechanism designed
to stimulate the export trade.[2]

IV

In these circumstances of ambiguity, the administration of the
Act became decisive. In the first test of strength, Hull repulsed
Peek's attempts to take over the program. Under Sayre and later
under Henry F. Grady, with Alvin H. Hansen of the University of
Minnesota as chief economist, an interdepartmental Committee on
Trade Agreements was set up to administer the Act. The State
Department then began a series of negotiations with foreign countries intended, in the main, to achieve the purpose which it had
not thus far clearly avowed and which Congress had certainly not
clearly endorsed — the purpose of producing an excess of imports
over exports, or, as Sayre put it in 1935, "increased exports with a
diminishing export balance." Peek kept up a stubborn flow of
protests against the Department's assault on the tariff structure.
At the same time, he tried himself to negotiate bilateral agreements of the horse-swapping kind.

The cold war between Peek and Hull continued through the
first half of 1935. Roosevelt, the eternal pragmatist, evidently
thought that the clash of policies was better than a surrender to
either extreme. Pressures within the administration mounted in

favor of Hull; in particular, Wallace and the Department of Agriculture maintained a powerful barrage of low-tariff argument. Peek's opponents grew ever bolder. "If the act is utilized merely to gain advantageous 'horse trades' at the expense of other nations," Sayre said pointedly in a speech in December 1934, "to trade off special privilege for special privilege, to bargain discrimination against discrimination, to outwit by clever deals one's trade competitors, the act had far better never have been passed." When Peek negotiated a barter deal to dispose of surplus American cotton to Germany, Hull denounced it as incompatible with the trade agreements program. Roosevelt, who had first approved the deal, was persuaded to change his mind. With this defeat, Peek and his policy went into permanent eclipse.

What remained was a rearguard action. Throughout 1935 Peek persisted in vain attempts to obstruct Hull's trade agreements. In July he tried to resign; Roosevelt asked him to withhold his resignation for the time being. In the meantime, Peek continued as president of the Export-Import Bank, a government corporation set up in 1934 to promote foreign trade by making or guaranteeing private loans. But he could no longer suppress his growing indignation; and on Armistice Day, 1935, speaking before the War Industries Board Association in New York, he defined the choice in trade policy as between Americanism and internationalism, strongly hinting that the administration had taken the un-American road. By now, Roosevelt's patience was trickling away. In late November he wrote Peek a strong letter denouncing what he regarded as Peek's misrepresentation of the administration policy. A few days later he accepted Peek's resignation.

Peek, a battler to the last, left the government with a notification to the President that he planned to continue his fight. Continuation took the form of collaborating with Samuel Crowther in writing a book, *Why Quit Our Own,* serialized in the anti-administration *Saturday Evening Post* and distributed in thousands of free copies by the Chemical Foundation, a leading agency of protectionism. While Peek's earlier views had been far more moderate than the doctrinaire isolationism of Crowther's *America Self-Contained,* bitterness was now driving him into the extremist camp.

Peek's departure meant the triumph of the Hull philosophy. As far as foreign trade was concerned, the New Deal was definitely committed to internationalism. And once again a hard-boiled political infighter had fallen victim to the long knife of Cordell Hull.[3]

V

By the end of 1935, reciprocal trade agreements were in effect with 14 countries; by 1945, with 29 countries. The spread of the area of reciprocity was accomplished by steady increases in the volume and value of trade. It is impossible, however, to isolate the contribution of the trade agreements program to the world commercial revival. For example, for the first year or two, devaluation undoubtedly did more than trade agreements to stimulate American exports. The problem of judgment is further complicated by the confusion of purpose which continued to surround trade agreements policy. Even its advocates seemed uncertain whether its objective was to correct the imbalance in international accounts caused by America's position as a creditor nation, or only, through pushing exports equally with imports, to transfer that imbalance to a higher level. Thus Cordell Hull, writing his memoirs fourteen years after the passage of the Act, began his case for the policy by arguing that exports to trade agreement countries had risen faster than exports to other countries! And, indeed, in the thirties this increase in United States exports was not offset by a corresponding increase in imports. From 1934 to 1939, exports rose by over a billion dollars, while imports rose by less than $700 million. The excess of merchandise exports over imports, which had stood at $477 million in 1934, was (with devaluation, European recovery and the fear of war) over a billion in 1938 and just under a billion in 1939. The debt of the outside world to the United States grew steadily throughout the decade.

The trade agreements program thus did little in the thirties to meet the world's or America's balance-of-payments problem; nor is it even clear that all its supporters intended it should. In addition, it is probable that the program had limited effect on the level of domestic economic activity. In general, its advocates persistently exaggerated its economic achievements. Still, this was done not with an intent to deceive but out of an unconquerable evangelism.

If this evangelism led the Secretary and much of the Department into an absorption with the program to the neglect of many more important matters, it nevertheless had its role in a world plunging blindly ahead into economic nationalism. With quiet intensity Hull and Sayre resurrected the vision of a freely trading civilization, opposed it to the image of totalitarian control, and thereby laid the foundation for one more effort in the forties and fifties to liberate world trade. The very confusion of objectives in the reciprocity policy of the thirties mirrored a time of transition. What emerged in the end was the appealing objective of an expanding world economy.

The early New Deal thus began by accepting world tendencies toward economic nationalism. It looked homeward and saw both the depression's cause and its cure in the national economy. Some New Dealers — Peek, Moley, Frank, Beard, Baruch — extended this idea almost into a form of economic autarchy; they desired a nation where external controls could render internal planning safe from the economic tempests of the world outside. But others, while equally rejecting the international theory of the depression, saw in the revival of foreign trade an indispensable element of national recovery. For them, the first step was to seek a national monetary policy. When the government could control the value of money and interest rates, there was no reason why it should not lower its tariffs and increase its foreign trade. Hull offered the multilateral doctrine in its nineteenth-century form; but what he offered could blend (under the ministrations of Herbert Feis and Alvin Hansen) with the new economics of Keynes; and Hull gave it unique moral force.

The economic nationalism of the Hoover administration had sought to shelter American industry behind ever-rising tariffs while at the same time it proposed to surrender American finance to the workings of the international gold standard. The result had been deflation and stagnation. In the end, as the New Deal redefined the economics of nationalism, it came out with the reverse policy — one which aimed at securing national control over finance while at the same time it sought to unfetter and increase world trade. Only on these terms, it seemed, was a policy of expansion, at home and abroad, possible.[4]

IV

The Cry
in the Streets

16. The Rise of Federal Relief

THE NEW DEAL thus launched in 1933 a series of experiments in agricultural, industrial, commercial, and monetary policy. These programs were addressed both to the immediate task of recovery and to the larger task of reconstruction. Yet they could not, in the best of circumstances, be expected to take effect overnight. There remained in the meantime the problem of the millions of men and women who had no work and could find none. No one knows how many there were on Inauguration Day — at least 12 to 15 million, over a quarter of the labor force — subsisting wanly and desperately on relief. How to keep these people going until jobs were available again?

The existing system of public relief, largely improvised in the course of depression, was itself breaking down. Private charity had long since become inadequate; municipal and state relief fell far below the need, and the Emergency Relief and Construction Act, passed by Congress in July 1932 and appropriating $300 million of federal funds for loans to state and local authorities, had little effect because of the meagerness of the appropriations, the commitment to the loan principle, and the cumbersome administrative procedures. The average relief stipend was now about fifty cents per day per family. In some states 40 per cent of the people were on relief; in some counties the figure rose to 80 or 90 per cent. Everywhere funds were running out.

Most people close to the subject had long since concluded that the only hope was a federal program. During the short session before Inauguration, a parade of experts — social workers, munici-

pal officials, representatives of charities — came to Washington to
testify for Senator Costigan's federal relief bill. None spoke more
authoritatively than Harry L. Hopkins, head of Franklin Roosevelt's Temporary Emergency Relief Administration in New York.
Hopkins dismissed the idea of loans to penniless states as unreal-
istic and called for a federal welfare agency — not a banking
agency, like RFC — to make direct grants to states for relief
purposes.

Hopkins had already made the same points in a letter to the
President-elect in December 1932. But in the early weeks of 1933
the banking and agricultural crises shouldered the relief problem
out of Roosevelt's attention. Unable to get through to the President, Hopkins turned to his former Albany colleague, Frances
Perkins. Accompanied by William Hodson, a veteran social worker
and director of the Welfare Council of New York City, he met
Miss Perkins at the crowded Women's University Club on a March
evening. The only place they could find to talk was a cramped space
under the stairs. There Hopkins and Hodson tersely laid out a
federal relief program. Miss Perkins, impressed by the precision of
their knowledge, got them an appointment with the President.

Other members of the administration were arguing for action.
Even John Garner spoke up one day: "When we were campaigning," he said, "we sort of made promises that we would do something for the poorer kind of people, and I think we have to do
something for them." Roosevelt agreed, and on March 21, 1933,
sent a message to Congress requesting the establishment of the
office of Federal Relief Administrator. At the same time, he called
in Costigan, La Follette, and Wagner and asked them to draw up
a bill.

The bill proposed a Federal Emergency Relief Administration
with $500 million for grants-in-aid to states. It produced some
violent reactions. "I can hardly find parliamentary language,"
said Simeon D. Fess of Ohio, "to describe the statement that the
States and cities cannot take care of conditions in which they find
themselves but must come to the Federal Government for aid."
"Is there anything left of our Federal system?" asked John B.
Hollister of Ohio. "It is socialism," said Robert Luce of Massachusetts, adding with his scholarly meticulousness, "Whether it is

communism or not I do not know." "God save the people of the United States," said C. L. Beedy of Maine. These were minority views. The bill passed the Senate on March 30 by a vote of 55 to 17 and the House three weeks later by 326 to 42.

Roosevelt quickly decided on Hopkins as head of the new agency. He had a little trouble with Governor Lehman of New York, who was disinclined to let Hopkins go. Finally on May 19, Hopkins telegraphed Lehman: PRESIDENT STATES HE WAS WIRING YOU AND WANTS ME TO REPORT TO HIM MONDAY MORNING. Lehman wired Roosevelt in anguish: YOU HAVE THE ENTIRE COUNTRY FROM WHICH TO MAKE CHOICE. But Roosevelt knew what he wanted. On May 22, 1933, Harry Hopkins went to Washington.[1]

II

Harry Hopkins had already come a long way in forty-two years for "the son of a harness maker from Sioux City" — the somewhat romantic self-identification in which he took delight all his life. He had spent his boyhood in midwestern small towns, ending in Grinnell, Iowa, where his father, a wanderer from the middle border with a weakness for poker and bowling, finally settled down as proprietor of a harness store. His mother was a woman of ardent religious faith, active in the Methodist Missionary Society. From her, young Harry received a militant social conscience, as he took his easygoing gaiety from his father.

Hopkins himself went to Grinnell College, where he knew Chester Davis and Paul Appleby. For a while he considered working with Davis after graduation on a paper in Montana; but instead he got a summer job with the Christadora House, a settlement house in New York. (Appleby, taking Hopkins's place in Montana, was launched thereby on an agricultural career.) The summer's experience with New York slum children was a revelation for Hopkins. He had not imagined such squalor before, and the shock never left him. He plunged into social work on the lower East Side, and in the next years, climbed steadily in the social welfare world — supervisor for the Association for Improving the Condition of the Poor; executive secretary of the Board for Child Welfare; New Orleans manager for the Red Cross during the war;

assistant director of the AICP; director of the New York Tuberculosis and Health Association. His political views were radical but subdued. In the New York mayoralty election of 1917, he backed Morris Hillquit, the Socialist candidate, and he may even have registered for a time as a Socialist. But, on the whole, he kept to the life of a professional social worker. Only his relaxations were unusual — not only tennis and poker, but also a tendency on fragrant spring days to go out to the race tracks and bet on the horses.

Hopkins was a lean, loose-limbed, disheveled man, with sharp features and dark, sardonic eyes. He talked quickly and cockily, out of the side of his mouth; his manner was brusque and almost studiously irreverent; his language, concise, pungent, and often profane. "He gives off," noted one observer, "a suggestion of quick cigarettes, thinning hair, dandruff, brief sarcasm, fraying suits of clothes, and a wholly understandable preoccupation." He was at his best under pressure. Wearing what friends described as his hell's-bells or you-can't-put-that-over-on-me expression, he would screw up his face and fire a volley of short, sharp questions until he had slashed through to the heart of a problem. Understanding what had to be done, he wasted no time in formalities, but assumed responsibility, gave orders, and acted. He expended nervous energy carelessly and restored it by chain-smoking and by drinking cup after cup of black coffee. Beneath his air of insouciance and cynicism, he had a buoyant — almost gay — conviction that all walls would fall before the man of resource and decision. And underneath the hard-boiled pose, there lay a surprising quick sensitivity to human moods and relationships.[2]

III

Action was instantaneous. Before evening on the second day, Hopkins had thrown together a staff, begun the collection of information, alerted forty-eight state governors to set up state organizations, and sent emergency aid to seven states. He warned his staff that he would soon be the most unpopular man in America: he planned to keep reminding the nation of unemployment and poverty, "and they won't want to hear it." Still, for all his forebodings, he set to work with aplomb.

The Federal Emergency Relief Administration did not deal directly with relief applicants. It made grants to local public agencies. Half of its $500 million was to be assigned on a matching basis — one dollar of federal funds for every three dollars of state money spent for relief during the three months preceding. The other half was to go where need was urgent and the matching requirement could not be met. Exhorting, cajoling, scolding, threatening, Hopkins and a small field staff used their power to pump new life into the faltering state agencies. Where a local organization seemed hopelessly incompetent, Hopkins asked the governor to make the necessary changes. Most of the time, his evident disinterestedness won cooperation. In a few cases, FERA had to go into the state and appoint its own administration. Hopkins remained profoundly convinced of the values of decentralization. He kept his Washington staff small and gave great responsibility to state administrators, while at the same time holding them as well as he could to the national mark.

The critical problem of relief, as he saw it, was preserving the morale of people forced to live by government handouts. Men and women who lacked jobs for reasons far beyond their own control should not, Hopkins believed, be made to feel like paupers; it was necessary not just to feed them but to maintain their self-respect. "I don't think anybody can go year after year, month after month, accepting relief without affecting his character in some way unfavorably," he wrote in June 1933. "It is probably going to undermine the independence of hundreds of thousands of families. . . . I look upon this as a great disaster and wish to handle it as such."

A measure of degradation in relief seemed inescapable. Since limited funds had to go as far as possible, it was essential that no one obtain relief who could get along without it. Thus FERA could not escape the means test. Investigation was left to local case workers, who could presumably conduct it with least humiliation to the applicant. Once need was established, the problem became the form in which relief was to be granted. Some states had set up special commissaries where reliefers could go for food. This was a cheap enough form of relief; but Hopkins, feeling that it portended a ghetto for the unemployed, liquidated the commissary system as fast as he could. The grocery order removed those on relief less from normal society. Still, it placed the family under a paternalism, compelling them to buy what the nutritionists decided they needed. Hopkins much preferred giving straight cash, even if the reliefer used it for tobacco or liquor; on the whole, he felt, more damage was done to the human spirit by loss of choice than by loss of vitamins.[3]

IV

Basically, however, Hopkins objected to direct relief in any form. Keeping able-bodied men in idleness, he believed, could not help but corrode morale. In 1932 the mayor of Toledo, Ohio, said: "I have seen thousands of these defeated, discouraged, hopeless men and women, cringing and fawning as they come to ask for public aid. It is a spectacle of national degeneration." It was this which Hopkins wanted to avoid in demanding a more creative response to the catastrophe. Instead of putting the unemployed on the dole, why not offer the weekly government check in exchange for labor performed for the public welfare? Work relief, Hopkins said, "preserves a man's morale. It saves his skill. It gives him a chance to do something socially useful." Of course, it would cost more than the dole. But the advocates of economy in relief, Hopkins said, never counted in the cost of depriving citizens of "their sense of independence and strength and their sense of individual destiny."

Although FERA, thrown so suddenly into the breach, could not escape direct relief as its main instrument, a wide variety of work relief projects were devised under Hopkins's relentless prodding. Thus teachers on relief rolls were assigned to country schools which would otherwise have had to close their doors; by December 1933, about 13,000 teachers, paid from relief funds, were holding classes in rural areas. FERA too had a special program to take care of transients — the thousands of jobless men roaming the country in search of work and hope. There were provisions for drought relief, and for grants to local self-help and barter associations. Hopkins invited experiment, calling on state administrators to show "imagination." Some local organizations remained resistant. This was partly because of the added expense of work relief, partly because of the added administrative difficulties. And often, when they tried it, the projects were ill-conceived and unconvincing.

As the fourth winter of the depression approached, new unrest stirred among the jobless. According to a *Fortune* report, men and women on relief "do not like the dole. They are almost unanimous in demanding *work*." Radicals and Communists were tireless in exploiting disappointments and grievances. In August 1933 several thousand members of the Ohio Unemployed League marched on the State House at Columbus. "We must take control of the government," shouted Louis Budenz, one of the agitators, "and establish a workers and farmers republic." Was it safe to try and negotiate the winter of 1933–34 on the direct relief basis? It seemed more and more evident that a new and better federal effort would be necessary to meet the winter's challenge.[4]

v

Hopkins, in Chicago on a field trip late in October, pondered the next step. His staff wanted him to make an all-out fight for a federal works program. Hopkins agreed in principle. But he was not sure he could sell the idea at the White House, and he was disturbed by the threat of labor opposition. In his Pullman drawing room between Chicago and Kansas City (where he was to confer with the Federal Re-employment Director of Missouri, Judge Harry C. Truman), Hopkins brooded over the problem. In Kansas City he received word from Aubrey Williams, a top FERA aide, that Samuel Gompers himself had once favored a works program, a fact which might turn aside labor objections. Encouraged, Hopkins called Washington and asked for a White House appointment.

Hopkins outlined his scheme at lunch with the President on the day of his return. Roosevelt asked how many jobs he thought he could provide. Hopkins answered four million, if he could get enough money. Roosevelt, thinking aloud, remarked that Ickes's Public Works Administration was slow in getting under way; perhaps Hopkins could get funds out of the PWA appropriations. Indeed, the whole effort might be conceived as a means of tiding the unemployed over one more winter, by which time PWA could begin to take up the slack.

This was the beginning of the Civil Works Administration. By November 15, Hopkins announced his objective: "the employment of four million by December 15, 1933." He set himself a prodigious job. Though CWA, unlike FERA, was empowered to operate works projects directly, Hopkins had no planning staff, no shelf of light public works, no formulated program. CWA jobs, moreover, had to be easy to learn and short in duration; winter weather limited the type of project available; necessary tools were in short supply. Yet Hopkins, always at his best when confronted by impossibilities, allowed nothing to get in the way of rapid expansion. He immediately converted much of his FERA staff to CWA and adopted the existing state relief organizations as CWA's local arms. Project ideas, generated in the atmosphere of pressure, came both down from Washington and up from the field. Hopkins missed his first target date — by December 14, there were only 2,610,451 on CWA rolls — but by the middle of January he was well over the 4,000,000 mark.

CWA tackled a tremendous variety of jobs. At its peak, it had about 400,000 projects in operation. About a third of CWA personnel worked on roads and highways. In the three and a half months of CWA's existence, they built or improved about 500,000 miles of secondary roads. Next in importance came schools — 40,000 built or improved, with 50,000 teachers employed in country schools or in city adult education, and large numbers of playgrounds developed. CWA gave the nation nearly 500 airports and improved 500 more. It developed parks, cleared waterways, fought insect pests, dug swimming pools and sewers. Three thousand writers and artists found CWA employment utilizing their own skills ("Hell!" said Hopkins. "They've got to eat just like other people.") Above all, it supplied work to four million Americans who would otherwise have festered in humiliation and idleness.

Of course, Hopkins paid a price for speed. In money, the cost was considerable — in the end, nearly a billion dollars. And there were administrative lapses too which Hopkins characteristically exposed before his critics could discover them. In January 1934 he lashed out at evidence of political interference and graft in CWA operations. "I never anticipated anything of the kind," he told newspapermen. "I suppose I'm naïve and unsophisticated, but that's the truth. I didn't, and I feel very badly about it." He ordered investigations, shook up incompetent or tainted state organizations and began to bring in Army officers to strengthen the program against corruption.

Lieutenant Colonel John C. H. Lee, a stern West Point engineer assigned to study CWA for the War Department, watched Hopkins's unorthodox methods with astonished admiration. "Mr. Hopkins's loose fluidity of organization," he concluded, "was justified by the results achieved. It enabled him to engage for employment in two months nearly as many persons as were enlisted and called to the colors during our year and a half of World War mobilization, and to disburse to them, weekly, a higher average rate of wage than Army or Navy pay." CWA, Lee said, reached every county and town in the United States in a period of two months during one of the most severe winters on record.

> The accomplishments of the CWA were possible through the arduous efforts of the young Administrator and the group of able young assistants which he has assembled and inspired. They have worked daily long into the night with a morale easily comparable to that of a war emergency. These assistants address Mr. Hopkins fondly as "Harry." There is no rigidity or formality in their staff conferences with him, yet he holds their respect, confidence and seemingly whole-souled cooperation.[5]

VI

As for the reliefers themselves, FERA field investigators like Lorena Hickok and Martha Gellhorn provided graphic reports of their condition. Poignant images spilled out of these documents — the cry in September 1933 in Pennsylvania, "Our children must have shoes, or they can't go to school"; the Catholic priest in Scottville, Pennsylvania, begging for medical supplies to keep his people alive; the little boy in Houston, Texas, who refused to go to school wearing trousers of black-and-white-striped ticking because everyone would know his family was on relief; the man in Camden, New Jersey, explaining that he went to bed around seven at night "because that way you get the day over with quicker"; the South Dakota farm wife who had a recipe for soup made from Russian thistles — "It don't taste so bad, only it ain't very filling"; the sixteen-year-old girl keeping house for her family in a dark tobacco barn in Wilson County, North Carolina, the place scrubbed spotlessly clean, the girl saying sadly, "Seems like we just keep goin' lower and lower"; pinned on her bosom, as one wears a brooch, was a 1932 campaign button, a profile of Franklin Roosevelt.

In 1933 Lorena Hickok noticed evidences of Communist activity. "They are very, very busy," she wrote from Aberdeen, South Dakota, in November, "getting right down among the farmers and working like beavers." In Pennsylvania the unemployed, she felt, were "right on the edge"; "it wouldn't take much to make Communists out of them." Martha Gellhorn, moving around the country a year later, found less organized protest. The idolatry of Roosevelt, she thought, was taking the spirit out of opposition. "The problem," she wrote Hopkins, "is not one of fighting off a 'red menace' . . . but of fighting off hopelessness; despair; a dangerous feeling of helplessness and dependence." Everywhere there seemed a spreading listlessness, a whipped feeling like the hitchhiker who said to Theodore Dreiser, "I'm going downhill. I'm going to hell, really. I don't care as much as I used to." Miss Gellhorn was disturbed most of all by this smell of defeat: "I find them all in the same shape — fear, fear driving them into a state of semicollapse; cracking nerves; and an overpowering terror of the future . . . each family in its own miserable home going to pieces."

The relief rolls were changing in character. First, there had been the unemployables; then had come the working-class unemployed; but now, increasingly, white-collar workers, their savings exhausted by four years of depression, their scruples conquered by want, their self-respect eroded by fear, were going on relief. They hated it, but in the end they saw no alternative. "I simply had to murder my pride," an engineer told Lorena Hickok. "We'd lived on bread and water three weeks before I could make myself do it." "It took me a month," said a lumberman. "I used to go down there every day or so and walk past the place again and again. I just couldn't make myself go in." And with white-collar relief there came new tensions. Above all, the compulsion to cling to some semblance at least of past ways of life complicated relationships with the relief administration. "We can provide overalls, but not tailored business suits," said Miss Hickok. "We can't keep those white collars laundered."

FERA and CWA had at least kept conditions from becoming worse. On the whole, there was less revolt, less starvation, and less Communism than might have been expected. As Hugh Charles Boyle, the Roman Catholic Bishop of Pittsburgh, told Lorena Hickok, "Inadequate though it may be, the emergency unemployment relief has been and is the most stabilizing force we have. . . . The Federal Government will have to put up the money, or — well, God help us all!" And CWA, because it provided work, was received by the unemployed — or at least by those who could get on its rolls — with special gratitude. Miss Hickok was in Iowa on the first CWA pay day. "And did they want to work?" she wrote Hopkins. "In Sioux City they actually had fist fights over shovels!" "It was pathetic to watch some of the reactions," reported a CWA administrator. "I saw a few cases leave the office actually weeping for sheer happiness."

Still, Hopkins's view was that federal relief was doing only a minimal job. "We have never given adequate relief," he said in 1936. Many social workers and public officials agreed. Thus Lawrence F. Quigley, mayor of Chelsea, Massachusetts, wrote Hopkins in January 1934 that only 155 people in his town could get CWA jobs; another 2000 were congregating sullenly in City Hall; "a spark might change them into a mob." "I believe," said Mayor Quigley, "that the Federal Government, once having acknowledged its responsibility by giving jobs merely for the sake of a job, must now put every unemployed man to work doing the most useful task that can be found for him. . . . If some such remedial measure is not immediately adopted I make bold to predict fundamental and sweeping changes in the structure of our government before the end of the present year." [6]

VII

This was one view. Other Americans believed that any national relief program at all was too much. As the economic situation began to improve in 1934, some of this opinion began to be vocal. When someone asked him about the homeless boys riding the rails in search of employment, Henry Ford said equably, "Why, it's the best education in the world for those boys, that traveling around. They get more experience in a few months than they would in years at school." Even a liberal businessman like Robert E. Wood of Sears, Roebuck could identify relief as the New Deal's "one serious mistake." "While it is probably true that we cannot allow everyone to starve (although I personally disagree with this philosophy and the philosophy of the city social worker)," Wood wrote, "we should tighten up relief all along the line, and if relief is to be given it must be on a bare subsistence allowance." Winthrop Aldrich of the Chase National Bank called for the elimination of work relief. Lincoln Colcord, reporting to Hopkins in 1934 on talks with businessmen, summed up business opinion as one of opposition to work relief, not only because of its cost but because all work projects — even ditch digging — were deemed competitive with private industry.

There was considerable resentment too in farm areas, especially in the South. Planters complained that relief made it impossible to get cheap Negro farm labor. "I wouldn't plow nobody's mule from sunrise to sunset for 50 cents per day," as one aggrieved farmer wrote to Governor Eugene Talmadge of Georgia, "when I could get $1.30 for pretending to work on a DITCH." (Talmadge forwarded this letter to Roosevelt, who dictated a biting reply. "I take it, from your sending the letter of the gentleman from Smithville to me," the President said, "that you approve of paying farm labor 40 to 50 cents per day." Figuring in the seasonal character of the employment, Roosevelt reckoned this to be $60 to $75 a year. "Somehow I cannot get it into my head that wages on such a scale make possible a reasonable American standard of living." On reflection, Roosevelt decided to send the letter under Hopkins's signature.)

Most pervasive of all was the feeling that the whole theory of federal relief was incompatible with American individualism. Much of this concern was doubtless the rationalization of objections to high taxes, to high wages, and to any increase in federal power; but much too reflected authentic anxieties over what dependence on government handouts might do to the American people. "Our present efforts in the direction of relief," wrote the banker Frank A. Vanderlip in a statement repeated ten thousand times by business leaders in these years, "have broken down self-reliance and industry. I profoundly believe that society does not owe every man a living."

It was easy to ridicule such arguments. When Hoover attacked federal aid to the unemployed for weakening the "moral fiber" of the people, Harold Ickes retorted that Hoover as President had not hesitated "to weaken the moral fiber of banks and insurance companies and manufacturing and industrial enterprises" by handing them millions of dollars. Hoover's policies no doubt justified Ickes's retort. Yet the issue raised by conservatives was a real one. Hopkins himself worried about moral effects: that, of course, was why he preferred to offer the unemployed jobs rather than the dole. Lorena Hickok was alarmed when she heard little boys in Salt Lake City boasting about whose father had been on relief longer. Some people on relief, she commented sorrowfully, became "gimmies"; "the more you do for the people, the more they demand." Social workers said, "They are beginning to regard CWA as their due — [they feel] that the Government actually owes it to them. And they want more." Some projects were themselves too obviously sham to help the morale of either the workers or the public. The term "boondoggling" arose to describe the most futile of the leaf raking or ditch-digging efforts.[7]

VIII

Yet what was the answer? Hopkins and the administration considered relief of some sort inevitable; the alternative was revolution. If this were the case, work relief seemed the form most compatible with self-respect and individualism. And the argument for work relief was more compelling in 1933–34 than it might be later. At a time when morale was low and before other spending programs were showing results, an emergency works program could have marked stimulative effect, both economically and psychologically.

For their part, the businessmen had no clear alternative to present. Some doubtless wished to abolish relief altogether. But few were prepared to avow this as their objective. This left most in the unsatisfying position of deploring the moral consequences of relief while advocating the form of relief which by their own theory was morally most deleterious — the cash handout, the detested dole. This contradiction did not, however, notably restrain many from doing all they could to forestall a works program.

Work relief really presupposed a national effort, since forty-eight separate works programs were inconceivable. Consequently returning relief to the states would effectively doom the works idea. And it would save money over-all; since state governments could not create the market for their own securities, the resources available to them for relief were limited. Best of all, such a policy would diminish the power of the national government. So the restoration of relief to the local communities became the key conservative issue. In December 1934, for example, a group of business leaders meeting at White Sulphur Springs under Chamber of Commerce and N.A.M. auspices, demanded that the states take over relief. But when *Today* magazine wired state governors asking them what they thought about this proposal, only one of the thirty-seven replying — Gene Talmadge — agreed. Thirty-three said that their states had already reached the limit of their contributions.

The fiscal point was only one of the arguments for federal relief. Many observers in addition considered a national program better proof against waste and graft. "Turning federal funds over to the states for administration," as Senator James F. Byrnes of South Carolina put it, "would mean more politics instead of less politics in administration." "If the relief system were not centralized where centralization is necessary," said the political writers Joseph Alsop and Turner Catledge in the *Saturday Evening Post*, "the inevitable result would be the greatest pork-barrel riot Congress has ever seen."

Still, some wanted a pork-barrel riot. Others wanted to kill work relief. Others wistfully hoped that defederalization might bring on a new access of local responsibility. And so a debate began which continued through the rest of the decade.[8]

IX

The first phase of the debate boiled up over the extension of CWA in January and February 1934. Criticism of CWA had been muted at first — a fact plausibly explained by Al Smith in December 1933 on the ground that "no sane local official who has hung up an empty stocking over the municipal fireplace is going to shoot Santa Claus just before a hard Christmas." (The embattled Hopkins replied with feeling, "The hell they won't. Santa Claus really needs a bullet-proof vest.") But the charges of waste and corruption — despite the fact that Hopkins was the first to reveal them — strengthened the hands of those who had disliked the works program all along. More important, Roosevelt, under pressure from southern Democrats and from his Director of the Budget, Lewis Douglas, was beginning to feel that the expensive CWA operation must end for the sake of the budget.

Hopkins, and most social workers and liberal Democrats, disagreed with this decision. So too did many Republicans; Governor Alfred M. Landon of Kansas, for example, wrote Roosevelt, "This civil-works program is one of the soundest, most constructive policies of your administration, and I cannot urge too strongly its continuance." To the left of the New Deal, Norman Thomas organized a march on Washington to protest against termination. In a single week nearly 60,000 letters and wires deluged the CWA office and the White House. CWA workers engaged in strikes and demonstrations. Yet, once the President had made his decision, Hopkins accepted it and, with his usual brusque efficiency, destroyed the organization he had so brilliantly built up. Roosevelt, in the atmosphere of neurotic administrators weeping on all available shoulders — the Johnsons, Richbergs, Peeks, Hulls — was grateful for Hopkins's uncomplaining loyalty.

What remained of CWA was transferred to the Emergency Work Relief Program of FERA, though work relief continued here only in diminished form. Where CWA had offered jobs at regular wages both to reliefers and to jobless persons who, for whatever reason — probably pride — had refused to go on relief rolls, FERA had to confine itself to those on relief and pay them only substandard wages; and, where CWA had planned and operated its own projects,

FERA could finance only state activities. FERA nonetheless carried on substantial parts of the CWA program, including the white-collar projects.

In addition, FERA developed new programs of its own during 1934. An experiment of special interest was the Federal Surplus Relief Corporation, first conceived in the fall of 1933 as a means of circumventing the irony whereby crops piled up in the country-side while the cities went hungry. "Will you and Peek and Harry Hopkins," Roosevelt wrote Henry Wallace in September, "have a talk and possibly prepare a plan for purchase of surplus commodities such as butter, cheese, condensed milk, hog products and flour, to meet relief needs during the course of the winter?" Jerome Frank proposed doing it through an independent corporation; and, starting in December, the Federal Surplus Relief Corporation began to acquire surplus commodities with the double purpose of helping the farmer by removing price-depressing stocks from the market and of helping the unemployed by giving him food. The Corporation began with pork from the martyred pigs and soon moved from food to surplus cotton, blankets, and even coal.

As FSRC operations expanded in 1934, some businessmen began to charge it with the sin of competing with private enterprise. When FSRC purchased cotton and sent it to FERA workrooms to be made into mattresses for the unemployed, the mattress manufacturers erupted in indignation; nor were they satisfied by FERA's demonstration that the mattresses went only to people who, because they had no money, could not possibly subtract from the mattress market. The drought of 1934 intensified both FSRC activities and business criticism. Taking over cattle which otherwise would have perished uselessly in the drought areas, FSRC proposed that they be converted into canned beef and shoes for men and women on relief. These plans provoked a storm of denunciation. Shoe manufacturers virtuously refused to rent the government the necessary machinery. Such adverse reaction restricted the scope of FSRC activities. In the two years before it was transferred to AAA in 1935, the total value of surplus commodities which FSRC was permitted to distribute amounted to only about 265 million dollars.[9]

X

FERA's support of self-help production roused equally strong business resentment. The self-help movement had sprung up spontaneously in the early depression. People who had no money could still work, and it seemed logical to some to try to trade what they could make for what they needed. In time, it began to seem similarly logical for state governments to provide facilities to enable the unemployed to manufacture things necessary for their own subsistence. FERA was consequently authorized by Congress to make capital grants to states to promote the "barter of goods and services."

In June 1934 the State Relief Commission of Ohio set up the Ohio Relief Production Units, Incorporated; and in a few months the state leased a dozen factories, in which unemployed men and women made dresses, overalls, furniture, and stoves for their own use or for exchange with relief agencies in other states. Half a dozen more states were similarly preparing to bring together idle labor and idle factories (often mattress factories or canning plants) to produce for the unemployed. It was estimated in the summer of 1934 that probably 50,000 families through the nation were members of self-help groups, some organized privately, some under state sponsorship. In the fall, these production projects accounted for 15 per cent of the employment under the Emergency Work Relief Program.

As these programs developed, however, the phrase "production-for-use" began to acquire sinister connotations. The impression grew in business circles that the self-help program was the entering wedge of socialism. The "Ohio Plan" was suspicious enough; and when Upton Sinclair, running for governor in California, envisaged production-for-use by the unemployed as the nucleus for a radical reconstruction of the economy, reaction was vigorous and unequivocal. FERA, because of business hostility, could grant in two years only a little more than three million dollars to self-help cooperatives (this figure does not, however, include the rather more significant support production-for-use received in the works programs). By 1935 the production-for-use and the self-help programs were both on their way out. (Only the President himself remained interested as when, confronted with new supplies of electric power from the new federal dams, he asked Ickes and Hopkins in the spring of 1935 to consider the government's going into the business of producing aluminum, nickel, or magnesium with unemployed labor).[10]

XI

FERA's Rural Rehabilitation Division was charged with the responsibility of relief on the countryside. Its most useful efforts went to what was known as "rehabilitation in place" — that is, loans to farm families for seed, fertilizer, livestock, or farm tools. It also engaged less profitably in attempts to set up rural communities, based on Roosevelt's old dream of decentralized industry and subsistence homesteads. Eventually these activities were absorbed by the Resettlement Administration in 1935. The Transient Division of FERA continued through 1934 to deal with the still large numbers of men on the road; this program disappeared in 1935.

Some of FERA's most striking successes were in particular localities. Thus imaginative FERA leadership saved Key West, Florida, from decay and probable extinction. In 1934 two-thirds of the inhabitants of Key West were on relief. The town government was bankrupt, and local services had wholly broken down, leaving the streets cluttered with garbage and rubbish. J. F. Stone, Jr., the regional FERA administrator, persuaded the governor of Florida to declare a state of "civil emergency," under which municipal powers in Key West were to be delegated to the Florida Emergency Relief Administration. It was an act of dubious legality, but it was enough. The Key West Volunteer Work Corps was then organized to clean up the streets and beaches; houses were painted and renovated, hotels reopened, an air service subsidized (by FERA funds), a federal art project set up, the FERA Marimba Band formed — and Key West entered a new, profitable and perhaps ultimately even more ruinous phase as a resort town.

Following the demobilization of CWA, FERA in 1934 resumed its efforts to hold the relief line, at the same time continuing under Hopkins's driving leadership to diversify and improve the quality of its projects. If much of FERA activity at this point had the air of marking time, it was because the relief picture could not be clear until the Public Works Administration swung into full operation.[11]

17. The Fight for Public Works

THE PUBLIC WORKS ADMINISTRATION had been established in June 1933 with an appropriation of $3.3 billion under Title II of the National Industrial Recovery Act. But PWA and NRA, conceived by Hugh Johnson as Siamese twins, were separated at birth. Snatched by the President from Johnson's waiting arms, PWA was confided to an interdepartmental Special Board for Public Works whose chairman was Secretary of the Interior, Harold L. Ickes. Colonel Donald H. Sawyer was named Acting Administrator of the new agency.

The President, who had hardly heard of Ickes in February, was viewing him with considerable respect by June. The new Secretary, it was evident, was a formidable figure. Now just under sixty, he was the scarred and doughty veteran of a thousand battles, and of very nearly a thousand defeats. But no setback had diminished his fighting spirit. He had wielded sword and buckler so long against evil — first in reform politics in Chicago, then with T.R. in the Bull Moose party, then in the guerrilla warfare he and his law partner Donald Richberg had waged against Samuel Insull and Big Bill Thompson in Chicago — that he had become almost the incarnation of lonely, righteous, and inextinguishable pugnacity.

The world took him at his face and considered him tough, reckless, and impervious. His rhetoric, extravagant and bellicose in the Bull Moose manner, supported this impression. But in action Ickes was characteristically careful and cautious. And in his inner self, by the evidence of the diary into which he regularly discharged his most private thoughts, he was a quivering mass, sensitive as a girl, suspicious as a moneylender. The years of battle had hardened his skin rather than his sensibility. There were softer strains within: the dry, deadpan humor; the deep concern for friendless groups like Indians; the delight in dahlias; the gourmet's fondness for good food and liquor; above all, the touching, desperate need for private affection and public reassurance. A nagging mastoid ailment and chronic insomnia increased his internal tensions. Wanting everyone to love him but trusting no one, he was convinced that mankind was engaged in an unrelenting conspiracy against him. He questioned everyone's motives, regarded disagreement as sabotage and vindictiveness (at least his own) as virtue. His impertinence toward his superiors was matched only by his arrogance toward his subordinates. Honesty was for him a rare and fleeting commodity, of which he had the good fortune to command the American monopoly. His egotism was so massive that he remained personally unconscious of its existence. With the best will, he could not but conclude that anything which extended his power served the republic.

Still, if he had defects, he had to a magnificent degree the virtues of these defects. Bellicosity implied boldness; self-righteousness implied rectitude; ambition implied energy; mistrust implied vigilance. With all the testiness and vanity, there radiated from the chunky, bristling, glowering figure the honest, old-fashioned individualism of the prewar Progressive movement. Stouthearted and incorruptible, he was at his best a superb public servant. His callers had to wait their turn under the stuffed buffalo heads at one end of his large walnut-paneled office in Interior. At the other end, the Secretary received them, one by one, at his desk. A public official, he seemed to say, should have nothing to conceal from the public. Seated solidly in his chair, gold-rimmed spectacles above his heavy nose, darting gloomy glances of intelligent distrust at his visitors, shuffling papers and fidgeting during long, aimless recitals, cutting to the core of issues with rasping questions, he was an indomitable defender of the national interest.[1]

II

The Public Works Administration had several kinds of authority. It could initiate its own projects as a construction agency. It could make allotments to enable other federal agencies to carry on construction work. It could offer a combination of loans and grants to states and other public bodies to stimulate nonfederal construction. And, for a time, it could make loans to certain private corporations. It worked, in the main, through private contractors, and it was not, like most of the work relief programs, restricted to the use of labor from relief rolls. The Public Works Board continued to meet each week to pass on allocations. Within PWA, the National Planning Board, composed of Frederic A. Delano, Roosevelt's uncle and an eminent city planner, Charles E. Merriam of the University of Chicago and Wesley C. Mitchell of Columbia, advised on long-range policies. The President himself, with his vast knowledge of the nation and its needs, kept up a lively interest, not just in broad issues, but in the most minute engineering and topographical details of PWA blueprints.

For a few weeks, from his eminence as chairman of the Public Works Board, Ickes hovered hungrily over PWA, watching Colonel Sawyer with disapproval and preparing his own plans for reorganization. The Acting Administrator, handicapped by his temporary status and doubtless unnerved by the specter of Ickes over his shoulder, showed a conspicuous lack of executive force. When the President returned from a short holiday in July, Dan Roper, as a member of the Special Board, proposed that Ickes be appointed Administrator. Ickes, who obviously yearned for the job, accepted without perceptible surprise (though he later wrote with innocence, "I had not been a candidate for the position and had never for a moment harbored the thought that the President was considering me").

If to Hugh Johnson the object of public works was to stimulate the heavy industries, and if to Harry Hopkins its object was to provide relief and re-employment, to Ickes its object was to beautify the national estate through the honest building of durable public monuments. To Lewis Douglas, it had no object at all. These various conceptions clashed at the meetings of the Public Works Board during the sweltering summer of 1933, its members sitting, coats off, on leather-cushioned chairs around the polished oval table in Ickes's office. "I feel," Douglas astonishingly said on July 1, 1933, "that apparently the spiral of deflation has come to an end, and the direction of events has turned; that the necessity for injecting an artificial factor into the situation no longer exists . . . that therefore we should put on the brakes." To this Rex Tugwell commented curtly, "Of course Mr. Douglas's suggestion is that we should not spend what is provided for in the bill." Douglas said that if the depression had been caused in some measure by excessive debt, how was it to be ended by increasing the thing that caused it? Ickes intervened: "But after all, the Act has been passed and we are called upon to administer it." "Yes, that is right," said Douglas; "but the Act is entirely permissive, Mr. Secretary, and not mandatory at all. I disagree with Dr. Tugwell on that." [2]

III

Tugwell, seeing PWA primarily in its economic function, advocated full speed ahead — a fast start on federal projects, low-interest loans to encourage local projects. Ickes showed little interest in PWA as a direct economic stimulant; one of his first acts when the agency was set up had been to instruct Sawyer *not* to consult Johnson. His concern was that projects be worthwhile and that spending be free from all suspicion of corruption. He well understood that the new program afforded limitless opportunity for graft, small and large. And he understood too that the whole future of public works as a federal function depended on a rigorously honest administration of PWA. The Teapot Dome affair, barely ten years old, was a horrid memory in everyone's mind. Ickes had no hesitation, as fairy godmother, in endowing PWA with incorruptibility rather than speed. "We set before ourselves at the outset," Ickes later wrote, "the perhaps unattainable ideal of administering the greatest fund for construction in the history of the world without scandal."

The decision meant that every PWA contract and plan was agonizingly reviewed all the way to the top. Ickes read every line of everything and often fired documents back with demands for revision and correction. With a thoughtful sense of historical retribution, he hired as head of the PWA division of investigation the same Louis R. Glavis whose pertinacity in charging Alaska coal land frauds had led to the Ballinger-Pinchot row in Interior a quarter-century before. Glavis set up an enormous staff of agents, tapped wires or at least listened to phone conversations, and shadowed doubtful employees and suspected contractors. Ickes meanwhile called on PWA employees to report on each other, denounced them for coming late to work or taking too long for coffee, and even promulgated an edict against pulling down shades over the windows in office doors.

In conducting this pitiless supervision, Ickes had the efficient support of E. K. Burlew, a deceptively mild old-time bureaucrat who had once worked for a firm of private detectives and now was Ickes's assistant in Interior as well as chief of personnel for PWA. The secretarial inquisition unquestionably lowered morale in both PWA and Interior. At the same time, it also did eliminate scandal in what had been traditionally the most corrupt of government departments and in what seemed potentially the most corruptible of emergency agencies. Any government agency with something to give away becomes the target of irresistible pressures. In Ickes these pressures met their irresistible force. His achievement deserves full credit; perhaps gentler methods would not have brought it about. For Ickes himself it produced the sobriquet of "Honest Harold." ("This title has always made me squirm," he wrote in his diary. ". . . I simply hate it. Besides, it makes me a target for sharpshooters.") ³

IV

And there were other reasons, too, why PWA was slow in getting under way — reasons which would have held it up even if demonic activists like Johnson or Hopkins had been in charge. For one thing, public works projects presupposed advance planning, specifications, engineering surveys, blueprints, cost sheets. Despite its cordial words about public works, the Hoover administration in four years had done almost nothing in the way of producing operating plans. PWA, beginning three months after Roosevelt took over, had to start almost from scratch, except for a few projects government departments had worked out on their own. In addition, PWA's effort to stimulate local projects often had to await legal action, such as the change of statutes to permit a city to borrow or the voting of bond issues to provide local funds. There was often delay in clearing title to land, in advertising for bids and letting contracts, and in ironing out the details of procedure. As a consequence, nearly all of the $900 million of contracts awarded by the beginning of 1934 (of which about $110 million was actually expended) went for ready-to-go federal projects like naval construction.

Nor can it be said that Roosevelt brought any driving sense of urgency to PWA. According to Ickes's recollection, the President minimized complaints about tardiness, even saying, "I do not want you to move faster." Explaining that recovery might come more swiftly than anticipated, Roosevelt observed that a "more deliberate carrying out of the Public Works program would mean money saved to the Treasury." And very likely Roosevelt, grateful to be spared any Teapot Domes, did say to the cabinet late in 1934, "When Harold took hold of Public Works, he had to start cold. He had no program and he had no organization. It was necessary to develop both. A lot of people thought that all he would have to do would be to shovel money out of the window. There have been a good many complaints about the slowness of the Public Works program and Harold's caution. I never expected it to be any faster than it has been and we can stand criticism of caution. There hasn't been even a minor scandal in Public Works, and that is some record." [4]

v

And, in time, there were other things to boast of. PWA may have missed out somewhat in its economic function because of its slowness to get under way; but, perhaps in part for this very reason, it scored superbly on its social function. It built roads and highways, sewage systems and water systems, gas plants and electric power plants; schools and courthouses, hospitals and jails; dams and canals, reclamation and irrigation projects, levees and flood control projects, bridges and viaducts, docks and tunnels. It started to rebuild the Navy — the aircraft carriers *Yorktown* and *Enterprise* were PWA projects, in addition to four cruisers, four heavy destroyers, and many light destroyers, submarines, planes, engines, and naval instruments. It helped the Army modernize and mechanize, built more than fifty military airports, gave planes to the Air Corps and improved thirty-two Army posts. (PWA's direct contributions to defense came to an end, however, in 1935, when Congress on the demand of Senator Borah expressly forbade the use of appropriations "for munitions, warships, or military or naval material.")

After considerable argument, Ickes persuaded the Pennsylvania Railroad to borrow more than $80 million to complete the electrification of its line between New York and Washington and to finish the 30th Street Station in Philadelphia — one of the luckiest investments the railroad ever made. PWA made it possible, despite bitter internecine warfare between Ickes and Robert Moses, to put up the Triborough Bridge in New York. PWA created the port of Brownsville in Texas. PWA gave Chicago (on the loan-grant arrangement) a new sewage system, Kansas City a great municipal auditorium, Denver a water supply system, the University of Washington a set of buildings, the Muskingum Valley of Ohio a flood control project. It rebuilt the schools of Los Angeles after the earthquake of 1933, and it built roads and bridges connecting Key West with the mainland in Florida. It helped build the Tennessee Valley Authority, the Grand Coulee and Bonneville Dams on the Columbia, Fort Peck Dam on the Upper Missouri, and Boulder Dam on the Colorado.

Between 1933 and 1939, PWA helped in the construction of about 70 per cent of the nation's new educational buildings; 65 per cent of the courthouses and city halls and the sewage disposal plants; 35 per cent of the hospitals and public health facilities; and 10 per cent of all the roads, bridges, subways, and similar engineering structures. It spent about $6 billion, created about a billion and three-quarters man-hours of labor on the site of construction, and generated another three billion man-hours of employment in the production of materials, fabrication, and transportation. No one ever convincingly accused the PWA of boondoggling or of fraud. It was a prodigious accomplishment; and it left behind, as Ickes so passionately wished, a splendidly improved national estate.[5]

VI

Harry Hopkins liked spending money and considered it essential to recovery. Harold Ickes was willing to spend money, so long as he was certain that the nation received full value in return. But some members of the administration abhorred the whole idea of spending. Of these, the most influential in 1933 was Lewis Douglas, the Director of the Budget.

The events of 1933 had not altered Douglas's fervent conviction that government retrenchment and a balanced budget were necessary not only for recovery but for human freedom itself. If circumstances forced him to acquiesce in the National Industrial Recovery Act, including its public works provisions, he soon grew to detest the NRA. If he reluctantly acknowledged the necessity for relief, again doctrine required that this should be in its cheapest form — direct relief. As for PWA, he was sure that public works spending would retard recovery far more by unbalancing the budget than it could promote recovery by stimulating the economy.

Douglas's arguments were conventional and doctrinaire; but their apparent clarity, reinforced by the considerable charm of his personality, had for a moment impact on the President. As 1933 wore on, however, Douglas saw that he was losing his influence. Events seemed to be sweeping the New Deal into an inflationary tide. The new monetary policy deeply upset Douglas. So too did the unfolding public works effort. Ever more insistently Douglas sought, as he conceived it, to bring Roosevelt back to his senses. For the Budget Director, Roosevelt's senses were defined by the Pittsburgh speech in the 1932 campaign. To others, Douglas's tone toward the President appeared increasingly hectoring. Once in Morgenthau's presence, Douglas sharply rebuked Roosevelt for not having carried out the Pittsburgh pledge. In response the President turned cold and cutting; it was one of the very few times Morgenthau ever saw Roosevelt angry. After hearing Douglas hold forth in cabinet on another occasion, Ickes noted in his diary, "In arguing with the President he went a little far both in the substance of what he said and the manner of its expression."

Yet Roosevelt's personal fondness for Douglas lingered. And believing that creative government was, in part, a debate, he also valued Douglas's role as a counterweight against the spenders. "Douglas' job," he explained to a press conference in December 1933, "is to prevent the Government from spending just as hard as he possibly can. That is his job. . . . Somewhere between his efforts to spend nothing . . . and the point of view of the people who want to spend ten billions additional on public works, we will get somewhere." But Douglas was not satisfied by the privilege of filing dissenting opinions. On December 30, 1933, he sent Roosevelt what he described as "this last plea" against further government spending except for direct relief. He reminded the President of the projected borrowing and refunding operations of the government over the next year. "I do not believe," Douglas said, "you can now under conditions existing as they are today, successfully borrow this amount of money. I do not believe the credit of the Government will stand the strain." It therefore followed, Douglas continued, that the government would plunge into paper inflation: this "I believe to be an inevitable consequence, quite irrespective of how much you may resist, of the expenditures which you have authorized for the fiscal year 1934."

Douglas recalled discussions with the President concerning the 1935 budget. "We cannot always have what we want," he told Roosevelt, perhaps a trifle sententiously: "we must deny ourselves in the interest of the general public welfare; and so, desirable as some of these things may appear to you, if the consequences of undertaking them means setting in motion the destructive forces of paper inflation, then, in the public interest, they should not be undertaken." Douglas therefore opposed giving the Reconstruction Finance Corporation authority to make loans to industry ("exclusive occupancy of the field of credit by the Federal Government is the last step toward complete state capitalism, and may develop into the medium by which we convert the economic system of this country into a communistic or fascistic one") ; he opposed public works; he opposed the Civilian Conservation Corps. "I wonder whether you thoroughly appreciate the implication of the steps which you have taken," Douglas concluded.

I see Government expenditures piled upon expenditures, so that paper inflation is inevitable, with a consequent destruction of the middle class. I see efforts to make the Government the exclusive occupant of the field of credit. I see inferences that the Government proposes and intends to plan for each individual economic activity. . . . The issue, then, it seems to me, is clearly drawn — either we will change our social order and deliberately abolish all private enterprise, replacing it with Government enterprise and employment, or we must maintain the credit of the Government so that confidence may be restored. . . . This can be accomplished only by a cessation of borrowing.

If Douglas's insistence began to irritate Roosevelt, so too did the Budget Director's new habit of submitting elaborate briefs in writing as if to build a dossier for his own future protection. "There is something I want to say here in the family in case I should die," the President remarked a few months later. "After I fired Dean Acheson as Under Secretary of the Treasury, Lew Douglas set out to make a written record. . . . If things go wrong he wants to be in position so he can show that on such and such a date he advised the President not to do thus and so." [6]

VII

Throughout this period Douglas persisted in trying to bring federal spending under the control of the Bureau of the Budget. Roosevelt, impressed perhaps more by his administrative than his substantive arguments, went along. Early in January 1934, the President issued an executive order requiring emergency agencies to obtain Budget Bureau approval before further funds could be obligated. Ickes, interpreting this order as giving Douglas veto power over emergency matters, rebelled; so did other cabinet members and agency chiefs; and in three days the order was revoked.

Yet Douglas did not give up the fight. He made it clear to PWA in January that he was determined not to allow more than $500 million for public works. Early in February he told a conference of state directors of the National Emergency Council, "The time is approaching, if it has not already arrived, when the United States Government proposes to gradually remove itself from the field of emergency expenditures." In the spring he was recommending to the President that specific PWA projects be canceled. But he was steadily losing ground. In early summer he went on a prolonged holiday. By August, Roosevelt could remark irritably to Morgenthau that Douglas had been "entirely wrong in what he has been telling me the last year."

A few days later, at the end of August, Douglas conferred with Roosevelt at Hyde Park. The next day Roosevelt summoned Morgenthau over from Hopewell Junction. The Secretary of the Treasury found the President taking a bath. When Morgenthau entered, the President sat up straight in the tub, looked his visitor fiercely in the eye and said, with emphasis, "Henry, in the words of John Paul Jones, we have just begun to fight." Douglas, it appeared, had resigned. The President had appealed to him, first as a patriot, then as a Democrat, to stay on until December (i.e., until after the congressional elections), but Douglas had righteously refused. Roosevelt then told Douglas that ten years from now he would be sorry for what he had done. To Morgenthau, the President seemed upset and hurt.

What next? To Morgenthau's horror, Roosevelt asked him what he thought of Tom Corcoran as Douglas's successor. Morgenthau replied that this was out of the question: Corcoran was far too much of an operator. The Secretary, fearing more presidential bright ideas, quickly proposed as Acting Director Daniel W. Bell, a veteran civil servant who had entered the Treasury Department twenty-three years before as a stenographer and had risen to be Commissioner of Accounts and Deposits. Roosevelt welcomed the suggestion and wrote out in his own hand a press release drawn to emphasize Bell's appointment rather than Douglas's resignation, timed to be lost in the confusion of the Labor Day weekend. ("He took great delight," observed Morgenthau, "in thinking this out.")

For his part, Douglas played the game; and, though the *New York Times* commented editorially that he seemed not to have received the usual White House letter of gratitude, Douglas held his peace through the elections. Late in November, he made a final attempt to rouse the presidential conscience. "One more word," he wrote Roosevelt, "which may bring back, through the mist of the past, a recollection of the days when I was your resisting Director of the Budget. I hope, and hope most fervently, that you will evidence a real determination to bring the budget into actual balance, for upon this, I think, hangs not only your place in history but conceivably the immediate fate of western civilization.". . . It was not until the next spring that Lew Douglas in a series of lectures at Harvard began to denounce the "deadly parallel" between Franklin Roosevelt's fiscal policies and those of the Soviet Union.[7]

VIII

But getting rid of Douglas by no means got rid of the viewpoint for which Douglas stood. For most in the administration, the balanced budget remained sacred, and inflation continued the overhanging threat. Those who felt it necessary to spend did so, on the whole, guiltily, against the grain of accepted economic doctrine. Moreover, the internal momentum of the Bureau of the Budget would lead any conscientious Director to seek control over government spending; and Daniel W. Bell was a conscientious Director. And, Henry Morgenthau, whose man Bell to some degree remained, had already exhibited deep concern of his own over the spending policies.

Two weeks before Douglas departed, Morgenthau showed Roosevelt a speech draft which said, among other things, that the administration was looking forward in the near future to a balanced budget. (Roosevelt commented unhappily, "I just don't see how you can make a statement like that because of course we are not going to be able to balance our budget in 1936.") Now, with the Budget Bureau under his control, Morgenthau felt he had a better chance to achieve his cherished objective. For the next three years, indeed, this was his ruling purpose. Yet the purpose was always deflected by his own instinctive compassion when confronted by human misery. Years later Hopkins wrote Morgenthau, "Many times when the days seemed pretty dark you were the one who helped influence a favorable decision on behalf of the millions who were out of work. I want particularly to say this to you because during those early years many people said publicly and privately that you were opposed to relief. . . . I presume people will never know what a great friend you have been to those who have little in life."

And there was more than enough in the relief situation in the summer and fall of 1934 to compel Morgenthau's sympathy. In mid-1934, about one out of every seven Americans — over 18 million people — were still receiving relief; and the total would rise again to 20 million by winter. Nearly 7 million children under 16 were on the rolls. In 39 states more than a tenth of the population, in 9 states more than a fifth, and in one state — South Dakota, seared by drought — more than a third were kept alive by public funds. Relief payments, though larger than in 1933, were still pathetic. In May 1934, the average monthly grant *per family* was $24.53 — an increase of $9 in a year, but still far from adequate. (In Kentucky the figure was $6.78 — which meant that Kentucky families with a monthly income of more than $6 could not qualify for relief.) There was no indication that the improvement in national income was immediately lessening the burden, partly because the increase in productivity meant that fewer workers were required than in 1929 to produce the same amount of goods, partly because the attrition of five depression years had brought more and more people to the point where relief was the only recourse. "Industry is not absorbing the unemployed," said an FERA report, "as rapidly as the number of those whose resources are exhausted is increasing."

It was imperative to continue federal relief. But it was also imperative, Morgenthau thought, to bring coherence into the spending programs — in particular to provide a single point of review for all relief and public works spending. A week after Douglas's resignation, Morgenthau and Bell, in a budget conference with the President at Hyde Park, proposed restoring in some form the executive order of the previous January which had given Douglas (for seventy-two hours) control over spending by the emergency agencies. Roosevelt resisted this but accepted a subsequent Morgenthau suggestion for a conference with Hopkins and Ickes to discuss the coordination of spending programs. At the first meeting of this group, on October 1, 1934, the President summed up his general view: that federal direct relief should come to an end on a specified date; that all direct relief thereafter would be the pauper relief supplied by local government; and that Washington should concentrate on giving every employable worker a job through a massive public works effort, costing perhaps $5 billion the first year and less in succeeding years. Such a program would serve both economic and social ends: it would prime the pump of recovery and tide the unemployed over until they could be absorbed in private employment.

Hopkins and Ickes both favored this policy, though to one "public works" doubtless meant an emphasis on light projects of the Civil Works Administration type, while to the other it meant heavy investment in the manner of PWA. But they agreed enough for Ickes to support a Hopkins memorandum outlining a national work and relief program. Roosevelt rejected the memorandum as excessively vague, and Morgenthau announced that the whole program left him cold. (Roosevelt observed, "You sound like Leffingwell [of Morgan's]." To which Morgenthau replied, "I wish I had half his brains.") A third meeting produced a more detailed memorandum, concentrating on the transfer of employables from relief rolls to public works jobs in housing, slum clearance, highways, railroads, water development, and rural electrification. Morgenthau again criticized the program as vague and said he could make no estimate about financing until he saw the engineering reports. And, despite Roosevelt's attempts to shush him up, he kept talking about the need for a centralized works organization. "I absolutely agree with you," the President explained the next morning, "but I did not want Ickes and Hopkins fighting over this at this time." [8]

IX

Russell Leffingwell was only one of a great number of businessmen urging on Roosevelt the sharp reduction of federal expenditures. There were pressures on the other side too. Thus Bernard Baruch wrote him on October 11, 1934: "Taking care of the needy is the first consideration and until that is done, we cannot move towards the balanced budget." Even more, the unemployed themselves, confronting the fifth depression winter, were increasing their agitation for larger benefits. The Unemployed Councils, controlled by the Communist party, persuaded Ernest Lundeen, a left-wing Farmer-Labor congressman from Minnesota, to introduce a bill providing unemployment benefits at prevailing wages for all workers, to be administered by commissions composed of rank-and-file members of workers' and farmers' organizations. (Benjamin Gitlow, by no means a reliable source but still a top Communist who had been his party's candidate for Vice-President, later said that Lundeen was a paid undercover Communist agent who often came to Communist headquarters to get his directives from the party's general secretary. Israel Amter, a Communist, told a congressional committee at the time that "the original writer of the workers' [Lundeen] bill was the Communist Party.") For a moment, the Lundeen bill became the focus of radical demands.

Roosevelt felt as keenly as anyone the defects of the existing system. Early in November he reported to his press conference that, according to Jim Townsend, the Democratic chairman of Dutchess County, 15 to 20 per cent of the relief workers were chiselers. "There is a general feeling," Townsend had told the President, ". . . that the people who are in charge of them almost give the order, 'Do not exert yourselves. Do not push yourselves. Spread it out as long as you can.'" "If that is true in Dutchess County," said the President, "it is true in every state of the Union." To reorganize the program, Roosevelt contemplated a twofold reform — the elimination of the 15 or 20 per cent of unemployables who ought not to be on federal relief, and the shift of the rest to genuinely useful work. "What I am seeking," he explained a few days later, "is the abolition of [federal] relief altogether. I cannot say out loud yet but I hope to be able to substitute work. . . . There will, of course, be a certain number of relief cases where work will not furnish the answer but it is my thought that in these cases all of the relief expenditures should once more be borne by the States and localities as they used to be."

By November 1934, the broad design was thus set for the next phase of federal relief. What remained were a series of troubling decisions over the actual composition of the works program.[9]

18. The Birth of Social Security

AT BEST, WORK relief was an emergency effort, designed only for those who could not find employment. It had little to offer to men and women who still had jobs but worried nonetheless about their homes, their futures, and their old age. It could be only a part of the New Deal's total attack on economic and social insecurity.

During the Hundred Days, Roosevelt had taken one notable step to assure a larger measure of general security. Few things were more demoralizing to the middle class in 1933 than the threatened loss of homes through mortgage foreclosure. In 1932, over 250,000 families lost their homes; in early 1933, foreclosures were taking place at a rate of more than a thousand a day. The mounting foreclosure rate weakened the position of savings banks and insurance companies. By mid-1933, homeowners were finding it increasingly difficult to negotiate new mortgages or even to renew old ones. The real estate market and the construction industry alike seemed to be headed toward collapse.

Hoover's Federal Home Loan Bank Act of 1932, designed to encourage banks to make loans to mortgagors, had little effect. In April 1933, Roosevelt consequently asked Congress for new legislation to protect small homeowners from foreclosure. The proposed legislation, modeled on the farm mortgage bill, called for government refinancing of mortgages for distressed small owners who had lost their homes as far back as 1930 or could not obtain present financing through normal channels. The Home Owners' Loan Corporation, which went into action in the summer of 1933, bought mortgages from holders who could carry them no longer, financed the immediate payments for taxes and repairs, and rewrote the mortgages to provide for easy repayment over a long term and at relatively low interest rates. The ceiling for an HOLC loan was $14,000.

According to careful estimates, the owners of about one-fifth of the nation's non-farm dwellings sought HOLC loans. Of these requests, more than a half were granted. In the end, one out of every five mortgaged urban homes in the country was an HOLC beneficiary; HOLC actually held about one-sixth the total urban home mortgage debt. Its lending operations involved HOLC in difficult problems of appraisal, loan criteria, loan servicing, and even, in time, foreclosures of its own. After an uncertain start, John H. Fahey, a newspaper publisher, took over the direction of HOLC; and it began to discharge its complex responsibilities with efficiency and economy.

In a short time, HOLC averted the threatened collapse of the real estate market and enabled financial institutions to begin to return to the mortgage-lending business. Its example simplified and liberalized methods of real estate financing everywhere in the nation. Most important of all, by enabling thousands of Americans to save their homes, it strengthened their stake both in the existing order and in the New Deal. Probably no single measure consolidated so much middle-class support for the administration.[1]

II

HOLC, by restoring the morale of a vital section of the middle class, contributed to the attack on insecurity. Still, this represented only a marginal gain. The fight for a general security program had to be conducted on a broader front. And in this fight the central figure was the Secretary of Labor, Frances Perkins.

Miss Perkins was fifty years old when she came to Washington in 1933. She was born in Boston, reared in Worcester, and educated at Mount Holyoke. A lively young lady with opinions of her own, she found herself bored after college by the staid society of Worcester and abandoned it for the slums of Chicago. Here she lived with Jane Addams at Hull-House and was initiated into the inner circle of the powerful social work apparatus; then transferred to Philadelphia, where she studied economics with Simon Patten ("one of the greatest men America has ever produced") ; then, in 1910, became executive secretary of the Consumers' League in New York and active in its lobbying activities in Albany.

Two people beside Patten particularly influenced her. One was Florence Kelley, the Joan of Arc of the Consumers' League; the other was Big Tim Sullivan of Tammany. From the one, she caught a crusading passion; from the other, she learned that even professional politicians had hearts and could be enlisted in good causes. Operating in the area where social work and politics intersected, a friend not only of the "dedicated old maids" but of the Bob Wagners and Al Smiths, she became an enormously effective woman in New York in the next two decades — director of investigations of the State Factory Commission, chairman of the State Industrial Board, Franklin D. Roosevelt's Industrial Commissioner.

Brisk and articulate, with vivid dark eyes, a broad forehead and a pointed chin, usually wearing a felt tricorn hat, she remained a Brahmin reformer, proud of her New England background (phrases like "New England common sense" and "Yankee thrift" studded her conversation) and intent on beating sense into the heads of those foolish people who resisted progress. She had pungency of character, a dry wit, an inner gaiety, an instinct for practicality, a profound vein of religious feeling, and a compulsion to instruct — the last of which sometimes led her to lecture her colleagues in her patrician Boston accent at what they considered wearying and sometimes intolerable length. In 1913, she married Paul C. Wilson, a New York statistician who was then secretary to John Purroy Mitchel, the reform candidate for Mayor. She had one daughter; but she fiercely guarded her privacy and fought off press intrusions. "We New Englanders like to keep ourselves to ourselves."

III

Frances Perkins had a keen sense of responsibility about being the first woman member of the cabinet. She had been incongruously given that most masculine of departments, the Department of Labor, redolent of big men with cigars in their mouths and feet on the desk; but she took over with her usual quick competence. The Department seemed to her to have gone to pieces: the offices were dirty, files and papers were missing, there was no program of work, there was an internal spy system, and everyone tried to get into her good graces by telling tales about the others. When the retiring Secretary, William Nuckles Doak, introduced her to the bureau chiefs, seven of them, as she told the story later, said, "I am in charge of immigration"; and the one who didn't say it bore the title of Commissioner of Immigration. On her first day, she sent for a dustcloth and personally cleaned her desk and chair, removing all traces of her dubious predecessor. When Emil Ludwig visited the new Department of Labor some years later, he said he could tell instantly from the wooden wainscoting and green leather furniture that it was managed by a woman.

When subordinates asked her how she should be addressed, she replied, "Call me Madam Secretary." The press inquired how she felt as a woman in the cabinet. "I feel odd. That's a New England word, like Calvin Coolidge's 'choose.' Mr. Coolidge would have known what I mean by 'odd.' " Someone persisted: Was being a woman a handicap? "Only in climbing trees," she crisply replied. In cabinet, she won the respect of her colleagues, impressing conservatives like Hugh Johnson and Jesse Jones ("I liked her very much") rather more than she did liberals like Ickes and Morgenthau, who thought she was too officious and talked too much. From the beginning, she was treated as an equal. Once Secretary of the Navy Swanson wondered whether he should tell a story because there was a lady present. "Go on, Claude," said Roosevelt, "she's dying to hear it."

Before accepting appointment, she laid before Roosevelt an extensive agenda, including unemployment and old-age insurance, minimum wages and maximum hours; and he told her to go ahead. For Miss Perkins, this opportunity was the culmination of a lifetime's hope and labor. Her background as a social worker inclined her, on the whole, to be more interested in doing things for labor than enabling labor to do things for itself; and her emphasis as Secretary was rather on the improvement of standards of work and welfare than on the development of labor self-organization. But this was in part a result too of the long indifference of the labor movement to improving its position through legislative action. The middle class had always had to fight labor's legislative battles for it. In any case, for Madam Secretary the overriding objective, once emergency problems of hunger and want had been met, was to construct a permanent system of personal security through social insurance.[2]

IV

"We advocate," the Democratic platform of 1932 had remarked, "unemployment and old-age insurance under State laws." This declaration, with all its limitations, recognized the rising interest in both forms of public insurance — an interest visible for more than a generation in Europe and detectable for at least a decade in America. It recognized probably too the rising influence of Franklin Roosevelt, the single national political leader to identify himself with the social insurance cause.

Of these two forms of social insurance, unemployment compensation, though it had a shorter history in the United States, had become in 1933 the more urgent issue. From the onset of the depression it had been earnestly discussed among economists and social workers and within the American Association for Labor Legislation. The discussion largely turned on the merits of the only existing unemployment compensation plan in the United States — the one adopted by Wisconsin in 1932 under the prodding of Governor Philip F. La Follette. This scheme, originally worked out by Professor John R. Commons in 1921 and revised a decade later by Harold R. Groves and Paul A. Raushenbush, required each corporation to build up its own unemployment reserves in order to take care of its own employees. Involved in this was the notion of "experience rating" or "merit rating," under which the size of the employer's contribution was determined by his own success in maintaining employment; thus companies with the most unemployment had to pay the highest rates. This combination of employer-financed company reserve funds with experience rating, it was argued in Wisconsin, was the pattern most likely to encourage business to do its best to stabilize employment.

Its adherents billed the Wisconsin plan as the "American plan" and took great care to distinguish it from the British system of compulsory unemployment insurance. But there was also sentiment in America for a scheme based more directly on the insurance principle. In 1932 the Ohio Commission on Unemployment Insurance came up with a proposal which differed from the Wisconsin plan in two important particulars. Instead of a system of separate reserves held by individual concerns, the Ohio plan proposed that contributions be pooled in a single fund; and it called for contributions from both employers and workers instead of from employers alone. The Ohio plan differed from the British plan, however, in not envisaging government contributions.

Some American experts felt that even the Ohio plan was inadequate. Of these the most influential was Abraham Epstein, who was executive secretary of the American Association for Old Age Security, and a fluent and powerful writer in the social security field. Epstein not only favored pooled funds as against individual employer accounts but also could see no escape from government participation on the British model. In this, he was joined by other experts, notably Professor Paul Douglas of the University of Chicago. For Epstein and Douglas, the Wisconsin plan was particularly defective in its assumption that an individual firm could sufficiently control economic conditions as to deserve reward or punishment for its employment record; it seemed evident by 1933 that mass unemployment was the result of conditions beyond the control of a single firm or a single industry.

Yet the Wisconsin plan, despite its critics, enjoyed the advantage of being in operation. Moreover, it had devoted and eloquent apostles, especially Paul A. Raushenbush and his wife Elizabeth, the daughter of Mr. Justice Brandeis. In the fall of 1933 the Raushenbushes met in Washington (the meeting was in the Brandeis apartment; the Justice was absent) with a group of liberal businessmen, like Henry Dennison and Edward A. Filene, and young New Dealers, among them Charles E. Wyzanski, Jr., and Thomas H. Eliot of the Labor Department, and Thomas G. Corcoran. The Raushenbush mission was to persuade the administration to induce other states to adopt unemployment compensation acts along the line of the Wisconsin law. To achieve this, Raushenbush submitted an ingenious plan invented by Brandeis — a payroll tax on employers with the provision that in states where unemployment compensation laws had been passed employers' contributions for that purpose could be deducted from the federal tax. Under this approach, states could have unemployment insurance systems without new costs to handicap employers in interstate competition. The proposal set certain minimum standards but in the main left ample room for local experimentation in the Brandeis tradition. Frances Perkins showed a lively interest in the idea; and Eliot and Raushenbush soon drew up a bill which Senator Wagner and Representative David J. Lewis of Maryland introduced into Congress, in February 1934.[3]

V

In the meantime, corresponding progress was being made toward provision for the aged. Here there was a longer tradition of national concern. The Progressive platform of 1912 had called for old-age pensions, and in the years following a number of states investigated the possibility of pension laws. In the twenties, eight states passed optional laws, and with the depression there was a great swing to mandatory legislation. In 1933 alone, ten states passed mandatory acts. Yet in all these laws payments were based on need; coverage varied tremendously; and nearly half the states had no laws at all. To Epstein and his Association for Old Age Security, as well as to many others, there seemed a pressing need for federal action.

Epstein's proposal was that the government offer states grants-in-aid equal to a third of the sum spent for pensions. Senator Clarence C. Dill of Washington and Representative William P. Connery, Jr., of Massachusetts introduced a bill to this effect in 1932; and by 1934 the House had passed the bill and the Senate Pensions Committee had given it a favorable report.

By the spring of 1934, then, both the Wagner-Lewis and the Dill-Connery bills had developed momentum. It was clear that if the administration did not take action soon its hand would be forced. Roosevelt, indeed, had endorsed the Wagner-Lewis bill in March. But, though committed to the principle of both bills, he was not yet convinced on details; and he was strongly pressed, especially by Tugwell, who disliked the Wagner-Lewis approach, to allow time for further study. Moreover, the President was beginning to believe that the social security program should be striven for not piecemeal but as a single package. In this way, he evidently believed, the program would have its maximum political effect — enough both to overcome the opposition of the right to the whole idea of social insurance and to drown out the growing clamor on the left for larger benefits than the country presumably could bear.

On June 8, 1934, therefore, he sent a message to Congress, vigorously reaffirming his faith in social insurance ("among our objectives I place the security of the men, women and children of the Nation first") but suggesting that legislation be deferred until the next winter. At the same time, he laid down what he regarded as the principles of a sound program: it should be a state-federal program, actuarially sound, and financed by contribution rather than by an increase in general taxation. Three weeks later he appointed a cabinet Committee on Economic Security, with Frances Perkins as chairman, charged with formulating a program to be submitted to the President before December.[4]

VI

From Frances Perkins's point of view, the Committee's job was to consider the whole field of economic security. Unemployment compensation might be the most important issue; but the Committee, in addition, had to review problems of old-age assistance and insurance; health insurance; workmen's compensation; and specialized types of public assistance for certain groups now on relief rolls, especially the aged, the blind, and dependent children. "As I see it," she observed in 1934, "we shall have to establish in this country substantially all of the social-insurance measures which the western European countries have set up in the last generation." (But, she warned, social insurance by itself could not "promise anything like complete economic security. More important than all social-insurance devices together is employment.")

Though the Committee accepted the full mandate, it devoted more time to the problems of unemployment compensation than to anything else. The executive director of the Committee's staff was Professor Edwin E. Witte of the University of Wisconsin, and the chairman of the Technical Board on Economic Security was Arthur

J. Altmeyer of Wisconsin. Both Witte and Altmeyer had been involved in the Wisconsin plan and had therefore a natural inclination toward its basic principles. This, of course, corresponded with Roosevelt's belief in state experimentation in this field. In a meeting late in August with Miss Perkins, Witte, and Altmeyer, the President made clear his preference for state administration of unemployment insurance.

On the other hand, many experts — and at the start a majority of both the Technical Board and the staff — favored a national system. Under such a system, the federal government would impose the tax, set up the administering agency, and distribute the benefits. A national system, its advocates contended, alone would insure uniformity of standards throughout the country with regard both to contributions and to benefits; it would meet the needs of a national economy, where workers, for example, often tended to move from state to state; and it would mean more efficient and economical administration than a miscellany of state systems. But the Wisconsin group was deeply opposed to the national system. Their essential argument against it was the Brandeis argument — the importance of encouraging local experimentation, especially when so many basic questions remained to be worked out. Experts, as Frances Perkins pointed out, were divided among themselves over such questions as pooling versus separate accounts and whether or not there should be employee contributions. "This bill," she said, "allows these different problems to be solved by the different States according to their own particular genius and to be administered locally by those States in the best interests of all of the people."

There were two variations of the state approach. One — the so-called "subsidy" plan — would have the government impose the tax and then provide subsidies equal to a stated percentage of the tax to states whose unemployment compensation laws met specified federal standards. The other employed the tax-offset method used in the original Wagner-Lewis bill, under which the states would collect their unemployment compensation funds directly. Of the two, therefore, the subsidy plan lent itself to the establishment of a greater degree of national control. The Wisconsin group consequently favored the Wagner-Lewis approach in the belief that this would best protect their own experiment. And they were able by invoking the constitutional issue to rally to their side some who, on the merits, might have favored the national or subsidy plan. For, if the Supreme Court struck down the national plan, there would be nothing left, and, if it struck down the subsidy plan, state laws would remain, but these laws, lacking means of raising revenue, would be inoperative; whereas if it struck down the federal features of the Wagner-Lewis plan, operating state laws would survive.

The argument swayed back and forth through the summer and fall. An Advisory Council on Economic Security, headed by Dr. Frank Graham of North Carolina, voted 9 to 7 for the subsidy plan, though several members of this majority really favored a thoroughgoing national plan. The Technical Board, under the Wisconsin influence, came out for the Wagner-Lewis plan. A National Conference on Economic Security, convened in Washington in November 1934, contained much nationalist sentiment, though the President, when he addressed it, advocated a state system. Observers noted that the Committee staff seemed to be steering clear of unemployment insurance experts, like Epstein, Paul Douglas, I. M. Rubinow, and Eveline M. Burns, known for their advocacy of the national system.

Within the Committee itself, Wallace, spurred on by Tugwell, kept up the fight for a national approach. Still, the preference of the President for a state system, the anticipated resistance in Congress to a national approach, the presumed constitutional vulnerability of such an approach — these considerations influenced a group under strong pressure to achieve a unanimous recommendation. On November 9 the Committee decided to abandon thought of an exclusively federal system. Yet this did not settle matters; a few weeks later it about agreed to recommend such a system after all. Finally, in Christmas week, confronting a presidential deadline, it voted unanimously, but, said Miss Perkins, "reluctantly and with mental reservations," in favor of the Wagner-Lewis approach.[5]

VII

When the Committee on Economic Security came to the question of the aged, it adopted a national system of contributory old-age and survivors insurance without anxiety or fuss. In so doing, it took a venturesome step which contrasted strikingly with the caution shown in the case of unemployment compensation — and in spite of the fact that much more thought had been given to a national system for the unemployed than for the aged. One reason why the Committee could be more audacious here was the absence of state old-age insurance projects; there was no Wisconsin plan to create vested intellectual interests. Another was the fierce outside agitation for old-age pensions; though the Committee on Economic Security had started work before Dr. Townsend's plan for $200 a month for everyone over sixty had developed momentum, yet the mounting Townsendite clamor in late 1934 and early 1935 certainly improved the opportunity for inserting sweeping old-age insurance recommendations in the social security bill. Another — and perhaps decisive — reason was the conviction of the actuaries that old-age insurance on a state basis would be infeasible because of the great mobility of workers in the course of a lifetime.

In addition to the old-age insurance system, the Committee called for a program of assistance to the states for the needy aged. This recommendation was based on the provisions of the Dill-Connery bill of 1934. Parallel recommendations were made for federal aid to the states for the blind and for dependent children; and federal grants were proposed for maternal and child-health aid, and for child welfare and public-health services. On health insurance, the Committee made no recommendations for immediate legislation. For a moment in 1934 there had been a flurry of optimism on this point: Harry Hopkins had declared himself convinced that "with one bold stroke we could carry the American people with us, not only for unemployment insurance but for sickness and health insurance." But the usual pressure from the American Medical Association succeeded in killing staff proposals in the medical field.[6]

VIII

There remained the problem of coordinating the long-term proposals with the emergency relief program. When it became apparent that unemployment compensation would be on a state basis, Hopkins and Tugwell lost interest in it and argued instead that the main emphasis should be on the provision of jobs through public works. Thus in the fall and winter of 1934, while Frances Perkins's Committee was work-

ing out the social security program, Hopkins and Ickes were developing their plans for work relief. For a time both Miss Perkins and
Hopkins seemed to feel that these proposals were in competition;
but Roosevelt saw them as complementary. If the federal government was to get out of the business of relief, then the works program
would take care of the employables after their unemployment compensation had run out, while the social security program would help
take care of the unemployables.

On January 15, 1935, the Committee on Economic Security trans-
mitted its reports to the President. Roosevelt already had his own
views on social security. "There is no reason why everybody in the
United States should not be covered," he once said to Miss Perkins.
"I see no reason why every child, from the day he is born, shouldn't
be a member of the social security system. . . . I don't see why not,"
he continued as Miss Perkins, appalled by the administrative problems of universal coverage, shook her head. "I don't see why not.
Cradle to the grave — from the cradle to the grave they ought to be
in a social insurance system."

He had in addition specific views about the character of a social
insurance program. Thus he believed that public insurance should
be built upon the same principles as private insurance. "If I have
anything to say about it," he once remarked, "it will always be contributed, and I prefer it to be contributed, both on the part of the
employer and the employee, on a sound actuarial basis. It means no
money out of the Treasury." This meant a self-supporting system,
financed by contributions and special taxes rather than out of the
general tax revenue. Frances Perkins, arguing against employee contributions, pointed out that the employer shifted the payroll tax to
the consumer in any case, so that employees were already paying their
share; Tugwell, arguing against the payroll tax, pointed out that
this amounted to a form of sales tax and meant that the system
would be financed by those who could least afford it; but none of this
argument availed. "I guess you're right on the economics," Roosevelt explained to another complainant some years later, "but those
taxes were never a problem of economics. They are politics all the
way through. We put those payroll contributions there so as to give
the contributors a legal, moral, and political right to collect their
pensions and their unemployment benefits. With those taxes in

there, no damn politician can ever scrap my social security program."[7]

IX

On January 17, 1935, Roosevelt sent a message to Congress requesting social security legislation. On the same day Wagner introduced the draft bill in the Senate and Lewis, jointly with Congressman Robert L. Doughton of North Carolina, introduced it in the House. A few days later hearings began in both Senate and House. Early in February, the administration made an important change of front when Secretary Morgenthau, testifying before the House Ways and Means Committee, advocated a new financing plan for the old-age insurance system.

The Committee on Economic Security, confronting the problem of the aged, proposed a compulsory system of contributory payments by which workers could build up gradually their rights to annuities in their old age. This left the problem of persons on the verge of retirement who had had no past opportunity to contribute to their own old-age pensions. The best way in which these aging workers could be taken care of, the Committee concluded, was through the federal government's paying a share of the cost. By 1980, according to its estimate, the government would have to contribute to the old-age system around $1.4 billion a year. The Committee conceded that the creation of this commitment would impose a burden on future generations. But the alternative would be to increase reserves at a far higher rate and thus impose a double burden on the present generation, which would have to contribute not only to its own annuities but to the unearned annuities of people middle-aged or over. "The plan we advocate," said the Committee, "amounts to having each generation pay for the support of the people then living who are old."

Morgenthau had accepted the Committee plan and signed the report. Yet as he meditated the financing scheme, he began to feel a certain immorality, as he told the Ways and Means Committee, in the notion of "borrowing from the future to pay the costs." Roosevelt shared Morgenthau's disapproval. "It is almost dishonest," he told Frances Perkins, "to build up an accumulated deficit for the

Congress of the United States to meet in 1980. We can't do that. We can't sell the United States short in 1980 any more than in 1935."

The Treasury alternative was to raise the rates of contribution and thereby build a much larger reserve fund, so that future needs could be met from the fund rather than by levies on current general revenue. This fund, Morgenthau suggested, could be applied to the reduction of the national debt. Roosevelt even supposed that it might eventually serve as the sole customer for federal bonds, thus freeing the government from reliance on private bankers. Under the original plan, the maximum size of the reserve fund would have been less than $12 billion; under the Treasury plan, it would amount to $50 billion by 1980. The Treasury plan had obvious disadvantages. It shifted the burden of providing for currently aging workers from the population as a whole to the younger wage-earners. "Our programs," said Abraham Epstein, "actually relieve the wealthy from their traditional obligation under the ancient poor laws." Moreover, the creation of so large a fund involved economic risks. As Alvin Hansen on the Technical Board and Marion Folsom of the Eastman Kodak Company on the Advisory Council pointed out, it would divert a large amount of money from consumer purchasing power; "that is bound," Folsom said, "to have a depressing effect on general conditions." And the problem of finding ways to invest $50 billion seemed packed with difficulties.

The self-sustaining theory of social insurance meant in effect that the poor had to pay most of the cost of keeping the poor. Yet, whether because of this or in spite of this, the House Committee quickly adopted the reserve system; probably the idea that private insurance should serve as the model was too compelling. Moreover, there was the political advantage which so impressed Roosevelt. Under the original plan, the old-age insurance system would be at the mercy of each succeeding Congress; while, with a vast reserve fund built up out of contributions, the people were in a sense creating a clear and present equity in their own retirement benefits. The existence of the reserve thus undoubtedly strengthened the system politically. Yet the impact of the reserve on the business cycle — the withdrawal of large sums of money from the spending stream and the reliance on regressive taxation — doubtless added deflationary tendencies which later in the decade weakened the whole nation economically. In time, it appeared that the administration and the Congress had made the wrong decision in 1935.[8]

X

While the friends of social security were arguing out the details of the program, other Americans were regarding the whole idea with consternation, if not with horror. Organized business had long warned against such pernicious notions. "Unemployment insurance cannot be placed on a sound financial basis," said the National Industrial Conference Board; it will facilitate "ultimate socialistic control of life and industry," said the National Association of Manufacturers. "Industry," observed Alfred Sloan of General Motors, "has every reason to be alarmed at the social, economic and financial implications. . . . The dangers are manifest." It will undermine our national life "by destroying initiative, discouraging thrift, and stifling individual responsibility" (James L. Donnelly of the Illinois Manufacturers' Association); it begins a pattern which "sooner or later will bring about the inevitable abandonment of private capitalism" (Charles Denby, Jr., of the American Bar Association); "the downfall of Rome started with corn laws, and legislation of that type" (George P. Chandler of the Ohio Chamber of Commerce). With unemployment insurance no one would work; with old-age and survivors insurance no one would save; the result would be moral decay, financial bankruptcy and the collapse of the republic. One after another, business leaders appeared before House and Senate Committees to invest such dismal prophecies with what remained of their authority.

Republicans in the House faithfully reflected the business position. "Never in the history of the world," said Congressman John Taber of New York, "has any measure been brought in here so insidiously designed as to prevent business recovery, to enslave workers, and to prevent any possibility of the employers providing work for the people." "The lash of the dictator will be felt," cried Congressman Daniel Reed. "And twenty-five million free American citizens will for the first time submit themselves to a fingerprint test." Even a respectable Republican like James W. Wadsworth of New York could only see calamity ahead. "This bill opens the door and invites the entrance into the political field," he darkly exclaimed, "of a power so vast, so powerful as to threaten the integrity of our institutions and to pull the pillars of the temple down upon the heads of our descendants." On a crucial test, all Republicans in the House save one voted to recommit the bill to committee. But, in the end, the opposition collapsed; and, fearing reprisal at the polls, most Republicans, after resisting every step along the way, permitted themselves to be recorded in favor of catastrophe. On April 19, the House passed a somewhat revised bill by a vote of 371 to 33.

In the Senate conservatives continued a desultory resistance. Most of the debate in both Houses was over the old-age rather than the unemployment compensation provisions. Hastings of Delaware, who predicted that the bill might "end the progress of a great coun-try and bring its people to the level of the average European," offered a motion to strike out old-age insurance. Twelve of nineteen Republican senators supported this move. But again, on the final show-down, political prudence triumphed, and the bill passed on June 19, 1935, by a vote of 76 to 6. Difficulties still remained: the Senate had adopted an amendment to exempt employers with industrial pension plans from coverage under the government system. The administration opposed this both as bad in principle and impractical in operation; but argument over this issue delayed Senate-House agreement for seven more weeks until the Senate conferees yielded.

Perhaps out of dissatisfaction with the Labor Department's presentation of the bill, the House, in redrafting, had removed the Social Security Board from the Labor Department and set it up as a separate agency. The Senate restored the Board to Labor; but in conference it was decided to keep it independent. A Huey Long filibuster in August then prevented an appropriation bill for the new Board from coming up for passage. Roosevelt, after clearing with congressional leaders of both parties, decided to give the Social Security Board funds from NRA and WPA appropriations to tide it over till the next session of Congress.

For chairman, Roosevelt selected John Gilbert Winant, a former governor of New Hampshire. Winant, a tall, earnest, inarticulate man, whose high cheekbones, gaunt features, and unruly black hair gave him a Lincolnian appearance, was a Bull Mooser of 1912 who had kept the Progressive faith. As governor, he had fought for minimum-wage regulation, old-age assistance, and emergency relief; and he had made a strong impression as a member of the Advisory Council of the Committee for Economic Security. Roosevelt, who had known Winant as a fellow governor, liked and trusted him. The other two members of the Board were Arthur Altmeyer and an Arkansas lawyer named Vincent Myles.[9]

XI

The Social Security Act in its final form was far from a perfect piece of legislation. In important respects it was actually weaker than the Wagner-Lewis bill of the year before. It failed to set up a national system and even failed to provide for effective national standards. It left to the states virtually every important decision and thus committed the nation to a crazy quilt unemployment compensation system, with widely varying benefits distributed under diverging standards by forty-eight separate state agencies.

This result was not wholly to be ascribed to the Wisconsin philosophy. Congress itself was even more deeply opposed to federal standards. For example, the original bill required states to select administering personnel on a merit basis. Congress rejected this proposal and, in addition, specifically prohibited the Social Security Board from requiring states to establish proper personnel practices in connection with any of the titles of the act. Similarly, under the leadership of Byrd of Virginia, the Senate cut from the bill attempts to set minimum standards in old-age assistance.

And, though the merit-rating idea derived from the Brandeisian desire to intensify individual employer responsibility for the operation of the economy (even if it appeared in some form in each of the three plans considered by the Committee on Economic Security), it was Congress which gave the idea full scope. The Committee, debating whether the states should have a pooled fund or an individual employer accounts system, adopted a compromise suggestion of Altmeyer's that all employers be required to contribute at least 1 per cent on their payrolls to a pooled fund. Had Congress accepted this, it would have greatly limited merit rating, since the average rate of employers' contributions had never been higher than 1.5 per cent. But Congress turned it down. For all its attraction (and

Roosevelt himself, who inserted a sentence into Altmeyer's draft of his social security message strengthening the case for merit rating, was among those attracted), the effect of merit rating was to modify the whole unemployment compensation system, not only reducing rates but promoting the very kind of interstate competition which the federal law was designed to eliminate. As a result of merit rating, states with low standards and low tax rates tended to enjoy a competitive advantage over states with higher standards. Moreover, merit rating increasingly placed the burden of unemployment compensation on the industries least able to bear it; costs which might better have been socially distributed were instead assessed in a way which further weakened the already weak. And merit rating, by leading to the possibility of tax reductions in times of full employment and tax increases in times of unemployment, could aggravate rather than moderate the swings of the business cycle.

It is hard to escape the impression that the Committee on Economic Security, correctly anticipating hostility in Congress and the courts and perhaps unduly influenced by the Wisconsin experience, felt obliged to adopt the least good of the plans of unemployment compensation before it. Indeed, after watching the federal Act in operation, Arthur Altmeyer, himself a veteran of the Wisconsin experiment, came to the conclusion not only that merit rating was a mistake but that the subsidy plan was better than the tax-offset plan and that a straight federal system would be best of all.[10]

XII

In the next months the Social Security Board swung into action with quiet efficiency. Facing an administrative challenge of staggering complexity, it operated with steady intelligence and competence. No New Deal agency solved such bewildering problems with such self-effacing smoothness. The old-age insurance program went into quick effect; within two years all 48 states passed unemployment compensation laws in response to the federal tax-offset principle; and the programs of categorical assistance gave state governments new resources to deal with their needy citizens. No government bureau ever directly touched the lives of so many millions of Americans — the old, the jobless, the sick, the needy, the blind, the mothers, the children — with so little confusion or complaint. And the overhead costs for this far-flung and extraordinary operation were considerably less than those of private insurance. For this prodigious achievement, founded on millions of records, clerks, and business machines, major credit went to Altmeyer.

For all the defects of the Act, it still meant a tremendous break with the inhibitions of the past. The federal government was at last charged with the obligation to provide its citizens a measure of protection from the hazards and vicissitudes of life. One hundred and ten years earlier, John Quincy Adams had declared that "the great object of the institution of civil government" was "the progressive improvement of the condition of the governed." With the Social Security Act, the constitutional dedication of federal power to the general welfare began a new phase of national history.[11]

V

The Battle
for Public Development

19. Remaking the Tennessee Valley

PART OF THE NEW DEAL IMPULSE was defensive — the determination to protect the freedom and opportunity of Americans from the ravages of unemployment and despair. But part too was a desire to build a better America — a desire which existed long before the depression, even if the depression gave it new vigor and possibility. Much of the Hundred Days was a frenzied effort to keep the system from falling apart. One event, however, stood out as an earnest of the better America which dedicated men might create. This was the enactment on May 18, 1933, of the Tennessee Valley Authority Act.

Perhaps no law passed during the Hundred Days expressed more passionately a central presidential concern. The concern arose only in part from Roosevelt's old absorption with land, forests, and water. It arose equally from his continued search for a better design for national living. Utopia still presented itself to him in the cherished image of Hyde Park — tranquillity in the midst of rich meadows and farmlands, deep forests, and a splendid, flowing river. America, he felt, was overcommitted to urban living. In the twenties he had discussed the possibility of keeping people on the land by combining farming with part-time local industry. As Governor of New York, he had talked of redressing the population balance between city and countryside — taking industry from crowded urban centers to airy villages, and giving scrawny kids from the slums opportunity for sun and growth in the country. The depression and the Presidency provided new opportunity to move toward a "balanced civilization."

Roosevelt saw other reasons for seeking this better balance. Clarence Pickett of the Society of Friends, presently working for the Subsistence Homestead Division of the Department of the Interior, told the President on returning from Vienna in 1934 that the Socialists who dwelt on one-acre garden plots around the city had refused to join their urban comrades in resisting the violence of the Dollfuss regime. This stolidity, which Roosevelt oddly admired, came, the President thought, from the fact that they were landowners. His hope, he said, was to avert a proletarian psychology in America by giving factory workers a stake in the land and at the same time to avert a peasant psychology by giving subsistence farmers part-time jobs in factories. People might call the New Deal socialistic, he added, but the New Deal aim was simply to multiply the number of American shareholders. "Is this socialistic?" the President asked Anne O'Hare McCormick, crinkling his eyes and throwing back his head in a hearty laugh.[1]

II

The basin of the Tennessee River spilled over seven southern states — Tennessee, Alabama, Georgia, Mississippi, North Carolina, Kentucky, and Virginia. The streams began high up in the mountains — in the Great Smokies and in the Blue Ridge, in the Iron Mountains and in the Unakas — and flowed into the valleys below. Near Knoxville the Holston and the French Broad Rivers joined to form the Tennessee; and for six hundred and fifty miles the Tennessee straggled and meandered across the state, now narrow and rushing, now wide and placid, curving south, then west, across northern Alabama to touch Mississippi, then turning north again through Tennessee and Kentucky to flow finally into the Ohio at Paducah. Together with its tributaries, it drained an area of forty thousand square miles.

There was a wide variety of life and landscape in the Valley, from the soaring trees of the Great Smokies through the bare, bleak hills of eastern Tennessee and the lazy cotton country of Alabama to the flat red lands of the west. But one condition united the Valley — poverty. Before the Civil War, a few great planters had lived in magnolia-scented affluence. These had been the exception; most people in the Valley had no slaves and scratched their living from

a reluctant soil. After the war, northerners came into the region and
eyed its stands of virgin timber. They set up logging mills, cut up the
hardwood forests, changed a small farming country into a lumbering
country, and then departed, leaving the natives stranded amidst
abandoned lumber camps. This was the start of a pattern of exploitation and retreat. "Three fortunes had been taken off that
country," said Arthur E. Morgan, an eminent civil engineer with
whom Roosevelt discussed the Tennessee problem, " forests,
oil and gas." Only poverty remained — poverty, with thousands
on thousands of families who never saw $100 cash income a year;
with meager industrial development and little investment capital;
with the decay of schools and the deterioration of government; with
the spread of tuberculosis and pellagra.

And there appeared no way out. Each year fifty-two inches of rain
fell, swelling rivers into angry torrents, flooding the land and carrying away strength and fertility from the soil. The forests, so sadly
thin and overcut, were further depleted by burning. Income was less
than half the national average. Only two out of every hundred farms
had electricity. In the fall of 1933, over half the families in the high-
land counties were on relief; in one county the rolls included 87 per
cent of the families. There seemed no protection against flood, fire,
or erosion — no alternative to further descent into squalor. "The
wreckage of rugged individualism," said Morgan, "has been handed
to us with a request that we try to do something about it." [3]

III

Yet a frail hope had centered for a dozen years around the dam
on the Tennessee River near the little town of Muscle Shoals in
Alabama. Here, in a foaming turbulence of rocks and rapids, the
river dropped over one hundred and thirty feet in a wandering drop
of forty miles. As a power site Muscle Shoals had attracted attention since the turn of the century; as early as 1903 Theodore Roosevelt vetoed a bill which would have delivered it to private hands.
In the second decade, war in Europe increased interest in Muscle
Shoals, though less from the viewpoint of electric power than of
the production of synthetic nitrates, which could be used both for
explosives and fertilizers. In 1916 Cotton Ed Smith of South Caro-

lina introduced a bill providing for the public construction and operation of nitrate plants.

The synthesis of nitrates required power; so the National Defense Act of 1916 authorized the government also to construct dams and powerhouses. Then the end of the war raised the problem of the future of the government installations. A group of southern congressmen wanted Muscle Shoals to guarantee the farmer a cheap and abundant supply of fertilizers. George Norris, skeptical about fertilizer because of the high cost of the Muscle Shoals process, was more interested in Muscle Shoals as a source of electric power. And businessmen were quite ready to take over Muscle Shoals power and manufacture fertilizer if government made them sufficiently favorable terms.

There followed a protracted guerrilla war over the disposition of Muscle Shoals. No issue, it has been estimated, consumed so much time in Congress during the twenties. Norris, as chairman of the Senate Agriculture Committee, dominated the fight. Under his leadership the fertilizer issue was subordinated and the power issue acquired major importance. Beginning in 1921, he introduced a series of bills providing for government operation of hydroelectric plants on the Tennessee River. At the same time, he led the fight against the attempts of private interests, among them Henry Ford, to take over Muscle Shoals. "The most effective help to save the people from such a monopoly," Norris argued, "would be to have the Federal Government own at least some of the power-producing elements that enter into such a system." Government operation would reduce prices to the consumer; and the rates offered by the public authority could serve as a "yardstick" to test the fairness of rates charged by private utilities.

Norris's bills passed Congress twice — in 1928 and 1931; but Coolidge and Hoover vetoed them. The proposal authorizing government operation at Muscle Shoals, said Hoover with passion, was "the negation of the ideals upon which our civilization has been based." On the other hand, Norris's patient determination did succeed in preserving the site for public development. This was only in part the result of aroused opinion. It was also in part a failure of imagination on the part of businessmen. "The trouble with Muscle Shoals," said James B. Duke, the tobacco king and president of the Southern Power Company, "is that it is in no situation to reach or establish industries to absorb its power and pay interest on the investment under fifty years development. . . . I would not take it as a gift today. Completed by the Government I would take it on Ford's basis, where the Government gives him $50,000,000 and he only pays 5 per cent on $28,000,000 or $1,400,000 a year." Such terms were too extortionate for Congress even in the age of business. And so, throughout the twenties, the mighty Wilson Dam remained largely idle, water dashing uselessly through its spillways, the nitrate plants nearby silent and deserted.[3]

IV

For George Norris, then, power was the issue at Muscle Shoals. For many southerners, needing fertilizer for their cotton and tobacco, nitrates remained the heart of the matter: "I care nothing for the power," said Hugo Black. "It is infinitesimal in importance." And other questions were involved: the prevention of floods and erosion, the navigability and purity of the river, the strength of the forests and the land. Franklin Roosevelt considered all these elements part of a single whole. The logic was plain — a multipurpose approach to the Tennessee Valley. And for Roosevelt this meant more than simply the combined development of physical resources. With Arthur E. Morgan he discussed how social planning might meet the problems created by overpopulation in the cities and by overproduction on the farms. "Is it possible," Roosevelt said to Morgan, "especially down in this region, where people never have had adequate incomes, is it possible for us to develop small industries, where the people can produce what they use, and where they can use what they produce, and where, without dislocating the industry of America, we can absorb a lot of this unemployment, and give population a sound footing on which it can live, possibly with restricted standards, but still live soundly and in a self-supporting way until we can work our way into a new economy?"

This went far beyond traditional congressional preoccupations with the production of power or fertilizer. During the interregnum Roosevelt and Norris made their trip to the Valley. Afterward at

Warm Springs the President confided to a press conference his grandiose scheme for Valley development. Someone asked Norris on his return to Washingon, "Is he really with you?" The old man, who had waited so long, answered with pride and incredulity, "He is more than with me, because he plans to go even farther than I did."

"As soon as this rush of emergency legislation is over," Roosevelt wrote Norris eight days after his inauguration, "I hope you will come in and have a talk with me about Muscle Shoals and the Tennessee Basin development." The result was a presidential recommendation far bolder than anything considered in Congress during the years of wrangle. Muscle Shoals, Roosevelt told Congress on April 10, 1933, represented only a "small part" of the potential usefulness of the Tennessee River. Envisioned in its entirety, such use would transcend "mere" power development: it would include flood control, soil conservation, afforestation, diversification of industry and retirement of marginal farm land. To provide unified direction, Roosevelt proposed that Congress create "a corporation clothed with the power of Government but possessed of the flexibility and initiative of a private enterprise." The new Tennessee Valley Authority would have "the broadest duty òf planning" in the Valley for the general good of the nation. "In short," the President concluded, "this power development of war days leads logically to national planning for a complete river watershed involving many States and the future lives and welfare of millions. It touches and gives life to all forms of human concern." George Norris, watching the culmination of an ancient dream, called it "the most wonderful and far-reaching humanitarian document that has ever come from the White House."

When Roosevelt had broached the idea before inauguration, he had had a foretaste of conservative reaction. "A fantastic pipe dream," said the Manchester *Union* in New Hampshire; "a super pork barrel," declared another paper. Even the *New York Times* was moved to stately protest. "Enactment of any such bill.at this time," it declared, "would mark the 'low' of Congressional folly." The House Military Affairs Committee held the only hearings on the bill. "The power that can be generated at Muscle Shoals," said Representative John E. Rankin of Tupelo, Mississippi, "now exceeds the physical strength of all the slaves freed by the Civil War." But an impressive parade of utility executives questioned whether the Tennessee Valley could use all this slave-power. The group included top officials of the Georgia Power Company, the Alabama Power Company, and the Tennessee Electric Power Company; and it was shepherded by the President of Commonwealth and Southern, the holding company which controlled the three operating companies, a New York lawyer named Wendell L. Willkie.[4]

V

Wendell Willkie was forty-one years old in the spring of 1933, a big, genial, confident man, with dark, rumpled hair, an open manner, sprawling posture, and slouching gait. He was born in Indiana, had practiced law in Ohio during the twenties, and had moved on to New York a few months before the crash. He had been general counsel of Commonwealth and Southern from its inception and in January 1933 became its president. A Democrat, he had voted for Roosevelt in 1932, though he had favored Newton D. Baker for the nomination. Among utility executives, he stood for progressive management.

"I want to say, Mr. Chairman," he began, "that no one has read or referred with more gratification than we have of this magnificent proposed development of the Tennessee Valley." He strongly objected, however, to the building of government transmission lines. "To take our market," he told the Committee, "is to take our property." Let government make cheap power at Muscle Shoals, Willkie contended, but let it be sold to the utilities at the bus bar and distributed through privately owned transmission lines. Unless this change were made, Willkie must oppose the bill. "I can say to you, as my deliberate judgment, that if this bill passes, this $400,000,000 worth of [Commonwealth and Southern] securities will be eventually destroyed."

Willkie's further contention was that the Tennessee Valley, in any case, was, as he put it, "more than adequately served" by the existing Commonwealth and Southern system. There was, he later said, an excess generating capacity of 66 2/3 per cent in the Valley.

His supporting cast spelled out the argument that the Valley was absorbing all the power it could use in the foreseeable future. "I do not think we need additional lines, and no power is needed to serve that territory," said the president of the Georgia Power Company. ". . . If this plan is carried through there will be an additional excess capacity." "I can see no market whatever for this power," said E. A. Yates, who, as vice-president of Commonwealth and Southern, of the Alabama Power Company, of the Georgia Power Company, of the Tennessee Electric Power Company, of the South Carolina Power Company, and of the Gulf Power Company, should perhaps have known.

In the House itself, the bill faced strong criticism. Congressman Joe Martin of Massachusetts led the Republican attack, declaring that the TVA was "patterned closely after one of the soviet dreams." "No, Mr. Speaker," said Martin, "I think I can accurately predict no one in this generation will see materialize the industrial-empire dream of the Tennessee Valley." "This bill, and every bill like it," said Representative Charles A. Eaton of New Jersey, "is simply an attempt to graft onto our American system the Russian idea." "The development of power in that particular locality of the Nation," said Representative Everett Dirksen of Illinois, "or of fertilizer for that matter, can be of no general good." In the end, the House passed by 306 to 91 a modified bill limiting the government's power to build dams and transmission lines and in other ways reducing the original conception.

But in the Senate, George Norris took personal charge of the fight, effectively backed by Kenneth McKellar of Tennessee. On May 3, by a vote of 63 to 20, the Senate passed the Norris bill without the limiting provisions inserted in the House. In conference the President intervened in favor of the Senate version, the House accepted his decision, and on May 18 Roosevelt signed the Tennessee Valley Authority Act. "It is emblematic," said George Norris, "of the dawning of that day when every rippling stream that flows down the mountain side and winds its way through the meadows to the sea shall be harnessed and made to work for the welfare and comfort of man." [5]

VI

Roosevelt had already made his choice for the chairmanship of the three-man board set up under the Act to run the new Tennessee Valley Authority. This was Arthur E. Morgan. Indeed, few American engineers had had so much experience with flood control projects, beginning with the famous Miami Conservancy District, which he designed before the First World War to prevent a recurrence of the Dayton flood. And Morgan joined to his technical talents unusual personal qualities. He was a tall, rangy, gray, impressive man of fifty-five, a Yankee moralist and mystic, honest and righteous, given to ethical meditations of a somewhat jejune but uplifting kind, a social thinker touched with utopianism. Since 1920 he had been president of Antioch College in Ohio.

Part technician, part prophet, Morgan was possessed by an earnest passion to remake man and remake society. Noting that man's control of the physical world, after growing with imperceptible slowness for centuries, had taken a great leap forward in the last two hundred years, he considered it reasonable to suppose that man's control over human nature was on the verge of a similar leap. "There is no traditional line," Morgan once said, "at which men must stop in their efforts to bring order out of a chaos; no limits need be set on our hopes for a more inclusive and masterly synthesis." It was no accident that he devoted years of his life to a biography of Edward Bellamy. Morgan thus was well prepared to respond to Roosevelt's dream of the Valley. "The TVA," Morgan observed, "is not primarily a dam-building job, a fertilizer job or power-transmission job. . . . We need something more than all these." It was an experiment in social reconstruction; "the improvement of that total well being, in physical, social, and economic condition, is the total aim."

But movement toward "an integrated social and economic order" could not come about, Morgan believed, through conflict and hatred. It had to come by "the democratic process of voluntary general agreement." "I want to tell you one thing," Morgan remarked to Judson King, the veteran public power advocate, a few days after his appointment, "I am not going to fight the power companies." His hope was that the utilities would develop a "sense of trusteeship" which would enable them to pull their weight in the progress toward a better life. He rejected "that frequent short-coming of revolutionists — a feeling that the destruction of what exists must be the first and major part of their program." [6]

VII

While Morgan was laying his plans for the reordering of life in the Valley, Roosevelt named as his colleagues on the three-man board Harcourt A. Morgan of Tennessee and David Lilienthal of Wisconsin. Harcourt Morgan was an agricultural scientist, sixty-six years old in 1933, who had been for fourteen years president of the University of Tennessee. He had promoted agricultural activities in the South since the nineties; and his work as Dean of the College of Agriculture at Tennessee and then as President brought him into close relations with the Extension Service which strongly urged his appointment. The people of the Valley trusted Harcourt Morgan, with his lean, weather-beaten face and his laconic ways.

The third member of the Board was only thirty-four years old — over twenty years younger than Arthur Morgan and nearly half the age of Harcourt Morgan. Like Wendell Willkie, David Lilienthal was born in Indiana. After graduating from DePauw University, Lilienthal had moved on to the Harvard Law School, where his crisp personality and incisive intelligence attracted the attention of Felix Frankfurter. When Lilienthal left Cambridge, Frankfurter strongly recommended him to Donald Richberg, who was just then setting up a new firm in Chicago. Lilienthal worked with Richberg in drafting the Railway Labor Act and soon became a successful lawyer in his own right, specializing in public utility regulation.

When Philip La Follette became governor of Wisconsin in 1931, he tried to persuade Richberg to accept the chairmanship of the Wisconsin Public Service Commission. Richberg declined but suggested Lilienthal; and, to Richberg's amazement, Lilienthal gave up a profitable law practice and moved to Madison. His distinguished record on the Commission made him an obvious choice for the TVA. A quiet, solid man, with a round face, spectacles, receding sandy hair, a deceptive gentleness of manner, and

a hard precision of mind, Lilienthal had a vocation of public service and a steely determination to protect the public interest. And
he had, in addition, a vivid sense of the meaning of electricity for
the national welfare. "We are just at the beginning of the power
age," he liked to say. "The future possibilities are as limitless as
the practical imagination of our scientists and the ingenuity of our
inventors." The conclusion seemed to him inescapable. "No wonder, then, that it is so vital that we maintain the strictest public
control over this great natural resource."

H. A. Morgan was given charge of fertilizer production and of
agricultural policy; Lilienthal, of power policy; and Arthur Morgan of dam construction and of the broader aspects of education,
rural living, and social and economic planning. The three men
seemed to make up a commission of admirably complementary
talents. In a high spirit of idealism and hope, the great adventure
in the Valley began.[7]

VIII

Yet uncertainties remained — not over the division of immediate
responsibilities, but over the broad conception of the undertaking.
In the fall of 1933, the directors on a visit to Washington asked
Tugwell what he thought Roosevelt meant TVA to be — a public
corporation confined to specified tasks, or a planning and coordinating agency, or a new kind of regional government. Tugwell
replied that TVA, in his view, must approximate a government. In
certain matters, it might even supersede the states.

In so responding, Tugwell was endorsing the Arthur Morgan
thesis that nitrates, phosphates, and electric power would never
by themselves solve the problem of the Valley. Years before, near
Memphis, Morgan had helped reclaim thousands of acres of arable
land. "The philosophy of that development was that if you give
people the means for creating wealth and comfort they will work
out the situation without further help. Yet today that most fertile
land in America is the locus of the most miserable sharecropper
tenantry, where poverty and bitterness are general, and violence
appears." He did not wish to repeat that experience in Tennessee.
"We might build a dam at every site in the valley," he said, "make

every farm fertile, put electricity in every home, and protect every city from floods, and yet we might not stabilize or permanently benefit the country."

Morgan therefore wanted a comprehensive social and economic plan. He saw no escape from benevolent paternalism. Under his plan he would not only produce power and fertilizer: he would stimulate small industry; he would promote self-help cooperatives, endowing them if necessary with a local currency of their own; he liked the idea of subsistence homesteads; he had in mind ambitious educational projects; he was much concerned with issues of health and housing; he wanted a change in the land laws so that land could be taken away from farmers who failed to adopt reasonable conservation practices. He even would prefer the Valley dwellers to give up alcohol and tobacco. His vision appealed to other planners in Washington. "This work of his," Tugwell wrote, "carries more significance for the future than any other single attempt of the administration to make life better for all of us."

The appropriations under the Act, however, made little provision for regional planning. Most TVA funds were tied to specific tasks — dams, transmission lines, fertilizer, navigation, flood control. And it soon became apparent that Arthur Morgan's colleagues had less exalted notions of TVA's role and responsibility. Where Arthur Morgan had strong utopian propensities, both H. A. Morgan and Lilienthal were fundamentally realists.

H. A. Morgan in his long life had seen too many strangers come into the Valley with benign schemes for local improvement. He regarded many of Arthur Morgan's ideas as impractical and visionary. "Too many of us," as another southerner, Jonathan Daniels, wrote after visiting Arthur Morgan's model town of Norris, "will prefer a sloppy South to a South planned in perfection by outlanders. We know out of our past that the worst carpetbaggers were the ones who came down here to improve us." And H. A. Morgan had additional reasons for opposing too aggressive a conception of the power of the Authority. As former president of a land-grant college and an old friend of the Extension Service, he did not welcome restrictions on the traditional power of the conservative hierarchy which had so long dominated American agriculture — that hierarchy which Arthur Morgan condemned as "a powerful political bureaucracy."

As for Lilienthal, he had doubtless imbibed from Frankfurter a distrust for overhead planning. "There is something about planning," he once said, "that is attractive to that type of person who has a yen to order the lives of other people. It has an attraction for persons of a vague and diffuse kind of mind given to grandiose pictures not of this world. Planning is a subject that attracts those who are in a hurry but are rather hazy as to where they want to go." And he believed in particular that Arthur Morgan's enthusiasm for folk industry ran against the grain of the power age. Lilienthal could see no turning back from the machine: "I am against 'basket-weaving' and all that implies. . . . We cannot prepare for the 'second coming of Daniel Boone' in a simple handicraft economy."

In addition, Lilienthal was alarmed by intimations of Arthur Morgan's conciliatory attitude toward the power companies. Viewing the utilities with the sharp aversion of a man reared in the tradition of Brandeis and La Follette, he could see only the ugly past — the "disgraceful looting" of the twenties, the bold attempt to purchase the public opinion of the country, the record of mismanagement and corruption. Let TVA stand, Lilienthal said, as a reminder that, when power companies fail in their responsibility to the public interest, "the public, at any time, may assume the function of providing itself with this necessity of community life." [8]

IX

A common suspicion of uplift thus thrust Lilienthal and H. A. Morgan into a coalition against Arthur Morgan. Concern for their own programs consolidated the alliance. Lilienthal was prepared to concede H. A. Morgan a free hand in the agricultural field if he could gain for himself a free hand in power policy. As early as August 1933, by a 2 to 1 vote, the two realists succeeded in winning autonomy for their own operations. There began at this point a quiet, protracted, and increasingly bitter civil war in the heart of the great experiment in unified development.

In opposition to Arthur Morgan's instinct for overhead control, his colleagues developed a theory of what they liked to call "grass-roots democracy." H. A. Morgan, according to Lilienthal, invented the idea; but Lilienthal himself became its most articulate exponent. The theory took its start from what Lilienthal described as "the danger implicit in vast size, the disaster consequent when power is exercised far from those who feel the effect of that power." While power units grew, Lilienthal observed in Brandeisian accents, men continued to come about the same size. Yet, Lilienthal conceded, the nature of the modern economy made centralization in industry and thus in government inevitable. How then to prevent centralization from turning into tyranny? To this question, Lilienthal, borrowing a distinction from Tocqueville, argued that the centralization of authority was one thing and the centralization of administration another. In the "decentralized administration of centralized authority" he saw the means of taking the curse off bigness. And he regarded the TVA as "the boldest and perhaps most far-reaching effort of our times to decentralize the administration of Federal functions."

Grass-roots democracy did not mean only the devolution of decision from Washington to the regional agency. It had a positive side, calling for an active partnership between the regional agency and the regional community. As H. A. Morgan construed this partnership, it meant that TVA should be "shaped by intimate association with long-established institutions." In other words, instead of seeking to carry out its program by independent TVA action, as Arthur Morgan in many instances desired, it should seek wherever possible to work with and through existing local organizations. In the case of the agricultural program, this meant the land-grant colleges, the Extension Service, and the county agents. In other cases, it might mean local power boards, school committees, planning commissions, agricultural experiment stations, or a variety of private organizations — nearly everything, in short, except private power companies, which Lilienthal refused to acknowledge as being local in any true sense. This was the paradoxical issue: here almost alone Arthur Morgan favored working through "local" institutions; here almost alone Lilienthal favored direct and independent TVA operations .

Through grass-roots democracy, then, the people of the Valley would be drawn into the program as participants from the start, giving them, in Lilienthal's words, "the fullest opportunity for the release of the great reservoir of human talents and energies." The method would be not coercion but persuasion, encouragement, incentives, contracts — methods based on the people's confidence in TVA's good faith. Lilienthal feared "the smooth-talking centralizers, the managerial elite." In the end, he felt, "the price of arbitrary enforcement of planning is nothing less than our freedom." Where Arthur Morgan would pass a law depriving a farmer of land he has misfarmed, Lilienthal and H. A. Morgan would offer him inducements to use his land more wisely. "A man must be given a free choice," Lilienthal said, "rather than compelling a choice or having super-men make the choice for him." By each means the people would regain the responsibility of choice; and only through choice was growth possible. "The often flabby muscles of community and individual responsibility will never be invigorated unless the muscles are given work to do. They grow strong by use; there is no other way."

The Tennessee Valley Authority thus became another battlefield in the struggle which divided the early New Deal — the struggle between the social planners, who thought in terms of an organic economy and a managed society; and the neo-Brandeisians, who thought in terms of the decentralization of decision and the revitalization of choice.[9]

X

For the moment, the conflict remained beneath the surface. Arthur Morgan built his dams and pressed his planning and educational programs. Harcourt Morgan pushed the production and distribution of his fertilizers. Lilienthal developed his power policy. From time to time, George Norris came on visits to the Valley. His coat on his arm, his vest unbuttoned, his hat shoved to the back of his head, he would stand for half an hour at a time in quiet content watching the steam shovels and the cement mixers as the work went forward.

New energy was pouring into the Valley. In the first instance, it was the electricity produced at the dams, brought from the great generators along gleaming copper and aluminum wires to factories and farms in the farthest corners of the Tennessee basin. It was the clearing of the rivers, the rebuilding of the forests, the replenishment of the soil, the improvement of agricultural methods, the spread of schools, the development of recreation. But beyond this there was something less tangible yet even more penetrating: the release of moral and human energy as the people of the Valley saw new vistas open up for themselves and for their children. The jagged river, flowing uselessly past worn-out fields, overcut forests, ramshackle huts, its muddy waters reflecting the dull poverty of the life around — all this was giving way to a shimmering network of green meadows, blue lakes, and white dams. The river, the destroyer, was becoming man's servant. The beaten and sour land was stirring with new hope. It was an eloquent symbol of the time — a symbol of man's capacity through the use of political and technical intelligence to change the conditions of life and transform defeat into possibility.

20. Saving the Land

TVA REPRESENTED a dramatic attack on one facet of the problem of natural resources. Other facets were not so accessible to the regional approach. There remained, for example, the great question of the future of the land itself — a question given ghastly significance in 1934 when the drought blighted the plains and the whirling dust storms darkened western skies. The explosion of the dust bowl was a signal that the nation could no longer evade the threat of erosion.

In some aspects of the resources problem, like power development or agricultural adjustment, Roosevelt, for all his long-time interest, was still dependent on experts. But when it came to the land he was an expert himself. From the days of Theodore Roosevelt and Gifford Pinchot, he had fought to protect soil and forest against private waste and greed. He knew the areas of vulnerability — the overgrazed grasslands of the Great Plains; the overcut timberlands of the Appalachians; the long white gashes across the Southeast; the farming land where the settler's plow had ripped off the protective cover and, as Roosevelt once put it, "the top soil in dry seasons is blown away like driven snow." He felt the scars and exhaustion of the earth almost as personal injuries.

Hyde Park itself provided an object lesson, and he used it often to prove his point. The Hyde Park farm had grown prize corn as late as 1840. By 1910, when he took it over, spring floods and summer cloudbursts had largely washed away the topsoil, and it grew about half of what it had grown before. "I can lime it, cross-plough it, manure it and treat it with every art known to science," he once said, "but it has just plain run out — and now I am putting it into trees in the hope that my great grandchildren will be able to try raising corn again — just one century from now."

The trees symbolized his desire to renew the land. From his bedroom window at the south end of the Hyde Park house he could look out at a magnificent yellow poplar, soaring one hundred and twenty feet into the sky, its crown almost as wide as its height, astir in spring with nesting birds. For a time, he planted twenty to fifty thousand trees a year on the estate — Norway pine, Scotch pine, poplar, hemlock. He knew the qualities of each — whether they grew fast or slow, needed shade or sunlight. And he found profound consolation in their shaded tranquillity.

Driving his own car by means of special mechanical devices, he liked to stop by the rippling pond near the top of the hill above his cottage, or in the deep hemlock glades below, or in the thick green plantings of spruce and larch along the side roads — stop and absorb the stillness of the forest. And his delight in trees was not merely aesthetic or sentimental: it was rather a passionate response to the marvelous intricacy of nature. He called the forest "the most potent factor in maintaining Nature's delicate balance in the organic and inorganic worlds." Trees held the soil on the slopes and the moisture in the ground, they controlled the flow of water in the streams, they moderated the extreme fluctuations of climate. "The forests," he said, "are the 'lungs' of our land, purifying our air and giving fresh strength to our people." [1]

II

Against the backdrop of drought and dust, Roosevelt hoped to awaken in the American people a sense of urgency about their ultimate basis in nature. "Unlike most of the leading Nations of the world," he observed a trifle bitterly in 1934, "we have so far failed to create a national policy for the development of our land and water resources." Here plainly was a major objective for his administration, even if it had to take second place to the war against depression. And surely depression itself offered opportunities to promote the cause of resource development.

Most immediately, why not contribute at once to conservation and to relief by sending jobless men to labor in the forests? In his last year as governor of New York he had set 10,000 unemployed to work on reforestation. In his acceptance speech he held forth the possibility of using a million men in forest work across the nation — a claim which stirred Hoover's Secretary of Agriculture to lofty derision. But, after his election, Roosevelt, undeterred by the Hoover administration's scorn, talked the plan over with Professor Nelson C. Brown of the New York State College of Forestry, and dispatched Tugwell to Washington to discuss it with Major R. Y. Stuart, the chief of the Forest Service.

As soon as the banking crisis was under control, the President turned to the idea of emergency conservation work. On the morning of March 14, 1933, he outlined to Moley his scheme for putting an army of unemployed youth to work in the forests. "I think I'll go ahead with this," he said, " — the way I did on beer." A week later Roosevelt sent a message to the Congress requesting the establishment of the Civilian Conservation Corps.

The mechanics were vague in the President's mind, and, occupied with a hundred other problems, he turned it over to Louis Howe to work out. Howe began with a romantic picture of a large-scale recruiting effort, bands playing and flags flying, leading to a mass exodus of the unemployed to the forests. Frances Perkins and Tugwell helped reduce the idea to practical proportions. As an operating plan emerged from the discussions, it was decided to have the Labor Department recruit the men, the War Department run the camps, and Agriculture and Interior organize and supervise the work projects.

Reaction was mixed. Some cabinet members felt that it might be dangerous to collect large groups of jobless and presumably resentful men in the woods. The labor movement professed to believe that the plan would mean the militarization of labor and the reduction of wages to a subsistence level. "It smacks, as I see it," William Green told a joint House-Senate committee, "of fascism, of Hitlerism, of a form of sovietism." A Communist witness was even more vehement. "This bill," said Herbert Benjamin, "undertakes to establish and legalize a system of forced labor." John Dewey's Committee on Unemployment denounced the idea.

But the opposition melted away, and the bill, with some useful revisions, passed Congress on March 31. To keep labor happy, Roosevelt appointed as director an acquaintance from the Wilson administration, Robert Fechner, vice-president of the Machinists. The President then issued immediate orders for the CCC to get under way: 250,000 men in the camps by early summer was the goal. Congress, as usual, had left much of the administrative detail to the discretion of the Executive; and it was quickly decided to limit the Corps to unmarried men between 18 and 25 from families on relief. The Labor Department set up the machinery for recruitment in three days, the Army sent out a hurry call for reserve officers to operate the camps, and the Forest Service and the National Park Service began to plan useful things for the Corps to do and to recruit civilian foremen to supervise the actual work. (When someone complained that this complicated setup violated the principles of sound organization, Roosevelt replied, "Oh, that doesn't matter. The Army and the Forestry Service will really run the show. The Secretary of Labor will select the men and make the rules and Fechner will 'go along' and give everybody satisfaction and confidence.")

III

By the middle of June 1300 camps were established; by the end of July over 300,000 boys were in the woods. They discharged a thousand conservation tasks which had gone too long unperformed. They planted trees, made reservoirs and fish ponds, built check dams, dug diversion ditches, raised bridges and fire towers, fought blister rust and pine-twig blight and the Dutch elm disease, restored historic battlefields, cleared beaches and camping grounds, and in a multitude of ways protected and improved parks, forests, watersheds, and recreational areas.

They did more, of course, than reclaim and develop natural resources. They reclaimed and developed themselves. They came from large cities and from small towns, from slum street corners and from hobo jungles, from the roads and the rails and from nowhere. One out of every ten or eleven was a Negro. Some had never seen mountains before, had never waded in running brooks or slept in the open air. Boys from the East Side of New York found them-

selves in Glacier Park, boys from New Jersey at Mount Hood in
Oregon, boys from Texas in Wyoming. Their muscles hardened,
their bodies filled out, their self-respect returned. They learned
trades; more important, they learned about America, and they
learned about other Americans.

More than 2.5 million boys passed through the camps (the top
enrollment was over 500,000 in 1935). Most stayed from six months
to a year. Their statements to interviewers expressed their pride
in the experience. "I weighed about 160 pounds when I went there,
and when I left I was 190 about. It made a man of me all right."
"It helps you to get along with other people in general, because it
helps you to get over being selfish." "Here they teach them how
to pour concrete and lay stones and drive trucks, and if a boy wants
to go and get a job after he's been in the C's, he'll know how to
work." Or (from a Cleveland boy who had been west for the
CCC): "I feel almost as if I owned that land. Some day when those
trees I planted grow large I want to go back and look at them."

The CCC had its share of difficulty. The Army's practical contribution was temperate and effective. (One of the most successful
officers associated with the CCC was a Colonel George Catlett
Marshall, who organized 17 camps in the Southeast.)   But War
Department brass sometimes cast covetous eyes on the Corps. The
brash Assistant Secretary of War, Harry H. Woodring of Kansas,
wrote early in 1934 that "whether or not it is true, as many hold,
that the CCC camps are the forerunners of the great civilian labor
armies of the future, I believe that this activity should be expanded
and put under the control of the Army." The Army, Woodring
added, was prepared to organize the CCC along with the veterans
of the World War and the people on relief into a system of "economic storm troops" — a singularly unfortunate phrase for a
nation which was just beginning to dislike Hitler. The White
House reprimanded Woodring.

On the whole, Fechner, with the adroitness of an old-time trade
unionist, managed to keep relations equable among the collaborating departments, and — as a result in part of the patronage generated when new camps were set up — with congressmen. But he
seemed more inclined to coast along than to develop new possibilities in the CCC idea. Tugwell considered him unimaginative.

and Harry Hopkins once said that, if he had the CCC camps, he could run them for 60 per cent less than Fechner.

Yet, for all the difficulties, the CCC was unquestionably one of the most fortunate of New Deal inventions. "The CCC camp activity," Roosevelt told a meeting of the National Emergency Council in 1934, "has probably been the most successful of anything we have done. There is not a word of complaint — rap on wood." For the President, who had mused about the possibility of setting up some form of universal service for youth since the First World War, CCC remained particularly close to his heart. "His knowledge of its details," said the chief of the Forest Service in 1937, "is almost uncanny." Roosevelt once told Hopkins that every boy should have the opportunity to go to the woods for six months. He intended to make the CCC "a permanent part of the policy of the United States Government." Unforeseen events destroyed Roosevelt's hope. But the CCC left its monuments in the preservation and purification of the land, the water, the forests, and the young men of America.[2]

IV

The CCC remained only an instrument of conservation, a brilliant instrument, yet not a policy. The United States required something more than this. It required the coordination of many efforts on many levels if the land was to recover from the generations of abuse. Americans, Tugwell said, had wasted their heritage in "riotous farming." "I doubt if even China," said Henry Wallace, "can equal our record of soil destruction." The time had come, Roosevelt felt, to mobilize every resource to arrest the decay of the land.

In October 1933, Major Stuart, the Chief Forester, harassed by overwork, killed himself. For his successor, Tugwell and Wallace turned to Ferdinand Silcox, once a career forester, more recently a labor relations expert. Silcox conceived his job as far more than simply protecting the forests already in existence. Under his strong and imaginative direction, the Forest Service, the most powerful of the conservation agencies, expanded its programs and tirelessly explored new problems and new techniques.

In particular, when Roosevelt pressed his tree-planting idea after the dust storms, the Service showed itself willing to undertake a job that no one else wanted. Roosevelt had in mind the construction of a "shelterbelt" to break wind, snow, and dust in a hundred-mile-wide zone stretching along the 100th meridian from Canada to Abilene, Texas. Critics insisted that if God would not grow trees in the Great Plains, there was no reason to suppose the New Deal could. Technicians rather doubted the effectiveness of the program. But the Service took on the job. In the next years, with CCC assistance, it planted over 200,000,000 trees as part of a barrier against a new eruption of the dust bowl.[3]

V

For the specific problem of soil erosion, Tugwell favored the creation of a separate bureau. And he saw on hand in government the man to head it — Hugh Hammond Bennett, a big, broad-shouldered, slow-spoken, hearty North Carolinian, fifty-two years old, who had been crusading on behalf of the American topsoil since he first started working for the Department of Agriculture thirty years before. In 1933 Bennett was running the erosion experiment stations of the Bureau of Soils. Hearing that five million dollars had been earmarked for terracing programs under the Public Works Administration in the name of soil conservation, Bennett made a furious descent on Tugwell's office. The attack on erosion, he said, called for a balanced program involving strip cropping and contour plowing and crop rotation and grassed waterways as well as terraces. He added that farmers under proper encouragement would do a good deal of the job themselves.

Tugwell, who knew Bennett's work, was impressed; and he persuaded Ickes to give him a special bureau in PWA to tackle the erosion problem. But Ickes, who never missed an opening in the traditional struggle between Interior and Agriculture for control over conservation, instead set up the new bureau directly in Interior, where it was known as the Soil Erosion Service. (When Tugwell reproached Ickes, the Secretary impenitently replied, "I'm going to get the Forest Service too. Why don't you come over here and run the whole thing?")

For Bennett soil conservation was almost a religion; and he preached the consequences of defiance with Old Testament wrath. Of the 600 million acres of arable land in the United States, he warned in a famous statement, 50 million were already ruined, another 150 million had declined to the point where farming was becoming unprofitable, and the rest was being steadily undermined by sheet erosion or skimmed off by water or wind. At least 3 billion tons of solid material, by his estimate, were washed out of the fields and pastures of America every year; over 700 million tons were discharged annually into the Gulf of Mexico by the Mississippi River. The annual cost of erosion, he calculated, was at least $400 million in terms of lost productivity alone. Unless it altered its ways, America was on the road to geological suicide.

Other experts, including some in Bennett's old Department regarded his statistics as overwrought. It was thought, in addition, that Bennett's approach concentrated too exclusively on erosion as a physical problem and omitted the social and economic factors which led to the depletion of the land, especially the vicious circle of low-income farming and soil abuse. Bennett no doubt felt that one bureau could not do everything, and that the engineering approach, by avoiding the politically sensitive problem of rural poverty, could gain conservation a broader support. And no one could deny that Bennett, aided by the dust storms, was doing a unique job in awakening the nation. Under the slogan that land should be used according to its capability and treated according to its need, his specialists scattered across the country, conducting demonstration projects and instructing farmers and CCC boys in the arts of soil conservation.

At the same time, AAA lent encouragement to the conservation effort by requiring farmers accepting benefit payments to devote part of their acreage to soil-improving crops and to adopt other conservation practices. In 1934, Wallace created a planning division in AAA under Howard Tolley to promote better land use and farm management. And Wallace, unreconciled to the loss of soil conservation to Interior, also brought continuing pressure on Roosevelt and on Ickes for the return of a function which seemed to him plainly to belong to Agriculture. Though Ickes confessed privately that he was half inclined to agree with Wallace, he maintained an unyielding public position. But in 1935, while he was on holiday in Florida (taken, he later complained, at the urging of his supposed friends Wallace and Tugwell), the President ordered the transfer of the Soil Erosion Service to Agriculture, where it was re-established as the Soil Conservation Service.

With the passage of the Soil Conservation Act in April 1935, Congress for the first time accepted the prevention of soil erosion as a national responsibility. The subsequent enactment of state soil conservation acts on a model provided by the SCS gave the Service, working through local soil conservation districts, new effectiveness. Wallace in 1933 had looked forward to the time when people would think of "this whole country as a good farmer thinks of his farm." The moment at last seemed at hand.

For the President, it must have seemed a recapitulation of thirty years, carrying him back to the old days when the young senator from Dutchess County with his gold *pince-nez* served as chairman of the Forest, Fish and Game Committee of the New York State Senate. "The nub of the whole question," F.D.R. wrote to Henry Wallace in 1937, "is this: if a farmer in up-State New York or Georgia or Nebraska or Oregon, through bad use of his land, allows his land to erode, does he have the inalienable right as owner to do this, or has the community, i.e., some form of governmental agency, the right to stop him?" He had first raised the question a quarter of a century before, when he affirmed the "liberty of the community" against the selfishness of the individual in his brave outburst of youthful progressivism at Troy, New York. Now his own administration was beginning to provide workable answers. And he himself was focusing the nation's attention on its soil and water and forests as no one had since Uncle Ted.[4]

VI

Harold Ickes meanwhile brooded over the conservation effort like a dark and glowering cloud. For years as a private citizen he had battled for the national domain. What could be more logical now than to give his Department the guardianship of the nation's common property? Yet for nearly a century Interior had had the reputation of being the most venal of Executive departments. No doubt this reputation was the result of the responsibility assigned it by Congress to dispose of the public domain: no agency charged with giving away valuable resources could escape the intense pressure of private interests. Still conservationists viewed its depravity not as functional but as inherent. "Every natural resource, without exception, that has been held for disposal by the Interior Department — public lands, Indian lands, coal, oil, water power, and timber — has been wasted and squandered at one time or another," said Gifford Pinchot, a high priest of conservation and Ickes's comrade from Bull Moose days. "It is one long story of fraud in public lands, theft in Indian lands, and throwing the people's property away. Most of the fights for conservation have been made to save natural resources belonging to the people which the Interior Department was throwing away."

In 1905, Theodore Roosevelt had launched the conservation movement by removing the national forests from Interior and presenting them to Pinchot and the Forest Service in Agriculture. From that moment, Agriculture stood as the conservationist citadel, while Interior seemed more and more the appointed avenue by which the stockmen, the oilmen, the mineowners, and the land speculators conducted their raids against the nation's resources. Pinchot himself had fallen victim to Interior when the Forest Service (in collaboration with Louis R. Glavis of Interior) tried to defend the Alaskan coal fields against Taft's Secretary of the Interior, Richard A. Ballinger. A decade later Harding's Secretary of the Interior, Albert B. Fall, not only auctioned off some of the nation's prize oil reserves but did his best to recapture the Forest Service from Henry C. Wallace in order to increase the available loot. Pinchot's conclusion was concise and bitter. "The tradition of the Interior Department is to put private interests first. The tradition of the Agricultural Department is to put public interests first."

This was what Interior seemed to stand for, and this was what Harold Ickes was determined to change. He had actually favored Pinchot for the Republican nomination in 1932; and one of his first acts as Secretary of the Interior had been to bring Glavis back to the Department. "I want to assure you gentlemen," Ickes once remarked to a congressional committee, "that the Secretary of the Interior is as hard-boiled and enthusiastic a conservationist as there is in this country." [5]

VII

The problem of grazing on the public range soon provided
Ickes with an opportunity to demonstrate his conservationist passion. As long as western ranchers could remember, they had used
the public lands to graze their cattle or sheep without supervision
or payment of fee. The predictable consequence had been overgrazing, with the gradual destruction of the grass cover and the
spread of desert. For some time, conservationists had urged public
regulation of private grazing in order to check erosion. But the
stockmen had always successfully fought such subversive proposals.

The depression, however, thrust the cattle industry into a predicament of its own. With beef prices falling and with cattle
outside the AAA system, it seemed necessary to do something to
stabilize the industry. One obvious way to protect cattlemen from
the wildcatters, from overproduction, and from each other was to
control grazing on the public range. This shift in the view of the
cattle industry was reflected in the conversion of Congressman
Edward T. Taylor of Colorado to national regulation. For years
an enemy of federal conservation policies, Taylor now suddenly
perceived malevolent consequences in unrestrained free enterprise
on the public range. "The basic economy of entire communities
was threatened," he later explained. ". . . Erosion, yes, even human
erosion, had taken root. The livestock industry, under circumstances beyond its control, was headed for self-strangulation."

The first bill to regulate grazing was introduced in 1932 with
the backing of Hoover's Departments of the Interior and Agriculture. Reintroduced as the Taylor bill the next year, Ickes and
Wallace led the fight for it on the Hill. The measure proposed to
vest with Interior the responsibility for regulation. Since the Forest
Service was already regulating grazing in the national forests, there
were those who considered it better equipped to do so on the public
lands. But Ickes argued that because Interior had always administered the public lands it ought to administer grazing on these lands.
He added that he could do it at a figure far below the estimate
offered by the Forest Service. What was doubtless persuasive to
Taylor and to the cattle industry, however, was their supposition
that Interior would be more amenable to pressure than the Forest

Service. In any case, the Forest Service and Wallace in a mood of magnanimity finally decided that the important thing was to establish the principle of regulation. Agriculture remained unhappy over provisions in the bill which they believed diminished federal rights in the national domain; but Ickes overrode the objections. When Congress passed the Taylor Act in 1934, Ickes promptly set up the Grazing Service in his own Department.[6]

VIII

For Ickes, the Soil Erosion Service and the Grazing Service were only the first steps in a larger design. His consuming ambition was to transform the Department of the Interior into a Department of Conservation, containing within it all the federal authority necessary for the preservation and development of natural resources. The keystone for such a department, as he saw it, had to be the Forest Service. From his first days in Interior, Ickes therefore embarked on an interminable campaign of intrigue, persuasion, and pressure designed to recapture Forestry from Agriculture.

This campaign quickly aroused the opposition of the Department of Agriculture and especially of the Forest Service itself, an agency almost unique in its independence, its pride, and its capacity to mobilize members of Congress with national forests in their states. More than that, Ickes soon provoked Gifford Pinchot into a defense of his beloved child against the ambiguous embraces of this old friend, now sitting in the chair of Ballinger and Fall. The Pennsylvania election of 1934 first caused strain between the two old Bull Moosers. Pinchot, though detesting Senator David A. Reed (they had always fought, Ickes said, "like two tomcats on a back fence") and defeated by him in the primaries, nonetheless supported him against Joseph Guffey, the Democratic candidate, in the election. Ickes, campaigning for Guffey, pointedly refrained from mentioning Pinchot. "He really is too fine a man to be attacked," Ickes wrote in his diary, adding, "except as a matter of ultimate necessity."

As late as 1935, arguing against the transfer of Forestry to Interior, Pinchot said, "Ickes is sincere and honest, but he cannot live forever." Relations rapidly deteriorated, however, and Ickes's

point of "ultimate necessity" was all too soon reached. As befitted
men for whom Theodore Roosevelt was a political hero, both
Ickes and Pinchot were violent and uninhibited controversialists,
and they fell on each other with fury. By 1937, Ickes was denouncing Pinchot as "the Lot's-wife of the conservation movement," and
the "self-anointed Messiah of conservation" who had posed too
long "as the infallible, the impeccable and the omnipotent conservationist of all time." "The Gifford Pinchot of today," he concluded, "is not the Gifford Pinchot of twenty-five years ago."

In time, though, Ickes began to wonder whether he might not
have been wrong twenty-five years ago. He had already fallen out
with Louis Glavis ("I will no longer put up with his high-handed
methods. . . . These investigators have become persecutors, man
hunters, and they are just as eager to hunt and drag down members
of my staff as they are lobbyists and crooked contractors"). Soon,
no doubt, it began to occur to him that Richard A. Ballinger had
found Pinchot and Glavis equally intolerable in 1910. Encouraged
by Henry F. Pringle's account of the Ballinger-Pinchot affair in
his biography of Taft, Ickes, with his new insight into Ballinger's
enemies, reopened the case, studied the records in the Department
files, and concluded that Ballinger was "an American Dreyfus,"
cruelly destroyed by a conspiracy organized by Pinchot.[7]

IX

Ickes's fight with Pinchot was a sideshow, however, compared
to his less spectacular but far more serious fight with Henry Wallace. At first, Ickes hoped to achieve his ambitions for Interior
by negotiation. He was prepared to trade such bureaus as Reclamation, General Land Office, Grazing, Soil Erosion, and Subsistence
Homesteads to Agriculture in exchange for Forestry, Roads, and
the Biological Survey, and he proposed making Tugwell Undersecretary of Interior in charge of conservation activities. For a
moment in March 1934 Wallace seemed inclined to go along. Then
the opposition of the Forest Service stiffened Wallace, and he soon
turned against the package deal.

In 1935 Ickes thereupon decided on a different approach. His
new strategy was to persuade Congress to change the name of his

Department to the Department of Conservation and Works. If the United States was to have a conservation policy, Ickes contended, it should have an agency to administer that policy; and the natural agency was Interior. This thesis brought Agriculture into open opposition. Conservation, Silcox and Wallace declared, was not a specific function; it was a broad purpose, running across all the departments. Setting up a Department of Conservation, Wallace suggested, "would be a little like setting up a Department of Prosperity." The true distinction between the Departments, he added, was in terms of resources. Organic resources — anything which grew — belonged to Agriculture; inorganic, nonrenewable resources — minerals, oil, and the like — belonged to Interior. Conservationists, testifying against the bill, added that they considered forests, wild life, and grazing to be safe only in Agriculture.

Agriculture's obstinacy goaded Ickes into a characteristic performance. He told Congress with mock sadness that he had looked on this bill as a family affair of no interest to the neighbors, like naming a baby. "You members who sit on these committees of Congress and see the kaleidoscope of witnesses that pass before you," he said reflectively, "must often ponder the selfish and meddlesome characteristics of humanity. No matter what somebody wants, there is always somebody else who does not want him to have it. You have an opportunity to study human nature at its worst." He was sorry, he added, if the bill offended the "lexicographical sensibilities" of Agriculture; but what was Agriculture, to tell other departments what to do? "I have heard of various kinds of government, such as oligarchies, monarchies, and democracies, but this is the first time that I have ever heard of a farmocracy." In any case, he concluded, "our act really was one of self-abnegation." Interior seemed too inclusive a term; he was only trying to limit the name and function. Indeed, "the name 'interior' has become more of an epitaph than a designation. Until two years ago, the Department had been operated on so successfully that only a few of its vital organs remain. . . . By a fortuitous circumstance, practically all of the remnants left to us by jealous and predatory colleagues relate directly to conservation and public works." Pleading, joking, arguing, shifting from sarcasm to logic to denunciation, Ickes employed all his wiles; but in the end the bill was defeated in the House Committee. In 1936 a similar bill passed the Senate, only to die in the House.[8]

X

The President did his best to stay out of the fight. But he rejected Agriculture's argument that the crucial distinction was between organic and inorganic resources. Interior was set up, he believed, to take care of the public lands, Agriculture to serve the needs of those farming privately owned lands. The logic of this position placed Forestry in Interior, and as early as 1934 Roosevelt seems to have conceded to Ickes that that was where Forestry ought eventually to go. "The days have passed," as he later told Pinchot, "when any human being can say that the Department of the Interior is utterly black and crooked."

But Roosevelt refused to endorse the Conservation Department bill; and, though he repeatedly told Ickes he would order Agriculture to stop lobbying against the proposal, he seems never to have done so. "In his heart I think the President does want it," Ickes wrote ruefully in 1935, "but apparently he doesn't want it enough to help me get it." This was undoubtedly an accurate statement. Weighing the fights he had to make, Roosevelt evidently did not propose to invest his always limited political resources in this one. Still, if Ickes could win the fight for himself then the President was all for it.

The contest for the control of conservation thus remained inconclusive; and the feud between Interior and Agriculture became a depressing feature of the Washington landscape. Once in 1937, when Ickes and Hopkins were on a fishing vacation in Florida, Hopkins jocosely wired the President, WHEN HAROLD GOT A STRIKE THE OTHER DAY . . . FIRST THE ROD AND REEL AND THEN HAROLD WENT OVERBOARD AND WE HOPED FOR A BRIEF MOMENT THAT WE HAD LOST THE BEST FISHERMAN IN THE CABINET BUT NO LUCK HE CAME UP WITH A COUPLE OF HENRY WALLACES BUREAUS. Yet, for all the troubles this competition created, it also spurred each Department to redouble its efforts in the conservation cause — a fact which may too have entered into Roosevelt's calculations.[9]

XI

So much converged in the resources problem — land, water, forests; erosion control, flood control, navigation, irrigation, reclamation; dams, power, poverty, politics. Here, if anywhere, central coordination seemed necessary. The indiscriminate pressure for flood control appropriations in the winter of 1933–34 helped force the issue. "We have been going ahead year after year," Roosevelt remarked, "with rivers and harbors bills and various other pieces of legislation which were more or less dependent, as we all know, on who could talk the loudest. There has never been any definite planning." What was necessary now, he believed, was to "put the physical development of the country on a planned basis." To this end, he was thinking in terms of a "permanent long-range planning commission" which could lay out a twenty-five- or fifty-year program for national development.

Such a commission already existed in rudimentary form in the PWA's National Planning Board. Here Frederic A. Delano, Wesley C. Mitchell, and Charles E. Merriam were charged with keeping track of public works projects and helping fit them into a national plan. The Board, chafing perhaps under Ickes's tight reins, was more than responsive to Roosevelt's idea of a permanent commission. In its report of June 1934, it recommended the establishment of a continuous national planning agency; and Charles W. Eliot II, the Board's executive officer, drew up a presidential order setting up the Board as an independent agency. Ickes rose in wrath when he saw the Eliot proposal. Eventually the irate Secretary succeeded in whittling the idea down to an interdepartmental committee, for which the Delano group would serve as an advisory committee.

At a meeting with Roosevelt in June 1934, the planning group discussed how its mission could best be defined. The President groped for a phrase like "land and water planning." Eliot suggested natural resources, and Mitchell commented that human beings were perhaps America's most important resource. Merriam then suggested the phrase "national resources." The President repeated the phrase several times, liked its sound and remarked, "That's right, friend Eliot, get that down, because that's settled." [10]

On June 30, 1934, the National Resources Board was established with Ickes as nominal chairman.

The Delano Committee, however, retained control of the Board's technical staff and directed its programs. Few Americans had had more impressive experience in city and regional planning than Delano. Chicago, New York and Washington all bore his mark in their programs for urban development. In 1927 the Committee on the Bases of a Sound Land Policy under his chairmanship had drawn up a basic report in the development of land-use policies. Eliot had been his director of planning for the National Capital Park and Planning Commission of the District of Columbia. Much, indeed, of the planning enthusiasm of the thirties derived from the experience of city planning. Ickes himself was a veteran of the fight for honest city government in Chicago; so were Merriam, Richberg, and Jerome Frank.

Mitchell and Merriam had served, in addition, as chairman and vice-chairman of Herbert Hoover's Committee on Recent Social Trends. This Committee had advocated what it called planning, though all it really meant was the systematic consideration of problems rather than the systematic execution of programs. For Mitchell in particular, planning was essentially an exercise in research rather than decision. "National planning," he could write, "is inevitable. [Our] only choice is whether it shall be piecemeal and inspirational or systematic and technically thorough." But, in practice, he felt that planning required the patient, exact, detailed accumulation of knowledge far beyond anything yet amassed — a conception of planning to which even Hoover (as he told Mitchell in 1934) had no objections. From the viewpoint of a practical planner like Tugwell, the activities envisaged by Mitchell could be more accurately called "pre-planning."

XII

After 1935, when the Board was once again reorganized into the National Resources Committee, Mitchell retired. Thereafter Beardsley Ruml and Henry Dennison functioned in his place. But Merriam emerged increasingly as the dominant figure. A political scientist of energy, imagination, and high character, Merriam had undergone a series of embittering experiences in Chicago politics which filled a normally genial personality with a certain harassing suspicion of his colleagues. "Even those who worked loyally with him," wrote his friend Donald Richberg, "were constantly annoyed and discouraged by his attitude." On the Committee, Merriam's doubts focused with particular intensity on Charles Eliot. The tension between them, mounting through the thirties as Delano's advanced age weakened his leadership, handicapped the Committee's work. The personal tension both reflected and aggravated differences in approach. Merriam and Mitchell, the scholars, tended to favor long-term research projects; Delano and Eliot, the planners, wanted to shape current policies and programs. Moreover, the Board's efforts at regional planning won it the mortal enmity of the Army Engineers, which conceived it to be poaching on sacred preserves.

Nevertheless, the Board did effective work both in stimulating local planning and in formulating regional plans. And its concern with the planned development of natural resources constantly spilled over into an interest in the planning of the general economy. Especially after Gardiner Means joined its staff in 1935 as director of the Industrial Section, the National Resources Committee became the arsenal for those in the administration who still believed in industrial planning and a managed economy. But in the end, various factors — deficiencies of authority and leadership on the Committee as well as resistance both in Executive departments and on the Hill — prevented the Committee from achieving coordination even in the field of resources planning.

Still, if the conservation effort was not to be controlled by a mechanism, it was magnificently held together by a common spirit. TVA, CCC, rural electrification, the great dams of the West, the work in soil conservation and reforestation and grazing control — all were changing the face of the land. In 1930, the American earth, the foundation of all American life, was crumbling away under the lash of wind and water, while the national government stood idly by, haltered by ignorance, by indifference, by commitments to private groups, by a conviction of its own constitutional impotence. By 1934, a massive national effort was at last under way, aimed at checking erosion, at strengthening the soil and purifying the water, at securing the physical basis of American civilization. Patches of green were appearing where the earth had been scarred and brown, ponds and streams where once the water had eaten its way through gullies and ravines, fertility where all had been parched and sterile. Emerging were the lineaments of a new land.[11]

21. The Revival of Community

FROM HIS FIRST DAYS as Assistant Secretary of Agriculture in 1933, Rexford G. Tugwell had been a central figure in the conservation revival. Brisk and energetic, disdainful of custom or precedent or vested interest, he was ready to mobilize all the powers of government to achieve his new America — "a land in order, wisely used, with the hills green and the streams blue." The protection of physical resources — soil, water, forests — he considered only part of the job. Beyond this, Tugwell saw an urgent human dimension. Conservation, he believed, had to take account above all of the men and women who wore themselves out working tired and barren soil. Submarginal land produced submarginal people, and submarginal people produced submarginal land. A national conservation policy could never succeed, Tugwell thought, until it moved to break this vicious circle.[1]

II

For Tugwell, rural poverty thus stood high on the conservationist agenda. Before he could mount his attack on this problem, however, he found himself diverted to a fight on another front — a fight in the end so protracted and damaging that his reputation never recovered from it. As Assistant Secretary, Tugwell had the special responsibility for the old-line bureaus of Agriculture; and, as a man with a profound belief in an expert civil service, he regarded it as his obligation to give the Department's scientists and technicians the wholehearted official support which previous administrations had denied them. As he had seized the opportunity to back Hugh Bennett in the soil conservation field, so in the spring of 1933 he recalled the Food and Drug Administration from the exile to which it had been consigned during recent Republican administrations. The Food and Drug Administration was still operating, in substance, under the law passed at Theodore Roosevelt's behest in 1906. More than a quarter-century's experience had revealed limitations and loopholes in the basic statute. Tugwell now encouraged the Food and Drug experts to prepare a new law. Before the end of the Hundred Days, a draft bill was ready for the Senate.

The atmosphere seemed propitious. As Upton Sinclair's *The Jungle* had helped stir the demand for the original Food and Drug Act, so a book published in January 1933 and in its eleventh printing by May seemed capable of doing the same for a new act. This was *100,000,000 Guinea Pigs*, a harsh exposé of the perils of foods, drugs, and cosmetics. One of its authors was F. J. Schlink, a physicist and mechanical engineer who had once worked for the Bureau of Standards and who, after writing *Your Money's Worth* with Stuart Chase in 1927, had set up Consumers' Research, Inc., as a testing service for consumers. His collaborator, Arthur Kallet, was an electrical engineer and a director of Consumers' Research. In vivid journalistic prose, Kallet and Schlink told Americans that every day they were plastering poisons on their faces and pouring them down their stomachs. The book named products, quoted records, and documented its charges with appalling cases of disfigurement or death following the use of misbranded or adulterated goods. If at times Kallet and Schlink gave the impression that eating, drinking, and primping were as dangerous as crossing no man's land in the midst of a gas attack, nonetheless a residue of hard and shocking truth emerged from their drastic indictment.

The issue of food and drug standards made a strong appeal to Tugwell. Desiring efficiency in the economy, he saw in what he called "the robbery of consumer deception" a major source of waste. Desiring to bring prices down, he wanted to deflate phony advertising claims and mobilize consumers as an organized economic interest. With his general animus against business dishonesty, he aimed at winning the nation "freedom from fakes."

Rushing somewhat impetuously into the situation in the spring of 1933, Tugwell issued an administrative order designed to reduce the amount of poisonous residue which could be left on fruits and vegetables after they had been sprayed to kill insects and fungus.

The legal lead arsenate tolerance thus dropped from 0.02 grain to 0.014 grain — a level still above that regarded as safe by the British Royal Commission on Arsenical Poisoning, but well below that to which American fruit growers were accustomed. The result was a wail of anguish from the International Apple Association and, the apple being a notably bipartisan fruit, an uprising of congressmen, Republicans and Democrats, from apple districts. Thus, almost before it was started, the fight for food and drug reform was transferred from a scientific to a political contest.[2]

III

Tugwell's status as a professor intensified the suspicions of businessmen; and the business community considered the new Pure Food and Drug bill, filed just before the end of the special session, sweeping enough to justify the gloomiest apprehensions. The new bill had several alarming features. It covered cosmetics for the first time. It extended regulation from labels on the bottle to newspaper and magazine advertising. It required that labels themselves contain definite information. It demanded grade labeling for foods. More than this, the Food and Drug Administration, to dramatize the need for the measure, put on a public exhibition of adulterated foods, poisonous patent medicines, corrosive hair dyes, and other concoctions which it lacked power to ban under existing law. These exhibits told the stories of deluded men and women who had paralyzed themselves by using mislabeled rat poison to remove superfluous hair or who had burned out their insides trying to lick obesity with dinitrophenol; or of pathetic idiots who sought to cure tuberculosis by rubbing horse liniment on their chests or to cure cancer by drinking a vile mixture of ammonia, turpentine, and eggs; or, most affectingly, of the once pretty matron, displayed in before-and-after photographs, who had blinded herself by using Lash-lure, an eyelash dye.

The press called the show the "Chamber of Horrors," and businessmen considered it a subversive attack on the sacred theory of consumer choice. For the naïve Tugwell, however, the conditions displayed were unreasonable and intolerable; and what was unreasonable and intolerable had to be changed. But he found it hard to enlist public interest. He tried Thomas Beck of *Collier's,* who had played so powerful a role in Theodore Roosevelt's similar crusade a quarter of a century before; Beck's crusading days were evidently over. For a moment Father Coughlin seemed interested; then he demanded a provision in the bill prohibiting contraceptives. And when the bill itself came up for hearings in the winter of 1933–34, it encountered a storm of opposition which only confirmed Tugwell's view that business sacrificed everything to profits. While Food and Drug Administration officials, public health officers, and doctors gave devoted expert testimony about the dire need for a new law, the drug, food, and cosmetic industries, supported by publishers and advertising associations, declared with stately rhetoric that fundamental principles of capitalism, of the free press, and self-medication would be destroyed if they were not free to continue poisoning their customers.

As H. B. Thompson of the Proprietary Association put it, "I never have in my life read or heard of a bill so grotesque in its terms, evil in its purposes, and vicious in its possible consequences as this bill." The Proprietary Association numbered among its members such firms as Bristol-Myers, Sterling Products, McKesson and Robbins, Merck, and Bayer's Aspirin, and its influence was felt in every corner drugstore in the country. C. C. Parlin of the Curtis Publishing Company, on behalf of the National Publishers Association, declared that the grade-labeling proposal threatened "the very existence" of American newspapers and magazines. Letters and telegrams poured out from patent medicine and drug manufacturers demanding that newspapers denounce what was beginning to be known as "the Tugwell bill"; plainly implied was the threat of cancellation of advertising contracts. Though Tugwell had contributed nothing to the bill except encouragement, its opponents missed no opportunity of portraying him as an enemy of the American system who had probably picked up the idea on his visit to Russia in 1927. As David F. Cavers, a main author of the bill, put it in a moment of exasperation before the Senate Subcommittee, "If one quarter of the interest, one quarter of the vigor which has been expressed in opposition to this bill had been expended by the industries themselves in the support of measures in the past to remedy these defects, these hearings would not be in session this afternoon."

IV

Caught in the cross fire was the nominal sponsor of the bill, Senator Royal S. Copeland of New York. A physician himself, a former commissioner of health in New York City, he was an easygoing man in his middle sixties, a carnation forever in his lapel, given to accommodation and compromise, but still possessed of some vague professional recognition of the need for new legislation. A flexible ethical sense enabled him to accept broadcasting fees from Fleischmann's Yeast, Eno Fruit Salts, and Phillips Milk of Magnesia while the legislation was under discussion; and more radical proponents of control, like Schlink and Kallet, dismissed him as a tool of the drug interests. Yet, while conceding a good deal to the trade, Copeland still kept the bill alive, sought to protect its central features and, on occasion, even denounced the "conspiracy on the part of the patent-medicine men" with impassioned sincerity.

The first draft had been perhaps unduly rigorous. Under Copeland's management, it suffered a series of dilutions. The process deeply pained Tugwell (who complained to Roosevelt early in 1934 that Copeland "apparently thought he had a mandate from you to kill every provision of the Food and Drug bill which would be of any use") but, in the end, the Department went along with Copeland in the belief that his bill was still better than nothing at all. The Consumers' Research group, however, had regarded even the first version as fatally weak; and it turned savagely against the revision. "By passing this bill," Kallet exclaimed of the 1935 version, "the Senate has made itself, knowingly or not, an accessory to thievery and murder."

But Consumers' Research was currently consumed with internal troubles of its own. Kallet's crusade against adulteration and misbranding had consolidated his contempt for the economic system which seemed to reward such abuses. "The jeopardizing of a dozen lives to save a few pennies," he wrote in 1934, "is entirely normal in a profit economy." In this mood, he was an obstreperous and insulting witness before congressional committees; and, as the mood grew upon him, he found himself acting in ever closer concert with the Communist party. In 1935 a bitter strike tore Consumers' Research apart. Kallet sided with a Communist attempt to organize the operation, while Schlink, along with J. B. Matthews, the Social Gospel fellow traveler who had become a Consumers' Research official, opposed the strikers. The result was the expulsion of Kallet, who went on to found a rival organization of his own, Consumers' Union in 1936. (Twenty one years later, Kallet, himself grown conservative, was displaced as director of Consumers' Union.)

As for the bill, whether for fear of lost advertising revenue or for other reasons, the press subjected it to an almost total blackout, except for splenetic denunciations of Tugwell. Even the *New York Times,* in the five years of the struggle, put the story only once on the front page (and this because of a disturbance made by a spectator in the Senate galleries). And, though President Roosevelt sent a message to Congress in 1935 calling for legislation (page 2 in the *Times*), he never threw full White House support behind the measure, presumably because he thought he should hold his fire for issues he deemed more important. From the viewpoint even of Wallace and the Department of Agriculture, this was a city dwellers' bill, and far from a top priority. Still the Food and Drug Administration and Copeland kept plugging away. Industry opposition diminished as the bill lost some of its stringency and even more as executives began to calculate the public relations consequences of their continued obstruction. Finally in June 1938, a sort of bill was at last passed. The grade-labeling provisions had long since been dropped; the enactment of the Wheeler-Lea Act in 1938, giving the Federal Trade Commission (rather than the Food and Drug Administration) control over advertising, drastically reduced the penalties. It was, said Tugwell sadly, "discredit to everyone concerned in it." Four days later, in June 1938, Senator Copeland died.[3]

V

By the time the bill became law, Tugwell was out of government. But his reputation was an early casualty of the long fight. The smears of 1934 and 1935 created an indelible image of the professorial Bolshevik. Hugh Johnson might call him "about as red as a blue hen"; his critics in the business community knew better. Tugwell's own occasional cockiness or condescension of manner only compounded his difficulties. His impatience with fools and bores and members of Congress (categories he sometimes found indistinguishable), his chilly refusal to accept businessmen at their own evaluation, his addiction to academic language and to soaring social speculation — all this complicated his position in Washington.

His efforts to reach the people hardly helped. His language was too often abstract and unintelligible. Consider Maury Maverick of Texas confronted by Tugwell's table talk:

> He used more professorial language and said something about "averting a revolution." I was going blind.
> Then, to prove the point, he said: "And the workers and farmers, combining their genius and (another word I couldn't get), and they shall form a nodule. . . ."
> I blew up completely.
> I said: "Rex, I am sore and insulted, and do not want to hear any more."
> "Why?" he asked.
> "What in God's name is a nodule?" I said.
> "A nodule is — " began Rex.
> "Stop! Stop!" I shouted. "Don't tell me. Whenever you use a word that I don't understand, it makes me mad. I am an American! The word nodule is not understood by the American people, nor it is understood by me, which makes it worse — and I do not want to know what it means. Nobody wants to listen to your academic phrases. Nodule my eye! Put your speech in simple language. I never heard of a 'nodule' before, so I don't like it. Besides," I continued, "it sounds like sex perversion."

For a while in 1934 Tugwell actually conducted a newspaper column, sometimes filled with improbable dialogue between himself and two fictitious figures, "Senator Progressive," and "Beauregard Boone." In due course the column spoke out on the food and drug bill ("People are still being swindled, poisoned and chucked under the chin. I don't like it"), whereupon most papers hastily dropped it. "I seem to have a certain faculty for running into trouble," he wrote in his diary in March 1934.

Still, his private influence continued. As Moley receded from White House circles, Tugwell became for a season the chief presidential confidant. In the spring of 1934, Roosevelt and Wallace decided to move him up from Assistant Secretary of Agriculture to the newly created post of Undersecretary. This caused some consternation among the husbandmen of the Hill — "He is not a graduate of God's Great University," said Cotton Ed Smith of South Carolina — but Tugwell, making all he could of his boyhood farm experience, presented himself as a dirt farmer with mud on his boots. "Tell Rex," Roosevelt is supposed to have said to Wallace later, "that I was surprised to hear he was so dirty." Eventually Roosevelt induced Smith to report Tugwell favorably by agreeing to appoint as United States Marshal a South Carolinian with a homicide record whom the President described to the cabinet as Smith's "favorite murderer." After this it seemed fitting that Sinclair Lewis should give a party in Washington to celebrate Tugwell's victory.

Tugwell, so ambiguously confirmed, remained more than ever a controversial figure. Whatever he touched ran into trouble, even when — as was so often the case — posterity would find him brave, sensible, and right. In particular, the stereotype which rose out of the food and drug fight gravely handicapped his cherished program for the conservation of the land and of the men and women who lived upon it.[4]

VI

Of Tugwell's bonds with Roosevelt, the most intimate was their shared passion for the earth. For many Americans, this became an enveloping nostalgia. "The land!" exclaimed Henry Ford in 1932. "That is where our roots are. No unemployment insurance can be compared to an alliance between a man and a plot of land. With one foot in industry and another foot in the land, human society is firmly balanced against most economic uncertainties." For a moment, even the population flow was reversed; more people were going back to the farms than coming to the cities. "We were raised on a farm in Illinois," one town dweller wrote in a typical scrawl to Washington. "I know how to farm. I would much rather work than beg the welfare workers for something to eat each week this way I have no work and not land to raise anything. . . . Most any where or any thing will beat this way of living during the last two weeks they gave us one dollar and twenty five cents grocery order."

The back-to-the-land movement, moreover, had acquired a publicist in Bernarr Macfadden of *Liberty Magazine* and the *New York Graphic;* and it even found a prophet in Ralph Borsodi, who during the twenties had conducted a lonely crusade against the mass production economy in the name of a new gospel of family self-sufficiency. Borsodi himself had moved his family to the country, where they grew their own food, ground their own flour, made their own clothes, and won thereby, he believed, rare spiritual fulfillment. With depression, Borsodi thought that the escape for the individual might be a solution for society. In his book of 1933, *Flight from the City,* Borsodi elaborated a program of subsistence homesteads to be organized into communities where men and women could secure their satisfactions from creative and self-expressive activities instead of from conspicuous consumption and vicarious play. Already he was serving as adviser for such a community near Dayton, Ohio.

Even Franklin Roosevelt was somewhat infected by this dream, though not in its more extreme forms. It was this hope which had helped transform TVA from a power and fertilizer project into an experiment in regional planning. As the President perceived that the recovery of production even to 1929 levels would still leave unemployment in the cities, he felt more strongly than ever the need to strike a better balance between city and country. Before his inauguration he spoke privately of putting a million families into what he called, a little unhappily, "subsistence farming" — that is, supplying them land on which they could raise crops for their own support near factories which could give them part-time work. After inauguration his figures became less ambitious, but his hope persisted. "I really would like to get one more bill," he wrote George Norris in the midst of the Hundred Days, "which would allow us to spend $25 million this year to put 25,000 families on farms, at an average cost of $1000 per family. It can be done. Also we would get most of the money back in due time. Will you talk this over with some of our fellow dreamers on the Hill?" The fellow dreamers responded, and Senator John H. Bankhead of Alabama wrote a $25 million appropriation for subsistence homesteads into the National Industrial Recovery Act. The back-to-the-land movement, Bankhead said, offered "a new basis for American society, in the restoration of that small yeoman class which has been the backbone of every great civilization." [5]

VII

The appropriation, falling under the second title of the National Industrial Recovery Act, became the responsibility of Harold Ickes as head of the Public Works Administration; and Ickes promptly set up a Subsistence Homestead Division in Interior with M. L. Wilson as chief. The statute envisaged these projects primarily as a means of draining off "the overbalance of population in industrial centers." But Wilson considered them in addition as a means of shifting poverty-stricken farm families from submarginal land. Instead of slums, urban and rural, Wilson now saw the possibility of establishing American society on a new and sounder basis.

The desire for community life close to the soil represented, he thought, a revolt "against the crass materialism and the shallowness of the Jazz Age" and a return to more abiding values. "I want to destroy all this," he once said of the cities. ". . . This is no way for people to live. I want to get them out on the ground with clean sunshine and air around them, and a garden for them to dig in. . . . Spread out the cities, space the factories out, give people a chance to live." In Utah he found an answer — the Mormon village, with its farmsteads neat and clean along the streets, enjoying the urban conveniences of power and plumbing, but still possessing an organic relationship with the soil. "Nowhere in the United States," Wilson wrote in 1933, "will be found as high a standard of living in relation to income as obtains in the Mormon villages today. The solution of the problem is the decentralization of industry and the development of a new type of suburban industrial city now made possible by the machine age."

The homestead *mystique*, with its image of roots in the land, was momentarily compelling. "I can't help thinking," said Henry Wallace, "that the self-subsistence homesteads, if experimented with sufficiently by men of scientific, artistic and religious understanding, will eventually lead us a long way toward a new and finer world. If I were a young man with no other job in prospect [a typical Wallace reservation], I would try desperately to get into the self-subsistence homestead movement." George Russell, the Irish poet and agricultural philosopher, was imported by Mary Harriman Rumsey to elaborate the homestead ethic. In hushed séances, Æ told the Subsistence Homestead Division that men could find wholeness of living only as they hugged the soil; otherwise they were condemned to be cogs in the industrial machine. "We had forgotten," said the Quaker Clarence Pickett, "that the hearth where the family gathers and where neighbors are welcomed is at the very heart of human life. We were trying again to put the welfare of the home and the individuals who live in it in the center of our national interest." Eleanor Roosevelt and Louis Howe were enthusiastic. Even hard-boiled characters like Hugh Johnson, Harry Hopkins, and Bernard Baruch viewed variations of the idea with approval.

And so the dream grew: placid communities made up of small white houses with green shutters in which families stranded by urban or rural poverty would find shelter and peace, engaging in hand-weaving or woodworking or small manufacturing, and growing their food on their own garden plots. The homestead movement, M. L. Wilson told Ickes, was "laying the basis for a new type of civilization in America." [6]

VIII

Limited in its funds, the best the Subsistence Homestead Division could hope to do was to demonstrate the value of the idea through pilot projects. The theory was that the government would buy the land, build the houses, acquire the livestock and farm machinery, bring in roads, water, and utilities, and then arrange to sell to the homesteaders over a period of thirty years. But M. L. Wilson was more a philosopher than a manager. In crisis he tended to be vague and elusive. And the interventions of Eleanor Roosevelt and Louis Howe did not contribute to orderly administration.

Eleanor Roosevelt's experience with her furniture factory at Hyde Park had given her an eager interest in the possibilities of small handicraft production. A visit to the depressed soft coal region of West Virginia in the autumn of 1933 renewed this interest. Not yet a familiar newspaper face, Mrs. Roosevelt was able to move around without recognition. As Quaker workers took her through small villages in the neighborhood of Morgantown, she was confronted by pathetic scenes — heads of families who had been on relief for three to five years; children who did not know what it was to sit down at table and eat a proper meal; rickety shacks black with coal dust. She took a businessman into one cabin; he came out, his face white, and vomited. In a company house, a man showed her his weekly pay slips: with the deductions for rent, oil, and his bill at the company store, he had less than a dollar in cash left each week for his family. His six pale, frightened children lived on the scraps which other American families fed to their dogs. One little boy clutched a pet white rabbit in his arms. His sister turned to Mrs. Roosevelt and said, "He thinks we are not going to eat it, but we are." At that, the boy fled down the road, clutching the rabbit closer than ever. (When Mrs. Roosevelt later told the story at a White House dinner, Bill Bullitt sent her a check the next day, saying he hoped it might help keep the rabbit alive.)

The conditions convinced Mrs. Roosevelt that something approaching revolution might break out. But one flicker of hope gleamed forth. The Quakers, casting about for ways of helping people to help themselves, had set up small factories in an attempt to tap local handicraft skills. A foundation thus seemed laid for a subsistence homestead effort; and on her return to Washington, Mrs. Roosevelt, ardently backed by Howe, did her best to hurl the Subsistence Homestead Division into the breach.

The first project was set up at Reedsville in the Scott's Run area. Howe rashly told the President that work would begin in three weeks. The result was a plunge into activity before planning could be completed. Eager to get things under way, Howe sent out a hurry call for fifty prefabricated houses. What he got were light knockdown houses, designed for summer on Cape Cod and wholly inadequate to a West Virginia winter. Faced with the choice of rebuilding or discarding the prefabs, Howe and Mrs. Roosevelt called in a team of New York architects who supervised an expensive process of redesigning and enlarging the houses to fit on new foundations. Howe bravely defended the mounting costs of Reedsville — or Arthurdale, as the new community was renamed — on the ground that this was the price of experiment. "Sparing no expense is the first rule, and must be the first rule, in the development of any new product," he said. ". . . Perfection of the first model means minimum costs in the production of the units to follow."

Wilson, with his passion for decentralization, had set up operations in terms of independent local corporations; but Ickes, restless at local waste and fecklessness, centralized administration in Washington in the spring of 1934. Wilson thereupon resigned. And, in the meantime, Ickes was growing particularly restive over Arthurdale. Told that it was to be a model for other homestead projects, Ickes asked acidly what it could be a model of; obviously not low-cost housing. In his diary, Ickes noted that, since Mrs. Roosevelt had taken Arthurdale under her wing, "we have been spending money down there like drunken sailors — money that we can never hope to get out of the project." And, again: "I don't see how we can possibly defend ourselves on this project." And, again: "I told the President that this was the only phase of my administration that I felt apologetic for." When he complained to the President, Roosevelt agreed, but added, a little helplessly, "My missus, unlike most women, hasn't any sense about money at all."

In time, however, after much premature flourishing of trumpets, the community began to emerge. Wesley Stout of the *Saturday Evening Post,* in a hostile article in 1934, reported that Arthurdale had the look of a "superior real-estate development," with its small houses spick in new white paint, pleasantly varied in form, well placed and spaced. A national committee, with John Dewey among its members, designed a progressive educational program to meet the community's vocational and recreational needs. There were agricultural and animal husbandry projects, industrial arts and crafts, music, drama, and folk dancing. "You should have seen those people's faces," exclaimed an ecstatic Bernard Baruch. "It was really the most remarkable thing I ever saw." The homesteaders were carefully recruited for their competence and stability — "the very men," remarked Stout, "likely first to get back on their feet with a revival of business" — and plans were under way for the development of local industry. The first thought was that Arthurdale might manufacture equipment for the Post Office. Senator Kenneth McKellar of Tennessee led the fight for this proposal; but the idea was bitterly attacked. "Its enactment," said Representative Louis Ludlow of Indiana, " . . . would lead the Government God knows where in the direction of sovietizing all industry . . . would sound the death knell of individual liberty in America." In the end Congress, fearing "unfair" competition with private industry, specifically banned the use of Post Office funds for such purposes. For the next few years, Arthurdale had to stagger along with a furniture factory and several abortive manufacturing projects.[7]

IX

Arthurdale was both the most costly and the most publicized of the homestead communities. There were many others — indeed, by the middle of 1935 about twenty were in operation or under construction and forty more had received Ickes's somewhat grudging approval. In Granger, Iowa, in another soft coal area, the local Catholic priest was the leader in organizing a community. Near Hightstown, New Jersey, Jewish needleworkers set up a community combining subsistence gardening with a clothing factory. In Dayton, Ohio, the Division took over Ralph Borsodi's Dayton Homestead Unit. Dayton much impressed Lorena Hickok, out on a field trip for Hopkins. "These families are of the same type as the white collar people I've been talking with," she wrote. ". . . And what a contrast! Instead of hopeless, afraid, whipped people, yes-

terday I found people busy, smiling, planning — actually happy."
For individuals, such communities scattered across the country
did provide for a moment a spurt of morale. But the nation as
a whole was not affected: the completion of all projects approved
by mid-1935 would take care of only about 6500 homesteaders.

In the meantime, the Rural Rehabilitation Division of the
Federal Emergency Relief Administration was conducting less
spectacular but more effective efforts on the countryside. Hopkins
had decided in 1934 that rather than pay out direct relief to
farmers, he would try to plan for their "rehabilitation in place"
through long-term loans and the provision of seed and equipment,
or, if the land was hopeless, to arrange for resettlement. Hopkins
also experimented with what he called "rural industrial communities" (only for stopgap purposes, however; "even though it is
eminently successful for many families," he noted in 1936, ". . .
such a plan can never offer a large-scale solution"). Where the
Subsistence Homestead Division had only $25 million to spend,
FERA by mid-1935 had expended $60 million — most of it repay-
able — for rehabilitation and (carrying out an old Department of
Agriculture program) another $25 million for land acquisition and
improvement.

Since Interior's Subsistence Homestead Division and FERA's
Rural Rehabilitation Division were attacking the same problem,
it seemed increasingly anomalous that they should be separate
undertakings. In April 1935 Roosevelt accordingly combined them
along with the FERA Land Program and AAA's Land Policy Section in a new agency called the Resettlement Administration. Here
at last a concentrated effort could be made to attack the grinding
agricultural cycle which had worn down land and men alike and
where, in last analysis, issues of conservation and poverty were
indistinguishable. And, for Resettlement Administrator, Roosevelt
turned to the man who had agitated these issues most persistently
and had proposed this solution — Rexford G. Tugwell.[8]

22. War against Rural Poverty

For Tugwell the Resettlement Administration was a perplexing as well as a gratifying assignment. "Redistribution of our essential wealth, the land, in order that the more tangible wealth of money, health, education and useful possessions may flow into the hands of these disadvantaged farm families," he wrote shortly after becoming Resettlement Administrator, "is the clearest mandate our society has received from the economic necessities of the present depression." Yet much of what he found in RA he did not like. In particular, he fundamentally disapproved of the whole subsistence homestead approach. The family farm seemed to him as much a monument of a primitive past as the small business; both were structural defects in an economy committed to large-scale units. Where M. L. Wilson laid it down as a basic principle that "technological efficiency alone is seldom or never all-important," Tugwell felt that to go against technology was to go against history. If the family farm or the subsistence homestead had a role, it was at best peripheral, exacting a far higher economic cost than social value justified.

As for the self-contained community, this seemed even more of an anachronism. "I am inclined to believe," Tugwell observed late in 1933, "that such settlements will function merely as small eddies of retreat for exceptional persons; and that the greater part of our population will prefer to live and work in the more active and vigorous main stream of a highly complex civilization." While he was always willing to humor Roosevelt by chat about the advantages of decentralization, he did his best to deflate the Rooseveltian belief that the land could absorb the urban unemployed and to diminish the Rooseveltian fantasy of a new rural-urban society. Agriculture's need was not the spinning wheel, but the ruthless application of the technical innovations which had already revolutionized industry.[1]

II

As Tugwell saw it, then, the problem was the massive retirement of exhausted land and the massive resettlement and retraining of exhausted farmers — an operation which would strike simultaneously at the nerves of physical and human erosion. Nonetheless, the administrative inheritance of the Resettlement Administration had a momentum of its own, both from the projects to which it was already committed and from the personnel which it had already attracted.

Receiving nearly a hundred rural communities, in process or in prospect, from Subsistence Homesteads and FERA, Tugwell confronted the problem of giving them an economic basis which would save them from decaying into rural slums. They had not attracted local industry, as M. L. Wilson had hoped. Congress had forbidden them publicly owned factories. The remaining solution, in Tugwell's view, was commercial agriculture. The most likely way to produce a salable surplus was through mechanized farming, and this could only be possible through collective operation of the land. Thus at Casa Grande, Arizona, at Lake Dick, Arkansas, in Jefferson and Walker Counties, Alabama, near New Madrid, Missouri, the Resettlement Administration organized cooperative farming projects. Bringing in a project manager, a farm manager, and a home supervisor, the agency cleaned up unsanitary conditions, replaced filthy shacks with simple cottages, formed medical and consumers' cooperatives, purchased heavy farm machinery for the community, and made individual loans for operating stock.

In addition, Tugwell backed a new form of community development, known in RA as Suburban Resettlement. He had long been interested in the notion of satellite cities. "My idea," he wrote early in 1935, "is to go just outside centers of population, pick up cheap land, build a whole community and entice people into it. Then go back into the cities and tear down whole slums and make parks of them." Suburban Resettlement set up shop in the Evalyn Walsh McLean mansion on Massachusetts Avenue. The high-ceilinged rooms with their brocaded walls and splashes of sentimental fresco were now a confusion of drafting boards, blueprints and diorama. From this there emerged the brilliant conception of the Greenbelt towns — garden suburbs, protected by encircling belts of farm and woodland, easily accessible to cities, but with the space and tranquillity of the countryside. Four model projects were contemplated: Greenbelt, near Berwyn, Maryland, half an hour outside Washington; Greendale, near Milwaukee; Greenhills, near Cincinnati; and Greenbrook, near New Brunswick, New Jersey.

III

Looking back on the RA communities fifteen years later, Tugwell wrote, "We were doomed to failure from the start." The cause of failure did not, he believed, lie in defects of conception or of technique; rather "it was character which failed. And that was not because the human stock was feeble; it was because the environment was hostile to the development of character." By this Tugwell meant that the participants had neither the commitment nor the self-discipline to make the communities work. He attributed this in part to the reactionary influence of press and pulpit.

The trouble surely lay deeper. The atmosphere in the new agency had become a little heady. Resettlement, wrote Marquis W. Childs of the St. Louis *Post-Dispatch*, was "a cozy conspiracy of good will to remake America on a cleaner, truer, more secure pattern." The aspirations could not have been more benevolent, and much hard thought went into plans and programs. But somehow, as Childs observed, the conspirators neglected to take the American people into their confidence. The whole effort skipped too many basic attitudes. M. L. Wilson used to talk about the "white-lighters, never satisfied, but excited," who could not bear to be by themselves in rural solitude. The trouble lay basically in the fact that most Americans were white-lighters, children of an individualistic and competitive culture, lacking any faith in the community idea. Observers repeatedly commented on the want of community spirit. Nor could government make up the deficit. Excessive outside supervision would only have enfeebled local initiative. Strong local leadership might theoretically have solved the problem. Yet "to convert all the large farms of the United States to cooperatives on the order of Casa Grande," as E. C. Banfield has noted, "would involve an investment of leadership far in excess of any possible return."

Most participants regarded community life as no more than a depression makeshift. They struck Lorena Hickok as "a little wistful, — still hoping against hope that they might be able to get their 'real jobs' back." The other life, the life outside, remained the "real" life. Dr. Will Alexander, Tugwell's chief aide in Resettlement, visiting a cooperative plantation in Arkansas, heard the chairman, an old Arkansas farmer, recount with apparent satisfaction the development of the cooperative. Later Alexander got him off by himself and asked what he really thought. The farmer replied, "I believe a man could stick around here for five or six years and save enough money to go off and buy himself a little hill farm of his own." The communitarians of the 1930's were making the same discovery that Albert Brisbane, the Fourierite, had made a century before; the aspirations of the individual could not find a satisfying outlet in the self-contained community. It finally seemed inevitable, Brisbane had written, that "members, perceiving that there existed outside of their little community a field of action more in harmony with personal requirements and ambitions, should turn their backs on the ideals of youth to mingle again with the outside world in broader and more complex spheres of action."

Yet there could be no question that, in backing Suburban Resettlement, Tugwell understood, perhaps prematurely, a tendency in American life which in another decade and a half would be compelling — the flow of population from the cities to the suburbs. The Greenbelt idea of the thirties found a kind of distorted realization in the suburban developments of the fifties. Ironically for the Resettlement planners, when success at last took place, even in their own projects, it only completed the defeat of the original conception of an autonomous community. Many of the Resettlement projects were bailed out by the war; in time, the government got back good returns on the original investment. But such communities, instead of laying the basis for a new type of civilization, only saw the reabsorption of their inhabitants into the main pattern of American life.

There were subsidiary difficulties. The Resettlement communities lacked a political constituency. Farm organizations were indifferent or hostile. Business was suspicious. Labor feared a chain of rural sweatshops. Bad administration and high costs made the projects politically vulnerable and killed Roosevelt's sympathy for the whole idea. "Frankly," the President wrote rather irritably to Will Alexander in 1936 concerning a project near Wichita Falls, Texas, "I think we have no right to finance Resettlement farm projects on any basis such as this. The unit cost of $7524 is in itself about $3000 too high and when you add to it the supplementary items, giving a total unit cost of $9273, I do not think we have a leg to stand on." A few months later Roosevelt observed sourly to Wallace, "The location of some of the projects does not appear to be such that those families for whom they are intended can ever become self-supporting." When Resettlement was succeeded in 1937 by the Farm Security Administration, most community projects were marked for liquidation.[2]

IV

Communitarianism was only the minor part of Resettlement's mission. The major part was the protection of land and forests through a determined attempt to save that 50 per cent of the farm population which received barely 10 per cent of total farm income. Too many Americans still lived in shacks or cabins on rocky hillsides, in barren gulches, in bleak cutover timberland, in exhausted mining areas, where housing, sanitation, and diet were as vile as anything in the most noisome city slum. Tugwell's objective was to take poor people off poor land and settle them where good land, good organization, good tools, and good advice might give them and their children a new chance.

The explosion of the southern tenant problem in 1934 dramatized the problem. After the Civil War, the southern plantation system acquired a semifeudal structure in which landlords surrounded themselves with a cluster of share tenants and sharecrop-pers — that is, dependent farmers who paid for the use of the land, as well as for food and clothes, not in cash, of which they had little, but in a lien on what they hoped to grow. Where the feudal relationship had at least a permanence and a sense of reciprocal obligation, however, the landlord-tenant relationship was casual, tense, and insecure. The landlord kept the record and figured the earnings — too often, as the croppers said, with a "crooked pencil." The cropper, who was the lowest form of tenant, had little legal or economic recourse against the landlord and not much hope, save in exceptional circumstances, of ever getting enough ahead of the "riding boss" or the local merchant or planta-tion commissary to be able to break out of the system. All he could do was move wearily from one place to another; about one out of three tenants changed farms every year. "The agricultural ladder, for these American citizens," Roosevelt once put it, "has become a treadmill."

It was a gray and hopeless life, and it seemed to be steadily engulfing the South. In 1880 hardly more than a third of southern farms were operated by tenants; in 1920 the proportion had grown to almost half. By 1930, nearly three-quarters of Mississippi farmers were tenants, and only slightly fewer in Georgia and Louisiana. Depression only spread tenancy and worsened the conditions of tenure. By the early thirties, there were over a million white tenant families and nearly seven hundred thousand Negro tenant families in the South. This meant that nearly eight and a half million persons were trapped in the system. Of these, more than a third (and more than half the Negroes) were croppers.

Life, particularly for the croppers, was gaunt and necessitous. Whole families labored in the fields from dawn to dusk (as they said in Arkansas, "from can to can't"). One observer saw a two-week-old baby wrapped in quilts and laid in a furrow while the mother worked the cotton. Frazier Hunt, traveling through the South for the New York *World-Telegram*, was reminded of Chinese coolies working along the South Manchuria Railroad, except that in China he had never seen children in the field. The croppers, Hunt wrote, "seemed to belong to another land than the America I knew and loved."

When not working, they lived in ramshackle cabins, unpainted and weather-beaten, roofs leaking and walls out of alignment. There were no screens, no plumbing, no sanitation. They lived on sowbelly, meal, and molasses, drank branch water from contaminated creeks, and suffered from pellagra, malaria, and ague. Their babies languished and died of "summer complaint," while the old folks shivered with what they called "weakness" or "spells" or sank into sodden apathy. Many families even lacked outhouses. When a newcomer started to build privies for his croppers in Arkansas, a neighbor protested: "All that a sharecropper needs is a cotton patch and a corn cob." Erskine Caldwell in early 1935 visited a two-room shack near Keysville, Georgia, occupied by three families with one to four children each. "In one of the two rooms a six-year-old boy licked the paper bag the meat had been brought in. His legs were scarcely any larger than a medium-sized dog's leg, and his belly was as large as that of a 130-pound woman's. . . . On the floor before an open fire lay two babies, neither a year old, sucking the dry teats of a mongrel bitch."

Across the South it stretched, an endless belt of dirt, drudgery, and despair, where worn-out people, whom disease made feeble and lack of hope made shiftless, scratched at life against the background of overcrowded shacks, rusting Model T Fords, children with hookworm, clothes falling into rags, tumble-down privies, the cotton patch and the corn cob. It was a fortunate cropper who received $200 cash income a year. Enmeshed in the single-crop system, most could not even raise garden crops to supply their own wants. There were no distractions — only sleep, filth, corn likker, and an occasional lynching. "I have traveled over most of Europe and part of Africa," said Naomi Mitchison, the English novelist in 1935, "but I have never seen such terrible sights as I saw yesterday among the sharecroppers of Arkansas."

At the end of 1936, when Henry Wallace was considering whether to bring the Resettlement Administration into the Department of Agriculture, Tugwell urged him to take a look for himself at Resettlement's problems in the South. The Secretary returned from the trip badly shaken. "I have never seen among the peasantry of Europe," he wrote soon after, "poverty so abject as that which exists in this favorable cotton year in the great cotton States from

Arkansas on to the East Coast. . . . I am tempted to say that one third of the farmers of the United States live under conditions which are so much worse than the peasantry of Europe that the city people of the United States should be thoroughly ashamed." [3]

V

For half a century the sharecropper situation had been a local scandal. Now AAA made it the nation's business. The plow-up and the acreage reduction uprooted cropper families and cast them onto the roads, the rivers, and the swamps. Despite provisions in AAA contracts, little federal money filtered through to the tenants. When croppers protested at the violation of contracts, they got nowhere. The landlords dominated not only the local administration of AAA but the sheriffs at the county courthouse and the congressmen in Washington. It was this situation that drove the AAA legal staff to the reinterpretation of the contract which led to the agricultural purge of 1935.

Yet the New Deal awoke new emotions among the croppers and laborers. Letters pouring into Washington exuded both despair and hope. Thus one to Harry Hopkins from a Georgia farmer:

I have Bin farming all my life But the man I live with Has Turned me loose taking my mule all my feed. . . . I have 7 in family. I ploud up cotton last yeare I can rent 9 acres and plant 14 in cotton But I haven't got a mule no feed. . . . I want to farm I have Bin on this farm 5 years. I can't get a Job So Some one said Rite you.

And, out of despair and hope, there began to rise further emotions: a sense of solidarity and a sense of militance. In July 1934, in a dingy schoolhouse outside Tyronza in Poinsett County, Arkansas, under the light of kerosene lamps, a group of croppers and laborers, white and black, met together and organized the Southern Tenant Farmers' Union. "The same chain that holds my people holds your people too," said a snowy-haired old Negro. "If we're chained together on the outside we ought to stay chained together in the union. . . . The landlord is always betwixt us, beatin' us and starvin' us and makin' us fight each other. There ain't but one way for us to get him where he can't help himself and that's for us to get together and stay together."

At first, the planters declined to take the STFU seriously. Then, under the devoted leadership of H. K. Mitchell, a Tyronza businessman, the STFU began to make progress. Howard Kester, a tall, thin, intense young minister, born and trained in the South, came into the state to help organize the croppers. Gardner Jackson and others in Washington provided encouragement. Functionaries of the Socialist and Communist parties began to appear. Radicals established Commonwealth College at Mena, Arkansas, to train young men for the struggle; the president of the Student Association at Commonwealth in the spring of 1935 was an Arkansas youth named Orval E. Faubus. Foreign visitors, like Jennie Lee, a Labour Member of Parliament, and Naomi Mitchison, toured the area. Most shocking of all, Norman Thomas, the Socialist leader, entered Arkansas and started to deliver his fiery, slashing speeches.

The atmosphere quickly changed. As a preacher of Marked Tree, Arkansas, told Raymond Daniell of the *New York Times*, "It would have been better to have a few no-account, shiftless people killed at the start than to have all this fuss raised up." The planters and riding bosses issued threats, loaded shotguns, broke up meetings, manhandled and whipped union organizers. At a mass meeting at Marked Tree, a young Methodist minister, responding to the campaign of intimidation, said, "I could lead a mob to lynch every landlord in the county if these people are not fed, but we do not want to resort to violence, we have carried our grievance to the courts." He was promptly arrested, charged with anarchy, blasphemy and an attempt to usurp the government of Arkansas, and sentenced to six months in jail.

VI

Some of the outside agitation — particularly that of the Communists — was calculated to inflame emotions rather than to improve conditions. But the landlords' attack against the STFU was motivated primarily by outrage over the uppityness of men and women who had so long and so properly slaved in silence. "We have had a pretty serious situation here," a leading citizen of

Arkansas told Daniell, "what with the mistering of the niggers and stirring them up to think the Government was going to give them forty acres." In March 1935, there were outbursts of terror and violence across the state — cabins riddled with machine gun bullets, organizers mobbed and murdered, union members beaten, terrorized, and jailed. "I talked to some of these men," wrote Frazier Hunt, "and listened to their incredible tales of how they were being beaten, thrown in jail, hounded and hunted down like runaway slaves. To all intents and purposes they were still slaves." At a town in Mississippi County bearing the euphonious name of Birdsong, a drunken mob of armed planters and sheriff's deputies slugged Norman Thomas, knocked him from the speaker's platform and ran him out of the county ("We don't need no Gawd-damn Yankee Bastard to tell us what to do with our niggers").

Thomas left Arkansas determined to awaken the national conscience. He reported the Birdsong incident in writing to Roosevelt, adding that the state of mind in Arkansas was "potentially the most dangerous situation I have seen in America." Roosevelt at first referred the matter to Chester Davis, who assured the President that surveys were going forward to improve AAA enforcement of the acreage reduction contracts; to Thomas, Davis wrote, "Obviously the right of free speech and assembly in Arkansas is a matter which state authorities must protect." But Thomas persisted. Henry Wallace characteristically refused to see him; and he got little satisfaction from Tugwell or from Aubrey Williams, Hopkins's deputy in FERA. Tugwell felt that he had a vast program under way to mitigate the abuses about which Thomas merely wanted to agitate; he knew, in addition, how thin a support the program had in Congress as it was. Thomas complained to Roosevelt that both Tugwell and Williams were "frankly in fear of the powers of Southern Senators." In a candid conversation with Thomas, the President made it clear that he agreed with Tugwell and Williams: he did not like the tenancy situation but could see little to be done at the moment. Roosevelt rejected Thomas's proposals as impractical, saying, "Norman, I'm a damned sight better politician than you are." "Well, certainly, Mr. President," Thomas replied. "You are on that side of the table and I'm on this." Roosevelt added: "I know the South, and there is arising a new generation of leaders in the South and we've got to be patient."

Patience was poor consolation to the croppers. It was no better for the migratory agricultural workers of the West, who were also outside the AAA system and were also responding to the new currents generated by the New Deal. The wanderers expelled from the cotton lands by AAA were joined in 1934 and 1935 by fugitives from the dust bowl — Arkies from Arkansas, Okies from Oklahoma, others from Texas and Kansas and Nebraska. Obeying a traditional American impulse, they moved toward the setting sun; their needles, like Thoreau's, settled west ("the future lies that way to me, and the earth seems more unexhausted and richer on that side"). A ragged army in broken-down Fords, they pushed on toward greener frontiers — the fruit ranches, the onion fields, the lettuce fields of distant California. Here they swelled the already overcrowded ranks of fruit tramps and stoop labor roaming from ranch to ranch through the Imperial Valley. Here too they began organizing to demand adequate housing and wages and working conditions; here too the ranchers organized against them, seeking through beatings, kidnapings, and false arrest to destroy the leadership and decapitate the movement.[4]

VII

Roosevelt was moved by their plight. But he would not take action. Under Roosevelt, said the *Sharecropper's Voice*, the organ of the STFU, "Too often the progressive word has been the clothing for a conservative act. Too often he has talked like a cropper and acted like a planter." Yet Roosevelt, while feeling the bitter injustice of the situation, recognized that federal power had its limits and that the process of change had to be gradual. More than this, to back the STFU would have been too unmistakable an affront to the conservative southern leadership in Congress on which he relied for so much of his legislative program — an affront in particular to the Senator from Arkansas, whom the *Sharecropper's Voice* called "Greasy Joe" Robinson and who was the Democratic leader of the Senate.

His plea for patience was not insincere. The Resettlement Administration was doing as much as it could. In perhaps its most important work, RA's Land Utilization Division bought up many millions of acres of submarginal land and transferred them to states or to the Park or Forest Services to be converted into pasture or forest. The Rehabilitation Division, determined not to use credits to perpetuate country slums, developed a program of farm-and-home loans by which farmers struggling to keep land and families together could receive money and supervision for specific improvements. The Resettlement Division relocated displaced and stranded persons. And new legislation was under consideration based on the experience in rural rehabilitation and aimed directly at the problem of tenancy. In 1935, Bankhead of Alabama, still seeking to restore the small yeoman class, introduced a bill to help tenants and farm laborers become owners through government loans at low interest with long terms for repayment. The Bankhead bill envisaged a Jeffersonian economy, with a wide distribution of small freeholds, every man secure under his own vine and figtree. "I know of no better means of reconstructing our agriculture on a thoroughly sound and permanently desirable basis," said Henry Wallace in 1935, "than to make as its foundation the family-size, owner-operated farm."

Not all his advisers shared Wallace's enthusiasm for the family farm. Tugwell, in particular, denied that tenancy, as such, was the problem, or ownership the solution. Ownership, after all, could be as precarious a condition as tenancy, the mortgage as harassing as the landlord. And the small farm, by reducing the use of machinery, generally meant high-cost farming; with the impending technical changes, "a forty-acre farm may well be a survival of inefficiency." So far as Tugwell could see, what Bankhead projected was little more than "a contented and scattered peasantry." Rather than worry about ownership, Tugwell would have concentrated on assuring tenure, whether for tenants or mortgaged owners, and at the same time on providing the farm family with a mule, seed, and fertilizer, better diet for children, treatment for illness, and a helping hand in crisis.

But Tugwell's influence was already beginning to fade. And the faith in the family farm was too deeply rooted in the national folkways to be upset by argument. Theodore Bilbo of Mississippi spoke for many southern politicians when he wired Roosevelt in August 1935: THE BANKHEAD TENANT SHARE CROPPER BILL IS NOT ONLY ONE OF THE MOST CONSTRUCTIVE BILLS THAT HAS BEEN BEFORE CONGRESS

THIS SESSION BUT WITH IT WE CAN DRIVE HUEY LONG OUT OF THE SOUTH. That year the bill passed the Senate but did not come to vote in the House. In 1936, Roosevelt appointed a special Committee on Farm Tenancy to report early in 1937. When the Bankhead bill was finally enacted in the summer of 1937, Wallace, following the recommendations of the Committee on Farm Tenancy, terminated the Resettlement Administration and set up the Farm Security Administration to carry out the Bankhead Act. With the establishment of FSA, under the direction of Dr. Will W. Alexander, who had long been concerned with tenancy, the attack on rural poverty entered a new phase.[5]

VI

Transformation
of a Labor Movement

23. The Travail of Labor

THESE WERE YEARS of awakening. New ideas and new hopes were set free in America. They penetrated everywhere — in time even to the sleepy headquarters of the American labor movement. For a decade that movement had been in a steady decline. From its top point in 1920, when it included 12 per cent of the labor force, it shrank in strength, year by year, till in 1933 it had barely two million members — less than 6 per cent of American workers. With Section 7a of the National Industrial Recovery Act, however, a new epoch seemed to be beginning. Across the country workers were determined to make good on the government's pledge that they could bargain collectively through unions of their own choosing.

In 1933 three times as many workers went out on strike as in 1932 — taxi drivers in New York, shipyard mechanics in New Jersey, aluminum workers in Pennsylvania, copper miners in Montana; from grocery clerks to lumberjacks, from East to West. There were more strikes still in 1934. And where, before 1934, the main cause of strikes had been the desire of the already organized to raise wages or to reduce hours (or, since the depression, to prevent wage cuts), now the right to organize was itself becoming the crucial issue. For the workers, union recognition was basic to everything else. For at least a strong minority of employers, to concede that right meant, they believed, irretrievable disaster. Each side felt it was fighting for its life. The result in some communities approached civil war.[1]

II

Minneapolis, the sturdy city, grew up where the Mississippi tumbled through its narrow gorge by St. Anthony Falls. The River made the community from the start a center of communication and marketing; the railroads, winding into the city from all directions, confirmed this destiny. From the countryside around — from Minnesota and Wisconsin and the Dakotas — wheat poured into Minneapolis mills. From Minneapolis stores, more tractors and farm tools went to the country than from any other city in the country. Here was a processing center, a distribution center, a financial center; here were the wheat elevators and the flour mills and the grain exchange of the great Northwest.

In 1934 Minneapolis was, in addition, a citadel of the open shop. For almost a generation, the Citizens' Alliance, an association of Minneapolis employers, had used its money, its staff, and its secret informers to hold the line against unionism. Minneapolis businessmen were not, as they put it, against collective bargaining: the only trouble, as Charles W. Pillsbury said, was that "labor leaders have interpreted it to mean that collective bargaining can come only through belonging to a union." Or, as the founder of the Citizens' Alliance, A. W. Strong, said, "I can conceive of dealing with a conservative and responsible labor leader, but certainly not with any of the AF of L leaders in Minneapolis."

Then NRA and Section 7a came to Minneapolis. In 1933, with encouragement from the Farmer-Labor governor, Floyd B. Olson, the truck drivers of the city began to organize. Their leaders were three brothers named Dunne, born in Little Falls, Minnesota, of Irish-Catholic stock, committed to a life of agitation and rebellion. Of the Dunne brothers, Vincent Raymond was the leader. He had started driving a team for a lumber company at the age of fourteen. A reliable worker, he became in turn weigh-master, dispatcher, and finally superintendent for a Minneapolis coal company. At the same time, he was a dedicated radical. A Wobbly, then a Communist, then too honest and independent to survive Communist discipline (the party expelled him as a Trotskyite in 1928) he remained a thoroughgoing class-conflict revolutionary Marxist, who nonetheless, because of his personal traits, dominated his local of the Teamsters Union and kept the confidence of the mass of drivers in the city.

As a distribution center, Minneapolis lived or died by transportation. For the business community, the plan to unionize the truckers seemed labor's attempt to gain a stranglehold over the city. The

Citizens' Alliance had smashed labor before, and it could do so again. It therefore declined in the spring of 1934 to deal with Local 574 of the Teamsters Union. The Regional Labor Board appealed to the employers to respect the provisions of 7a. This appeal had no effect. The workers responded on May 12, 1934, by calling a strike.

The Dunne brothers left little to chance. From strike head-quarters, Ray Dunne and Farrell Dobbs deployed their forces with military efficiency. The union had its own newspaper, its own sound trucks, its own intelligence network. It even provided its own hospital, knowing that for wounded strikers, city hospitals were often only a stopping place on the way to jail. In a short time, the strike was about 95 per cent effective. The city, as they put it locally, was tied up as tight as a bull's eye in flytime.

Negotiations continued. The union moderated its demands, and Governor Olson threatened to call out the National Guard if a settlement were not reached. But the employers, anticipating that public opinion would shift in their direction as the community began to feel the pinch of the strike, stiffened their position and prepared to go on the offensive. This meant a resumption of Citizens' Alliance tactics which had worked so well in the past. An Alliance agent in union ranks was directed to lead a group of pickets into a police trap. The phase of violence now began.

At a meeting of businessmen, Totten Heffelfinger called for a "mass movement of citizens" to end the strike. A "citizens' army" was mobilized on fashionable Lowry Hill to start the trucks rolling again in the streets of Minneapolis. Over 155 upper-class figures were sworn in as "special officers," a title accepted with Skull and Bones high spirits. As the sense of class strife mounted, other labor unions, which at first had hung back, affirmed solidarity with the truckers. The Central Labor Union endorsed the strike. Both sides began to arm themselves with lead pipes and baseball bats.

III

On the morning of May 22, 1934, after twenty-four hours of gathering tension, over twenty thousand people crowded into Minn-eapolis's central marketplace. Many were police and special dep-uties, determined to clear the market for trucks. Others were workers, determined to keep the trucks off the streets. There was an ominous interval of waiting. Then a scuffle: a striker tossed a crate of tomatoes through a plate-glass window; and, in a moment, the square dissolved into a melee. Clubs rose and fell, people screamed and cursed and ran. Two special deputies were killed: one a graduate of Hotchkiss and Yale and counsel for the Citizens' Alliance.

Governor Olson now ordered the mobilization of the National Guard. After the shock of what came to be known as the "Battle of Deputies Run," an agreement was proposed on the basis of indirect union recognition. The Dunne brothers persuaded the workers to accept this compromise (the local Communist party denounced them for selling out to the Alliance). But peace was only temporary. A series of wrangles broke out over an interpretation of the terms. Finally the employers, who still hoped to smash the union, broke off the talks. On July 16, 1934, the truckers voted again to strike.

Once more, the trucks stopped rolling; once more, tension began to build in the silent streets. The police, determined to start the trucks moving and apparently resolved on precipitating an incident, sent out a truck with an armed convoy. When a strikers' truck, manned by unarmed pickets, tried to block its way, the police without warning let loose a barrage of shotgun fire at the second truck and into a gathering crowd. In ten minutes they had shot sixty-seven persons, many in the back; two lay dying. "Suddenly I knew," wrote young Eric Sevareid, covering the scene for the Minneapolis *Star*. "I understood deep in my bones and blood what Fascism was." His father had the opposite reaction: "This — is *revolution!*" The sense of class war was tearing families and the city itself in two. When they buried one of the victims a few days later, a vast funeral procession of workers, marching somberly across the city, stopped all traffic.

Floyd Olson considered himself a radical and a friend of the workers. But he was also governor of the state of Minnesota and determined to uphold the public authority. Federal mediators had worked out a new plan of settlement. Olson now declared that unless both sides accepted the plan he would impose martial law. The union agreed but the employers refused and the National

Guard took over the embattled city. Olson promptly ordered a reduction of picketing and gave certain categories of trucks permission to move. The leaders of Local 574, regarding this as strikebreaking, demanded in an angry interview that Olson let them advise on the issuance of special truck permits; otherwise they would close down the city again. Olson's response was swift and brutal. He ordered a dawn raid of strike headquarters and an arrest of the strike leaders. Two days later, he ordered a similar raid of the Citizens' Alliance.

As time passed and negotiations resumed, a few employers began to sign up with the union on the basis of the federal plan. Finally on August 21 the Citizens' Alliance suddenly accepted the plan, giving the strikers, said Ray Dunne, "substantially what we have fought and bled for since the beginning." After a civil conflict stretching over four months, wide loss in property and wages, violence, death and martial law, the employers of Minneapolis conceded the right of the truckers to be represented by their own union. When the working men and women of Minneapolis heard the news they filled the streets for twelve hours of riotous cele-bration.[2]

IV

San Francisco, rising in splendor above the Bay, was the loveliest of American cities. But its veiled and shining beauty concealed a history of violence. With gambling and shooting and vigilantism, with fires and earthquakes, with riots and bomb outrages, San Franciscans had always lived near the line where death came casually.

San Francisco labor was strong-minded and turbulent; San Francisco employers were tough and unyielding. The sea offered a hard life at best, and it gave labor relations a savage character. "You can put me in jail," Andrew Furuseth, the sailor, said bitterly to those who tried to stop him from organizing his mates. "But you cannot give me narrower quarters than as a seaman I have always had. You cannot give me coarser food than I have always eaten. You cannot make me lonelier than I have always been." And longshoremen were equally bitter, awaiting the freighters in dawn shape-ups along foggy wharves or gathering in shabby hiring halls where the independent or rebellious faced an employers' blacklist. Harry Bridges of Australia, who had been both sailor and longshoreman and had lived in San Francisco since 1920, had soaked up the bitterness in his bones. Many, like him, who had lived harried lives along the waterfront now looked for work, for recognition, and for revenge.

Labor had once been powerful in San Francisco — powerful enough before the First World War to elect its own mayor. Then came the Preparedness Day bombing of 1916 — the bombing for which in 1934 Tom Mooney on imperfect evidence still lingered in the penitentiary. In the twenties, the employers formed an Industrial Association, established a company union, and tried to drive all national unions off the waterfront. By the early thirties, their control seemed secure.

But NRA came to San Francisco, as it came to Minneapolis. A local of the International Longshoremen's Association sprang into existence. A new militancy pervaded the Embarcadero, the longshoremen's boulevard winding along the waterfront. Harry Bridges was emerging as the dockers' leader. A slight, thin, tense man, dressed in cheap clothes and a worn overcoat, he was hard, suspicious, and reticent, without scruples and without illusions. Few people knew whether he was a card-holder in the Communist party: "I neither affirm nor deny that I am a Communist," he himself said. In his combination of cynicism and dedication, his lack of self-regard, his determination to stay close to the masses, he was an archetype of the Communist hero; and he rarely deviated from the Communist line. "We as workers have nothing in common with the employers," he told one audience in his sharp cockney voice. "We are in a class struggle."

For the employers, the class struggle was quite as real in fact, if not so explicit in theory. As the ILA began to seek recognition in the early spring of 1934, George Creel, the old Wilsonian, now serving on the Regional Labor Board, warned Roosevelt that the bosses wanted a showdown; any money they might lose as a result of a dock strike, Creel said, would be more than worth it in their view if the union were destroyed. In the negotiations, the employers bluntly refused to recognize the union. On May 9, 1934, the longshoremen denied other recourse, went out on strike.[3]

V

The strike opened in an atmosphere of violence. When the police tried to break up picket lines, other San Francisco unions, including the Teamsters, joined the walkout. A federal mediating team, led by Assistant Secretary of Labor Edward McGrady, worked out a compromise, accepted by Joseph Ryan, international president of the ILA, providing for union recognition with joint control of the hiring halls. The local leadership, however, feared that joint control would not do away with the blacklist, and turned down the plan. As the sympathetic strike spread within the city and as the dock strike crept up the coast toward Seattle, a sense of panic began to arise.

Early in July, the Industrial Association decided to open the port by force. On July 3, trucks with police convoy began to roll out of the docks toward company warehouses. Hostilities were adjourned over the holiday. But on Thursday, July 5, the effort to break the strike was resumed with full energy. Violence raged up and down the Embarcadero, as strikers tried to overturn trucks and dump goods in defiance of the police escorts. Bricks, stones, clubs, firehoses, tear gas, and finally guns came into play. At the end of Bloody Thursday, two strikers were dead and many more on both sides were injured. At midnight the National Guard marched into San Francisco to restore order.

Bloody Thursday sent a wave of shock through all San Francisco labor The local Communist party put out a call for a general strike, and Bridges carried the slogan to the unions. On July 12 the Teamsters, who had already struck the docks, now struck the whole city. In the next days, new groups of workers walked out. Even the most conservative unions joined the exodus. On July 16 the San Francisco general strike formally began, the first in America since Seattle in 1919.

By now, panic on the West Coast was reaching new intensity. HERE IS REVOLUTION NOT ONLY IN THE MAKING BUT WITH THE INITIAL ACTUALITY, Senator Hiram Johnson, the old radical, wired Harold Ickes. . . . NOT ALONE IS THIS SAN FRANCISCO DISASTER BUT IT IS POSSIBLE RUIN OF THE PACIFIC COAST. Governor Julius Meier of Oregon told the President: GOVERNOR OF CALIFORNIA INDICATES HE WILL ASK

FOR FEDERAL TROOPS AND I WILL DO SAME . . . TO PREVENT INSURREC-
TION WHICH IF NOT CHECKED WILL DEVELOP INTO CIVIL WAR. At this
point, Hugh Johnson arrived in San Francisco on an NRA inspec-
tion tour. Unable to resist the temptations of melodrama, the General at once delivered himself of a characteristic denunciation. The
strike, he said, "is a threat to the community. It is a menace to
government. It is Civil War. . . . If the Federal Government did
not act, this people would act to wipe out this subversive element as
you clean off a chalk mark on a blackboard with a wet sponge."
Responsible unions, said the General, "must erase this sinister bar
from their escutcheons. They must run these subversive influences
out from their ranks like rats."

In Washington, in the meantime, with the President away on the
U.S.S. *Houston* in the Pacific, there was a division of counsel.
Homer Cummings and Cordell Hull favored drastic measures.
Frances Perkins, on the other hand, refused to regard the San Francisco tie-up as a general strike in any serious sense; it seemed to her
a spontaneous demonstration to vindicate the right of collective
bargaining. Cummings and Hull wanted Roosevelt to break his
cruise and order the strike put down by force. But Louis Howe
cabled him reassuringly for Miss Perkins, ONLY DANGER SAN FRAN-
CISCO STRIKE IS THAT MAYOR IS BADLY FRIGHTENED AND HIS FEAR HAS
INFECTED ENTIRE CITY. Howe and Miss Perkins urged the President
not to cut short his trip; such action would only START THE VERY
PANIC IT IS NECESSARY TO AVOID. "Everybody demanded that I sail
into San Francisco Bay," Roosevelt later said, "all flags flying and
guns double shotted, and end the strike. They went completely
off the handle."

They *had* gone off the handle: Miss Perkins's estimate was much
closer to the truth. Far from being a triumph of revolutionary
syndicalism, the strike, in spite of its measure of Communist direction, was ill-considered and improvised. "What we see," said Walter Lippmann justly, "is a revolutionary weapon being wielded
by men who do not want revolution." The leadership, having
shut down the city, had no idea what to do next. "When the means
of food supply — milk to children, necessities of life to the whole
people — are threatened," said Johnson, "that is bloody insurrection." In fact, the so-called general strike stopped short of con-

trolling food, light, power, water supply, communications, or the press; no one went hungry; essential services continued. "About the only real deprivation endured by the general public," said one observer, "was the inability to go to the theater, eat in a hotel dining room, ride in a taxi or a Market St. Railway car, get clothes cleaned or washed, and get a hair-cut." Lacking a defined political objective, the general strike succeeded in provoking the community without intimidating it. In four days it collapsed. Over Bridges's opposition, the longshoremen accepted arbitration. In the end they gained union recognition and most of their specific demands.[4]

VI

Minneapolis and San Francisco were more bloody and spectacular than the rest. They were not alone. In Toledo in the spring of 1934, strikes for union recognition at the Electric Auto-Lite Company and the Toledo Edison Company led to police violence and to labor demands for a general strike. On a spring day late in May, Ohio National Guardsmen, in tin hats and khaki, carrying gas bombs, rifles, bayonets, and machine guns, marched into the Auto-Lite plant to evacuate strikebreaking workers. Pickets showered the Guardsmen with bricks and beer bottles and broke the windows of the factory ("now you have your open shop"). When the soldiers fired into the crowd, two people were killed, hundreds more wounded and gassed. Confronted by the threat of general strike, the employers agreed under federal mediation by Charles P. Taft II to settle on terms which met most of the union demands.

The issue in Minneapolis, San Francisco, and Toledo was labor's right to self-organization and collective bargaining. In each case, an inflexibly anti-union employer policy thrust the leadership of labor into radical hands — Trotskyites in Minneapolis, Stalinists in San Francisco, Musteites in Toledo. Indeed, Dan Tobin, international president of the Teamsters, actually disavowed the strike leadership in Minneapolis as Joe Ryan of the ILA disavowed it in San Francisco. Employer immoderation in this period of grass-roots unionism made labor immoderation inevitable.

And so it continued through the turbulent summer. Late in July in Kohler, Wisconsin, a company town, special deputies shot down two pickets when the Kohler Company refused to bargain with an AF of L union. On August 31, 1934, the United Textile Workers called a strike, which in the next weeks left violence in its trail from Georgia to Rhode Island. In Georgia, Gene Talmadge set up a concentration camp for unruly pickets. Sheriff's deputies killed six strikers at Honea Path, South Carolina. In North Carolina, old Josephus Daniels wrote Franklin Roosevelt, "Mill men put arms in the hands of the men in the mills and the Governor called out the State Guard, at the request of the owners. . . . In nearly every instance the troops might as well have been under the direction of the mill owners." In Rhode Island strikers and troops clashed in the streets. "A few hundred funerals," observed the New England trade journal *Fibre and Fabric,* "will have a quieting influence." Late in September, the union leaders, pulling back in alarm, called the strike off on terms which meant disastrous defeat.[5]

VII

Defeat, indeed, was the keynote for labor in 1934. There were local successes as in Minneapolis, San Francisco, and Toledo; but the main story was failure, and, most crucial of all, failure in the mass production industries. Labor failed in textiles, failed in the automobile industry, failed in steel, failed in rubber.

Part of the failure was labor's own fault — the result, in particular, of the weakness of the American Federation of Labor's leadership and, even more, of the irrelevance of the AF of L philosophy to the particular organizing circumstances of the 1930's. Thus in the automobile case the first mistake was Green's acceptance of reservations in the Automobile Code which seriously limited the application of 7a to the industry. Then the Federation showed little initial interest in organizing the auto workers under the Code. When it belatedly accepted the challenge, it sent in organizers who, reared in craft traditions, spent as much time discouraging militancy among the workers as in exhibiting it toward the bosses. In February 1934, when Hugh Johnson reinterpreted the Automobile Code to establish proportional representation in place of majority rule, Green went along; and he acquiesced in the supersession of the National Labor Board by the Automobile Labor Board under Leo Wolman. When the Federation finally decided to contest the Wolman Board, it did so timidly and ineffectually. In the meantime, by ignoring the auto workers, thwarting their organizing efforts, and sabotaging their strikes, the AF of L leadership of the auto union succeeded in reducing its membership from perhaps 100,000 in 1934 to 10,000 by the winter of 1935.

In the case of steel, there had existed before NRA a venerable union with about 5000 members under Michael F. Tighe, a seventy-six-year-old leader known, whether affectionately or not, as "Grandmother" Tighe. After NRA, the steelworkers began to call strikes, which Tighe mostly denounced, and to organize locals of his union, which Tighe mostly resented. Through 1934 the old man tried to wrestle with the embarrassments of young impatient followers who wanted their union to do something. He was fairly successful: by the fall of 1934, he could tell the AF of L convention that of the 100,000 who had applied for membership in 1933 and 1934 only 5300 were still in the union.

When Akron rubber workers set up a union on a plant basis, an AF of L organizer split it up into nineteen separate craft locals, from Blacksmiths through Metal Workers to Teamsters. And so on, through other mass-production industries. Old-line leaders, used to organizing skilled workers by crafts, could not face the vast explosion of energy involved in organizing unskilled workers by industries. The premonitory stirrings from below frightened them; they feared releasing forces with which they could not deal. Moreover, they remembered other times — most recently in 1919–21 — when emotionalism had overextended the labor movement only to weaken it in the face of new crises. For them the problem was less to get new unions than to keep old ones strong enough to weather adversity. So concern for the movement as well as for their own position in it made them do everything they could to keep the new energies from overturning the old structure. The result, in a time when workingmen wanted to organize from below, was frustration.

There were outside reasons too for labor's defeat in 1934. Employers, believing that everything depended on smashing the drive for recognition, were fighting back as never before. Thus in steel, automobiles, and rubber, while the AF of L frittered its opportunity away, there was an unprecedented development of company unionism. This was only the first line of defense. Fundamentalist employees prepared to fight it out, if necessary, on the barricades. Never had American businessmen hired so many private police, strikebreakers, thugs, spies, and *agents provocateurs*. Never had they laid up such stores of tear gas, machine guns, and firearms.

Beyond this, there was the federal government itself, more uncertain than ever before about its own labor policy. Officially it stood committed to the program of self-organization announced in 7a. But, in administering 7a, it could not outrun the actual power situation. Where labor leadership was strong, as in coal and the needle trades, 7a benefited labor. Where labor leadership was weak, as in steel and automobiles, 7a could not make up the deficit. Moreover, the ambiguities of 7a left room for discretion within the administration. In practice, government became less the impartial administrator of a law than a battleground of conflicting forces, some favoring the rise of an independent labor movement, others reflecting the apprehensions of the employers. The struggle centered increasingly around the new agency created in June 1934 under Public Resolution No. 44 — the National Labor Relations Board.[6]

24. Development of a National Labor Policy

THE CHAIRMAN of the National Labor Relations Board was Lloyd K. Garrison, Dean of the Wisconsin Law School. Garrison, a bright, pink-cheeked man of thirty-six, had the liberal convictions without the fanaticism of his abolitionist ancestor. His two colleagues were Professor Harry A. Millis of the University of Chicago, a labor economist, patient, knowledgeable, and mellow, and Edwin S. Smith, the Commissioner of Labor and Industries of Massachusetts, whose long fight for decent working conditions had evidently instilled a bitter conviction that no substantial improvement was possible within the capitalist order. When Garrison resigned in November 1934, he was succeeded as chairman by Francis Biddle, a Philadelphia lawyer, Groton and Harvard, who beneath his social and legal respectability had a sharp and inquiring mind and a lively interest in pioneering in the uncharted area of labor law.

II

The new Board had more status and power than the National Labor Board which it superseded. It was independent of NRA; it had explicit authority to interpret Section 7a and to hold elections; for this purpose, it could subpoena company payrolls, as its predecessor could not. But it inherited the NLB's two major problems. One was the question of majority rule — the principle, that is, that when a majority of workers chose a union, the employer must bargain exclusively with that union as representing all workers. Without this principle, the NLRB believed, collective bargaining was a farce. And the related question was that of the enforcement of NLRB decisions.

Like the NLB, the NLRB was dependent for enforcement either on an appeal to the NRA to withdraw the Blue Eagle or on an appeal to the Department of Justice to institute legal action. In August 1934, when the Board found the Chicago Motor Coach Company guilty of violating Section 7a, Garrison asked the NRA to remove the Blue Eagle. Johnson refused, partly because he thought removal would be ineffectual and NRA could secure compliance without it, partly because he resented Garrison's intervention. He did not believe, he told Garrison, "that you have been on this job or — for that matter — on this planet long enough to advise me about the sensitive, subtle and serious situation with which we are dealing. . . . It is like a boy who had ridden a raft out of the Johnstown Flood lecturing Noah about the Ark."

Garrison persisted despite Johnson's lectures; and for a time, as Johnson faded from the NRA picture, he succeeded in getting from NRA fairly automatic execution of NLRB recommendations. In the meantime, the Board went ahead to reaffirm the principle of majority rule. Its decision in the Houde Engineering Corporation case of September 1, 1934, rejected the proportional-representation interpretation of Section 7a laid down by Johnson and Richberg in February and presumably endorsed by the President during the automobile dispute in March. The Houde company announced that it would not obey the decision, and the National Association of Manufacturers urged all employers to disregard it. The Board replied by asking NRA to withdraw the Blue Eagle from Houde, which was done, and then by asking the Department of Justice to institute a suit against the company.

III

In the fall of 1934, as Richberg returned to influence in NRA, the moment of cooperation with the NLRB came to an end. By November Richberg was undertaking a public campaign against the majority rule principle. Then a new problem appeared to make the issue sharp between the two agencies. A year before a group of newspapermen, headed by Heywood Broun, the columnist, had or-

ganized the American Newspaper Guild to improve working conditions and job security in the newspaper field. Dean Jennings,
fired from Hearst's San Francisco *Call-Bulletin* for Guild activity,
appealed to the San Francisco Regional Labor Board. The Board
accepted the case; but the *Call-Bulletin* refused to appear, saying
that jurisdiction properly belonged to a special board set up under
the Newspaper Code Authority. The Newspaper Industrial Board
had been deadlocked on every important issue since its inception,
and reference of the case to it could only mean that nothing would
ever happen. So Jennings persisted in applying to the NLRB machinery, and by late November the case reached Washington. Millis,
anticipating trouble, doubted whether the Board should accept it.
But Biddle felt that there was no point in trying much longer to
avoid a showdown with Richberg.

So Biddle, the former counsel for the Pennsylvania Railroad,
contended for labor organization against Richberg, the former
counsel for the railroad brotherhoods. On November 26 Biddle
said that he saw no reason to surrender the case to NRA at this
late date. On December 6 Richberg complained to the White
House, "The Newspaper Guild representatives are not acting in
good faith, but simply trying maliciously to make trouble." On
December 12 the NLRB ordered Jenning's reinstatement. The next
day Richberg predicted that if the NLRB continued to take cases
away from boards set up under code authorities, the result would
be the disintegration of efforts to adjust labor relations under the
codes. "When a federal agency not only disregards suggestions of
the 'Commander,'" Richberg added insinuatingly in a note to the
White House, "but issues a public attack upon him, the matter
requires the attention of higher authority." By the end of the
month, Richberg could hardly contain himself about the NLRB.
In handwritten notes to Roosevelt, he accused it of "arrogant self-
assertion," demanded its reorganization, and complained of having been "viciously" libeled by Heywood Broun. "The Board,"
he concluded, "is today doing much more harm than good. It's
[*sic*] power for mischief should be curbed."

Richberg's protests were backed up by a great outcry from newspaper publishers, who affected to see in the NLRB acceptance of
the Jennings case an assault on the First Amendment and a threat

to the freedom of the press. Roosevelt was prevailed upon to intervene; and in January he sent Biddle a letter telling the NLRB to
stay out of cases where labor relations machinery existed under the
codes. This included automobiles, newspapers, soft coal, and other
industries. With relish, Richberg called up Biddle, who had not
been consulted, to inform him of the presidential decision. Millis
and Smith thought the Board should resign. But Biddle, judging
the situation to be in flux, argued that there still might be value
in a fight, and Senator Wagner backed him up.

By March 1935, however, the NLRB seemed to have come to the
end of its tether. Much of its jurisdiction had gone. In fields
where its jurisdiction was not yet challenged, it was finding it
harder and harder to secure compliance. Enforcement through
NRA was not only increasingly problematic but increasingly ineffective; and, of the thirty-three cases the NLRB had referred to
the Department of Justice, practically nothing was heard of most
of them again. On top of all this, a federal district court decision
late in February in the long postponed Weirton case held Section
7a itself to be unconstitutional.

The Board well understood its own weaknesses. It had power
to subpoena witnesses and records only in connection with elections. Every time it ordered an election, the employers could stall
by securing an injunction. Its findings, in last analysis, were nothing more than recommendations; and, as Biddle bitterly observed to
a Senate committee, "the recommendation of the National Board is
nothing more than an opinion." "The Board," its members concluded, "is powerless to enforce its decisions." [1]

IV

A year before, Senator Wagner had perceived the difficulty and
proposed a remedy. In 1934, Roosevelt had been able to sidetrack
the Wagner bill. Now the New York senator, dismayed by the
NLRB's growing troubles, determined to try again. Leon Keyserling, his counsel, together with Calvert Magruder, general counsel of the Board, set to work on a new bill. Francis Biddle in
speeches and statements began to build public support for new
labor legislation. And the labor movement, seeing 7a on the verge

of collapse, backed the campaign. On February 21, 1935, Wagner introduced the bill into the Senate.

Behind the bill lay Wagner's belief that economic stability could be achieved only through a wider distribution of the proceeds of industry. In the twenties, without a strong labor movement, the gains of productivity had gone into plant, profits and speculation rather than into the support of demand; the inevitable result, Wagner said, was depression. The best way to secure "that fair distribution of purchasing power upon which permanent prosperity must rest" was through strengthening collective bargaining. His bill proposed to give the NLRB new power — power to order elections; power to define and prohibit unfair labor practices (such as the employer-dominated company union, the discriminatory discharge of union members, or the refusal to bargain in good faith); power to enforce decisions through machinery modeled on that of the Federal Trade Commission. The aspirations of Section 7a at last had the promise of becoming enforceable realities.

But the administration, despite its mild approval of a similar bill a year before, now took a strict hands off attitude. Frances Perkins warily described the measure as "very interesting." Richberg, the most influential labor adviser at the White House was actively hostile; and his persisting, if no longer justified, pro-labor reputation made his views the more compelling with the President. Roosevelt himself seemed to partake of the antilabor mood. "Labor's public enemy No. 1," cried Heywood Broun, still aggrieved over the Jennings case, at a New York mass meeting, "is Franklin D. Roosevelt." [2]

v

For Roosevelt, labor was not, like conservation or social welfare, a field in which he had primary experience or clear-cut views. He approached it quite without the preconceptions of his class — with, indeed, sympathy for the idea of organized labor as a makeweight to the power of organized business. But he sympathized with organized labor more out of a reaction against employer primitivism than as necessarily a hopeful new development in itself. This attitude spared him hysteria over incidents like San Francisco, without giving him great general confidence in the unions. "I am fairly certain," he wrote of San Francisco, "that the Manufacturers Association and some of that crowd did everything they could do to foment the general strike, knowing that a general strike can never be successful and that when it failed it would end the days of organized labor." Similarly, when the steel barons refused to sit around a table with William Green, Roosevelt was indignant. "That kind of autocratic attitude on the part of a steel company official," he said, "does not make for working things out." "On the other hand," he quickly added, "there are other people on the other end of the camp, the labor end, who are just as autocratic."

He saw himself as holding the balance between business and labor; and he viewed both sides with detachment. Though during the First World War and as governor of New York Roosevelt had prided himself on affable relations with labor leaders. Tugwell was undoubtedly right in noting that he showed with them little of the instinctive rapport he displayed at once when farm leaders sat across his desk. Both Frances Perkins and Francis Biddle have testified to his indifference to the technical problems of unionism — in marked contrast to his detailed interest in problems of agriculture or conservation. As late as 1944, he could not remember — or perhaps under the stress of war had forgotten — whether the International Ladies' Garment Workers' Union was "Sidney Hillman's or Dubinsky's outfit." Reared in the somewhat paternalistic traditions of prewar progressivism and of the social work ethos, Roosevelt thought instinctively in terms of government's doing things for working people rather than of giving the unions power to win workers their own victories.

Above all, the President's primary concern in 1934 and 1935 was economic recovery. He seems to have been impressed by the argument that production might get ahead faster if labor decisions could be postponed until business was on its feet again. While he sympathized with the grievances which drove labor to strike, he was often irritated by strikes themselves, especially when they complicated his pursuit of other political or economic objectives. During the strike wave in the summer of 1934 a memorandum from Homer Cummings told him how he might, if necessary, call out federal troops. At the height of the textile strike, six weeks later,

Steve Early sent him language for this purpose, recommending a Harding proclamation as "the most appropriate to follow in the present emergency." Roosevelt, of course, did not take such drastic action; yet it was evidently under consideration at the White House.

Nor, indeed, did New Dealers in general have much expectation in 1934 of creative contributions from labor. In Frances Perkins's experience, the unions never had any ideas of their own; most labor and welfare legislation in her time had been brought about by middle-class reformers in face of labor indifference. Tugwell declared that labor "seems always to be in opposition, to be resisting progress. . . . In this they are perhaps worse than most other American groups." A labor renaissance, he added, appeared unlikely; yet "strange things have happened before in history; perhaps this too may occur." Perhaps; but few New Dealers counted on it in 1933 or 1934. Edmund Wilson found it hard to find anybody in the administration in 1934 who "knows anything of the way that the American world looks and feels to labor." Neither politically nor intellectually was the New Deal much interested in the labor movement during Roosevelt's first years.[3]

VI

Wagner was almost alone among liberal Democrats in placing a high value on trade unions; and it was Wagner who was almost singlehandedly forcing a reluctant administration into a national labor policy. Hearings on the revised Wagner bill began before the Senate Labor Committee in March 1935. The main issue among the bill's supporters was whether the new Board should be independent of the Labor Department. Wagner and Biddle thought it should, and so for a time did William Green, until, as he later said, Frances Perkins fixed him with her eye and persuaded him that he thought she should have it. Miss Perkins's own testimony was benign, remote, and somewhat inconclusive. For the rest, Wagner, Biddle, the labor leaders, some labor relations experts like Garrison, Millis, William M. Leiserson, and Will H. Davis, along with a few businessmen, argued for the bill.

In general, they contended that labor's right to organize was essential to democratic society, not only as "a matter of simple justice" (Garrison) but as a means of achieving economic and social balance. Only a strong labor movement could uphold wages and preserve purchasing power from "this continually shrinking shriveling process that is going on today" (Biddle). Even more important, only a strong labor movement could give the workers a feeling that their grievances could be redressed within the capitalist system. As Garrison said, he was for the bill "as a safety measure, because I regard organized labor in this country as our chief bulwark against communism and other revolutionary movements."

As for the bill itself, Wagner suggested, nothing new was involved; it simply gave effect to principles long established in labor law. "It seems to me," Professor Sumner Slichter of Harvard had remarked in the testimony a year earlier, "to be a bill which ought to arouse very little controversy." Wagner denied that it was "one-sided" because it imposed obligations on employers and not on workers. "No one would assail a traffic law because it regulates the speed at which automobiles run and not the speed at which people walk. . . . No one feels that the Securities and Exchange Act is iniquitous because it places duties upon brokers but not upon buyers." Experience had shown that the only way to give Section 7a meaning was to set up machinery which could enforce it.

But for the business community, Section 7a, as an aspiration, was one thing; the idea of enforcing it was quite different. "The bill," said the *Commercial and Financial Chronicle*, "is one of the most objectionable, as well as one of the most revolutionary, pieces of legislation ever presented to Congress." Lewis Brown of Johns-Manville, Charles R. Hook of the American Rolling Mill Company, George H. Houston of Baldwin Locomotive, and eleven other durable-goods magnates, claiming to employ over half the manufacturing force of the country, denounced the bill as inviting unions to use "without restraint or responsibility, the most dangerous weapons of social coercion." Henry I. Harriman predicted that it would have a "disastrous effect upon the economic life of the country." "It would result," said the National Automobile Chamber of Commerce, "in giving a labor union official virtual domination over American industrial life." Ernest T. Weir called it "one of the most vicious pieces of legislation ever proposed"; "it will mean," he added, "the end of the fine spirit of cooperation between employers and employees, which has been growing through employee-representation plans." Walter Lippmann said that, "if the bill were passed it could not be made to work," adding that it was a "legal monstrosity" and "one of the most reactionary measures of our time." According to the Associated Industries of Oklahoma, it "would out-STALIN Stalin, out-SOVIET the Russian Soviets, create a despotism from which none could escape or appeal . . . the most amazingly vicious and daring attack upon industry and the liberty of individual conduct in the history of American government!" Alfred P. Sloan, Jr., of General Motors summed up the sense of panic: "Industry, if it has any appreciation of its obligations to future generations, will fight this proposal to the very last." David Lawrence's *United States News* described the National Association of Manufacturers campaign against the bill as "the greatest ever conducted by industry regarding any Congressional measure."

The one group which exceeded the leaders of American business in their hatred of the bill was the American Communist party. The new NLRB, the Communists said, would be "a weapon to destroy the power which the workers have gained through their economic organizations." [4]

VII

While the debate raged, the Senate Labor Committee, dominated by Wagner, considered the bill and on May 2, 1935, reported unanimously in its favor. Southern Democrats made last-minute efforts to persuade Roosevelt to ask for delay. But Wagner induced him to let nature take its course. On May 15, the New York senator brought the bill to the floor of the Senate in an eloquent speech. After a scattering of debate, the bill came up for roll call the next day. Even southern Democrats like James F. Byrnes, Walter George, and Tom Connally backed it. Eight Republicans, led by Warren Austin and Arthur Vandenberg, joined four conservative Democrats in opposition. The vote was 63–12.

There was still the possibility of a presidential veto. Secretary of Commerce Roper wrote on May 22, "It seems almost inevitable that the Administration would have much to lose in public support if it could be represented as taking steps designed to impose such labor control by a single organization in the country." Roosevelt, influenced by the Senate vote, and probably losing faith in the wisdom of Richberg, kept his counsel. On May 24 he convened a White House conference where Wagner and Richberg debated the measure. In the course of the discussion, Roosevelt made it at last clear that he wanted the Wagner bill in some form.

In the middle of June the bill came on the floor of the House. Here southern Democrats led the attack. Eugene Cox of Georgia declared that the bill carried on its face "the most terrible threat — and I speak deliberately and advisedly — to our dual form of government that has thus far arisen." Howard Smith of Virginia, seconded by many Republicans, joined in the onslaught. But most congressmen clearly favored the bill, whether because they were impressed by the vigorous work of the American Federation of Labor in the lobbies, or because they hoped that the Supreme Court might eventually declare it unconstitutional. On June 19, the bill passed the House without a roll call. After differences between the House and Senate had been ironed out in conference, the bill went to the President, who signed it on July 5, 1935.

On the same day, Francis Biddle, under pressure from his law partners to rejoin his firm, submitted his resignation. A few weeks later Roosevelt appointed as his successor J. Warren Madden, a sweet-tempered and unpretending professor of law from the University of Pittsburgh. Edwin S. Smith continued as a member of the new Board, and John M. Carmody of the National Mediation Board replaced Millis, who was eager to return to Chicago.

Two weeks later the American Liberty League, an organization of businessmen and conservatives, published a brief signed by fifty-eight lawyers pronouncing the Wagner Act invalid, "a complete departure from our constitutional and traditional theories of government." A reporter asked Earl F. Reed, counsel for the Weirton Steel Company and chairman of the Liberty League Committee, whether he would now advise a client to obey the Wagner Act. "I feel perfectly free," answered Reed, "to advise a client not to be bound by a law that I consider unconstitutional."

Labor's struggle for recognition had not ended It was only entering a new period.[5]

25. Emergence of the CIO

WHILE CONGRESS EVOLVED a national labor policy, the labor movement itself was struggling to clarify its purposes. The failure of the organizing drive of 1934 fortified doubts concerning both the old-time leadership and the old-time philosophy of the American Federation of Labor.

Samuel Gompers, on his death in 1924, had bequeathed to his successors a clear-cut theory of labor organization. In the hard experience of forty years, the Federation seemed to have made its enduring gains in a single way — through the organization of strategic workers and, by this means, the organization of employers. There had been times, as in the turbulent eighties, when working people themselves got religion and organized from below. But reliance on grass-roots evangelism had produced the excesses and vulnerabilities of the Knights of Labor. The essence of the Gompers philosophy was a distrust of rank-and-file revivalism and a belief that solid gains came only by organizing from above.

The strategy of organizing key workers implied two other doctrines — voluntarism and craft unionism. Voluntarism was the doctrine that labor had nothing to gain from the intervention of the state. Craft unionism was the doctrine that workers should be organized by the skills they possessed and the tools they used rather than by the product they created or the plant in which they worked. Only by remaining faithful to these tenets, the old-line leaders felt, could they build unions strong enough to resist the pressure of employers and government and to survive economic adversity.

The depression had caused certain inroads on the old faith. The Federation found itself endorsing unemployment insurance and hailing Section 7a and the Wagner bill. Moreover, the leaders could hardly ignore the new clamor for organization from below. William Green, an amiable man who would have liked to keep everyone happy, told the AF of L convention in October 1933 that the new slogan must be "Organize the Unorganized in the Mass Production Industries" and spoke of raising the membership of the Federation to ten ("the next step"), even twenty-five, million. These were brave words, and they struck terror in the hearts of editorial writers. Yet, when the time came to act, something held him back. He seemed to feel about the unorganized workers in the heavy industries, in Ben Stolberg's cruel phrase, "as an old and impotent man feels about a young and desirable woman. He wants her, yet he is afraid." [1]

II

What held him back, above all, was the collection of tough and clear-sighted men in the ruling hierarchy of the AF of L. These men looked with dismay on the emerging tendencies in labor — the movement for unionization from below; the resort to government; above all, the demand for organization by industrial units.

This last raised particularly critical issues. Though the AF of L contained industrial unions, such as the United Mine Workers and the Amalgamated Clothing Workers, it was committed to a constitutional theory of the exclusive jurisdiction of craft unions, a jurisdiction extending even to those who were only potentially union members. The craft tradition was thus imbedded in the very structure of the movement. It had given the Federation its peculiar stamp. It had kept it essentially an association of skilled workers from older immigrant stocks — Yankees, Irish, Germans, Scandinavians. The history of the Federation, indeed, was the history of one attempt after another to repulse the heresy of industrial unionism, whether espoused by the Knights of Labor in the eighties, by Eugene V. Debs and the American Railway Union in the nineties, by the Industrial Workers of the World after the turn of the century, by Daniel De Leon with his conception of the industrial union as "at once, the battering ram with which to pound down the fortress of capitalism, and the successor of the capitalist social structure itself," by the Communists. To the old-timers, the craft idea seemed constitutionally, politically, and socially the very guarantee of union strength and stability.

Against this, industrial unionism as a general policy meant the denial of the exclusive jurisdiction of existing unions. It challenged the hierarchy of rights from which the movement derived its integrity. It threatened a barbarian invasion of Eastern Europeans and Negroes boiling up from the unskilled and unwashed depths of the labor market. No one could foretell the calamitous consequences of such a departure. The old-timers recurred to the wisdom of Gompers thirty years before: "The attempt to force the trade union into what has been termed industrial organization is perversive to the history of the labor movement, runs counter to the best conception of the toilers' interests now and is sure to lead to the confusion which precedes dissolution."

But the onset of depression and then of the New Deal had brought the older philosophy into question. Once again, a mass demand for organization was surging up from below. In addition, a benevolent government was offering labor new opportunities. In the mass-production industries, the attempt to divide a working force along craft lines seemed particularly artificial; it succeeded only in weakening the bargaining position of workers against an increasingly concentrated organization of business. With NRA, it was the industrial unions which made the spectacular gains. By 1935, indeed, on the basis of their reports to the Federation, craft unions showed a growth in membership of only 13 per cent since 1933 as against 132 per cent for the Federation's four industrial unions and 126 per cent for the semi-industrial unions. Such statistics, combined with the collapse of the AF of L's mass-production campaigns, seemed to attest the impotence of the craft idea. If, said John L. Lewis of the Mine Workers, "the labor movement in this country cannot fulfill its mission unless the basic, mechanized, mass production industries are organized upon an industrial basis, it is clear that the American Federation of Labor, so long as it permits craft unions to possess jurisdiction over skilled workers in these basic industries, cannot meet the proper requirements of an organized labor movement in America." [2]

III

The fight for industrial unionism took off from the problem of the "federal unions," set up in 1933 as catchalls in unorganized areas until workers could be apportioned among the established craft unions. Such unions were by definition temporary and powerless. Yet they represented too great a gesture toward industrial unionism for the older leaders. In the 1933 convention Frey and other old-timers condemned the federal-union policy. But at a meeting of the Executive Council in January 1934, the federal unions showed an equal determination to survive. The argument continued inconclusively through the year until the annual convention at San Francisco in October.

After nearly a week of wrangling in committee, Charles P. Howard of the Typographical Union, who, while representing a craft union, favored industrial unions in the mass-production industries, contrived a compromise. The Howard resolution began by pledging existing unions full protection in their jurisdictional rights. It went on, however, to assert the special needs of the mass-production industries; and it called on the Executive Council to issue charters in the automotive, cement, aluminum, and other unspecified industries and to launch an organizing campaign in iron and steel. At the same time, the resolution concluded that the Federation itself for a provisional period would have to direct the policies of the new unions in order to safeguard the rights of the old.

On the surface, the industrial principle seemed to have gained a victory; certainly it had never won such explicit recognition in an AF of L convention. Even John L. Lewis spoke for the resolution with apparent enthusiasm. But the old-line leaders consoled themselves by reflecting that the industrial charters, if construed in terms of the guarantee of exclusive craft jurisdiction, could not mean very much. And, in any case, the Executive Council showed little disposition to carry out the resolution. It first delayed the issue of charters — ten months after San Francisco for automobiles, eleven months for rubber — and then hedged them round with reservations to protect the sacred rights of the crafts. It showed no disposition to promote serious organizing campaigns in automobiles and rubber, and no disposition to act at all in steel.

Through 1935 the industrial-union bloc — Lewis, Howard, Sidney Hillman of the Amalgamated, David Dubinsky of the ILGWU, George L. Berry of the Pressmen — grew increasingly dissatisfied. Theirs was a curious coalition. Lewis was himself an old-timer, for many years a member of the ruling clique; yet he headed an industrial union and now saw limitless possibilities in the industrial idea. Hillman and Dubinsky represented the newer immigrants seeking status in an alien society. Howard and Berry were astute veterans who perceived the need of the times.

Opposed were the stalwarts of the Federation — Green, Matthew Woll of the Photo-Engravers, John P. Frey of the Molders, and the labor barons: Dan Tobin of the Teamsters, Arthur O. Wharton of the Machinists, Dan Tracy of the Electricians, T. A. Rickert of the United Garment Workers, and, above all, Bill Hutcheson of the Carpenters. These men were business unionists, concerned only with the interests of their own membership, indifferent to ideology, contemptuous as good Irishmen of the late-coming Italians, Slavs, Negroes, and poor whites — the "rubbish," as Dan Tobin called them — crowding into the movement from the heavy industries. (It was Bill Collins of the New York Federation of Labor who remarked to Norman Thomas, "My wife can always tell from the smell of my clothes what breed of foreigners I've been hanging out with.") [3]

IV

In October 1935, as the delegates gathered at Atlantic City for the annual convention, both sides were maneuvering toward a showdown. The resolutions committee, confronted with twenty-one proposals on the subject of industrial unionism, brought in a majority report by Frey making decisive the San Francisco guarantee of exclusive craft jurisdiction and a minority report by Howard demanding a clear-cut policy of industrial organization with "unrestricted charters" in the mass-production industries.

In the ensuing debate, Howard gave a cool and judicious explanation of the need for a new departure. Matthew Woll then assailed industrial unionism, along with the Wagner Act, as betrayals of the heritage of Gompers. Next John L. Lewis, rising in majestic indignation, denounced the Federation's "twenty-five years of constant, unbroken failure" in the basic industries. President Green, "in a moment of exuberance," had talked of organizing twenty-five million workers; "perhaps President Green's arithmetic was wrong and he meant twenty-five thousand, because the total results are nearer the twenty-five thousand than the twenty-five million." So long as the craft philosophy remained dominant, even the new unions could only die "like the grass withering before the Autumn sun."

Lewis spoke with irony of the resolution adopted the year before. "At San Francisco they seduced me with fair words. Now, of course, having learned that I was seduced, I am enraged and I am ready to rend my seducers limb from limb, including Delegate Woll. In that sense, of course, I speak figuratively." With eloquence, he reminded the delegates that the labor movement was organized on the principle that the strong should help the weak. "Heed this cry from Macedonia that comes from the hearts of men. Organize the unorganized and in doing this make the American Federation of Labor the greatest instrument that has ever been forged in the history of modern civilization to befriend the cause of humanity." Let no one underestimate the issue. "Methinks that upon this decision of this convention may rest the future of the American Federation of Labor."

In the evening, the convention voted 18,204 to 10,993 for the craft position. But this vote did not settle the fight. In subsequent days the craft and industrial blocs warred over new aspects of the issue. John Frey solemnly invoked ancient AF of L precedents, identified industrial unionism with Debs, De Leon, Stalin, Mussolini, and Hitler and declared, "The American Federation is going to carry on just as it has in the past." Philip Murray, Lewis's ablest lieutenant in the Mine Workers, drew a comic portrait of Frey, "with poetry on his lips and tears coursing down his cheeks," and vigorously reaffirmed the industrial case. Toward the end of the convention, as delegates from the new automobile and rubber unions tried to gain the floor, Big Bill Hutcheson, the head of the Carpenters, signaled for a point of order, contending that the industrial-union question had already been settled.

William Green, who was presiding, conceded the point well taken. Lewis rose angrily and spoke for the right of the industrial delegates to be heard. "This thing of raising points of order all the time on minor delegates," he concluded, "is rather small potatoes." Hutcheson, his face flushed, leaped again to his feet, his six feet three inches overshadowing even Lewis's formidable bulk. "I was raised on small potatoes," he said with ponderous sarcasm. "That is why I am so small."

Lewis, on his way down the aisle to his own seat, paused by the towering Hutcheson and muttered, "Pretty small stuff." "We could have made you small," said Hutcheson furiously: "could have kept you off the executive council, if we wanted to." Then he mumbled a contemptuous phrase of which only the word "bastard" came through. Lewis's face tightened; and, while delegates idly watched the two men arguing, Lewis suddenly swung on Hutcheson, hitting him square on the side of the face with all the force of his 225 pounds. Hutcheson fell heavily against a long table. In a moment, the antagonists mixed again and delegates scrambled to separate them.

Hutcheson, raised to his feet, made his way to the washroom, blood streaming down his face. John P. Frey, nervously kneading his hands on the dais, said to Green, "This will wreck the labor movement." Straightening his clothes and smoothing his hair, Lewis placed a cigar in his mouth and strolled casually to the platform. "You shouldn't have done that, John," Green said to him. "He called me a foul name," Lewis replied. "Oh," said Green, always willing to accommodate, "I didn't know that." John L. Lewis stared thoughtfully ahead.[4]

V

Lewis, for all the thunder of his rhetoric, was not a man of ungovernable temper. Hutcheson, Lewis said later, "represented symbolically the kind of leadership in the American Federation of Labor that the workers of this country detested." With one blow, Lewis coolly dramatized the split in the Federation. That night, the convention adjourned. The next morning, Lewis convened the leaders of the industrial bloc for a Sunday breakfast at the Hotel President.

The group which sat around the table at the President were in a grim mood. From the Mine Workers there were Lewis, Phil Murray, Thomas Kennedy, and Lewis's ancient enemy John Brophy, now returned to the fold; from New York there were Hillman and Dubinsky, along with Max Zaritsky of the Hatters; in addition, there were Thomas McMahon of the Textile Workers and Charlie Howard. If the Executive Council of the Federation would not organize the mass-production industries, then why not set up a committee within the Federation to promote such organization? Three weeks later in Washington, the Committee for Industrial Organization was formally established. And in another fortnight, Lewis, without consulting his CIO colleagues, wrote briefly to Green: "Dear Sir and Brother, Effective this date, I resign as vice-president of the American Federation of Labor." To a press conference he explained, "I have neither the time nor the inclination to follow the council in its seasonal peregrinations from the Jersey beaches in the summer to the golden sands of Florida in the winter." Labor's civil war had begun.

Green replied by calling on the new Committee to disappear. But Lewis prodded his more cautious associates, and the CIO responded by harassing the session of the Executive Council at Miami in January 1936 with new demands for industrial charters. The Council pronounced the CIO "a challenge to the supremacy of the American Federation of Labor" and demanded its dissolution. "The mountain has labored and brought forth a mouse," said Lewis, adding genially that he would see the Council members "wearing asbestos suits in hell" before he would disband the CIO. Green mingled appeals and intimidations in his efforts to end the schism. But he was fighting outside his class. When Green spoke softly, Lewis commented, "Alas, poor Green, I knew him well. He wishes me to join him in fluttering procrastination, the while intoning O tempora, O mores!" When Green tried to sound tough, Lewis observed, "I fear his threats as much as I believe his promises."

For six months, the war of nerves continued. In July 1936 the Council formally charged the CIO with fomenting insurrection and summoned the erring brethren to a heresy trial. The CIO leaders declined to appear. The trial nevertheless proceeded on schedule. John P. Frey, prosecutor, compared Howard to Machiavelli and Lewis to Mussolini ("like a volcano he spouts flame and burning lava, spreading poisonous gases over the countryside"). By a vote of 13 to 1, the Executive Council gave the CIO unions a month to choose between recantation and suspension. Lewis denounced the proceeding as "incredible and crass stupidity" and threatened to retaliate

by expelling Green from the UMW. Green unwarily replied that
this would not affect his position in the labor movement; after all,
he was an honorary member of the musicians' union. "That," Lewis
said with relish, "is appropriate. Like Nero, Green fiddles while
Rome burns." "The American Federation of Labor," Lewis concluded, "is standing still, with its face toward the dead past." ⁵

VI

It was not only the CIO's defiance which had driven the Federation
to its extreme decision; it was even more the CIO's activity. The exposed situation of miners in the "captive" coal mines — that is, in
the coal mines owned by steel companies — had long given the Mine
Workers an interest in organizing the steel industry. For Lewis, this
was the prime CIO objective. In February 1936, he made one last
effort to needle Green and the Federation into a steel drive. A. O.
Wharton expressed the craft union sentiment when he replied that
there was no need for a general campaign and that his Machinists
always stood ready to organize "the men eligible to join our organization in the steel industry."

Lewis then made a direct offer of CIO assistance to Grandmother
Tighe and his battered Amalgamated Association of Iron, Steel and
Tin Workers. Green countered by proposing to the Amalgamated
a campaign based on a recognition of existing craft jurisdictions.
"This business about steel workers clamoring to get into unions,"
Green said, "is all nonsense." For a few weeks, Tighe and the Amal
gamated tried to dodge the decision. But the pressure from below
was too strong, and on June 13, 1936, with Tighe's acquiescence,
Lewis set up the Steel Workers' Organizing Committee with Phil
Murray as director. In a short time, the SWOC had nearly 500 organizers working their way through the steel towns. When Green
said that he would watch developments with interest, Lewis wrote
him magnanimously, "I overlook the inane ineptitude of your statement. . . . Perchance you were agitated and distraught." He added
that he found it inconceivable that Green should now choose "to sit
with the women under an awning on the hill-top while the steel
workers in the valley struggle in the dust and agony of industrial
warfare."

The *ad hoc* organizing committee became the CIO's chosen weapon. Such committees were brilliantly designed to pour money and organizing talent into unorganized industries, furnishing inexperienced unions a concentration of seasoned leadership when they most needed it. Similar committees were soon set up in textiles, in utilities, in petroleum. Where, as in the automobile industry, the industrial union felt that it had passed beyond the organizing stage. the CIO provided money and manpower. In the wake of the CIO drive an almost evangelical fervor began to sweep over large sections of American labor. The awakening of 1936 had, indeed, many of the aspects of a revival. Organizers labored endless hours and braved unknown perils, like missionaries; workers crowded labor halls to hear the new gospel; new locals sprang out of communion and dedication to pass on the good news. And they sang their sardonic, wistful hymns; it was, to a great extent, a singing movement. Thus "Mammy's Little Baby Loves a Union Shop":

> Rush, says the boss,
> Work like a hoss;
> I'll take the profits and you take the loss,
> I've got the brains, I've got the dough
> The Lord Himself decreed it so.

What the CIO brought for this moment was a rush of hope for those who had resigned themselves to being beyond hope. Hope came to the unskilled worker in the mass-production industry, to the east- or south-European immigrant who had never been accepted in the American labor movement, to the Negro, to millions who felt themselves shut out, not only by their bosses but by their fellow workers. In union, there was faith. In union, there was strength. And they sang, to the melody of the "Battle Hymn of the Republic":

> They have taken untold millions, that they never toiled to earn,
> But without our brain and muscle not a single wheel could turn;
> We can break their haughty power, gain our freedom when we learn —
> That the Union makes us strong.
>
> *Solidarity Forever,*
> *Solidarity Forever,*
> *Solidarity Forever,*
> *For the Union makes us strong.*[6]

Presiding over the revival there remained the massive, enigmatic figure of John L. Lewis. His postures, always histrionic, now had almost a prophetic quality. He seemed to see his shadow falling across the continent. "I salute the members of my own union as they listen tonight," he said in a radio speech in 1936. ". . . From the Warrior River in the southland up through the great Appalachian range to the island of Cape Breton, they listen. Across our parched midwestern plains to the slopes of the Rockies and the Cascades, and to the far province of Saskatchewan, they are at attention." The organizing drive of 1933 had restored him to his union. More than that, it had made vivid to him again the memories of his own life in the mines a quarter-century before — the overhanging pall of black dust cutting off the coal towns; the tedium and loneliness and danger in the dark tunnels under the earth; the blasted faces and the broken bodies; the pride and the bitterness. Now depression had generalized the miner's predicament to all America.

Lewis, suddenly responsive to the suffering of working people, was no longer the hard-boiled AF of L bureaucrat of the twenties. As he spoke, his somber grandiloquence lost its ham quality; the issues seemed at last to justify the rhetoric. His utterances gave the sorrows and aspirations of all labor a new dignity. Across the country, people recognized in him — some with hope, some with fear — the authentic voice of a great social force. And yet a puzzle remained: "What makes me tick?" he is said to have asked an aide late one afternoon, as he rocked in a red-leather swivel chair behind his large walnut desk, a cigar in his mouth, in his paneled office in Washington. "Is it power I'm after, or am I a Saint Francis in disguise, or what?"

What indeed! "It takes every man some time to find himself in this world, to decide what he wants to do with his life," he told one interviewer. "It took me longer than most people." Had he now found himself? What were his ideas, beyond the passion to organize the unorganized? Politically he had become the champion of the working class in its struggle against the bosses. Yet in November 1935 he told Selden Rodman with emphasis, "I'm not interested in classes. . . . Far be it from me to foster inferiority complexes among the workers by trying to make them think they belong to some special class. That has happened in Europe but it hasn't happened here yet." Rodman mentioned that equality of opportunity was vanishing in America. "It is conceivable," conceded Lewis, "that if this dangerous state of affairs is allowed to continue there will not only be 'class-consciousness' but revolution as well. But it can be avoided. The employers aren't doing much to avoid it. But the United Mine Workers are doing everything in their power to make the system work and thereby avoid it. We'll see."

Similarly, he had presumably become the great champion in the labor movement of economic planning. Yet, when Rodman reminded him of his obeisance to the free play of natural economic laws in his book of 1925, *The Miners' Fight for American Standards*, Lewis replied, a trifle defensively, "Well, I still more or less agree with that." How, then, could he justify his support of NRA? After a moment, Lewis replied, "When natural economic law doesn't operate in hard times for the best interests of industry and the public, then" — a sly look from behind the shaggy eyebrows — "then perhaps the time comes for a bit of regulation."

VIII

Essentially he wanted to increase labor's power, not to alter the system. "Labor does ask for and demand," he said, "a voice in the determination of those policies that affect the human element in industry . . . It wants a place at the council table when decisions are made that affect the amount of food that the family of a worker may eat, the extent of the education of his children, the kind and amount of clothing they shall wear, the few pleasures they may enjoy." He had no more serious desire for social reconstruction than Sam Gompers; like Adolph Strasser of the old Cigar Makers Union in his famous statement before a Senate committee half a century before, Lewis was going on from day to day, fighting for immediate objects, without ultimate aims. Even in desolate mining towns, his only remedy was higher wages and improved mine safety; not for him the cooperatives, the schools, the health plans, the housing projects of Hillman and Dubinsky, the labor leaders in the Socialist tradition. He saw himself as preserving the system, standing, as he said, "between the rapacity of the robber barons of industry of America and the lustful rage of the Communists who would lay waste to our traditions and our institutions as with fire and sword." The difference between Lewis and the AF of L mandarins was that where they remained faithful to the letter of the Strasser-Gompers doctrine Lewis sought to transpose its spirit to a new age.

If he had few ideas, he had a burning vision — the vision of a mass workers' movement, bringing "industrial democracy" to the nation by giving labor its deserved stature in American society. And the very intensity of this vision introduced a new militancy into the life of labor. "The time has passed in America," said Lewis, "when the workers can be either clubbed, gassed, or shot down with impunity. I solemnly warn the leaders of industry that labor will not tolerate such policies or tactics." His old-fashioned militancy opened the way for new ideas and ideologues — Socialists or ex-Socialists like Hillman and Dubinsky, or like the young Reuther brothers, struggling to build a union in Detroit; Trotskyites, Lovestonites, Stalinists. With the tolerance of a man indifferent to ideas, Lewis welcomed them all, confident that he could turn the zeal of each to his own purposes. Needing manpower for the battles of steel and rubber, he even suspended his old hatred of Communism. "Industry should not complain if we allow Communism in our organization," he observed. "Industry employs them." "Never refuse to work with anybody," he told the Newspaper Guild, "who's willing to work with you." He went so far as to declare an agnosticism about the Soviet Union. "To determine what is actually taking place in Russia is quite impossible — at least for me," he told Selden Rodman with unwonted modesty, adding, "I think we will solve our own difficulties in our own way." Lee Pressman left his government job and became Lewis's counsel in the CIO. Communists went into the field as CIO organizers. When someone expostulated to Lewis about the Communist influx, he is said to have replied, "Who gets the bird, the dog or the hunter?"

The CIO had a spirit of its own, however, diverging both from the Communists and from Lewis. Unlike the Communists, the CIO militants wanted a free and democratic America; unlike Lewis, they wanted a new America. But for the moment all united in their adherence to the Lewis gospel: "Let the workers organize. Let the toiler assemble. Let their crystallized voice proclaim their injustices and demand their privileges. Let all thoughtful citizens sustain them, for the future of labor is the future of America."[7]

VII

Resurgence
on the Right

26. The Bridge to Business

THE FIRST MONTHS of the New Deal were to an astonishing degree
an adventure in unanimity. Though the business community had
in the main gone for Hoover in 1932, prominent businessmen had
supported Roosevelt; and neither Roosevelt's platform nor his personality seemed to hold any special problems for business after the
election. The assassination attempt at Miami, followed by the banking crisis, only increased the sentimental unity behind the new
President. And most of the measures of Roosevelt's first month —
in particular, the reopening of the banks, the cutback in government
spending, and the return of beer — strengthened his conservative
support. Even New Deal planning was for a moment acceptable.
After all, few businessmen cared what happened in agriculture; and
NRA not only drew on ideas long urged by business leaders but
depended on close business-government collaboration.

II

Business, moreover, was hardly in a position to hold out against
the President. Its claim to national leadership had long since collapsed. The Senate inquiry into stock exchange operations was displaying (in the words of one leading financier, Joseph P. Kennedy)
"practically all the important names in the financial community in
practices which, to say the least, were highly unethical." Not only
the political but the moral authority of business was gone. "The belief that those in control of the corporate life of America were motivated by honesty and ideals of honorable conduct," said Kennedy,

"was completely shattered." Governor Alfred M. Landon of Kansas, a Republican, even singled out by name three well-known business leaders as "racketeers" who would be "driven out of finance and industry by the scorn of honest people and the strong arm of the government." Walter Lippmann reported that by early 1933 people had so lost confidence in business "that men asked themselves seriously whether the private direction of industry would not have to be supplanted by public management." Thoughtful businessmen had not failed to note that Franklin Roosevelt drew his first notable applause during his inaugural address when he assailed the money-changers, and the next, and even louder applause, when he promised an end to business misconduct. The business community, in short, needed Roosevelt a good deal more in 1933 than he needed it.

Nor was it just that people had lost confidence in business. Even more demoralizing, business was losing confidence in itself. For the first time American businessmen were questioning their own judgment, methods, and goals. Frances Perkins later recalled how some of the most powerful among them, like Alfred Sloan of General Motors, unmanned by the dangerous fact that the Secretary of Labor was a woman, poured into her ears long, tormented confessionals to justify careers which, for a moment, baffled even the men themselves. Never had the business community felt such a sense of its own fallibility; only the bankers remained immune. In consequence, when the President, instead of exploiting the resentment against capitalism, invited capitalists to Washington as partners in national planning, businessmen responded with heartfelt gratitude. "In the first months of NRA," Donald Richberg said, "it seemed as though a considerable part of the business world had 'got religion.' " A prominent businessman informed John T. Flynn that he regarded Roosevelt as the greatest leader since Jesus Christ; he hoped God would forgive him, he said, for voting for Hoover.

Both Wall Street and Main Street shared this initial enthusiasm. "Except in war time," John J. Raskob wrote Roosevelt in April, "few Presidents have accomplished as much in a whole term as you have in a single month." And in October, from Russell Leffingwell of Morgan's: "I want to congratulate you upon what you have accomplished in the seven months since you took office. The country today is scarcely recognizable as the same country it was on March 4th." Three months later, William Allen White urged that Congress grant Roosevelt more power. "If ever a servant deserved commendation of his masters," White said, "the American people through their Congress should give it to Franklin Roosevelt. . . . Our one fortress in this hour is the President." *Fortune* summed up Roosevelt's first year as proving it "possible for a democratic government retaining at least the democratic forms to act more rapidly and decisively than either Hitler or Lenin was able to act at the moment of assuming power." [1]

III

The National Recovery Administration was the first bastion of government-business cooperation. Though in the end NRA produced more friction than fusion, in 1933 and 1934 it offered businessmen their most important bridgehead in Washington. In the meantime, Daniel C. Roper, as Secretary of Commerce, tried to improve cooperation by setting up the Business Advisory Council of the Department of Commerce in June 1933. Among the members of the Business Advisory Council in its first five years were Averell Harriman of Union Pacific, Edward R. Stettinius, Jr., of United States Steel, William L. Batt of S.K.F. Industries, W. L. Clayton of Anderson, Clayton, and other businessmen who later made contributions to government. But Roper came to view his experiment with disappointment. "I seemed to be able neither to bring businessmen to indorse the plans of the New Deal nor to get the Administration to counsel with these businessmen as frequently as I thought necessary." The President in particular showed little interest in the Business Advisory Council — perhaps because, as he once remarked to Missy LeHand, he felt that Roper had succumbed to big business influences.

The most enduring stronghold of government-business cooperation came to be, appropriately enough, an agency inherited from the Hoover administration — the Reconstruction Finance Corporation. Its new chairman was Jesse H. Jones of Texas. Jones had begun as a lumberman in Dallas in the nineties, then moved to Houston and branched out into banking, real estate, and news-

papers. "I had been brought up," he once said, "in the belief that
the three most necessary things to a satisfactory life were family,
religion, and money." Some might wonder whether this accurately
stated the priority; but people learned not to fool with Jesse Jones.
He was now almost sixty, a great monument of a man, his face
square and hard, his lips compressed, his erect seventy-five inches
topped by a mass of silver-white hair. He was profane and taciturn
in the Texas manner, loved power, was indifferent to ideology, never
read books, had no sentimental illusions about the underdog, and
kept his word. He could do business with anybody, even New
Dealers, even Wall Street.

Jones had always been a Democrat, if of the type which opposed
Bryan in '96. During the First World War, as director of military
relief for the Red Cross, he met both Woodrow Wilson and Franklin
Roosevelt. His check for $200,000 brought the Democratic conven-
tion to Houston in 1928. The gesture was splendid; but the thrifty
Jones, who took few chances, later (as Senator Tom Connally put
it) "scurried about Texas raising money in order to reimburse himself." Nevertheless a grateful Texas delegation made him its
favorite-son candidate. Though Jones always denied that this was
serious, pamphlets were prepared presenting his claims, and once
when a huge bag, attached by ropes to the roof of the convention
hall, was opened by mistake, red and gold balloons drifted down
to the delegates marked "Jesse H. Jones for President." [2]

IV

In 1932 Hoover brought him to Washington as one of the Democrats required by statute for the bipartisan board of the RFC. Jones
found this a trying experience. He felt that Eugene Meyer, the RFC
chairman, abetted by Ogden Mills, Hoover's Secretary of the Treasury, treated the Democratic members as second-class citizens. Moreover, RFC lending policies seemed to reflect the cautious views of
the New York financial community — an attitude which Jones, a
Texas promoter with big ideas and faith in growth, rejected. Jones
disagreed too with Hoover's insistence on secrecy for RFC loans.

Most of all, he wanted a far bolder use of RFC as an instrument
of inflation. Hoover and Mills considered RFC primarily a psycho-

logical weapon. Convinced that the depression was about over, they supposed that the gesture of establishing a lending agency, perhaps supplemented by a few emergency loans, would be enough to revive confidence. "The sooner it is created," Mills actually said of RFC, "the less use we will have to make of it." Thus the agency was set up for only one year; and its loans were limited to banks, insurance companies, and other financial institutions (plus railroads, included because so many financial institutions held railroad securities; the point here was to support the railroad debt structure, not to keep the trains running). The act did not permit loans for business, for public works, or for relief; nor did it provide for putting capital into financial institutions. The Hoover idea of RFC was essentially defensive — to protect the credit machinery of the country from liquidation.

Some on Capitol Hill wanted to make it an instrument of economic stimulation. When Congress in July 1932 passed a bill widening the authority of RFC to allow loans to states, municipalities, corporations, and individuals, Hoover returned an angry veto. "This proposal," he said, "violates every sound principle of public finance and of government. Never before has so dangerous a suggestion been seriously made to our country." [3]

v

It was evident to Jones that the original RFC had both misconceived and underestimated its task. The debacle of February 1933, when RFC proved helpless before the Michigan banking panic, underlined its failure. When Roosevelt appointed him chairman, Jones set out to lead the agency into a new phase dedicated not just to defense but to reconstruction and expansion.

The banking crisis itself made possible the first steps toward a new RFC. The Hoover theory had been to save the banks by lending them money. Jones considered this exactly the wrong medicine; what the banks needed was not more debt but more capital. As Russell Leffingwell summarized the Hoover policy, "For a fatal year and a half the Reconstruction Finance Corporation continued to lend money to the banks on adequate collateral security and gradually bankrupted them in the effort to save them." The bank holiday now provided the opportunity for a new start. The emergency banking legislation gave RFC authority to purchase preferred stock in banks. In this way public funds could strengthen the capital structure of the banks and incidentally provide the basis for an expansion of commercial credit. "A dollar spent in the purchase of preferred stock," as Leffingwell said, "ought to do as much as $5 or $10 spent in making adequately secured loans."

To many bankers, however, the investment policy implied the threat of government control of the banking system. Almost unique in the business community in retaining illusions of power and prestige, they declined to collaborate now with such a program, even if it was designed to rescue them. By July only five banks had taken advantage of the RFC offer. With the NRA blanket code going into effect in August, Washington began to worry about the bankers' resistance. Small firms, their working capital already depleted after three years of depression, urgently needed loans to meet the increased payrolls. Late in August, Roosevelt called on Jones and on Eugene R. Black, Governor of the Federal Reserve Board, to get the banks to loosen up on credit. But the bankers, still largely oblivious to the change in the atmosphere, gave no ground. When the American Bankers Association convened in Chicago in September, Francis H. Sisson of the Guaranty Trust, the ABA's president, haughtily dismissed attacks on banking policies as "absolutely unjustified." Then Jesse Jones brought a new note into the self-congratulatory deliberations. In a hectoring speech, he advised the banks to improve their capital position by letting RFC buy their preferred stock. He added significantly, "Banks must provide credit . . . otherwise the government will." "Be smart, for once," Jones harshly told the resentful audience. "Take the government into partnership with you."

That evening the bankers held their annual party, complete with dinner and floor show. Jones, called on again, said that he had already spoken once that day and no one liked what he said. All he would add now, he observed grimly, was that half the banks represented in this jolly gathering were insolvent. "Those of you representing these banks know it better than anyone else." [4]

VI

Jones followed up his blunt language by offering low-interest RFC loans to financial institutions to stimulate short-term relending. At the same time, the Federal Reserve Board continued through open-market purchases to enlarge the basis for credit expansion. But the financial community remained unmoved. "There is no doubt in my mind," Roosevelt wrote the Secretary of the Treasury in October, "that you and I are being subjected to all sorts of silent pressure by some members of the banking fraternity who do not want to make loans to industry. They are in a sullen frame of mind, hoping by remaining sullen to compel foreign exchange stabilization and force our hands. If you and I force these funds on them they will have to act in accordance with our desires." The President told the cabinet a few days later that the bankers were conspiring to block the ad-ministration program and that it might be necessary to extend federal credit directly to business.

This proposal had the support not just of New Deal planners but of the growth-minded wing of the business community, the men on the make in the South and West, of whom Jones was the representa-tive in Washington. The hard-money, *rentier* businessmen, speaking through Lewis Douglas, defended the bankers and sharply opposed the notion of giving RFC authority to make direct loans to industry (for similar reasons, Douglas opposed and Jones supported the gold-purchase policy). Indeed, in the fall of 1933, Douglas, backed by Eugene Black, actually tried to take the bank rehabilitation program away from RFC with the idea of putting it in the charge of a New York banker. Jones was bungling his job, Douglas and Black told Roosevelt, and the nation was heading into another banking debacle. Jones, seeing another attempt by Wall Street to resume its control over the nation's credit system, responded with vigor that RFC could and would do the job. Roosevelt said, "Boys, I am going to back Jess."

The need for a certificate of solvency in order to qualify for the recently-adopted deposit insurance program finally broke the bank-ers' resistance to RFC. At the end of October, the Manufacturers Trust of New York accepted $25 million from the RFC in exchange for preferred stock. In the next weeks other bankers followed this example. But even this capital transfusion was not enough to make all shaky banks solvent. As the deadline for deposit insurance approached, Jones flinched from the prospect of informing the nation that some two thousand banks could not qualify — a bulletin which might well start another panic. With characteristic resourcefulness, Jones suggested that if Morgenthau would certify borderline banks as solvent he would guarantee to make them solvent in six months. Morgenthau went along. Jones later wrote, "He really had no choice." In this way, the doubtful banks came quietly in under the Federal Deposit Insurance Corporation, and in another six months RFC, as Jones promised, made most of them solvent.

This injection of new capital — which meant that by 1935 RFC owned over a billion dollars of preferred stock in about half the banks of the country — stopped the liquidation, made possible the guarantee of bank deposits, and saved the banking system.[5]

VII

Jesse Jones's empire was only beginning to expand. A collection of RFC subsidiaries soon carried his authority into diverse fields. The Commodity Credit Corporation, backing up AAA, supported prices for agricultural commodities through its loan and storage facilities. The Electric Home and Farm Authority, backing up the Rural Electrification Administration, financed the purchase of electrical appliances, especially on the countryside. The RFC Mortgage Company and the Federal National Mortgage Association, backing up the Federal Housing Administration, created in effect a new market for first mortgages. The Export-Import Bank sought through its loan policy to stimulate the export trade. RFC loans to eighty-nine railroad companies, owning two-thirds of the nation's tracks, helped avert the collapse of railroad securities. In addition, RFC helped finance the public works program, drove down interest rates, provided aid for flood and hurricane victims, refinanced drainage, levee, and irrigation districts, offered loans for mining, smelting, agricultural marketing and rural electrification, put (or kept) American Airlines, Tennessee Gas Transmission, and El Paso Natural Gas in business, and financed school construction and payment of teachers' salaries.

Jones's control of this empire was absolute. Men like Adolf Berle,

Jerome Frank, and Thomas G. Corcoran were from time to time on the RFC payroll; and, though Jones was too shrewd to cramp their style, he kept them from running away with any of his authority. His six colleagues on the RFC board regarded him with awe. "When Mr. Jones favored something," one of them once said, "it never occurred to any of us to oppose it." Congress indulged him almost as much. "I think Mr. Jones more generally holds the confidence of Congress," said Senator Arthur Vandenberg of Michigan, "than any other member of the Roosevelt Administration." (And Jones took care to sweeten congressional reactions by thoughtful attention to pet congressional projects.) Under his direction, RFC established a unique position in the government. Existing largely outside the budget, financed by its own revolving fund and by its power to sell notes to the public through the Treasury, self-supporting in its day-to-day operations, headed by a man who commanded business and legislative confidence, the agency enjoyed a notable freedom of action. Its financial independence, its political immunity, and its free-floating status as a public corporation gave it, in addition, a flexibility which tempted Roosevelt to toss new jobs to it, such as gold purchase or foreign trade credits, when the problem of getting specific legislative authority seemed too chancy or time-consuming.

Toward the President, Jones remained tolerant if a little remote. "Whenever we did anything of importance, that was on the border line of our authority, I would try at first opportunity to tell the President about it, but after the fact. He was always interested, and he never criticized." For his part, the President respected Jones's ability and valued him as an anchor to rightward. "Your conservatism is a good thing for us in this Administration," he told Jones on occasion.

Under Jones's leadership, the operation envisaged by Hoover and Mills, strictly limited to bailing out financial institutions, had grown into a powerful instrument of state capitalism. The New Deal RFC was virtually a new agency; it grew into essentially the plan Hoover had so indignantly vetoed in the summer of 1932. "No one in February, 1932, at which time this Corporation was set up," Jones said in 1935, "had the faintest idea as to the extent that it would be called upon to assist business." By January 1, 1934, it had disbursed two-thirds again as much money in its short twenty-three months of existence as the House of Morgan and its syndicates had disbursed in aggregate underwritings from 1919 to 1933. It was by far the largest single investor in the American economy as well as the biggest bank in the country. By 1938, at the end of its first seven years, it had disbursed $10 billion. Of this, nearly $4 billion went to financial institutions, nearly $1.5 billion to agriculture, and nearly $1 billion each to railroads and self-liquidating public works — and nearly all was eventually paid back.[6]

VIII

If Jones had changed RFC a great deal, some administration liberals — notably Adolf Berle — wanted to change it still more. They conceived of RFC not just as an intelligent public bank, but as the key agency in the institutional reconstruction of the economy. As Berle saw it, RFC had taken "financial control of the country away from the hands of a group which did not enjoy public confidence, putting it into the hands of a government which could command the necessary trust." Its position as the senior long-term finance agency in the country gave it vast powers. "As long as additional capital is needed through the Reconstruction Finance Corporation," Berle pointed out, "just so long there must be acquiescence in the views which it happens to express." In addition, its ownership of preferred stock, as well as its legal powers when its loans were in default, gave it means of direct control of the policy of individual banks. It could influence capital policy, dividend rates, personnel, and even salaries.

Berle wanted RFC to use these powers for social purposes. And he wanted to complete its work by setting up new public lending institutions. Thus he proposed to revitalize entrepreneurship and small business by establishing a chain of "capital credit" banks which would actively seek out new investment opportunities and stake men of initiative to the creation of enterprises of benefit both to the enterpriser and to the community. "Outside of the large corporations," Berle said, "men who have ideas for new enterprise cannot expect to find much assistance in the commercial banking system." Following somewhat this conception, Roosevelt in March 1934 recommended the establishment of a dozen credit banks "for the small or medium-size industrialist."

Jones quickly blanketed this when he gained for the RFC in June 1934 authority to make direct loans to business and industry, thereby keeping government credit operations under his own control. Where Berle was interested in economic organization, Jones was interested in economic enterprise. On occasion Jones might force changes in management and install his own men as executives; in 1933 he even imposed salary limitations on officials of railroads and insurance companies borrowing from RFC. But these interventions, though often brusque and forceful, were strictly *ad hoc.* "There is no thought," he said, "of dictating management nor of coercion as to bank policies or bank investment." In 1933 Berle said that the possibilities of direction inherent in the RFC mechanism were "as yet only barely conceived." By 1935 he was obliged to write, "I am not aware that the Reconstruction Finance Corporation has yet endeavored to exercise any control save in very rare cases."

RFC, in short, took on the character not of the First New Deal but of Jesse Jones. Instead of providing a basis for economic planning, it became an enormously astute and versatile financial exercise conducted on private banking principles if under public auspices and with public money. Still, if Jones's RFC differed from Berle's, it also differed from the Ogden Mills-Lewis Douglas-Wall Street RFC. Mills never wanted RFC to do much; by 1935 Douglas wanted to abolish it. They saw it as an emergency backstop for the *rentier* class — for people anxious to insure steady returns on stakes they already had and were not certain they could make again. Jones, on the other hand, saw it as a continuing instrumentality for assisting a rising class of new men like himself, promoters and entrepreneurs, to make their initial stake. Only a man of what Thomas G. Corcoran called his "extraordinary bull-strength energy, practical shrewdness and technical competence" could have withstood the Wall Street drive to dominate government lending.

Along with the new monetary policy, the new RFC and Jesse Jones thus played an indispensable role in shifting the economic and financial direction of the country from the hard-money, gold-standard, coupon-clipping groups of the East to those who, for better or worse, were prepared to risk monetary inflation because they deeply believed in economic growth.[7]

27. Alienation of the Financial Community

THOUGH THE PRESIDENT himself seemed ready enough in the spring of 1933 to welcome the money-changers back to the temple, the popular mood toward business remained irascible. One reason was the almost daily reminder in newspaper headlines of the squalid ethics of the men who had been the nation's financial leaders. Each day reporters crowded into the Senate caucus room, where, under the tall windows and the glittering crystal chandeliers, Ferdinand Pecora, as counsel of the Senate Banking and Currency Committee, genially and inexorably pressed his investigation into banking, stock exchange, and security practices.

Ironically, the idea of an investigation of Wall Street had begun with Herbert Hoover, who had come to believe by early 1932 that bear raids conducted by short sellers were an important factor in demoralizing the securities market. Public exposure, Hoover thought, might check such speculative manipulation. When a group of bankers led by Thomas W. Lamont of Morgan's opposed the investigation, Hoover rejected their protests. Under the chairmanship of Senator Peter Norbeck of South Dakota, hearings began in April 1932. After the election, Norbeck, on the recommendation of Frank L. Polk, hired Pecora, a Theodore Roosevelt Progressive, now a Democrat, who had served a dozen years as assistant district attorney of New York County. When Pecora took over the investigation in January 1933, he assembled a staff of experts, among them John T. Flynn, a skilled and hard-working financial journalist, and Max Lowenthal, a lawyer who specialized in unraveling corporate mystification. With the new Democratic Congress, the scope of the inquiry expanded, and Senator Duncan U. Fletcher of Florida assumed the chairmanship. Though seventy-five years old, Fletcher presided over the hearings day after day and gave Pecora unwavering support.[1]

II

The investigation continued through the winter and spring of 1933, into the summer and fall, and on into 1934. Pecora, the Sicilian immigrant, swarthy and tough, with his flashing black eyes and defiant pompadour of gray-black hair, examined witnesses all day, then stayed up half the night to prepare for the next day's session. "I looked with astonishment," John T. Flynn later wrote, "at this man who, through the intricate mazes of banking, syndicates, market deals, chicanery of all sorts, and in a field new to him, never forgot a name, never made an error in a figure, and never lost his temper." The eminent financiers of the age, flanked by their hundred-thousand-dollar-a-year lawyers, took the stand: Charles Mitchell, for whom interrogation was a preliminary to indictment; A. H. Wiggin, Clarence Dillon, and Winthrop Aldrich; Thomas W. Lamont and George and Richard Whitney. Above all, there was J. P. Morgan, the younger, son of the titan and a near-titan himself, his face unknown to the people of his native land but his signature still able to make or break governments across the world. Flushed at last out of his clubs and yachts and shooting boxes, he stepped politely from the shadows, with his great head, bushy white mustache, and massive nose, a gold watch chain gleaming on his waistcoat.

Unperturbed by the lordly apparition, Pecora ($255 a month) consulted his notes and pursued his inquiries. One afternoon he asked whether Morgan had paid any income tax in 1930. The room, alive a moment before with a hum of whispers, grew abruptly silent. Reporters near Morgan seemed to hear his heavy gold watch ticking the seconds away. After a pause, Morgan replied, "I cannot remember." Pecora, with dispassionate scorn, showed that Morgan had — quite legally — paid no income tax in the United States in 1930 or, for that matter, in 1931 or 1932. (He had paid taxes in Great Britain these years.) Indeed, the aggregate income tax paid by all Morgan partners in 1930 had amounted to less than fifty thousand dollars; in 1931, the members of the firm, skillfully canceling out gains by real or technical losses, had paid no income tax at all. "I really do not know anything whatever about the income tax statements of the office," said Morgan shortly, tugging at his watch chain.

Still worse was the unveiling of the Morgan "preferred list" — an enumeration of the friends to whom the House of Morgan occasionally sold stock at figures far below market price. Thus, when shares of the Alleghany Corporation, a Van Sweringen holding company, were selling on the exchange at from $31 to $35, friends of Jack Morgan — "good, sound, straight fellows," as he described them — were invited to buy at $20 a share. One such sound, straight fellow, by selling his allotment a short time after he made the purchase, realized $229,411 — a sum which measured the proportion of the favor and implied the size of the future obligation. Among those who accepted Alleghany stock at Morgan's bargain rates in the booming days of 1929 were such leading conservative Democrats as Owen D. Young, Newton D. Baker, John J. Raskob, and William G. McAdoo, such national heroes as General Pershing and Charles A. Lindbergh, such respected figures as Owen J. Roberts, whom Hoover had subsequently appointed to the Supreme Court, and William H. Woodin, whom Roosevelt had subsequently appointed to the cabinet. A list of Morgan's favored subscribers for Standard Brands included most of these names and, in addition, Calvin Coolidge, Norman H. Davis, John W. Davis, and Bernard Baruch.

The preferred list disconcerted even the *New York Times*, not a notably anti-Wall Street paper. In a stern editorial condemning the "gross impropriety" of Mr. Morgan's system, the *Times* wondered why the most powerful banking firm in the world should practice "the small arts of petty traders." As for those eminent citizens who accepted the Morgan *douceur*, their role was even more puzzling. "Those favored by Morgan," as the Kansas City *Times* said concisely, "were placed under obligation to him." Thus Raskob expressed to a Morgan partner the cordial hope that the future would hold "opportunities for me to reciprocate." "It is nothing more or nothing less than bribery," said Governor Alfred

M. Landon of Kansas of the preferred list. ". . . I confidently expect the President to demand the resignation of Secretary of the Treasury Woodin."

Woodin did raise this question with the cabinet and the President. Garner, with his Texas banker's dislike of Wall Street, thought Woodin should resign. Ickes and Cummings, however, disagreed. Ickes was much more concerned about Norman Davis, who, unlike Woodin, had taken Morgan's favors while engaged in the public business, and, indeed, was still in the spring of 1933 in debt to the firm. Roosevelt minimized the incident, saying that many people had done things in 1929 they would not think of doing now. In the end, both Woodin and Davis stayed.

Before he finished, Morgan was subjected to a final humiliation. A Ringling Brothers Circus press agent popped a female midget on his lap: "The smallest lady in the world wants to meet the richest man in the world." Times had indeed changed: men like James F. Byrnes, who had heard the elder Morgan testify twenty years before at the Pujo hearings, remarked on the contrast between the overwhelming old man, tapping the floor impatiently with his cane, responding to Samuel Untermyer's questions with massive dignity, ("The first thing is character. . . . Before money or anything else. Money cannot buy it.") and the son, affable and deferential, who, when it came to sound, straight fellows, could get it for them wholesale.[2]

III

Coldly Pecora made his witnesses recollect the gilded past — the stupendous bonuses they had received and the taxes they had avoided, the stock market pools they had rigged, the holding companies they had launched, the bad investments they had palmed off on a trusting nation. From their reluctant testimony emerged the portrait of a world of insiders where for years businessmen had greedily stuffed their own pockets at the expense of the innocent and dumb American citizen.

Thus, when a syndicate of American bankers proposed floating an issue of Peruvian bonds in 1927 and 1928, the consortium's own investigator (a sardonic figure named Lawrence Dennis) advised against the project in the most unqualified terms and predicted default in five years. Undeterred by this and by other expert warnings, the bankers, after paying bribes of over four hundred thousand dollars to the son of the President of Peru, unloaded the securities on the American people. The bankers took their profits, the government of Peru defaulted in 1931 a little ahead of schedule, and the American investors were left with worthless paper. Or, when the National City Company considered a bond issue on behalf of the Brazilian state of Minas Gerais, its own experts reported adversely, noting that the laxness of the state authorities bordered on the "fantastic" and emphasizing their "complete ignorance, carelessness and negligence" with respect to external long-term borrowing. But National City floated the issue just the same, stating calmly in the prospectus that the finances of Minas Gerais had been characterized by "prudent and careful administration." Minas Gerais did not default until 1932.

Pecora filled out the picture with broad, vigorous strokes. Too much became, perhaps, an indictment of individuals when it might better have been an indictment of a national state of mind. When Senator Couzens asked George Whitney of Morgan's why he had done something, Whitney could only reply helplessly, "I don't know, Senator Couzens. It is hard to answer why we did things. It is even harder to say why we didn't." To Pecora's question why he had gone into stock-jobbing, Albert Wiggin replied, "I think the times. . . . There were a great many people who began to think you did a great injustice to everybody if you did not have equity stocks." (In another mood, Wiggin placed the responsibility even higher up, describing the boom of 1929 as "a 'God-given' market." Senator Adams of Colorado, astonished, asked, "Are you sure as to the source?") Otto H. Kahn, of Kuhn, Loeb, while conceding that the bankers had not tried very hard to restrain the speculative mania, added, "But when it had taken full sway of the people and there was an absolute runaway feeling throughout the country, I doubt whether anyone could have stopped it before calamity overtook us."

The better bankers, contending in effect that they were being judged by the standards of one age for acts committed in another, won a kind of public absolution as the victims of the hallucinations

of their times. As for some of the others, tempted beyond irresponsibility into criminality, they ended up in the dock and
the penitentiary. But not many; Huey Long sarcastically complained that the American people were taking care that the only
lions they pulled out of the den were the dead ones. "First we prod
them, kick them, poke them, and make sure they're dead. Then,
once we're sure of that, we all shout together. 'Let's go after them,'
and we do. They never went after Insull until he was in Greece." [6]

IV

Through interrogations, questionnaires, and interviews, the
Senate Committee amassed more information about what was wrong
with the stock exchanges than anyone had ever collected before.
Obviously one trouble was that the sellers of securities had no com-
punction about misrepresenting their wares; the answer to this
was to compel full and complete disclosure. Another trouble was
that commercial banks had gone into the stock-jobbing business;
the answer to that was to compel commercial banks to divorce
themselves from their security affiliates. Another trouble was that
private banks, like the House of Morgan, were trying both to
float securities and to accept deposits; the answer to that was to
compel them to concentrate on one or the other. These seemed
rudimentary measures. But at least they would offer safeguards
against some excesses of the New Era.

There were ample precedents for such a program. Great Britain
had supervised its securities issues for nearly a century under the
Companies Act. Many American states, beginning in 1911, had
passed blue-sky laws to protect investors against misrepresentation
in the sale of securities. The revelations of the Pujo investigation
before the First World War had made people wonder whether this
was not a federal problem as well. The experience of the Capital
Issues Committee during the war led to the introduction of the
Taylor bill setting standards for securities issues. Roosevelt himself had called for a program of financial regulation in his Columbus speech during the 1932 campaign.

Such a program, moreover, commanded the vigorous support of
two groups among his followers: the opponents of bigness in the

Brandeis tradition, led by Felix Frankfurter; and the rural progressives, long fearful of Wall Street domination of the economy, led by men like Sam Rayburn of Texas and Burton K. Wheeler of Montana. Indeed, in 1914, in an early version of the alliance of 1933, Brandeis and Rayburn had collaborated on a bill to give the Interstate Commerce Commission control over the issue of new railroad securities. In tackling the problem again twenty years later, liberals were returning to unfinished business.[4]

V

Already, during the interregnum, Moley had asked Samuel Untermyer, the Pujo veteran, to work on possible stock-exchange and securities legislation. Early in January 1933, Untermyer came up with a bill which, among other things, proposed to make the Post Office Department the agency of regulation. This feature of the draft, as well as the doubtful constitutionality of other provisions and Untermyer's chronic disposition to build himself up to the press as a presidential adviser, annoyed Roosevelt. Without saying anything to Moley, the President asked Cummings and Roper to prepare alternative legislation: and Cummings and Roper turned the job over to their old friend from Wilson days, Huston Thompson, a former chairman of the Federal Trade Commission.

Thompson's bill, on the model of state blue-sky laws, proposed to give the Federal Trade Commission power to review and disapprove the issuance of securities. Not only did this seem to impose excessive responsibilities on government; but the actual draftsmanship of the bill was unconvincing. Roosevelt, confronted with two unsatisfactory bills, characteristically asked all parties to work it out around a table. The flamboyant Untermyer found collaboration difficult, however, and the conference proved a failure. The President now solved the problem by splitting the assignment. Thompson, he said, should draft a bill regulating the issue of new stocks and bonds, and Untermyer a bill regulating the exchanges.

Securities legislation had the priority; and, on March 29, 1933, in a message to Congress Roosevelt called for a law based on "the ancient truth that those who manage banks, corporations and other agencies handling or using other people's money are trustees acting for others." The doctrine of *caveat emptor* had to be supplemented; "let the seller also beware." The law, Roosevelt said, must put "the burden of telling the whole truth on the seller."

Sam Rayburn dropped the Thompson bill into the hopper of the House. But the draft soon aroused strong criticism, even among those friendly to the idea of regulation. W. Averell Harriman, a liberal businessman who had voted for Smith and Roosevelt and whose investment banking house of Brown Brothers, Harriman had notably escaped Pecora's criticism, protested the measure to Moley with some cogency as unworkable. Rayburn finally dismissed the Thompson draft as hopeless and told Moley that only a new bill would save the situation. Moley thereupon sent a distress signal to Frankfurter at Harvard. Two days later, on April 7, Frankfurter showed up in Washington with two grave young men who, he said, would help in the drafting process.

One was a shortish, wiry, hawk-faced man of thirty-three named James McCauley Landis, professor of legislation at the Harvard Law School. The other was a tall, gentle figure of thirty-nine, whose voice rose and fell in melancholy cadences, named Benjamin V. Cohen. Landis, born in Tokyo, son of a Presbyterian missionary, had gone to Princeton, led his class at the Harvard Law School, and served as a Brandeis law clerk before joining the Law School faculty. His sharp features and what one reporter described as his "bright, scowling eyes" expressed a missionary intensity of personality. He combined this with a detached, incisive, almost cold intelligence. Cohen, a man of deep and sensitive idealism, was a brilliant draftsman and sagacious counselor. For all his unworldliness of manner, he well understood the stock market and, indeed, had made a good deal in the twenties, getting out safely before the crash.

The principle, as Frankfurter saw it, was that a corporation, when it sought funds from the public, became "in every true sense" a public body, and its managers and bankers public functionaries. His group therefore favored a bill on the model of British legislation, requiring full disclosure of all material elements but conferring no general power, as under the Thompson draft, to disapprove issuance. In certain respects Landis and Cohen proposed going beyond the British legislation — in the degree of disclosure required and particularly in adding the so-called "stop order" mechanism by which issuance could be held up in cases where full disclosure was not made in the registration. Working feverishly from Friday morning to Monday morning, the two men turned out a draft along these lines and defended it successfully before Rayburn's subcommittee of the House Commerce Committee. With a green light from Rayburn, Landis and Cohen, joined by Middleton Beaman, the legislative counsel of the House, and (in the evenings) by Thomas G. Corcoran of the RFC, started to perfect their work.

Wall Street, awaiting developments with understandable nervousness, insisted on a chance to criticize the bill before it went up to the full Committee. Moley finally prevailed on a reluctant Rayburn to listen to a group of Wall Street lawyers, led by John Foster Dulles of Sullivan and Cromwell. But Dulles, as Landis and Cohen had no trouble demonstrating, was ill-informed about the problem; and the subcommittee was not impressed by his presentation. In the next weeks the Committee and then the House as a whole accepted the Cohen-Landis draft. Though the Senate had meanwhile passed the Thompson version, Rayburn obtained the substitution of the House bill in conference.

On May 27, 1933, the President signed the Securities Act. In a few months, Landis was appointed to the Federal Trade Commission to administer the new law.[5]

VI

The Pecora Committee also had recommendations concerning banking practices — especially the divorce of commercial banks from their security affiliates and of investment banks from their deposit business. The financial community liked these proposals no more than it did securities legislation. "What American banking needs," President Francis H. Sisson of the American Bankers Association had said in January 1933, "is the abolishment of special laws placing it under public regulation and supervision, rather than more statutes for its restriction and control." In March, it is true, Winthrop Aldrich, succeeding the unfortunate Wiggin as head of the Chase, made an unexpected demand for the separation of commercial and investment banking. This represented, however, very much a minority view on Wall Street; Aldrich's action was interpreted as a Rockefeller assault on the House of Morgan; and for a time he achieved almost the dignity of a traitor to his class. W. C. Potter of the Guaranty Trust characterized his proposals as "quite the most disastrous" he had "ever heard from a member of the financial community"; and J. P. Morgan himself predicted that separation of deposit and investment banking would have the most dire effects on his firm's future ability to supply capital "for the development of the country."

Congress nonetheless enacted the Glass-Steagall bill embodying the banking divorce in June. What was even worse, it added to the law a federal guarantee of bank deposits. The American Bankers Association itself led the fight — "to the last ditch," in its president's words — against the guarantee idea as "unsound, unscientific, unjust, and dangerous." Roosevelt himself was hardly more enthusiastic. Some members of the administration, however, notably Jones and Garner, favored the idea; and members of Congress, especially Arthur H. Vandenberg of Michigan, were determined to put it over. Finally Roosevelt accepted the proposal, hoping to use it at least as a means of unifying the banking system; the law provided that after 1936 state banks had to join the Federal Reserve System to qualify for deposit insurance.

The deposit insurance system turned out, of course, to be one of the most brilliant and successful of the accomplishments of the Hundred Days. Undeterred by the categorical predictions of disaster, the Federal Deposit Insurance Corporation entered into a markedly placid and effective existence. In the end, the total bank suspensions for the entire rest of the decade were less than those in any year of the twenties — and were less than 8 per cent of those in the single year of 1933, when the American Bankers Association fought so hard to prevent the new system from going into effect.[6]

VII

The attempts in 1933 to regulate finance implied a conception of business quite different from that involved in NRA — business not as a power to be propitiated or, at the very least, as a partner to be cajoled, but as an erratic and irresponsible force requiring strict social discipline. And the program of financial control introduced a new cast of characters — men lacking the faith of the Brain Trust, even of a Tugwell, in the virtues of bigness and of industrial self-government, and proposing instead to use the federal power to revitalize and police the competitive economy.

If this disciplinary approach was hard enough for the average businessman to accept, it was hardest of all for the bankers. No business group was more proud and powerful than the bankers; none was more persuaded of its own rectitude; none more accustomed to respectful consultation by government officials. To be attacked as antisocial was bewildering; to be excluded from the formation of public policy was beyond endurance. When one remembered both the premium bankers put on inside information and the chumminess they had enjoyed with past Presidents and Secretaries of the Treasury, the new chill in Washington was the cruelest of punishments. The bitter resentment flowing out of Wall Street after the financial legislation infected a large share of the business community. For the first time, businessmen began to wonder aloud about the New Deal. "There is no greater murmuring in the land," said the St. Louis *Post-Dispatch* in November 1933, "than that which rises in protest against the Securities Act."

Yet financial regulation seemed in 1933 a marginal part of the New Deal, and Frankfurter, Landis, Corcoran, and Cohen peripheral figures. Even Moley, for all his activity in getting the Securities Act drafted and passed, really regarded this approach as futile. What was needed, he believed, was not negative prevention but positive federal action to bring about a harmonious relationship among the factors involved; government "should participate freely rather than regulate as a policeman." Adolf Berle noted that the Securities Act would have stopped few of the financial transactions condemned in the Pecora investigation; all it did was to patrol one front when it ought to have aimed at reconstructing the system. Tugwell, dismissing the bill as better suited to 1910 than to 1933, wanted a government mechanism to control investment, like the wartime Capital Issues Committee. "The Act," said Professor William O. Douglas of the Yale Law School, "is a nineteenth-century piece of legislation." It ignored the need to manage investment; it ignored the problem of capital structure; instead of facilitating economic planning, it aimed at restoring a lost world of freely competing small units. It was "of a decidedly secondary character," Douglas said, so far as correcting the evils of high finance was concerned, and, more than that, it was "wholly antithetical to the programme of control envisaged in the New Deal and to the whole economy under which we are living." [7]

28. Crisis in the Skies

IF THE IDEA of a minatory government attitude toward business was not central to the New Deal of 1933, yet it certainly corresponded to the popular emotions of the year. The Pecora hearings remorselessly continued. And in the fall and winter of 1933–34, a Senate investigation into shipping and airplane subsidies, headed by Hugo Black of Alabama, dug up additional evidences of sharp business practice. Before it was finished, the Black Committee precipitated a chain of events which brought relations between government and business to a new point of tension.

II

Hugo Black, who was forty-seven years old in 1933, had served in the Senate since 1927. He was deceptively mild in appearance and manner, concealing a keen mind behind a placid unlined face, soft blue-gray eyes, and an unhurried Alabama drawl. Born in Clay County, the son of a country storekeeper, he grew up when the red-clay country of east-central Alabama was swept by Populism. Though Black's own family was, by Clay County standards, well-to-do, his father flirted briefly with the Populists, and the boy took away a strong sense of identification with the poor whites as against the Bourbon Democrats of Alabama's rich cotton counties. He went to the University of Alabama Law School, then practiced law in Birmingham, became police court judge and prosecuting attorney, and, with a politician's instinct, joined every fraternal order in sight — the Masons, the Knights of Pythias, the Odd Fellows, and in September 1923 the Robert E. Lee Chapter of the Ku Klux Klan.

The Klan was for Black one more means of political advancement; it was also perhaps one more means of striking out at the social elite of Alabama. He could have had few illusions about the group he was joining: the flogging of a county health officer by the Klan in Birmingham had caused a local outcry the year before. Yet, in a disorderly and degraded way, the southern Klan carried a strain of the Populist inheritance. Tom Watson, across the border in Georgia, had shown how Populism could degenerate into racism and xenophobia. When Black joined the Alabama Klan, its main opponent was Senator Oscar W. Underwood, whose opposition to bigotry possibly cost him a place on the Democratic ticket in 1924; still, Underwood, the embodiment of old-fashioned southern conservatism, was also the ancient foe of William Jennings Bryan, of women's suffrage, and of public power at Muscle Shoals. For Black in 1923, it seemed less important to be for freedom than to be for the people.

In 1925 Black announced his intention of running against Underwood the next year. His candidacy led him to resign from the Klan, because some Klansmen deemed it inappropriate for a member to stand for office. Black's personal attitude toward the organization evidently remained unchanged. Underwood, an old man, decided to withdraw. In the election that followed, Black, described in his circulars as "the candidate of the masses," undertook a whirlwind campaign. His chief organized backing came from the Women's Christian Temperance Union, some trade unions, and the Klan; and he defeated better-known opponents in the election.

Afterward he attended a Kloreo of the Birmingham Klan to hear an address by the Imperial Wizard, Hiram Evans of Georgia. Following the speech, Black, to his surprise, was given a Grand Passport, which meant an honorary life membership in the Klan. The Passport was good, he was told, "as long as you are good." Responding, Black said that he realized he had been elected to the Senate "by men who believe in the principles that I have sought to advocate and which are the principles of this organization." Then he added, "The great thing I like about this organization is not the burning of crosses, it is not attempting to regulate anybody." Beyond the Klan, he said, he saw a bigger vision — the vision of America "as it remains true to the principles of human liberty." He never attended another Klan meeting. Years later, his wife, coming across the Grand Passport in a drawer, destroyed it.

In Washington, Black began a new career. Aware of the deficiencies in his preparation, he read prodigiously in the classics of law, history, and political theory. His important friendships were with Senate liberals — with Norris, Tom Walsh, La Follette, Wheeler, Costigan. He ostentatiously kept away from his Alabama colleague, Tom Heflin, who whiled away dull days with passionate excoriations of the Pope. There were occasional recurrences to Clay County. Thus Paul Y. Anderson of the St. Louis *Post-Dispatch* reported as late as 1932 that Black "became hysterical over the prospect of a federal relief plan which might feed Negroes as well as whites, and gave an exhibition which brought a blush to the face of Tom Heflin, lurking in the rear of the chamber." Still, hard work, mastery of information, trenchancy in debate, and an increasing concern for fundamental principles of government won him the growing respect of his colleagues. The more generous aspects of his Populism remained. He broadened his solicitude for the poor folk to include the trade unions; this gained him prominence as the sponsor of the thirty-hour-week bill. And he was always ready to bring his hard-driving and suspicious intelligence to bear on the claims of business to special privileges from the state.[1]

III

The Black Committee was set up by special resolution during the lame-duck session of Congress before Roosevelt's inauguration. Black's first intention had been to concentrate on the mail contracts by which the government subsidized the merchant marine. Then Senator King of Nevada insisted that air mail subsidies be included in the investigation, and preliminary exploration soon convinced Black that this was by far the richer field.

Checking about in the air mail problem, Black heard that a Hearst reporter named Fulton Lewis, Jr., had accumulated explosive material on the assignment of air mail contracts — material which his newspaper was withholding from publication. Two years before, it developed, Lewis had caught Herbert Hoover's Post Office Department awarding a contract for the transport of air mail between New York and Washington at a rate three times as high as that proposed in a rejected bid from a much smaller company. His interest piqued by this discrepancy, Lewis concluded after months of investigation that Postmaster-General Walter F. Brown was systematically using government subsidies as a means of favoring the big companies and freezing out the independent shoestring operators in the air transport field.

Brown, who was in some respects the ablest member of Hoover's cabinet next to Henry Stimson, saw the problem differently. Finding American commercial aviation in what he regarded as a state of anarchy, he conceived it his mission as Postmaster-General to coordinate and consolidate American airlines in order to lay the foundations for a national air transport system. Ruthless and overbearing, he used all the stated powers of his office — and no doubt others too — to realize this imperial conception. Air mail subsidies were his most potent weapon for compelling large companies to expand their services and, at the same time, for driving bothersome and impecunious independents out of business. To attain the flexibility he needed in working out an integrated system, Brown was particularly eager to get away from the system of competitive bidding. Brown's program naturally enraged the independents, some of whom had more initiative and experience than their wealthier rivals but could not get the subsidies they needed for their own expansion.

As the hearings began, Black, well armed with information from Lewis, from the independents and from company files, summoned a selection of airlines executives. His technique was to persuade witnesses that he already had the facts and merely wanted confirmation for the record. Courteous, smiling, puffing gravely on his cigar, he undertook to "refresh" their memories, leading them imperceptibly into admissions which enabled him to conclude with incisive and damaging summations of their testimony.

As Black patiently reconstructed the story, a dismally familiar picture emerged — immense salaries, bonuses, and speculative profits; dubious relations between the industry and the government officials who dealt with it; the avoidance of competitive bidding; the covert destruction of official records — all in all, an ex-

ceptionally blatant case, it seemed, of an industry using government
to exploit the public. Black made a good deal of a closed meeting
of airline executives at the Post Office Department in the spring of
1930. Even participants had wondered whether they were violating the Sherman Act; one reassuringly remarked, "If we were holding this meeting across the street in the Raleigh Hotel, it would
be an improper meeting; but because we are holding it at the
invitation of a member of the cabinet, and in the office of the Post
Office Department, it is perfectly all right." A representative of an
independent airline who tried to crash the meeting was thrown
out; the Superintendent of Air Mail later told him that his line
was too small to qualify. As a result of Brown's policies, it became
apparent three large aviation holding companies — United Aircraft, Aviation Corporation of Delaware, and North American-
General Motors — were given 24 of the 27 federal air mail contracts.

IV

Undoubtedly Brown was neither so selfless and farseeing as he
presented himself to the Committee nor so wicked as Black proclaimed him to the press. In his desire to bring order to a disorganized industry, Brown too easily mistook size for efficiency and
financial backing for engineering skill. Given his passion for stability, he naturally favored Wall Street combines, however ignorant
of aviation, to penniless air pioneers, however skilled at flying.
But he was not the agent of a profiteering conspiracy, even if his
methods permitted others to make huge profits; he was always the
active force in promoting coordination, not the companies themselves, which remained inveterately suspicious of one another.

For his part, Black was prepared to agree that subsidies were
necessary in the national interest to build the air system. But they
required, he felt, the check of competitive bidding. And he particularly condemned the concentration of government favor on
what seemed to him Wall Street escadrilles, formed less to fly
planes than to kite securities. "The control of American aviation,"
Black said, "has been ruthlessly taken away from the men who could
fly and bestowed upon bankers, brokers, promoters and politicians,

sitting in their inner offices, allotting among themselves the tax-payers' money." Someone had to bring the racket to a halt. Late in January 1934, Black, lunching at the White House, pointed out to the President that the Postmaster-General had power to cancel contracts obtained by fraud or conspiracy. In the Post Office Department Solicitor Karl Crowley was also urging cancellation. On February 8 Roosevelt asked Homer Cummings to look into the matter. The next morning Cummings reported that the evidence was sufficient to justify cancellation.

There were differences of opinion about timing. The Post Office Department wanted to postpone cancellation until June 1 and use the intervening time to advertise for new bids; in this way, they could avoid interruption in air mail service. As the President saw it, however, if the contracts were crooked, they ought to be cancelled forthwith. But what about air mail service in the interim? An Assistant Postmaster-General now asked General Benjamin D. Foulois, chief of the Army Air Corps, whether his pilots could take over the delivery of the mail — a mission the Army had not undertaken since 1918. Foulois gave a confident yes in reply. Two hours later, on February 9, 1934, the President issued an order annulling the contracts and directing the Air Corps to carry the mail during the emergency.[2]

v

The same week the Air Corps assumed responsibility for the mails, savage February weather lashed the country — blizzards in the West, gales, sleet, fog, and intense cold in the Middle West and East. Army pilots were not trained for bad-weather flying; many were not even prepared for night flying; and few knew the transcontinental routes they were suddenly ordered to follow. Weather and inexperience brought tragedy. One plane, far off its course, crashed in flames near Jerome, Idaho. Another, its wings coated with ice, thundered helplessly into a mountain in Utah. An Army seaplane landed in freezing spray and high seas off Rockaway Point and was soon crumbled to pieces by the waves. At the end of the first week of Army operations, five pilots were dead (three were killed in test operations before the Army officially took over), six were injured, eight planes were wrecked. The country was appalled. Eddie Rickenbacker, a First World War ace, now vice-president of Eastern Airlines, denounced it as "legalized murder."

The national shock suddenly gave the pent-up dissatisfaction with the New Deal a seemingly legitimate outlet. Moreover, the aviation industry was ready to fight back. And in taking on the administration, it had the unique advantage of presenting as its voice the single American personality who might match Franklin Roosevelt in national popularity. This was the Lone Eagle, Colonel Charles A. Lindbergh, the one authentic American hero of the 1920's, still a young man of thirty-two. In the years since *The Spirit of St. Louis* had soared across the Atlantic, his hard work and quiet modesty had preserved the purity of his popular image. The frightful kidnaping and murder of his baby son in 1932 had deepened his place in the nation's affections. In these years, too, Lindbergh had become thoroughly identified with the air industry. In 1929 he had become a technical consultant for Transcontinental Air Transport. At that time he had received a check for $250,000, which, according to a previous agreement, he immediately exchanged for 25,000 shares of TAT stock. In 1933, as technical adviser for Pan American, he accepted stock warrants which brought him profits of $150,000, all of which he reinvested in the company. When the administration canceled the contracts, Lindbergh was a logical figure to express the industry's resentment.

He promptly sent the President a sharp telegram. With calm precision, he addressed himself to the weak part of Roosevelt's case: the fact that the contracts were canceled without hearings. YOUR PRESENT ACTION, said Lindbergh, DOES NOT DISCRIMINATE BETWEEN INNOCENCE AND GUILT AND PLACES NO PREMIUM ON HONEST BUSINESS. . . . YOUR ORDER OF CANCELLATION OF ALL AIRMAIL CONTRACTS CONDEMNS THE LARGEST PORTION OF OUR COMMERCIAL AVIATION WITHOUT JUST TRIAL. George W. Norris, who had fought alongside Lindbergh's father to keep the United States out of the First World War, observed, "Now Colonel Lindbergh is earning his $250,000." And Steve Early was swift to complain that Lindbergh had released the telegram to the press without allowing the President the courtesy of receiving it. But none of these jabs made much impression against the casualty lists and Lindbergh's apparently invincible prestige.

The brunt of the attack settled on Postmaster-General Farley as the man who had technically canceled the contracts. One newspaper cartoon depicted him guiltily waving away the accusing skeletons of twelve dead air mail pilots. In actual fact, Farley played little role in the decision. In his appearances before the Black Committee, he showed meager knowledge of the subsidy problem. Indeed, his predecessor, Walter Brown, testified that Farley told him he had no sympathy with "these investigations." Farley added (according to Brown; Farley denied these remarks) that he considered Black "a publicity hound — but don't tell anybody I said so, because I have to get along with him." Still, pushed by Crowley and Black, Farley went along with cancellation. When the storm broke, he took uncomplaining public responsibility for the decision. Privately, as he later wrote, "I was hurt that the President had not seen fit to divert the wrath."

The conflict between Roosevelt and Lindbergh might have presented many Americans a hard choice. But the collapse of the Air Corps made the decision easy. As accidents continued, protests mounted. By February 25, 1934, Arthur Krock wrote in the *New York Times* that, for the first time since the inauguration, the administration "seems really on the defensive." Early in March Roosevelt told Secretary of War Dern, "The continuation of deaths in the Army Air Corps must stop." The Air Corps reduced its mail flights until the weather improved. At the same time, Roosevelt asked Congress to enact new legislation which would let private air mail contracts on the basis of competitive bidding. And, in a conciliatory gesture, Dern invited Lindbergh to serve under Newton D. Baker on a War Department board to review the Air Corps.

Lindbergh was in no mood to be placated. He rejected Dern's offer in another brusque communication: "I believe that the use of the Army Air Corps to carry the air mail was unwarranted and contrary to American principles." A few days later he came to Washington to testify before the Senate Post Office Committee. Crouched in a big red-leather chair, his youthful face intent and grave, he assailed the presidential action in terse and self-possessed manner before the fascinated Caucus Room. "Whenever his face flashed in the familiar, winsome smile," reported the *New York Times*, "a murmer of approval ran through the hall." Eddie Rickenbacker, following Lindbergh to the stand, made the same case in more lurid language, ending in a plea to Roosevelt to "purge his official family of those traitorous elements, few in number, I presume, who have misadvised or advised without giving full facts and cause him to act contrary to American principles."

VI

By May the commercial airlines were once again carrying the mail. But the industry, for all its apparent triumph, emerged from this experience somewhat chastened. Jim Farley, in reopening bids for air mail contracts, stipulated that the companies which had enjoyed Walter Brown's favor must reorganize before their bids were acceptable. This took place, bringing a measure of responsibility to the industry; and, under the new dispensation, the air mail subsidies fell from $19.4 million in 1933 to less than $8 million in 1934. Moreover, the experience showed the deficiency of existing aviation legislation and led to the Air Mail Act of 1934, introduced by Black and Kenneth McKellar (and eventually to the Civil Aeronautics Act of 1938, sponsored by Senator Pat McCarran of Nevada and Representative Clarence Lea of California, and to the Civil Aeronautics Authority).

As for the government, it too was shaken by the experience. For those who believed that air power might be decisive in future wars, the need for an overhauling of the aviation industry and the Air Corps could not be more apparent. Thus General Billy Mitchell, the dedicated prophet of American air power, vigorously backed Hugo Black in his air mail investigation. "If the Government spends money on aviation," he told a House committee, "it should make sure that it gets the best results for that money, and not allow that money to be handled principally for gambling on the stock exchanges." Nor was Mitchell impressed by Lindbergh's intervention. "Lindbergh has disclosed himself as the 'front man' of the Air Trust," said Mitchell. ". . . He is a commercial flyer. His motive is principally profit."

Mitchell believed that the Air Corps should fly the mails permanently. "It would result in a much more efficient Air Corps and it would aid in the proper development of aviation as a means of national defense." The disastrous outcome of the experiment of

1934 he blamed on the private airlines. "The United States could not use their radio system nor their radio equipment nor their planes. . . . The Army Air Corps, which was not properly equipped for any kind of duty, due to the machinations of these aviation profiteers and service politicians, undertook to carry the mail under these conditions." How could pilots who had only about one hundred hours of flying a year be expected to make good? "The army has lost the art of flying," he said angrily. "It can't fly. If any army aviator can't fly a mail route in any sort of weather, what would we do in a war?"

Like most of Billy Mitchell's questions, this one was uncomfortably penetrating. The air mail fiasco made it impossible even for the War Department to dodge the question further. "I think it is excellent," said Mitchell, "that this matter has come up at the present time, although, unfortunately, lives have been lost. I think we will be better for it in the end." And so, indeed, the nation was. As Major H. H. Arnold, who was in charge of air mail operations in the Pacific Coast area, later wrote, "It gave us wonderful experience for combat flying, bad weather flying, night flying; but, best of all, it made it possible for us to get the latest navigational and night-flying instruments in our planes." And the experience produced the Baker Board, which, though it resisted Mitchell's theories of an independent air force, did advocate the establishment of a General Headquarters Air Force, out of which an independent air force might eventually come.

The air mail fight flared up in January 1934, died down by April, and was largely forgotten by summer. Yet its significance far outweighed its brevity. The fight dented the myth of Roosevelt's invulnerability and strengthened the business community's dislike of what it considered personal and arbitrary actions by the New Deal. It quickened the pace and intensity of criticism of the administration. It had its effect too on personalities: it brought Hugo Black into new prominence, planted a first seed of resentment in the breast of Jim Farley, and uncovered in Charles Lindbergh a man who perhaps appealed to more American hearts that anyone save Franklin Roosevelt. Above all, it set in motion reforms in the aviation industry and in the Army Air Corps — reforms for which the nation would have cause for gratitude in future crises.[3]

29. Controlling the Stock Exchanges

THE AIR MAIL crisis was reaching its height in March 1934, when relations between the New Deal and the business community took a new turn for the worse. Prominent in the unfinished business left over from the Hundred Days was the companion piece to the Securities Act, the bill to regulate the stock exchanges. The 1933 draft of the stock exchange bill, prepared by Samuel Untermyer, had now been discarded. In December 1933, Ferdinand Pecora and Max Lowenthal, anticipating a congressional request for a new bill, asked Ben Cohen to produce a draft. Cohen, busy for the moment on railroad loans, set two younger men, Telford Taylor and I. N. P. Stokes, to work on preliminary drafting. Then over the Christmas holidays, with the help of Thomas G. Corcoran and James M. Landis, Cohen completed the bill.

The Cohen-Corcoran mandate to work on a stock exchange bill at all was vague. Their assignment from Pecora and Lowenthal was wholly informal. While a display of interest on Raymond Moley's part in December gave them a hope of White House sponsorship, Moley, fearful of their "exuberance," did not tell them that Roosevelt had expressly asked to have a bill prepared. Operating more or less in the dark, Cohen and Corcoran could only go ahead on their own. They consulted extensively with Pecora and his aides, particularly John T. Flynn; some work had already been done on a bill under Landis's direction in the FTC; and Winfield Riefler of the Federal Reserve Board helped on the margin provisions. By the first week in February, when Senator Duncan Fletcher of Florida, the chairman of the Senate

Banking Committee, asked for a bill, the draft was in fair shape.

On February 9, Roosevelt sent a message to the Hill calling for stock exchange legislation. The Cohen-Corcoran bill, promptly introduced by Fletcher in the Senate and Sam Rayburn in the House, was an intricate document, fifty pages long, recondite in its technical detail, but clearly dedicated to three main objectives. The first was to protect investors from insiders' manipulations of the securities market — matched orders, washed sales, market rigging, pools, options — by placing trading practices under federal supervision. The second was to protect investors from misrepresentation by requiring the registration not only of new securities but of all securities traded on the exchanges. The third was to reduce speculation by controlling the amount of borrowed money in the market through the regulation of margin requirements. The Federal Trade Commission was to administer the law. The broad hope was that the stock exchanges, properly regulated, would serve thereafter as a place of investment rather than of speculation and gambling. This reform, it was believed, would not only save the individual investor but would contribute significantly to general economic stability.[1]

II

For the next weeks, business leaders condemned the bill in steady procession before the House Interstate and Foreign Commerce Committee. Most of the attack was along familiar lines: regulation of the exchanges was unnecessary, impractical, and dangerous; its only effect would be to deter investment. Then on March 23, 1934, James H. Rand, Jr., of Remington, Rand, chairman of the Committee for the Nation, adorned the case against stock exchange regulation with new and more thrilling arguments. The bill, he said, was deliberately designed to push the nation "along the road from Democracy to Communism." To support this remarkable accusation, Rand produced a manuscript written by Dr. William A. Wirt, an educator who for a quarter-century had been superintendent of schools in Gary, Indiana.

In the summer of 1933, according to the manuscript, Dr. Wirt had asked a group of "brain trusters" how they planned to bring about their proposed overthrow of the social order. They replied that by holding back recovery they could prolong the country's troubles until the people would realize that the government had no choice but to take over everything. What about the President? Wirt asked. Roosevelt, the "brain trusters" said, was in the middle of a swift stream; the current was so strong that he could not turn back. "We believe that we can keep Mr. Roosevelt there until we are ready to supplant him with a Stalin. We all think that Mr. Roosevelt is only the Kerensky of this revolution." But would not the President see through their schemes? "We are on the inside," they told Wirt. "We can control the avenues of influence. We can make the President believe that he is making decisions for himself."

The Committee, hearing this extraordinary tale with skepticism, decided on further investigation. Early in April a Select House Committee called Dr. Wirt for direct testimony. Wirt began by identifying the occasion of the supposed remarks. It was a dinner party, he said, at the home of Alice Barrows, who had been Wirt's private secretary forty years before and had worked since 1917 for the Bureau of Education. The other guests included David Cushman Coyle, an engineer turned economist; Robert Bruere, a specialist in industrial relations; Laurence Todd, who was Washington correspondent of Tass; and two government women, Hildegarde Kneeland and Mary Taylor. It soon developed that no one at the party was a member of the Roosevelt circle or, indeed, prominent at all in the New Deal. After reconsideration, Wirt himself absolved Coyle, Bruere, and Miss Barrows from participation in the subversive talk. (Except for Todd, Miss Barrows was the only member of the group found in subsequent association with Communists; in 1953, she invoked the Fifth Amendment when asked whether she was herself a party member.) Wirt further conceded in his rambling and protracted testimony that no one had actually spoken of wanting to thwart business recovery — this was his own deduction; that most of the talk of radical change came from Wirt himself trying to recollect an old speech of Tugwell's — during which, he reported ominously, the others seemed to "nod approval"; and that the Roosevelt-Kerensky analogy had been made by Todd, the one person present beside Wirt who had no connection at all with the government.

His performance before the Committee may not have been unlike his performance at the Barrows dinner. "I agree," Wirt admitted of the dinner, "that I did a great deal of talking." In this statement, if in no other, he had the endorsement of his fellow-guests. Miss Barrows: "As a dinner, it was not a success, because Dr. Wirt talked practically all the time." Miss Kneeland: "It was impossible for either myself or anyone else to take considerable part in the conversation." Miss Taylor: "Dr. Wirt really had no conversation. The monologue continued." Todd: He "talked nearly five hours continuously." Coyle (as an engineer, he had fortunately specialized in wind resistance) : "Dr. Wirt did the talking." Bruere: "I had listened to Dr. Wirt for several hours discoursing on money."

III

It was Bruere's remark which was perhaps most significant. For Dr. Wirt was, above all, a monetary radical; and, in the tradition of those possessed by monetary hallucinations, he supposed that only a malign conspiracy could prevent the immediate application of so self-evident a solution. Where others of his faith identified the conspirators as international bankers or Jews, Wirt saw Communists. When the Committee for the Nation published his full manuscript, the balance of his preoccupations became evident. *America Must Lose* (the allusion, of course, was to Wallace's pamphlet) was a fifty-page argument for the reduction of the gold value of the dollar in foreign exchange as the one sure road out of depression. The tale of conspiracy, which Rand had brought to the House Committee, occupied half a dozen pages. Wirt's point in telling it was clearly not to make serious charges of subversion. It was rather to account in passing for the otherwise unaccountable failure of the administration to accept the exchange depreciation panacea.

Moreover, though Wirt, when the story first broke, referred to what he called "the whole communistic plot," and though his testimony before the Committee dealt a good deal in personal innuendoes, his more consistent picture was not of a treasonable conspiracy at all but of a philosophical campaign of an entirely public sort looking toward a planned economy. As he put it, "I have never said these people, or anybody, was planning to overthrow the government, I said the social order." Or, again: "For a year the leaders of the New Deal, the so-called 'Brain Trust,' have been making statements *publicly* . . . outlining in great detail their plans for a social and economic revolution in America." In the end, Wirt's testimony turned into a discursive monologue made up of vague allegations punctuated by self-convicting misstatements (such as having the group discuss Henry Wallace's *America Must Choose* six months before it was published). The fact that a Communist conspiracy was operating in Washington when Wirt spoke hardly vindicated what he said; for he had no such underground operation in mind, and his evidence for any sort of conspiracy was footling and absurd.

Donald Richberg summed up the Washington reaction:

> A cuttlefish squirt
> Nobody hurt,
> From beginning to end;
> Dr. Wirt.

The President himself lightly observed to a group of congressmen who met him at the station on his return to mid-April from a fishing trip to the Bahamas, "In Washington apparently you good people have been going from Wirt to Wirt." "Flatter than a crepe suzette," said *Time,* "fell the Red Scare of 1934."

Yet a residue remained. The Wirt affair helped shape a new stereotype — the theory of the New Deal as a subversive conspiracy. Mark Sullivan had already broached this hypothesis in a series of columns the previous December portraying Tugwell as the chief of a group of young intellectuals working to transform American society into one which, as Sullivan put it, "the word 'Russia' described more nearly than any other." By July 1934, the Hearst papers could editorialize, "As a matter of frank fact, much of the Administration is more Communistic than the Communists themselves." If some conservatives disdained this style of attack, others were more than ready to adopt the new weapon which Dr. Wirt had so confusedly flung into the national picture. "What will come of it no one knows," Tugwell noted in his diary in April. "If there is genuine strength in the present reaction, we may be thrown overboard." [2]

IV

The Wirt disclosure dissolved into bad farce. But, after the sideshow closed, the main event — the fight over the stock exchange regulation bill — still roused sufficient excitement on its merits. The more serious leader of the opposition to the Fletcher-Rayburn bill was, appropriately, the president of the New York Stock Exchange, Richard Whitney.

In October 1933, Pecora, in his pursuit of information about the stock market, had dispatched two emissaries to discuss with Whitney the sending of questionnaires to members of the Exchange. When they entered his office, Whitney recognized one of them as John T. Flynn, long Wall Street's virulent critic. Flushing, Whitney rose abruptly from his chair and walked from the room in a rage. Several moments passed before he regained control of himself sufficiently to return, and his anger soon flared up again. When his visitors asserted the need for federal regulation, Whitney turned sharply on them. "You gentlemen are making a great mistake," he said proudly. "The Exchange is a perfect institution."

Pride, indeed, was Whitney's essence — pride in the Exchange, pride in his class, pride in himself. He was tall and portly, with a large nose, prominent eyebrows, and heavily handsome features. He had attended Groton and Harvard; he had married the daughter of the president of the Union League Club; he had worked at Kidder, Peabody in Boston and then at Morgan's in New York. He was a sportsman, kept a stable of thoroughbreds on his New Jersey estate, was president of the Essex Fox Hounds and Treasurer of the New York Yacht Club. His clubs were the Links, the Turf and Field, the Racquet, and the Knickerbocker; from his watch chain there dangled the golden pig of Harvard's Porcellian. He saw himself as the guardian of aristocratic proprieties. When drunken graduates defaced the chapel at Groton, Whitney was said to have remarked that if any of these young men appeared as candidates for the Knickerbocker he would exert all his influence to keep them out. To outsiders, his manner, whether he was in a mood of affability or arrogance, seemed deeply condescending.

His economic philosophy was simple. "I claim that this country has been built by speculation," he told the Senate Banking Com-

mittee, "and further progress must be in that line." He admitted
the existence of abuses but denied that the "excesses of 1929 and
preceding years were to a material extent caused by or due to our
stock exchanges or the way in which they were operated." "When
does speculation become excessive?" a congressman asked. "That
I cannot tell you," said Whitney, adding that he was willing to
leave "that interpretation in the hands of those who control the
credit system of the country." The fight against speculation seemed
to him futile. "You are trying to deal with human nature," he
said. ". . . Speculation is always going to exist in this country just
as long as we are Americans." [3]

V

For Whitney the notion of federal regulation of the Stock Exchange was practically *lèse-majesté*. He repeatedly insisted that
Wall Street was perfectly capable of regulating itself. To prove his
point before a Senate committee, he once cited a rule adopted
two weeks earlier to prevent members of the Exchange from engaging in pools or other manipulative operations. Senator Costigan asked why it had taken so long to make such an obvious regulation. Whitney replied that many rules were adopted only after
years of discussion. "What was the argument against the rule?"
asked Senator Bulkley curiously. "I do not suppose, Senator Bulkley," Whitney replied, "that there was any argument." "It took
several years," said Bulkley. "I thought there must be some argument advanced against it." Whitney said again that there had been
no argument. "Is it one result of the stock-exchange investigation?"
said Costigan sharply. "It might be so construed," said Whitney
reluctantly.

He had every objection to the bill. He opposed the effort to
segregate the functions of brokers, floor traders, and specialists.
He opposed the provision forbidding brokers to trade on their
own accounts. Under the pretext of regulating the exchanges, he
said, the bill gave the FTC "an absolute power to manage and to
operate them." Under the guise of establishing sound practices,
it aimed "to establish indirectly a form of nationalization of business." He addressed a personal letter to Roosevelt warning that the

bill might result "in freezing the Stock Exchange, which is the market for liquid securities, just as effectively as the Securities Act has frozen the market for capital securities." If the bill passed, he told the House Commerce Committee, "the security markets of the Nation will dry up"; there would be "tremendous, if not universal, withdrawal" of corporations from the exchanges. More than this, the bill was unconstitutional. At bottom, indeed, he appeared to object not to this or that provision, but to the whole idea of federal regulation. Though Roland Redmond, the counsel for the Exchange, went through the motions of offering a weak regulatory measure, Redmond frankly confessed that the Wall Street substitute seemed to Whitney and himself as unconstitutional as the Fletcher-Rayburn bill.

Four days after Roosevelt's message Whitney called in representatives of the thirty principal wire houses to plan a campaign against the bill. In another two days he sent a letter to all members of the Exchange and to the presidents of eighty large corporations. When debate began, he rented a house in Washington in order to direct the fight in person. Businessmen across the country rallied to his leadership. George M. Humphrey of the Hanna Company, chairman of the Cleveland Committee on the Fletcher-Rayburn bill, called the measure "detrimental to industry as a whole, to the recovery of business, and to the reemployment of normal working forces." Gerard Swope and the Business Advisory Council of the Department of Commerce said its enactment would be a "national disaster." It would result, said Eugene Meyer, "in state control of industry." Twenty-eight leading industrialists, led by Edgar M. Queeny of Monsanto, Sewell Avery of United States Gypsum, Thomas M. Girdler of Republic Steel, and Frank Phillips of Phillips Petroleum, asserted in a display of solicitude for small business that the bill would bring nearly 500,000 firms with no Wall Street connections "under the strangling regulation of a Federal bureau." Eugene E. Thompson, president of the Associated Stock Exchanges, predicted "the wreck of the stock exchanges as institutions and . . . financial and industrial chaos." "The real object of the bill," said Republican congressman, Fred Britten of Illinois, "is to Russianize everything worthwhile." [4]

VI

The New Deal had not thus far confronted such an outburst of business indignation. Sam Rayburn called it "the most powerful lobby ever organized against any bill which ever came up in Congress." "Those old Wall Street boys," said Will Rogers on March 23, "are putting up an awful fight to keep the government from putting a cop on their corner." The complexity of their measure made things especially difficult for its sponsors. On the eve of the Senate hearings, Pecora startled Corcoran and Cohen by asking them to testify for the measure the next day. After a night's rehearsal of all possible questions and answers, Corcoran, anticipating an executive session of the Committee, emerged reasonably confident. The next morning he encountered not only a public hearing and a crowded room but also Redmond, who had somehow wangled from Fletcher the privilege, unusual in congressional hearings, of cross-examination. Corcoran faced the situation with limitless aplomb, however, and, matching technicality with technicality, answered everything Redmond asked him. (A few days later, Oliver Wendell Holmes, to whom Corcoran occasionally read aloud in the evenings, told him that another former secretary had protested to the old Justice that Corcoran was disgracing him by his role in the Stock Exchange fight. "I told him," Holmes said to Corcoran, "that I was proud to be even remotely associated with such a glorious row.")

As the row went on, opposition to the bill centered increasingly on two aspects: the provision setting fixed margin requirements; and the provision making the Federal Trade Commission the administering agency.

The friends of the bill, convinced that too much borrowed money in the market encouraged speculation, sought to impose rigid controls over the permissible loan value on securities. They wanted a 30 per cent margin requirement; and they wanted to write it into the statute instead of leaving margins to the discretion of the regulatory commission; for they were not sure that any commission could resist pressure from the exchanges to relax margin restrictions. Whitney was, of course, appalled at this approach to the margin problem. Such a requirement, he said, "totally prohibits what is commonly known as 'margin trading,' and will have the effect, as I see it, of eliminating all speculation from security markets." If speculation were eliminated, Whitney dourly continued, "there follows from that, in my opinion, the result that security markets will cease to exist." ("I believe in stock exchanges," Tom Corcoran told the Committee. "I do not believe you should kill them. I do believe you should regulate them.")

Whitney's other main effort was to take regulation out of the hand of the FTC. He favored a seven-member special commission, with two members representing the stock exchanges and one the Federal Reserve Banks. He remained unmoved when senators asked him whether he thought railroads should appoint members to the Interstate Commerce Commission. In the Senate, Carter Glass led the fight for a separate commission.[5]

VII

In the first weeks of March, Whitney's counteroffensive began to have effect, even within the administration. Senator Robinson of Arkansas, the Majority Leader, suggested publicly that the bill might not be pressed further that session. Tom K. Smith, a St. Louis banker who was serving as special assistant to Morgenthau at the Treasury, tried to dilute the bill from the inside; and Eugene Black of the Federal Reserve Board and Moley were tireless counselors of caution.

Yet, if the issue divided the administration, it also divided Wall Street. Whitney represented primarily the operators on the Exchange — the floor traders and specialists, men with little direct contact with the public who engaged in speculations on their own account and tended to regard the stock market as a sort of private club. But the large commission houses had fewer illusions about the state of national opinion; they were less likely to be traders on their own account; and they had long resented the Whitney regime. It became evident that their organization, the Association of Stock Exchange Firms, along with the New York Curb Exchange and the out-of-town exchanges, might be detached from the Whitney campaign. Such influential commission brokers as E. A. Pierce and Paul V. Shields, such men as James V. Forrestal of Dillon, Read and Robert A. Lovett of Brown Brothers, Harriman represented a moderate Wall Street group, hostile to market manipulation and reconciled to the need for regulation. Sensing this situation, Landis and Corcoran started to drive a wedge between the two groups. In time, the moderates, convinced that a frontal attack on the bill would fail, decided to work with the administration in an effort to get a law which would be both effective and sensible.

On March 20, Cohen and Corcoran submitted a thorough redraft to the House Committee. The new version, while far more acceptable to the Wall Street moderates, still went much too far for Whitney, who promptly said it was as bad as the original. On the other hand, the President, who had stood throughout for a rigorous approach, obviously meant to retreat no further. On March 26 Roosevelt, who had already disowned Robinson's musings about postponement, sent a strong letter to Senator Fletcher. He asserted that "a more definite and more highly organized drive" was being made against the stock exchange bill than against any other of his recommendations; he asserted too that an overwhelming majority of the people were determined to bring unregulated security speculation to an end. "I am certain," Roosevelt said, "that the country as a whole will not be satisfied with legislation unless such legislation has teeth in it." The present bill, he added, seemed to meet the minimum requirements. "I do not see how any of us could afford to have it weakened in any shape, manner or form."

By the end of April, the Senate and House Committees had more or less settled on a pattern of regulation by which the government would have power to compel the disclosure of information, to force investigations, to control margins, and even to induce the exchanges to alter their own rules. But important disagreements remained. Rayburn's bill, more faithful to the original, kept the FTC as the administrative agency and favored statutory margin requirements. The Senate version, on the other hand, provided for a new regulatory commission and wanted margin provisions to be set by the new commission and the Federal Reserve Board. The question of a separate commission was, in part, an unreal issue. Landis, on the basis of his FTC experience, actually favored a new commission; and Rayburn was going through the motions of opposing it primarily in order to gain leverage when it came to appointing the commissioners. On May 5, the House passed its bill by a vote of 280 to 84; a week later the Senate bill went through by the surprising margin of 62 to 13. Toward the end of the month, the differences were ironed out in conference, the House accepting the new commission and the Senate consenting to a nominal limitation of margins to 45 per cent with ample room for Federal Reserve intervention. The final bill in effect confided to the discretion of the new Securities and Exchange Commission much of the authority over the stock market which the earlier version had made mandatory in the statute.

The result owed a great deal to the parliamentary strength and skill of Rayburn, who stood off pressures with cool composure and an astute sense of political possibility. A few purists like John T. Flynn, convinced that the original measure had been sold out to Wall Street, denounced the President. But Landis, Cohen, and Corcoran were not unhappy about the increased flexibility and felt reasonably satisfied with the outcome. Roosevelt himself signed the Securities Exchange Act on June 6, 1934.[6]

VIII

The new Commission was charged with administering both the Securities Exchange Act of 1934 and the Securities Act of 1933. The next critical question was its membership. Having roused the financial community by the law, Roosevelt must now have hoped to compose it, to a degree, at least, by the administration. He was accordingly receptive to Moley's suggestion of Joseph P. Kennedy as chairman for the Securities and Exchange Commission. Kennedy knew Wall Street and might inspire its confidence; his knockabout business career had given him long experience in bringing mutually suspicious people together; and he had contributed generously to the Democratic campaign in 1932.

Kennedy, who was forty-six years old in 1934, was born and brought up in East Boston, where his father had been a successful businessman and politician. At Boston Latin and Harvard, Joe Kennedy seemed a bright, affluent, and aggressive young Irishman on the way up. By the age of 25 he was a bank president. During the First World War, he went into shipbuilding at Fore River;

it was then that he first met Franklin Roosevelt. After the war, he served for a time as the manager of Hayden Stone and Company, an investment banking house in Boston. In the twenties he pursued a varied and spectacular career in the world of finance, specializing in the film industry. Then came the crash. "I am not ashamed to record," Kennedy wrote in 1936, "that in those days I felt and said I would be willing to part with half of what I had if I could be sure of keeping, under law and order, the other half." But he continued to prosper. By 1932 this tough, impatient, healthy-looking man in heavy horn-rimmed glasses, surrounded by nine attractive children, owned homes in New York, Hyannisport, and Palm Beach, and was still active in Wall Street.

In 1932 he supported Roosevelt for the Presidency. In the summer of 1933 he participated in a pool in the stock of the Libby-Owens-Ford Company — precisely the kind of speculative manipulation the SEC was designed to prevent. For this and other reasons, rumors of his appointment as SEC chairman provoked violent opposition. The New Dealers, mostly favoring Landis or Pecora for the chairmanship, were incredulous. "I say it isn't true," John T. Flynn wrote. "It is impossible. It could not happen." Roy Howard of Scripps-Howard protested personally to the President and had the Washington *News* say editorially that Roosevelt could not "with impunity administer such a slap in the face to his most loyal and effective supporters." But Roosevelt, as he told the cabinet on June 29, had confidence in Kennedy as a man who could do the job because he knew the tricks of the trade.

The New Dealers found consolation in the rest of the commission, which included Landis, Pecora, and two liberal Republicans — George C. Mathews, a La Follette man from Wisconsin, then on the FTC, and Robert Healy of Vermont, the FTC's chief counsel. When Moley told Corcoran about the SEC nominations, Corcoran, after complaining about Kennedy, said, "Oh well, we've got four out of five anyhow." "What do you mean by that?" said Moley. "What I mean," said Corcoran (as Moley later recalled it), "is that four are for us and one is for business." Moley replied with heat that he conceived the economy as an arena for collaboration, not for conflict, and that he would like to know if Corcoran and his friends thought differently. Corcoran, looking, Moley wrote, "like a misunderstood cherub," said in mollifying accents that Moley had got him wrong. Still, it seemed to Moley a portentous remark, symbolic of the transition from the First to the Second New Deal.[7]

IX

As chairman, Kennedy moved cautiously but firmly. If the SEC had the cooperation of the moderates in Wall Street like Pierce and Shields and such younger men as Forrestal, Lovett, and Ferdinand Eberstadt, it still faced the irreconcilable opposition of Richard Whitney and the old guard. Kennedy's hope was to give responsible people on the Street reason to cooperate with the SEC and, at the same time, to cajole the Exchange into reform through self-regulation. Though his gestures were conciliatory, he did nothing to diminish the Commission's authority. He backed Landis's efforts to develop the administrative law of the SEC; and, when Landis asked William O. Douglas of Yale to head what became an exceedingly tough investigation into corporate reorganization, both Landis and Douglas received Kennedy's full support.

In the meantime, he worked hard to bring about the resumption of new financing. Business blamed the slowdown on capital issues on the new legislation; Kennedy argued that corporations simply did not see opportunities to employ long-term money profitably. The outcome justified Kennedy: as the business situation improved, corporations began to float issues quite happily despite the new laws. In the early spring of 1935, Swift and Company broke the log jam with a $43 million bond issue. By September, the new financing rose to about $800 million.

Kennedy, whose objective had been to secure the adoption of new trading rules and to restore the capital market, now resigned. Roosevelt appointed Landis his successor, and SEC moved into a new and sterner phase. Yet Kennedy's contribution had been substantial. He had achieved the acceptance of SEC without sacrifice of principle, and he had given its administrative operations invaluable momentum.

It was already beginning to be apparent that the Securities Act and the Securities Exchange Act, far from destroying the securities

business, were offering it a new lease on life. It was not only that
they gave disillusioned investors new reasons for confidence. Even
more, they removed the whole process of capital investment from
the realm of guess and gamble and rested it — through the detailed
and continuous disclosure required by the SEC — on the solid
basis of reliable fact. One result, as Corcoran later pointed out,
was to educate the financial community itself in the arithmetic of
its own business. In a short time, few men in Wall Street would
wish the repeal of this legislation which, when proposed, they had
so desperately resisted.[8]

30. The Rise of Conservative Opposition

WILLARD M. KIPLINGER, the writer of an influential newsletter for businessmen, later gave March 1, 1934, as the date when business reaction against Roosevelt began to be significant. "It seems clear that the honeymoon is over," Harlan F. Stone wrote Herbert Hoover that month, "and that we may witness the beginning of real political discussion." By September 1934, *Time* reported, "Private fulminations and public carpings against the New Deal have become almost a routine of the business day."

The partial economic recovery — national income rose by over 20 per cent in 1934 — had ended the sense of national crisis. The mood of deathbed contrition, which had spread over the business community in 1933, was giving way in 1934 to a revived self confidence and a renewed mistrust of Washington. At the same time the NRA experience, compounded by the securities and stock exchange legislation, had raised the specter of bossy and regulatory government. And the militance of organized labor, under apparent New Deal incitement, was rousing particularly deep resentment. Edward A. Filene, after a study of business conditions in fourteen large cities, reported in March 1934 that the "severest" criticism he encountered had to do with government labor policy. He was convinced that "employers generally, and especially the large national corporations with branches throughout the country, do not intend to allow labor to successfully organize." The *Commercial and Financial Chronicle* brooding over William Green's euphoric prediction of a membership of ten million for the AF of L, concluded that this would mean "a class dictatorship to which all would have to submit and from the rule of which no one could escape . . . the extinction of freedom."

American businessmen had lived for years in a happy condition of psychic security, their authority unchallenged in an economy they ran and a social order they dominated. "When you and I first began to practice law," Frederic R. Coudert of New York wrote to James M. Beck of Philadelphia, "one hardly needed to know that there was a Federal Government until one went abroad." One had to know even less about the labor movement. Now businessmen faced the rise of big government and big labor — forces once contemptible, now grown aggressive and threatening. It was the psychological rather than the economic cost of regulation which was crucial — the reduction of the businessman's power in the community, the contraction of his freedom of choice, and the denigration of his picture of himself and of his status in society. The process of adjustment to the new reality was painful in the extreme. Understandably, many clung to the memories of the past and regarded the developments of 1933 and 1934 as a frightful aberration, to be cured by exhortation and a return to first principles.[1]

II

The attempt to exorcise the nightmare began to produce in 1934 a literature in which businessmen and their political champions set forth a deeply felt picture of the New Deal and of themselves. The business leaders, as usual, tended to be inarticulate, with the conspicuous exception of James P. Warburg, whose *The Money Muddle* and *It's Up to Us* both appeared in 1934. The politicians were more voluble. Herbert Hoover's *The Challenge to Liberty*, in 1934, provided a comprehensive statement of the conservative position. Ogden Mills in three books between 1935 and 1937 — *What Of Tomorrow?*, *Liberalism Fights On*, and *The Seventeen Million* — amplified the business thesis. And a number of newspaper commentators, especially David Lawrence, Frank Kent, and Mark Sullivan, became faithful spokesmen of the cause.

The image of the New Deal, as it emerged from these writings, was that of the totalitarian state — in the words of Ogden Mills, "an all-powerful central government to which all men must look for security, guidance and assistance, and which, in turn, undertakes to control and direct the lives and destinies of all." The actions of the New Deal, Mills said, "abolish the sovereignty of the States. They make of a government of limited powers one of unlimited authority over the lives of us all. . . . We have to turn back many centuries to the days of absolute autocrats to find so great a power over the lives of millions of men lodged in the hands of a single fallible being." For Hoover the New Deal was "the most stupendous invasion of the whole spirit of Liberty that the nation has witnessed since the days of Colonial America." This "maelstrom of centralized order-giving," said David Lawrence, ". . . more strongly resembles the dictatorship of the Fascistic and Communistic states of Europe than it does the American system."

How had this monstrous usurpation come about? As most of the conservative critics saw it, the means was the shrewd exploitation of the economic crisis by a collection of impractical intellectuals — "third rate college professors and unsuccessful welfare workers," in the words of Frank Kent — allied with a group of political bosses and an amiable but reckless President. Since Roosevelt in 1934 was still a little popular for direct attack, hostile fire concentrated at first on the brain trusters. The nation's "most immediate danger," said Eugene Meyer in the spring of 1934, lay in "the inexperience of the young intellectuals who are now apparently directing the policy of the administration." "The major policies of agriculture and foreign trade," said George Peek, "are in charge of men who have never earned their livings in industry, commerce, finance or farming." "If they are as a class competent to plan and run the business of the country," said the *Saturday Evening Post*, "then practical experience and training in industry have lost their meaning." This "coterie of visionaries," in Raoul Desvernine's phrase, was running wild, while "competence and enterprise," as Merle Thorpe complained in *Nation's Business*, "cool their heels in the anteroom of authority." The prominence of the college professor was particularly distressing. "Regardless of how we look at it," said another writer in *Nation's Business*, "the differences between the man of thought and the man of action seem fundamental and irreconcilable." "After all," said the

Saturday Evening Post, "it is our country and not a laboratory for a small group of professors to try out experiments that bid fair to result in an explosion and a stink." "The day will come," said Bruce Barton, the advertising man, "when, compared to the word 'professor,' the word 'banker' will be a term of endearment."

The starry-eyed academic represented the comic half of the image of government; his more sinister partner was the power-hungry bureaucrat. "The human animal," said Hoover, ". . . has two forms of greed — the greed for money and the greed for power. The lust for power is infinitely the worse." Many businessmen doubtless shared the view expressed some years earlier by one of their number in *Nation's Business* that the best public servant was the worst one: "the better he is and the longer he stays, the greater the danger. If he is an enthusiast — a bright-eyed madman who is frantic to make this the finest government in the world — the black plague is a house pet by comparison." There seemed too many bright-eyed madmen in Washington now. "In all bureaucracies," declared Hoover, "there are three implacable spirits — self-perpetu-ation, expansion, and an incessant demand for more power." The inevitable result of bureaucratic rule, he suggested, was "this host of government agents spread out over the land, limiting men's honest activities, conferring largess and benefits, directing, inter-fering, disseminating propaganda, spying on, threatening the people and prosecuting for a new host of crimes." [2]

III

Having established the picture of dreamy intellectuals and power-mad bureaucrats in charge of a government of unlimited authority, the conservative philosophers proceeded to trace out the consequences. In its economic aspect, this condition, as they saw it, set up obstacles to business recovery. In its moral aspect, it meant the undermining of the qualities of initiative and self-reliance which had made America great. In its political aspect, it promoted personal government, capricious and vengeful, leading ultimately to the establishment of despotism if not of Communism.

Most businessmen believed that recovery was bound to come in time as a result of natural economic forces. The one prerequisite was business confidence. "Where political uncertainty is the rule," Merle Thorpe wrote in *Nation's Business,* "businessmen cannot make long term contracts; they cannot plan ahead; they cannot expand." And the New Deal, with its mania for meddling and spending, was keeping business in a perpetual insecurity. Businessmen did not know how much the dollar might be worth tomorrow. They were frightened about the national debt. They were equally frightened at the idea of taxation to pay off the debt; when Harry Hopkins lightly said in 1934, "This country does not know what real heavy taxation is," he sent a chill of horror through the business community. They were alarmed about government competition. They claimed not to know which of their actions or policies, once innocent, might now be criminal offenses; as Warburg said, "In its anxiety to prevent a recurrence of the unfortunate experience of investors in the past, the Government has practically destroyed the investment machinery." They felt, in short, that they were playing a game in which the rules were being constantly and mysteriously changed. What Frank Kent called "the whole dizzy New Deal procedure" was creating what Walter Lippmann called "an economy of bedlam." So long as "artificial risks created by political action" continue, said Harper Sibley of Rochester, New York, "capital will be reluctant to invest, industry will hesitate to expand."

As for the moral consequences, many conservatives earnestly believed that the New Deal was destroying the historic pattern of American life — a pattern of local initiative and individual responsibility. "The last remnant of local self-government will have vanished," Frank Kent wrote in February 1935, "if and when the present Roosevelt program is enacted." The states, Kent thought, were already "in process of being obliterated except as to name, form and geographical lines." As the independence of the local community faded away, "the sense of community responsibility," said Hoover, "has been turned to greed for Federal money." Worst of all, the individual himself was losing his pioneer qualities of sturdiness, resourcefulness and courage. Boyden Sparkes in the *Saturday Evening Post,* condemned the do-gooders' campaign against child labor on the ground that "the surest prescription for starting an American boy toward outstanding success is to let him go to work before he is fully grown." Newton D. Baker, writing on "The Decay of Self-Reliance," feared that the younger generation wanted only "secure equality in a State which does all our planning and thinking and providing for us." To an exceptional youth who wished to become a trapper in the Arctic Circle, Baker said mournfully, "I wonder whether you are not in fact the last young man I shall ever see who is not afraid of the dark and of hardship, and wants to stand on his own feet and force his own way by the vigor of his own spirit and the strength of his own hands." President Ernest M. Hopkins of Dartmouth agreed that "initiative, courage, hardihood, frugality, and aspiration for self-betterment" were being penalized, and their fruits taken from those who had "undergone self-sacrifice to attain them and bestowed upon those who have never developed the qualities to possess themselves of rewards." In consequence, he said, the country was "inducing a deterioration in our national character to a point little short of self-destruction." [3]

IV

The political consequences of the New Deal aroused perhaps the gravest concern — in particular, the conviction that affirmative government was destroying American freedom. Government was coming to seem, first of all, arbitrary and personal; in a phrase much revived in these years, it appeared a government of men and not of laws. In a thoughtful article in 1935, *Fortune* suggested that, although no businessman ever liked regulation, what really infuriated him about New Deal regulation was "the sense of personal action, personal will; the feel of the human interferer." Across the fingers of the businessman, it now seemed, fell not a statute but the intellectual pride of a Bright Young Man.

What was to *Fortune* an alarming tendency appeared to others the living actuality of personal despotism. "Government by personal whim," William Randolph Hearst called it: and so much of the whim — as in the cancellation of the air mail contracts, or in Hugh Johnson's crackdowns, or in Pecora's investigations — appeared vindictive in its purpose. No one should be deceived, said Herbert Hoover, by the fact that such acts were ostensibly directed against business abuses: "other freedoms cannot be maintained if economic freedom is impaired . . . because the maximum possible economic freedom is the most nearly universal field for release of the creative spirit of men." The New Deal, he concluded, was an attack on "the whole philosophy of individual liberty." "To me the Bill of Rights is the heart of the American Constitution," said Hoover's Undersecretary of State, William R. Castle, in February 1934, "and in eleven months the Bill of Rights has almost ceased to exist." More and more, the notion began to be expressed that the New Deal was "communist," though the word was used in a broadly objurgatory sense rather than as implying complicity in a specific conspiracy. By 1935, Merle Thorpe — who in late 1933 had been chiding friends for mourning the passing of individualism — wrote: "We have given legislative status, either in whole or in part, to eight of the ten points of the Communist Manifesto of 1848; and, as some point out, done a better job of implementation than Russia." One aggrieved man of wealth exclaimed of Roosevelt, "He is a communist of the worst degree. . . . Who but a communist would dare persecute Mr. Morgan and Mr. Mellon?" [4]

v

The business community — or, at least, its appointed spokesmen — thus began to see the New Deal as an agency of totalitarian tyranny, remorselessly enlarging its control over all aspects of American life. The moments of self-doubt and of penitence of 1933 were behind them. "We might just as well say that the world failed," said Albert W. Atwood, a *Saturday Evening Post* editorial writer, "as that American business leadership failed." Business now seemed a target of unfair attack, "the country's No. 1 whipping boy," in the words of Merle Thorpe, "the butt of every demagogue who looks on mud as the nation's greatest natural resource." The *Saturday Evening Post* found the air full of unjust epithets — "tory, reactionary, cannibal, obscene, adherent to the law of tooth and claw." "You are the selfish obstructionists in the way of the multitudinous, altruistic and celestial plans which, if unimpeded, would make everything right," as Ernest T. Weir told the Union League Club of Chicago with elaborate sarcasm. People recognized that Kreisler had a peculiar ability to play the violin, Will Rogers a peculiar ability to entertain; why would they not recognize, asked *Nation's Business,* that "a small group has likewise been given a peculiar ability to direct the energies of other men in the economic field?" So long as the antibusiness campaign continued, the country was in danger. "Probably the failure of business to get fully back on the job," said the *Saturday Evening Post,* "has been due to the persistent attacks on it." "The swing upward," one businessman said, "lacks only a hearty and a friendly gesture from the Administration."

What, beyond kind words from Washington, did business require to get fully back on the job? In private, many capitalists seemed deeply pessimistic about American capitalism. D. W. Brogan, touring America in 1934, concluded that businessmen, in numbers big enough to be significant, were beginning to sell America short. They told him that there were ten million superfluous people in the country who could never earn their keep. "This city has stopped growing," one said, "it will never get any bigger, the best we can hope to do is to slow down its decay, and we can't do that if labor troubles keep on recurring." But the official philosophy remained one of economic expansion. "We have been told," Herbert Hoover said, referring to Roosevelt's Commonwealth Club address of 1932, "that our industrial plant is built, that our last frontier has long since been reached. . . . That is a false assumption, for the frontiers of science, invention, and the inspirations of human behavior are as yet but barely penetrated by men."

On the question of means by which economic expansion would be resumed and the new frontiers penetrated, the business community was less clear. In general, it reiterated the old prescription of 1932: cut government spending; balance the budget; restore the gold standard; remove government sponsorship from labor; end experimentation; get rid of the brain trusters. "The business and banking community," said one businessman, "awaits some sincere assurance that there will be less interference by government agencies with the law of supply and demand." Richard Whitney summed up the business program: "Provide adequate incentives for private enterprise! Grant management the maximum of freedom! Restore confidence to capital! With these three great fundamentals achieved, then indeed is true recovery assured." [5]

VI

Until Whitney's great fundamentals could be achieved, the nation seemed well down the road to totalitarianism. With American freedom in jeopardy, business leaders began to see themselves as the last defenders of the faith, against fearful odds. They were fighting, it seemed, for much more than their own interests; or, at least, the interests of business *were* the interests of all. As Hoover suggested, "Corporations are not a thing apart from the people, for they are owned by somewhere between six and ten million families." The issue created by the war on business, Hoover said, was "orderly individual liberty and responsible constitutional government as opposed to un-American regimentation and bureaucratic domination." Businessmen, in short, were fighting for civilization itself. "If you destroy the leisure class," J. P. Morgan told a Senate committee, "you destroy civilization." (When reporters asked him to identify the leisure class, he replied, "All those who can afford to hire a maid.")

In the conservative view, the worst fallacy of all was the idea that a stopping-place was possible between capitalism and socialism. "We can have a free country or a socialistic one," said Ogden Mills. "We cannot have both. Our economic system cannot be half free and half socialistic. . . . There is no middle ground between governing and being governed, between absolute sovereignty and liberty, between tyranny and freedom." Hoover was equally vehement. "Even partial regimentation cannot be made to work," he said, "and still maintain live democratic institutions." There was, he said, a borderline in the activities of free government. "When these boundaries of Liberty are overstepped, America will cease to be American."

A Republican congressman, delivering a Lincoln's birthday address in 1934, provided an only slightly heightened statement of the conservative case.

I have seen constitutional government ravished and reduced to a travesty. I have seen hitherto boasted State sovereignty offered up on the Moloch of centralized power. I have seen the Congress of the United States absolutely abdicate its authority to the Executive. I have seen a dictatorship spring up which must have made the noses of Herr Hitler, Stalin, Mussolini, and Mustapha Kemal of Turkey turn green with envy. Independence in private business is a thing of the past, and individual liberty is only a memory.[6]

VII

As this sense of catastrophe grew, it sought its natural outlet in the Republican party. But the Republicans in 1934 were still in a state of shell shock. In 1932 the party had elected only 5 senators and 117 congressmen. The Democratic sweep, followed by the Hundred Days, left it disunited and demoralized. The new Senate leader, Charles McNary of Oregon, hero of the agricultural wars of the twenties, was an urbane political professional who, in his weather-beaten and cynical way, tried to keep alive the tradition of Theodore Roosevelt. McNary had been too much the party regular to follow the example of Cutting, Johnson, and La Follette in supporting Roosevelt in 1932; but he thwarted attempts to expel these heretics from the party caucus and looked on the New Deal with wary sympathy. On the other hand, the House leader, Bertrand H. Snell, an upstate New York businessman, was a rigid ideological conservative who had reached by June 1934 the conclusion that "the purpose of the Roosevelt administration is not the healing of our economic ills but the destruction of our economic system" — its goal, the imposition of "a Russianized form of government."

Yet even Snell seemed a moderate compared to Republicans out of Congress. The state bosses who composed the party's Old Guard — men like Charles D. Hilles of New York and J. Henry Roraback of Connecticut — had many points of difference with the group around Herbert Hoover; indeed, the Old Guard was currently involved in trying to get rid of Everett Sanders, Hoover's choice as Republican national chairman. But the Old Guard and the Hoover group agreed in demanding root-and-branch warfare against the New Deal and all its works. By November 1933 the Republican National Committee began to put out violent anti-New Deal tracts (one bore the title, "Tories, Chiselers, Dead Cats, Witch Doctors, Bank Wreckers, Traitors"). This eruption of activity appalled the congressional Republicans, who hastily set up their own House and Senate campaign committees. Thereafter the National Committee relapsed into inactivity, spending considerably less money in 1934 and 1935 than the Democrats.

In the meantime, the issue between liberalism and conservatism inside the Republican party was being fought out in influential states. In the spring of 1934 Governor Pinchot of Pennsylvania, announcing his desire to "stand beside President Roosevelt in his fight for the forgotten man," challenged the re-election effort of David A. Reed, one of the Senate's most wholehearted conservatives. Reed was renominated in May with a comfortable margin of more than 100,000, though Pinchot polled about 40 per cent of the vote. A similar, if less spectacular fight took place in New York, where W. Kingsland Macy, the state chairman, exhilarated by the victory of the Progressive Republican Fiorello H. La Guardia in the New York City mayoralty contest, now proposed to run Samuel Seabury for governor, and reform the whole state party. The Old Guard, led by Hilles, James Wadsworth, Hamilton Fish, John Taber, and the young Herbert Brownell, battled Macy desperately and, by September, succeeded in driving him from the chairmanship.

Within the National Committee, the Old Guard seemed equally successful. Sanders finally agreed to resign in May 1934. In June, the Committee rejected Senator Borah's proposal that it take a progressive westerner as the new chairman and instead chose Henry P. Fletcher of Pennsylvania, a retired diplomat nominated by the Hoover faction. The platform committee, dominated by Hilles, expressed the party's official evaluation of the New Deal in lugubrious terms. "A small group in Washington, vested with temporary authority, is seeking covertly to alter the framework of American institutions," it declared. ". . . In place of individual initiative they seek to substitute government control of all agricultural production, of all business activity." It went on to describe "an unassailable national credit and a balanced budget" as "indispensable foundations of national well-being." "American institutions and American civilization," it somberly concluded, "are in greater danger today than at any time since the foundation of the republic." A few weeks later, at the eightieth birthday celebration of the Republican party, Fletcher said that Roosevelt wielded powers "comparable to those possessed by Mussolini and Hitler." In this mood of heroic resistance the Republicans began the arduous labor of preparing for the fall congressional election.[7]

VIII

This sense of catastrophe was also pervading conservatives in Democratic ranks. After all, the Democratic party had in the past welcomed business support. Under Smith and Raskob, it had even made a systematic effort to give businessmen prominence in party councils. Democratic victory in 1932 seemed to hold out the hope that such men might now insure sound leadership in Washington. But the New Deal had disappointed this hope. In 1933, *Fortune* published a fairly considerable list of Democratic industrialists. In April 1934, it declared that, with negligible exceptions, "there is not now to be found within hailing distance of Mr. Roosevelt a single prominent Democratic industrialist named in *Fortune's* list." Conservative Democratic politicians were equally aggrieved. "It is difficult today," wrote Frank Kent, himself an old-line Democrat, "to name any outstanding Democratic leader of the pre-New Deal period who is in sympathy with the Roosevelt policy. . . . Except in the most perfunctory manner, none of them have been consulted by the President. Most of them have been completely ignored. Yet until two years ago, they were the most conspicuous and respected leaders of the party."

The reasons for this situation were apparent enough. Nearly all the conservative Democrats had opposed Roosevelt's nomination. Most of them had little sympathy with his policy or purposes. There were few whose advice he respected or whose talents he could profitably employ. And for their part they believed, forgetting Bryan and Wilson, that the New Deal was betraying the whole historic mission of the Democratic party — a mission they saw in fundamentalist Jeffersonian terms as the defense of states' rights and resistance to enlargement of the federal authority. "The Roosevelt policies," said Kent in 1935, "clash head on with the historic party doctrines upon which every Democratic campaign, including the last one, has been waged." Some Democrats, like Kent and Arthur Mullen, blamed it all on the infiltration into the administration of Progressive Republicans bearing wicked Hamiltonian ideas. David Lawrence, another old-time Democrat, suggested that the two wings of the party be hereafter known as the Constitutional-Democratic party and the Socialist-Democratic party. "If Roosevelt is a Democrat," said former Senator Charles S. Thomas of Colorado, "I am not and never was." "Democrats, Democrats," said Carter Glass of the New Dealers. "Why, Thomas Jefferson would not speak to these people."

Most of the party's living presidential candidates shared this view. James M. Cox was the exception. Roosevelt had offered him the ambassadorship to Germany and the chairmanship of the Federal Reserve Board and finally persuaded him to head the delegation to the Economic Conference; and, if Cox was no ardent New Dealer, he declined to enter into the campaign against his onetime running mate. But John W. Davis looked on the Roosevelt administration with horror. "The world is in more danger of being governed too much than too little," he wrote. The Democratic party "cannot accept the doctrine that the State is the universal almoner or the distributor of special grants of money or of privilege to chosen persons or selected classes." Newton D. Baker, a leading contender for the nomination in 1932, regarded most of the New Deal as unconstitutional; he even refused to recommend a friend for employment in the Rural Electrification Administration, "since I have a deep conviction that the Federal Government has no power to interest itself in rural electrification."

Al Smith was most vehement of all. "I am in favor," he declared, "of restoring conditions which make business leadership possible." Donald Richberg reminded Smith of Stalin; and the New Dealers in general filled him with disgust. "If I must choose between the leaders of the past, with all the errors they have made," he said, ". . . and the inexperienced young college professors . . . I am going to be for the people who have made the country what it is." The traditional role of the Democratic party had been to oppose "highly centralized Federal control"; the more Smith looked at Washington, the less it seemed to him to have anything to do with the Democratic party as he knew it.

"Who is Ickes? Who is Wallace? Who is Hopkins, and, in the name of all that is good and holy, who is Tugwell, and where did he blow from? . . . Is La Guardia a Democrat? If he is, then I am a Chinaman with a haircut." [8]

IX

As conservatives lived on into 1934, they felt increasingly the need for an organization through which they could carry on their fight for American principles. The Republican party was too much identified with misrule and defeat; in any case, it showed few signs of coming out of the shock of 1932 and 1933. The party, said James M. Beck early in 1934, "seems to be asleep . . . and I am not sure that it is not the sleep of death." The National Association of Manufacturers increased its dues and its budget; in the four years after Roosevelt's inauguration, its income increased nearly sixfold. But a truly effective conservative organization required a broader base. It must, as Dr. Henry Hatfield, Republican senator from West Virginia, urged to Beck, "draw the friends of liberty and the Constitution from both parties."

A nucleus for such a bipartisan movement was already in existence. This was the American Association Against the Prohibition Amendment, set up some years earlier by Captain William H. Stayton of the Baltimore Steamship Company and other businessmen in the hope that repeal, by producing new revenue from alcohol taxes, would lighten the tax load on the rest of business. Jouett Shouse had become its president a few weeks after leaving the Democratic National Committee. A leading backer was Pierre S. du Pont, who had actually tried to get it to support Roosevelt in 1932; the du Ponts were traditional Democrats from the time that Jefferson had befriended the first Pierre S. du Pont, the physiocratic economist, and helped establish his son Irénée in his gunpowder factory on the banks of the Brandywine outside Wilmington, Delaware.

With the Eighteenth Amendment repealed, members of the Association began to dream of new worlds to conquer. Some now wanted to move on to the income tax amendment. Others agreed with Stayton, who wrote Beck in August 1933, that while prohibition had long been the great threat to America, "what we have had since March 4th (and I am an ardent Democrat)" seemed now even a greater threat. When the Association started to go out of business at the end of the year, its directors resolved that individual members consider "the formation of a group, based on our old membership in the Association, which would in the event of danger to the Federal Constitution stand ready to defend the faith of the fathers." In the winter of 1933–34 there seemed to be growing convergence on this point. Thus Beck began writing to friends in December 1933 that "property interests without respect to party" ought to start a counter movement against the New Deal.

Moreover, the experience of life under the terror was awakening more and more rich Americans to the need for counterrevolution. In March 1934, Robert R. M. Carpenter, a du Pont vice-president and son-in-law, sent a poignant letter to John J. Raskob describing the ordeal to which he had been subjected under the Roosevelt administration. "Five negroes on my place in South Carolina," he wrote, "refused work this spring, after I had taken care of them and given them house rent free and work for three years during bad times, saying they had easy jobs with the Government. . . . A cook on my houseboat at Fort Myer quit because the Government was paying him a dollar an hour as a painter." If one person had undergone such experiences, said Carpenter, how many thousands of times — presumably on how many thousands of South Caroline plantations and Florida houseboats must they have been repeated? Yet no one knew the awful facts: "through some method unknown the President has strangled free speech both over the radio and by daily papers."

Carpenter, who believed that Senator Elmer Thomas of Oklahoma was "even more radical than Lenin," was a man of extreme views. But Raskob, himself a du Pont product, responded sympathetically and spoke of "trying to induce the du Pont and General Motors groups, followed by other big industries, to definitely organize to protect society from the suffering which it is bound to endure if we allow communistic elements to lead the people to believe that all business men are crooks, not to be trusted, and that no one should be allowed to get rich." There should be, Raskob emphasized, "some very definite organization that would come out with some plan for educating the people." After all, he added, the du Pont group "controls a larger share of industry through common-stock holdings than any other group in the United States." 9

X

And so the American rich brooded among themselves. By the midsummer of 1934 their whispered discussions produced the decision to set up an organization to be called the American Liberty League. In its essence, this was a group of conservative Democrats — Al Smith, Jouett Shouse, John J. Raskob, John W. Davis, Bainbridge Colby, the du Ponts — backed by a number of wealthy businessmen — Alfred P. Sloan and William S. Knudsen of General Motors, Ernest T. Weir, Will L. Clayton, the Texas cotton broker (though Clayton lasted only a few months), Edward F. Hutton and Colby M. Chester of General Foods, J. Howard Pew of Sun Oil, Sewell L. Avery of Montgomery Ward, and others. In August, Shouse, slated to be the League's president, called on Roosevelt to inform him of what was intended. Pulling a piece of paper out of his pocket, Shouse read aloud the League's two objectives — to teach respect for the rights of persons and property, and to teach the duty of government to encourage private enterprise and protect the ownership and use of property. Roosevelt suavely commented that every American citizen could subscribe to these objectives. Shouse then asked whether he had any objection to the organization. Roosevelt replied of course not; it was none of his business, and he had no objection anyway to a private group working for axiomatic principles of American life.

But, as he later observed to his press conference, the principles of the League, while unimpeachable, were perhaps incomplete. "An organization that only advocates two or three out of the Ten Commandments," the President said, "may be a perfectly good organization in the sense that you couldn't object to the two or three out of the Ten Commandments, but that it would have certain shortcomings in having failed to advocate the other seven or eight Commandments." Thus the League said nothing about the need for teaching respect for the right of individuals against those who sought to enrich themselves at the expense of their fellow citizens, nor about the duty of government to find jobs for all who wished to work. A few days later, Roosevelt wrote to Bill Bullitt in Moscow, "All the big guns have started shooting — Al Smith, John W. Davis, James W. Wadsworth, du Pont, Shouse, etc. Their organization has already been labelled the '*I Can't Take It Club.*'" Someone asked whether Shouse had invited him to join. "I don't think he did," said Roosevelt, laughing. "Must have been an oversight."

Raskob did ask Herbert Hoover to join, much to the former President's indignation. "This is the group that financed the Democratic smearing campaign," Hoover said with understandable bitterness. ". . . They are, therefore, hardly the type of men to lead the cause of Liberty." He added that he had "no more confidence in the Wall Street model of human liberty, which this group so well represents, than I have in the Pennsylvania Avenue model upon which the country now rides." But other conservatives responded with more enthusiasm. Wall Street, the *New York Times* reported, regarded the League as "little short of an answer to a prayer" (a reaction which, Roosevelt told his press conference, made him laugh for ten minutes in bed that morning). "The American Liberty League," wrote David Lawrence reverently for the *United States News*, "is a call to arms." [10]

VI

There was no question about the earnestness with which the League dedicated itself to the new crusade. Its declaration of principles and purposes was a grave and stately rendition of the ideas which the conservatives of 1934 deeply believed they believed. Hardly a cliché was overlooked; the phrases of Herbert Spencer and William Graham Sumner, worn smooth with time, slipped around in meaningless order; and the result was a clear, if tedious, exposure of the meagerness of conservative philosophy.

In only one area did the League's appeal connect with vital American sentiment. Its special contribution to political debate was its emphasis on the Constitution. As Captain Stayton, a member of the executive committee, said in August, "I do not believe

that many issues could command more support or evoke more
enthusiasm among our people." Even if few knew the Constitution in detail, "nevertheless, there is a mighty — though vague —
affection for it. The people, I believe, need merely to be led and
instructed."

Still, even the Constitution seemed for the League only a half-
way covenant. Thus the League's National Lawyers Committee
was criticized for intervening only on behalf of the embattled
wealthy. Seeking to silence such criticism, James M. Beck rashly
offered its services to all who felt their constitutional rights in
jeopardy. The American Civil Liberties Union took the League
up on this offer; so too did the Hod Carriers Union of York, Pennsylvania, one of whose members had been arrested for speaking
on the public common. The League's libertarian ardor promptly
languished. Beck, receiving the plea from the Civil Liberties
Union, sent it along to Shouse; and nothing was heard of it again.
At no point on record did the American Liberty League construe
"liberty" as meaning anything else but the folding stuff. At no
point did it show convincing interest in the sufferings of people
who lacked plantations in South Carolina or houseboats on the
Caloosahatchee.

For the time being, the League restrained its activities. Shouse
kept asserting its nonpolitical character; as Raskob told Farley
in November, "This League shall be absolutely non-partisan, just
as much so as the Association Against the Prohibition Amendment
was." Beck explained privately, however, that the League was marking time until the fall congressional elections. Then it would
throw itself into "the coming struggle to preserve our Constitution." [11]

31. The Verdict of 1934

THROUGHOUT 1934 the abstractions, the syllogisms, the cries of alarm and woe thundered down upon the country. But the conservative arguments were not always received with the gravity with which they were propounded. Phrases cast forth with heartfelt seriousness by the American Liberty League struck many Americans as pompous hypocrisies. What was to be made, for example, of the passion for constitutional liberties suddenly declared by men who up to this point had successfully dissembled their solicitude? William E. Borah was not impressed. "They were deeply moved about the Constitution of the United States," he sourly said. "They had just discovered it." So too William Allen White on the emergence of Theodore Roosevelt, Jr., as a fighting libertarian: "The Bill of Rights, I fear, in the bright lexicon of young Teddy, is to be the bulwark of privilege rather than a defense of democracy."

Most people simply could not accept the portrait of the American government as a totalitarian dictatorship. "The hysterical conservatives," said Walter Lippmann, "ought to know by this time that in a contest at the level of mere epithets they have not the ghost of a chance to win." The wild statements of calamity corresponded to nothing in the popular experience. Franklin Roosevelt's questions in a fireside chat in June 1934 seemed far more to the point. "Plausible self-seekers and theoretical diehards," he told his audience, "will tell you of the loss of individual liberty. Answer this question . . . out of the facts of your life. Have you lost any of your rights or liberty or constitutional freedom of action and choice?" Turn to the Constitution, he said, read each provision of the Bill of Rights, "and ask yourself whether you personally have suffered the impairment of a single jot of these great assurances."

In any case, so far as history was a guide, totalitarianism came about not because affirmative government did too much but because negative government did too little. Thus Thurman Arnold denounced "the absurd idea that dictatorships are the result of a long series of small seizures of power on the part of a central government." The exact opposite was true: "every dictatorship which we now know flowed into power like air into a vacuum because the central government, in the face of a real difficulty, declined to exercise authority." Beyond this, people who knew what the totalitarian idea really implied considered its application to the New Deal outrageous. "To compare Roosevelt's effort with that of Hitler," said Winston Churchill, "is to insult, not Roosevelt, but civilization. The petty persecutions and Old World assertions of brutality in which the German idol has indulged only show their smallness and squalor compared to the renaissance of creative effort with which the name of Roosevelt will always be associated."

Nor were people much more inclined to regard the New Dealers as a collection of incompetents, especially when the picture came from men who themselves had just steered the country into depression. The "fear of brains," said Donald Richberg, was an "insanity" running through the business community. He repudiated the whole conception of a "brain trust" as "mythical"; men with brains were too independent-minded to be trustified — though, of course, "men accustomed to organizing hog trusts are unable to realize that brains cannot be herded together in the same way." "When any man ventures to scoff at the use of brains in government," said Richberg conclusively, "he should be asked to explain by what part of the anatomy he believes human affairs should be conducted." [1]

II

Nor was the theory that the New Deal was killing American individualism too persuasive. Walter Lippmann thought that the conservatives had long since killed individualism themselves. The men who declaimed loudest about freedom of enterprise, he said, were the same men who had organized the industrial life of the country into a highly centralized corporate system; this had imperiled the older American style of individualism, he suggested, far more than anything which had happened in Washington since March 4, 1933. Russell Leffingwell of Morgan's had already given the Pecora Committee a more honest picture of the condition of American self-reliance: "The growth of corporate enterprise has been drying up individual independence and initiative. . . . We are becoming a nation of hired men, hired by great aggregates of capital."

Similarly, was it the Social Security Act or was it laissez-faire capitalism itself which, as one writer put it, taught "great numbers of careful, long-headed, hard-working, thrifty, highly-skilled families that their years of planning, skill-getting and self-denial have . . . gone for naught"? Far from being the enemy of individualism, might not government be the only agency means of giving the individual a solid basis in industrial society? Nor did a government policy of helping everyone toward a fair start in life seem likely to eradicate all human initiative. As Winston Churchill had said of the British dole, there would remain, even with the government guarantee of a few shillings a week, quite enough grindstone in human life to keep us keen. "When the community," wrote Jerome Frank, "exercising intelligent choice and acting through the Government, puts a solid material foundation under the individual, it does not intrude on individual freedom and dignity; it makes them possible." [2]

III

The conservative conviction that the New Deal, by tampering with natural economic laws, was blocking recovery similarly failed to move a people who had suffered too long by government inaction. In 1935, Herbert Hoover sought to reassure the graduating class of Drake University about the future.

Did it ever occur to you that all the people who now live in these houses, who conduct this vast complex of life and civilization are going to die? And that just as sure as death, you will take over their jobs?

The former President's consolation seemed a trifle mortuary. In any case, as Walter Lippmann warned, when business leaders told the youth that economic forces were beyond human control and there was nothing to do but wait, they preached "a gospel of frustration" which inevitably drove young men to communism, to fascism, to "almost anything which is emphatic and bold and positive." More and more people regarded an intelligent governmental effort to master economic forces as the only hope. The "new imperative," said Lippmann, was that government accept responsibility for the living standards of the people. No one could seriously believe any longer in the neutral state; "one may declare that laissez-faire is dead," Lippmann said, "and that the collective principle is now generally accepted." "An organized functioning society," observed Joseph P. Kennedy, "requires a planned economy. The more complex the society the greater the demand for planning."

Nor were many persuaded by the argument that government intervention destroyed "business confidence," and that until confidence was restored recovery was impossible. A national debt of about $30 billion with annual carrying charges well under $1 billion might terrify the financial community; but the nation as a whole refused, quite rightly, to suppose that the republic was at an end. The people could not be told to suffer, said Lippmann, "like Chinese coolies in a famine, until, for some mysterious reason, the warm blood of confidence rises once more in the veins of bank directors and corporation executives." Adolf Berle questioned the whole argument that business could be induced to expand by exhortation and reassurance. "If it is profitable, it will do so; if it is unprofitable it will not do so." In any case, what was the need for new capital investment when existing productive capacity was so dismally underutilized?

Nor could many people see the justice in guaranteeing profits in advance, as some businessmen seemed inclined to demand. Indeed, if businessmen considered security so demoralizing for the workers, why should they deem it so invigorating for themselves?

Richberg, trying to persuade the Congress of American Industry to take risks, hoped that American businessmen might soon begin to display that zest in adventure and uncertainty which they so strongly recommended for their employees.[3]

IV

The image of business protest in 1934 was not, in short, impressive. Tom Connally of Texas summed up a popular reaction in October. "If the Government had not got into business," he said, "there would be no business today. As soon as the businessman sees a slight improvement he keeps shouting, 'The Government must get out of business.' Businessmen do nothing but bellyache."

Some businessmen agreed. The contribution of business — in particular the call for total trust in business leadership — struck not a few business leaders as unconvincing. "The capitalist system," Milo Perkins, a bag manufacturer from Houston, Texas, wrote in 1934, "can be destroyed more effectively by having men of means defend it than by importing a million reds from Moscow to attack it." The American people, Perkins added, had a right to jobs and to homes fit for their children. "The whole private ownership of production is failing as a system to provide those fundamental things for our people." Unless capitalism could meet this challenge, it was through, and time was running out. "Grab the torch, men of means, grab the torch!"

There were other voices of business dissent. In Chicago, E. G. Shinner, after twenty-five years of success in the retail meat business, wrote in *The Forgotten Man* that he regarded the chain system as "basically wrong" and believed that it should be changed "notwithstanding the fact that it may materially affect my own personal affairs." "God grant," Shinner concluded, after a trenchant analysis of the problems of the small-unit operator, "that Franklin D. Roosevelt may enjoy the health and strength to pursue the course he knows to be right." In Texas, Will L. Clayton, now out of the Liberty League, tried to explain to his fellow businessmen why capitalism was on the defensive. "A highly industrialized society, used to the amortization of machinery and plant," he said, "must now make provision for human obsolescence and for recurring periods of unemployment." He added: "The private ownership of property is a permissive, not an inherent right."

In Massachusetts, Henry S. Dennison, long known as a progressive manufacturer, decided that government was the only hope. "All of my old notions of being able to do anything through preachment as to good management," Dennison said, "have gone to the winds. Five percent of a trade can knock them all into a cocked hat, and we could never manage even to get five percent interested, much less ninety-five percent." "It has not been the United States Chamber of Commerce," said Edward A. Filene, the Boston department store owner, ". . . but President Roosevelt who has been representing the true interests of business." Filene accepted New Deal taxes with equanimity: "Why shouldn't the American people take half my money from me? I took all of it from them." *Fortune,* summing up Roosevelt's first three years, called it "fairly evident to most disinterested critics" that the New Deal "has had the preservation of capitalism at all times in view" 4

v

Thoughtful elder statesmen shared the suspicion that the predominant conservative line might be fallible. Henry L. Stimson spoke with regret in 1934 of the Republicans and "their rather stupid policy of indiscriminate opposition." When Herbert Hoover asked his old friend Justice Harlan F. Stone of the Supreme Court to read the manuscript of *The Challenge to Liberty,* Stone wondered gently whether Hoover understood "the perpetual, and to some extent, irreconcilable conflict between the demands of individual liberty and the necessities of an increasingly complex civilization, in which every individual and every group within the state becomes increasingly interdependent with every other." Things had changed since the time of Jefferson. "Personally," Stone told Hoover, "I like the Jeffersonian state better, but I have to recognize that because I live in a highly industrialized modern state, in order to make the system work, I have to suffer restrictions on individual liberty which Jefferson would probably have regarded as intolerable." When the individual was at the mercy of economic forces beyond his control, then surely the community was entitled to intervene. "The issue cannot be settled," Stone emphasized, "by an appeal to the eighteenth century philosophy of individualism in the abstract, for that philosophy cannot be completely adapted to the twentieth century state." Stone urged Hoover not to publish the book. "The country is convinced that the time has come for sweeping reforms, and that these are being, and will be, resisted for selfish reasons by those who have an excessive stake in things as they are." Invocation of an abstract doctrine of "individual liberty" would not avail. "Even the man in the street is aware that every important reform in the past seventy-five years has been resisted and assailed as an infringement of individual liberty."

Stone wrote to other correspondents in the same vein, arguing that the problem of the hour was to reconcile the principles of liberty with industrial society, and that this meant a search for "a way of securing a better distribution of income." But, in 1935, he wrote dispiritedly, "I can see no recognition of this truth on the part of any important Republican leader." The Stones and Stimsons, the Dennisons and Filenes and Shinners remained an impotent minority in the conservative community; few businessmen rushed to seize Milo Perkins's torch. Instead, most accepted the leadership of the Republican party, the Chamber of Commerce, the National Association of Manufacturers, and the American Liberty League.

Reliance on this leadership only confirmed the popular notion that business was stupid and greedy. There were many legitimate criticisms to be made of the Roosevelt administration — in particular of the cocky New Deal assumption, repeated in so many contexts, that any government official was wiser than any private person. But such criticism could not be made responsibly or persuasively by talking about the imminent imposition of a totalitarian state. The conservative publicists created a lurid and ultimately boring fantasy of doom, which struck most other Americans as outrageously hypocritical or as hopelessly comic.

Donald Richberg called it a "post-depression psychosis." These businessmen had seen their prestige and power melt away. They had heard men who fawned upon them jeer at their stupidities.

They had seen former associates stripped of fortune and honor, some retiring to a well-earned obscurity, some ending as fugitives from justice. The only way they could maintain their self-esteem, Richberg suggested, was by developing delusions of persecution, in which they saw themselves defending freedom against a sinister conspiracy of college professors. The spectacle of the rich men of the nation declaring that America was in the grip of revolution because their servants were no longer content with their wages was not one which deeply moved many of their fellow countrymen. The calamity-howlers were stuffed shirts in a familiar mold, and their every pronouncement seemed only to document the charges made against them. "The campaign of the League of Stuffed Shirts," said Richberg, "is the greatest menace to our economic recovery today."

Was there not something else involved? Something less easy to dismiss, something with a nastiness of its own? James Boyd caught an aspect of it in his comment on Miami. "Like the rest of the country," Boyd said, "it is divided into the people Roosevelt ruined and the people he saved — those he ruined still living in Byzantine palaces in more than Oriental luxury, and those he saved still living in tar-paper shacks." Was there not, in the end, something indecent when those who suffered so little pretended to suffer so much, and did their best to prevent the government from helping the real sufferers? The performance of the American rich in 1934 lacked even the dignity of hubris. Like the struggle in Britain before the First World War between the House of Lords and the Asquith government, it had a fatuous intensity which the rich themselves could look back on a few years later only with astonishment and disbelief.[5]

VI

One American who was not much surprised was the President. He had known the rich too long and too well to take them very seriously. His upbringing as a Hudson River Squire had given him a sense of superiority over mere millionaires; and nothing he had seen in the years since Hyde Park and Groton led him to suppose that money conferred wisdom. He declined to pay the rich the compliment of fearing them. He thought rather that they inclined to be ignorant and hysterical. For a moment, perhaps, he had hoped that the humility induced by depression might endure. Certainly his attempt at business-government cooperation in 1933 was sincere enough. The "challenge to industry" implied in the National Industrial Recovery Act was still for him, in March 1934, "a great test" to see how business leaders could operate for the general welfare. But, in the meantime, he was losing faith in business motives. "Now that these people are coming out of their storm cellars," he complained, "they forget that there ever was a storm." He believed that a "rather definitely organized effort" had been made in the fall of 1933 to destroy the New Deal; and it seemed to him that this drive was being renewed in the spring of 1934. Speaking at Green Bay, Wisconsin, in August 1934, Roosevelt suggested that for a certain kind of businessman confidence could evidently be restored only by repealing all regulatory laws; "if we were to listen to him and his type, the old law of the tooth and the claw would reign in our Nation once more." And business talk about "liberty" left him equally cold. "I am not for a return to that definition of liberty," he said crisply in October, "under which for many years a free people were being gradually regimented into the service of the privileged few." [6]

VII

As the 1934 congressional elections approached, business criticism became more insistent. Roosevelt, who had left Washington on July 1 for a fourteen-thousand-mile cruise on the U.S.S. *Houston* through the Caribbean and the Canal to Hawaii, returned to the country in August to find new signs of discontent. The summer surge of strikes, followed in September by the resignation of Lewis Douglas, was increasing business apprehension. In mid-September one hundred and fifty leading industrialists, led by George Houston of Baldwin Locomotives and Lewis Brown of Johns-Manville, gathered in secret session at Hot Springs, Virginia. Though their deliberations were never unveiled, Louis Stark of the *Times*, who saw a copy of the program under discussion, reported that, if it were carried out, "every outstanding piece of emergency legislation enacted by the last Congress would have to be abandoned or so modified as to make it worthless." More than a thousand firms told the New England Council that lack of confidence was making them "negate, defer or curtail normal operations and commitments." When a speaker at a Boston conference on distribution made a violent attack on the New Deal, Julius Rosenwald of Sears, Roebuck urged that the opinions be sent directly to the President as expressing "not only the sense of the meeting but of the national business world." In late September the United States Chamber of Commerce demanded that Roosevelt make a "definite statement" on whether and when he intended to balance the budget, stabilize the currency, and encourage business initiative.

The increasing strain between government and business worried conservative friends of the administration. Raymond Moley, in particular, favored a "sympathetic effort" to relieve the tension, even granting that many business complaints were purely imaginary. He therefore responded to a business suggestion that he arrange a series of dinners where New Dealers and business leaders could talk things out face to face. About the same time Floyd Carlisle of Niagara Hudson gave a dinner where Harry Hopkins discussed the relief problem with Thomas W. Lamont, Gerard Swope, Lewis Brown, and other business leaders. Lamont told Hopkins that he had known Roosevelt for many years, that he thought Roosevelt would be President at least till 1940 and "probably" till 1944, that business must look upon Roosevelt as "the only hope and as a bulwark for sane policies," and that he, Lamont, was trying to be helpful in every way possible. "When people complain to me of the amount of money that the Government has been borrowing," Lamont said, "I always answer it by saying: 'Well, if the country was willing to spend thirty billion dollars in a year's time to try to lick the Germans, I don't see why people should complain about its spending five or six billion dollars to keep people from starving.'" And Roosevelt himself invited a long list of business leaders to Hyde Park in September for private talks.[7]

VIII

One result was a conciliatory fireside chat on September 30, in which Roosevelt proclaimed his faith in "the driving power of

individual initiative and the incentive of fair private profit,"
though he added that this faith must be "strengthened with the
acceptance of those obligations to the public interest which rest
upon us all." Some businessmen still objected that he had said
nothing about sound money and a balanced budget, but others
were apparently relieved to discover that the administration actually believed in the profit system. In the meantime, the 1934
meeting of the American Bankers Association in Washington in
the third week of October seemed to provide a signal opportunity to
clinch the new mood of government business amity. Chastened by
their experience a year before in Chicago, the Wall Street bankers
in particular hoped for a negotiated peace. As Winthrop Aldrich
disarmingly suggested in a phone call to the White House, if the
President would only take this opportunity to "rebuild the confidence of the public in the bankers," then everything would be all
right.

But Moley, summoned to Washington to help on the speech to
the bankers, discovered that the reconciliation project had enemies
within the administration. Tom Corcoran had already told him
that the younger New Dealers were disturbed over his New York
dinners. Morgenthau and Hopkins shared these suspicions; and,
at a conference in the President's study the day before the ABA
speech, they repeated one needling story after another of business
antagonism in an effort — as Moley saw it — to put the President
in an antibusiness mood. Morgenthau seemed especially indignant
over the speech of introduction, to be made by Jackson Reynolds of
the First National Bank of New York. Reynolds proposed to begin
by discussing Scipio's refusal to negotiate with Hannibal and re-
calling its consequences — the destruction of both armies and the
death of both commanders in exile. Morgenthau found this passage offensive because it assumed that the bankers and the government were both sovereign powers, as well as because of its ambiguous personal allusions. Later on, Reynolds planned to reminisce
about his days as a professor at the Columbia Law School when
he had "an eager youth named Franklin Roosevelt" in his classes;
"I was accustomed to put to him a series of questions," Reynolds
intended to say, "and I am going to be so far guilty of a breach of
confidence as to tell you that he did not always answer all of them
correctly." Though these remarks were obviously friendly in intent,

Roosevelt, who felt on the defensive because he had never taken his Columbia degree, resented them. Still Moley argued the need for harmony and urged Morgenthau to ask Reynolds to take out the offending passages. The President, however, seemed infected by the Morgenthau-Hopkins attitude. When he began to dictate his first draft, the result seemed to Moley hopelessly bellicose. During the night, Moley tried to give the President's draft a more conciliatory note. Roosevelt accepted the softened version in the morning.

Constitution Hall was overflowing with bankers the next day. Most of the audience, especially the small-town bankers, were bitterly anti-New Deal — far more so than their sophisticated colleagues in New York. Reynolds in a fair-minded talk acknowledged that the bankers might have put undue pressure on the administration for firm commitments on budget balancing and on monetary stabilization. "The banking fraternity in the last two years," he told the President, "has endured enough mass punishment so that it is now in such a chastened and understanding mood that you can accept with hospitality any overture of cooperation." And he paid tribute to Roosevelt as the man who in March 1933 "contributed more to rescue and rehabilitate our shattered banking structure than any of us did individually and collectively."

Roosevelt, without commenting on Reynolds's remarks, denied that the bankers and the government could be considered as equal and independent units; "government by the necessity of things must be the leader, must be the judge of the conflicting interests of all groups in the community, including bankers." He then called upon the bankers to assume more of the burden of lending, offering to curtail public credit as the bankers showed themselves able to take up the slack. When he came to the phrase "what we call the profit system," he encouraged his audience by changing it in delivery to "what we call — and accept — as a profit system"; and he concluded by urging "an alliance of all forces intent upon the business of recovery . . . business and banking, agriculture and industry, and labor and capital. What an all-America team that would be!" Though the New York Times reported that the address was greeted with an "ovation," Moley later remembered it as "perfunctorily delivered" in a "frigid" atmosphere. The tone of the speech, on the whole, was rather cold and correct; and the bankers could derive only a modicum of comfort.[8]

IX

It seems probable that Roosevelt, though persuaded that pacific gestures were nice on the eve of an election, had by this time given up real hope of the kind of constructive partnership with business he had envisaged in NRA. Evidently nothing had discouraged him more than his futile efforts to get ideas from business leaders. To every problem they offered a single answer — the restoration of "confidence" through balancing the budget, halting reform, and reducing government regulation. When the World's Fair opened in Chicago in May, Alfred P. Sloan, presiding over a dinner conference on industrial progress, released a series of messages from some three hundred bankers and industrialists. Isador Lubin, analyzing the result for Frances Perkins, reported that only a dozen or so showed any sympathy for the administration's objectives, that most moaned about "taxation, government regulation, elimination of freedom," and that in general they provided "outstanding evidence that American business has not the slightest conception of what the New Deal is about."

After receiving a letter from W. B. Donham, Dean of the Harvard Business School, on how to restore business confidence, Roosevelt bid the Dean to Hyde Park. "I put several problems up to him," Roosevelt later wrote, "and he had not one single concrete answer to any of them!" He called in the most intelligent representatives of the business community — for one, Leffingwell of Morgan's. Leffingwell told Roosevelt, "You cannot feed people with aphorisms" and disclaimed any interest in the "old incantations about a balanced budget." Yet even Leffingwell in two long letters had little to offer, except opposition to public works spending and to government controls. "Somehow I feel strangely cold," Roosevelt wrote of Leffingwell to Frankfurter, "because I cannot see one constructive thought in either of his letters." The apparent bankruptcy of business thought contrasted strangely with the inexhaustible resourcefulness of his academic advisers. He summed up his feelings in a letter to Congresswoman Mary Norton of New Jersey in October:

Confidentially, it has been extremely interesting to observe the constant storm of requests that "you say something reas-

suring to business, Mr. President." Just what should be said
that would be reassuring to business no one seems to know.
At least not one of those who have urged it have had any practical suggestions.

I believe that what is being done and the results that are
being obtained is not only the best, but the only means of reassuring those timid souls. . . . Action and results are the things
that will count and I do not believe that any mere statement
would have any particular effect in "reassuring business."

Roosevelt tried to discriminate among his critics. After reading
a letter from Henry L. Stimson, he penciled a chit to himself: "Prevent union of those seeking economic feudalism with those people
who are honest but *afraid* of what is happening." In an effort to
explain what he considered the flagrant unreality of so much business thinking, he ascribed it to ignorance of what conditions actually were. When James P. Warburg sent him a copy of *The Money
Muddle,* Roosevelt replied that he hoped Warburg would someday
bring out a second edition, but not till he had put on his oldest
clothes, bought a secondhand Ford, and toured the country, "undertaking beforehand not to speak on the entire trip with any banker
or business executive (except gas stand owners) , and to put up at
no hotel where you have to pay more than $1.50 a night." What he
could not abide were those who seemed to be trying deliberately to
frighten the nation. In September 1934 he amended his inaugural
statement to say that, even more than fear itself, it was necessary
to fear those who sought to instill fear into the American people.

The experience of his Presidency thus confirmed his mistrust of
business. When the Dean of Freshmen at Harvard wrote Roosevelt
in August asking whether he had any counsel about his youngest
son John, who was just entering college, the President replied that
freshmen need "instruction along lines which may best be described
as the exact opposite of Chamber of Commerce posters and lectures
on *'How To Succeed in Business.'* " The business ethos — its ideas,
its assumptions, its goals, its vanities — just seemed to him absurd.
He hated the whole thing. It could not, he thought, interpret the
experience of most Americans. It did not understand the higher
values and ideals of American civilization. It could not even intelli-

gently advance its own interests. "One of my principal tasks," Roosevelt wrote in November, expressing a deeply-held conviction, "is to prevent bankers and businessmen from committing suicide!" [9]

X

In the meantime, the administration was preparing for its first national test at the polls. Roosevelt's fireside chat in late June had set the keynote for the Democratic campaign. "The simplest way for each of you to judge recovery," he said, "lies in the plain facts of your individual situation. Are you better off than you were last year? Are your debts less burdensome? Is your bank account more secure? Are your working conditions better? Is your faith in your own individual future more firmly grounded?" Roosevelt added to this appeal a private determination to give the fall campaign a predominantly nonpolitical cast. "The situation we are to bear in mind," he told the National Emergency Council in June, ". . . is that the Government is being run less for political purposes and more for the general good than it has been in some time. . . . In other words, we are thinking about Government, and not merely about party; and the more we emphasize that fact, the more it will really be brought home to the public that we are trying to do service regardless of mere party or political reasons." He added, as if an afterthought, "Incidentally, from the political point of view we catch more votes doing it that way than the other."

There can be no question that Roosevelt's political tactic in 1933 and 1934 was to present himself as above the party battle. He declined to participate in the traditional Democratic feasts on Jefferson Day, suggesting "non-partisan Jefferson dinners" in their stead with Republicans as well as Democrats on the banquet committees. "Our strongest plea to the country in this particular year of grace is that the recovery and reconstruction program is being accomplished by men and women of all parties — that I have repeatedly appealed to Republicans as much as to Democrats to do their part." He made the Democratic National Committee withdraw in early 1934 a review of the year written in Charles Michelson's best style; and when someone asked in a press conference how he meant to vote in November, Roosevelt replied, "Well, Stevie, it would be amusing if anybody knew how often I have voted for individual Republicans." An irritated Iowa congressman actually wrote Marvin McIntyre in 1936 to inquire "whether or not the President has ever mentioned the Democratic party or ever used the word 'Democrat' since, as the Democratic party's nominee, he took office." "He took the role," James M. Burns has brilliantly argued, "of national father, of bipartisan leader, of President of all the people."

The question remained whether he really believed in this role and looked toward some form of national rally as a permanent thing; or whether his nonpartisan stance was not put on to attract Progressive Republicans and independents into the existing Democratic party as a first step toward rebuilding the party system along liberal-conservative lines. There are many indications that his real objective was a liberal party rather than a national party. From the days of T. R., he had been particularly sympathetic to the Progressive strain in Republicanism. "His consistent ambition for many years prior to his election to the Presidency," wrote Ernest Lindley, who knew him well in these years, "was to form a new liberal party by attaching the Republican Progressives and miscellaneous liberals to the Democratic party." Wilson had attempted this in 1916, Smith in 1928, but obviously a Democrat bearing the name of Roosevelt would be best equipped to bring home the Bull Moose for good. Moreover, as a man who had made his first mark in politics by opposing the machine, Roosevelt was exceptionally sensitive to the independent vote. "People tell me . . . that I have too many people in my Administration who are not active Democrats," he once told party leaders at a Jackson Day dinner. "I must admit the soft impeachment." He added that the future lay with politicians who realized "that the great public is more interested in government than in politics . . . that vast numbers of people consider themselves normally adherents of one party and still feel perfectly free to vote for one or more candidates of another party, come election day." One night in 1932 before the fire at Albany, Roosevelt mused to Tugwell, "Rex, we shall have eight years in Washington. At the end of that time we may or may not have a Democratic party; but we will have a Progressive one." This was, Tugwell wrote later, his "fondest hope." In 1936 Roosevelt told Ickes that he looked forward to a "realignment of parties," by which he seems to have meant a revitalization of the Democratic party by a blood transfusion of Progressive Republicanism.

Though he proposed to push nonpartisanship as far as it was politically profitable to go, he was essentially using it as a cover to woo not all Republicans but precisely the Progressive Republicans indispensable to the dream of realignment. He appointed two Progressive leaders to the cabinet. He surrounded himself with ex-Bull Moosers like Richberg and Frankfurter. He kept on excellent terms with George Norris. He buttered up Hiram Johnson at every opportunity. He offered Phil La Follette eight government posts (or so Bob La Follette stated publicly in 1934). He was less a sincere bipartisan leader in this period than he was a man working astutely under the guise of bipartisanship toward a national liberal party.[10]

XI

The campaign opened informally when, after a vacation trip on the U.S.S. *Houston* in July, Roosevelt landed on the West Coast early in August. There followed a triumphal tour across the country. Though newspapers by this time had become critical of many aspects of the New Deal, the same editorials which attacked the experiments often praised the experimenter. And the people seemed to have no doubts. The presidential train went slowly across Montana, North Dakota, Minnesota, Wisconsin, Illinois, through land baked by the summer sun and blistered by drought. Thousands drove hundreds of miles across the dusty plains, waited around bonfires beside the tracks, clustered at every crossing, hopeful for a glimpse of the President, grateful for the chance to wave and shout as the train raced by. Newspapermen wrote they had never heard such cheers. As Roosevelt himself told Garner, "Coming across the continent the reception was grand and I am more than ever convinced that, so far as having the people with us goes, we are just as strong — perhaps stronger — than ever before."

The organized business drive against the New Deal gave some Democrats pre-election jitters. The President remained calm. "Taking it by and large," he said to the National Emergency Coun-

cil on his return, "we have to remember to keep our tempers in the
next couple of months." The problem, as he saw it, was to put
across the idea — "and I believe it comes pretty close to being true"
— that opposition came mostly "from about ten to fifteen per cent
of people whose mental slant is what might be described as being
at the extreme right of modern philosophy, and the rest of it is
from ten to fifteen percent of the mental slant that belongs to
the extreme left." ("Of course," he added, "there is a great deal
of perfectly legitimate criticism from which we can derive satisfaction and help.") To Garner he remarked in late September, "I
am inclined to believe that the voters as a whole are pretty well
satisfied that we are going some place and that they still want
action."

In October Roosevelt took his steps to foil business criticism by
arranging the appearance of a truce with the bankers. And he carefully refrained from taking an active party role in the campaign.
Moreover, he forbade cabinet members (save for the Postmaster-
General) to make campaign speeches, except in their own states; and
he gave specific orders that no Democrat should try to make partisan
capital out of relief. As a consequence, the administration's appeal
continued somewhat above the party battle. And the image of the
President appeared more potent and more adored than ever. When
a Republican congressional nominee in Wisconsin referred to him
as "a man who can't stand on his own feet without crutches," there
were cries of resentment from a Republican audience, and the Republican candidate for senator walked off the platform. Jim Farley,
as local reports poured into national headquarters, could not contain his optimism. On the Saturday before election, he wrote the
President predicting a great Democratic victory. Democrats would
win twenty-six out of the thirty-five senatorial contests, Farley declared, including the Republican stronghold of Pennsylvania; in the
House, the administration would do what administrations did so
rarely in off-year elections — "we will stand about even." [11]

XII

Roosevelt thought the forecast recklessly optimistic. It turned
out to be overcautious. In the Senate, Farley was right; among the

Republican casualties were such leaders of the right wing as David A. Reed of Pennsylvania (defeated by Joseph F. Guffey), Arthur R. Robinson of Indiana (defeated by Sherman Minton), Simeon D. Fess of Ohio (defeated by Vic Donahey), and Roscoe C. Patterson of Missouri (defeated by Harry S. Truman). In the House, Democratic gains exceeded Farley's estimate: the Democratic strength rose from 313 to 322, largely as a result of the sweep in Pennsylvania, while the Republicans declined from 117 to 103. In the total popular vote cast for congressmen, the Democratic percentage actually rose (if only from 50.0 to 50.8 per cent) — an almost unprecedented phenomenon in an off-year election. And in the state capitals, the Republicans after the election retained but 7 governorships, against 39 for the Democrats and one each for the Progressives and the Farmer-Laborites.

The New Deal, Arthur Krock said in the *New York Times*, had won "the most overwhelming victory in the history of American politics." "There has been no such popular endorsement since the days of Thomas Jefferson and Andrew Jackson." William Randolph Hearst wrote Roosevelt. "It shows how faithful the American people are to the true spirit of democracy. . . . The forgotten man does not forget." William Allen White, musing on the Roosevent triumph, said, "He has been all but crowned by the people." [12]

VIII

Evolution
of the Presidency

32. The Dynamics of Decision

FRANKLIN ROOSEVELT's two years in the White House had done much to transform potentiality into actuality. On the verge of power, he had been a man of charm, courage, craftiness, and faith who had survived a terrible personal ordeal but so far had been untried by ultimate public responsibility. Now he had undergone the testing of crisis. The result was a process of hardening and deepening which was changing a genial and enigmatic gentleman into a tough, forceful and still profoundly enigmatic President.

II

The White House routine had not altered much from 1933. The day still began for the President soon after 8 o'clock with breakfast on a tray in his bedroom. Beside the narrow white iron bedstead was a plain white table, covered with telephone, pencils, memoranda, ash trays, cigarettes, nose drops, and a glass of water. Ship prints and seascapes, old Roosevelt treasures, hung on the wall. Over the fireplace, on top of the marble mantelpiece with its grape carvings, was an assortment of family photographs, toy animals, and whatever other mementos had caught the President's fancy. Like every room in any Roosevelt house, the presidential bedroom was hopelessly Victorian — old-fashioned and indiscriminate in its furnishings, cluttered in its décor, ugly and comfortable.

While breakfasting, the President looked rapidly through half a dozen leading newspapers, half of them bitterly critical of his administration (the New York *Herald Tribune*, the Washington

Times-Herald, and the Chicago *Tribune*). He usually wore a sweater or cape; a dressing gown was too much trouble for a crippled man. The breakfast conferences of the Hundred Days were now pretty well abandoned, except in moments of emergency. Even Eleanor Roosevelt, pausing to see her husband on her way out, usually said no more than good morning; "he liked no conversation at this hour." The newspaper scanning was the first phase in Roosevelt's unceasing effort to get the feel of the government and the nation.

Between 9 and 9:30 his secretaries — Steve Early and Marvin McIntyre, with Louis Howe, until he became ill, and then usually Colonel Edwin M. Watson, better known as Pa, the President's military aide — came in to discuss the day's schedule. In the next half-hour Roosevelt dressed and shaved. Often he combined this with business. Thus Harold Ickes:

> When I got to his study, his valet ushered me into his bedroom, telling me that the President was shaving. He waved toward the bathroom and the President called out to me to come in. There he was, sitting before a mirror in front of the washstand, shaving. He invited me to sit on the toilet seat while we talked. When he was through shaving he was wheeled back to his room where he reclined on his bed while his valet proceeded to help him dress. . . . I was struck all over again with the unaffected simplicity and personal charm of the man. He was the President of the United States but he was also a plain human being, talking over with a friend matters of mutual interest while he shaved and dressed with the help of his valet. His disability didn't seem to concern him in the slightest degree or to disturb his urbanity.

Around 10:30 he was ordinarily pushed in his wheelchair along the newly constructed ramps to the executive office in the west wing of the White House. Here, in the lovely oval room, he held his official appointments and spent most of his working day. The room had the usual Rooseveltian country-house informality. "You would think," said Emil Ludwig, "you were in the summer residence of the general manager of a steamship company, who has surrounded himself with mementoes of the days when he was captain." On the wall hung Hudson River prints by Currier and Ives; ship models stood on the mantel: a litter of memoranda, government reports, books, toy pigs, donkeys, and ship's rudders lay on his desk; on the floor, at the President's side, occasionally rising to be patted, were two fine Irish setters. The symbols of high office — the presidential flag, the Great Seal in the ceiling — were subdued and inconspicuous. Behind the President, light streamed softly in through great glass windows running down to the floor, and to the east, briefly glimpsed, were the quiet rose garden and the porticoes and the magnolia trees. In the commotion of Washington, this bright and open room had an astonishing serenity.

Most presidential appointments took place here in the two hours before lunch. The President aimed at seeing people at fifteen-minute intervals, but often fell behind, while visitors waited in the anteroom and McIntyre and Watson did their soft-spoken best to hurry things up. Lunch took place at his desk, with food served from a metal warming oven; it was often hash with a poached egg (when two eggs came, Roosevelt sometimes sent word to the housekeeper that this was a waste of food); lunch too was usually combined with business. In the afternoon there might be more appointments; then, about midafternoon, the President usually called in Grace Tully for an hour or two of dictation. About five o'clock during the first term, the office staff was briefly summoned for what he called "the children's hour," an interlude of relaxation and gossip. Soon after 5:30, the office day ended; and the President took twenty minutes in the White House swimming pool, installed as a result of money raised in a campaign sponsored by the New York *Daily News*. Refreshed by exercise, the President prepared for dinner, ordinarily preceded by a martini or an old-fashioned. After dinner, he often went to his private study, a genial oval room on the second floor next to his bedroom, and dictated some more or read papers or held further conversations. Usually in bed before midnight, he quickly threw off the concerns of the day and in five minutes was deep in sleep. Unlike other Presidents, Roosevelt never allowed the Secret Service to lock the doors of his room at night.[1]

III

Roosevelt's immediate staff was loyal and efficient. The longest in point of service, of course, was Louis Howe, who had worked for Roosevelt nearly a quarter of a century. Howe was only in his early sixties, but, frail and wizened, he was older than his years. His devotion to the President was more proprietary than ever, and his waspishness toward everyone else more insistent. But both Franklin and Eleanor Roosevelt cherished him. On certain matters, especially politics and patronage, Roosevelt continued greatly to value Howe's counsel; and on most matters he welcomed his opinions. "I am going to talk this over with Louis," he would say. "He has forty ideas a day and sometimes a few good ones." While the President often dodged Howe's advice, if he had to bypass his old friend he did so with incomparable tact.

As for Howe, he did not allow his protégé's eminence to constrain their relationship. Once McDuffie, the President's valet, brought him a message to which he replied snappishly, "Tell the President to go to hell." McDuffie, appalled, told his wife Lizzie, one of the White House maids, that he could not possibly deliver such a message to the President. Lizzie said she would fix it up; "Mr. President," she said, "Mr. Howe says that is a hell of a thing to do." The President laughed skeptically: "That isn't what Howe said, Lizzie. He told me to go to hell." Roosevelt's feeling toward Howe, as Richberg discerningly remarked, was that of a middle-aged son who still appreciated father's wisdom but was also impatient at father's efforts to keep him under parental guidance.

By the end of 1934, Howe's health, never good, grew steadily worse. He spent more and more of his time in his suite on the second floor of the White House. In February 1935 bronchial complications brought about a collapse. He was rushed to the Naval Hospital and put under an oxygen tent. Doctors despaired of him. "He seems to cling to life in the most astonishing manner," Eleanor Roosevelt wrote sadly to Molly Dewson, "but I am afraid it is the end." She underestimated his vitality. He rallied and, though he never left the hospital for long, he stayed alive another year. Much of this time he spent in bed, doubled up in an effort to reduce the pain; he let his beard grow into a straggling goatee which made his appearance more peculiar than ever. He continued to follow politics with sharp-eyed attention, sending out a flow of confusing directives to the National Committee and to cabinet members. The Roosevelts visited him regularly. But he knew in his heart that he had not long to live. One day a friend told him that everyone counted on him for the 1936 campaign. "No," the old man said. "No, they'll have to run this campaign without me." He paused for a moment; then said, "Franklin's on his own now." In mid-April 1936, Louis Howe died.

Eleanor Roosevelt always felt that Howe's death left an irreparable gap in Franklin's life. Howe was almost alone, she believed, in being ready to follow through an argument with her husband, forcing him by peevish persistence to see unpleasant sides of an issue: "After Louis' death," she wrote, "Franklin frequently made his decisions without canvassing all sides of a question." Harold Ickes said the same thing: "Howe was the only one who dared to talk to him frankly and fearlessly. He not only could tell him what he believed to be the truth, but he could hang on like a pup to the root until he got results." Moreover, Howe unscrupulously organized campaigns to press his views; at his instigation, Eleanor Roosevelt, Farley, Ed Flynn, and others would suddenly converge on the President and, as if by accident, make the same point. Eleanor Roosevelt felt in addition that her husband saw a better cross section of people and heard a greater variety of views when Howe was alive.

These things were probably true. Yet Howe's range was limited. "Louis knows nothing about economics," Roosevelt once said; in fact, he knew little of any aspect of public affairs, and was only vaguely aware what the New Deal was all about. Howe would have saved Roosevelt from mistakes in politics, but hardly from mistakes in policy. Still the subtraction of the most vehement nay-sayer from the entourage was certainly a misfortune.[2]

IV

Roosevelt had named Howe his Chief Secretary as a testimonial to his years of service. His other secretaries, Early and McIntyre, received the same salary as Howe and, as time went on, took over more and more of the day-to-day responsibility. Early, a tough, hard-driving, profane newspaperman just under fifty who had been for many years an ace for the Associated Press, had press relations as his main job. McIntyre, a gentle, agreeable man in his middle fifties, with a long and not especially distinguished background in newspaper work and public relations, was more or less in charge of political appointments (though, as in any Roosevelt operation, this seemed at times everybody's responsibility). Both Early and McIntyre were southerners, Early from Virginia, McIntyre from Kentucky. Both had worked for Roosevelt in the 1920 vice-presidential campaign. Both were aggressively non-ideological. Each preferred the political and business types with which they were familiar to the odd new breed of New Dealers; in McIntyre's case, an innocent fondness for the company of lobbyists was more than once a source of embarrassment to the White House. Both were loyal to Roosevelt rather than to his philosophy. But they kept out of policy questions and each strove to do as fair a job as possible.

Pa Watson, the military aide, who ran the general appointment schedule, was a more complex and subtle figure. An Alabaman in his early fifties who had been an aide to Wilson at Versailles, Watson was a man of winning personal charm. "I have never known anyone just like him," Ickes once said. ". . . He could be relied upon to keep us all in a mellow humor, and this without any effort on his part, but simply by being himself." People so adored the bubbling good nature that they sometimes missed the sophisticated awareness which lay beneath the quips and stories. Not a New Dealer, Watson had a greater understanding than Early and McIntyre of what the New Deal was about.

Of all the staff, Marguerite LeHand, the President's personal secretary, was undoubtedly closest to him and had most influence upon him. Missy was now in her late thirties, a tall, slender woman, prematurely gray, with a lovely face and attractive gray-blue eyes. She had worked for Roosevelt so long that she knew intimately his every expression and mood; his fondness for her was so great that he would listen to her as to few others on questions of appointments and even policy ("Mr. President, you really *must* do something about" so-and-so or such-and-such). She lived on the third floor of the White House, and, when Eleanor Roosevelt was away, acted as White House hostess, inviting people who she thought might divert the President. Eleanor Roosevelt, while respecting Missy's abilities and understanding her value to her husband, felt that "occasionally her social contacts got mixed with her work and made it hard for her and others." People like Bill Bullitt and Tom Corcoran, she suggested, "exploited Missy's friendship" for their own purposes. But "though occasionally someone fooled her for a time, I always waited for enlightenment to come, with confidence born of long experience." Missy was pretty and gay and liked lively company; there can be no question that she brought an essential femininity as well as a sympathetic common sense into Roosevelt's life, and there is no evidence that she ever abused the affection and trust he reposed in her. An attack of rheumatic fever in 1926 had strained Missy's heart; and more and more of the office work, as, for example, taking dictation, fell to Grace Tully, another pretty and lively girl, who had worked for Roosevelt since the 1928 campaign. Both girls were Catholics, Miss LeHand of French, Miss Tully of Irish descent. They both cared deeply about the objectives of the New Deal. Both were exceptionally able and devoted women.

One other key White House figure was the executive clerk, Rudolph Forster, who had been there since the McKinley administration. His responsibility was the channeling of state papers, and he did this with an austere and frightening efficiency. For him the job was an end in itself; Presidents came and went, but papers went on forever. "You would be terrified," he once said to a Roosevelt assistant, "if you knew how little I care." (Yet even Forster, in the end, succumbed. In the 1944 campaign, as Roosevelt was leaving the White House on a political tour, Forster, with what Robert E. Sherwood described as "the air of one who was willfully breaking all of the Ten Commandments but prepared to take the consequences," shook the President's hand and wished him luck. Roosevelt, astonished and moved, said as the car drove away, "That's practically the first time in all these years that Rudolph has ever stepped out of character and spoken to me as if I were a human being instead of just another President.") [3]

V

The next concentric circle beyond the White House staff in the President's constellation was the cabinet. In the American system this had always been an ambiguous and unsatisfactory body. At the beginning of the republic, some conceived it as a sort of executive council. All grave and important matters, it was supposed, would be submitted to a cabinet vote in which, as Jefferson put it, "the President counts himself but one." But Presidents, even Jefferson, recoiled from such a conception; and Jackson, in his general process of revolutionizing the Presidency, decisively redefined the relationship between the President and his cabinet.

Jackson flatly declined, for example, to submit questions to vote. "I have accustomed myself to receive with respect the opinions of others," he said, "but always take the responsibility of deciding for myself." Lincoln, going even further, found cabinet meetings so useless that he often avoided them and at one time seemed on the verge of doing away with them altogether. As for voting: "Ayes one, noes seven. The ayes have it" — or so the old story went. "There is really very little of a government here at this time so far as most of the cabinet are concerned," complained Gideon Welles, Lincoln's Secretary of the Navy; "certainly but little consultation in this important period." Or again: "But little was before the Cabinet, which of late can hardly be called a council. Each Department conducts and manages its own affairs, informing the President to the extent it pleases." Theodore Roosevelt ignored his cabinet on important issues. Woodrow Wilson did not even bother to discuss the sinking of the *Lusitania* or the declaration of war with it. "For some weeks," wrote his Secretary of the Interior, Franklin Lane, "we have spent our time at Cabinet meetings largely telling stories."

Roosevelt remained generally faithful to this tradition, though he made rather more effort than Lincoln or Wilson to recognize the cabinet's existence. At first, he planned two cabinet meetings a week, on Tuesday and Friday afternoons. Effectively he had only one, however; the Tuesday meeting was first enlarged to include the heads of the emergency agencies and then dropped almost entirely. Sessions took place in an atmosphere of characteristic Roosevelt in-

formality. The President ordinarily began with a recital of pleasan-
tries, telling stories which tickled him or joshing cabinet members
about their latest appearances in the newspapers. Then he might
throw out a problem for a generally rambling and inconclusive decision. Or, turning to the Secretary of State, he might say without
ceremony, "Well, Cordell, what's on your mind today?" Then he
would continue around the table in order of precedence.

The men — and one woman — sitting around the table were of
varying qualities and abilities. They had conspicuously one thing
in common — a high degree of personal rectitude. "For integrity
and honesty of purpose," wrote Raymond Clapper after twenty
years of covering Washington, "I'll put this Cabinet against any
that has been in Washington since the war. It is one thing that does
truly distinguish this group. There is not a shady one in the lot."
Beyond that, the people around the table represented a variety of
viewpoints and temperaments, held together only by a loyalty to,
or at least a dependence on, the President. There was Garner
(whom the President, to his later regret, invited to attend cabinet
meetings) with his complacent country sagacity; Hull, courteous and
grave, always vigilant to defend his authority against real or fancied depredation; Henry Morgenthau, closest personally to the
President, earnest, devoted, and demanding; the testy and agres-
sive Ickes; the preoccupied and thoughtful Wallace; Homer Cummings, bland, canny and unperturbed; Jesse Jones, wary and self-
contained, the intelligent and articulate Miss Perkins (whose protracted discourses appeared to fascinate the President, but bored
most of the others and at times enraged Ickes — "she talks in a
perfect torrent, almost without pausing to take breath"); the amiable
Farley, reacting only when politics came into the discussion — they
were all forceful personalities, regarding each other with a show of
conviviality which often only barely concealed depths of suspicion.
For the most part, they chose problems of only middling — or else
of highly general — significance to communicate to the group. This
was partly because, in the inevitable jostling of bueaucracy, each
felt that every man's hand was against him, and none wanted to
expose vulnerabilities. It was also because the conviction grew that
some members would "leak" tasty items — Garner to his cronies on
the Hill, or Ickes to the columnist Drew Pearson. Questions that

really troubled them they reserved for private discussion with the President afterward, a practice which Garner used to call "staying for prayer meeting." "Then you would stay behind," as Morgenthau described it, "and whisper in his ear and he would say yes or no."

The members of the Roosevelt cabinet, as usual, suffered frustration and, as usual, thought their experience unique. In private, they echoed the familiar laments of Gideon Welles and Franklin Lane. "Only the barest routine matters were discussed," burst out Ickes in his diary after a meeting in 1935. "All of which leads me to set down what has been running in my mind for a long time, and that is just what use the Cabinet is under this administration. The cold fact is that on important matters we are seldom called upon for advice. We never discuss exhaustively any policy of government or question of political strategy. The President makes all of his own decisions. . . . As a matter of fact, I never think of bringing up even a serious departmental issue at Cabinet meetings." "It seemed to me," wrote William Phillips, sitting in occasionally for Hull, "that a great deal of time was wasted at Cabinet meetings and much of the talk was without any particular import." "The important things were never discussed at Cabinet," said Morgenthau. "The President treats them like children," Tugwell wrote in his diary, "and almost nothing of any importance was discussed."

The meetings evidently retained some obscure usefulness for the President. The reaction he got from this miscellany of administrators perhaps gave him some idea of the range of public opinion. It also helped him measure the capacity of his subordinates. Grace Tully reports, for example, that he preferred Henry Wallace's willingness to speak out on a wide variety of problems "to the reticence or indifference of some Cabinet members." But, like all strong presidents, Roosevelt regarded his cabinet as a body of department heads, to be dealt with individually — or, sometimes, as a group of representative intelligent men, useful for a quick canvass of opinion — not as a council of constitutional advisers.[4]

VI

Beyond the cabinet there stretched the Executive Branch of the government — an endless thicket of vested usage and vested interest, apportioned among a number of traditional jurisdictions, dominated by a number of traditional methods and objectives. This was, in the popular understanding, the government of the United States — the people and departments and agencies whose office it was to carry out the national laws and fulfill the national policies. The President had few more basic responsibilities than his supervision and operation of the machinery of government. Little fascinated Franklin Roosevelt more than the tasks of presidential administration. And in few things was he more generally reckoned a failure.

This verdict against Roosevelt derived ultimately from a philosophy of public administration — a philosophy held for many years after by Civil Service professionals, expounded in departments of political science, and commending itself plausibly to common sense. This school's faith was in logical organization of government, founded on rigid definitions of job and function and maintained by the sanctity of channels. Its weapons were the job description and the organization chart. Its unspoken assumption was that the problems of administration never change; and its consuming fear was improvisation, freewheeling or unpredictability — which is nearly to say creativity — in the administrative process. From this point of view, it need hardly be said, the Roosevelt government was a textbook case of poor administration. At one time or another, Roosevelt must surely have violated every rule in the sacred texts of the Bureau of the Budget.

And this conventional verdict found apparent support in much of the literature written by men who worked for Roosevelt. Though these reports differed on many other things, one thing on which they very often agreed was in their complaint about Roosevelt as an administrator. They agreed on one other thing too — the perspective from which they were written. Nearly all exhibited the problems of the Presidency from below — from the viewpoint of the subordinate rather than from that of the President. The picture created by this mass of individual stories, while vivid and overwhelming, was inevitably distorted and too often querulous. For no subordinate ever got what he wanted or thought he needed. In later years, George C. Marshall would talk of "localitis" — the conviction ardently held by every theater commander that the war was being won or lost in his own zone of responsibility, and that the withholding of whatever was necessary for local success was evidence of blindness, if not of imbecility, in the high command. "Localitis" in one form or another was the occupational disease of all subordinate officials; and, in a sense, it had to be, for each of them ought to demand everything he needed to do the best job he can. But "localitis" offered no solid ground for judgment of superiors, whose role it must inevitably be to frustrate the dreams of subordinates. The President occupied the apex of the pyramid of frustration. The essence of his job was to enforce priorities — and thereby to exasperate everybody. And, in Roosevelt's case, there is little left in the literature to emphasize the view from the summit, where any President had to make his decisions. As Grace Tully (whose book does something to redress the balance) commented on other memoirists, "None of them could know that for each minute they spent with the President he spent a hundred minutes by himself and a thousand more with scores of other people — to reject, improvise, weigh and match this against that until a decision was reached on a public policy."

The question remains whether the true test of an administrator may be, not his ability to design and respect organization charts, not his ability to keep within channels, but his ability to concert and release the energies of men for the attainment of public objectives. It might be argued that the essence of successful administration is: first, to acquire the ideas and information necessary for wise decisions; second, to maintain control over the actual making of the decisions; and, third, to mobilize men and women who can make the first two things possible — that is, who can provide effective ideas and information, and who can reliably put decisions into effect. It is conceivable that these things may be more important than preserving the chastity of administrative organization — that, indeed, an excessive insistence on the sacredness of channels and charts is likely to end in the stifling of imagination, the choking of vitality, and the deadening of creativity.[5]

VII

Franklin Roosevelt, at any rate, had some such philosophy of administration. The first task of an executive, as he evidently saw it, was to guarantee himself an effective flow of information and ideas. And Roosevelt's first insight — or, at least, his profound conviction — was that, for this purpose, the ordained channels, no matter how simply or how intricately designed, could never be enough. An executive relying on a single information system became inevitably the prisoner of that system. Roosevelt's persistent effort therefore was to check and balance information acquired through official channels by information acquired through a myriad of private, informal, and unorthodox channels and espionage networks. At times, he seemed almost to pit his personal sources against his public sources. From the viewpoint of subordinates, this method was distracting when not positively demoralizing. But Roosevelt, with his voracity for facts and for ideas, required this approach to cross-check the official system and keep it alert as well as to assure himself the balanced and various product without which he could not comfortably reach decisions.

The official structure, of course, maintained a steady flow of intelligence. Roosevelt was, for a President, extraordinarily accessible. Almost a hundred persons could get through to him by telephone without stating their business to a secretary; and government officials with anything serious on their minds had little difficulty in getting appointments. In addition, he read an enormous number of official memoranda, State Department cables, and government reports, and always tried to glance at the *Congressional Record*. The flow was overwhelming, and he sought continually to make it manageable. "I learned a trick from Wilson," he remarked to Louis Brownlow. "He once told me: 'If you want your memoranda read, put it on one page.' So I, when I came here, issued a similar decree, if you want to call it that. But even at that I am now forced to handle, so the oldsters around tell me, approximately a hundred times as many papers as any of my predecessors." Certainly his subordinates paid little attention to the one-page rule.

What gave Roosevelt's administrative practice its distinctive quality was his systematic effort to augment the official intelligence. The clutter of newspapers on his bed each morning marked only the first stage in his battle for supplementary information. In this effort, reading was a useful but auxiliary weapon. Beyond government documents and newspapers, he read little. So far as current magazines were concerned, the President, according to Early, "sketches the field," whatever that meant. As for books, Roosevelt evidently read them only on holiday, and then not too seriously. When Frances Perkins sent him the Brookings study *America's Capacity to Produce*, he replied, "Many thanks. . . . I am taking it on the trip and will guarantee to browse through it but not of necessity to read every word!" On the whole, he preferred to acquire both information and ideas through conversation.

Many visitors, it is true, left Roosevelt with the impression that he had done all the talking. This was markedly less true, in his first term, however, than it would be later. Indeed, Henry Pringle, reporting the Washington view in 1934, wrote, "He is a little too willing to listen." And the complaint against Roosevelt's overtalk- ing meant in some cases only that a visitor had run into a deliber- ate filibuster (thus William Randolph Hearst's baffled lament after a session with Roosevelt in 1933, "The President didn't give me a chance to make suggestions. He did all the talking"). "Words are a good enough barrage if you know how to use them," Roosevelt told one visitor. Like many talkers, moreover, Roosevelt absorbed atti- tudes and ideas by a mysterious osmosis on occasions when the visitor complained he hadn't got a word in edgewise.

Conversation gave him an indispensable means both of feeling out opinion and of clarifying his own ideas. He talked to everybody and about everything. His habits of conversation out of channels were sometimes disconcerting. He had little hesitation, if he heard of a bright man somewhere down the line in a department, about summoning him to the White House. Ickes complained bitterly in his diary about "what he does so frequently, namely, calling in members of my staff for consultation on Department matters, with- out consulting me or advising with me." And often he bewildered visitors by asking their views on matters outside their jurisdiction. "He had a great habit," said Jesse Jones, "of talking to one caller about the subject matter of his immediately preceding interview." "I would go to see the President about something," wrote James P. Warburg, "and the fellow who was there before me talking about cotton would be told by the President, 'Well, why don't you stay.' Before we were through the guy who was there talking about cotton was telling him what to do about gold." All this, irritating as it was to tidy minds, enlarged the variety of reactions available to him in areas where no one was infallible and any intelligent person might make a contribution.

Moreover, at this time, at least, conversation around him was unusually free and candid. Always sensitive to public criticism, Roosevelt could take a large measure of private disagreement. Moley describes him as "patient, amenable to advice, moderate and smilingly indifferent to criticism." "In those days," wrote Richberg, "he enjoyed the frankness and lack of deference with which the original 'brain trusters' and I discussed problems." When people disagreed, they said so plainly and at length. "I had numerous quarrels with him," wrote Ed Flynn, who once (in 1940) hung up on him in the midst of a phone conversation. "However, as with sincere friends, the quarrels never impaired our friendship." [6]

VIII

In seeking information, Roosevelt took care not to confuse the capital with the nation. "Pay no attention to what people are saying in Washington," he once told Molly Dewson. "They are the last persons in the country to listen to." He loved going out to the country himself and got infinite stimulus from faces in crowds, from towns quietly glimpsed out of the windows of slow-moving trains, from chance conversations with ordinary people along the way. But polio and the Presidency limited his mobility. Instead, he had to urge others to get out of Washington. "Go and see what's happening," he told Tugwell. "See the end product of what we are doing. Talk to people; get the wind in your nose."

His first reliance was on his wife. From the first days after his disability, he trained her to do his looking for him. "That I became, as the years went by, a better and better reporter and a better and better observer," she later wrote, "was largely owing to the fact that Franklin's questions covered such a wide range. I found myself obliged to notice everything." While he sometimes doubted her judgment on policy and especially on timing, he had implicit faith in her observations. He would say at cabinet, "My Missus says that they have typhoid fever in that district," or "My

Missus says that people are working for wages way below the minimum set by NRA in the town she visited last week." "It was not unusual," said Grace Tully, "to hear him predicate an entire line of reasoning upon a statement that 'my Missus told me so and so.'" In addition, he liked detailed reports of the kind Lorena Hickok and Martha Gellhorn rendered on the situation of people on relief. And he listened with interest to any reasonably succinct account of human conditions anywhere.

Another great source of information was the mail. Five to eight thousand letters a day came normally to the White House; in times of anxiety, of course, many more. The mail was regularly analyzed in order to gauge fluctations in public sentiment. From time to time, the President himself called for a random selection of letters in order to renew his sense of contact with raw opinion. As the White House mail clerk later wrote, "Mr. Roosevelt always showed a keen interest in the mail and kept close watch on its trend."

In all these ways, Roosevelt amassed an astonishing quantity of miscellaneous information and ideas about the government and the country. "No President," wrote Alben Barkley, "has ever surpassed him in personal knowledge of the details of every department"; and he could have added that probably no President surpassed him in specific knowledge of the geography, topography, and people of the nation. Roosevelt took inordinate pride in this mastery of detail and often displayed it at length when those around him wished to get down to business. But, at the same time, the information — and the pride in it — signified the extraordinary receptivity which was one of his primary characteristics.

This receptivity produced the complex of information systems by which he protected himself from White House insulation. It oriented the administrative machinery away from routine and toward innovation. It made possible the intellectual excitement of the New Deal; it helped provoke a tempest of competing ideas within government because everyone felt that ideas stood and fell at the White House on their merit, not on whether they arrived through the proper channels. Good ideas might pop up from anywhere. "You sometimes find something pretty good in the lunatic fringe," Roosevelt once told his press conference: after all, America today was remade by "a whole lot of things which in my boyhood

werc considered lunatic fringe." Anyone with new theories had a
sense that they were worth developing because, if good, they would
find their way to the center. Sometimes this caused problems:
Roosevelt was occasionally sold on harebrained ideas which more
orderly procedures would have screened out and which taxed responsible officials before he could be unsold. But, on balance,
benefits far outweighed disadvantages. H. G. Wells, who saw in
Roosevelt's union of openness of mind and resolution of will the
realization of his old dream of the Open Conspiracy, wrote with
admiration in 1934, "He is, as it were, a ganglion for reception,
expression, transmission, combination and realization, which I
take it, is exactly what a modern government ought to be." [7]

                              IX

If information was the first responsibility of the executive, the
second was decision. American Presidents fall into two types: those
who like to make decisions, and those who don't. One type de-
signs an administrative system which brings decisions to him; the
other, a system which keeps decisions away from him. The second
technique, under its more mellifluous designation of "delegation of
authority," is regarded with favor in the conventional theory of
public administration. Yet, pressed very far, "delegation of authority" obviously strikes at the roots of the Presidency. One can
delegate routine, but one cannot delegate any part of the serious
presidential responsibility. The whole theory of the Constitution
makes the Chief Executive, in the words of Andrew Jackson, "accountable at the bar of public opinion for every act of his Administration," and thus presumably accountable in his own conscience
for its every large decision.

Roosevelt, in any case, was pre-eminently of the first type. He
evidently felt that both the dignity of his office and the coherence
of his administration required that the key decisions be made by
him, and not by others before him. He took great pride, for example, in a calculation of Rudolph Forster's that he made at
least thirty-five decisions to each one made by Calvin Coolidge.
Given this conception of the Presidency, he deliberately organized
— or disorganized — his system of command to insure that im-

portant decisions were passed on to the top. His favorite technique was to keep grants of authority incomplete, jurisdictions uncertain, charters overlapping. The result of this competitive theory of administration was often confusion and exasperation on the operating level; but no other method could so reliably insure that in a large bureaucracy filled with ambitious men eager for power the decisions, and the power to make them, would remain with the President. This was in part on Roosevelt's side an instinct for self-preservation; in part, too, the temperamental expression of a restless, curious, and untidy personality. Co-existence with disorder was almost the pattern of his life. From the day of his marriage, he had lived in a household of unresolved jurisdictions, and it had never occurred to him to try to settle lines finally as between mother and wife. As Assistant Secretary of the Navy, he had indulged happily in the kind of administrative freewheeling which he was not much concerned to penalize in others now. As his doctor once said, Roosevelt "loved to know everything that was going on and delighted to have a finger in every pie."

Once the opportunity for decision came safely into his orbit, the actual process of deciding was involved and inscrutable. As Tugwell once put it, "Franklin allowed no one to discover the governing principle." He evidently felt that clear-cut administrative decisions would work only if they expressed equally clear-cut realities of administrative competence and vigor. If they did not, if the balance of administrative power would not sustain the decision, then decision would only compound confusion and discredit government. And the actualities of administrative power were to be discovered, not by writing — or by reading — Executive orders, but by apprehending through intuition a vast constellation of political forces. His complex administrative sensibility, infinitely subtle and sensitive, was forever weighing questions of personal force, of political timing, of congressional concern, of partisan benefit, of public interest. Situations had to be permitted to develop, to crystallize, to clarify; the competing forces had to vindicate themselves in the actual pull and tug of conflict; public opinion had to face the question, consider it, pronounce upon it — only then, at the long, frazzled end, would the President's intuitions consolidate and precipitate a result.

Though he enjoyed giving the impression of snap decisions, Roosevelt actually made few. The more serious complaint against him was his weakness for postponement. This protraction of decision often appeared a technique of evasion. And sometimes it was. But sometimes dilemmas did not seem so urgent from above as they seemed below — a proposition evidently proved when they evaporated after the passage of time. And Roosevelt, in any case, justified, or rationalized, delay in terms of his own sense of timing. He knew from hard experience that a person could not regain health in a day or year; and he had no reason to suppose that a nation would mend any more quickly. "He could watch with enormous patience as a situation developed," wrote his wife, "and would wait for exactly the right moment to act." When people pressed proposals on him, he often answered (as he did to Frank Walker in 1936), "You are absolutely right. . . . It is simply a question of time." The tragedy of the Presidency in his view was the impotence of the President. Abraham Lincoln, Roosevelt said, "was a sad man because he couldn't get it all at once. And nobody can." He was responding informally to an important young questioner. "Maybe you would make a much better President than I have. Maybe you will, some day. If you ever sit here, you will learn that you cannot, just by shouting from the housetops, get what you want all the time."

Yet his caution was always within an assumption of constant advance. "We must keep the sheer momentum from slacking up too much," he told Colonel House in 1934, "and I have no intention of relinquishing the offensive." Woodrow Wilson had given him a cyclical conception of social change in America. Roosevelt told Robert H. Jackson that he had once suggested that Wilson withhold part of his reform program for his second term. Wilson replied in substance: We do not know that there will be a second term, and, if there is, it will be less progressive and constructive than the first. American history shows that a reform administration comes to office only once in every twenty years, and that its forward impulse does not outlast one term. Even if the same party and persons remain in power, they become complacent in a second term. "What we do not accomplish in the first term is not likely to be accomplished at all." (When Roosevelt told this story to his press conference in the first year of his second term, he lengthened the period of possible accomplishment from four to eight years.) [8]

X

This technique of protraction was often wildly irritating to his subordinates, enlisted passionately on one side or another of an argument and perceiving with invincible clarity the logic of one or another course. It was equally irritating to his opponents, who enjoyed the advantages of oversimplification which come from observation without responsibility. But the President's dilatory tactics were, in a sense, the means by which he absorbed country-wide conflict of pressures, of fears, of hopes. His intelligence was not analytical. He did not systematically assess pros and cons in his own mind. What for others might be an interior dialogue had to be externalized for Roosevelt; and it was externalized most conveniently by hearing strong exponents of divergent viewpoints. Listening amiably to all sides, watching the opposing views undergo the test of practice, digesting the evidence, he gradually felt his way toward a conclusion. And even this would not often be clearcut. "He hated to make sharp decisions between conflicting claims for power among his subordinates," noted Francis Biddle, "and decided them, almost always, in a spirit of arbitration: each side should have part of the morsel." Quite often, he ordered the contestants to work out their own compromise, as in NRA and on farm policy. In this connection he liked to cite Al Smith: "He said if you can get the parties into one room with a big table and make them take their coats off and put their feet up on the table, and give each one of them a good cigar, you can always make them agree."

With the conclusion, however reached, a new phase began. When Garner once tried to argue after Roosevelt had made up his mind, the President said, "You tend to your office and I'll tend to mine." ("I didn't take offense at that," said Garner, "because he was right.") "You could fight with Roosevelt and argue with him up to a certain point," said Morgenthau, "— but at no time during his waking hours was he anything else but a ruler." Wayne Coy, who was a Roosevelt assistant for some years, observed that one could say exactly what one thought to Roosevelt, so long as he was saying only "in my judgment" or "I think." When he said "The President thinks," the time for discussion was over. To another assistant, James Rowe, who insisted that he should do something in a particular way, Roosevelt said, "I do not have to do it your way and I will tell you the reason why. The reason is that, although they may have made a mistake, the people of the United States elected me President, not you."

Often he announced his decisions with bravado. He liked to tell advisers, "I'm going to spring a bombshell," and then startle them with novel proposals — or rather with proposals novel to them, not perhaps to another set of advisers. "He delights in surprises — clever, cunning and quick," said Hugh Johnson. "He likes to shock friends as well as enemies with something they never expected." But he seems rarely to have supposed that any particular decision was in a final sense correct, or even terribly important. "I have no expectation of making a hit every time I come to bat. What I seek is the highest possible batting average." He remembered Theodore Roosevelt's saying to him, "If I can be right 75 per cent of the time I shall come up to the fullest measure of my hopes." "You'll have to learn that public life takes a lot of sweat," he told Tugwell, "but it doesn't need to worry you. You won't always be right, but you mustn't suffer from being wrong. That's what kills people like us." After all, Roosevelt said, suppose a truck driver were doing your job; 50 per cent of his decisions would be right on average. "You aren't a truck driver. You've had some preparation. Your percentage is bound to be higher." And he knew that the refusal to decide was itself a form of decision. "This is very bad," he said to Frances Perkins, "but one thing is sure. We have to do something. We have to do the best we know how to do at the moment." Then, after a pause: "If it doesn't turn out right, we can modify it as we go along."

This dislike of firm commitments, this belief in alternatives, further reduced the significance of any single decision. As Miss Perkins observed, "He rarely got himself sewed tight to a program from which there was no turning back." The very ambiguity of his scheme of organization — the overlapping jurisdictions and duplicated responsibilities — made flexibility easy. If things started to go bad, he could reshuffle people and functions with speed which would have been impossible in a government of clear-cut assignments and rigid chains of command. Under the competitive theory, he always retained room for administrative maneuver.

Only a man of limitless energy and resource could hold such a system together. Even Roosevelt at times was hard put to keep it from flying apart. But he did succeed, as no modern President has done, in concentrating the power of executive decision where the Constitution intended it should be. "I've never known any President," said W. M. Kiplinger, "who was as omnipresent as this Roosevelt." "Most people acting for Roosevelt were messenger boys," said Ed Flynn. "He really made his own decisions." [9]

33. The Control of Government

As a President's conquest of the problem of information makes decision possible, so his conquest of the problem of decision leads on to the third responsibility of administration: execution. Success in administration obviously stands or falls on skill in execution. Execution means, above all, the right people — it means having men and women capable of providing the information and carrying out the decision. Nothing is more important for a President than to command the necessary abundance of understanding, loyalty, and ardor on the part of able and imaginative subordinates.

Different Presidents want different things from their subordinates. Some want fidelity, some diligence, some flattery, some no more than the undemanding competence which will take things off their own back. Roosevelt no doubt wanted all of these at various times. What he evidently wanted most was liveliness, vitality, vision. He sought out men who had ideas and drive; and he designed the kind of administrative system which would bring him the men he wanted. Again, as in the case of information, the competitive approach to administration best served his purposes. The men around Roosevelt were not easily contented or contained. They were always fanning out, in ideas and in power. A government well organized in the conventional sense would have given them claustrophobia. The looseness of the New Deal gave them the feeling of scope and outlet which made public service for them tolerable and amusing.

II

To guarantee the scope, Roosevelt had to revamp the structure of government. By orthodox administrative theory, the antidepression activities should have been brought in under the appropriate old-line departments — Agriculture, Commerce, Labor, the Treasury. But Roosevelt felt that the old departments, even with new chiefs, simply could not generate the energy and daring the crisis required. "We have new and complex problems. We don't really know what they are. Why not establish a new agency to take over the new duty rather than saddle it on an old institution?" Hence the resort from the start to the emergency agency, an essential instrument in the Rooseveltian technique of administrative improvisation. If the obvious channel of action was blocked and it was not worth the political trouble of dynamiting it open, then the emergency agency supplied the means of getting the job done nevertheless. And the new agencies simplified the problem of reversing direction and correcting error. "We have to be prepared to abandon bad practices that grow out of ignorance. It seems to me it is easier to use a new agency which is not a permanent part of the structure of government. If it is not permanent, we don't get bad precedents."

The New Dealers, particularly those of the Brandeis-Frankfurter school, talked a good deal about the importance of a first-class Civil Service on the British model. Roosevelt accepted this as an aspiration. "Public service," he said proudly in 1934, "offers better rewards in the opportunity for service than ever before in our history." But in practice the professional civil service often seemed an arsenal of obfuscation. It had become, said Tugwell, "a way of choosing and keeping 'the best of the worst,' of making certain that, barring revolution, war or economic disaster, the chosen dullards could have a long, uneventful, thoroughly secure working life." More than that, the Civil Service register for upper-grade positions reflected the generally Republican character of the professional and business classes. Mathematics thus indicated that staffing the New Deal through the Civil Service would fill key positions with anti-New Dealers. In consequence, the new agencies did their best to bypass the Civil Service. By 1936 the proportion of employees under the "merit system" had materially declined.

The new agencies were plainly indispensable. They tended to have an administrative dash and *élan* which the old departments, sunk in the lethargy of routine, could not match. Yet the theory could be pushed too far. At times Roosevelt acted as if a new agency were almost a new solution. His addiction to new organizations became a kind of nervous tic which disturbed even avid New Dealers. By 1936 we find Tugwell pleading with him not to set up new organizations. "My experience — and Harry's — is that it takes almost a year to perfect a country-wide administrative organization and that while it is being done there is political turmoil over the jobs, criticisms of procedure from the field, jealousy on the part of old organizations which fancy their prerogatives are threatened and other sources of irritation."

Each new agency had its own distinct mission. But in many cases jurisdictions overlapped each other and even spilled into cabinet departments. This was sloppy and caused much trouble. Yet this very looseness around the joints, this sense of give and possibility which Henry Stimson once called the "inherently disorderly nature" of Roosevelt's administration, made public service attractive to men of a certain boldness and imagination. It also spurred them on to better achievement. Roosevelt liked the competitive approach to administration, not just because it reserved the big decisions for the President, but perhaps even more because it enabled him to test and develop the abilities of his subordinates. How to tell which man, which approach was better? One answer was to let them fight it out. This solution might cause waste but would guarantee against stagnation. "There is something to be said," Roosevelt once observed, " . . . for having a little conflict between agencies. A little rivalry is stimulating, you know. It keeps everybody going to prove that he is a better fellow than the next man. It keeps them honest too. An awful lot of money is being handled. The fact that there is somebody else in the field who knows what you are doing is a strong incentive to strict honesty." One can see, for example, in the diaries of Harold Ickes how the overhanging presence of Hopkins and Morgenthau caused Ickes to spend hours and days in intrigue and invective. One can also see how the feuding stimulated him and them to more effective accomplishment and kept every part of the relief and public works effort forever on its toes.

Sometimes the competitive theory could meet political needs too. Roosevelt, as the leader of a coalition, had to keep a variety of interests satisfied, or at least hopeful. What better way than to give each representation where decisions were made? Some agencies seemed to be staffed on the ancient Persian theory of placing men who did not trust each other side by side, their swords on the table. Everywhere there was the need to balance the right and the left — let Cohen and Corcoran write the act establishing the Securities and Exchange Commission, but let Joe Kennedy administer it, but flank him with Jim Landis and Ferdinand Pecora. Rather than sitting on creative vitality anywhere, give each faction something of a head and try to cope with the results. "He had an instinct," wrote Frances Perkins with insight, "for loose, self-directed activity on the part of many groups."

Competition in government, inadequately controlled, would mean anarchy. Adequately controlled, it could mean exceptional creativity. One consequence under the New Deal was a darkling plain of administrative confusion, where bureaucrats clashed by night. Another was a constant infusion of vitality and ideas. In a quieter time, when problems were routine, there would have been every reason to demand tight and tidy administration. But a time of crisis placed a premium on initiative and innovation — and on an organization of government which gave these qualities leeway and reward.[1]

III

Getting bold and imaginative subordinates, however, by itself hardly solves the problems of execution. The worst error a President can make is to assume the automatic implementation of his own decisions. In certain respects, having able subordinates aggravates that problem, since strong personalities tend to have strong ideas of their own. Civil government operates by consent, not by command; the President's task, even within his own branch of government, is not to order but to lead. Students of public administration have never taken sufficient account of the capacity of lower levels of government to sabotage or defy even a masterful President. Somehow, through charm, cajolery, and the communication of ideals, as well as through pressure, discipline, and coercion, the President must make the Executive Branch *want* to carry out his policies.

The competitive approach to administration gave Roosevelt great advantages. It brought him an effective flow of information; it kept the reins of decision in his own hands; it made for administrative flexibility and stimulated subordinates to effective performance.

At the same time it exacted a price in morale. It placed those close to him under incessant strain. Even for men who could have operated in no other way, it was at best nerve-wracking and often positively demoralizing. Yet this too Roosevelt turned to his own purposes of control. Their insecurity gave him new opportunities for manipulation, which he exploited with cruel skill, while looking blandly in the opposite direction. He pretended not to know what was going on around him; but, said Tugwell, "those who knew his weakness for not grasping really nasty nettles knew from small signs that he was peeking through his fingers." In a way he liked the agony below: "he gave" said Cordell Hull a bit dolefully, "the impression almost of being a spectator looking on and enjoying the drama." "If he seemed to ignore the heaving bosoms presented to him," said Tugwell, "it did not mean that he did not know all about the agitation, or . . . did not enjoy it."

"You know," Harry Hopkins once said, "he is a little puckish." Puckish at times must have seemed an inadequate description. What Roosevelt could regard with equanimity from his place at the summit was often unbearable for those beneath. And it was not just that he seemed oblivious or entertained; at times he appeared to take a light and capricious pleasure in intensifying anxieties. His sometimes unfeeling ribbing of his associates expressed a thin streak of sadism of which he was intermittently aware and for which he was intermittently remorseful. "However genial his teasing," said Francis Biddle, "it was often . . . pointed with a prick of cruelty, because it went to the essence of a man, hit him between the ribs into the heart of his weakness, which might often be his unreasonable affection for his chief." Others shared Biddle's apprehension "that if we came too close I might suffer from his capacity to wound those who loved him."

No one came closer than Henry Morgenthau, and no one suffered more. Selfless devotion, as Biddle observed, sometimes became a bore; "one had to dissipate the irritation — the mild irritation — by stroking Henry against the grain in public now and then. One could not tease a man in private." Roosevelt himself once confessed to Morgenthau, "I was so tired that I would have enjoyed seeing you cry or would have gotten pleasure out of sticking pins into people and hurting them." As almost a member of the family, Morgenthau bore more than his share of Roosevelt's excess irritability. But the President had his way of tormenting everybody. Against others, indeed, the very closeness to Morgenthau was itself a weapon. The intimacy demonstrated in their weekly Monday luncheons created heartburning and indignation among other top officials who saw (or affected to see) nothing of talent or interest in the underrated Secretary of the Treasury. As Richberg said, "This relationship between the President and Secretary Morgenthau caused a great many jealousies." "For one thing," said Tugwell, "everyone else by contrast felt himself neglected; for another, no one could understand it."

And so the President went around the cabinet table. He played Ickes like an expert fisherman, giving him plenty of line, watching him fight and flap with fury and occasionally hauling him in. To each Attorney-General he would at some point outline an objective and say: "If you are a good Attorney General tell me how I can do it." "They always give him a silly laugh," said Morgenthau, "and go out and tell him how to do it." He bypassed Hull, limited his relations to Farley, kept Wallace at arm's length, and blew hot and cold on a dozen others. "He watched his subordinates at their games," said Tugwell, "checked them when necessary, contributed to their build-up when it was convenient, reprimanded them effectively by non-recognition, rewarded them by intimacies."

No one ever could be sure where he stood. Ickes once burst out at him: "You are a wonderful person but you are one of the most difficult men to work with that I have ever known." Roosevelt said, "Because I get too hard at times?" "No," Ickes replied, "you never get too hard but you won't talk frankly even with people who are loyal to you and of whose loyalty you are fully convinced. You keep your cards close up against your belly. You never put them on the table." (Roosevelt, Ickes added, "took all of this frank talk in a perfectly friendly manner.")

As Roosevelt saw the Presidency, no President could ever afford to lay his cards on the table. His way of playing the game frightened his subordinates. He had a genius for being indirect with people.

Nearly all around him had the chilling fear, generally shoved to the back of their minds, that he regarded them as expendable. As Frances Perkins said, "He reserved the right not to go out and rescue you if you got into trouble." "It was your battle," said Tugwell, "and you were expected to fight it. If you ran to the President with your troubles, he was affable and even, sometimes, vaguely encouraging, but he never said a public word in support." In a bitter moment, Jerome Frank proposed a principle of liberal politics: "A liberal leader can always count on the active support of certain persons, because of their belief in his major policies, regardless of how badly he treats them. (Item: Some of them are masochists who apparently work harder when they are ill-treated.) Therefore rewards should not be wastefully bestowed upon them but should be saved for potential enemies."

The more self-centered among Roosevelt's subordinates furiously resented this attitude and took it out on the President when their time came. The more philosophical regarded it as inevitable. "If this made you indignant," said Tugwell, "and it practically always did, there was nothing you could do and, when you thought it over, nothing of any use that you could say. The President was not a person; he was an institution. When he took political chances, he jeopardized not himself but the whole New Deal. And the New Deal could not afford to be responsible for practitioners who threatened its life — that is, who might lose it votes." It was up to the President to judge what endangered his essential objectives, and he made the judgment "in the recesses of his own considering apparatus which no one ever penetrated." Morgenthau, looking back, observed with insight, "He never let anybody around him have complete assurance that he would have the job tomorrow." Morgenthau added, "The thing that Roosevelt prided himself the most about was, 'I have to have a happy ship.' But he never had a happy ship." [2]

IV

Yet, as Morgenthau in other moods would freely admit, it was not altogether an unhappy ship either; for, if the manipulation of insecurity was part of Roosevelt's method, the provision of charm and consolation was an equally indispensable part. Probably no President was ever more skilled in the art of persuasion. He used every trick in the book, and most of them with the relish of a virtuoso. He had, as Biddle said, an intuitive grasp of people's weaknesses; and he employed this with stunning effect, not only to make them sad or scared, but to make them happy as well. As William Phillips put it, "He had a rare capacity for healing the wounded feelings which he had inadvertently caused." Roosevelt called this process "hand-holding." To it he devoted considerable energy and talent. "The maintenance of peace in his official family," Grace Tully reports, "took up hours and days of Roosevelt's time."

Hand-holding emerged as naturally from his complex personality as did the instinct to tease. His concern for people was perfectly spontaneous and genuine — and immensely disarming. After telling Morgenthau that he had been so tired he would have enjoyed seeing him cry, he added, "We both must take regular vacations . . . and never permit ourselves to get so tired again." Such messages were addressed again and again to all his associates. "When he detected signs of nerves or overwork," said Grace Tully, "he was quick to propose rest trips to Warm Springs or irregular vacations. More than once, he picked up substantial doctors' bills for members of his personal staff." Thus in January 1934 we find him urging Ickes and Wallace to go away. "He was quite insistent about it," Ickes reported. "He told me that it was beginning to worry him just to look at me and that if I didn't go away he would get mad." In May he ordered Wallace and Ickes to go to Santa Fe for a few days' rest ("This continued concern for my well-being," said Ickes, "really touched me"). In June, he ordered Hopkins on a trip abroad for his health. In December he wrote Richberg, "I am terribly sorry that you are still feeling so wretchedly and all I can do is to give you a definite order from old family Doctor Roosevelt. . . . Don't think about my 'problems' until you have a chance to come and talk them over with me." (Richberg commented, "The calming influence of such a communication as this can be imagined.")

He could not bear to fire anybody — perhaps his best noted and most conspicuous administrative failing. He shrank from disagreeable personal interviews and pronounced himself "a complete softy" in face-to-face relations. In 1936 he described as "probably much the hardest decision I have had to make since coming to Washington," not any great issue of domestic or foreign policy, but his failure to reappoint his old friends Adolph Miller and Charles Hamlin to the reconstituted Federal Reserve Board. In addition, he could hardly bear to have people resign. Harold Ickes, who resigned often, came fuming away from one conference with Roosevelt, "The reason I wanted to send in my resignation right away was because I was afraid the President would do just what he did do. He side-tracked me. It is almost impossible to come to grips with him." Richberg, another chronic resigner, once was defeated when Roosevelt said gently to him, "You aren't going to let the old man down, are you, Don?"; and was equally defeated another time when Roosevelt, who thought his grievance trivial, said satirically, "I have just had some bad news, Don. Secretary Hull is threatening to resign. He is very angry because I don't agree with him that we ought to remove the Ambassador to Kamchatka and make him third secretary to the Embassy at Svodia." ("I felt thoroughly chastened after this conversation," said Richberg, "and very grateful that the President had betrayed only friendly amusement instead of the stern displeasure which a Chief Executive with a poorer understanding of human nature or less of a sense of humor might well have shown.")

The President spent a good deal of time dealing with what he called his "prima donnas" — the people who felt neglected and kept demanding attention and sympathy. Ickes and Morgenthau, of course, were pre-eminent in the cabinet. The Secretary of the Interior, whom Roosevelt used to refer to privately as "Donald Duck," at times made himself so unbearable with his self-righteous insistence that Roosevelt for long periods avoided seeing him; at other times, the President soothed his hurt feelings with flattery. As for Morgenthau, if the Secretary of the Treasury took more punishment than most, he also received more balm. Once when Roosevelt was telling his staff how he wanted his naval prints in his office, Marvin McIntyre said, "You are right, Mr. President, you ought to have them hung to suit yourself. After all, you are in this office more than anyone else except Henry Morgenthau."

There were always minor personal squabbles requiring attention.

Once Morgenthau denounced Ickes in cabinet for some jurisdictional transgression. Roosevelt scribbled on a piece of paper, "You must not talk in such a tone of voice to another cabinet officer," showed it to Morgenthau and tore it up. But the argument continued, Roosevelt finally saying, "Don't you understand, Henry, that Harold said he knows nothing about it and that ends the matter." Morgenthau replied, "I am afraid that I am very dull, Mr. President, I do not understand." Roosevelt answered coldly, "You must be very dull." That evening Roosevelt called Morgenthau and was, as Morgenthau put it in his diary, "most sympathetic and kind." He finished by saying, "Stop worrying, Henry, go to bed and get a good night's rest." He made a similarly tranquilizing call the same evening to Ickes, deprecated Morgenthau's attitude and hoped Ickes hadn't minded; "he was plainly," Ickes noted in *his* diary, "trying to apologize for Morgenthau." By such efforts, Roosevelt kept the peace.[3]

v

There were other prima donnas. Roosevelt complained particularly about Joe Kennedy ("the trouble with Kennedy is you always have to hold his hand . . . he calls up and says he is hurt because I have not seen him") and Moley ("he usually gets upset once a month") ; about Johnson and Richberg. Still, for all the irritation and drain, Roosevelt obviously enjoyed the role of assuming people's burdens and keeping them happy. John Gunther has perceptively noted that he liked to refer to himself as "Papa." After a speech or a press conference, he would say, "How did Papa do?"; or, to administrators, "If you do get into trouble, come back to Papa." Grace Tully heard him say more than once to subordinates, "All right, send it over to me. My shoulders are broad. I can carry the load." His doctor used to protest in vain that too many people ran to him with their problems. "Instead of giving these 'leaners' the boot," McIntyre later wrote, "the President encouraged them in the habit." "Instead of being vexed by appointees returning for advice and consultation," said George Creel, "he *loved* it."

At times he certainly did love it. At other times, as was often the case with this bewildering personality, he loved the opposite. Once, discoursing on the problem of prima donnas, Roosevelt held up Tugwell as an example to the contrary. No one, the President said, had been subjected to such criticism. "Yet Rex has never whimpered or asked for sympathy or run to anyone for help. He has taken it on the chin like a man." (Ickes, to whom this lesson was addressed, listened solemnly and wrote it all down later without supposing any application to himself.) Roosevelt liked Hopkins for the same reason.

And, indeed, for all his insistence on controlling big decisions and for all his fascination with detail, Roosevelt's intervention into the administrative affairs of his subordinates was rarely petty or nagging. He did, of course, constantly pass along ideas that struck his fancy, scribbling laconic chits on White House memo pads. But, in the main, he gave his appointees wide discretion — even to the point of overlooking their disregard of presidential directives — so long as they seemed on top of their responsibilities. (As one presidential assistant, Jonathan Daniels, commented, "Half of a President's suggestions, which theoretically carry the weight of orders, can be safely forgotten by a Cabinet member.") "He would give you a job to do," testified General Philip Fleming, who did a succession of jobs for him, "and leave you free to do it by yourself. He never told you how to do it." "He never meddled in Selective Service matters," said Lewis B. Hershey. "He gave me a job to do and he let me do it without ever breathing down my neck." "If he asked me to do something which in my opinion we could not or should not do — and that happened only a few times — " said Jesse Jones, "we just did not do it." As Frances Perkins put it, "He administered by the technique of friendship, encouragement and trust. The method of not giving direct and specific orders to his subordinates released the creative energy of many men." "He gives them a *blank check,*" said Frederic A. Delano, "and even when they nearly *ruin* him, he shows no outward evidence of anger. . . . On the whole his method has developed lots of men who otherwise would never have been heard from."

One way or another, he managed people. He was prepared to pay the price in time and temper to hold the loyalty of men of drive and ideas. Everyone who worked for him went through periods of disillusion and despair, questioned his integrity, contemplated bitter letters of resignation; in the end the President talked most of them around. "Never in my experience," said Colonel House, "have I known a man who could handle men as well as Roosevelt."

Yet it would be a great error to regard Roosevelt's success with people as essentially a triumph of technique. He was unquestionably a great operator; but he did not finally succeed because he was an operator. His greatest resource lay not in charm of manner or skill at persuasion. It lay in his ability to stir idealism in people's souls. "His capacity to inspire and encourage those who had to do tough, confused, and practically impossible jobs," wrote Frances Perkins, "was beyond dispute. I, and everyone else, came away from an interview with the President feeling better." And his tendency to make himself personally felt on all levels of government, however destructive to orthodox theories of chain of command, had a wonderful effect in permeating the administration with his hopes and ideals. The President, instead of being a shrouded and remote figure at the peak of an unintelligible bureaucracy, was a leader whose personality and ethos touched and galvanized most officials of government.

Roosevelt had decided early that he wanted an inventive government rather than an orderly government. It was as if, given the need to arrive quickly at a destination, he chose, not a team of reliable work horses, but a miscellany of high-spirited and sensitive thoroughbreds. One sees him trying to ride herd over this rearing, tossing, jostling collection. His horses are overflowing with temperament, and he spends an unconscionable amount of time combing their manes, stroking their brows, and feeding them lumps of sugar. More tractable horses would not have pulled so far or run so fast. The proof of his control was the way, once the reins fell from his hand, the horses plunged wildly in all directions.[4]

VI

Yet the supervision of a government could not be altogether a personal matter. Roosevelt went as far as he could in trying to make it so. The fact remained that he was not driving a team of horses. He was attempting to run a great and multifarious country. The size and variety of the problems crowding in on him were bound to defeat him. There had to be some means beyond the personality of the President to bring coherence into the formulation of policy and coordination into its execution.

From an early point in his administration he played around with one after another person or structure hopefully designed to improve coordination among the departments and agencies. Indeed, the word coordinator had fallen into such disrepute as early as September 1933 that Louis Howe could sourly reassure Morgenthau, "Henry, when you have been in the Government service as long as I have, you will recognize that coordinators come and coordinators go, and that furthermore sometimes it is good business to place so much work on a man that he cannot handle any of it." The theoretical instrument of coordination during the first six months was a body known as the Executive Council, established on July 11, 1933, and composed of the heads of departments and agencies. Its executive secretary was Frank Walker, a Montana lawyer of exceptional evenness of temper and fairness of mind, deeply devoted to Roosevelt and always in demand as an arbiter in New Deal disputes. "Everyone trusted and liked him," Tugwell said. "He was one character in the New Deal cast without taint of self-interest, of ambition, or of vindictiveness." But what Walker possessed in sweetness he more than made up for by absence of force; and the Executive Council, though its weekly meetings superseded the Tuesday cabinet meeting, was largely ignored by the demonic administrators of the day, especially Johnson and Peek. Lacking both an agenda and aggressive leadership, it came to life only when the President attended it himself. As Johnson summed up its impact, "It left the situation about where it was before."

In November 1933, Roosevelt tried again, this time creating the National Emergency Council, a less inclusive body designed to coordinate the recovery agencies. Frank Walker was also its director. The National Emergency Council absorbed the Special Industrial Recovery Board and eventually (in October 1934) the Executive Council itself. At its first meeting, on December 19, 1933, Roosevelt explained that, when Congress was in session, he had "probably on the average of between three or four hours a day of conferences with congressional leaders" and consequently could not devote enough time to the administrative end of government. On the whole, he thought the recovery program was going along well; "it is quite remarkable to me that we have not had more overlapping and clashes"; but the time had come "when I have got to have somebody to act as sort of *alter ego* for me during the congressional session, going around and acting as my legs and ears and eyes and making certain — what might be called suggestions . . . working out these things in such a way that they will not come up to me during the session of Congress."

The National Emergency Council did at least have an agenda. But its membership — it rapidly grew from ten to thirty-three persons — was far too large for effective discussion; and its meetings consisted largely of the reading of mimeographed reports already rendered by the various agencies to the executive director. "I never saw a real question of major importance arise until the end of each of these meetings" wrote Johnson later, "when the President came in. . . . From the moment, things would begin to happen." This was certainly true. The minutes of the National Emergency Council remain, next to the press conferences, the most spectacular exhibit of Roosevelt's range and mastery in face of problems of governmental administration.

In the middle of 1934, Walker had to retire to look after his private affairs. Roosevelt, seeking to put new energy into his mechanisms of coordination, handed both of Walker's jobs on to Donald Richberg. Richberg, nervous and ambitious, was far more vigorous than Walker. At one time, according to Richberg, Roosevelt even contemplated appointing him to a new office, that of Assistant to the President. On October 29, 1934, the Executive Council and the National Emergency Council were finally consolidated, with Richberg the apparent beneficiary in terms of power. The *New York Times* headline was typical of the reaction: RICHBERG PUT OVER CABINET IN NEW EMERGENCY COUNCIL . . . NOW NO. 1 MAN. Newspaper stories spoke of Richberg as Assistant President. Roosevelt was always jealous of the presidential prerogative; and his reaction was prompt and explosive. "Get hold of Krock," he said to Steve Early, "and tell him . . . that this kind of thing is not only a lie but that it is a deception and a fraud on the public. It is merely a continuation of previous lies such as the headlines that Moley was running the government; next that Baruch was Acting President; next that Johnson was the man in power; next that Frankfurter had been put over the Cabinet and now that Richberg has been put over the Cabinet. . . . This whole story is made out of whole cloth and illustrates why the public is believing less and less the alleged news columns of the newspapers." To the cabinet, which thoroughly shared Roosevelt's dismay, the President explained that Richberg was, in Ickes's rendition, no more than "an exalted messenger boy." [5]

VII

The National Emergency Council gradually built up a formidable administrative apparatus of its own. Each state had its own NEC director, and the Council soon developed a set of divisions to service its field operations. But in its formal operations the Council was dependent on the accuracy of the reports made to it. More and more, these became public relations blurbs rather than candid accounts of problems and difficulties. Furthermore, as the NEC grew in size, it became too unwieldy for frank exchange. "In the end," Roosevelt said, "I couldn't take it any more because I found myself making stump speeches to the council instead of listening to its members."

Still, certain tangible gains were made toward coordination. The President found the weekly meetings useful in amplifying his "feel" of things in government. "The whole NEC," he once said, "was a wonderful essay in democracy. It was exactly like a New England town meeting. It gave everybody a chance to blow off. I learned many things there — many things that those who were reporting never suspected that I learned and some that they wouldn't have liked me to know anything about. They also learned a lot about each other."

In a more specific sense, the NEC enabled the President to begin to gain control of the administration's legislative program by providing for central clearance of all legislative proposals coming out of the Executive Branch. All requests for appropriations, he said, should go through the Bureau of the Budget, all requests for new legislation through the NEC. During the previous session, he explained in 1934, he had been "quite horrified — not once but half a dozen times — by reading in the paper that some department or agency was after this, that, or the other without my knowledge." "If you are going to ask for any legislative action," he continued, "it has got to come through Donald Richberg and up to me if necessary."

Roosevelt was perfectly frank about his purposes. Legislative proposals, as he explained to a later meeting of the Council, fell from his point of view into three categories: those which he could not possibly support; those which the department or agency might press for but could not be adopted as major administration bills; and the so-called *must* legislation, to which "I have to confine myself." "If I make every bill that the Government is interested in *must* legislation, it is going to complicate things. . . . Where I clear legislation with a notation that says 'no objection,' that means you are at perfect liberty to try to get the thing through, but I am not going to send a special message. It is all your trouble, not mine." Centralized clearance through the Council and the Budget, in other words, was an essential means by which the President preserved his initiative and defended his authority.

The new system was by no means an immediate success. The President, indeed, was in practice one of its main saboteurs. Thus few major bills in the 74th Congress passed through the new machinery. The President even on occasion thwarted the Budget's attempt to bring order into the allocation of funds already voted. Morgenthau describes, without too much exaggeration, an incident early in 1935: "He assured me and Harry Hopkins that he would not allot any more money until we had another meeting. I understand a couple of weeks ago he allotted Hopkins $125,000,000 secretly. Next Tugwell appeals to him directly and he gives him what he wants. The result is that everybody is angry and frothing at the mouth. Then when I draw his attention to it, instead of doing the straightforward thing and cancelling Tugwell's authorization which could not have yet reached him, he double crosses Tugwell by telling me to tell Bell [the Director of the Budget] that Tugwell cannot have one cent until the Budget passes on it. This makes a complete circle and everybody will be sore." Morgenthau added, "This is so typical of the President."

Nevertheless, the National Emergency Council established certain principles; and these principles, in time, created precedents which in a few years, as the Bureau of the Budget increased its power, were converted into practices. Though the Council itself, especially after Richberg's departure from government in 1935, withered away, it left its imprint on the Roosevelt administration in the shape of a new desire for the unification of policy.[6]

VIII

Still, the first experiments in structural coordination failed. Lacking a mechanism, or, to put it more precisely, disliking a mechanism, Roosevelt fell back on people as the means of coordination. From time to time, he would talk about the existence of an "inner Cabinet." In late 1934 he defined it to Ickes as Morgenthau, Cummings, Ickes, Miss Perkins, Wallace, Hopkins, Chester Davis, and the man who would head NRA. But even this was too cumbersome a group for his purposes. As a lone operator, Roosevelt could best find the extension of his personality — the long sought *alter ego* — in an individual. And, as a lonely man, Roosevelt could best find the intimacy of exchange he occasionally needed not in a council but in a person.

Howe, of course, had been that *alter ego* for many years. But age, ill health, and new issues outmoded him by the time Roosevelt reached the White House. The President thereafter looked endlessly for a substitute. As Eleanor Roosevelt commented, "For one reason or another, no one quite filled the void which unconsciously he was seeking to fill; and each one in turn disappeared from the scene, occasionally with a bitterness which I understood but always regretted."

Moley was the first to come and the first to go. Even after he left the government to become editor of *Today*, he continued throughout 1934 and 1935 to visit the White House and to work on speeches. Yet he began increasingly to doubt the new directions of the New Deal; and he regarded himself — and Roosevelt regarded him — less and less as a confidant on policy. "I was summoned, in such cases," Moley later wrote, "as a technician at speech construction, just as I'd be called in if I were a plumber and a pipe needed fixing." He came in time to take a perverse pride in giving forceful expression to ideas with which he disagreed.

In 1934 Tugwell began to take Moley's place as policy confidant.

Tugwell lacked Moley's skill as a middleman of ideas and as an organizer of talent. However, his brow rarely needed to be stroked, and his loyalty was invincible. By Tugwell's theory of discipline, he must follow Roosevelt whether or not he agreed; "nothing could be done at all unless we hung together under a leader . . . we had no real right to make [independent] judgments." Tugwell had, in addition, a glowing enthusiasm for the forests and the land and for America as a great estate, to be nurtured and cherished; this passion was, of course, deep in the President, and it was something he shared with few of his urbanized associates. Above all, at precisely this moment, before the horizons of possibility had really begun to close in, Roosevelt was probably drawn by the challenging, questioning bent of Tugwell's mind, forever stimulating the presidential imagination to new visions of things to be done. "There was nothing we could not discuss with him," said Tugwell in retrospect of 1933 and 1944, "and the opportunities were sufficient for the purpose."

Tugwell was perhaps the least pliant of the Roosevelt intimates. He conceived his role, not to try and find out what the President wanted, but to tell him what he ought to want — to serve as a sort of conscience, representing to Roosevelt his "more consistent self." Standing for coordination in economic policy, he tried always to use the logic of coordination as the measure of the New Deal. Looking back, Tugwell felt that he must sometimes have seemed insistent and stubborn. "He must have had many impatient hours with me. [Yet] he seldom showed any irritation." In 1935, however, the philosophy of coordination began to recede. Tugwell, moreover, had none of Moley's facility as a speech technician to keep him useful beyond his time. His new assignment as head of the Resettlement Administration occupied him more; and, with a mutually delicate appreciation of the changed situation, he and the President talked less, though their friendship remained undiminished.[7]

IX

For the present, Roosevelt himself, as the essential ganglion for reception, transmission, and realization, had to serve as the substitute for a structure of coordination. He did it with zest and energy. His instinct for the basic general issue, his flypaper mastery of detail, his capacity to carry a large variety of problems in his mind, his ability to shift with speed from one problem to another, his appetite for long hours of plain hard work, his "vast and gracious tolerance" (in a phrase of Adolf Berle's) for a whole series of forces and people, from the noble to the self-seeking and from the decent to the corrupt — all this enabled him to stay more or less ahead of crisis. Perhaps he could have done it in no other manner. "He, more than any man," wrote Hugh Johnson, "is almost utterly incapable of acting organizationally or any other way than individually." He succeeded, said Johnson, "not as a master of planning or knowledge, but as a master of dexterity."

An account of his Presidency which deals topically with the problems Roosevelt confronted (and which, in this volume, omits foreign policy) does scant justice to his skill as an executive. To visualize Roosevelt in action, one must conceive these things happening all at once, in chaos and urgency, from NRA, AAA, relief, conservation, and monetary policy to disarmament, the Good Neighbor policy, Manchuria, Ethiopia, and Hitler, an incessant series of explosions, minor and major, at the presidential desk, with the President nearly always in touch, generally in command, and never disturbed. His patience, his personal solicitude, his fantastic grasp of detail, his instinct for timing, his jocose and evasive humor, his lightheartedness, his disingenuousness, his reserve, his serenity, his occasional and formidable severity, his sense of his office, his sense of history — these were the means by which he ordered and dominated the crises of his administration. One understands why most who worked for him had to burst out from time to time against him. But one understands too why most of them submerged indignation in a larger sense of admiration. In the end, one doubts whether the Presidency can ever be effectively bureaucratized. Its essence is an independence, initiative, and creativity which requires and relies on its own lines of communication to the world outside. Vigorous government under the American system would seem almost impossible without something like the Rooseveltian sleight-of-hand at the center.

Harold Smith, who became the Director of the Budget in 1939

and shared his Bureau's prejudices in favor of order and symmetry in government, once reflected on Roosevelt's concept of administration. Nothing had seemed more maddening at the time, but in retrospect Smith wondered whether Roosevelt's apparently erratic methods did not produce exceptional results. "I think I'd say," Smith concluded, "that Roosevelt must have been one of the greatest geniuses as an administrator that ever lived. What we couldn't appreciate at the time was the fact that he was a real *artist* in government." [8]

34. The Anatomy of Leadership

LEADING THE Executive Branch of government was only part of the job. The President had also to lead the Congress; beyond this, he had to lead the electorate. If leadership in the Executive Branch meant management, leadership in the other areas meant politics. For Roosevelt, of course, this was a natural medium. He had been a politician all his life; it was far more his profession than the law. Sometimes he listened silently to discussions of *what* should be done; but when the conversation shifted to *how* it should be done, he would say, "Now that's a question of politics and as to that I claim to speak with some authority." Politics could mean the high politics of education and persuasion; or it could mean the low politics of pressure, manipulation, and intrigue. Roosevelt played both with equal skill.[1]

II

Both were involved in his relations with Congress. High politics was the more important: despite myths to the contrary, the most powerful incentive to members of Congress to support his legislative program came not from pap or pressure but from the appeal of the measures themselves. Roosevelt's main formal reliance in making this appeal was, of course, on his messages. "He has discussed in his messages and addresses," Charles A. Beard once said, "more fundamental problems of American life and society than all the other Presidents combined." Beyond this, Roosevelt worked largely through the regular party leadership — Robinson, Harrison, Byrnes, and Barkley in the Senate, Rainey, Byrns, Bankhead, Rayburn, and

Doughton in the House. While these men (except for Barkley and Rayburn) had far less innate sympathy with the New Deal than the Senate and House progressives, they had greater personal loyalty to the President, a better sense of party discipline, and a wider influence in their own chambers. Where some progressives made difficulties about proposals whose general purport they favored, Robinson often carried the fight for proposals he personally disliked. The 1934 election strengthened the presidential influence on the Hill by bringing into Congress a new breed of New Deal Democrats — men like Schwellenbach of Washington, Minton of Indiana, Guffey of Pennsylvania, Truman of Missouri in the Senate and the more responsible members of the Maury Maverick group in the House — who combined the party regularity of the older Democrats with the liberal fervor of the older progressives.

During sessions of Congress, Roosevelt held frequent conferences with the party leaders. He also spent long hours, in his office and over the telephone, persuading, reassuring, mollifying, and disciplining individual senators and congressmen. He had to be tough, or he would have no control; but he could not afford to be vengeful, or he would turn occasional dissenters into permanent enemies. Senator Tom Connally of Texas, an occasional opponent of the New Deal, reports, "He glossed over my opposition to the NRA in 1933 as a matter of honest personal differences. He was not hard to deal with, for he made it a point to be frank about anything we discussed." (Candor too could be a Rooseveltian weapon.) He was a master at the art of providing congressional gratification — at the easy first name, the cordial handshake, the radiant smile, the intimate joke, the air of accessibility and concern, the quasi-confidential interview, the photograph at the White House desk, the headline in the home-town newspaper. His own estimate of three to four hours a day spent on congressional relations during the session was probably not too great an exaggeration.

The contemporary cliché about "rubberstamp" Congresses should not conceal the fact that the national legislature at this time contained strong, independent-minded, and intelligent men and on crucial occasions itself assumed the legislative initiative. Far from being a tame and servile body, it played a vital and consistently underestimated role in shaping the New Deal. A number of important measures — the federal deposit insurance system, the National Labor Relations Act, the public housing legislation — were entirely of congressional origination. At other times, congressional initiative forced the administration into action, as when Black's thirty-hour bill precipitated NRA, or when Elmer Thomas gave the administration an unsought flexibility in its monetary powers, or when the constant pressure of La Follette, Costigan, and Wagner helped increase appropriations for relief and public works. In these early years, Congress was as often to the left of Roosevelt as to the right.

Sometimes, as in the case of the bonus, congressional initiative went too far. Then Roosevelt had in his veto power a constitutional response. He used the veto purposefully, as Richard Neustadt has suggested, to enforce respect for the President's policies and prerogatives. Sometimes he cast about for bills to veto; once, as he sent back a packet of proposed statutes to the Bureau of the Budget, he said, "The Budget is getting too soft; tell them to stiffen up." "If the decision is close," he told the National Emergency Council, "I want to veto." No President ever vetoed such a variety of measures. Though Cleveland maintained a slim numerical lead over Roosevelt, most of Cleveland's vetoes were of private pension laws. It was calculated at the end of Roosevelt's second term that Cleveland and Roosevelt between them were responsible for two-thirds of the vetoes since Washington first employed the power in 1792. Of the 505 bills vetoed in Roosevelt's first eight years, only seven were repassed by Congress over his veto.

Because Congress was made up of proud men who had been longer in Washington than any President and were jealous of their prerogatives, the President had to avoid an appearance of dictation, even when members of Congress pleaded for it (as Samuel B. Pettengill, for example, did in 1934: "Our people are so darn tired of the depression and so anxious to get out of it that they would welcome strong party discipline in the House which we certainly do not have now.") Thus we find Roosevelt in 1936, at the request of Cordell Hull, urging Robert Doughton, the powerful chairman of the House Ways and Means Committee, to refuse hearings of certain tariff proposals. "If the world were to know that I was writing you about hearings on tariff bills," Roosevelt said, "they would say that I was once more cracking the whip of a dictator over the House of Representatives.

I know that neither you nor Jere Cooper will have that feeling if I send you this delightful memorandum from Cordell Hull. It speaks for itself and I think he is wholly right." He concluded by asking Doughton to show the note to Cooper and destroy it. Someone on the White House staff objected even to this delicate approach: "I think it is *very* unwise to do this — You know he will *not* destroy it — and you know how congressmen talk! Can't you telephone or have Mac *see* him." Roosevelt, acceding, did not send the note to Doughton.

Sometimes members of Congress could not be persuaded: they had to be manipulated or coerced. In the application of low politics to the Hill, the President took less of a personal role. Here he worked through White House emissaries, who used a variety of techniques. Patronage per se has always been a somewhat over-rated item in the presidential management of Congress. Nonetheless, on occasion it might become necessary to trade a Rex Tugwell for a murderer, and marginal votes were always to be won or lost by dangling or canceling postmasterships or dams. But the harder skill was perhaps the reverse — denying loyal followers what had to be denied and still keeping them happy. Here, occasionally, it was necessary for the President to intervene and supply healing poultices.

Once Joe Robinson was backing an unsuitable candidate for the Indian Commissionership. To settle the matter, Roosevelt asked Robinson and Ickes — who had his own more qualified candidate — over to the White House for tea. Then the President set Robinson talking about his recent defense of the administration against Huey Long, spurring him on by exclamations of wonder and admiration. As the apparently aimless talk continued, Ickes began to doubt whether Roosevelt would ever reach the point; "I felt that, for some reason, the President had decided to put off the operation." Finally, as dinner was announced and the two men rose to leave, Roosevelt said, "By the way, Joe, I would like to talk with you about the Indian Commissionership. You have a man from Arkansas. . . . I have had a lot of protests about him from women's organizations, Indian rights associations and reformers generally. Now, I don't suppose that you and I want to go up against that kind of opposition." Caught off guard, Robinson mumbled a reply. "Well, I thought that you would feel that way about it," the President said suavely. "I have been under pressure to name John Collier. And Harold Ickes, here, does not want Meritt. He does not believe that he can work with him. He wants Collier. Since he is to be responsible, I suppose that the thing to do is to let him have the man he wants."

Roosevelt enjoyed his virtuosity at such things. He once boasted to Morgenthau of his skill in indicating to a senatorial delegation that he was prepared to accept a bill on silver to which the administration was formally opposed: "I was good. I saw Barkley and the others, and with my right arm I said, 'Not one inch will I give in, not an inch!' But with my left hand I said, 'Boys, come and get it.'" Charles Taussig, waiting in the presidential anteroom, caught a glimpse of the President after he had succeeded in calming down an angry congressional delegation. Roosevelt, not aware that he was observed, leaned back, slowly picked out a cigarette, stuck it in his holder, lit a match, and took a long puff. "A smile of complete satisfaction spread over his face." [2]

III

One wonders whether the smile of satisfaction was really complete. Though Roosevelt played both high and low politics with equal skill, he really did not play them with equal relish. He greatly enjoyed low politics as a game — but only up to a point. Certainly he loved to outwit the professionals at their own specialty ("I am a little nervous with regard to the political situation," as Key Pittman wrote him admiringly in 1933. "Of course, you have no nerves"). But, while he often played at being Machiavelli, he was not really Machiavellian. Endicott Peabody had done his work too well. The rather simplehearted idealism which lay so near the core of Roosevelt's personality could not indefinitely support the experiments in smart-aleckness and trickiness. "When he did something cheap," Tom Corcoran once said, "he was basically ashamed of himself. He would never admit it — but he would show it instead in his attitude toward something else." "While he played politics with skill and gusto," wrote Adolf Berle, "the President with one lobe of his brain regarded it as unpleasant, corrosive business."

What he really cared about was high politics — not politics as intrigue, but politics as education. Nothing government could do mattered much, he deeply believed, unless it was firmly grasped by the public mind. He once said, "I want to be a *preaching President* — like my cousin." "The whole fate of what the Government is trying to do," he told the National Emergency Council, " . . . depends, regardless of the election, on an understanding of the program by the mass of the people." And future possibilities of leadership similarly depended on what the people thought and wanted — or could be induced to think and want. As Roosevelt said to Upton Sinclair, "I cannot go any faster than the people will let me." Very little pleased Roosevelt more about the New Deal than its accomplishment in raising the level of concern about public policy. "I believe our biggest success," Roosevelt wrote H. G. Wells in 1935, "is making people think during these past two years. They may not think straight but they are thinking in the right direction." (Roosevelt added, "And your direction and mine are not so far apart; at least we both seek peaceable conveyances in our travels.") The Presidency he conceived as "the most important clearing house for exchange of information and ideas, of facts and ideals, affecting the general welfare." "Politics, after all," he once said, "is only an instrument through which to achieve government."

If politics was essentially an educational process, deeds, of course, were the most important teacher. The New Deal itself became a great schoolhouse, compelling Americans to a greater knowledge of their country and its problems. Thus Roosevelt told Anne O'Hare McCormick that NRA was valuable above all as an educational agency, forcing those within and without the codes to do some hard thinking on the central problems of the economy. Laws which remade people's lives through such new things as social security, railroad pensions, home mortgage refinancing, rural electrification, works relief, farm ownership, and the like brought with them — in the period before they became part of the landscape — a quickening of popular interest in public affairs.

Roosevelt was alert to cultivate the interest his administration aroused. Thus he seized on the radio as a revolutionary new medium of person-to-person communication. "Time after time, in meeting legislative opposition in my own state," Roosevelt wrote before he entered the Presidency, "I have taken an issue directly to the voters by radio, and invariably I have met a most heartening response. Amid many developments of civilization which lead away from direct government by the people, the radio is one which tends on the other hand to restore direct contact between the masses and their chosen leaders." Of the various forms of radio address, the "fireside chat" proved most effective. The "fireside" phrase (actually invented by Harry C. Butcher, manager of the Columbia Broadcasting System office in Washington) conveyed Roosevelt's conception of himself as a man at ease in his own house talking frankly and intimately to neighbors as they sat in their living rooms. He gave eight such talks in his first term, of which six came in 1933 and 1934.[8]

IV

The preparation of a Roosevelt speech was a complex process. First the President himself mused about the general tone, topic and purpose of the speech. If he had time, he dictated a number of sample passages ("to give something for the boys to get their teeth into"); but he rarely wove them into a consecutive draft ("well — something along those lines — you boys can fix it up"). Then he would turn over to his chief writer (generally Moley in this period) an assortment of ideas and "scraps," along with any relevant suggestions in a speech-material file kept by Miss LeHand. The writer would then go away and put together a connected text, consulting the people whose views he believed the President would want to know. In due course, the draft would be ready for submission to the President. Then followed an intensive and sometimes exasperating period of writing and rewriting. The President would redictate the speech to Grace Tully in order to insert his own jokes, remove complexities of construction and language and get the text into his own cadences; the writers would argue for the restoration of paragraphs which Roosevelt wanted to drop and would themselves quietly drop presidential inspirations to which they objected; everyone would struggle for compression and vividness and seem to achieve prolixity and tedium. At some moment

in the composition of every speech, as they sat around the big
table in the Cabinet Room, strewn with sheets of paper, books,
clippings, cigarette stubs, sandwiches, and bottles of ginger ale and
beer, the text appeared hopeless beyond all possibility of redemp-
tion. But in time, with the President himself beginning to concentrate on the job, something would begin to emerge. Though he
rarely originated much of the language, Roosevelt by the end had
participated as intimately as anyone in the creative process. His
revisions and interpolations generally succeeded in giving his
speeches the homely directness and the unmistakable personal imprint which survived any number of changes in his speech-writing
teams. "I was never present when a big speech was born," wrote
Charlie Michelson, "that the President did not take the political
viands offered and cook them in his individual way. . . .Roosevelt
is a better phrase maker than anybody he ever had around him."

Finally, the time came for delivery. These moments always
found him perfectly calm and businesslike. If it was a fireside
chat, the President was wheeled into the Diplomatic Reception
Room on the ground floor of the White House. He sat at a desk,
waved genially at the technicians and guests, opened the black-
leather looseleaf notebook containing his speech, borrowed a
watch from the announcer, and generally sent someone upstairs for
a removable bridge which he disliked wearing but which cut down
on the sibilances in his voice. Once on the air with his invariable
"My friends," he spoke in an even, relaxed way, averaging about
one hundred words a minute and always finishing within his time.
When it was over, he would ask with some interest how it had all
gone; then, in a few moments would go off cheerfully to bed.[4]

v

His other great instrument of public education was the press.
Roosevelt approached newspapers with initial advantages. He
liked reporters and, in the main, respected the job they had to do.
He learned their first names, read their stories, solicited their
ideas, kidded them about their hangovers, made news for them,
invited them to Sunday evening supper at the White House, and
gave them a status in the presidential household. His particular

triumph was in the press conference. This was, he once said, "a special art all by itself," and while at times he irritated reporters by acting as if his editorship of the *Harvard Crimson* had disclosed to him all the secrets of the profession, no one ran a conference with more charm and skill.

If Theodore Roosevelt was the first President to see the importance of the newspapers as a means of reaching the people, Wilson was the first to hold regular press conferences in the modern sense. With the Harding administration the custom fell into decay, reaching its nadir in the last dismal days under Hoover, when conferences, already reduced to impotence by Hoover's insistence on written questions, were practically abandoned. Roosevelt, remembering the family conferences he had held with newspapermen in Albany, determined to meet the press twice a week, on Tuesdays and Fridays, and to a surprising degree succeeded. In his first term, he held 337 press conferences; in his second, 374.

The newspapermen jammed into his office, often over a hundred of them, crowding into the oval room all the way up to the President's desk. There he sat, his cigarette fixed in his holder, his eye friendly but vigilant, his manner jovial but ever so slightly on guard, his whole bearing that of a man awaiting with relish an impending battle of wits. Then the questions began to fly. The President answered some plainly and soberly, used others as pretexts for a display of his grasp of administrative or topographical detail, turned away others with jokes or diplomatic avowals of ignorance, put others off the record, on occasion reproached or scolded reporters for asking others. John Dos Passos noted that the President responded "simply and unhurriedly as if he were sitting at a table talking to an old friend"; "his voice is fatherly-friendly, without strain, like the voice of the principal of a first-rate boy's school." As the conference proceeded, the President ran through a variety of expressions and gestures — throwing back his head, puffing out his cheeks, rubbing his nose, pursing his lips, projecting successively good humor, astonishment, perplexity, concern, intelligent awareness, stern rectitude. Then, with "Thank you, Mr. President," the conferences broke up, and reporters scrambled for the phones in the White House press room.

A special Roosevelt innovation was the budget press conference.

Where previous Presidents, like Hoover, had explained their budgets in mimeographed handouts prepared in the Bureau of the Budget, Roosevelt held a seminar for the press. "We go over the Budget message that is to go up to Congress the following day," as Roosevelt described it, "and take it apart. Anybody can ask any question he wants about it." The result, in addition to confirming the respectful impression of Roosevelt's grip on the details of government, assured a sympathetic presentation of the budget in the newspapers.

For Roosevelt, the press conference was a rare opportunity to discover how policies could be most effectively expounded as well as to set the tone for their newspaper interpretation. More than that, the conference enabled him to some degree to guide the whole movement of public discussion, spotlighting some issues, minimizing others. And it allowed him to say things he might not wish to say in a more formal setting. Nor was the communication by any means one-way: the character and intensity of the newspapermen's questions let him know what the public was asking and, on occasion, even forced new issues on his attention.

By according the press the privilege of regular interrogation, Roosevelt established the presidential press conference in a quasi-constitutional status as the American equivalent of the parliamentary question period — a status which future Presidents could downgrade to their peril. And the presidential example produced an open-door policy throughout the administration, with cabinet members and agency heads generally holding regular conferences of their own. One result was an enormous increase in the volume of news out of Washington. By 1934, the United Press wires were carrying three times as much Washington news as in 1930, and one quarter of all Associated Press news was originating in Washington. Another result was to give newspapermen, long used to being dismissed as snoopers, a sense of having a stake in the New Deal. Many, indeed, went to work for the government. As Raymond Clapper wrote in 1934, most newspapermen felt that "the administration from President Roosevelt down has little to conceal and is willing to do business with the doors open."

Apart from the conference, Roosevelt used newspapers with skill as a sounding board for public reactions. He became particularly adept at the clandestine manipulation of the press — the release of trial balloons, the planting of rumor in order to watch the popular response. Such feed-back devices played an important part in the system by which he informed himself about the national mood. And, in addition, he set forth his general philosophy from time to time in exclusive interviews with people like George Creel of *Collier's* or Anne O'Hare McCormick of the *New York Times.*

For their part, newspapermen watched Roosevelt with a mixture of delight, mistrust, and professional admiration; but the element of mistrust was not too important; they were seeking to use him, as he was seeking to use them; and success on either side was one of the risks of the game. The general impact of the Roosevelt approach was of free communication, even when the actuality was — as it occasionally was — evasion. Newspapermen had never seen anything like this accessibility, dexterity, and intermittent candor on the part of a President. Theodore G. Joslin, Hoover's press secretary, ascribing to "a former President" the remark that no Chief Executive could satisfy the press until he was dead and buried, added, "Roosevelt has come nearer than any of them to meeting the expectations" of the press corps. One working newspaperman gave even more adoring testimony. "Never have I encountered a subject of this type who lays it on the line as Mr. Roosevelt does," wrote Westbrook Pegler in 1934. ". . . I am afraid I couldn't be trusted around Mr. Roosevelt. For the first time in my life in this business I might find myself squabbling for a chance to carry the champion's water bucket." [5]

VI

On the whole, Roosevelt returned the affection of the working press. But he had occasional doubts about the final product. When a paper ran a photograph of Roosevelt with a caption describing a beauty queen, the President passed it on to Steve Early with the penciled comment: "Accuracy of the American press." And, like most men in public life, Roosevelt found newspaper criticism less desirable in practice than it had seemed in theory. Some critics stung him to a violent (though, on the whole, private) reaction. On Frank Kent:

This Kent man not only has no regard for truth but uses the kind of poison pen and poison tongue which has alienated practically all of his friends.

On Arthur Krock (in a letter to Adolph Ochs, the publisher of the *New York Times* and Krock's boss):

This is not the first occasion on which Mr. Krock has rendered a real disservice . . . I am making this the first — literally the first — exception to my general rule of not writing to any Editor of any paper in regard to stories which their people send out from Washington.

Again on Krock, four years later:

Wasn't Krock terrible? However, I got passed [*sic*] the stage of writing him, correcting his articles about five years ago. It got to the point where I would have had to write him once a week!

On Walter Lippmann:

He writes so lucidly and charmingly that we are apt to overlook the fact that he is, to say the least, not always consistent. I wish sometime that he could come more into contact with the little fellow all over the country and see less of the big rich brother!

On the editorial staff of the *New York Times:*

About fifteen years ago I attended one of the famous luncheons in the French mahogany carved sanctum of the New York *Times.* In that rarefied atmosphere of self-anointed scholars, I had the feeling of an uneducated worm under the microscope.

He did not like the press to get away with things. Thus friends in the cabinet told Drew Pearson that Roosevelt personally urged Douglas MacArthur to file a libel suit against Pearson and Robert S. Allen in order to put the "Washington Merry-Go-Round" column out of business. (MacArthur did so and eventually settled out of court, agreeing to pay the defendant's costs; Pearson and Allen made no retraction.) At a famous Gridiron dinner, Roosevelt repaid one of his most biting critics, H. L. Mencken, by engaging in what appeared to be a mad diatribe against the American press — as shot through with "stupidity, cowardice and philistinism," staffed by men "who do not know what a symphony is or a streptococcus . . . who could not pass the entrance examination for Harvard and Tuskegee, or even Yale" — until the audience gradually and joyously perceived that he was quoting Mencken's own essay on "Journalism in America." ("I'll get the son of a bitch," Mencken, his sense of humor suddenly failing, said furiously to Governor Ritchie, who was sitting next to him. "I'll dig the skeletons out of his closet.")

Believing in the inherent virtue of working newspapermen, Roosevelt explained the increasing hostility of the newspapers (which, by 1935, were 60 per cent against the New Deal) as a result of the prejudices of the publishers. "It is not the man at the desk in most cases," he would say. "It is not the reporter. It goes back to the owner of the paper. . . . You know perfectly well that special bureau chiefs down here write what the owner of the newspaper tells them to write, and they leave out half the truth." As owners became richer, Roosevelt felt, they associated less and less with average people, they thrilled "over their membership in social circles"; "soon the check book and the securities market supplant the old patriotism and the old desire to purvey straight news." Roosevelt brooded darkly over what he called the "fat-cat newspapers": "I think they have been more responsible for the inciting of fear in the community than any other factors." On his old friend Hearst:

> I sometimes think that Hearst has done more harm to the cause of Democracy and civilization in America than any three other contemporaries put together.

On Henry R. Luce:

> Beginning with the first number of *Time*, I discovered that one secret of their financial success is a deliberate policy of either exaggeration or distortion. Pay no attention to them — I don't.

On the Chicago *Tribune* (Ickes speaking):

> He agreed with me that it was the rottenest newspaper in the whole United States.

Nothing exasperated him more than charges that the New Deal was contemplating restrictions on the press. "Verily, the freedom of the press is in jeopardy, not from the Government, but from certain types of newspaper owners." When Ickes denounced the pattern of press ownership in his *Freedom of the Press Today,* Roosevelt scribbled in his copy, "This is a really worthwhile book."

There is no evidence to sustain the charge occasionally voiced at the time that the New Deal planned to crack down on the newspapers. No President, however, ever offered more advice about how stories should be written and newspapers run; and few grew more indignant over the alleged obliquity of the press. "Forget it," William Allen White once said to him. "That is the way they make their money and that is the way they want to run their paper. It cannot hurt you, and it gives them some comfort." Roosevelt should have paid more attention to such advice. Still, no President in history has ever accepted criticism with the philosophic calm recommended by those not in the line of fire, and Roosevelt was taking more of a pounding from the press than any President had had to take since Andrew Jackson.

In the main, Roosevelt was persuaded to keep his growing resentment out of public discussion. A document exists at Hyde Park dated in June 1935: "I, Franklin D. Roosevelt, party of the first part, do solemnly agree to submit, in ample time for full discussion to Marguerite LeHand and Felix Frankfurter, parties of the second part, any and all proposed attacks direct or indirect, upon the press"; scribbled below is the derisive rejection: "Nerts — Franklin D. Roosevelt." And, while he had pretty well lost the editorial pages by 1936 and suffered an undue amount of distortion and misrepresentation in the news columns, he succeeded nonetheless in using the press much more than it succeeded in abusing him. Few papers dared deny space to the President of the United States. By the brilliant but simple trick of making news and *being* news, Roosevelt outwitted the general hostility of the publishers and converted the press into one of the most effective channels of his public leadership.[6]

VII

Through his handling of government and his handling of Congress, through his speeches and his press conference, through his style and manner as a public figure, Roosevelt projected what a more public-relations-conscious age would call his image upon the country. In 1933, it was an image of fatherly purpose which reassured and unified a panicky nation. Thereafter it became an image increasingly divisive in its effects. Some Americans grew to hate the public *persona* of Roosevelt with a ferocious and unappeasable hatred. Others — a far larger number — began to balance that hate with a passionate and equally uncritical adoration.

The hatred of Roosevelt began to be noticeable by 1934 and acute by 1935. The sentiment of Roosevelt-hatred was something different from honest opposition, however strong and deep. It was an emotion of irrational violence, directed against Roosevelt's personality rather than his program, incoherent in its argument, scandalous in its illustrations, sometimes scatological in its imagery. It had a variety of expressions. Nearly all its manifestations shared, however, not just a common psychopathological impulse but a common social source.

That source was the American upper class. "A consuming personal hatred" of the President, as Marquis W. Childs wrote in the spring of 1936, was beginning to permeate the whole upper stratum. "Regardless of party and regardless of region, today, with few exceptions," said *Time* in April, "members of the so-called Upper Class frankly hate Franklin Roosevelt." The family of J. P. Morgan used to warn visitors against mentioning Roosevelt's name in the august presence lest fury raise his blood pressure to the danger point. Indeed, the name of any Roosevelt was dangerously inflammatory. When someone spoke of Theodore, the old man once cried with heartfelt passion, "God damn all Roosevelts!" And Morgan's reaction was comparatively restrained. Through the channels of the rich — the clubs, the banks, the brokerage offices, the Park Avenue salons, the country club locker rooms, the South Carolina shoots, the Florida cabanas — there rushed a swelling flood of stories and broadsides, many unprintable, depicting Roosevelt as a liar, a thief, a madman given to great bursts of maniacal laughter, an alcoholic, a syphilitic, a Bolshevik. There was the humorous business card: "If you don't give me an order, I'll vote for That Man again!" There was the gay doggerel, Franklin and Eleanor in duet:

> You kiss the negroes
> I'll kiss the Jews,
> We'll stay in the White House,
> As long as we choose.

Or a more ambitious attempt:

> When the organizers needed dough
> I closed up the plants for the CIO
> I ruined jobs and I ruined health
> And I put the screws on the rich man's wealth.
> And some who couldn't stand the gaff
> Would call on me and how I'd laff.
> When they got too strong on certain things
> I'd pack and head for old Warm Springs.
> I ruined their country, their homes and then
> I placed the blame on the NINE OLD MEN.

Occasionally the stories encountered resistance. A dining car steward once attempted to tell Herbert Hoover a Roosevelt joke. Hoover said feelingly, "I don't like stories about Presidents." But much of the time they were heard and repeated with relish. Reasonable people argued in vain that most Roosevelt haters were far better off after March 4, 1933, than before; that, far from destroying capitalism, Roosevelt had probably saved it. Those possessed by the obsession saw the truth too clearly and fanatically to be deterred by their own experience or that of society. One self-styled Roosevelt hater wrote in *Harper's* that any future historian surprised at the tone of his piece would no doubt be equally "astonished because General Sherman was not popular in Georgia and because Mussolini has not gone over big in Addis Ababa. He certainly will never understand why Germany has never taken to the Treaty of Versailles, or why Jews feel antipathy toward their Führer." The tie which bound Roosevelt haters together, this writer frankly added, was the consciousness "that as a social and economic class we, who have lived or tried to live in any part on money saved, are being liquidated."

This was the basis of the mania. It was a disease of the *rentier* class. Depression and the New Deal had knocked the pinnings from under them; accustomed to security, they were adrift; accustomed to power, they were frightened as new forces boiled up from the lower depths. Everything they stood for seemed under mortal attack — and, worst of all, the man leading the barbaric onslaught was one of their own. They consequently saw him as a failure at law and business and society, seeking compensation in the applause of the masses, a traitor to his class, hiding his apostasy under a Boy Scout's grin and a hypocrite's talk about moral principles. Peter Arno summed it up in his famous *New Yorker* cartoon where one group of beleaguered aristocrats exhorted another through the windows of a club: "Come along. We're going to the Trans-Lux to hiss Roosevelt." (When Early showed this to Roosevelt, he scribbled on it the single word: "Grand.") [7]

VIII

Perhaps no incident contributed more to this indignation than the government's attempt to prosecute Andrew Mellon for income tax evasion. Mellon was, after all, one of America's great businessmen, "the greatest Secretary of the Treasury since Alexander Hamilton," one of the revered symbols of the lamented New Era. Patiently Robert H. Jackson, the government counsel, tried to unravel the intricate family transactions by which, he asserted, the Mellons had registered fictitious gifts and losses and thereby succeeded in dodging their obligations to the government. Dramatically he produced a memorandum to Mellon as Secretary of the Treasury from his Commissioner of Internal Revenue outlining a dozen ways of tax avoidance; Mellon on the stand had to claim that it was only coincidence that he had subsequently employed a Treasury tax expert and five of the recommended methods to reduce his tax liability. To the New Dealers the case was a matter of basic principle. As Morgenthau told Jackson, "I consider that Mr. Mellon is not on trial but democracy and the privileged rich and I want to see who will win."

To the Roosevelt haters, it was a matter of basic principle, too, and of vile persecution, with profound social implications. Mellon's lawyer actually took a *New York Times* reporter to task, not because his stories contained factual errors, but because they provided "ammunition for the radicals." When a federal grand jury rejected the government's case, the conservatives rejoiced. When, after Mellon applied for a refund, the Bureau of Internal Revenue reopened the case before the Board of Tax Appeals, it seemed further evidence of Roosevelt's personal vindictiveness. "If I consulted my personal comfort," Homer Cummings said, "I would be disposed to drop the matter — but I do not see how I can do this unless the whole attempt to stop 'wash sale' devices is to be given up. . . . I haven't the disposition to get after the little fellows and treat the big fellows on a different basis." Eventually the Board found for Mellon on some counts, for the government on others. As *Fortune* summed it up, "The plain fact of the matter was that Mr. Mellon had made out his tax return in one economic era and was being prosecuted for it in another." But the Roosevelt haters refused to accept the new age. Hatred was supplying a retreat for the baffled rich, where they found in anti-Roosevelt fantasies a means of renewing their sense of potency.

The hatred of Roosevelt even overcame the old school tie. Outraged Grotonians wrote in to the Rector, harshly denouncing the only Groton alumnus ever to become President of the United States. Endicott Peabody had himself voted for Hoover in 1932. Now he defended Roosevelt and the New Deal. To those who questioned Roosevelt's sincerity, he gave a headmaster's endorsement: "He was at Groton for four years, and so far as I can remember, there was no suspicion of untruthfulness or insincerity during his entire course." To those who said he was violating the Constitution, Peabody observed that many of those now professing such deep respect for the Constitution had themselves broken the Eighteenth Amendment; "the opinions of such men in regard to the Constitution seem to me negligible." To those who inveighed against New Deal policies, Peabody said, "At the time Franklin Roosevelt became President, things were in the worst kind of doldrums owing to the inefficiency of Mr. Hoover as President. Change of a drastic nature was called for, and Franklin answered the call. Some of his policies have been mistaken. He prophesied

that they would be. . . . Many have in my judgment contributed
to the benefit of the people at large and have saved this country
from the serious attacks made upon it by extreme radicals." To
Roosevelt himself, whose portrait now stood on the mantel of his
study, Peabody wrote, "It is a great thing for our country to have
before it the leadership of a man who cares primarily for spiritual
things."

All the Rector's passion was unavailing: this was the only thing
he could not persuade his old boys to accept. At a dinner tendered
him by Groton men at the Union Club in New York, an occasion
interspersed with the laughter and applause of a happy family
party, Peabody, with a sudden change of tone, said that something
had been troubling him lately. "In national crises like the present
one," he said, "we get pretty excited and perhaps we give vent to
expressions that later on we are sorry for. I believe Franklin
Roosevelt to be a gallant and courageous gentleman. I am happy
to count him as my friend."

Among the graduates of Franklin Roosevelt's old school there
was bleak silence.[8]

IX

The Rector saw more deeply than his boys. If one per cent of
Americans regarded Roosevelt with unrelenting hatred, a far larger
proportion regarded him with keen and grateful affection. Never
had any President been so vivid a presence in American homes and
hearts. The White House mail provided one test. Up to March
1933, one man had handled the entire presidential mail — even
during the First World War, even during the anxious days of 1931
and 1932. But within a week after Roosevelt's inauguration, the
mail clerk, with nearly half a million unopened letters stacked in
his office, rapidly and permanently enlarged his staff. As things
settled down, Roosevelt averaged about ten times as much daily
mail as Hoover.

People wrote him because they saw him as a friend, deeply and
personally responsive to their troubles. They cut his picture out
of the paper, framed it in gilt cardboard and put it on their tables.
When he spoke, they clustered around the radio, nodding in agree-

ment and relief. Martha Gellhorn, writing from North Carolina in 1934, found the President's portrait in every house; he was "at once God and their intimate friend; he knows them all by name, knows their little town and mill, their little lives and problems. . . . He is there, and will not let them down." Lorena Hickok reported from New Orleans: "People down here all seem to think they know the President personally! . . . They feel he is talking to each one of them." They told her in Los Angeles: "He makes us all feel that he is talking directly to us as individuals." "I have heard him spoken of with an almost fanatical fervor," wrote Walter Davenport of *Collier's*. ". . . I have been where unemployed men have knocked down a possible employer who had sneered, 'Go ask your friend Roosevelt for a job.'" "More than any man who has been President within the memory of any of us now living," said Sherwood Anderson, "he has made us feel close to him."

Some, including a few who supported his policies, found the simplicities of the fireside chat a bit patronizing, even false. "There is a man leaning across his desk," John Dos Passos observed of the radio voice, "speaking clearly and cordially to youandme, explaining how he's sitting at his desk there in Washington, leaning towards youandme across his desk, speaking clearly and cordially so that youandme shall completely understand that he sits at his desk there in Washington with his fingers on all the switchboards of the federal government." But this was a sophisticated reaction. Most people thought the communication spontaneous and authentic. He came through to people because they felt — correctly — that he liked them and cared about them: one form of sentimentality reached out to another. Frances Perkins, watching him deliver a fireside chat, noted how unconscious he was of those around him at the White House as he concentrated on visualizing the plain folk listening at the other end. As he talked, his head would go up and down and his hands move in simple, natural gestures. "His face would smile and light up as though he were actually sitting on the front porch or in the parlor with them. People felt this, and it bound them to him in affection." They saw him primarily in personal terms, not only as strong and effective, but as warm and understanding, carrying an authority to which they were glad to submit and a humanity in which they felt total trust. And they saw him in addition as a gay and confident champion of their cause, a man who loved a fight and feared no one. As Westbrook Pegler remarked with surprise, Roosevelt had shown himself "a tremendously tough rough-and-tumble fighter, who will use any hitch that comes to mind, and expects to be used the same way." F.D.R. cared for the people, battled for them, and exulted in the battle.

It was the image of human warmth in a setting of dramatic national action which made people love him, not any special necromancy as a politician. Can the political art in any case be practiced apart from objectives? As a politician per se, Roosevelt has been overrated. While he worked hard and handled political problems with general skill and efficiency, he showed no evidence of supernatural talent. Any Democrat could have been elected President in 1932; given the New Deal, any Democrat stood a chance of election in 1936. In a later period, when the going got harder, Roosevelt would commit egregious political errors. It was not any technical wizardry as a politician but rather his brilliant dramatization of politics as the medium for education and leadership which accounted for his success. Beyond the backdrop of the depression and the deeds of the New Deal, Roosevelt gained his popular strength from that union of personality and public idealism which he joined so irresistibly to create so profoundly compelling a national image.[9]

35. Behind the Mask

But the public image was one thing. The question remained: what was he really like underneath? Nothing more preoccupied and frustrated those around him than the search for an answer. If on the eve of the Presidency Franklin Roosevelt had seemed a baffling mixture of Eagle Scout optimism and hard-bitten resolve, two years in the White House only gave every facet of the contradictory character a higher polish and deeper and more inscrutable gleam.

II

Physically he changed little. His health was excellent, save for his continued susceptibility to the common cold and his chronic sinus trouble (for which he received almost daily treatment from the White House physician, Dr. Ross McIntire). He had pretty much abandoned his old effort to restore motion in his leg muscles and operated most of the time from his wheelchair — except for speeches, when he wore leg braces, or special occasions like the Sunday evening devotional service after Thanksgiving at Warm Springs in 1935 (described here by General Evans Carlson):

We had placed a chair at the roadside for the President's use, but when he drove up he waved the chair aside. Descending from the car he drew himself up and with magnificent dignity and superb will he walked down the ramp, through the door and forward to his seat amid the patients. Never will I forget

that walk, which was performed in utter silence. No explanation was ever given for what must have been a supreme effort.
But I sensed, and I felt that others present must have sensed,
that it was made for the purpose of giving hope and inspiration to the assembled patients.

His energy rarely flagged. Sometimes a sustained bout of work
darkened the circles under his eyes and accentuated the occasional
trembling of his hands ("My boys' hands shake like that," Roosevelt would say. "It is a family trait"); but a few days under the
sun at Warm Springs or sailing on blue water always restored
his abundant vitality. Anne O'Hare McCormick reported in 1937,
"Of all the leaders of his time, he is perhaps the least variable."
Where the rulers of Europe seemed to her to have shriveled and
aged under the glare of power, Roosevelt was more himself than
ever — his hair perhaps a trifle thinner, his face and figure thicker,
but the gestures, the warmth, the composure, the tempo the same.
"Mr. Roosevelt is a unique figure in the modern world: the one
statesman this writer has seen who seems able to relax."

Yet was not his air of relaxation itself a way of disarming and
confusing those who sought to penetrate behind the mask? The
surface, as Tugwell said, was all charm, or puckish humor, or absorption in fascinating detail, or delight in maneuver; only one
thing seemed certain — that the significant area of operations was
taking place a good way below. This area, Roosevelt plainly conceived, was no one's business save his own. "It was part of his
conception of his role," remarked Tugwell, "that he should
never show exhaustion, boredom, or irritation." He would rather
have posterity believe that decision was simple for him, that he
selected goals with careless ease and pursued them with serenity,
than to admit to misgiving or foreboding. "The serious student,"
said Tugwell, "is forced to conclude that this man deliberately
concealed the processes of his mind." It was partly this; it was
partly too, as Herman Kahn has suggested, the Ivy League convention of casualness, now exhibited for the first time in the Presidency.

On one level, this became pure theatrics, sometimes of an obvious kind. Peggy Bacon commented on the bright, direct look,

the frank, clear gaze of craft, "clever as hell but so innocent . . . a grand old actor." He turned on his dazzling smile, said one unimpressed White House functionary, "as if somebody had pressed a button and sent a brilliant beam from a lighthouse out across the sea"; to this man, who had served every President since McKinley, Roosevelt's private and public selves seemed more alike than those of any other President because his performance never stopped — because "he never failed to present himself as the lead-ing actor on whatever stage was available at the moment." Those who saw him at close range tried forever to peer into what Robert Sherwood vividly described as "his heavily forested interior." Most of them concluded with Sherwood: "I could never really understand what was going on in there."

His first defense was the cordial, winning but essentially im-personal courtesy which both tantalized and defeated intruders. Dr. Hjalmar Schacht described him as "for all his frankness, pos-sessed of a peculiar reticence." Mary Colum, visiting the White House on a literary occasion, noted "the amazing smile that was a combination of so many kinds of smile, and none of them evoked by any of the people he was addressing," the intelligent, unim-passioned face that seemed incapable of betraying anything but conventional graciousness — yet the hint of "untried intensity" within. "It is difficult to imagine stone or steel under that smooth, bright flow," Anne O'Hare McCormick once said; but she knew it was there. "Make no mistake," said Dr. C. G. Jung after seeing Roosevelt in 1936, "he is a force — a man of superior but impene-trable mind, but perfectly ruthless, a highly versatile mind which you cannot foresee." [1]

III

These were chance visitors. Those who saw him enough to get behind the wall of conventional courtesy encountered next his sense of unassailable internal dignity. One or two interpreted this as snobbishness; but Roosevelt was not a snob. If it is true that people's backgrounds registered on his mind — that he had, for example, an odd weakness for European titles, however seedy — it is also true that lack of background made no difference. "Roosevelt, in his personal relationships," said Stanley High, "is whole-heartedly a democrat" of that "genuine and uninhibited sort" of pa-tricians who had nothing to lose by friendliness or to gain by patron-izing. "Snooty people are as much on his black list as prima donnas." His letters to Harvard deans show an evident anxiety to save his sons from "the lack of individuality and the narrowness" which he considered to mark "the club and Boston life of the average private school freshman." His three closest friends were a middle-class newspaperman, a Jew, and the son of a harness maker. "There was a quiet reserve about him," said a White House maid, "but Mr. Roosevelt never made me 'feel like a servant' or 'feel like a Negro.'" Jim Farley, the main source of the snobbishness story, tried to support it by ascribing to Eleanor Roosevelt a quotation ("Franklin finds it hard to relax with people who aren't his social equals") which she subsequently denied and which, in any case, was demonstrably untrue — as Ed Flynn said, "just silly. The Roosevelts were all gregarious to the point of foolishness." Before personal disappointment had embittered him, Farley himself rendered quite different testimony. "There isn't a snobbish bone in his body," he wrote in 1938. If some men born to high social po-sition conveyed feelings of superiority, "I can honestly say I have never observed anything of the kind in Roosevelt. . . . His friends and personal companions are not chosen from any particular group of class."

It was not snobbishness at issue: it was Roosevelt's intense pro-tection of his own interior privacy. "He never was 'one of the boys,'" wrote Mike Reilly of the Secret Service, "although he frequently made a good try. It was such a good try that it never quite came off." No one could be permitted to glimpse the wheels at work. "He never did let down the bars beyond a certain point," said Henry Morgenthau. "I would be the last to claim," said Donald Richberg, "that I ever became well acquainted with that inner man." Harold Ickes reached the conclusion that, however open and smiling the surface, "the core underneath was self-contained, and perhaps even inclined to reserve to the point of coldness." "Roosevelt," said Stanley High, "has a great many intimates, few close friends and no cronies." "Nobody that I know," said Hugh Johnson, "has ever really gotten within the aristocratic reserve of his inherently proud, even haughty, and, I will venture to say, lonely spirit."

Even his wife, to whom he was profoundly devoted, did not share his interior hopes or tribulations. She has written that he did not even tell her when he decided to run for the Presidency; this she learned from Louis Howe. "Franklin," she has said, "did not talk a great deal about the work that he was doing, either at meals or in private family conversation." Tugwell's summary of their relationship seems compassionate and exact: "Eleanor shared everything with Franklin that she was allowed to share and opened her faithful heart completely to his desires and needs. But Franklin himself did not possess the key to his own unconscious reticences, and there was very imperfect reciprocation." They were "linked by indissoluble bonds but not lost in each other as husband and wife might sometimes be." [2]

IV

Some people who do not reveal themselves at work reveal themselves at play. But whose relaxation could have been less revealing than Franklin Roosevelt's?

The White House, of course, imposed new circumspections on a life already drastically limited by steel braces and a wheelchair. It was almost impossible to escape the atmosphere of official responsibility, even in the family rooms upstairs. And, though the Roosevelt regime brought a gay informality the presidential mansion had not seen since Roosevelts last lived there, the White House still had defects from the viewpoint of thoroughly relaxed living. Most notable of all, perhaps, was the food. Mrs. Nesbitt, whom Mrs. Roosevelt had brought from Hyde Park as housekeeper, described herself as "small-town and a homebody" and believed in "plain foods, plainly prepared." This was fine for Mrs. Roosevelt, who could not care less what she ate; but the President, who enjoyed good cooking, spent his years in the White House in a state of ill-suppressed dissatisfaction. The most powerful man in the country, he could not command a good dinner. His guests were even more indignant. Tugwell described White House food and drink as "pretty awful." "On only one other occasion," wrote Ickes bitterly after a White House dinner, "have I ever tasted worse champagne."

In the White House, Roosevelt sought diversion above all in people and talk. He demanded to be informed and entertained; and he liked people who could pleasantly take his mind from what Francis Biddle once called "the horrible ennui of that wholly impersonal life." Old friends who knew nothing of official affairs here served a purpose — thus Vincent Astor or Henry Hooker. Among associates in government, he could relax only with those who shared his capacity to turn their backs on the daily routine. This is why Jim Farley failed to achieve intimacy — not because he was not in the *Social Register* but because he could talk of nothing except politics. In contrast, as Moley has noted, Ed Flynn was in the personal circle because he "always seemed bored with politics, had read widely and could amuse Roosevelt with items far from statecraft."

As a relief from the White House, Missy LeHand began in 1936 to arrange occasional parties at Harold Ickes's secluded house out beyond Chevy Chase Lake. Ickes, a gourmet, served excellent dinners; and Missy would select an entertaining group — Corcoran, perhaps, with his accordion; or Watson, Early, Hopkins, Morgenthau, McIntyre, later Bill Douglas and Bob Jackson, for an evening of poker. These evenings consisted mainly of idle, easy, kidding chat. They relaxed the President, but disclosed nothing and fitted admirably into his system of defense. "It is delightful to see how the President can enter in at a party," Ickes once wrote. "He had as good a time as anyone there, laughing and talking and joking. . . . Yet, in spite of all his fun-making, no one ever presumes to treat him with familiarity."

If the President's hobbies were more revealing, what they revealed was a set of contradictory traits. In some favorite diversions — the playing of cards, the mixing of drinks, the making of jokes — his habits were conspicuously broad and disorderly. At the poker table (thought he played for tiny stakes, "just for conversation," as the Vice-President, a serious poker player, said patronizingly) he adored reckless variations like seven-card stud with deuces and one-eyed jacks wild or improbable improvisations like "spit in the ocean." His style at rummy, according to Molly Dewson, was similarly "bold, dashing, high-spirited." When he mixed drinks, he always overdid the vermouth in the martinis and the bitters in the old-fashioneds. His humor was slapdash, lacking wit and consisting mostly of corny remarks which no doubt sounded funnier at the time than they do in cold print. From a press conference:

> Q: Mr. President, does the ban on the highways include the parking shoulders?
> Roosevelt: Parking *shoulders?*
> Q: Yes, widening out on the edge, supposedly to let the civilians park as the military goes by.
> Roosevelt: You don't mean necking places? *(Prolonged laughter)*

Once when George Dern read the cabinet a long report on beet sugar, Morgenthau could stand it no more and scribbled a note to the President: "May I sing some soft music?" The note promptly came back: "Yes, *chamber* music, or a *pot*pourri." When coins were pouring into the White House for the campaign against polio, Roosevelt sent a characteristic message to the mail clerk: "I hope you are having a good dime." His match books for a time bore the legend "Stolen from Franklin D. Roosevelt."

His attitude toward baseball sums up this cluster of traits: "I am the kind of fan who wants to get plenty of action for his money." Pitchers' duels, he supposed were all right, but "I get the biggest kick out of the biggest score — a game in which the batters pole the ball to the far corners of the field, the outfielders scramble, and the men run the bases. In short, my idea of the best game is one that guarantees the fans a combined score of not less than fifteen runs, divided about eight to seven."

Yet despite all this, nothing absorbed him more than his stamp collection; and stamp collecting obviously called on an entirely opposite set of psychological characteristics. He spent many happy evenings in his upstairs study, an album open before him, magnifying glass, tweezers, and hinges by his side; he found infinite pleasure in leafing through philatelic catalogues and ordering new items. In the 1920's Roosevelt had begun to specialize in stamps from North, Central, and South America and Hong Kong.

By the thirties he had about 25,000 stamps in some forty albums. Following the example of Hoover, who had also been a collector, Roosevelt asked the White House mail clerk to rescue unusual stamps from the incoming mail. The philatelic passion would seem to attest to a particular personality type with classic characteristics of meticulousness, tidiness, parsimoniousness, and obstinacy. Obviously such a hobby suited Hoover perfectly; but how to reconcile it with the disorderly, generous, and flexible Roosevelt? Yet it gave him more relaxation than almost anything else he could do in the White House and it clearly corresponded to some need in his bewildering personality.[3]

v

Still, for truly effective relaxation, he had to get away. Travel much improved the opportunities for rest and for privacy. In 1933 he spent 92 days away from Washington; in 1934, 149; in 1935, 145. He liked moving around by automobile or slow train, refreshing himself by watching the countryside unroll before him. His favorite objectives were the places he knew best and which soothed him most — Hyde Park and Warm Springs. There he could give the slip to official cares, even to official supervision. Despite the assassination attempt at Miami in 1933, Roosevelt continued to chafe at the vigilant protection of the Secret Service. Where Hoover kept his White House under incessant patrol by four operatives on the ground floor and two on every floor above, Roosevelt ordered them all to stay in the Usher's office. Away from Washington he was even more insouciant. "I certainly do not want a high wire fence around the Warm Springs cottage!" Roosevelt told Chief Moran in early 1933. "The simplest protection would be, as before, a flood light covering each side of the house and front." "Nothing pleases my husband more, in Hyde Park or Warm Springs," Eleanor Roosevelt said, "than to lose the Secret Service car which always follows him." When Colonel Starling, the head of the White House unit, wanted to cancel a trip in 1934 because of reports of an assassination plot, Roosevelt called the idea "absurd." "Every public appearance of a chief executive entails an element of risk; but . . . if anyone wants to kill me, there is no possible way to prevent him. About all that can be done is to guard against a second shot." The only thing that worried him was fire. Shortly after moving to the White House, he worked out a system for escape, involving even a canvas chute on which he could slide to safety. Starling later wrote, "His absolute lack of fear made it difficult at times for him to understand the safeguards with which we surrounded him. He liked to feel completely free, and he saw no reason why he should not be."

He could never feel completely free; but he found momentary refreshment observing the rose garden at Hyde Park, or driving his specially fitted car along the twisting woodland roads beside the Hudson, or looking at the view from the ridge where he would soon build his beloved Hilltop Cottage, or watching the blue herons at dusk at the Val-Kill pond, or picnicking on the Knob at Warm Springs, with its illimitable view of quiet green country receding dimly into the distance, or pausing a moment among lovely southern pines at twilight. Then the implacable round started again, and he returned to the memoranda, the cables, the phone calls from Washington, and the important guests.

The best escape of all was the sea: Roosevelt once told Ickes that sailing was the only way he could really rest. Except for swimming, it was the one exercise which remained to him after polio; combined with fishing, it gave him deep excitement and almost inviolable privacy. On his own boat, the *Amberjack*, he wore his oldest sweater and his dirtiest flannels and never shaved. Cruises on Vincent Astor's *Nourmahal* with nonpolitical friends (Ed Flynn, watching them embark, once observed sardonically, "The Hasty Pudding Club puts out to sea") were a cheerful antidote to the Presidency. And there were more formidable expeditions, like the one which Hopkins and Ickes never forgot on the *Houston* in the autumn of 1935 to Cocos Island, a densely flowered islet of vivid green rising two thousand feet out of the brilliant blue Pacific off the shores of Costa Rica. Lowered to the chair in the stern of his special fishing launch, fighting sailfish and pompano in the choppy Pacific, using all the power of his massive arms and shoulders to reel in the fish, Roosevelt cast off weariness and irritability under the healing beneficence of sun and spray and salt.[4]

VI

At work or at play, the defenses remained intact. He appeared almost deliberately to surround himself by incurious people — the Earlys, McIntyres, Watsons — as if to preserve his inner sanctuaries. "It sometimes seems," Tugwell has perceptively noted, "that those who were closest to him for the longest time were kept there because they did not probe or try to understand but rather because they gave an unquestioning service."

Some pressed too hard, of course. They were too curious or insensitive or cared too much. It was when Roosevelt was thus pressed that he resorted — almost, it would seem, as if he considered himself entitled to do so — to deviousness and to deceit. Those who did not press rarely complained of being cheated. "I knew Roosevelt for twenty years," said Molly Dewson, "and never once did he give me double talk. In human intercourse, if a person shies off from a subject, it is common sense not to press him and force him into an evasive answer." Frances Perkins, who ordinarily restrained herself, said, "It is my final testimony that he *never let me down.*" Those who plunged ahead invited their own punishment. "It was evident," wrote Richberg, "that he often regarded the use of a deceptive statement as justified, particularly in discussions with someone who was trying to get him to commit himself to a position he did not wish to take."

There is no question that he took a certain relish in misleading those who seemed to him to deserve it. What may have begun as a necessity became on occasion a pleasure. "He was apt to see the importance of immediate ends," said Tugwell acutely, "more readily than the consequences of doubtful means" — and this myopia became a pervading weakness of his Presidency. For Roosevelt, the result tended to grow more essential than the method; and he never adequately recognized that casualness over methods might jeopardize or corrupt results. "Never let your left hand know what your right is doing," he once told Morgenthau. "Which hand am I, Mr. President?" Morgenthau asked. Roosevelt said, "My right hand, but I keep my left under the table." ("This is the most frank expression of the real F.D.R. that I ever listened to,"

Morgenthau noted, "and that is the real way he works — but thank
God I understand him.") Once, rehearsing a speech, Roosevelt read
a passage in what he called the T.R. manner. Tom Corcoran
spoke up (as Richberg recalled it): "Oh, but Mr. President, the
difference between you and T.R. is that you never fake." Roosevelt replied, "Oh, but Tommy, at times I do, I do!"

He did, of course; it became the last resort of his system of
defense. Those who impaled themselves on it felt bitter resentment in consequence. Some never forgave him. Others, who
adored him, were deeply upset and angry. "It is pretty tough
when things like this can be said about the President of the United
States," wrote Harold Ickes after a Democratic congressman remarked to him that Roosevelt might have a hard time disproving
Huey Long's charge that he was a liar, "and when members of his
own official family and of his own party in Congress feel that his
word cannot be relied upon. It hurts me to set down such a fact,
but it is the fact, as I have had occasion to know more than once."

Roosevelt enjoyed mystification too much. But perhaps a
measure of mystification is inherent in the Presidency. "There
isn't enough time," Tom Corcoran once said, "to explain everything to everyone, to cajole everyone, to persuade everyone, to
make everyone see why it has to be done one way rather than
another. If a President tried to do this, he would have no time
left for anything else. So he must deceive, misrepresent, leave false
impressions, even, sometimes, lie — and trust to charm, loyalty
and the result to make up for it. . . . A great man cannot be a good
man." [5]

VII

There are two sorts of greatness — the foursquare, all-of-a-
piece, unitary, monolithic kind, possessed by Washington, Jackson, Winston Churchill; and the glittering, elusive, pluralistic,
impalpable kind, possessed by Jefferson, Henry Clay, Lloyd George,
where levels of personality peel off with the delusive transparence
of the skins of an onion, always frustrating the search for a hard
core of personality underneath. The greatest statesman may perhaps, like Lincoln, combine both kinds: in the phrase of Archi-

lochus, he is both hedgehog and fox. Franklin Roosevelt clearly
belongs in the second category. He had, not a personality, but a
ring of personalities, each one dissolving on approach, always revealing still another beneath.

Yet one cannot exhaust the Roosevelt mystery by saying that
he was complicated. For, though the central core of personality
remained impossible to pin down, one felt, nevertheless, beneath
the dazzling variety on the surface, behind the succession of
masks, a basic simplicity of mind and heart. His complexity was
infinite, but it all pertained to tactics. On questions of essential
purpose, he retained an innocence which was all the more baffling
because of its luminous naïveté. "He sometimes tries to appear
tough and cynical and flippant," Hopkins once told Sherwood, "but
that's an act he likes to put on. . . . You and I are for Roosevelt
because he's a great spiritual figure, because he's an idealist." This
was true. It was his tactical deviousness which got him into trouble;
it was the fundamental, tantalizing, intermittent but ultimately
indestructible idealism which saved him.

He was complicated everywhere except in his heart of hearts.
There he perceived things with elementary, almost childlike, faith.
"What is your philosophy" asked the young man. "Philosophy?"
Roosevelt replied. "Philosophy? I am a Christian and a Democrat — that's all." And for him, his church and his party implied
a series of lucid commitments — respect for persons, respect for
nature, respect for freedom. He held to these commitments with
a confidence he never questioned and a serenity which never
faltered.

This inner well of serenity was the unending source of spiritual
refreshment. Anne O'Hare McCormick called him "apparently
the least worried man in the country." Gerard Swope once said to
him that he marveled at the calm with which he carried the presidential load. "I'll tell you, Gerard," Roosevelt replied, "at night
when I lay my head on my pillow, and it is often pretty late, and
I think of the things that have come before me during the day
and the decisions that I have made, I say to myself — well, I have
done the best I could, and turn over and go to sleep." "More than
any other person I have ever met," said Dr. McIntire, ". . . he had
equanimity, poise and a serenity of temper that kept him on the

most even of keels." As Eleanor Roosevelt summarized his attitude: "You made up your mind to do a thing and you did it to the
best of your ability. If it went sour, why then you started in all
over again and did something else, but you never spent time re-
pining." And she added significantly: "I have never known a man
who gave one a greater sense of security. . . . I never heard him
say there was a problem that he thought it was impossible for
human beings to solve." "Roosevelt was a man," said Tugwell,
"with fewer doubts than anyone I had ever known."

What was the source of this serenity? He himself offered no
clues; he was, he used to say, "the least introspective man in the
world." In part, of course, it was character, temperament, experience, triumph over catastrophe. "F.D.R. was very tough," said
Francis Biddle. "He had got on top of life. Nothing could touch
him." But it was something more than this. "He had," said Tugwell, "a source of detached exaltation which could not be touched
by the outcome." "He felt guided in great crises," said Eleanor
Roosevelt, "by a strength and wisdom higher than his own." Hugh
Johnson put it more forcibly, perhaps too forcibly: "That he has
some sort of messianic complex, none who is near him will deny."

Roosevelt unquestionably had a deep sense of religious assurance, though its character remains a puzzle. His faith was un-
analyzed, nontheological, a matter of tradition and propriety,
something which he felt but did not care to formulate. "I think it
is just as well not to think about things like that too much!" he
admonished his wife. He was by no means a regular churchgoer;
"by the time I have gotten into that pew and settled down with
everybody looking at me, I don't feel like saying my prayers at all."
The divisiveness of dogmatic theologies bothered him: "in our religious worship we should work together instead of flying off on
different tangents and different angles." Though a Senior Warden
of St. James's Church at Hyde Park, he personally preferred Presbyterian, Methodist, or Baptist sermons to Episcopalian, and on
Christmas tended to go to one of the big Methodist or Baptist
churches in Washington ("What's the matter? I like to sing hymns
with the Methodys"). For a time, he had even omitted his Episcopalian affiliation from his biography in *Who's Who*, not restoring
it until 1924. Yet, as Robert Sherwood said, "his religious faith

was the strongest and most mysterious force that was in him." He once wrote, "I doubt if there is in the world a single problem, whether social, political, or economic, which would not find ready solution if men and nations would rule their lives according to the plain teaching of the Sermon on the Mount." If nothing ever upset him, if his confidence seemed illimitable, it was because he deeply believed, with full reverence and humility, that he was doing his best in the eyes of God, that God was blessing his purposes, that he was at one with the benign forces of the universe.[6]

VIII

In the end, a President of the United States must stand or fall by his instinct for the future as well as by his understanding of the past and his mastery of the present. Implanted within him, there must be an image, not necessarily — or even desirably — explicit or conscious, but profoundly rich, plastic, and capacious, of the kind of America he wants, of the vision of the American promise he is dedicated to realize, of the direction in which he believes the world is moving. Without such a sense, his Presidency will be static and uncreative. As Franklin Roosevelt's successor once put it, "The President's got to set the sights." This vision of the future becomes the source of his values; it justifies his strivings; it renews his hopes; it provides his life with its magnetic orientation.

It was this astonishing instinct for the future which above all distinguished Roosevelt, his extraordinary sensitivity to the emergent tendencies of his age and to the rising aspirations of ordinary people — a sensitivity housed at the same time within a personality and intelligence sufficiently conventional to provide in itself a bridge holding together past and future. Indeed, his very position on the breaking point between an old world and a new one gave him a special freedom and spontaneity which only a man can possess who is nourished by older values. When Roosevelt accepted the inevitability of change, he did so, not by necessity, but by conscious choice. He had made a deliberate decision, both temperamental and intellectual, in favor of adventure and experiment. "My impression of both him and of Mrs. Roosevelt," wrote H. G. Wells, "is that they are unlimited people, entirely modern in the openness of their minds and the logic of their actions." Nothing could daunt him, very little surprised him, he was receptive to everything, and not in a passive sense either, he received, not to accumulate, but to act; the future which he perceived was (this he deeply believed) to be in part his own creation. Wells summed him up: "The most effective transmitting instrument possible for the coming of the new world order. He is eminently 'reasonable' and fundamentally implacable. He demonstrates that comprehensive new ideas can be taken up, tried out and made operative in general affairs without rigidity or dogma. He is continuously revolutionary in the new way without ever provoking a stark revolutionary crisis."

The essence of Roosevelt, the quality which fulfilled the best in him and explained the potency of his appeal, was his intrepid and passionate affirmation. He always cast his vote for life, for action, for forward motion, for the future. His response to the magnificent emptiness of the Grand Canyon was typical: "It looks dead. I like my green trees at Hyde Park better. They are alive and growing." He responded to what was vital, not to what was lifeless; to what was coming, not to what was passing away. He lived by his exultation in distant horizons and uncharted seas. It was this which won him confidence and loyalty in a frightened age when the air was filled with the sound of certitudes cracking on every side — this and the conviction of plain people that he had given them head and heart and would not cease fighting in their cause.[7]

Notes

IN ORDER to avoid a hopelessly large number of notes, I have followed the practice of collecting the references necessary to a particular passage in a single note. The full citation of each title is to be found on the first mention in each chapter, with the exception of the following works, which receive abbreviated citation throughout:

Franklin D. Roosevelt, *Public Papers and Addresses*, S. I. Rosenman, comp. (New York, 1938–50), cited as F.D.R., *Public Papers*, with the year covered by the volume in parenthesis.

Franklin D. Roosevelt, *His Personal Letters: Early Years*, Elliott Roosevelt, ed. (New York, 1947); *His Personal Letters: 1905–1928*, Elliott Roosevelt, ed. (New York, 1948); *His Personal Letters: 1928–1945*, Elliott Roosevelt, ed. (2 vols., New York, 1950), cited as F.D.R., *Personal Letters*, I, II, III, IV.

Franklin D. Roosevelt Collector, cited as *F.D.R. Coll.*

Annals of the American Academy of Political and Social Science, cited as *Annals*.

Bureau of the Census, *Historical Statistics of the United States, 1789–1945* (Washington, 1949), cited as *Historical Statistics*.

Harold L. Ickes, *The First Thousand Days, 1933–1936* (New York, 1953), cited as Ickes, *First Thousand Days*.

Raymond Moley, *After Seven Years* (New York, 1939), cited as Moley, *After Seven Years*.

Henry Morgenthau, Jr., Diary, Morgenthau Papers, cited as Morgenthau, Diary; Farm Credit Administration Diary, Morgenthau Papers, cited as Morgenthau, Farm Credit Administration Diary.

Rexford G. Tugwell, "A New Deal Memoir: Early Days, 1932–1933," Tugwell Papers, cited as Tugwell, "New Deal Memoir"; and Diary, Tugwell Papers, cited as Tugwell, Diary.

Additional abbreviations are:

AAA, for the Agricultural Adjustment Administration
FERA, for the Federal Emergency Relief Administration
NRA, for the National Recovery Administration.

Of the manuscript collections cited, the following are at the Roosevelt Library at Hyde Park, New York: Franklin D. Roosevelt Papers, Franklin D. Roosevelt, Press Conferences; Roosevelt Foundation Papers; Mary W. Dewson Papers; Harry L. Hopkins Papers; Henry Morgenthau, Jr., Papers; Herbert Claiborne Pell Papers. The following are at the National Archives, Washington, D.C.: Department of Agriculture Papers; Agricultural Adjustment Administration Papers; Bureau of the Budget Papers; National Recovery Administration Papers; Federal Emergency Relief Administration Papers; Proceedings of the Executive Council, National Emergency Council, Special Industrial Recovery Board, and the National Resources Committee. The E. M. House Papers and the Henry L. Stimson Diary are at the Sterling Library, Yale University; the Jay Pierrepont Moffatt Diary is in the Moffatt Papers at the Houghton Library, Harvard University. I consulted the Norman H. Davis Papers at the Council on Foreign Relations in New York City; they are now in the Library of Congress. The Oral History Research Office is at Columbia University. The papers of Adolf A. Berle, Jr., Francis Biddle, Herbert Feis, Leon Henderson, Raymond Moley, Blackwell Smith, and Rexford G. Tugwell are in the personal possession of the persons named.

CHAPTER 1 (Pages 1-23)

1. F.D.R., *Public Papers* (1933), 16; R. L. Hazlet, "Will There Be an FDR Legend?" *F.D.R. Coll.*, May 1953; *New York Times*, March 5, 1933.
2. Cordell Hull, *Memoirs* (New York, 1948), I, 167-68; R. G. Tugwell, *The Democratic Roosevelt* (New York, 1957), 270-71; Woodrow Wilson, *Constitutional Government in the United States* (New York, 1908), 73; *New York Times*, Feb. 8, March 27, 1933, Aug. 4, 1936. I use the version of Governor Landon's remarks contained in the stenographic record of the Department of the Interior rather than the more succinct (and otherwise identical) version reported contemporaneously in the *Times*.
3. W. S. Myers and W. H. Newton, *The Hoover Administration: A Documented Narrative* (New York, 1936), 338-41, 351; "Memorandum of Treasury Conference[s]," March 5-6, 1933, Berle Papers; Moley, *After Seven Years*, 148-50; Tugwell, "New Deal Memoir," Ch. 1; F.D.R., Diary, March 5-6, 1933, La Follette and Costigan to F.D.R., March 9, 1933, Roosevelt Papers; M. W. Childs, *I Write from Washington* (New York, 1942), 21; Bronson Cutting, "Is Private Banking Doomed?" *Liberty*, March 31, 1934; R. G. Tugwell, "The New Deal in Retrospect," *Western Political Quarterly*, Dec. 1948; Franklin D. Roosevelt, *On Our Way* (New York, 1934), 3-8; *New York Times*, March 5-8, 1933.
4. Moley, *After Seven Years*, 150-55; Moley, *27 Masters of Politics* (New

York, 1949), 187–88; Charles Michelson, *The Ghost Talks* (New York, 1944), 55–58; Tugwell, *Democratic Roosevelt*, 264; A. A. Ballantine, "When All the Banks Closed," *Harvard Business Review*, March 1948; F.D.R., *Public Papers* (1933), 46; S. K. Bailey and H. D. Samuel, *Congress at Work* (New York, 1952), 229–35; *New York Times*, March 9, 10, 19, 1933.

5. F.D.R. to J. A. Simpson, May 20, Wallace to F.D.R., May 16, 1933, Roosevelt Papers; *Amherst Student*, Oct. 14, 1937; Morris Markey, "He's Got His Hand in Your Pocket," *American Magazine*, June 1933; Turner Catledge, "A Hard-Hitter Strikes at the Budget," *New York Times Magazine*, March 19, 1933; *New York Times*, April 28, 1933; L. W. Douglas, "Economy in Federal Government," *Review of Reviews*, April 1933: F.D.R., *Public Papers* (1928–32), 807–8, *Public Papers* (1933), 49–50.

6. F.D.R. to House, April 5, 1933, Roosevelt Papers; Moley, 27 *Masters*, 31; *New York Times*, May 19, 1933; Tugwell, Diary, May 31, 1933; E. K. Lindley, *The Roosevelt Revolution* (New York, 1933), 90–95.

7. F.D.R., *Public Papers* (1933), 30, 65; Grace Tully, *F. D. R., My Boss* (New York, 1949), 89–91; F.D.R. to Helen W. Reynolds, Oct. 30, 1933, in *Dutchess County Historical Society Yearbook* (Hyde Park, 1933), XVIII; A. A. Berle, Jr., Diary, Sept. 19, 1939, Berle Papers; Michelson, *Ghost Talks*, 56–57; Ballantine, "When All the Banks Closed"; Stimson to F.D.R., March 14, Hearst to F.D.R., n.d., Roosevelt Papers; *New York Times*, March 19, 31, May 13, 1933; Will Rogers, *Sanity Is Where You Find It*, Donald Day, ed. (Boston, 1955), 167; Rogers, *Autobiography*, Donald Day, ed. (Boston, 1949), 312–13; Walter Lippmann in *Review of Reviews*, May 1933.

8. E. W. Starling, *Starling of the White House* (New York, 1946), 306–7; S. J. Woolf, *Here Am I* (New York, 1941), 198; *New York Times*, March 10, May 16–22, 1933; Jo Davidson, *Between Sittings* (New York, 1951), 275; Tugwell, "New Deal Memoir," Ch. 3; Tully, *F. D. R.*, 64–65; Eleanor Roosevelt, "My Day," *New York Post*, May 19, 1958; interview with Thomas G. Corcoran, Oct. 21, 1957; *Nation*, May 31, 1933; *Time*, May 22, 29, 1933; Frances Perkins, *The Roosevelt I Knew* (New York, 1946), 112; Eleanor Roosevelt, *This I Remember* (New York, 1949), 112–13; Jack Douglas, *Veterans on the March* (New York, 1934), 324.

9. George N. Peek, with Samuel Crowther, *Why Quit Our Own* (New York, 1936), 20, 114; W. M. Kiplinger, "What's Ahead in Washington," *Nation's Business*, June 1934; Krock in Hanson Baldwin and Shepard Stone, eds., *We Saw It Happen* (New York, 1938), 5, 9; A. T. Mason, *Harlan Fiske Stone* (New York, 1956), 384; Anne O'Hare McCormick, *The World at Home* (New York, 1956), 177; Ray Tucker, "The National Air," *Collier's*, Jan. 27, 1934; Henry James, *The American Scene* (New York, 1946), 343; J. P. Moffatt, Diary, May 16, 1933; Herman Kahn, "What Happened to the First New Deal, 1933–34,"

Roosevelt Library; Francis Biddle, "The Labor Board," Biddle Papers; Tugwell, "New Deal Memoir," Ch. 2; T. L. Stokes, *Chip off My Shoulder* (Princeton, 1940), 362.

10. R. B. Fosdick, *Chronicle of a Generation* (New York, 1958), Ch. 10; O. G. Villard, "Mr. Roosevelt's Two Months," *New Statesman and Nation,* May 13, 1933; Tugwell, Diary, May 6, 1933; F.D.R., *Public Papers* (1933), 302; H. S. Johnson, "Pied Pipers," *Vital Speeches,* March 11, 1935; R. G. Tugwell, "The Ideas behind the New Deal," *New York Times Magazine,* July 16, 1933; Walter Lippmann in New York Herald Tribune Forum, *This Crisis in History* (New York, 1933), 15–16; Krock in *New York Times,* March 12, 1933; Mason, *Stone,* 344; J. G. Frederick, *Primer of "New Deal" Economics* (New York, 1933), 281–82; McCormick, *World at Home,* 174; Ray Tucker, "Ickes — and No Fooling," *Collier's,* Sept. 30, 1933; editorial in *Collier's,* Sept. 23, 1933; Winston S. Churchill, "While the World Watches," *Collier's,* Dec. 29, 1934.

CHAPTER 2 *(Pages 27–39)*

1. *Historical Statistics,* Ser. E93, 95, 104; Senate Agriculture and Forestry Committee, *Agricultural Adjustment Relief Plan: Hearings,* 72 Cong., 2 Sess. (1933), 15; Anne O'Hare McCormick, "Roosevelt's View of the Big Job," *New York Times Magazine,* Sept. 11, 1932; E. D. Coblentz, *William Randolph Hearst* (New York, 1952), 147.

2. Russell Lord, *The Wallaces of Iowa* (Boston, 1947), especially 167, 589; H. A. Wallace, *Statesmanship and Religion* (New York, 1934), especially 8, 22, 44–47, 71, 79–80, 102, 125; Wallace, *New Frontiers* (New York, 1934), especially 11, 17, 269; Wallace, *The Price of Freedom* (Washington, 1940), especially 1, 76, 105; Jack Alexander, "Henry A. Wallace: Cornfield Prophet," *Life,* Sept. 2, 1940; E. D. Graham, Jr., "Henry Wallace: Modern Prophet" (seminar paper, Harvard University); Hubert Herring, "Henry III of Iowa," *Harper's,* Feb. 1943; Daniel Seligman, "Henry Wallace" (research memorandum; author's possession).

3. Wallace, *Statesmanship,* 77–78; Wallace, *New Frontiers,* 279; Wallace to Roerich, June 17, to F.D.R., Sept. 18, Hull to F.D.R., Oct. 11, Wallace to F.D.R., Oct. 27, to Marvin McIntyre, Nov. 10, 1933, Roosevelt Papers; Henry Morgenthau, Jr., "The Morgenthau Diaries: III," *Collier's,* Oct. 11, 1947; J. P. Moffatt, Diary, Dec. 4, 1933; *Newsweek,* March 22, 1948; Westbrook Pegler in the *New York Journal-American,* March 1948, *passim;* purported Wallace texts in *New York Journal-American,* Oct. 22, 1948; National Emergency Council, Proceedings, Jan. 23, 1934; Wallace to Lawrence Westbrook, Jan. 27, 1937, Hopkins Papers; Gardner Jackson, "Henry Wallace: A Divided Mind," *Atlantic,* Aug. 1948; Dwight Macdonald *Henry Wallace: The Man and the Myth* (New York, 1948), Ch. 7.

4. Sherwood Anderson, "No Swank," *Today*, Nov. 11, 1933; Jackson, "Henry Wallace"; George Creel, *Rebel at Large* (New York, 1947), 313; Donald Richberg, *My Hero* (New York, 1954), 245; Tugwell, "New Deal Memoir," Chs. 1, 2; H. F. Pringle, "Our Unknown Dictator," *Red Book*, Sept. 1933; H. A. Wallace, "Address . . . before the Democratic Women's Club, Philadelphia . . . May 9, 1933" (Department of Agriculture release), 2; Wallace to F.D.R., Feb. 19, 1933, Roosevelt Papers; K. L. Butterfield, "Wanted — Farm Life," *World Tomorrow*, March 1, 1933; M. O. Sillars, "Henry A. Wallace's Editorials on Agricultural Discontent, 1921–1928," *Agricultural History*, Oct. 1952; Wallace, *New Frontiers*, 111; Ferner Nuhn, "Wallace of Iowa," *New Republic*, March 15, 1933; W. G. Shepherd interviewing Wallace, "Why the Farmer Doesn't Like Our Dollar," *Collier's*, April 1, 1933.

5. House Agriculture Committee, *Farm Marketing Program (Voluntary Domestic Allotment Plan): Hearings*, 72 Cong., 1 Sess. (1932), 2–5; M. L. Wilson, *Farm Relief and the Domestic Allotment Plan* (Minneapolis, 1933), 26–28; Russell Lord, "M. L. Wilson: Pioneer," *Survey Graphic*, Oct. 1941; Lord, *Wallaces*, 295–312; Tugwell, "New Deal Memoir," Ch. 1; G. C. Fite, *George N. Peek and the Fight for Farm Parity* (Norman, Okla., 1954), 230–32; Chester Davis, "Toward Planned Harvests," *Review of Reviews*, Dec. 1933; Senate Agriculture Committee, *Farm Relief: Hearings*, 72 Cong., 1 Sess. (1932), 56–59; House Agriculture Committee, *Agricultural Adjustment Program: Hearings*, 72 Cong., 2 Sess. (1932), 139–41; O. E. Baker, Ralph Borsodi, and M. L. Wilson, *Agriculture in Modern Life* (New York, 1939), 215, 244.

6. W. I. Myers, "Confidential Memorandum of Discussion on Emergency Farm Relief Legislation . . . Washington, D. C., Dec. 12–14, 1932," Morgenthau Papers, C. V. Gregory, "Birth of the AAA," *Bureau Farmer*, Aug.–Sept. 1933; Wallace, "Address . . . Democratic Women's Club"; F.D.R., *Public Papers* (1933), 74; *New York Times*, March 19, 1933.

CHAPTER 3 *(Pages 40–54)*

1. *Congressional Record*, 73 Cong., 1 Sess., 669, 693 (March 21, 1933); E. K. Lindley, *The Roosevelt Revolution* (New York, 1933), 97; J. E. Reeve, *Monetary Reform Movements* (Washington, 1943), especially Chs. 4, 9, 10; Moley, *After Seven Years*, 159–60.

2. Milo Reno, "What the Farmer Wants," *Common Sense*, Feb. 1934; *New York Times*, March 13, April 28–May 4, 1933; Harlan Miller, "Watchfully the Farmer Awaits Events," *New York Times*, May 7, 1933; *Chicago Tribune*, April 28, 1933; *Time*, May 8, 1933; "Prairie Fire," *Nation*, May 17, 1933; Karl Pretshold, "Do Farmers 'Revolt'?" *North American Review*, July 1933; Frazier Hunt, *One American* (New York, 1938), 378–79.

3. *New York Times,* April 23–May 13, 1933; H. E. Gaston to L. M. Howe, "Progress of Farm Mortgage Refinancing through the Farm Credit Administration," Dec. 1, 1933, in Morgenthau Diary; Farm Credit Administration, *Cooperative Farm Mortgage Credit, 1916–1936* (Washington, 1936); Henry Morgenthau, Jr., "The Paradox of Poverty and Plenty," *Collier's,* Oct. 25, 1947.

4. Mordecai Ezekiel, "Agricultural Adjustment: First Phase," *New Republic,* June 23, 1937; George N. Peek, with Samuel Crowther, *Why Quit Our Own* (New York, 1936), 14–17, 39, 43, 46, 78, 83, 90, 97; Russell Lord, *The Agrarian Revival* (New York, 1939), 155; Tugwell, Diary, April 3, 1933; Tugwell, "New Deal Memoir," Ch. 2; Senate Agriculture and Forestry Committee, *Agricultural Emergency Act to Increase Farm Purchasing Power: Hearings,* 73 Cong., 1 Sess., (1933), 82; G. C. Fite, *George N. Peek and the Fight for Farm Parity* (Norman, Okla., 1954), 244–57; Morgenthau, Farm Credit Administration Diary, May 3, 1933: Wallace to F.D.R., May 15, 1933, Roosevelt Papers; interview with John D. Black, 1956; Chester Davis to author, Aug. 10, 1956.

5. I am indebted to Richard H. Rovere for access to his notes for a profile of Jerome Frank and have drawn particularly on a letter from Abe Fortas to Mr. Rovere, Oct. 25, 1946; Tugwell, "New Deal Memoir," Ch. 2; Peek, *Why Quit Our Own,* 14, 21–22, 112; Russell Lord, *The Wallaces of Iowa* (Boston, 1947), 346–47; Lord, *Agrarian Revival,* 156; Fite, *Peek,* 260–61.

6. It should be noted that both Nathaniel Weyl and Whittaker Chambers have identified Alger Hiss as a member of the Ware Group: Lee Pressman, however, although naming Abt, Witt, and others, declared of Hiss, "I have no knowledge regarding the political beliefs or affiliations of Alger Hiss. . . . For the period of my participation in that group, Alger Hiss was not a member of the group." Weyl, "I Was in a Communist Unit with Hiss," *U.S. News & World Report,* Jan. 9, 1953; Whittaker Chambers, *Witness* (New York, 1952), 332–47; testimony of Pressman, John Abt, House Committee on Un-American Activities, *Hearings Regarding Communism in the United States Government,* 81 Cong., 2 Sess. (1950), especially 2845, 2926; testimony of Weyl, Senate Judiciary Committee, *Institute of Pacific Relations: Hearings,* 82 Cong., 2 Sess. (1952), 2799–2800; Ella Reeve Bloor, *We Are Many* (New York, 1940), 279; Jerome Frank to Charles J. Brand, Aug. 10, 1933, AAA Papers; *Time,* Feb. 14, 1955; Tugwell, "New Deal Memoir," Ch. 3; H. A. Wallace, "The Rules of the Game," *Survey Graphic,* July 1934; Gardner Jackson to author, May 2, 1957.

CHAPTER 4 *(Pages 55–67)*

1. George N. Peek, with Samuel Crowther, *Why Quit Our Own* (New York, 1936), 101–3; Special Industrial Recovery Board, Proceedings,

Sept. 25, 1933; E. G. Nourse, *Marketing Agreements under the AAA* (Washington, 1935), Chs. 1–2.

2. Nourse, *Marketing Agreements*, Chs. 2, 5; Peek, *Why Quit Our Own*, Ch. 8; G. C. Fite, *George N. Peek and the Fight for Farm Parity* (Norman, Okla., 1954), 254–66; Tugwell, "New Deal Memoir," Chs. 2, 4.

3. Russell Lord, *The Agrarian Revival* (New York, 1939), 161–62; Lord, *The Wallaces of Iowa* (Boston, 1947), 381–82; Grant McConnell, *The Decline of Agrarian Democracy* (Berkeley, 1953), 74–75.

4. H. I. Richards, *Cotton and the AAA* (Washington, 1936), especially Chs. 7, 8, 11, 14; J. S. Davis, *Wheat and the AAA* (Washington, 1935), especially Chs. 3, 4, 11; Jesse H. Jones, with Edward Angly, *Fifty Billion Dollars* (New York, 1951), Ch. 6; statement by Davis in National Emergency Council, Proceedings, Feb. 20, 1934; H. A. Wallace, "American Agriculture and World Markets," *Foreign Affairs*, Jan. 1934; Chester Davis, "Toward Planned Harvests," *Review of Reviews*, Dec. 1933; Fite, *Peek*, 254–55; Peek, *Why Quit Our Own*, 127; H. A. Wallace, *New Frontiers* (New York, 1934), 171.

5. D. A. Fitzgerald, *Corn and Hogs under the Agricultural Adjustment Act* (Washington, 1934), especially Chs. 2–3; Fitzgerald, *Livestock under the AAA* (Washington, 1935), Chs. 4–5, 12; Wallace, *New Frontiers*, 138–39, 178–83, 200; Wallace, "The Farm Situation," *Vital Speeches*, Dec. 3, 1934; Executive Council, Proceedings, Aug. 15, 1933; H. F. Pringle, "The Secretary of Agriculture Takes the Stand," *American Magazine*, July 1934; Lord, *Wallaces*, 329, 363–66; J. K. Galbraith, "An Economic Aspect of Farm Crop Restriction," *Plan Age*, April 1939; *Historical Statistics*, Ser. J49; H. A. Wallace, *America Must Choose* (New York, 1934), 8, 23; Wallace, "American Agriculture and World Markets"; Mordecai Ezekiel, "Can We Starve Ourselves Rich?" *Today*, Nov. 11, 1933; R. G. Tugwell, "The Price Also Rises," *Fortune*, Jan. 1934.

6. Wallace to F.D.R., Sept. 11, 1933, Floyd Olson to F.D.R., March 19, F.D.R. to Olson, April 16, 1934, Roosevelt Papers; E. C. Owen to F.D.R., Oct. 16, 1933, Department of Agriculture Papers; Lorena Hickok to Harry Hopkins, Nov. 7, 23, 1933, Hopkins Papers; Morgenthau, Diary, Nov. 4, 1933; Wallace, *New Frontiers*, 56–58; William Hard, "Reno and Revolt in Iowa," *Today*, Nov. 11, 1933; "Bryan! Bryan!!" *Fortune*, Jan. 1934; F. A. Pearson, W. I. Myers, and A. R. Gans, "Warren as Presidential Adviser," *Farm Economics*, Dec. 1957.

CHAPTER 5 *(Pages 68–84)*

1. Department of Agriculture, "The Drought Situation, June 1, 1934," and Drought Coordinating Committee, "The Drought of 1934, A Report of the Federal Government's Assistance to Agriculture," Roosevelt Papers; National Emergency Council, Proceedings, Aug. 21, 1934;

M. L. Cooke, "Twenty Years of Grace," *Survey Graphic*, June 1935; H. H. Bennett, "The Vague, Roaming 'Dust Bowl,'" *New York Times Magazine*, July 26, 1936; R. G. Tugwell, "No More Frontiers," *Today*, June 22, 1935; Tugwell, "New Deal Memoir," Ch. 4; Russell Owen, "Where Drought Sears Land and People," *New York Times Magazine*, Feb. 15, 1931; Lawrence Svobida, *An Empire of Dust* (Caldwell. Idaho, 1940), especially Chs. 6–7; Harlan Miller, "When Searing Drought Smites the Farm," *New York Times Magazine*, May 27, 1934; Miller, "Dust Rides the Winds," *New York Times Magazine*, March 31, 1935; Sherwood Anderson, "War of the Winds," *Today*, Feb. 23, 1935; Lorena Hickok to Harry Hopkins, Aug. 24, 1934, Hopkins Papers; Russell Lord, *The Wallaces of Iowa* (Boston, 1947), 370–72; P. B. Sears, *Deserts on the March* (Norman, Okla., 1947); Sears, "The Black Blizzards," in Daniel Aaron, ed., *America in Crisis* (New York, 1952), 287–302.

2. Murphy to F.D.R., Sept. 5, 1934, Roosevelt Papers; *Historical Statistics*, Ser. E88, 91, 104, 244–49; F. C. Mills, *Prices in Recession and Recovery* (New York, 1936), 238; E. G. Nourse, J. S. Davis, and J. D. Black, *Three Years of the Agricultural Adjustment Administration* (Washington, 1937), especially Chs. 10, 11.

3. Tugwell, Diary, Jan. 6, 1933; H. A. Wallace, *New Frontiers* (New York, 1934), 219, Chs. 19, 20; M. L. Wilson, "Agricultural Adjustment," *Harvard Business Review*, Summer 1935; R. G. Tugwell and E. C. Banfield, "Grass Roots Democracy — Myth or Reality?" *Public Administration Review*, Winter 1950; Tugwell, *The Battle for Democracy* (New York, 1935), 198; L. V. Howard, "The Agricultural Referendum," *Public Administration Review*, Winter 1942; Raymond Moley, "'Never-Never Land,'" *Today*, June 29, 1935. With regard to Moley's comment, it should be noted, however, that an early Gallup poll in December 1935 reported that the country was 59 per cent against AAA and 41 per cent for it. But this poll evidently left out the "no opinion" group; and there is internal evidence to suggest that it miscalculated the relative balance of Democrats (who were 70 per cent for AAA) and Republicans in the nation. See Hadley Cantril, ed., *Public Opinion, 1935–1946* (Princeton, 1951), 135.

4. Lord, *Wallaces of Iowa*, 395–409; George N. Peek, with Samuel Crowther, *Why Quit Our Own* (New York, 1936), 91; Chester Davis, "Toward Planned Harvests," *Review of Reviews*, Dec. 1933; Appleby to J. D. LeCron, July 20, 1934, Department of Agriculture Papers; Natl. Emer. Council, Proceedings, Feb. 20, 1934; Tugwell, Diary, April 8, 1934; J. D. Black, *The Dairy Industry and the AAA* (Washington, 1935), 128–30; E. G. Nourse, *Marketing Agreements under the AAA* (Washington, 1935), 47–48; Gardner Jackson, "Henry Wallace: A Divided Mind," *Atlantic*, Aug. 1948; interviews with Chester Davis, Jerome Frank, Gardner Jackson; Paul A. Porter to author, March 28, 1958.

5. H. I. Richards, *Cotton and the AAA* (Washington, 1936), Ch. 9; Lord, *Wallaces*, 395–409; Appleby to C. B. Baldwin, March 7, 1935, Dept. of Agr. Papers; F.D.R. to E. P. Costigan, Feb. 13, 1935, Roosevelt Papers; Jackson, "Wallace: A Divided Mind"; Tugwell, Diary, Feb. 6–13, 1935; *New York Times*, April 22, 1935; Chester Davis to Wallace, Jan. 12, 1951, in *Freeman*, May 7, 1951; "Mr. Wallace Replies," *Freeman*, Feb. 26, 1951; H. A. Wallace, "No Final Answer to the Farm Problem," *U.S. News & World Report*, Jan. 8, 1954; W. R. Amberson, "The New Deal for Share-Croppers," *Nation*, Feb. 13, 1935; R. G. Swing, "The Purge at the AAA," *Nation*, Feb. 20, 1935; Gardner Jackson to Burton K. Wheeler, March 11, Wheeler to Chester Davis, March 21, 1935, AAA Papers; Ickes, *First Thousand Days*, 292–93, 302–3; interviews with Davis, Frank, Jackson; Davis to author, Aug. 10, 1956; Porter to author.

6. Morgenthau, Diary, Oct. 28, 1935; H. A. Wallace, "The Next Four Years in Agriculture," *New Republic*, Dec. 2, 1936; speeches by Wallace and Tolley in Appendix B of Nourse, Davis, and Black, *Three Years*.

7. H. A. Wallace, *America Must Choose* (New York, 1934), 16–18, 20, 23–25, 28; Wallace, *New Frontiers*, 78.

CHAPTER 6 (*Pages 87–102*)

1. *Historical Statistics*, Ser. H3, J30, J49; Senate Finance Committee, *Investigation of the National Recovery Administration: Hearings*, 74 Cong., 1 Sess. (1935), 2409–11; Moley, *After Seven Years*, 185; H. S. Johnson, *The Blue Eagle* (New York, 1935), 93, 101, 114, 153–55, 169, 172, 187–88; C. F. Roos, *NRA Economic Planning* (Bloomington, Ind., 1937), Ch. 11 A. M. Schlesinger, Jr. *The Crisis of the Old Order* (Boston, 1957), 181.

2. Raymond Moley, "Changing the NRA," *Today*, June 2, 1934; G. B. Galloway et al., *Industrial Planning under Codes* (New York, 1935), 21–23; J. T. Flynn, "Whose Child Is the NRA?" *Harper's*, Sept. 1934; Schlesinger, *Crisis*, 182–83; Ickes, *First Thousand Days*, 24; Frances Perkins, *The Roosevelt I Knew* (New York, 1946), 230; House Labor Committee, *Thirty-Hour-Week Bill: Hearings*, 73 Cong., 1 Sess. (1933), 198–99 (Harriman); Sen. Finance Com., *Investigation of Economic Problems: Hearings*, 72 Cong., 2 Sess. (1933), 299–301 (Lewis), 875–76 (Hillman).

3. Matthew Woll and W. E. Walling, *Our Next Step — A National Economic Policy* (New York, 1934), 80; Sen. Finance Com., *Investigation of Economic Problems*, 875 (Hillman); Mary W. Dewson to F.D.R. [Feb. 1933], in Mary W. Dewson, "An Aid to the End," I, 104–5, Dewson Papers; Josephine Goldmark, "The New Menace in Industry," *Scribner's*, March 1933; Senate Judiciary Committee, *Thirty-Hour*

Work Week: Hearings, 72 Cong., 2 Sess. (1933), especially 2–11, 21–22, 285; House Labor Committee, *Six-Hour Day — Five-Day Week: Hearings,* 72 Cong., 2 Sess. (1933), especially 14, 17; Ralph E. Flanders, "Limitations and Possibilities of Economic Planning," *Annals,* July 1932; John Chamberlain, "Panaceas for the Depression: Solving It with a Thirty-Hour Week," *New Republic,* March 29, 1933; J. P. Frank, *Mr. Justice Black* (New York, 1949), 89; Charlotte Williams, *Hugo Black* (Baltimore, 1950), 47–49.

4. Donald Richberg, "Trying to Bury the Big Stick," *Survey Graphic,* Sept. 1929; Richberg, *Tents of the Mighty* (New York, 1930), 196–203; Senate Committee on Manufacturers, *Unemployment Relief: Hearings,* 72 Cong., 1 Sess. (1932), 340; Sen. Com. on Man., *Federal Aid for Unemployment Relief: Hearings,* 72 Cong., 2 Sess. (1933), 453–55; Sen. Finance Com., *Investigation of Economic Problems,* 643–48; Moley, *After Seven Years,* 184; R. G. Tugwell, *The Industrial Discipline* (New York, 1933), 212–16; Tugwell, "New Deal Memoir," Ch. 2; Tugwell, "America's War-Time Socialism," *Nation,* April 6, 1927; Jerome Frank, *Save America First* (New York, 1938), 341–43; Schlesinger, *Crisis,* Ch. 2, pp. 224–26.

5. J. T. Flynn, "The New Capitalism," *Collier's,* March 18, 1933; Johnson, *Blue Eagle,* 153; Alexander Sachs, "National Recovery Administration Policies," in Clair Wilcox *et al.,* eds., *America's Recovery Program* (New York, 1934), 117; Perkins, *Roosevelt I Knew,* Chs. 16, 22; Perkins, letter in *Washington Post,* April 20, 1933; *Time,* April 17, 1933; House Labor Com., *Thirty-Hour-Week Bill,* especially 3–7; Frances Perkins, "Eight Years as Madame Secretary," *Fortune,* Sept. 1941; Ickes, *First Thousand Days,* 21; Tugwell, Diary, March 31, April 2, 3, 1933; Moley, *After Seven Years,* 184–90.

6. Moley, *After Seven Years,* 184–90; Johnson, *Blue Eagle,* 193–204; J. P. Warburg, "Reminiscences" (Oral History Research Office, 1952), 213, 216, 248, 369–70, 378–80, 493; Tugwell, Diary, April 21, May 30, 1933, and "New Deal Memoir," Ch. 2; Press Conference #11, April 12, 1933, #18, May 5, 1933; H. I. Harriman to F.D.R., May 11, 1933, Roosevelt Papers; F.D.R., *Public Papers* (1933), 157, 164–65; Donald Richberg, *The Rainbow* (New York, 1936), 106–10; "The Birth of the NRA," unsigned memorandum, NRA Papers; Perkins, *Roosevelt I Knew,* Chs. 17, 22; Donald Richberg, *My Hero* (New York, 1954), 163–65; Flynn, "Whose Child is the NRA?"; H. S. Johnson, "Background of NRA," *Saturday Evening Post,* June 30, 1934; Roos, *NRA Economic Planning,* 36–40; E. K. Lindley, *The Roosevelt Revolution* (New York, 1933), 151–61; *New York Times,* May 4, 1933; *Time,* May 15, 1933; Leon Keyserling to author, April 9, 1958.

7. House Ways and Means Committee, *National Industrial Recovery: Hearings,* 73 Cong., 1 Sess. (1933), 72, 95–96, 117–22; *Congressional Record,* 73 Cong., 1 Sess., 5279–80 (June 7, 1933).

8. *Congressional Record,* 73 Cong., 1 Sess., 5153, 5244, 5245, 5307 (June

7, 1933), 5835, 5838, 5839, 5840, 5845, 5861 (June 13, 1933); F.D.R., *Public Papers* (1933), 246, 252, 256.

CHAPTER 7 *(Pages 103–118)*

1. H. S. Johnson, *The Blue Eagle* (New York, 1935), 197, 200, 206–11; Frances Perkins, *The Roosevelt I Knew* (New York, 1946), 201–3; Alexander Sachs to F.D.R., Sept. 14, 1936, Roosevelt Papers; Ickes, *First Thousand Days*, 52–55.
2. Johnson, *Blue Eagle*, especially 208; Matthew Josephson, "The General," *The New Yorker*, Aug. 18–Sept. 1, 1934; Jonathan Mitchell, "The Versatility of General Johnson," *Harper's*, Oct. 1934; Raymond Clapper, "Top Sergeants of the New Deal," *Review of Reviews*, Aug. 1933; Russell Owen, "General Johnson Wages a Peace-Time War," *New York Times Magazine*, July 30, 1933; Isabel Leighton, "The NRA — and General Johnson," *Red Book*, Nov. 1933; Margaret Marshall, "Hugh-and-Cry Johnson," *Nation*, March 12, 1938; Perkins, *Roosevelt I Knew*, 200–201; "No Climax," *Fortune*, Oct. 1933; Donald Richberg, *Tents of the Mighty* (New York, 1930), 128, 214; Richberg, *My Hero* (New York, 1954), 165–66; Jonathan Mitchell, "Grand Vizier: Donald Richberg," *New Republic*, April 24, 1935.
3. Johnson, *Blue Eagle*, 211, 368; Tugwell, Diary, May 30, 1933, and "New Deal Memoir," Ch. 3; Tugwell, "The Experimental Roosevelt," *Political Quarterly*, July–Sept. 1950; Tugwell, "America Takes Hold of Its Destiny," *Today*, April 28, 1934; Sachs memorandum in C. F. Roos, *NRA Economic Planning* (Bloomington, Ind., 1937), 84–85; Sachs to F.D.R., Sept. 14, 1936, Roosevelt Papers; Ickes, *First Thousand Days*, 52–55; Sidney Hyman, memorandum of conversation with Philip Fleming, Aug. 10, 1949, Roosevelt Foundation Papers; Mitchell, "Versatility of General Johnson"; Owen, "General Johnson"; Leighton, "The NRA"; Johnson at the Conference of State Directors of the National Emergency Council, Jan. 31–Feb. 3, 1934, Addresses and Minutes, NRA Papers; Johnson to Richberg, Dec. 26, 1933, NRA Papers; Johnson at the National Association of Manufacturers, Dec. 7, 1933, NRA Release #2126.
4. Johnson, *Blue Eagle*, Chs. 19–20; F.D.R., *Public Papers* (1933), 299; Bruce Bliven, "Washington Kaleidoscope," *New Republic*, Aug. 16, 1933; articles by Owen, Mitchell, Josephson, previously cited; *Time*, July 3, Aug. 21, 1933.
5. Special Industrial Recovery Board, Proceedings, July 18, 19, 1933.
6. Johnson, *Blue Eagle*, Ch. 21; F.D.R., *Public Papers* (1933), 298, 301; Donald Richberg, *The Rainbow* (New York, 1936), 159–62, 288, 295; *New York Times*, Sept. 14, 1933; *Time*, Sept. 18, 25, 1933; *Nation*, Aug. 30, 1933; Herbert Hoover, *Memoirs . . . The Great Depression, 1929–1941* (New York, 1952), Ch. 38.

7. Johnson, *Blue Eagle*, Ch. 20; E. K. Lindley, *The Roosevelt Revolution* (New York, 1933), 233–44; President's Committee of Industrial Analysis, *The National Recovery Administration* (multigraphed, Washington, 1937), 25; G. B. Galloway et al., *Industrial Planning under the Codes* (New York, 1935), especially Chs. 5–9, 16; Morgenthau, Diary, Aug. 16, 1933; Ford jottings, *New York Times*, May 7, 1953; Ickes, *First Thousand Days*, 91–92; J. A. Farley, *Jim Farley's Story* (New York, 1948), 42; Richberg, *Rainbow*, 162.

CHAPTER 8 *(Pages 119–135)*

1. Special Industrial Recovery Board, Proceedings, Aug. 21, 1933; E. K. Lindley, *The Roosevelt Revolution* (New York, 1933), 252–61; *New York Herald Tribune*, July 29, 1933.

2. H. S. Johnson, *The Blue Eagle* (New York, 1935), Ch. 21; George Leighton, "In Search of NRA," *Harper's*, Jan. 1934; Lorena Hickok to Hopkins, April 11, 1934, Hopkins Papers; Walter Lippmann, *Interpretations, 1933–1935*, Allan Nevins, ed. (New York, 1936), 98; Gerard Swope, statement at meeting of the Business Advisory Council, Department of Commerce release, Nov. 1, 1933; *Time*, Nov. 12, 30, Dec. 4, 1933; Donald Richberg, *The Rainbow* (New York, 1936), 159–63.

3. F.D.R., *Public Papers* (1933), 255; G. B. Galloway, "Genesis of NRA Price Policy and Practice," *Plan Age*, July–Aug. 1935; C. F. Roos, *NRA Economic Planning* (Bloomington, Ind., 1937), 93; Alexander Sachs, "National Recovery Administration Policies," in Clair Wilcox et al., eds., *America's Recovery Program* (New York, 1934), 178; Donald Richberg, "The Future of the NRA," *Fortune*, Oct. 1934; G. B. Galloway et al., *Industrial Planning under the Codes* (New York, 1935) Ch. 3; A. R. Burns, *The Decline of Competition* (New York, 1936), Ch. 10; Tugwell, Diary, April 23, 1934; Tugwell, "The Price Also Rises," *Fortune*, Jan. 1934; Tugwell, *The Battle for Democracy* (New York, 1935), 44; Tugwell to Johnson, June 29, 1933, Bureau of the Budget Papers; Spec. Indus. Recov. Bd., Proceedings, June 19, Aug. 21, Oct. 9, 16, Nov. 13, 1933; Wallace to F.D.R., Oct. 2, 1933, Roosevelt Papers; L. S. Lyon et al., *The National Recovery Administration* (Washington, 1935), 760.

4. Spec. Indus. Recov. Bd., Proceedings, Oct. 9, 1933; Johnson, *Blue Eagle*, 177–81; Leon Henderson, "Statement . . . on 'Price Provisions in Codes' in the Public Hearings on Price Provisions in Codes of Fair Competition," Jan. 9, 1935, NRA Papers; NRA, *Prices and Price Provisions in Codes* (multigraphed, Washington, 1934); Burns, *Decline of Competition*, Ch. 10; C. A. Pearce, *NRA Trade Practice Programs* (New York, 1939); William Hard, "Left, Right," *Red Book*, April 1935; H. L. Ickes, "The Function of Government," *New York Times Magazine*, Feb. 2, 1936; Persia Campbell, *Consumer Representation in the New Deal*

(New York, 1940), 113-14; NRA Report, April 3, 1935, Senate Finance Committee, *Investigation of the National Recovery Administration: Hearings*, 74 Cong., 1 Sess. (1935), 940, 2476; Eugene Grace, "Industry and the Recovery Act," *Scribner's*, Feb. 1934.

5. Tugwell, *Battle for Democracy*, 58; Spec. Indus. Recov. Bd., Proceedings, Nov. 13, 27, Dec. 12, 1933; G. S. Ferguson, Jr., to F.D.R., Dec. 30, 1933, Roosevelt Papers; Tugwell, "New Deal Memoir," Ch. 4.

6. S. J. Woolf, "Champion of the Consumer Speaks Out," *New York Times Magazine*, Aug. 6. 1933; Raymond Moley, "Mary Harriman Rumsey," *Today*, Dec. 29, 1934; *Time*, July 10, 1933; *New York Times*, Dec. 19, 1934; F. J. Schlink to F.D.R., Nov. 20, 1933, in Senate Commerce Committee, *Foods, Drugs and Cosmetics: Hearings*, 73 Cong., 2 Sess. (1934), 293-97; J. B. Matthews, *Guinea Pigs No More* (New York, 1936); F. J. Schlink, *Discovering Consumers* (New York, 1936), Chs. 1, 2; Clark H. Foreman and Michael Ross, *The Consumer Seeks a Way* (New York, 1935); Gardiner C. Means, "The Consumer and the New Deal," *Annals*, May 1934; Walton H. Hamilton, "Consumers' Interest in Price-Fixing," *Survey Graphic*, Feb. 1934; National Emergency Council, Proceedings, Jan. 9, 23, 1934; Sue White to Mary W. Dewson, Feb. 18, 1935, Roosevelt Papers; Campbell, *Consumer Representation*, 62-70; Frances Perkins, *The Roosevelt I Knew* (New York, 1946), 206.

7. Campbell, *Consumer Representation*, 31, 67-74; Johnson, *Blue Eagle*, 180, 272; *Congressional Record*, 73 Cong., 2 Sess., 866-71 (Jan. 18, 1934); *Time*, Jan. 29, 1934; P. H. Douglas, "The Role of the Consumer in the New Deal," and Dexter Keezer, "The Consumer under the National Recovery Administration," *Annals*, March 1934; F.D.R., *Public Papers* (1934), 123-31; *New York Times*, March 5-8, 1934; Leon Henderson to author, March 8, 1957; Lyon *et al.*, *National Recovery Administration*, Ch. 28.

8. Lowell Mason, "Darrow vs. Johnson," *North American Review*, Dec. 1934; Darrow Board reports, special and supplementary report by Darrow and Thompson, minority report by John F. Sinclair, April 14, 1934, Johnson to F.D.R., May 15, Thompson to F.D.R., June 13, 1934, Roosevelt Papers; *Congressional Record*, 73 Cong., 2 Sess., 9236-37 (May 22, 1934); Paul Y. Anderson, "The Darrow Report," *Nation*, May 30, 1934; NRA Release #6136, June 29, 1934; Irving Stone, *Clarence Darrow for the Defense* (New York, 1941), 507-14; Sen. Finance Com., *Investigation of NRA*, 305-9; Johnson, *Blue Eagle*, 272-74; *New York Times*, March 8, 1934; *Washington Post*, May 24, 1934.

9. Lyon *et al.*, *National Recovery Administration*, Ch. 24; Galloway, "Genesis of NRA Price Policy"; H. F. Taggart, *Minimum Prices under the NRA* (Ann Arbor, 1936); Sen. Finance Com., *Investigation of NRA*, 232-38, 1693-94; Leon Henderson to Frances Robinson, May 11, 1934, NRA Papers; Roos, *NRA Economic Planning*, 333; Henderson to author, March 8, 1957.

CHAPTER 9   (Pages 136–151)

1. R. S. Rubinow, *Section 7(a): Its History, Interpretation and Adminis-tration* (NRA, Division of Review, Work Materials No. 45, Wash-ington, 1936), 7–17; Francis Biddle, "Labor Boards," *New Republic,* Oct. 9, 1935; P. F. Brissenden, "Genesis and Import of the Collective-Bargaining Provisions of the Recovery Act," *Economic Essays in Honor of Wesley Clair Mitchell* (New York, 1935); Irving Bernstein, *The New Deal Collective Bargaining Policy* (Berkeley, 1950), Ch. 3.
2. James A. Wechsler, *Labor Baron: A Portrait of John L. Lewis* (New York, 1944), Chs. 1–5; S. D. Alinsky, *John L. Lewis* (New York, 1949), Chs. 1–3; S. J. Woolf, "Lewis Challenges Labor's Old Order," *New York Times Magazine,* March 15, 1936; Louis Adamic, "John L. Lewis' Push to Power," *Forum,* March 1937; "John Llewellyn Lewis," *Fortune,* Oct. 1936; Raoul de Roussy de Sales, "John L. Lewis," *Atlantic,* June 1937; Dale Kramer, "John L. Lewis: Last Bid?" *Harper's,* Aug. 1942; M. W. Childs, "The Illinois Mine Battle," *New Republic,* Sept. 14, 1932; John L. Lewis, "Labor and the NRA," *Annals,* March 1934; *United Mine Workers Journal,* June 1, 15, 1933; Kentucky State Federation of Labor handbill in Roosevelt Papers; McAlister Cole-man, *Men and Coal* (New York, 1943), Ch. 15.
3. Alinsky, *Lewis,* 67–70; Matthew Josephson, *Sidney Hillman: States-man of American Labor* (New York, 1952); George Soule, *Sidney Hill-man* (New York, 1939); R. H. Rovere, "Sidney Hillman and the House-broken Workers," *Reporter,* Feb. 17, 1953; Benjamin Stolberg, *Story of the CIO* (New York, 1938), 53, 58–59; M. D. Danish, *The World of David Dubinsky* (Cleveland, 1957), Ch. 6.
4. Frances Perkins, *The Roosevelt I Knew* (New York, 1946), Ch. 18; *New York Times,* Aug. 16, 1933; *Time,* Oct. 2, 1933; Leon Henderson to author, March 8, 1957.
5. C. F. Roos, *NRA Economic Planning* (Bloomington, Ind., 1937), Ch. 8; Senate Education and Labor Committee, *To Create a National Labor Board: Hearings,* 73 Cong., 2 Sess. (1934), 111–12; A. L. Bern-heim and Dorothy Van Doren, eds., *Labor and the Government* (New York, 1935), 78–79; Special Industrial Recovery Board, Proceedings, Aug. 14, Sept. 11, 1933; Rubinow, *Section 7(a),* Ch. 4; Cyrus S. Ching, *Review and Reflection* (New York, 1953), 41; Jonathan Mitchell, "The Versatility of General Johnson," *Harper's,* Oct. 1934; Donald Rich-berg, *The Rainbow* (New York, 1936), 287; E. K. Lindley, *The Roose-velt Revolution* (New York, 1933), 242; Perkins, *Roosevelt I Knew,* 232; Cyrus Sulzberger, *Sit Down with John L. Lewis* (New York, 1938), 68; Henderson to author.
6. L. L. Lorwin and Arthur Wubnig, *Labor Relations Boards* (Washing-ton, 1935), 88–108; Rubinow, *Section 7(a),* Chs. 4–5; Perkins, *Roose-velt I Knew,* Ch. 20; Sen. Ed. and Labor Com., *To Create a National Labor Board,* 102, 104–5, 758–63; E. T. Weir, "New Responsibilities

of Industry and Labor," *Annals,* March 1934; Hook to Johnson, March 8, 1934, Roosevelt Papers.

7. Lorwin and Wubnig, *Labor Relations Boards,* 107–13, 353–59; Rubinow, *Section 7(a),* 68–73; H. S. Johnson, *The Blue Eagle* (New York, 1935), 292–94; *New York Times,* March 8, 1934; "The President's Conference with the Senators" [on the Wagner Bill], April 14, 1939, Roosevelt Papers; Bernstein, *New Deal Collective Bargaining,* Chs. 5–6.

CHAPTER 10 *(Pages 152–176)*

1. Matthew Josephson, "The General," *The New Yorker,* Sept. 1, 1934; [J. F. Carter], *The New Dealers* (Washington, 1934), 36; Ickes, *First Thousand Days,* 197; Morgenthau, Diary, Aug. 7, 1934; Special Industrial Recovery Board, Proceedings, Sept. 11, 1933; Frances Perkins, *The Roosevelt I Knew* (New York, 1946), 206, 240–41; H. S. Johnson, "Future of NRA," *Saturday Evening Post,* July 21, 1934; memorandum of phone call from Secretary Perkins to Harry Hopkins, June 28, 1933, Hopkins Papers; H. S. Johnson, *Where Do We Go from Here?* (New York, 1935), 1; Johnson, *The Blue Eagle* (New York, 1935), x, 320, 343–44.

2. Johnson, *Blue Eagle,* 242, 371–75, 385–86; Donald Richberg, *My Hero* (New York, 1954), 174; Richberg, *The Rainbow* (New York, 1936), 182; Ickes, *First Thousand Days,* 147, 173.

3. Johnson, *Blue Eagle,* Ch. 29; *New York Times,* Oct. 2, 1934; Richberg, *My Hero,* 173–76; Richberg to F.D.R., Sept. 4, to McIntyre, Sept. 5, Tugwell to F.D.R., Sept. 5, Sept. 7, Johnson to F.D.R., Sept. 9, 24, F.D.R. to Johnson, Sept. 25, 1934, Roosevelt Papers, "Difficult or Controversial Matters Requiring Attention In Immediate Future," memorandum [for the President], Aug. 24, 1934, Blackwell Smith Papers; Ickes, *First Thousand Days,* 195; Blackwell Smith to author, April 24, 1957.

4. Early to F.D.R., Oct. 15, 1934, Roosevelt Papers; Richberg, *Rainbow,* 191; Tugwell, Diary, Nov. 22, 1934; Ickes, *First Thousand Days,* 198, 201, 209–11, 219–21, 235–36; *Washington Post,* May 24, 1934; M. W. Childs, *I Write from Washington* (New York, 1942), 229–30; Robert McCormick, "Where the Thinking Starts," *Collier's,* Jan. 7, 1939; Sam Lubell, "The Daring Young Man on the Flying Pri-cees," *Saturday Evening Post,* Sept. 13, 1941; Henderson to author, March 8, 1957; Henderson memorandum on NRA, June 27, 1934, Roosevelt Papers; Henderson to Johnson, May 14, 1934, and T. C. Blaisdell, Jr., to National Industrial Recovery Board, Jan. 5, 1935, NRA Papers; "Memorandum concerning Industrial Emergency Committee Meeting, Nov. 8, 1934," Howe Papers.

5. NRA Division of Research and Planning, "Trend Away from Code

Restrictive Provisions," April 3, 1935, in Senate Finance Committee, *Investigation of the National Recovery Administration: Hearings,* 74 Cong., 1 Sess., (1935), 940–41, 2461–62; *New York Times,* Jan. 10, 1935; *Time,* Jan. 21, 1935; C. A. Pearce, *NRA Trade Practice Programs* (New York, 1939), 121; Johnson, "Future of NRA"; Johnson, "Reorganization of NRA," Sept. 9, 1934, Roosevelt Papers; F.D.R., *Public Papers* (1934), 417–18; Blackwell Smith to author, April 24, 1957.

6. Ickes, *First Thousand Days,* 210, 221, 242, 247–48, 314; Donald Richberg, "NRA Ideals," *New York Times Magazine,* Feb. 25, 1934; Richberg, "The New Deal's 'Revolution' Defended," *New York Times Magazine,* Dec. 5, 1937; Richberg, Address at General Conference of Code Authorities, March 5, 1934, NRA release; Richberg, "The National Emergency Council," *Vital Speeches,* Oct. 22, 1934; Jonathan Mitchell, "Grand Vizier: Donald R. Richberg," *New Republic,* April 24, 1935; *New York Times,* Feb. 2, 5, 8, 23, 1935; Lewis before Senate Judiciary Committee, *Thirty-Hour Work Week: Hearings,* 74 Cong., 1 Sess. (1935), 67–68; L. L. Lorwin and Arthur Wubnig, *Labor Relations Boards* (Washington, 1935), 353–59, 376–81; H. S. Johnson, "Pied Pipers," *Vital Speeches,* March 11, 1935; [Carter], *New Dealers,* 40–41; Richberg to Early, Jan. 30, 1935, Roosevelt Papers.

7. Richberg to McIntyre, March 19, 1935, Roosevelt Papers; Richberg, *My Hero,* Ch. 16.

8. F.D.R., *Public Papers* (1935), 79–83; *New York Times,* March 8, 1935; Donald Richberg, "Planning and Controlling Business Activities," *Vital Speeches,* Dec. 17, 1934; Richberg, *Government and Business Tomorrow* (New York, 1943), 19; H. L. Ickes, "The Function of Government," *New York Times Magazine,* Feb. 2, 1936; Sen. Finance Com., *Investigation of NRA,* 127, 314, 609, 627–28, 2416, 2474; House Ways and Means Committee, *Extension of NIRA: Hearings,* 74 Cong., 1 Sess. (1935), 683; *United Mine Workers Journal,* May 1, 1934; Moley, "The NRA: Dead or Alive?" *Today,* March 2, 1935.

9. *New York Times,* Feb. 23, 25, March 11, 1935; Sen. Finance Com., *Investigation of NRA,* 9, 15 (Richberg), 651 (Black), 1112–17 (Mason), 1384-85 (Ryan), 2412, 2439, 2447 (Johnson); Johnson, "Future of NRA"; J. A. Ryan, *Social Doctrine in Action* (New York, 1941), 249–50; W. Averell Harriman, "Why the Little Fellow Needs the NRA," *Today,* May 18, 1935; Raymond Moley, "A House Divided," *Today,* June 2, 1934; Johnson, *Blue Eagle,* 279, 280; Johnson to F.D.R., June 26, 1934, Richberg to F.D.R., April 13, 1935, Roosevelt Papers; NRA Legal Division memorandum in House Ways and Means Com., *Extension of NIRA,* 725–50; C. F. Roos, *NRA Economic Planning* (Bloomington, Ind., 1937), Ch. 13; Committee of Industrial Analysis, *National Recovery Administration* (Washington, 1937), Chs. 13–14; Pearce, *NRA Trade Practice Programs,* 191; L. S

Lyon *et al., The National Recovery Administration* (Washington, 1935), Chs. 23, 34, 39.

10. Richberg at Conference of State Directors of the National Emergency Council, Jan. 31–Feb. 3, 1934, Addresses and Minutes, NRA Papers; Sen. Finance Com., *Investigation of NRA*, 8, 2415–16, 2450; Com. of Industrial Analysis, *NRA*, Ch. 20; Lyon *et al., NRA*, Ch. 40; Roos, *NRA Economic Planning*, Ch. 15; Leon Keyserling to author, Feb. 4, 1958; Perkins, *Roosevelt I Knew*, 207–12, 350; William Saroyan, *The Daring Young Man on the Flying Trapeze* (New York, 1934), 139.

CHAPTER 11 (Pages 179–194)

1. Theodore Roosevelt, *Works* (Natl. Ed., New York, 1925), XVI, 456–63, XVII, 12; R. G. Tugwell, *The Battle for Democracy* (New York, 1935), 7, 8, 153; Tugwell, "The Ideas behind the New Deal," *New York Times Magazine*, July 16, 1933; H. L. Ickes, *The New Democracy* (New York, 1934), 96.

2. Moley, *After Seven Years*, 162, 184; Moley, editorial, *Today*, Sept. 26, 1933; Moley, "An NRA for Finance," *Today*, Dec. 30, 1933; Moley, "The March of Circumstance," *Today*, July 13, 1935; Morgenthau, Diary, May 5, 1933; Tugwell, "New Deal Memoir," Ch. 2; E. K. Lindley, "War on the Brains Trust," *Scribner's*, Nov. 1933; Washington Observer, "A Brain Trust at Work," *Review of Reviews*, July 1933; Vincent Astor to Moley, June 25, 1957, Moley Papers; A. A. Berle, Jr., "What's behind the Recovery Laws," *Scribner's*, Sept. 1933; Berle, "The Trend of the Turn," *Saturday Review of Literature*, April 15, 1933; Tugwell, *Battle*, 14, 56, 259; Tugwell, "New Deal Memoir," Ch. 1; J. G. Frederick, *Primer of "New Deal" Economics* (New York, 1933), 276; E. K. Lindley, *The Roosevelt Revolution* (New York, 1933), 307–8; Raymond Moley, "On Reading Ecclesiastes," *Today*, July 13, 1935; R. G. Tugwell, "The Future of National Planning," *New Republic*, Dec. 9, 1936.

3. J. M. Keynes, "National Self-Sufficiency," *Yale Review*, June 1933; Keynes, "Proposals for a Revenue Tariff," *New Statesman and Nation*, March 7, 1931; Keynes in Arthur Salter *et al., World's Economic Crisis* (New York, 1932), 67; Keynes, *Essays in Persuasion* (New York, 1932), 279–89; Samuel Crowther, *America Self-Contained* (New York, 1933), 338.

4. Walter Lippmann, "The Second Reconstruction," *American Magazine*, Sept. 1933; Charles A. Beard, *The Open Door at Home* (New York, 1934), vii, 279, 287; John Chamberlain, "Youth and the Old Economics," *Common Sense*, Jan. 1934; F. W. Taussig, "Necessary Changes in Our Commercial Policy," *Foreign Affairs*, April 1933; Walter Lippmann, "An Economic Issue," *Fortune*, Aug. 1932; W. B. Donham,

"National Ideals and Internationalist Idols," *Harvard Business Review*, April 1933 (supplement); "Baruch," *Fortune*, Oct. 1933; H. S. Johnson, *The Blue Eagle* (New York, 1935), 116–17; Donald Richberg, *The Rainbow* (New York, 1936), 92; Moley, *After Seven Years*, 196; R. G. Tugwell, "Address . . . before the International Institute of Agriculture at Rome, Oct. 24, 1934," Roosevelt Papers.

5. Cordell Hull, *Memoirs* (New York, 1948), especially I, 3–4, 24, 37, 48–50, 52, 136–37; H. B. Hinton, *Cordell Hull* (New York, 1942), especially 32–33, 87, 119, 123, 136, 143, 159; "The Hulls of Tennessee," *Life*, March 18, 1940; W. R. Allen, "The International Trade Philosophy of Cordell Hull, 1907–1933," *American Economic Review*, March 1953; William Phillips, *Ventures in Diplomacy* (North Beverly, Mass., 1952), 185; Arthur Krock in *New York Times*, July 26, 1955; Jonathan Daniels, *Frontier on the Potomac* (New York, 1946), 21; Grace Tully, *F. D. R., My Boss* (New York, 1949), 174; H. B. Hinton, "Hull Describes Our Role in the World," *New York Times Magazine*, Sept. 29, 1935; Cordell Hull, address at Charlottesville, Virginia, July 14, 1932; Moley, *After Seven Years*, 113; Tugwell, "New Deal Memoir," Ch. 2.

6. Wallace to F.D.R., Sept. 28, F.D.R. to Blanshard, Aug. 4, 1933, to Hull, Nov. 19, 1934, Roosevelt Papers; E. D. Coblentz, *William Randolph Hearst* (New York, 1952), 147–51; F.D.R., *Public Papers* (1933), 14, 139, 157, 164; Tugwell, "New Deal Memoir," Ch. 1; Franklin D. Roosevelt, *On Our Way* (New York, 1934), x.

CHAPTER 12 *(Pages 195–212)*

1. A. M. Schlesinger, Jr., *The Crisis of the Old Order* (Boston, 1957), 453; G. G. Johnson, Jr., *The Treasury and Monetary Policy, 1933–1938* (Cambridge, 1939), 15; Press Conference #1, March 8, #10, April 7, 1933; F.D.R. to House, April 5, to Simpson, April 6, 1933, Roosevelt Papers; W. L. White, *Bernard Baruch* (New York, 1950), 82; J. P. Warburg, *How to Co-Exist without Playing the Kremlin's Game* (Boston, 1952), 68–69; Warburg to author, Jan. 25, 1957.

2. Irving Fisher with H. R. L. Cohrssen, *Stable Money: A History of the Movement* (New York, 1934), especially 104–22; I. N. Fisher, *My Father Irving Fisher* (New York, 1956), especially Chs. 12, 14; H. M. Bratter, "The Silver Episode: I," *Journal of Political Economy*, Oct. 1938; Bratter, "The Committee for the Nation," *Journal of Political Economy*, Aug. 1941; J. E. Reeve, *Monetary Reform Movements* (Washington, 1943), especially Chs. 4, 9, 10.

3. Walter Lippmann, *Interpretations: 1933–1935*, Allan Nevins, ed. (New York, 1936), 50–53; J. P. Warburg, "Reminiscences" (Oral History Research Office, 1952), 305–6, 495–99, 503–4, 507–8; Herbert Feis, memorandum of April 20, 1933, Feis Papers; Moley, *After Seven Years*, 159–60; Ickes, *First Thousand Days*, 659; J. P. Warburg, *The Money*

Muddle (New York, 1934), 92–96; Tugwell, Diary, May 6, 1933; Warburg to author, Jan. 25, 1957.

4. "No Climax," *Fortune*, Oct. 1933; White, *Baruch*, 79; Senate Finance Committee, *Investigation of Economic Problems: Hearings*, 72 Cong., 2 Sess. (1933) 555; Leffingwell to F.D.R., Oct. 2, 1933, Roosevelt Papers; Leffingwell, "Managing Our Economy," *Yale Review*, June 1945; Leffingwell, "The Gold Problem and Currency Revaluation," address before the Academy of Political Science, March 21, 1934; *New York Times*, April 20, June 11, 1933; Warburg, "Reminiscences," 1194–95; Warburg, *Hell Bent for Election* (New York, 1935), 67.

5. Schlesinger, *Crisis*, 442; Department of State, *Foreign Relations of the United States, 1932* (Washington, 1948), I, 809, 817, 827, 840; F.D.R. to Davis, Nov. 26, 1932, Davis Papers; Tugwell, Diary, Feb. 26, April 2, 1933, and "New Deal Memoir," Ch. 2; Stimson, Diary, Feb. 26, 1933, Stimson Papers; Moley, *After Seven Years*, 116; Moley to author, Aug. 5, 1957; Cordell Hull, *Memoirs* (New York, 1948), I, Ch. 18; *New York Times*, April 9, 1933.

6. For official statements pertaining to the Conference, Department of State, *Foreign Relations of the United States, 1933* (Washington, 1950), I, 452–825. See also F.D.R., *Public Papers* (1933), 140; *Time*, May 1, 1933; Tugwell, Diary, May 3, 1933; Herbert Feis, *The Sinews of Peace* (New York, 1944), 53; Jeanette P. Nichols, "Roosevelt's Monetary Diplomacy in 1933," *American Historical Review*, Jan. 1951; Winston S. Churchill, "The Bond between Us," *Collier's*, Nov. 4, 1933; Moley, *After Seven Years*, 206–10, 406–14; memorandum of March 29, 1933, confidential source; Hull, *Memoirs*, I, 247–49.

7. Moley, *After Seven Years*, 215–20; Hull, *Memoirs*, I, 259; Dept. of State, *Foreign Relations . . . 1933*, I, 620–27; Tugwell, Diary, May 31, 1933; Ickes, *First Thousand Days*, 42.

8. Dept. of State, *Foreign Relations . . . 1933*, I, 586, 597–98, 607; Moley, *After Seven Years*, 217; Hull, *Memoirs*, I, 250–55; W. D. Robbins to F.D.R., June 15, 1933, Roosevelt Papers.

9. Feis, memorandum of July 17, 1933, Feis Papers; Warburg, "Reminiscences," 486–87, 882, 895, 902–3, 929, 941–42; L. B. Wehle, *Hidden Threads of History* (New York, 1953), 112–15; J. M. Cox, *Journey through My Years* (New York, 1946), 373; Moley, *After Seven Years*, 135–37; Nichols, "Roosevelt's Monetary Diplomacy"; Harry Barnard, *Independent Man: The Life of Senator James Couzens* (New York, 1958), Ch. 40.

CHAPTER 13 *(Pages 213–232)*

1. Moley, *After Seven Years*, 224–38; Department of State, *Foreign Relations of the United States, 1933* (Washington, 1950), I, 631–54; House to Lothian, June 23, 1933, House Papers; Moley to author, Aug. 5, 1957; Leo Pasvolsky, *Current Monetary Issues* (Washington, 1933),

Ch. 4; Bingham to F.D.R., June 16, 1933, Roosevelt Papers; J. P. Warburg, "Reminiscences" (Oral History Research Office, 1952), 978,
1559–60; Morgenthau, Diary, June 29, 1933; J. M. Cox, *Journey
through My Years* (New York, 1946), 368; *Time,* June 26, 1933; Jeanette P. Nichols, "Roosevelt's Monetary Diplomacy in 1933," *American
Historical Review,* Jan. 1951.

2. Moley, *After Seven Years,* 238–56; Cordell Hull, *Memoirs* (New York,
1948), I, 259–62; Dept. of State, *Foreign Relations . . . 1933,* 656–72;
(London) *Times,* June 15–July 1, 1933; Moley to author, Aug. 5, 1957;
Morgenthau, Diary, June 29, 30, July 21, 1933; S. Gold, "London Eco-
nomic Conference," Dec. 13, 1943, in Morgenthau Diary, Vol. 683; Basil
Blackett, *Planned Money* (New York, 1933), 21, 91; Warren to F.D.R.,
July 12, 1933, Roosevelt Papers; F. Livesey to Feis, June 29, and Feis
memorandum of July 3, 1933, Feis Papers; Garet Garrett, "This
Thing of Trade," *Saturday Evening Post,* July 1, 1933; Raymond
Moley, "Heat Lightning or Dawn?" *Today,* Oct. 31, 1936; Herbert
Elliston, "Ties of Gold," *Atlantic,* March 1938; E. K. Lindley, *The
Roosevelt Revolution* (New York, 1933), Ch. 6; Charles Michelson, *The
Ghost Talks* (New York, 1944), 108–14; J. A. Farley, *Jim Farley's
Story* (New York, 1948), 40–41; Ickes, *First Thousand Days,* 76–77.

3. Dept. of State, *Foreign Relations . . . 1933,* I, 679, 680; J. P. Moffatt,
Diary, July 6, 1933; R. F. Harrod, *Life of John Maynard Keynes* (New
York, 1951), 445; Churchill in 280 *H.C. Deb.* 5 s., 787–88 (July 10,
1933); Winston S. Churchill, "While the World Watches," *Collier's,*
Dec. 29, 1934; *Time,* July 17, 1933; Meade, Harrod, *et al.* to F.D.R.,
Nov. 20, Baruch to F.D.R., July 5, Leffingwell to F.D.R., Oct. 2, 1933,
F.D.R. to Mrs. Eliot Cross, July 27, 1933, Roosevelt Papers.

4. Dept. of State, *Foreign Relations . . . 1933,* I, 681; Mary Heaton Vorse,
"The Gods Play Tiddlywinks," *Common Sense,* Aug. 1933; confidential
source (conversation with George V); MacDonald to Hull, July 5,
1933, Roosevelt Papers; Moley, *After Seven Years,* 259–69; Hull,
Memoirs, I, 262–69; Warburg, "Reminiscences," 1076–1105; Dept. of
State, *Foreign Relations . . . 1933,* I, 679–97; Lindley, *Roosevelt Revolution,* Ch. 6; Pasvolsky, *Current Monetary Issues,* Ch. 4.

5. Harrison to F.D.R., Dec. 12, and F.D.R. memorandum for the
historical record, Dec. 16, 1933, Roosevelt Papers; Gustav Cassel, *The
Downfall of the Gold Standard* (Oxford, 1936), 141; Dept. of State,
Foreign Relations . . . 1933, I, 743–45; Pasvolsky, *Current Monetary
Issues,* 86–87.

6. Dept. of State, *Foreign Relations . . . 1933,* I, 625, 687, 738; (London)
Times, June 27, 1933; *Manchester Guardian,* July 14, 1933; James
Couzens, "When Nations Talk Business," *Nation's Business,* Aug.
1933; J. M. Keynes, *The Means to Prosperity* (London, 1933), 25; Warburg, "Reminiscences," 351–54; Herbert Feis, "Synchronized Expenditure Program," April 4, 1933, Feis Papers; J. W. Beyen, *Money in a
Maelstrom* (New York, 1949), 95.

7. Dept. of State, *Foreign Relations . . . 1933*, I, 734, 680; Warburg, "Reminiscences," 1060; Hull to F.D.R., July 11, 1933, Roosevelt Papers; Moley, *After Seven Years*, 267–77; Michelson, *Ghost Talks*, 117; Welles to Davis, Sept 4, 1933, Davis Papers; [J. F. Carter], *The New Dealers* (New York, 1934), 294; Morgenthau, Diary, July 30, 1933; Vincent Astor to Raymond Moley, June 25, 1957, Moley Papers.
8. F.D.R. to MacDonald, Aug. 30, MacDonald to F.D.R., Sept 27, 1933, Roosevelt Papers; F.D.R. to George V, Nov. 5, 1933, in Harold Nicolson, *King George the Fifth* (New York, 1953), 501.

CHAPTER 14 (*Pages 233–252*)

1. J. P. Warburg, "Reminiscences" (Oral History Research Office, 1952), 1165–69, 1188–95; Warburg to F.D.R., July 24, 1933, Roosevelt Papers; Warburg, *The Money Muddle* (New York, 1934), 124–34; G. F. Warren and F. A. Pearson, *Prices* (New York, 1933), 125, 176; F. A. Pearson, W. I. Myers, and A. R. Gans, "Warren as Presidential Adviser," *Farm Economics*, Dec. 1957, 5621–27, 5643.
2. H. A. Wallace, "Money and Credit in Relation to Agricultural Prices," in E. A. Duddy, ed., *Economic Policy for American Agriculture* (Chicago, 1932), 114; Warren to F.D.R., April 24, 1933, Roosevelt Papers; Robert E. Wood to Henry Wallace, Sept. 1, 1933, Department of Agriculture Papers; H. A. Wallace to F. A. Pearson, Jan. 4, 1958, Wallace Papers; Warburg, "Reminiscences," 1251–54, 1376–78; Warburg, *Money Muddle*, 194–40; I. N. Fisher, *My Father Irving Fisher* (New York, 1956), 278–81; S. Gold, "London Economic Conference," Dec. 13, 1943, in Morgenthau Diary, Vol. 683.
3. Rayburn, Black, John Wood, Luther Johnson, W. B. Bankhead, W. J. Driver, D. D. Glover, Jed Johnson to F.D.R., Sept. 14, McKellar, Morris Shepard, Rankin, Doughton to F.D.R., Sept. 15, 1933, Roosevelt Papers; *Time*, Sept. 25, Oct. 2, 1933; F.D.R., *Personal Letters*, III, 366; Warburg, *Money Muddle*, 133, 146–48; F.D.R. to Woodin, Sept. 30, Warburg to F.D.R., Sept. 20, 1933, Roosevelt Papers; Warburg, "Reminiscences," 1458–63; Warburg to author, Jan. 15, 1957.
4. Warren to F.D.R., Sept. 20, 1933, Roosevelt Papers; Morgenthau, Farm Credit Administration Diary, Aug. 16, Sept. 26, Oct. 1, 18, 19, 1933; "Memorandum for the Attorney General with Respect to the Power of the President . . . to Purchase Gold" [1933], Department of Justice Papers, National Archives; Pearson *et al.*, "Warren," 5639; Philip Hamburger, "Mr. Secretary," *The New Yorker*, Nov. 19, 1949; Joseph Alsop and Robert Kintner, "'Henny Penny,' Farmer at the Treasury," *Saturday Evening Post*, April 1, 1939; Warburg, "Reminiscences," 1577–81, 1641–45; F.D.R., *Public Papers* (1933), 426–27; Ickes, *First Thousand Days*, 110.

5. E. K. Lindley, "Roosevelt in Print," *Southern Review*, Autumn 1939; Warburg, *Money Muddle*, 133, 144; Walter Lippmann, *Interpretations, 1933–1935*, Allan Nevins, ed. (New York, 1936), 160–65; Jesse Jones, with Edward Angly, *Fifty Billion Dollars* (New York, 1951), Ch. 20; Henry Morgenthau, Jr., "The Paradox of Poverty and Plenty," *Collier's*, Oct. 25, 1947; Jonathan Grossman, "The New Deal Grain and Gold Buying Programs, 1933–1934" (mimeographed); Grace Tully, *F. D. R., My Boss* (New York, 1949), 193; Pearson *et al.*, "Warren," 5620, 5638–44.

6. Morgenthau, Farm Credit Administration Diary, Oct. 27, 29, Nov. 13, 1933; John Gunther, *Roosevelt in Retrospect* (New York, 1950), 43–44; Tully, *F. D. R.*, 177–78; Hamburger, "Mr. Secretary"; Morgenthau, "Paradox of Poverty and Plenty."

7. "'One of Two of a Kind,'" *Fortune*, May 1934; Alsop and Kintner, "'Henny Penny'"; Josephus Daniels, *The Wilson Era: Years of War* (Chapel Hill, 1946), 214–15.

8. *New York Times*, Nov. 22, 23, 1931; Alfred E. Smith, "Sound Money," *New Outlook*, Dec. 1933; F.D.R., memorandum for the historical record, Dec. 16, 1933, F.D.R. to Woodin, Oct. 9, 1933, to Sprague [Nov. 1933], K. C. Blackburn to Louis Howe, "Public Reaction to the Gold Buying Policy," Roosevelt Papers; O. M. W. Sprague, *Recovery and Common Sense* (Boston, 1934), 18–22, 74; *Time*, Dec. 4, 1933; J. E. Reeve, *Monetary Reform Movements* (Washington, 1943), 58–60; Irving Fisher, *Stable Money* (New York, 1934), 364–67.

9. Seymour E. Harris, *Exchange Depreciation* (Cambridge, 1936), especially xxiii, xxvi, Chs. 8–10; G. G. Johnson, Jr., *The Treasury and Monetary Policy* (Cambridge, 1939), especially 4–6, 18; F.D.R. to House, Nov. 21, 1933, Leffingwell to F.D.R., March 3, 1934, Roosevelt Papers.

10. A. S. Everest, *Morgenthau, The New Deal and Silver* (New York, 1950), 39, Chs. 2–3; H. S. Johnson, *The Blue Eagle* (New York, 1935), 133; Raymond Moley, "Justice for Silver," *Today*, Jan. 6, April 28, 1934; Reeve, *Monetary Reform Movements*, Ch. 15.

11. Coughlin to F.D.R., Sept. 24, 1933, Roosevelt Papers; H. M. Bratter, "The Silver Episode," *Journal of Political Economy*, Oct.–Dec. 1938; Morgenthau, Diary, April 27, 1934, Dec. 12, 1935; Everest, *Morgenthau*, Ch. 3; R. G. Swing, "Father Coughlin," *Nation*, Jan. 2, 1935; "Discussion on Silver: The President's Conference with the Senators, April 14, 1934," Roosevelt Papers; Johnson, *Treasury and Monetary Policy*, Ch. 6; *Time*, May 14, 1934; *Statistical Abstract of the United States, 1943* (Washington, 1944), 720.

CHAPTER 15 *(Pages 253–260)*

1. Cordell Hull, *The Path to Recovery* (Washington, 1934), 12–13; *Congressional Record*, 73 Cong. 2 Sess., 9006–7, 9133, 9683, 9693 (May 17,

21, 28, 1934); H. B. Hinton, "Again the Vexatious Tariff," *New York Times Magazine*, Aug. 2, 1936; Joseph Alsop and Robert Kintner, "Sly and Able," *Saturday Evening Post*, July 20, 1940; H. L. Stimson and McGeorge Bundy, *On Active Service* (New York, 1948), 299–300; Cordell Hull, *Memoirs* (New York, 1941), I, 357.

2. Hull, *Memoirs*, I, 370; George N. Peek, "How to Sell Cotton," *Today*, May 18, 1935; Wallace to F.D.R. (draft), Nov. 27, 1934, Department of Agriculture Papers; George N. Peek, "World Market — Closed," *Today*, Oct. 24, 1936; Peek, with Samuel Crowther, *Why Quit Our Own* (New York, 1936), Chs. 1, 9, 10; G. C. Fite, *George N. Peek and the Fight for Farm Parity* (Norman, Okla., 1954), 268–79; F. B. Sayre, *Glad Adventure* (New York, 1957), Ch. 12; Raymond Moley, the following in *Today* for dates indicated: "Toward a Democratic Foreign Policy" (March 24, 1934), "Save Our Foreign Trade" (May 18, 1935), "Open Covenants, Limited" (Nov. 23, 1935); F. B. Sayre, *Tariff Bargaining* (Washington, 1934), 5, 8; Senate Finance Committee, *Reciprocal Trade Agreements: Hearings*, 73 Cong., 2 Sess. (1934), especially 5.

3. F. B. Sayre, *Increased Exports with a Diminishing Export Balance* (Washington, 1935); Sayre, *American Commercial Policy* (Washington, 1935), 17; Sumner Welles, *The Trade-Agreements Program* (Washington, 1934), 5–6; Peek, *Why Quit Our Own*, Chs. 1, 10–17; F.D.R. to Peek, Nov. 22, 1935, Roosevelt Papers; Fite, *Peek*, 277–90; F. B. Sayre, *The Way Forward* (New York, 1939), 54–59, 205; H. J. Tasca, *The Reciprocal Trade Policy of the United States* (Philadelphia, 1938), Chs. 3, 5; Hull, *Memoirs*, I, 370–77.

4. Hull, *Memoirs*, I, 376–77; *Historical Statistics*, Ser. M32, 52, 54, 55.

CHAPTER 16 (Pages 263–281)

1. H. L. Hopkins, "The War on Distress," *Today*, Dec. 16, 1933; Hopkins, "Employment in America," *Vital Speeches*, Dec. 1, 1936; Josephine C. Brown, *Public Relief, 1929–1939* (New York, 1940), Chs. 6–7, p. 249; Gertrude Springer, "The New Deal and the Old Dole," *Survey Graphic*, July 1933; Frances Perkins, *The Roosevelt I Knew* (New York, 1946), 167, 182–85; *Congressional Record*, 73 Cong., 1 Sess., 1038, 2108, 2114, 2118 (March 30, April 21, 1933); Hopkins to Lehman, May 19, Lehman to F.D.R., May 19, 1933, Frances Perkins to Hopkins, Aug. 26, 1940, Hopkins Papers; Press Conference #6, March 24, #22, May 19, 1933.

2. Robert E. Sherwood, *Roosevelt and Hopkins* (New York, 1948), Chs. 1–2; "Harry Hopkins," *Fortune*, July 1935; Thomas Sugrue, "Hopkins Holds the Bag," *American Magazine*, March 1936; Jonathan Mitchell, "Alms-Giver: Harry L. Hopkins," *New Republic*, April 10, 1935; Raymond Clapper, "Who Is Hopkins?" *Forum*, Dec. 1937; M. W. Childs, "The President's Best Friend," *Saturday Evening Post*,

April 26, 1941; George Creel, "One-Round Hopkins," *Collier's*, Nov. 9, 1935.

3. Corrington Gill, *Wasted Manpower* (New York, 1939), 152; Hopkins to André Maurois, June 27, 1933, Hopkins Papers.

4. H. L. Hopkins, "Federal Emergency Relief," *Vital Speeches*, Dec. 31, 1934; Hopkins, *Spending to Save* (New York, 1936), Ch. 4; Hopkins, testimony before House Appropriations Committee, *Federal Emergency Relief and Civil Works Programs: Hearings*, 73 Cong., 2 Sess. (1934), 3-28, and before Senate Appropriations Committee, *Federal Emergency Relief and Civil Works Programs: Hearings*, 73 Cong., 2 Sess. (1934), 3-18; J. L. Heffernan, "The Hungry City," *Atlantic*, May 1932; "On the Dole: 17,000,000," *Fortune*, Oct. 1934; Arnold Johnson, " 'Give Us Relief or We'll Take It,' " *Modern Monthly*, Feb. 1934; E. A. Williams, *Federal Aid for Relief* (New York, 1939), 107-11; J. A. Maxwell, *Federal Grants and the Business Cycle* (New York, 1952), 96-97.

5. House Appro. Com., *Federal Emergency Relief*, 20-28; Sherwood, *Roosevelt and Hopkins*, 51-59; "On the Dole"; *New York Times*, Jan. 23, 27, 1934; R. F. Post, "Grappling the Vast Problem of Relief," *New York Times Magazine*, July 8, 1934; Lt. Col. J. C. H. Lee, "The Federal Civil Works Administration: A Study Covering Its Organization in November 1933 and Its Operations until 31 March 1934," Hopkins Papers; Louis Brownlow, *A Passion for Anonymity* (Chicago, 1958), 286-88.

6. Lorena Hickok to Hopkins, Report on Pennsylvania, Aug. 7-12, 1933, Report on West Virginia, Aug. 16-26, 1933, Report on Eastern Kentucky, Aug. 31-Sept. 3, 1933, Letters to Hopkins, Oct. 28, Nov. 7, 25, 1933, April 2, 1934, to Katherine Godwin, Hopkins's secretary, Nov. 21, 1936, Martha Gellhorn to Hopkins, Nov. 5, 11, Dec. 1934, April 25, 1935, Hopkins Papers; Theodore Dreiser, "Keep Moving Or Starve," *Today*, March 3, 1934; Louise V. Armstrong, *We Too Are the People* (Boston, 1938), 162; G. H. Brooks, "White-Collar Workers on Relief," *Today*, Aug. 24, 1935; Hopkins, *Spending to Save*, 99; L. F. Quigley to Hopkins, Jan. 11, 1934, Hopkins Papers.

7. Kyle Crichton, "This Is the Day of Opportunity," *Collier's*, Nov. 10, 1934; R. E. Wood to Henry Wallace, June 29, 1934, Department of Agriculture Papers; Lincoln Colcord to Hopkins, Dec. 5, 1934, Hopkins Papers; William H. Matthews, "Relief Can Be Too Cheap," *Survey*, Jan. 1935; R. L. Andrews to Eugene Talmadge, Feb. 7, Talmadge to F.D.R., Feb. 11, F.D.R. to Talmadge (draft), Feb. 13, Grace Tully to Stephen Early, Feb. 21, Early to Hopkins, Feb. 21, 1935, Hopkins Papers; F. A. Vanderlip, with Boyden Sparkes, *From Farm Boy to Financier* (New York, 1935), 257-58; H. L. Ickes in *New York Times*, April 7, 1936; Lorena Hickok to Hopkins, Feb. 14, Sept. 2, 1934, to Aubrey Williams, Aug. 24, 1934, to Katherine Godwin, Nov. 21, 1936, Hopkins Papers.

8. Joseph M. Clark, "Relief: The Nation's Stepchild," *Today*, Jan. 12, 1935; James F. Byrnes, "Shall We Return Relief to the States?" *Vital Speeches*, May 1, 1939; Joseph Alsop and Turner Catledge, "Our Biggest Business — Relief," *Saturday Evening Post*, April 3, 1937.

9. Alfred E. Smith, "Civil Works," *New Outlook*, Dec. 1933; Clapper, "Who Is Hopkins?"; Sherwood, *Roosevelt and Hopkins*, 55–56; Williams, *Federal Aid*, 122; *Time*, April 16, 1934; F.D.R. to Wallace, Sept. 11, 1933, Roosevelt Papers; Tugwell, "New Deal Memoir," Ch. 4; "The Federal Surplus Relief Corporation," FERA, *Monthly Report*, July 1935; "On the Dole"; Williams, *Federal Aid*, 142–44; Hopkins, *Spending to Save*, Ch. 8.

10. Hopkins to Bronson Cutting, Feb. 20, 1935, *Congressional Record*, 74 Cong., 1 Sess., 3954–63 (March 19, 1935); F.D.R. to Ickes and Hopkins, April 16, 1935, Roosevelt Papers; Paul S. Taylor and Clark Kerr, "Putting the Unemployed at Productive Labor," *Annals*, Nov. 1934; Joanna Colcord, "Ohio Produces for Ohioans," *Survey*, Dec. 1934; P. A. Kerr, "Production-for-use and Distribution in Work Relief Activities," FERA, *Monthly Report*, Sept. 1935; Udo Rall, "Self Help — Practical and Proved," *Survey*, Nov. 1937; Williams, *Federal Aid*, 145–46; R. G. Swing, "EPIC and the Ohio Plan," *Nation*, Oct. 3, 1934.

11. Elmer Davis, "New World Symphony," *Harper's*, May 1935; Richard H. Rovere, "End of the Line," *The New Yorker*, Dec. 15, 1951.

CHAPTER 17 (Pages 282–296)

1. H. L. Ickes, *Autobiography of a Curmudgeon* (New York, 1943); P. H. Douglas, "Ickes of Chicago," *New Republic*, May 3, 1933; Donald Richberg, *My Hero* (New York, 1954), 62–64; R. G. Tugwell, *The Stricken Land* (New York, 1946), 656–57; *Time*, July 24, 1933; Walter Lippmann, "Ickes: American Fundamentalist," *New York Herald Tribune*, Feb. 7, 1952; S. J. Woolf, *Here Am I* (New York, 1941), 239; S. K. Padover, "Ickes: Memoir of a Man without Fear," *Reporter*, March 4, 1952; Jack Alexander, "Reformer in the Promised Land," *Saturday Evening Post*, July 22, 1939.

2. Ickes, *First Thousand Days*, 59; Ickes, *Back to Work* (New York, 1935), Chs. 1–3; Sidney Hyman, memorandum of talk with Philip B. Fleming, Aug. 19, 1949, Roosevelt Foundation Papers; Frances Perkins, *The Roosevelt I Knew* (New York, 1946), Ch. 22.

3. Ickes, *Back to Work*, Chs. 1–3; Ickes, "Precept — Then the Ax," *New Republic*, Dec. 24, 1951; Ickes to F.D.R., Dec. 27, 1934, Jan. 30, 1935, Roosevelt Papers; Ickes, *First Thousand Days*, 55, 159; Tugwell, *Stricken Land*, 17; Alexander, "Reformer"; Padover, "Ickes."

4. Corrington Gill, *Wasted Manpower* (New York, 1939), 208–9; R. L

Duffus, "Lifting America's Face," *New York Times Magazine*, June 13, 1937; H. L. Ickes, "My Twelve Years with F.D.R.," *Saturday Evening Post*, June 12, 1948; Ickes, *First Thousand Days*, 256.

5. Public Works Administration, *America Builds: The Record of PWA* (Washington, 1939); J. F. Isakoff, *The Public Works Administration* (Urbana, Ill., 1938); J. K. Williams, *Grants-in-Aid under the Public Works Administration* (New York, 1939); Ickes, "My Twelve Years"; Ickes, *Autobiography*, 286-94.

6. Lewis W. Douglas, *The Liberal Tradition* (New York, 1935), 72; Ickes, *First Thousand Days*, 115, 134, 174; interview with Henry Morgenthau, Jr., Oct. 12, 1954; Press Conference #77, Dec. 13, 1933; Douglas to F.D.R., Dec. 30, 1933, Roosevelt Papers.

7. Ickes, *First Thousand Days*, 134-36, 143; Douglas before the Conference of State Directors of the National Emergency Council, Feb. 2, 1934, Minutes; Williams, *Grant-in-Aid*, 130-32; Morgenthau, Diary, Aug. 20, 31, 1934; Douglas to F.D.R., Nov. 28, 1934, Roosevelt Papers; Douglas, *Liberal Tradition*, 53; *New York Times*, Aug. 30–Sept. 5, 1934.

8. Morgenthau, Diary, Aug. 13, 1934; Hopkins to Morgenthau, Sept. 6, 1940, Hopkins Papers; Hopkins, "Beyond Relief: The Larger Task," *New York Times Magazine*, Aug. 19, 1934; Josephine C. Brown, *Public Relief, 1929–1939* (New York, 1940), 234, 249; E. A. Williams, *Federal Aid for Relief* (New York, 1939), 82; E. W. Bakke, "Fifth Winter of Unemployment Relief," *Yale Review*, Winter 1935; Lorena Hickok to Hopkins (first page missing; evidently late 1934), Hopkins Papers; Morgenthau, Diary, Sept. 8, Oct. 1, 10, 16, 17, 18, 1934; Ickes, *First Thousand Days*, 194, 200–203, 206; Henry Morgenthau, Jr., "The Fight to Balance the Budget," *Collier's*, Sept. 27, 1947.

9. Baruch to F.D.R., Oct. 11, F.D.R. to E. M. House, Nov. 27, 1934, Roosevelt Papers; A. J. Muste and I. M. Rubinow, "The Lundeen Bill," *Survey*, Dec. 1934; Benjamin Gitlow, *The Whole of Their Lives* (New York, 1948), 260, 261; House Labor Committee, *Unemployment, Old Age and Social Insurance: Hearings*, 74 Cong., 1 Sess. (1935), 819; Press Conference #156, Nov. 7, 1934.

CHAPTER 18 *(Pages 297–315)*

1. C. L. Harriss, *History and Policies of the Home Owners' Loan Corporation* (New York, 1951); F.D.R., *Public Papers* (1933), 135–36, 233–37; *Historical Statistics*, Ser. H113–27.

2. Frances Perkins, "Eight Years as Madame Secretary," *Fortune*, Sept. 1941; C. M. H. Lynch, "Frances Perkins," *Mount Holyoke Alumnae Quarterly*, April 1929; Russell Lord, "Madame Secretary," *The New Yorker*, Sept. 2, 9, 1933; Herbert Corey, "Madame Secretary," *Today*, Jan. 27, 1934; Benjamin Stolberg, "Madame Secretary," *Saturday*

Evening Post, July 27, 1940; Frances Perkins, *The Roosevelt I Knew* (New York, 1946), 150–52; Emil Ludwig, *Roosevelt* (New York, 1938), 315; Jesse Jones, with Edward Angly, *Fifty Billion Dollars* (New York, 1951), 308–9.

3. E. E. Witte, "Development of Unemployment Compensation," *Yale Law Journal,* Dec. 1945; P. H. Douglas, *Social Security in the United States* (New York, 1936), Ch. 1; Abraham Epstein, *Insecurity: A Challenge to America* (3rd ed., New York, 1936), Ch. 18; Perkins, *Roosevelt I Knew,* Ch. 23; Perkins, "Unemployment and Relief," *American Journal of Sociology,* March 1934; Grace Abbott, *From Relief to Social Security* (Chicago, 1941) 248–56; P. A. Raushenbush, "The Wisconsin Idea," I. M. Rubinow, "The Ohio Idea," J. B. Andrews, "Prospects for Unemployment Compensation Laws," *Annals,* Nov. 1933; interview with Thomas H. Eliot, Nov. 10, 1947; Charles E. Wyzanski, Jr., "Brandeis," *Atlantic,* Nov. 1956.

4. Douglas, *Social Security,* 5–12; Epstein, *Insecurity,* Ch. 28; Tugwell to F.D.R., Feb. 24, 1934, Roosevelt Papers; F.D.R., *Public Papers* (1934), 161–62, 287–92, 321–22.

5. Frances Perkins, "The War of Security," *Survey Graphic,* Dec. 1934; House Ways and Means Committee, *Unemployment Insurance: Hearings,* 73 Cong., 2 Sess. (1934), 13–14 (Perkins); House Ways and Means Com., *Economic Security Act: Hearings,* 74 Cong., 1 Sess. (1935), 182–83 (Perkins), 372–73 (Hansen), 571 (Epstein), 874–82 (Report of the Technical Board); Senate Finance Committee, *Economic Security Act: Hearings,* 74 Cong., 1 Sess. (1935), 113–15 (Perkins), 468 (Epstein), 902–6 (Paul Kellogg), 1012 (Eveline Burns); Arthur J. Altmeyer to author, March 31, 1958; E. E. Witte, "An Historical Account of Unemployment Insurance in the Social Security Act," *Law and Contemporary Problems,* Jan. 1936; Witte, "Development of Unemployment Compensation"; Perkins, *Roosevelt I Knew,* 290–92; Tugwell, Diary, June 6, Dec. 28, 1934, Jan. 16, 1935; Abraham Epstein, " 'Social Security' under the New Deal," *Nation,* Sept. 4, 1935; Epstein, "Social Security — Where Are We Now?" *Harper's,* June 1940; Epstein, *Insecurity,* 696–718; Douglas, *Social Security,* 29–50; interview with Alvin H. Hansen, Oct. 17, 1955; M. T. Reynolds, *Interdepartmental Committees in the National Administration* (New York, 1939), 32–41.

6. J. Douglas Brown, "The Development of the Old-Age Insurance Provisions of the Social Security Act," *Law and Contemporary Problems,* April 1936; Altmeyer to author; Hopkins to John A. Kingsbury, April 16, 1934, FERA Papers.

7. Tugwell, Diary, Nov. 22, Dec. 31, 1934; Perkins, *Roosevelt I Knew,* 188–89, 282–84, 284–85; Press Conference #360–A, April 15, 1937; Luther Gulick, "Memorandum on Conference with Franklin D. Roosevelt . . . Summer 1941," Roosevelt Foundation Papers; R. G. Tugwell, "Roosevelt and Hoover," *Antioch Review,* Winter 1953–54.

8. House Ways and Means Com., *Economic Security Act*, 897–99 (Morgenthau), 242–43 (Brown), 993–1007 (Folsom); Committee on Economic Security, *Report to the President* (Washington, 1935), 25–37; Brown, "Development of the Old-Age Insurance"; G. M. Modlin, "The Old-Age Reserve Account and Its Economic Implications," *Law and Contemporary Problems*, April 1936; Abraham Epstein, "Government's Responsibility for Economic Security," *Annals*, Nov. 1939; Perkins, *Roosevelt I Knew*, 293–94; Douglas, *Social Security*, 168; interview with Alvin H. Hansen, May 4, 1957.

9. National Association of Manufacturers, *Annual Proceedings . . . 1930* (New York, 1930), 36; *Literary Digest*, Jan. 14, 1933; A. P. Sloan, Jr., "Industry's Responsibilities Broaden," *Vital Speeches*, Dec. 30, 1935; *Congressional Digest*, Feb., March, 1935; House Ways and Means Com., *Economic Security Act*, 1102 (Chandler); *Congressional Record*, 74 Cong., 1 Sess., 6054 (Taber), 6051 (Reed), 6061 (Wadsworth), April 19, 1935; J. K. Galbraith, *Economics and the Art of Controversy* (New Brunswick, N. J., 1955), 82–85.

10. Seymour E. Harris, "Priorities in Welfare Outlays" (mimeographed, 1955), 48–51; Arthur J. Altmeyer, "The Future of Social Security in America," *Congressional Record*, 83 Cong., 1 Sess., Appendix, 4491–93.

11. J. Q. Adams, First Annual Message to Congress.

CHAPTER 19 *(Pages 319–334)*

1. Anne O'Hare McCormick, "Roosevelt Surveys His Course," *New York Times Magazine*, July 8, 1934; McCormick, "Still 'A Little Left of Centre,'" *New York Times Magazine*, Nov. 25, 1934.

2. A. E. Morgan, *The Work of the Tennessee Valley Authority . . . Address before the Democratic Women's Luncheon Club of Philadelphia* (Philadelphia [1934]), 18–20; R. L. Duffus, *The Valley and Its People* (New York, 1946), 53.

3. C. H. Prichett, *The Tennessee Valley Authority* (Chapel Hill, 1943), Ch. 1; J. S. Ransmeier, *The Tennessee Valley Authority* (Nashville, 1942), Ch. 2; Norman Wengert. "Antecedents of TVA," *Agricultural History*, Oct. 1952; Herbert Hoover, *Memoirs . . . The Cabinet and the Presidency, 1920–1933* (New York, 1952), 304; Arthur Pound and S. T. Moore, eds., *They Told Barron* (New York, 1930), 51; Anne O'Hare McCormick, "The Great Dam of Controversy," *New York Times Magazine*, April 20, 1930.

4. Alfred Lief, *Democracy's Norris* (New York, 1939), 314, 415; Morgan, *Work of the TVA*, 11–12; Morgan, "Bench-Marks in the Tennessee Valley," *Survey Graphic*, Jan. 1934; Joint Committee on the Investigation of the Tennessee Valley Authority, *Investigation of the Tennessee Valley Authority: Hearings*, 75 Cong., 3 Sess. (1939), 313; T. R. B., *New Republic*, Feb. 15, 1933; F.D.R. to Norris, March 12, 1933, Roose-

velt Papers; F.D.R., *Public Papers* (1933), 122–23; E. B. Nixon, ed., *Franklin D. Roosevelt and Conservation, 1911–1945* (Hyde Park, 1957), I, 151–52; *Literary Digest*, Feb. 18, 1933; *New York Times*, April 27, 1933; House Military Affairs Committee, *Muscle Shoals: Hearings*, 73 Cong., 1 Sess. (1933), 1.

5. House Mil. Affairs Com., *Muscle Shoals*, 107, 115, 159, 223, 225; Wendell Willkie, "Government and the Public Utilities," *Vital Speeches*, Feb. 11, 1935; *Congressional Record*, 73 Cong., 1 Sess., 2178, 2179 (April 22, 1933), 2260 (April 24, 1933); Lief, *Norris*, 415–20; S. K. Bailey and Howard Samuel, *Congress at Work* (New York, 1952), Ch. 9.

6. (A. E. Morgan is the author of the first six following works.) *Edward Bellamy* (New York, 1944), 414–16; "The American Bent for Planning," *Survey Graphic*, April 1936; "Bench-Marks in the Tennessee Valley," *Survey Graphic*, Jan., Nov. 1934; "Not by Eastern Windows Only," *Antioch College Bulletin*, March 1936; "Sky Hooks," *Antioch Notes*, Jan. 1933; "The Community," *Atlantic*, Feb. 1942; Judson King, "Keep Your Eye on the Ball," *National Popular Government League Bulletin*, March 17, 1938; A. E. Morgan, *The Philosophy of Edward Bellamy* (New York, 1945), 67; Louis Adamic, *My America* (New York, 1938), 595–611.

7. Donald A. Richberg, *My Hero* (New York, 1954), 126–27; Willson Whitman, *David Lilienthal* (New York, 1948), Ch. 1.

8. Joint Committee, *Investigation of the TVA*, 102–3, 147, 233, 331; R. G. Tugwell and E. C. Banfield, "Grass Roots Democracy — Myth or Reality?" *Public Administration Review*, Winter 1950; Tugwell, *The Battle for Democracy* (New York, 1935), 24; Jonathan Daniels, *A Southerner Discovers the South* (New York, 1938), 57–59, 66–71; Daniels, "Three Men in a Valley," *New Republic*, Aug. 17, 1938; J. C. Poe, "The Morgan-Lilienthal Feud," *Nation*, Oct. 3, 1936; "Sweetness and Light vs. Power and Light," *Today*, Feb. 6, 1937; Willson Whitman "Morgan and Morgan and Lilienthal," *Harper's*, Sept. 1938.

9. Philip Selznick, *TVA and the Grass Roots* (Berkeley, 1949), Ch. 1; David E. Lilienthal, *TVA: Democracy on the March* (New York, 1953), Chs. 10, 13, 14, 18; Lilienthal, "Administrative Decentralization of Federal Functions," *Advanced Management*, Jan.–March 1940; Lilienthal, "The TVA and Decentralization," *Survey Graphic*, June 1940.

CHAPTER 20 (*Pages 335–353*)

1. F.D.R. to H. W. Van Loon, Feb. 2, 1937, Roosevelt Papers; Nelson C. Brown, "Personal Reminiscences of Franklin D. Roosevelt," Roosevelt Foundation Papers; Brown, "President Has Long Practiced Forestry," *New York Times*, April 30, 1933; F.D.R., *Public Papers* (1934), 290, *Public Papers* (1935), 65.

2. F.D.R., *Public Papers* (1934), 289; Senate Education and Labor Com-

mittee, House Labor Committee, *Unemployment Relief: Joint Hearings*, 73 Cong., 1 Sess. (1933), especially 46, 69; Civilian Conservation Corps, *Two Years of Emergency Conservation Work* (mimeographed, Washington, 1935); E. B. Nixon, ed., *Franklin D. Roosevelt and Conservation, 1911–1945* (Hyde Park, 1957), I, 138–51, 431–33, 591–93; Brown, "Personal Reminiscences"; Ferdinand Silcox, "Our Adventure in Conservation," *Atlantic*, Dec. 1937; C. P. Harper, *The Administration of the Civilian Conservation Corps* (Clarksburg, W. Va., 1939); Kenneth Holland and F. E. Hill, *Youth in the CCC* (Washington, 1942); H. M. Walker, *The CCC through the Eyes of 272 Boys* (Cleveland, 1938); Frances Perkins, *The Roosevelt I Knew* (New York, 1946), Ch. 14; Perkins, "The Builder of Roosevelt's Presidency," *New Republic*, June 21, 1954; Tugwell, "New Deal Memoir," Chs. 2, 3; National Emergency Council, Proceedings, Oct. 30, 1934; F.D.R. to F. C. Walcott, Oct. 22, 1934, to C. L. Peck, Sept. 7, 1935, Marguerite LeHand to I. Van Meter, July 15, 1939, Roosevelt Papers; Moley, *After Seven Years*, 173–74; Morgenthau, Diary, Dec. 9, 1937; D. C. Roper, *Fifty Years of Public Life* (Durham, N. C., 1941), 289; H. H. Woodring, "The American Army Stands Ready," *Liberty*, Jan. 6, 1934.

3.   H. A. Wallace, "New Vistas for Agriculture," *New York Times Magazine*, March 29, 1936; R. G. Tugwell, *The Battle for Democracy* (New York, 1935), 105–23; Tugwell, "The Planned Use of the Land," *Today*, Jan. 20, 1934; Tugwell, "No More Frontiers," *Today*, June 22, 29, 1935; E. W. Tinker, "The Plains Shelterbelt," Aug. 15, 1936, Harold Smith to F.D.R., Nov. 6, 1941, Roosevelt Papers; M. L. Cooke, "Shelterbelts — for Dustbowl Control," *Survey Graphic*, Sept. 1947.

4.   Tugwell, "New Deal Memoir," Ch. 4; Wellington Brink, *Big Hugh: The Father of Soil Conservation* (New York, 1951); H. H. Bennett, *Soil Conservation* (New York, 1939), especially viii–ix, 8, 9, 11, 55; Russell Lord, *The Wallaces of Iowa* (Boston, 1947), 372–74; C. M. Hardin, *The Politics of Agriculture* (Glencoe, Ill., 1952), 102–3, 239; F.D.R. to Wallace, March 17, 1937, Roosevelt Papers; Russell Lord, *The Agrarian Revival* (New York, 1939), 161; Mordecai Ezekiel, "Farm Aid — Fourth Stage," *Nation*, Feb. 26, 1938.

5.   Pinchot letter in *Washington Post*, July 17, 1935; House Public Lands Committee, *To Provide for the Orderly Use, Improvement and Development of the Public Range: Hearings*, 73 Cong., 1, 2, Sess. (1933, 1934), 134.

6.   House Pub. Lands Com., *Public Range: Hearings*, especially 26, 52, 56; E. L. Peffer, *The Closing of the Public Domain* (Stanford University, 1951), 214–24; Ickes, *First Thousand Days*, 169–70; Nixon, ed., *Roosevelt and Conservation*, I, 160, 296, 314; Marquis James, with Ickes, "The National Domain and the New Deal," *Saturday Evening Post*, Dec. 23, 1933.

7.   Ickes, *First Thousand Days*, 202, 203, 208, 551, 681; *Washington Post*, July 17, 1935; Ickes statement, Department of the Interior release,

May 2, 1937; Ickes speech at Evening Star Forum, May 31, 1937, Roosevelt Papers; Ickes, *The Lowering Clouds* (New York, 1954), 111, 118; Ickes, "Not Guilty! Richard A. Ballinger — an American Dreyfus," *Saturday Evening Post*, May 25, 1940; Ickes, *Autobiography of a Curmudgeon* (New York, 1943), 153.

8. Tugwell, Diary, March 30, 1934; Ickes, *First Thousand Days*, 250, 259, 350, 417, 542, 596; Senate Committee on Expenditures in the Executive Departments, *To Change the Name of the Department of the Interior and to Coordinate Certain Governmental Functions: Hearing*, 74 Cong., 1 Sess. (1935), especially 4, 5, 18-20; House Committee on Expenditures in the Executive Departments, *Change Name of Department of the Interior to the Department of Conservation and Works: Hearings*, 74 Cong., 1 Sess. (1935), 1-3, 122.

9. F.D.R. to Harold Smith, Jan. 24, 1940, to Pinchot, Jan. 15, 1940, Roosevelt Papers; Ickes, *First Thousand Days*, 151, 328, 417-18; Ickes, *The Inside Struggle* (New York, 1954), 8, 43, 311; Ickes, "My Twelve Years with F.D.R.," *Saturday Evening Post*, June 19, July 24, 1948; Tugwell, "New Deal Memoir," Ch. 4; Hopkins to F.D.R., April 18, 1937, Roosevelt Papers.

10. National Planning Board, Minutes, June 25, 1934, National Archives; Ickes, "The President made it perfectly clear that he intended under the term 'National Resources' to include both material and human resources." Senate Commerce Committee, *National Planning Board of 1935: Hearing*, 74 Cong., 1 Sess. (1935), 4.

11. Press Conference #98, Feb. 14, 1934; Ickes, *First Thousand Days*, 145-46, 171-72; Ickes, *Back to Work* (New York, 1935), 79-80; J. D. Millett, *The Process and Organization of Government Planning* (New York, 1947), 143-46; C. E. Merriam, "The National Resources Planning Board," *American Political Science Review*, Dec. 1944; Lucy Sprague Mitchell, *Two Lives* (New York, 1953), 369-76; Donald Richberg, *My Hero* (New York, 1954), 75-76; R. G. Tugwell, "The Utility of the Future in the Present," *Public Administration Review*, Winter 1948; Tugwell and E. C. Banfield, "Governmental Planning at Mid-Century," *Journal of Politics*, May 1951; Tugwell, "The Sources of New Deal Reformation," *Ethics*, July 1954.

CHAPTER 21 *(Pages 354-368)*

1. R. G. Tugwell, *The Battle for Democracy* (New York, 1935), 66.
2. R. G. Tugwell, "Freedom from Fakes," *Today*, Nov. 17, 1933; Tugwell, "America Takes Hold of Its Destiny," *Today*, April 28, 1934; Tugwell, Thomas Munro, and R. E. Stryker, *American Economic Life* (New York, 1930), 584-85; Tugwell, *The Industrial Discipline* (New York, 1933), 127, 173-74; Arthur Kallet and F. J. Schlink, *100,-000,000 Guinea Pigs* (New York, 1933).

3. Senate Commerce Committee, *Foods, Drugs, and Cosmetics: Hearings,*
73 Cong., 2 Sess. (1933), especially, 12, 172, 322, 394; Senate Commerce
Com., *Foods . . . Hearings,* 73 Cong., 2 Sess. (1934), especially 292, 411;
House Interstate and Foreign Commerce Committee, *Foods, Drugs,
and Cosmetics: Hearings,* 74 Cong., 1 Sess. (1935), especially 507, 523;
Tugwell, "New Deal Memoirs," Chs. 2, 4; D. F. Cavers, "The Food,
Drug, and Cosmetic Act of 1938," *Law and Contemporary Problems,*
Winter 1939; Ruth de F. Lamb, *American Chamber of Horrors* (New
York, 1936); Tugwell to F.D.R., Feb. 21, Marguerite LeHand to
Marvin McIntyre, Feb. 28, 1934, Roosevelt Papers; Arthur Kallet,
"Foods and Drugs for the Consumer," *Annals,* May 1934; R. G. Tug-
well, *The Democratic Roosevelt* (New York, 1957), 464–67; Arthur
Kallet, "Consumers' Research on Strike," *New Masses,* Sept. 17, 1935;
Don Wharton, "Arthur Kallet," *Scribner's,* Nov. 1937; *Consumer Re-
ports,* Aug. 1957; interview with D. F. Cavers, 1957.
4. H. S. Johnson, "Background of NRA," *Saturday Evening Post,* June
30, 1934; Maury Maverick, *A Maverick American* (New York, 1937),
235–36. Tugwell, Diary, March 22, 1934; Russell Lord, "Rural New
Yorker," *The New Yorker,* March 23, 30, 1935; Senate Agriculture
and Forestry Committee, *Confirmation of Rexford G. Tugwell: Hearings,* 73 Cong., 2 Sess. (1934), especially 166–67, 171; R. G. Tugwell,
"The Compromising Roosevelt," *Western Political Quarterly,* June
1953; *Time,* June 25, 1934; Ickes, *First Thousand Days,* 164.
5. Ford in *Time,* June 13, 1932; E. E. Peoples to Lawrence Westbrook,
May 21, 1934, FERA Papers; Bruce Bliven, "Mr. Borsodi's Way Out,"
New Republic, July 10, 1929; Ralph Borsodi, "One Way Out," *New
Republic,* July 17, 1929; Borsodi, *Flight from the City* (New York,
1933); Borsodi, "Subsistence Homesteads," *Survey Graphic,* Jan. 1934;
F.D.R. to Norris, April 17, 1933, Roosevelt Papers; E. D. Coblentz,
William Randolph Hearst (New York, 1952), 148; John H. Bankhead,
"The One Way to Permanent Recovery," *Liberty Magazine,* July 22,
1933.
6. Russell Lord and Paul H. Johnstone, eds., *A Place on Earth* (Bureau
of Agricultural Economics, Washington, 1942); Wallace to Lewis Douglas, June 5, 1933, Bureau of the Budget Papers; H. L. Hopkins, "Beyond Relief," *New York Times Magazine,* Aug. 19, 1934; H. S. Johnson, *The Blue Eagle* (New York, 1935), 198; M. L. Wilson, *Farm Relief
and the Domestic Allotment Plan* (Minneapolis, 1933), 49–50; Wilson,
"The Place of Subsistence Homesteads in our National Economy,"
address, Philadelphia, Dec. 27, 1933 (Department of Agriculture release), 5–6; Russell Lord, *The Wallaces of Iowa* (Boston, 1947), 300–
304; Lord, "The Rebirth of Rural Life," *Survey Graphic,* Dec. 1941;
C. E. Pickett, *For More Than Bread* (Boston, 1953), 52–53, 62; H. A.
Wallace, "We Are More Than Economic Men," *Scribner's,* Dec. 1934.
7. Eleanor Roosevelt, *This I Remember* (New York, 1949), 126–32; Ickes,
First Thousand Days, 129, 152, 154, 205–7, 218–19, 227–32, 253–54;

Louis Howe radio broadcast, Sept. 28, 1934, Roosevelt Papers; Pickett, *For More Than Bread*, 58–61; Wesley Stout, "The New Homesteaders," *Saturday Evening Post*, Aug. 4, 1934; Eleanor Roosevelt, "Subsistence Farmsteads," *Forum*, April 1934; W. E. Brooks, "Arthurdale — A New Chance," *Atlantic*, Feb. 1935; M. M. Rice, "Footnote on Arthurdale," *Harper's*, March 1940; Wilson, "Place of Subsistence Homesteads"; Subsistence Homestead Division, *Circular No. 1, General Information Concerning the Purposes and Policies of the Division of Subsistence Homesteads* (Washington, 1933); *Time*, June 18, 1934; Margaret Coit, *Mr. Baruch* (Boston, 1957), 690.

8. H. L. Ickes, *Back to Work* (New York, 1936), 191–94; Lorena Hickok to Hopkins, May 25, 1934, Hopkins Papers; R. P. Duggan, *A Federal Resettlement Project: Granger Homesteads* (Washington, 1937); H. L. Hopkins, *Spending to Save* (New York, 1936), 147; Hopkins to Lawrence Westbrook, Nov. 5, 1934, in *Rural Rehabilitation*, Nov. 15, 1934; Hopkins, "Hope for the Millions," *Today*, May 4, 1935; E. A. Williams, *Federal Aid for Relief* (New York, 1939), 140–41; Berta Asch and A. R. Mangus, *Farmers on Relief and Rehabilitation* (Works Progress Administration Research Monograph VIII, Washington, 1937).

CHAPTER 22 (*Pages 369–381*)

1. R. G. Tugwell, "No More Frontiers," *Today*, June 29, 1935; Tugwell, *The Battle for Democracy* (New York, 1935), 157; Tugwell, *The Stricken Land* (New York, 1946), 21, 35, 218; Tugwell, "The Preparation of a President," *Western Political Quarterly*, June 1948; Tugwell, "New Deal Memoir," Chs. 1, 2; O. E. Baker, Ralph Borsodi, and M. L. Wilson, *Agriculture in Modern Life* (New York, 1939), 74h.

2. E. C. Banfield, *Government Project* (Glencoe, Ill., 1951) with foreword by R. G. Tugwell; G. A. Warner, *Greenbelt: The Cooperative Community* (New York, 1954) with introduction by J. S. Lansill; Russell Lord and Paul H. Johnstone, eds., *A Place on Earth* (Bureau of Agricultural Economics, Washington, 1942); M. W. Childs, *I Write from Washington* (New York, 1942), 10–14; Lorena Hickok to Hopkins, May 28, 1934, Hopkins Papers; Tugwell, Diary, March 3, 1935; Tugwell, "The Meaning of the Greenbelt Towns," *New Republic*, Feb. 17, 1937; Baker, Borsodi, and Wilson, *Agriculture*, 255–56; G. G. Gross, "Greenbelt — the Boondoggle That Made Good," *Washington Post*, June 8, 1947; Jonathan Daniels, *Frontier on the Potomac* (New York, 1946), 135–36; Russell Lord, "The Rebirth of Rural Life," *Survey Graphic*, Dec. 1941; Redelia Brisbane, *Albert Brisbane* (Boston, 1893), 218; F.D.R. to Alexander, Aug. 28, 1936, to Wallace, Feb. 2, 1937, Roosevelt Papers.

3. Resettlement Administration, *The Resettlement Administration* (Washington, 1935); *Farm Tenancy: Message from the President of the United*

States Transmitting the Report of the Special Committee on Farm Tenancy, 75 Cong., 1 Sess., Hse. Doc. No. 149 (Washington, 1937); Howard Kester, *Revolt among the Sharecroppers* (New York, 1936); J. D. Black and R. H. Allen, "The Growth of Farm Tenancy in the United States," *Quarterly Journal of Economics,* May 1937; C. S. Johnson, E. R. Embree, and W. W. Alexander, *The Collapse of Cotton Tenancy* (Chapel Hill, 1935), 6–23; H. C. Nixon, *Forty Acres and Steel Mules* (Chapel Hill, 1938), 19–27; L. P. Davis, "Relief and the Sharecropper," *Survey Graphic,* Jan. 1936; C. T. Carpenter, "King Cotton's Slaves," *Scribner's,* Oct. 1935; *New York World-Telegram,* July 30, 1935; *Time,* March 4, 1935; H. A. Wallace, "Wallace Maps a Farm Program," *New York Times Magazine,* Jan. 3, 1937; Russell Lord, *The Wallaces of Iowa* (Boston, 1947), 459–62.

4. Kester, *Revolt;* Carpenter, "King Cotton's Slaves"; Essick Low to Harry Hopkins, April 9, 1934, FERA Papers; *Arkansas Gazette,* Aug. 3, 1954; *New York Times,* April 18, 1935; Frazier Hunt, *One American* (New York, 1938), 394; Thomas to F.D.R., March 15, April 9, 22, 23, Davis to F.D.R., March 19, to Thomas, March 19, 1935, Roosevelt Papers; Norman Thomas, *Plight of the Sharecropper* (New York, 1934); Thomas, "Reminiscences" (Oral History Research Office), 83, 88; P. S. Taylor and Clark Kerr, "Uprisings on the Farms," *Survey Graphic,* Jan. 1935; James Rorty, "Lettuce — with American Dressing," *Nation,* May 15, 1935.

5. *Sharecropper's Voice,* July, Oct., Nov. 1936; H. A. Wallace, "Wallace Points to the Danger of Tenancy," *New York Times Magazine,* March 31, 1935; Tugwell, Diary, Jan. 23, April 14, 1935; Tugwell, "Behind the Farm Problem: Rural Poverty," *New York Times Magazine,* Jan. 10, 1937; Bilbo to F.D.R., Aug. 18, 1935, Roosevelt Papers; W. W. Alexander memorandum of May 27, 1948, Roosevelt Foundation Papers; J. G. Maddox, "The Bankhead-Jones Farm Tenant Act," *Law and Contemporary Problems,* Oct. 1937; Paul V. Maris, *"The Land Is Mine": From Tenancy to Family Farm Ownership* (Washington, 1950), Ch. 1; Tugwell to author, April 14, 1958.

CHAPTER 23 *(Pages 385–396)*

1. Irving Bernstein, "The Growth of American Unions," *American Economic Review,* June 1954; *Historical Statistics,* D224–38; Edward Levinson, *Labor on the March* (New York, 1938), 55–57.

2. Charles Rumford Walker, *American City* (New York, 1937), Chs. 6–12; "Revolt in the Northwest," *Fortune,* April 1936; Herbert Solow, "War in Minneapolis," *Nation,* Aug. 8, 1934; C. R. Walker, "The Farmer-Labor Party of Minnesota," *Nation,* March 13, 1937; Herbert Lefkovitz, "Olson: Radical and Proud of It," *Review of Reviews,* May 1935; Eric Sevareid, *Not So Wild a Dream* (New York, 1946), 58; James P. Cannon, *History of American Trotskyism* (New York, 1944), Ch. 8.

3. "The Maritime Unions," *Fortune*, Sept. 1937; Creel to F.D.R., March 21, 1934, John Steelman to Frances Perkins, May 19, 1937, Roosevelt Papers; Louis Adamic, "Harry Bridges," *Nation*, May 6, 1936; G. P. West, "Labor Strategist of the Embarcadero," *New York Times Magazine*, Oct. 25, 1936; Bruce Minton and John Stuart, *Men Who Lead Labor* (New York, 1937), Ch. 7; Frances Perkins, *The Roosevelt I Knew* (New York, 1946), 316.

4. *Time*, June 25–Aug. 6, 1934; Perkins, *Roosevelt I Knew*, 312–15; H. S. Johnson, *The Blue Eagle* (New York, 1935), 321–26; Hiram Johnson to Ickes, July 16, Meier to F.D.R., July 16, Perkins to F.D.R., July 15, Howe to F.D.R., July 15, 1934, Roosevelt Papers; F.D.R., *Public Papers* (1934), 399; Lillian Symes, "Thunder over San Francisco," *Modern Monthly*, Aug. 1934; Miriam Allen De Ford, "Labor Bids for Power," *Nation*, July 18, 1934; "San Francisco: An Autopsy on the General Strike," *Nation*, Aug. 1, 1934; Minton and Stuart, *Men Who Lead Labor*, 181–89; Johnson, speech of July 17, 1934, NRA Release #6823, July 27, 1934; Larry O'Conner, "The Facts behind the San Francisco Strike," *Today*, Sept. 8, 1934; Maurice Goldbloom, John Herling, *et al.*, *Strikes under the New Deal* (New York [1936]), 44–52; Walter Lippmann, *Interpretations: 1933–1935*, Allan Nevins, ed. (New York, 1936), 139–40; W. Z. Foster, *Pages from a Worker's Life* (New York, 1939), 193–97.

5. "The Industrial War," *Fortune*, Nov. 1937; *Time*, June 4–Sept. 24, 1934; Daniels to F.D.R., Sept. 17, 1934, Roosevelt Papers; Levinson, *Labor*, Ch. 3.

6. Herbert Harris, *American Labor* (New Haven, 1938), 279–83; Harris, *Labor's Civil War* (New York, 1940), 31–32; Levinson, *Labor*, Chs. 3–4.

CHAPTER 24 *(Pages 397–406)*

1. Francis Biddle, "The Labor Board," Biddle Papers; Garrison to Johnson, Aug. 17, Johnson to Garrison, Aug. 18, Biddle to F.D.R., Dec. 6, Richberg to Marvin McIntyre, Dec. 6, 13, Richberg to F.D.R., Dec. 15, 18, 26, 1934, Roosevelt Papers; Senate Finance Committee, *Investigation of the National Recovery Administration: Hearings*, 74 Cong., 1 Sess. (1935), 1536–38; L. L. Lorwin and Arthur Wubnig, *Labor Relations Board* (Washington, 1935), 302–3, 309, 324–28, 439–40; Francis Biddle, "Labor's Status Today," *Nation*, June 26, 1935; L. K. Garrison, "The National Labor Board," *Annals*, March 1936; Garrison, "7–A and the Future," *Survey Graphic*, Feb. 1935; Garrison, "The National Labor Relations Act," *Survey Graphic*, Dec. 1935; *New York Times*, March 8, 1935; R. G. Swing, "Richberg Misinforms the President," *Nation*, Feb. 6, 1935.

2. Leon Keyserling, "Why the Wagner Act?" in L. G. Silverberg, ed., *The Wagner Act after Ten Years* (Washington, 1945); Irving Bernstein,

New Deal Collective Bargaining Policy (Berkeley, 1950), Ch. 7; Senate Education and Labor Committee, *To Create a National Labor Board: Hearings,* 73 Cong., 2 Sess. (1934), especially 7–13; Sen. Ed. and Labor Com., *National Labor Relations Board: Hearings,* 74 Cong., 1 Sess. (1935); Biddle, "The Labor Board"; Heywood Broun, "Labor and the Liberals," *Nation,* May 1, 1935.

3. F.D.R. to Garner, Aug. 11, Alice Winegar to William D. Hassett, Oct. 6, Cummings to F.D.R., July 20, Early to F.D.R., Sept. 13, 1934, Roosevelt Papers; Press Conference, #125, May 25, 1934; R. G. Tugwell, *The Industrial Discipline* (New York, 1933), 115, 134–35; Frances Perkins, *The Roosevelt I Knew* (New York, 1946), 303–4, 307–10, 325; R. G. Tugwell, "Franklin D. Roosevelt on the Verge of the Presidency," *Antioch Review,* Spring 1956; Bernstein, *New Deal Collective Bargaining,* 26, 99; Donald Richberg, "Rights and Wrongs of Labor," *Vital Speeches,* June 1, 1953; Edmund Wilson, *The American Earthquake* (New York, 1958), 561.

4. Senate Ed. and Labor Com., *NLRB: Hearings,* 125, 126, 581–87; House Labor Committee, *Labor Disputes Act: Hearings,* 74 Cong., 1 Sess. (1935), 174; Sen. Ed. and Labor Com., *To Create a National Labor Board,* 59, 496, 763, 972–92; L. H. Brown, Charles R. Hook, G. H. Houston, *et al.,* to F.D.R., March 21, 1934, Roosevelt Papers; *Commercial and Financial Chronicle,* March 24, 1934; E. T. Weir, "Present Relations of Business to Government," *Vital Speeches,* April 22, 1935; Walter Lippmann, *Interpretations: 1933–1935,* Allan Nevins, ed., (New York, 1936), 148, 153, 154; clipping from an Oklahoma City paper, April 19, 1934, Hopkins Papers; A. P. Sloan, Jr., "Comments on the Current Situation," *Vital Speeches,* April 22, 1935; Bernstein, *New Deal Collective Bargaining,* Ch. 8; Keyserling, "Why the Wagner Act?"

5. Bernstein, *New Deal Collective Bargaining,* Ch. 9; Roper to F.D.R., May 22, 1935, Roosevelt Papers; *New York Times,* May 25, 1935; *Congressional Record,* 74 Cong., 1 Sess. 9679 (June 19, 1935); Biddle, "The Labor Board"; Malcolm Ross, *Death of a Yale Man* (New York, 1939), 173–74; National Lawyers' Committee of the American Liberty League, *Report on the Constitutionality of the National Labor Relations Act* (Washington, 1935), xi.

CHAPTER 25 *(Pages 407–419)*

1. The general analysis owes much to conversations with John T. Dunlop. Compare also his paper "Structural Changes in the American Labor Movement and Industrial Relations System" (MS); Benjamin Stolberg, *The Story of the C.I.O.* (New York, 1938), 11; Edward Levinson, *Labor on the March* (New York, 1938), Ch. 4.

2. Theresa Wolfson and Abraham Weiss, *Industrial Unionism in the American Labor Movement* (New York, 1937), 8–19; Daniel De Leon,

Industrial Unionism (New York, 1935), 4; Arnold Petersen, *Daniel De Leon: Social Architect* (New York, 1941), 242; Marjorie R. Clark, "Recent History of Labor Organization," and John L. Lewis, "Adapting Union Methods to Current Changes," *Annals*, March 1936.

3. Levinson, *Labor*, Chs. 3, 4.

4. AF of L, *Proceedings of the Fifty-fifth Annual Convention* (Washington [1936]), 521–64, 727; *New York Times*, Oct. 20, 1935; Levinson, *Labor*, Ch. 5; James A. Wechsler, *Labor Baron: A Portrait of John L. Lewis* (New York, 1944), 50–54.

5. S. D. Alinsky, *John L. Lewis* (New York, 1949), 78; Levinson, *Labor*, Ch. 6; Wechsler, *Labor Baron*, 54–57; *New York Times*, Jan. 24, Aug. 5, 1936; *Time*, Feb. 10, 1936; Louis Stark, "The Crisis in the Labor Movement," *New York Times Magazine*, March 25, 1936; John L. Lewis, "Industrial Unionism Surveys the Future," *Forum*, April 1936; Walter Galenson, "Relationship between the A.F. of L. and the C.I.O., 1935–41" (MS); "The Great Labor Upheaval," *Fortune*, Oct. 1936.

6. Walter Galenson, "The Unionization of the American Steel Industry," *International Review of Social History*, I, 29; Levinson, *Labor*, Ch. 6; *Time*, June 15, 1936; Kermit Eby, "They Don't Sing Any More," *Christian Century*, Feb. 27, 1952.

7. John L. Lewis, the following in *Vital Speeches* for dates indicated: "The Battle for Industrial Democracy" (Aug. 1, 1936), "The Future of Labor" (Oct. 15, 1936), "I Solemnly Warn the Leaders of Industry" (Jan. 15, 1937); Selden Rodman, "Labor Leader No. 1," *Common Sense*, Jan. 1936; Wechsler, *Labor Baron*, 3, 73–83; Lewis before Senate Finance Committee, *National Industrial Recovery: Hearings*, 73 Cong., 1 Sess. (1933), 406; C. L. Sulzberger, *Sit Down with John L. Lewis* (New York, 1938), 51; Heywood Broun, "We Still Want the United Front," *Nation*, Jan. 1, 1936; Bruce Minton and John Stuart, *Men Who Lead Labor* (New York, 1937), 114.

CHAPTER 26 (Pages 423-433)

1. J. P. Kennedy, *I'm for Roosevelt* (New York, 1936), 93; *Topeka Capital*, May 26, 1933; *New York Times*, Sept. 14, 1936; Walter Lippmann, "Big Business Men of Tomorrow," *American Magazine*, April 1934; interview with Frances Perkins, Feb. 21, 1947; Donald Richberg, "The Future of the NRA," *Fortune*, Oct. 1934; J. T. Flynn, "Other People's Money," *New Republic*, Dec. 11, 1935; Raskob to F.D.R., April 4, Leffingwell to F.D.R., Oct. 2, 1933, Roosevelt Papers; W. A. White in *Emporia Gazette*, Jan. 3, 1934; "Mr. Roosevelt's Men," *Fortune*, April 1934.

2. D. C. Roper, *Fifty Years of Public Life* (Durham, N. C., 1941), 284, 346–47; Ickes, *First Thousand Days*, 542; Jesse H. Jones, with Ed-

ward Angly, *Fifty Billion Dollars* (New York, 1951), especially 290;
B. N. Timmons, *Jesse H. Jones* (New York, 1956); T. L. Stokes, *Chip
off My Shoulder* (Princeton, 1940), 232; Ray Tucker, "Texas Steerer,"
Collier's, Sept. 22, 1934; Dwight Macdonald, "Jesse Jones, Reluctant
Dragon," *Nation*, Feb. 7, 14, 1942; W. B. Huie, "Jesse Jones," *Ameri-
can Mercury*, April 1942; Tom Connally, with Alfred Steinberg, *My
Name Is Tom Connally* (New York, 1954), 131–32.

3. Jones, *Fifty Billion Dollars*, 73, 84, 290, 517–18; Timmons, *Jones*, 168,
174; Senate Banking and Currency Committee, *Creation of a Reconstruction Finance Corporation: Hearings*, 72 Cong., 1 Sess. (1932), 40;
Herbert Hoover, *State Papers* (New York, 1934), II, 228 ff.

4. Leffingwell to Alexander Sachs, Jan. 4, 1935, Roosevelt Papers; *New
York Times*, Sept. 5, 1933; Jones, *Fifty Billion Dollars*, 26–27; Timmons, *Jones*, Ch. 18; C. F. Roos, *NRA Economic Planning* (Bloomington, Ind., 1937), 383–86; Elliott V. Bell, "The Bankers Sign a
Truce," *Current History*, Dec. 1934.

5. F.D.R. to Woodin, Oct. 9, 1933, Roosevelt Papers; Ickes, *First
Thousand Days*, 108–9; Jones, *Fifty Billion Dollars*, 27–37.

6. Reconstruction Finance Corporation, *Seven-Year Report* (Washington, 1939); "The House of Jesse," *Fortune*, May 1940; Jones, *Fifty
Billion Dollars*, 261–62; Macdonald, "Jesse Jones"; M. W. Childs, *I
Write from Washington* (New York, 1942), 28; Timmons, *Jones*, Ch.
22; Jesse Jones, *Recovery Is Obvious . . . Address . . . May 10, 1935*
(n.p., n.d.), 5; Thomas G. Corcoran to author, April 1, 1958.

7. A. A. Berle, Jr., "High Finance: Master or Servant," *Yale Review*,
Autumn 1933; Raymond Moley, "Must the Government Take Over the
Banks?" *Today*, Feb. 3, 1934; A. A. Berle, Jr., *New Directions in the
New World* (New York, 1940), Ch. 5; F.D.R., *Public Papers* (1934),
152–54; C. B. Upham and Edwin Lamke, *Closed and Distressed Banks*
(Washington, 1934), 235–40; A. A. Berle, Jr., "The New Deal and
Economic Liberty," *Annals*, March 1935; Corcoran to author, April 1,
1958.

CHAPTER 27 *(Pages 434–445)*

1. Herbert Hoover, *Memoirs . . . The Great Depression, 1929–1941* (New
York, 1952), 125–30; J. T. Flynn, "The Marines Land in Wall Street,"
Harper's, July 1934.

2. Senate Banking and Currency Committee, *Stock Exchange Practices:
Hearings*, 73 Cong., 1 Sess. (1933), 53, 64, 175; *Report*, 73 Cong., 2
Sess., especially 125–33; Ferdinand Pecora, *Wall Street under Oath*
(New York, 1939), Chs. 1, 2; T. L. Stokes, *Chip off My Shoulder* (Prince-
ton, 1940), 345–50; Flynn, "Marines Land in Wall Street"; *New York
Times*, May 25–June 1, 1933, Sept. 14, 1936; *Topeka Capital*, May 26,
1933; *Time*, June 5, 12, 1933; Ickes, *First Thousand Days*, 45–46.

3. Pecora, *Wall Street,* 96–103; Sen. Banking and Cur. Com., *Stock Exchange Practices,* 388, 1010, 2834; *New York Times,* March 26, 1933.

4. J. M. Landis, "Should the Federal Securities Act of 1933 Be Modified?" *Congressional Digest,* May 1934; A. S. Link, *Woodrow Wilson and the Progressive Era* (New York, 1954), 68; Pecora, *Wall Street,* Ch. 13.

5. Moley, *After Seven Years,* 175–84; "The Legend of Landis," *Fortune,* Aug. 1934; Ray Tucker, "Wall Street's Boss," *New York Times Magazine,* Oct. 6, 1935; "SEC," *Fortune,* June 1940; F.D.R., *Public Papers* (1933), 93–94; Felix Frankfurter, "The Federal Securities Act," *Fortune,* Aug. 1933; Landis to author, Feb. 13, 1957.

6. F. H. Sisson, "Men, Not Laws, Make Sound Banks," *Nation's Business,* Jan. 1933; B. N. Timmons, *Jesse H. Jones* (New York, 1956), 177–78, 183, 187; *New York Times,* March 9, 1933; Pecora, *Wall Street,* 285, 295; *Historical Statistics,* Ser. N135.

7. Elliott V. Bell, "The Bankers Sign a Truce," *Current History,* Dec. 1934; Bell, "The Decline of the Money Barons," in Hanson Baldwin and Shepard Stone, eds., *We Saw It Happen* (New York, 1938); *St. Louis Post-Dispatch,* Nov. 5, 1933; Raymond Moley, "An NRA for Finance," *Today,* Dec. 30, 1933; A. A. Berle, Jr., "High Finance: Master or Servant," *Yale Review,* Autumn 1933; Tugwell, "New Deal Memoir," Ch. 2; W. O. Douglas, "Protecting the Investor," *Yale Review,* Spring 1934; Gardiner C. Means, "Protecting the Buyers of Securities," *New York Times,* April 9, 1933.

CHAPTER 28 *(Pages 446–455)*

1. J. P. Frank, *Mr. Justice Black* (New York, 1949), Chs. 1–3; Charlotte Williams, *Hugo L. Black* (Baltimore, 1950), Ch. 2; Paul Y. Anderson, "Democracy at Work," *Nation,* March 2, 1932; Raymond Clapper, "Hugo Black," *Review of Reviews,* April 1934.

2. H. L. Smith, *Airways* (New York, 1942), 212–68; M. R. Werner, *Privileged Characters* (New York, 1935), Ch. 6; Clapper, "Hugo Black"; Frank, *Black,* 52–53; *Time,* Feb. 19, 1934; Paul Tillett, "The Army Flies the Mails," Inter-University Case Program, No. 24 (1955), 1–29.

3. Senate Post Office Committee, *Revision of Air-Mail Laws: Hearings,* 73 Cong., 2 Sess. (1934), 114, 124, 220; House Post Office Committee, *Air Mail: Hearings,* 73 Cong., 2 Sess. (1934), 382–88; Tillett, "Army Flies the Mails," 30–69; *New York Times,* Feb. 9–March 17, 1934; *Time,* Feb. 19–March 19, 1934; Smith, *Airways,* 142–43, 249–77; J. A. Farley, *Jim Farley's Story* (New York, 1948), 47; Isaac Don Levine, *Mitchell: Pioneer of Air Power* (New York, 1943), 392–94; Emile Gauvreau and Lester Cohen, *Billy Mitchell* (New York, 1942), 211; H. H. Arnold, *Global Mission* (London, 1951), 109–11; Werner, *Privileged Characters,* 433; F.D.R., *Public Papers* (1934), 138–42.

CHAPTER 29 (*Pages 456–470*)

1. See testimony by Corcoran and E. A. Goldenweiser, Senate Banking and Currency Committee, *Stock Exchange Practices (National Securities Exchange Act): Hearings*, 73 Cong., 2 Sess. (1934), 6437–40, 6465–66; also House Interstate and Foreign Commerce Committee, *Stock Exchange Regulation: Hearings*, 73 Cong., 2 Sess. (1934), especially 85–86; Moley, *After Seven Years*, 284–85; Benjamin V. Cohen to author, Dec. 30, 1955; Landis to author, March 20, 1956.

2. Select House Committee, *To Investigate Charges Made by Dr. William A. Wirt: Hearings*, 73 Cong., 2 Sess. (1934), 8, 11, 39, 41, 50, 66, 72, 81, 88; William A. Wirt, *America Must Lose* (New York, 1934), 22–25, 33–37; Wirt, *Keeping America Safe for Democracy* (n.p., 1936); *New York Times*, March 25–April 11, 1934; House Interstate and For. Commerce Com., *Stock Exchange Regulation*, 755–73; *Time*, April 23, 1934; F.D.R., *Public Papers* (1934), 182; Mary Heaton Vorse, "Behind Dr. Wirt," *New Republic*, April 25, 1934; W. R. Hearst, *Selections from Writings and Speeches* (San Francisco, 1948), 109; Mark Sullivan in *New York Herald Tribune*, Dec. 12–28, 1933; Tugwell, Diary, April 8, 1954; Edmund Wilson, *The American Earthquake* (New York, 1958), 538–44; J. C. Malin, *On the Nature of History* (Lawrence, Kan., 1954), 237–62; Charles Collins, "The Ordeal of Dr. Wirt," *Chicago Tribune*, April 4, 1954.

3. Joseph Alsop and Robert Kintner, "The Battle of the Market Place," *Saturday Evening Post*, June 11, 1938; Matthew Josephson, "Groton, Harvard, Wall Street," *The New Yorker*, April 2, 1932; Whitney's testimony in Sen. Banking and Cur. Com., *Stock Exchange Practices*, 98, 6605, 7538, and House Interstate and For. Commerce Com., *Stock Exchange Regulation*, 195; S. J. Woolf, "Whitney Defends the Takers of Risks," *New York Times Magazine*, July 3, 1932; *Time*, Feb. 26, 1934; T. L. Stokes, *Chip off My Shoulder* (Princeton, 1940), 359.

4. Sen. Banking and Cur. Com., *Stock Exchange Practices*, 6583–84, 6606, 6609, 7000, 7486; House Interstate and For. Commerce Com., *Stock Exchange Regulation*, 495, 561, 731, 939; Whitney to F.D.R., Feb. 8, 1934, Roosevelt Papers; *Congressional Record*, 73 Cong., 2 Sess., 7944 (May 2, 1934), 8012 (May 3, 1934); *New York Times*, March 17, April 22, May 7, 1934; "Wall Street's Raid on the New Deal," *Today*, April 21, 1934.

5. Will Rogers, *Autobiography*, Donald Day, ed. (Boston, 1949), 339; Alsop and Kintner, "Battle of the Market Place"; *New York Times*, April 24, 1934; Corcoran to author, April 1, 1958; Sen. Banking and Cur. Com., *Stock Exchange Practices*, 6574, 6584, 6601, 6733; Landis to author, March 20, 1956.

6. F.D.R., *Public Papers* (1934), 170; *New York Times*, March 7, 8, 20, 21, May 5, 13, 27, 1934; Alsop and Kintner, "Battle of the Market

Place"; J. T. Flynn, "The Marines Land on Wall Street," *Harper's*, July 1934; Landis to author, Feb. 13, 1957.

7. Moley, *After Seven Years*, 286–89; J. P. Kennedy, *I'm for Roosevelt* (New York, 1936), 3; "Mr. Kennedy the Chairman," *Fortune*, Sept. 1937; Karl Schriftgiesser, "Mr. Ambassador Kennedy," *North American Review*, Winter 1938–39; J. T. Flynn, "Other People's Money," *New Republic*, July 11, 18, 1934; Ickes, *First Thousand Days*, 173; Corcoran writes, "I don't know whether I ever made this particular remark to Moley identifying the enemy as 'for business.' . . . I might have said, 'Four are for *us* and one is against *us*.' At the time, considering the kind of 'Communist' fight that had been waged against Ben and myself personally, we were probably in no dove of peace mood. . . . But there were no real rancors because there had been businessmen for us as well as against us." To author, April 1, 1958.

8. Landis to author, Feb. 13, 1957; Corcoran to author, April 1, 1958; Elliott V. Bell, "Wall Street's Life with SEC," *Banking*, Jan. 1939; Alsop and Kintner, "Battle of the Market Place"; "SEC," *Fortune*, June 1940; "Kennedy, Who Guards the Investor," *Nation's Business*, March 1935.

CHAPTER 30 *(Pages 471–488)*

1. W. M. Kiplinger, "What's Ahead in Washington," *Nation's Business*, May 1934; Stone to Hoover, March 27, 1934, in A. T. Mason, *Security through Freedom* (Ithaca, 1955), 74; *Time*, Sept. 24, 1934; E. A. Filene, "A Report of a Study Tour of Business Conditions in 14 Large Cities," March 1934, Roosevelt Papers; *Commercial and Financial Chronicle*, Oct. 7, 1933; Coudert to Beck, Dec. 30, 1933, in Morton Keller, "Journey to Disillusion: James M. Beck and the Course of Modern American Conservatism," Ph.D. thesis, Harvard University; for the concept of the "psychic cost" of regulation, see Robert E. Lane, *The Regulation of Businessmen* (New Haven, 1954), Ch. 1.

2. Ogden Mills, *What of Tomorrow?* (New York, 1935), 2, 7–11; Herbert Hoover, *The Challenge to Liberty* (New York, 1934), 85, 114–15; David Lawrence, *Stumbling into Socialism* (New York, 1935), 5; Frank Kent, *Without Grease* (New York, 1936), 33; *New York Times*, April 22, 1934; George N. Peek, with Samuel Crowther, *Why Quit Our Own* (New York, 1936), 11; "Smilin' Through!" *Saturday Evening Post*, Sept. 22, 1934; R. E. Desvernine, *Democratic Despotism* (New York, 1936), 158; Merle Thorpe, "The Supreme Court of Worth," *Nation's Business*, Dec. 1935; L. W. Lancaster, "The Professor's Place in Government," *Nation's Business*, June 1935; Heywood Broun, *It Seems to Me* (New York, 1935), 237; Homer Ferguson, "A Plea for Inefficiency," *Nation's Business*, Nov. 1928; Herbert Hoover, "The Towers of Babel," *Vital Speeches*, Feb. 24, 1936.

3. Merle Thorpe, "Speculating upon Speculation," *Nation's Business,* May 1934; *Time,* July 2, 1934; J. P. Warburg, *It's Up to Us* (New York, 1934), 194; Kent, *Without Grease,* 56, 76–77; Harper Sibley, "The Function of Government," *New York Times Magazine,* Feb. 2, 1936; W. M. Kiplinger, "Why Business Men Fear Washington," *Scribner's,* Oct. 1934; Raymond Moley, "Our Present Discontent," *Today,* Sept. 8, 1934; Hoover in New York Herald Tribune Sixth Annual Forum, *The New Way of Living and the Political Issues Which America Faces in 1936* (New York, 1936), 175; Boyden Sparkes, "Horatio Alger at the Bridge," *Saturday Evening Post,* May 2, 1936; N. D. Baker, "The Decay of Self-Reliance," *Atlantic,* Dec. 1934; E. M. Hopkins, "Thoughts Current," *Atlantic,* Oct. 1936.

4. "The Case against Roosevelt," *Fortune,* Dec. 1935; Thorpe, "Speculating upon Speculation"; Hoover, *Challenge,* 1, 33; Roger Burlingame, "Freedom and the Lone Wolf," *Harper's,* June 1934; Cornelius Vanderbilt, Jr., "Society Snubs Roosevelt," *Liberty,* July 14, 1934; Merle Thorpe, "Redefinition of Liberty," *Nation's Business,* July 1935; Elliott V. Bell, "Roosevelt and Business: The Wide Rift," *New York Times Magazine,* Aug. 16, 1936.

5. A. W. Atwood, "Has Business Leadership Failed?" *Saturday Evening Post,* Sept. 22, 1934; Merle Thorpe, "The First Order of Business," *Nation's Business,* Sept. 1936; "Smilin' Through!"; E. T. Weir, "Present Relations of Business to Government," *Vital Speeches,* April 22, 1935; Merle Thorpe, "Give Management Its Job!" *Nation's Business,* Jan. 1936; Forney Johnston, "Why Industry Hesitates," *Nation's Business,* Feb. 1935; D. W. Brogan, *American Themes* (New York, 1948), 32–33; Hoover, *Challenge,* 147–48; W. L. Garrison, Jr., "The Hand of Improvidence," *Nation,* Nov. 14, 1934; Richard Whitney, *Elements of Recovery: Address Delivered . . . Pittsburgh, Pa.,* Feb. 26, 1935 (n.p. [1935]), 16; New England Council, "The Extent, Causes and Suggested Remedies for the Current Lack of Confidence," Sept. 1934, W. B. Donham to F.D.R., Sept. 10, 1934, Roosevelt Papers; Colby M. Chester, "Industry and Recovery," *Vital Speeches,* April 6, 1936.

6. Hoover, *Challenge,* 5, 156, 198; Hoover, "A Call to Republicans," *Vital Speeches,* April 8, 1935; Ogden Mills, *Liberalism Fights On* (New York, 1936), 70; Mills, *What of Tomorrow?* 26, 41; *New Republic,* Feb. 19, 1936; J. W. Taylor in *Congressional Record,* 73 Cong., 2 Sess., 12595 (June 18, 1934).

7. *Congressional Record,* 73 Cong., 2 Sess., 11875, 11882 (June 15, 1934); *New York Times,* Nov. 1, Dec. 5, 1933, Feb. 9, April 10, June 7, July 8, 1934; Louise Overacker, "Campaign Funds in the Presidential Election of 1936," *American Political Science Review,* June 1937. I am also indebted to Mr. Richard E. Low's paper, written in my Harvard seminar, "The Republican Reaction to the New Deal, 1933–1938."

8. "Mr. Roosevelt's Men," *Fortune,* April 1934; Frank Kent, "Which

Way Will the Elephant Jump?" *American Magazine,* Dec. 1935; Kent, *Without Grease,* 8–10; Lawrence, *Stumbling into Socialism,* 63; C. S. Thomas to Elmer Thomas, April 15, 1934, in *Congressional Record,* 73 Cong., 2 Sess., 9836–37 (May 29, 1934); Arthur Mullen, *Western Democrat* (New York, 1940), 316–18; J. W. Davis, "The Torch Democracy Keeps Alight," *New York Times Magazine,* March 5, 1933; *New York Times,* Feb. 28, 1934; Baker to Russell Cook, Nov. 7, 1935, Roosevelt Papers; following articles by Alfred E. Smith in *New Outlook* for dates indicated, "Business Control" (July 1933), "On the Way to Repeal" (Aug. 1933), "Sound Money" (Dec. 1933), and "I Am an American Before I Am a Democrat," in *Vital Speeches,* Oct. 15, 1936.

9. A. S. Cleveland, "NAM: Spokesman for Industry," *Harvard Business Review,* May 1948; R. W. Gable, "NAM: Influential Lobby or Kiss of Death?" *Journal of Politics,* May 1953; Keller, "Journey to Disillusion," 417–20; Special Senate Committee Investigating the Munitions Industry, *Munitions Industry: Hearings,* 73 Cong., Recess (1934), 4424–27; Senate Committee To Investigate Lobbying Activities, *Investigation of Lobbying Activities: Hearings,* 74 Cong., 2 Sess., (1936), 2059; Mason, *Security through Freedom,* 93–95.

10. Press Conference #137, Aug. 24, 1934; F.D.R., *Personal Letters,* III, 417; *Time,* Sept. 3, 1934; Herbert Hoover, *Memoirs . . . The Great Depression, 1929–1941* (New York, 1952), 454–55; *United States News,* Aug. 27, 1934.

11. Mason, *Security through Freedom,* 95; Raskob to Farley, Nov. 5, 1934, Roosevelt Papers; Keller, "Journey to Disillusion," 427, 429; *American Liberty League: A Statement of Its Principles and Purposes* (Washington, 1934); Frederick Rudolph, "The American Liberty League, 1934–1940," *American Historical Review,* Oct. 1950.

CHAPTER 31 *(Pages 489–507)*

1. *New York Times,* April 11, 1936; W. A. White, *Selected Letters . . . 1899–1943,* Walter Johnson, ed. (New York, 1947), 346; Walter Lippmann, *Interpretations, 1933–35,* Allan Nevins, ed. (New York, 1936), 184; F.D.R., *Public Papers* (1934), 314–15; Thurman Arnold, "How They Are Voting," *New Republic,* Sept. 30, 1936; Winston S. Churchill, "While the World Watches," *Collier's,* Dec. 29, 1934; *New York Times,* April 11, 1934.

2. Walter Lippmann, *The New Imperative* (New York, 1935), 43–46; Lippmann, *The Method of Freedom* (New York, 1934), 27; Senate Banking and Currency Committee, *Stock Exchange Practices: Hearings,* 72 Cong., 1 Sess. (1932), 954; Whiting Williams, " 'But You Can't Let People Starve,' " *Survey Graphic,* Feb. 1932; J. G. Winant, "An Approach to Social Security," *Atlantic,* July 1936; Winston S. Church-

ill, "The Dole," *Saturday Evening Post,* March 29, 1930; Jerome Frank, *Fate and Freedom* (New York, 1945), 214.

3. *New York Times,* June 4, 1935; Lippmann, *New Imperative,* 1, 46–47; J. P. Kennedy, *I'm for Roosevelt* (New York, 1936), 14; Lippmann, *Method of Freedom,* 37; A. A. Berle, Jr., "The New Deal and Economic Liberty," *Annals,* March 1935; Donald Richberg, "Points of View," *Nation's Business,* Feb. 1935.

4. *Time,* Oct. 29, 1934, Nov. 9, 1936; Milo Perkins, "Grab the Torch," *Nation,* Nov. 28, 1934; E. G. Shinner, *The Forgotten Man* (Chicago, 1933), ix, 109; W. L. Clayton, "The Future of Capitalism," *Vital Speeches,* Oct. 1, 1936; H. S. Dennison to Ida Tarbell, March 14, 1935, courtesy of Mrs. Henry Dennison; Senate Finance Committee, *Investigation of the National Recovery Administration: Hearings,* 74 Cong., 1 Sess. (1935), 1431; "The Case against Roosevelt," *Fortune,* Dec. 1935.

5. H. L. Stimson and McGeorge Bundy, *On Active Service* (New York, 1948), 300; A. E. Mason, *Harlan Fiske Stone* (New York, 1956), 371–75; *New York Times,* April 11, 1934; Gerald Johnson, *Incredible Tale* (New York, 1950), 188; Roy Jenkins, *Mr. Balfour's Poodle* (London, 1954).

6. F.D.R., *Public Papers* (1933), 252, *Public Papers* (1934), 125, 420; F.D.R. to Edwin S. Smith, April 18, 1939, Roosevelt Papers; F.D.R., *Public Papers* (1934), 373, 422.

7. *New York Times,* Sept. 16, 25, 1934; *Time,* Oct. 8, 1934; Moley, *After Seven Years,* 294–95; Lamont to Norman Davis, Oct. 1, Davis to F.D.R., Oct. 10, 1934, Roosevelt Papers; Hopkins memorandum of talk with Lamont, Oct. 1, 1934, Hopkins Papers.

8. F.D.R., *Public Papers* (1934), 416–17, 435–40; *Time,* Oct. 8, Nov. 5, 1934; H. M. Kannee to Marvin McIntyre, Oct. 23, 1934, Roosevelt Papers; Moley, *After Seven Years,* 295–98; Arthur Krock, "The Bankers Were Suppliants in 1934," *New York Times,* Sept. 25, 1953; *New York Times,* Oct. 25, 1934.

9. Lubin to Frances Perkins, June 7, Donham to F.D.R., Sept. 10, F.D.R. to De Coursey Fales, Oct. 6, Leffingwell to F.D.R., Oct. 13, 30, F.D.R. to Frankfurter, Nov. 2, to Mary T. Norton, Oct. 22, Stimson to F.D.R., Sept. 5, F.D.R. to Warburg, May 23, 1934, Roosevelt Papers; Press Conference #141, Sept. 5, 1934; F.D.R., *Personal Letters,* III, 419, 429.

10. F.D.R., *Public Papers* (1934), 314, (1940), 28; National Emergency Council, Proceedings, June 26, 1934; F.D.R., *Personal Letters,* III, 394; James M. Burns, *The Lion and the Fox* (New York, 1956), 183–85; Press Conference #155, Nov. 2, 1934; Fred Biermann to McIntyre, April 28, 1936, Roosevelt Papers; E. K. Lindley, *The Roosevelt Revolution* (New York, 1933), 10; R. G. Tugwell, "Roosevelt and Hoover," *Antioch Review,* Winter 1953–54; Tugwell, "New Deal Memoir," Ch. 1; Ickes, *First Thousand Days,* 533; La Follette in *New York Times,* Oct. 25, 1934.

11. F.D.R. to Garner, Aug. 11, Sept. 25, to Claude Swanson, Oct. 25, 1934, Katherine Blackburn to Louis Howe, Aug. 10, 1934, "Supplementary Memorandum on Editorial Reaction to Recovery Administration," Roosevelt Papers; National Emergency Council, Aug. 21, 1934; *Time*, Aug. 20, 1934; *New York Times*, Oct. 15, 24, 1934; Ickes, *First Thousand Days*, 202; J. A. Farley, *Jim Farley's Story* (New York, 1948), 47–48.

12. *New York Times*, Nov. 7, 11, 1934; *Time*, Nov. 19, 1934.

CHAPTER 32 (*Pages 511–532*)

1. Eleanor Roosevelt, *This I Remember* (New York, 1949), 84; Frances Perkins, *The Roosevelt I Knew* (New York, 1946), 65–66; Grace Tully, *F. D. R., My Boss*, (New York, 1949), 71–81; Ickes, *First Thousand Days*, 421–22; Emil Ludwig, *Roosevelt* (New York, 1938), 290–94; R. G. Tugwell, "Must We Draft Roosevelt?" *New Republic*, May 13, 1940; Ross McIntire, *White House Physician* (New York, 1946), 65, 76; James W. Gerard, *My First Eighty-Three Years in America* (New York, 1951), 355; Drew Pearson and Robert S. Allen, "How the President Works," *Harper's*, June 1936; H. F. Pringle, "The President," *The New Yorker*, June 16, 23, 1934.

2. Interview with John Keller, Oct. 9, 1949; Keller, with Joe Boldt, " 'Franklin's on His Own Now,' " *Saturday Evening Post*, Oct. 12, 1940; Donald Richberg, *My Hero* (New York, 1954), 210–11; Henrietta Nesbitt, *White House Diary* (New York, 1949), 137; Eleanor Roosevelt to Molly Dewson, March 22, 1935, Dewson Papers; Eleanor Roosevelt, *This I Remember*, 113, 145, 167; Ickes, *First Thousand Days*, 552, 640; Pringle, "The President," *The New Yorker*, June 30, 1934; E. J. Flynn, *You're the Boss* (New York, 1947), 144–45; Lela Stiles, *The Man behind Roosevelt* (Cleveland, 1954), 236–301; John Gunther, *Roosevelt in Retrospect* (New York, 1950), 84–86; Raymond Moley, *27 Masters of Politics* (New York, 1949), 142.

3. Tully, *F. D. R.*, 150–55; Ickes, *First Thousand Days*, 398, 461; Eleanor Roosevelt, *This I Remember*, 108, 114, 170; Doris Fleeson, "Missy — to Do This — F.D.R.," *Saturday Evening Post*, Jan. 8, 1938; S. J. Woolf, "Roosevelt as His Secretary Sees Him," *New York Times Magazine*, June 10, 1934; Gunther, *Roosevelt*, 72–73; Jonathan Daniels, *Frontier on the Potomac* (New York, 1946), 49–50; Robert E. Sherwood, *Roosevelt and Hopkins* (New York, 1948), 207–9.

4. E. S. Corwin, *The President: Office and Powers* (New York, 1957), 19, 320, 323, 491–92; A. M. Schlesinger, Jr., *The Age of Jackson* (Boston, 1945), 40; H. L. Ickes, "My Twelve Years with F.D.R.," *Saturday Evening Post*, June 5, 1948; Ickes, *First Thousand Days*, 152, 308, 315, 407; William Phillips, *Ventures in Diplomacy* (North Beverly, Mass., 1952), 183; Tugwell, Diary, Feb. 16, 1935; Tully, *F. D. R.*, 187; interview with Morgenthau, Dec. 20, 1945, Morgenthau Papers; Perkins,

Roosevelt I Knew, 134–35; D. C. Roper, *Fifty Years of Public Life* (Durham, N. C., 1941), 288–89; Jesse H. Jones, with Edward Angly, *Fifty Billion Dollars*, (New York, 1951), 303–4; Cordell Hull, *Memoirs* (New York, 1948), I, 203–7; Pringle, "The President," *The New Yorker*, June 30, 1934; Raymond Clapper, *Watching the World* (New York, 1944), 154.

5. This section is an adaptation of a paper read before a session of the American Historical Association, Dec. 29, 1954. The Grace Tully quotation is from *F. D. R., My Boss*, xi.

6. Louis Brownlow, *The President and the Presidency* (Chicago, 1949), 61–62; Early to Eugene Lyons, Feb. 2, 1939, Frances Perkins to F.D.R., June 18, F.D.R. to Frances Perkins, June 19, 1934, Roosevelt Papers; Pringle, "The President," *The New Yorker*, June 30, 1934; E. D. Coblentz, *William Randolph Hearst* (New York, 1952), 154; Rosita Forbes, *These Men I Knew* (New York, 1940), 220; Ickes, *First Thousand Days*, 326; Jones, *Fifty Billion Dollars*, 261; J. P. Warburg, "Reminiscenses" (Oral History Research Office, 1952), 1299; Moley, *27 Masters*, 45; Richberg, *My Hero*, 160–61; Gunther, *Roosevelt*, Ch. 8; "More Candor," *The New Yorker*, Aug. 30, 1947; Flynn, *You're the Boss*, 214.

7. Mary W. Dewson, Appendix of "An Aid to the End," Dewson Papers; Tugwell, "New Deal Memoir," Ch. 3; Eleanor Roosevelt, *This I Remember*, 56, 125; Perkins, *Roosevelt I Knew*, 30, 68–70; Tully, *F. D. R.*, 107; Ira T. Smith and Joe Alex Morris, *"Dear Mr. President"* (New York, 1949), 150–51; Louis Howe, "The President's Mailbag," *American Magazine*, June 1934; Leila A. Sussmann, "FDR and the White House Mail," *Public Opinion Quarterly*, Spring 1956; Alben Barkley, *That Reminds Me* (New York, 1954), 144; Press Conference #952, May 30, 1944; H. G. Wells, *Experiment in Autobiography* (New York, 1934), 683; James Kieran, "The President Listens In on the Nation," *New York Times Magazine*, Oct. 3, 1937.

8. Andrew Jackson, Protest to the Senate of the United States, April 15, 1834; Louis Brownlow, *A Passion for Anonymity* (Chicago, 1958), 384; McIntire, *White House Physician*, 80; R. G. Tugwell, "Franklin D. Roosevelt on the Verge of the Presidency," *Antioch Review*, Spring 1956; Eleanor Roosevelt, *This I Remember*, 7; F.D.R., *Personal Letters*, III, 401, 554; Press Conference #360A, April 15, 1937, #649A, June 5, 1940; Robert H. Jackson to Arthur M. Schlesinger, Oct. 9, 1950.

9. Francis Biddle, "The Labor Board," Biddle Papers; F.D.R., *Public Papers* (1944–45), 232; interview with John N. Garner, *United States News & World Report*, March 8, 1957; interview with Henry Morgenthau, Jr., July 26, 1946; interview with Wayne Coy, May 10, 1949; Tully, *F. D. R.*, 172; H. S. Johnson, "Profile of a President," *Ladies' Home Journal*, March 1938; F.D.R., *Public Papers* (1933), 165; R. G. Tugwell, "The Experimental Roosevelt," *Political Quarterly*, July–Sept. 1950; Perkins, *Roosevelt I Knew*, 137, 164; W. M. Kiplinger,

"What's Ahead in Washington," *Nation's Business,* Feb. 1934; E. J. Flynn, "Reminiscences" (Oral History Research Office, 1950).

CHAPTER 33 *(Pages 533–552)*

1. Frances Perkins, *The Roosevelt I Knew* (New York, 1946), 359–60, 380, 385; F.D.R., *Public Papers* (1934), 315; R. G. Tugwell, "The New Deal: The Available Instruments of Governmental Power," *Western Political Quarterly,* Dec. 1949; *Time,* July 27, 1936; Tugwell to F.D.R., Dec. 21, 1936, Roosevelt Papers; H. L. Stimson and McGeorge Bundy, *On Active Service* (New York, 1948), 333; A. M. Schlesinger, Jr., "Curmudgeon's Confessions," *New Republic,* Dec. 7, 1953.
2. R. G. Tugwell, "The Experimental Roosevelt," *Political Quarterly,* July–Sept. 1950; Cordell Hull, *Memoirs* (New York, 1948), I, 205; Tugwell, "New Deal Memoir," Ch. 2; Francis Biddle, "The Labor Board," Biddle Papers; Morgenthau, Diary, Dec. 2, 1935, Aug. 5, 1942; Donald Richberg, *My Hero* (New York, 1954), 288; R. G. Tugwell, *The Democratic Roosevelt* (New York, 1957), 359, 442; Perkins, *Roosevelt I Knew,* 137; R. G. Tugwell and E. C. Banfield, "Grass Roots Democracy — Myth or Reality?" *Public Administration Review,* Winter 1950; H. L. Ickes, *The Inside Struggle* (New York, 1954), 659; Jerome Frank to Harry Hopkins, Aug. 22, 1937, Hopkins Papers; interview with Morgenthau, July 26, 1946.
3. Biddle, "The Labor Board"; William Phillips, *Ventures in Diplomacy* (North Beverly, Mass., 1952), 183–84; Grace Tully, *F. D. R., My Boss* (New York, 1949), 72, 170; Morgenthau, Diary, Feb. 15, April 13, Dec. 2, 1935; Tugwell, "The Experimental Roosevelt"; Ickes, *First Thousand Days,* 144, 165, 245, 295–96, 426; Robert E. Sherwood, *Roosevelt and Hopkins* (New York, 1948), 63; F.D.R., *Personal Letters,* III, 442; Richberg, *My Hero,* 291–92; Mary W. Dewson, "An Aid to the End," Dewson Papers; F.D.R. to A. A. Sprague, Jan. 29, 1936, Roosevelt Papers; W. O. Douglas, "Spoken Like a True American," *Virginia Quarterly Review,* Spring 1954.
4. Morgenthau, Diary, April 13, 1935; John Gunther, *Roosevelt in Retrospect* (New York, 1950), 49; Tully, *F. D. R.,* 66; Ross McIntire, *White House Physician* (New York, 1946), 80; George Creel, *Rebel at Large* (New York, 1947), 333; Ickes, *First Thousand Days,* 692; Jonathan Daniels, *Frontier on the Potomac* (New York, 1946), 31; Sidney Hyman, memoranda of conversations with Philip B. Fleming, Aug. 19, 1949, with Lewis B. Hershey, Oct. 9, 1949, Roosevelt Foundation Papers; Jesse Jones, with Edward Angly, *Fifty Billion Dollars* (New York, 1951), 262; Perkins, *Roosevelt I Knew,* 380, 385; Delano to H. S. Hooker, Oct. 28, 1936, Roosevelt Papers; James E. Abbe, "Revolutions Don't Grow Here," *Today,* Nov. 23, 1935.
5. Morgenthau, Diary, Sept. 27, 1933; Tugwell, *Democratic Roosevelt,*

380; H. S. Johnson, *The Blue Eagle* (New York, 1935), 370–71, 430–32; National Emergency Council, Proceedings, especially Dec. 19, 1933; Richberg, *My Hero*, 177–78; *New York Times*, Nov. 1, 1934; F.D.R. to Early, Nov. 3, 1934, Roosevelt Papers; Ickes, *First Thousand Days*, 220–21; Louis Brownlow, *A Passion for Anonymity* (Chicago, 1958), 318–22.

6. Brownlow, *Passion*, 321; Natl. Emer. Council, Proceedings, Dec. 11, 1934, Jan. 22, 1935; Morgenthau, Diary, Jan. 22, 1935; R. E. Neustadt, "Presidency and Legislation: The Growth of Central Clearance," *American Political Science Review*, Sept. 1954.

7. Ickes, *First Thousand Days*, 201, 596; Eleanor Roosevelt, *This I Remember* (New York, 1949), 145; Moley, *After Seven Years*, 283–84; Tugwell, Diary, March 26, 1934; Tugwell, "New Deal Memoir," Chs. 2, 3.

8. H. S. Johnson, "Profile of a President," *Ladies' Home Journal*, March 1938; S. J. Woolf, "Up the Ladder with F.D.R.," *New York Times Magazine*, Aug. 27, 1939; A. A. Berle, Jr., Diary, April 14, 1945, Berle Papers; Sherwood, *Roosevelt and Hopkins*, 73.

CHAPTER 34 *(Pages 553–573)*

1. Donald Richberg, *My Hero* (New York, 1954), 293.

2. National Emergency Council, Proceedings, Dec. 17, 1935; R. E. Neustadt, "Presidency and Legislation: The Growth of Central Clearance," *American Political Science Review*, Sept. 1954; George C. Robinson, "The Veto Record of Franklin D. Roosevelt," *American Political Science Review*, Feb. 1942; Charles A. Beard, "Roosevelt's Place in History," *Events*, Feb. 1938; Pettengill to McIntyre, Feb. 24, 1934, Hull to F.D.R., May 4, F.D.R. to Doughton [not sent], May 5, 1936, Roosevelt Papers; Tom Connally, with Alfred Steinberg, *My Name Is Tom Connally* (New York, 1954), 154, 184; H. L. Ickes, "My Twelve Years with F.D.R.," *Saturday Evening Post*, June 12, 1948; Morgenthau, Diary, June 29, 1939; Drew Pearson and Robert S. Allen, "How the President Works," *Harper's*, June 1936.

3. Interview with Thomas G. Corcoran, Oct. 21, 1957; A. A. Berle, Jr., "Roosevelt's Rendezvous with History," *New York Times Book Review*, June 4, 1950; interview with Herbert C. Pell, Aug. 30, 1957; Natl. Emer. Council, Proceedings, Dec. 17, 1935; Upton Sinclair, *I, Candidate for Governor and How I Got Licked* (Pasadena, 1935), 78; F.D.R. to R. W. Farrell, March 28, 1932, Pittman to F.D.R., Aug. 25, 1933, F.D.R. to Wells, Feb. 15, 1935, Roosevelt Papers; F.D.R., *Public Papers* (1940), 27, 31; Anne O'Hare McCormick, "Roosevelt Surveys His Course," *New York Times Magazine*, July 8, 1934.

4. John H. Sharon, "The Fireside Chat," *F.D.R. Coll.*, Nov. 1949; Charles Michelson, *The Ghost Talks* (New York, 1944), 13; Grace Tully, *F. D. R.,*

My Boss (New York, 1949), 98–100; Raymond Moley, 27 *Masters of Politics* (New York, 1949), 149; Eleanor Roosevelt, *This I Remember* (New York, 1949), 72–73; Press Conference #969, Sept. 22, 1944; Robert E. Sherwood, *Roosevelt and Hopkins* (New York, 1948), 212–18; Richberg, *My Hero*, 285.

5. James E. Pollard, *The Presidents and the Press* (New York, 1947), 773–818; "Washington, D. C.," *Fortune,* Dec. 1934; Raymond Clapper, "Why Reporters Like Roosevelt," *Review of Reviews,* June 1934; Natl. Emer. Council, Proceedings, Dec. 11, 1934; John Dos Passos, "Washington: The Big Tent," *New Republic,* March 14, 1934; F.D.R., *Public Papers* (1933), 38–45, *Public Papers* (1935), 509; Westbrook Pegler, "Fair Enough," *New York World-Telegram,* March 13, 1934; A. Merriman Smith, *Thank You, Mr. President* (New York, 1946), Ch. 2; Emil Ludwig, *Roosevelt* (New York, 1938), 283–84; John Gunther, *Roosevelt in Retrospect* (New York, 1950), 21–23; Geoffrey Hellman, "Roosevelt," *Life,* Jan. 20, 1941; W. D. Hassett, "The President Was My Boss," *Saturday Evening Post,* Oct. 17, 1953; William L. Chenery, *So It Seemed* (New York, 1952), 258; George Creel, *Rebel at Large* (New York, 1947), 290.

6. Mrs. Stephen Early, "F.D.R. — As My Husband Knew Him," *American Weekly,* April 24, 1955; F.D.R. to Ochs, Nov. 26, 1934, to B. P. P. Moseley, March 25, to Robert M. Hutchins, June 29, July 1, to Norman Hapgood, July 11, 1936, to Cleveland Rodgers, Aug. 11, 1936, to Claude G. Bowers, Aug. 3, 1937, to James W. Gerard, July 20, 1939, to Josephus Daniels, Sept. 28, 1940, Roosevelt Papers; Drew Pearson, "My Life in the White House Doghouse," *Saturday Evening Post,* Nov. 10, 1956; Edgar Kemler, *The Irreverent Mr. Mencken* (Boston, 1950), 268–72; F.D.R., *Public Papers* (1935), 512–13, *Public Papers* (1938), 278–81; Ickes, *First Thousand Days,* 204; Roosevelt inscription in Ickes, *Freedom of the Press Today* (New York, 1941), Roosevelt Papers; LeHand scrapbook, June 19, 1935, Roosevelt Papers.

7. M. W. Childs, "They Hate Roosevelt," *Harper's,* May 1936; *Time,* April 27, 1936; Nicholas Roosevelt, *A Front Row Seat* (Norman, Okla., 1953), 4–5; A. S. Karr, "The Roosevelt Haters," *F.D.R. Coll.,* May 1950; J. K. Wilcox, "Anti-FDR Checklist," *F.D.R. Coll.,* May 1954; for the longer doggerel I am indebted to Mr. W. P. Gillotte, who writes, "It was passed from hand to hand in the pre-war Republican underground"; Moley, *After Seven Years,* 301; Robert Hale, "But I, Too, Hate Roosevelt," *Harper's,* Aug. 1936; Mrs. Early, "F.D.R."; Esther Arthur, "Have You Heard about Roosevelt?" *Common Sense,* Aug. 1938; M. W. Childs, "They Still Hate Roosevelt," *New Republic,* Sept. 14, 1938; Stephen Early, "Below the Belt," *Saturday Evening Post,* June 10, 1939.

8. Morgenthau, Diary, May 8, 1935; *Time,* April 15, 1935; M. W. Childs, "Mr. Mellon in Court," *New Republic,* May 15, 1935; Raymond Daniell, "Land of the Free," in Hanson Baldwin and Shepard Stone,

eds., *We Saw It Happen* (New York, 1938), 83–84; Homer Cummings, *Selected Papers*, C. B. Swisher, ed. (New York, 1939), 247; "Robert H. Jackson," *Fortune*, March 1938; F. D. Ashburn, *Peabody of Groton* (New York, 1944), 295, 340–45; George Biddle, *An American Artist's Story* (Boston, 1939) 66–67.

9. Ira T. Smith and Joe Alex Morris, *"Dear Mr. President"* (New York, 1949), 12, 213–214; Lorena Hickok to Hopkins, April 8, July 1, Martha Gellhorn to Hopkins, Nov. 11, 1934, Hopkins Papers; Walter Davenport, "Recovery Throws Away a Crutch," *Collier's*, May 5, 1934; Sherwood Anderson, "Explain, Explain!" *Today*, Dec. 2, 1933; John Dos Passos, "The Radio Voice," *Common Sense*, Feb. 1934; Frances Perkins, *The Roosevelt I Knew* (New York, 1946), 72; Westbrook Pegler, *The Dissenting Opinions of Mister Westbrook Pegler* (New York, 1938), 152–53; F. H. Sanford, "Public Orientation to Roosevelt," *Public Opinion Quarterly*, Summer 1951.

CHAPTER 35 *(Pages 574–588)*

1. Evans Carlson to Marguerite LeHand, Jan. 4, 1940, Roosevelt Papers; Grace Tully, *F. D. R., My Boss* (New York, 1949), 273; Walter Tittle, *Roosevelt as an Artist Saw Him* (New York, 1948), 135; N. C. Fabricant, "Franklin D. Roosevelt's Nose and Throat Ailments" and "Franklin D. Roosevelt, the Common Cold and American History," *Eye, Ear, Nose and Throat Monthly*, Feb. 1957, March 1958; Jesse Jones, with Edward Angly, *Fifty Billion Dollars* (New York, 1951), 262; Anne O'Hare McCormick, "Still 'A Little Left of Center,'" "An Unchanging Roosevelt Drives On," and "As He Sees Himself," *New York Times Magazine*, June 21, 1936, Aug. 15, 1937, Oct. 16, 1938; "Peggy Bacon's Guillotine," *New Republic*, Dec. 12, 1934; Ira T. Smith and Joe Alex Morris, *"Dear Mr. President"* (New York, 1949), 6, 156; Robert E. Sherwood, *Roosevelt and Hopkins* (New York, 1948), 9; Hjalmar Schacht, *My First Seventy-Six Years* (London, 1955); Mary Colum, *Life and the Dream* (New York, 1947), 440–42; C. G. Jung in *London Observer*, Oct. 18, 1936.

2. Stanley High, *Roosevelt — And Then?* (New York, 1937), 27, 63; F.D.R., *Personal Letters*, II, 513–14, III, 418–19; J. A. Farley, *Jim Farley's Story* (New York, 1948), 68, and *Behind the Ballots* (New York, 1938), 64, 318, 349; Eleanor Roosevelt, "If You Ask Me," *Ladies' Home Journal*, Sept. 1947; "More Candor," *The New Yorker*, Aug. 30, 1947; interview with Morgenthau, July 26, 1946; Elizabeth McDuffie, "What I Miss Most about Franklin D. Roosevelt," *Look*, April 22, 1952; Michael F. Reilly, *Reilly of the White House* (New York, 1947), 57; Donald Richberg, *My Hero* (New York, 1954), 292; H. L. Ickes, "My Twelve Years with F.D.R.," *Saturday Evening Post*, July 24, 1948; H. S. Johnson, "Profile of a President," *Ladies' Home Journal*, March 1938; Eleanor

Roosevelt, *This I Remember* (New York, 1949), 65, 161; R. G. Tugwell, *The Democratic Roosevelt* (New York, 1957), 65–66.

3. Henrietta Nesbitt, *White House Diary* (New York, 1949), 3; Tully, *F. D. R.*, 4, 7, 115, 206; Tugwell, "New Deal Memoir," Ch. 3; Ickes, *First Thousand Days*, 50–51, 126–27, 240, 249, 449–52, 537, 633–35; Francis Biddle, "The Labor Board," Biddle Papers; Raymond Moley, *27 Masters of Politics* (New York, 1949), 113; Garner interview in *U.S. News & World Report*, March 8, 1957; Mary W. Dewson, "An Aid to the End," Dewson Papers; James Kieran, "How FDR Played Poker," *Look*, Aug. 19, 1947; John Gunther, *Roosevelt in Retrospect* (New York, 1950), 67–70; F.D.R. to J. P. Dawson, Jan. 25, to Early, June 18, 1937, Roosevelt Papers; Ross McIntire, *White House Physician* (New York, 1946), 78–79, 84–85; Smith and Morris, "Dear Mr. President," 144–45; Ickes, "My Twelve Years"; Henry Morgenthau, Jr., "The Paradox of Poverty and Plenty," *Collier's*, Oct. 25, 1947.

4. "What's to Become of Us?" *Fortune*, Dec. 1933; F.D.R. to W. H. Moran, May 27, 1933, Roosevelt Papers; *Time*, July 27, 1936; E. W. Starling, *Starling of the White House* (New York, 1946), 309–11; Margaret L. Suckley, "A Day at Hyde Park," *New Republic*, April 15, 1946; H. F. Pringle, "The President," *The New Yorker*, June 23, 1934.

5. Tugwell, *Democratic Roosevelt*, 97, 333; Dewson, "An Aid to the End"; Frances Perkins, *The Roosevelt I Knew* (New York, 1946), 162; Donald Richberg, *My Hero* (New York, 1954), 281, 285–86; Morgenthau, Diary, May 20, 1935; Ickes, *First Thousand Days*, 606; interview with Thomas G. Corcoran, Oct. 19, 1957.

6. Sherwood, *Roosevelt and Hopkins*, 9, 266; Perkins, *Roosevelt I Knew*, 145, 173, 330; McIntire, *White House Physician*, 77; Anne O'Hare McCormick, *The World at Home* (New York, 1956), 219, 324; Swope to Grace Tully, March 30, 1949, Roosevelt Foundation Papers; J. N. Rosenau, "Interviews with Mrs. Franklin D. Roosevelt," Appendix B of "An Estimate of Franklin D. Roosevelt Based upon His Personal Letters," senior thesis, Bard College, 1948; Eleanor Roosevelt, *This I Remember*, 67–69; R. G. Tugwell, *The Stricken Land* (New York, 1946), ix; Biddle, "The Labor Board"; R. G. Tugwell, "The Experimental Roosevelt," *Political Quarterly*, July–Sept. 1950; Eleanor Roosevelt, *This Is My Story* (New York, 1937), 150; Roosevelt, *Public Papers* (1933), 368, *Public Papers* (1938), 381–82; Johnson, "Profile of a President"; Tully, *F. D. R.*, 6; H. L. Ickes, *The Inside Struggle* (New York, 1954), 290.

7. The quotations are from R. E. Neustadt, "The Presidency at Mid-Century," *Law and Contemporary Problems*, Autumn 1956; H. G. Wells, *Experiment in Autobiography* (New York, 1934), 681–82, and Eleanor Roosevelt, "My Day," *New York World-Telegram*, April 20, 1945. See also two remarkable essays in the *Atlantic Monthly* by Sir Isaiah Berlin: "Mr. Churchill" (Sept. 1949) and "Roosevelt through European Eyes" (July 1955).

Index

Wallace's Farmer, 28
Walsh, Tom, 448
War Industries Board, 176
War Industries Board Association, 258
War Production Board, 176
Warburg, James P., 225, 228, 238; monetary policies of, 196, 214; and planning for London Conference, 200, 201, 204, 207, 209; on F.D.R., 203, 524–25; at London, 211, 214, 230; urged by Douglas to continue battle against inflation, 234; and Warren, 235, 236, 237; on Douglas's discouragement over gold-purchase program, 240; breaks with administration, 244; books by, 472, 502; on government and investment machinery, 475; F.D.R.'s reply to, *re The Money Muddle,* 502
Ware, Harold, 52
Warren, Dr. George F., 237; proposes increasing price of gold, 36; consulting economist for Committee for the Nation, 198; book, *Prices,* 219, 234–35; Roosevelt's discussions with, 219, 235, 236, 241; and the gold-purchase program, 238, 239, 240, 241
Washington *News,* 468
Washington *Times-Herald,* 511–12
Watson, Edwin M. (Pa), Colonel, 512, 513, 516
Watson, Tom, 447
Weir, Ernest T., and meeting with Green in Miss Perkins's office, 142; and union election dispute, 148–49; on the Wagner bill, 404–5; Chicago Union League Club speech of, 477; in American Liberty League, 486
Weirton Steel Company, 148
Welles, Gideon, 518, 520
Welles, Sumner, 232
Wells, H. G., 558; on F.D.R., 527, 587–88
Weyl, Nathaniel, 53
Wharton, Arthur O., 411, 415
What Of Tomorrow?, Mills, 472
Wheat prices, surpluses and, 61–62; effect of dust storms on, 70

Wheeler, Burton K., Senator, 448; wants action on silver, 41; supports Borah *re* antitrust laws, 100; silver amendment of, 199; on the necessity of bimetallism, 249; favors financial regulation, 440
Wheeler-Lea Act, 359
White, William Allen, 566; urges Congress to grant Roosevelt more power, 425; on Theodore Roosevelt, Jr., 489; on Roosevelt's triumph in 1934 elections, 507; advice to Roosevelt *re* the press, 566
White House staff, 15, 514–17
White Sulphur Springs meeting, 276
Whiteside, Arthur D., favors price-fixing, 131; member National Industrial Recovery Board, 157; candidate for chairman of NRA, 165
Whitney, George, 435, 438
Whitney, Richard, at Pecora investigation, 435; leads opposition to stock exchange legislation, 461, 462–63, 464–65, 466, 469; background, 461; economic philosophy of, 461–62; on margin requirements, 464–65; on the program for business, 478
Why Quit Our Own, Peek and Crowther, 258
Wiggin, Albert H., 435, 438, 443
Williams, Aubrey, 269, 378
Williams, Clay, 157, 158, 164
Williams, John Sharp, 189
Willkie, Wendell, 325–26
Wilson, Edmund, 403
Wilson, M. L., 82; and the domestic allotment plan, 36, 37, 38; as chief of Wheat Division, 49, 62; and marketing agreements, 55; proposes State Extension Directors for AAA administrators, 60; stresses planning *with* farmers, 72; as chief of Subsistence Homestead Division, 363–64, 365, 366, 369, 370; on Mormon villages, 363–64; on "white-lighters," 371
Wilson, Paul C., 299
Wilson, Woodrow, quoted, 3; and his Cabinet, 518; and F.D.R., 529; and the press, 561
Winant, John G., Governor, in Stable

Arthur M. Schlesinger, Jr., won the Pulitzer Prize for History in 1946 for *The Age of Jackson* and the Pulitzer Prize for Biography in 1966 for *A Thousand Days: JFK in the White House*. He is the Albert Schweitzer Professor in the Humanities at the City University of New York. A graduate of Harvard, Schlesinger also studied at Peterhouse, Cambridge, and has been a professor of history at Harvard. He lives in New York City.